Tom Hutton

SENSIBLE CRUISING DESIGNS

SENSIBLE CRUISING DESIGNS

by L. Francis Herreshoff

INTERNATIONAL MARINE PUBLISHING COMPANY

Camden, Maine

© 1973 by International Marine Publishing Company
Library of Congress Catalog Card Number 73-88019
International Standard Book Number 0-87742-035-1
Printed in U.S.A.
Eighth printing, 1981

Published by International Marine Publishing
Company, 21 Elm Street, Camden, Maine 04843

CONTENTS

PUBLISHER'S PREFACE

L. Francis Herreshoff created some great yacht designs. His designs are marked by clean, sweeping lines and a simplicity of hull and rig that shows that they have been drawn by a real artist. In each design, he strips away every nonessential and leaves the true elements of a masterpiece. His father, Nathanael G. Herreshoff, had this same genius, but whereas the work of the father emphasized engineering perfection, the work of the son emphasized artistic perfection.

Francis Herreshoff's work certainly shows the influence of his father, but his designs are tempered with an even older tradition. One of Captain Nat's famous designs was the little Buzzards Bay 12½-footer, which may be examined in the plans at the back of this book in the form of Francis Herreshoff's slightly enlarged copy, the Buzzards Bay 14-footer. It is interesting to note the influence of this design on L. Francis' H-28. But the schooner yacht *America,* which came out decades before Captain Nat began designing yachts, also had a great influence on several well-known Francis Herreshoff designs, such as the *Tioga II,* now *Ticonderoga,* and the *Nereia.* And L. Francis was obviously intrigued with the possibilities of the double-ender, an ancient form of hull.

The primary designs in this book are based on L. Francis

Herreshoff's series of articles in the *Rudder* magazine of the 1940's and 1950's detailing how to build many of his designs. It was a very popular series, and a considerable number of boats were built according to the plans and instructions L. Francis presented. We have included plans for forty-six additional small craft and cruising yachts designed by L. Francis at the back of the book. We could not have assembled and presented these designs without help from his devoted secretary, Mrs. Muriel Vaughn, and from Stuart James at the *Rudder,* and we thank these good folks for facilitating this publication.

Some minor hazards in L. Francis' text and plans may be worth bringing to the attention of the reader. In the text, specific recommendations for power plants may be out of date either because the engine specified may no longer be available or because a better engine may now be made. The same is true for manufactured fittings specified, and, of course, catalog numbers have changed. On the plans, scales such as "¼ inch = 1 foot" are accurate for L. Francis' original drawings but are obviously not for the reductions that appear in the book. Readers with an editorial eye will quickly note that L. Francis was more intent on the artistry of his lettering than on consistently choosing any particular letters to make up the words he needed. He seemed quite capable of giving a boat a leeboard on the port side, and a leaboard to starboard; both would be beautifully drawn and if built to the drawings would work extremely well on the boat.

In the course of assembling material for this book, a most interesting copy of a thirty-year-old letter was found, coincidentally relating to the very project on which we were embarked. It was addressed to the editor of the *Rudder* from W. Starling Burgess, one of the few men who could be called a true peer of L. Francis Herreshoff. Both men were sons of the very greatest yacht designers, Edward Burgess and Captain Nat Herreshoff, and both were themselves outstanding yacht designers.

Commenting on some articles he had recently read in the *Rudder,* now gathered in this book, Mr. Burgess wrote on November 24, 1943, as follows:

"The various articles of Mr. Herreshoff which you have published in the last few months are splendid. They are evoking the highest praise from all I meet who have read them. I have recommended them in turn to many more who have been unable to obtain copies of your magazine.

"May I suggest that you consider reprinting them together under one cover and offering them for sale. I am sure you will get a hearty response.

"Mr. Herreshoff's is the sort of writing which many people long for and seldom find. Personally I consider they may well prove to be of lasting literary value. Has it occurred to you that he writes as Thoreau would have written had he been a sailor?

"I have known Francis Herreshoff all my life and have the very greatest admiration for him." (signed, W. Starling Burgess)

We first got to know L. Francis Herreshoff when he generously donated back issues of many foreign yachting magazines to our school-boy boating club. That was twenty-five years ago. In the course of corresponding with him about the activities of the club and about boat design in general, we asked him about the prospects of becoming a naval architect.

He wrote back, "As for the training — if you want to become a yacht designer later, I think if you can draw as much as possible (particularly freehand drawing) it will give you a sense of proportion better than any other kind of training.

No doubt you have a course in freehand drawing, but besides this you should draw a great many things from your own imagination, for after all the designer must draw things before they exist. Sometimes I think the training in freehand drawing is more important than training in mechanical drawing, and if you really love freehand drawing this is a good indication of your later ability as a designer. Of course later on I think it is very necessary to serve your time in a boat shop, where boats are really built, as this is the only practical way to learn construction."

Not being able to draw or build well, we gravitated toward writing, editing, and publishing on boats, instead of designing them. We agree wholeheartedly with Starling Burgess' comments, and we have never published a book with more pleasure than this one.

L. Francis Herreshoff gave his blessing to this book project a few months before his death in December, 1972. The first part of the Introduction contains the last words he wrote for publication. It is our hope that this book will lead to the building of more and more boats from the designs of L. Francis Herreshoff. There could be no more fitting tribute to him.

Roger C. Taylor
International Marine

SENSIBLE CRUISING DESIGNS

INTRODUCTION

It is interesting that International Marine wanted to publish some of my small yacht designs, for many people think these designs are old-fashioned and expensive to build. The truth of the matter is that when a small vessel is carefully built from a good design she will hold her original value for a long time. I know of several boats over forty years old which will bring twice their original cost, so there is no doubt that their owners have done their yachting in the most economical way.

It might interest some of my readers to hear how the cost of a small auxiliary cruiser can be broken down or divided into its principal parts. When I first learned this, perhaps sixty years ago, I, too, was much surprised. Like many today, I thought the hull the principal expense, but I think anyone who has worked in the office of a yacht yard will agree that the following is a good approximation of the division of cost:

- The hull, including the ballast and deck — 25 per cent.
- The auxiliary power plant, including the engine, fuel tanks, exhaust line, propeller shaft, stuffing box, strut and propeller, the distant controls and the installation of their parts — 25 per cent.
- The interior (or cabin), including water tank, plumbing, sink, hand basin, W.C., stove, electrical wiring, berths, upholstery, hatches, skylights, marine windows (or portholes), bulkheads, cabin sole, etc. — 25 per cent. (This is the one place in a small yacht where simplicity can save much and complication cost much.)
- Sails, spars, rigging, ground tackle, deck hardware, and steering gear — 25 per cent.

If one thinks he makes a great saving by having the hull made of an unsuitable material, he is much mistaken. Suppose, for example, there is a saving in hull cost of 10 per cent; then the saving in total cost will be 2½ per cent. Is this worthwhile if the center of weight of the yacht (as a whole) has risen so much that she cannot carry a normal sail plan? If the hull is made of a heavy material to save money, one disadvantage is that it will damage itself when taking hard bottom in a seaway. However, if the ballast keel weighs 50 per cent or more of the displacement and this ballast is nearly all on the outside, then if the hull is of good structural design and made of materials having good elastic limits like wood and bronze, the vessel may come off the next tide without leaking. As an example, about fifteen years ago, the yacht, *Ticonderoga,* was in a race off Bar Harbor where there are several ledges. There was a good breeze and the *Ti* was under spinnaker and all when she was jumped over a ledge that was said to be three feet shallower than her draft. She was taken to Southwest Harbor, where she needed only minor repairs. *Ti* then went on to set records over twenty ocean race courses and won the Skaw race, one of the most important European races since World War II.

Yacht yard expense can be analyzed by looking at two different eras: before World War II and after World War II. Before World War II, in the well-equipped yard, charges would be divided about 30 per cent for materials, 30 per cent for labor, and 30 per cent for what is called overhead costs, which included taxes, insurance, heat, light, and depreciation of buildings and equipment. But you must understand that some operations which built rough ships in the open on land lightly taxed and had little office work other than making up the payroll perhaps only had 10 per cent overhead cost, while those that went in for advertising, etc., might have had an overhead cost of 40 per cent.

Since World War II, however, the building costs have changed, for taxation has risen so much that, so far as I know, no yacht builder has his own foundry pattern shop and well-equipped machine shop. As inventory (lumber, sheet metal, rods, tubes, etc.) is taxed, the cost of having the necessary materials on hand when needed is very great, so that while materials and labor are four or five times what they were in say 1914, the overhead cost has risen so much that yachts cost fifteen times as much as in 1914.

The principal disadvantage of plastic construction is that the necessary mold costs so much that many hulls must be made from the mold to pay for it, so to move this large number of boats, the builder has to use a distributor and salesmen, and pay for advertisements showing a commercial model clad in little more than a yachting cap, so that under these conditions the poor builder only gets about 30 per cent of the selling price of the boat, so that many essentials such as bow chocks and proper mooring cleats are left out.

As for ferrocement construction, which we used to call reinforced concrete, the metal reinforcement is so near the center of oscillation that it takes almost no strain when this composite construction is exposed to a bending condition. This construction also is not logical in that it is composed of two materials which differ greatly in their elastic limits, so the concrete is bound to give out before the metal reinforcement takes its part of the load. And you must remember that no structure can well stand severe strains or local concussions unless it is made of materials with a reasonable amount of elasticity.

Editor's Note. L. Francis Herreshoff was writing this introduction at our request, just a few words to put his work of the Forties and Fifties in perspective from the vantage point of the Seventies. This is as far in the Introduction as his life span allowed him to proceed. To round out his perspective of his own work, we present a piece of writing he did for the *Rudder* in 1945. This hypothetical conversation manifests many of his views — some would say prejudices — on yacht design. A few of his comments appear dated; most do not, and probably never will.

The Editor came up to call on me a short time ago, and when we settled down after supper the conversation took what I thought was a rather interesting turn, for it had to do with the present trend of yachting. The Editor is in a peculiar position for observing the truth of things which have to do with present thought, for he receives thousands of letters on this matter from all over the world and, because this trend is so different from what the advertisers would lead one to suppose, I thought you might like to hear about it. As for the advertisers — well, if they have been barking up the wrong tree all the time, they too might like to know it. Our conversation went about as follows:

Editor speaking: "I have come up to get another design for our 'How To Build' series."

"Well," I said, "it seems to me you want these designs pretty often."

"Now it's this way," said the Editor. "The H 28 plans have sold very well indeed; we have sold about a hundred and twenty of them already and there are about thirty-eight of these boats either built or under construction at the present time. This I consider quite remarkable considering wartime conditions. But you would be surprised if you knew how many letters I receive requesting a design either a little larger or smaller than the H 28 but of the same general hull shape."

"Well," I said, "I am surprised to say the least. I thought they all wanted some sort of preformed and geometrically developed shape which had no connection with usefulness. I thought they wanted streamlined hulls which cheated some rule that never existed."

"No," said the Editor, "and you would be surprised if you knew how sensible the average reader of THE RUDDER is. They write in to me from England, Australia, Sweden, South America and all of the islands in the various oceans, and all demand sensibleness."

"You don't say so," I said, "but you must get some crackpot letters too."

"Yes, of course," he replied, "we get our share of those too, but the one thing I like best about my job is the many, many letters we receive of sincere appreciation when we print something with common sense in it. I don't mind telling you they like your writing — it seems they like the plain horse sense of it."

"Well," I said, "I don't know whether it is horse sense or horse something else, but if they like it I know where there is a whole pile of it."

"But to get back to our subject," said the Editor. "You remember that design you made of a 22 foot 9 inch sloop; one of them was named *Button,* and we published the plans in the September, 1942, RUDDER.

"Yes," I said, "I remember those little sloops well enough, but they haven't got lapping jibs, winches or a lot of advertised claptrap."

"I know," said the Editor, "and that is the very thing I like about this design, for they will sail without all this what you call claptrap."

"I guess they will sail all right," I said, "but I thought people liked to make a lot of work out of sailing nowadays."

"Yes," he said, "some of them do, particularly if they think someone is watching."

"Kind of exhibitionist sailors," I said, "who have confused self advertising with sailing."

"Well," said the Editor, "you can't blame a young man for showing off a little."

"No," I said, "I suppose not, but it seems strange that those boys should leave the city or stray beyond the fringe of the village park; why they should ever take up sailing and cruising is still stranger, for these sports are generally practiced over the horizon so the red pants, swordfisherman's hats, lapping jibs and all are lost to the observer. Shades of Tom Day," I said. "It's a good thing the old man died before yachts made of veneering and manned with gigolo yacht jockies appeared."

"What do you mean, gigolo yacht jockies?" asked the Editor.

"Why I mean those young men who are kept by the owner to sail his yacht for him instead of a professional crew. Supposed to be Corinthians, you know."

"Well," said the Editor, "I guess if the city of Corinth had many like them there wouldn't have been many cigarettes or much liquor left in the Greek Archipelago."

"No," said I, "nor maidens either, for that matter."

"Well, what can be done about it?" queried the Editor.

"Plenty could be done," I said, "but if we continue with our present freaks (sometimes called ocean racers) we will only breed a lot of young parasites instead of sailors."

"Why does the type or design of the yacht affect the character of the crew?" asked the Editor.

"I'll tell you. If you have yachts that are so expensive to run that only the very rich can afford them, then the young man with a moderate income is out of luck, particularly if he has a wife and some children. Generally he can never hope to afford such an expensive toy, and if he did it would be a ridiculous waste of money, so under the present conditions about all he can be is some sort of a gigolo yacht jockey if he wants to go sailing."

"Do you mean to say," said the Editor, "that yachting was, or ever can be again, less expensive?"

"Most assuredly I say so," I replied. "Take boats like those 22 foot 9 inch sloops that you are talking about. The three or four of them that have been built can be sold for twice as much as they cost originally. You will find, also, that nearly all of the annual care of these boats can be done by the owner, so that his yachting for three or four years costs practically nothing. But you take one of these damn fool boats that have high narrow sails, lapping jibs, and a lot of what we call claptrap — well, when you come to sell her you won't get back twenty-five per cent of your investment, for she is no good to cruise in as she can't sleep the crew that is necessary to handle her. The cost of upkeep and depreciation of her sails is something terrific."

"Why do you call them 'damn fool boats'?" asked the Editor.

"Well, I dunno," I said, "but that is what every clam-digger from Sandy Hook to Machias, Maine, calls them when he looks over his shoulder and sees them half hove down and not making much progress. What do you say if we have a drink," asked I, "for I always feel uncommonly dry after supper."

"Go to it," said the Editor, "but as for my part, I can think just as well without any refreshment."

"Well, here's to the new 'How To' class for THE RUDDER," I said.

"By the way," said the Editor, "what do you think we should name this new class?"

"Well, I once designed a little sloop of about this size that was named *Prudence*."

"Hand me the dictionary please," said the Editor, "while I look up the definition . . . Here it is now — 'Prudence, 1, the quality of wisdom put into practice. 2, economy.' By George," he continued, "that is just the name we want, for it describes the only kind of a boat most of us can afford until we get through paying for this war racket."

"I don't know about the war," I said, "but I can tell you there is not a piece of waste timber shown on her construction, and I think most experienced builders will agree to this statement. Also, those boats with long straight keels always turn out the most economical when completed."

"I predict," said the Editor, "that there will be a whole flock of them built, perhaps as many as of the H 28."

"I doubt it," I said, "for you must remember you are dealing with a public which is advertisement minded. You know the average man likes to be fooled."

"That may be so with the general public," said the Editor, "but I doubt if it is so with many subscribers to THE RUDDER."

"Well, to look at some of your advertisements it would appear someone thought they were fools," I said.

"Why do you say that?" asked the Editor.

"Well," I said, "they generally show some girls in abbreviated costumes as their advertisement, as if that would cover up the defects of their product. One person I know calls this sort of thing Japanese advertising."

"I tell you," said the Editor, "they do that to please the boys in the armed forces."

"I don't doubt that is what they think," I said, "and they call them G.I.'s and think they are kind of simple, but did it ever occur to you that some of these boys have gone through more in six months than most people go through in a lifetime? Many of them have actually handled some of these advertised products and know at first hand just how accessible, reliable and long lived they are."

"We are pretty careful with our advertisements in THE RUDDER," said the Editor, "and we are determined to keep our advertising clean and of a high moral standard. Perhaps you have noticed that for the last fifty years or so we have not shown cigarettes, liquor or women's clothes."

"Oh, I see," said I. "So that's the reason the girls are only allowed a gasket and a couple of sail stops when they appear in the advertisements of THE RUDDER. Personally I think it would be an improvement to show women's clothes in some cases."

"I am sorry you don't like our ads," said the Editor, "but did it ever occur to you that some people are rather hurt at some of your writing?"

"No doubt," I said, "but take the cedar bucket, for instance; you told me you had received many complimentary letters on that subject."

"While that is true," he replied, "still some of our advertisers did not like it."

"Very likely not," said I, "but it is an ill wind that blows no one good. While the cedar bucket may have taken some work away from the machine shop, it has given work to some honest cooper."

"Yes," said the Editor with a sigh, "but *they* don't advertise in THE RUDDER."

"Well," I said, "the Prudence, too, is going to hurt some people's feelings. The plain straightforward simple honesty of her is the direct opposite to the aims of the manufacturers and hucksters who have tried to make people think they could not sail without a whole boat load of gadgets. Personally if I were to have a Prudence I would prefer her without even a motor, and depend on a white ash breeze if caught in a calm spot, for with the right length of oar or sweep a boat of this size can be rowed with little difficulty, and I must say I would prefer to row many hours rather than pay three or four hundred dollars — the cost of a motor including installation. When you consider the noise, smell and drag of the propeller, together with space used up and the dirty bilges — well, to be short, I would prefer occasionally to be a little late to supper."

"You don't seem to like motors or our modern motor boats," said the Editor.

"Yes and no," I said. "Take the modern motor. There is no doubt it is a fine piece of engineering; the power for the weight, size and cost is most astounding. In my childhood the weight of the power plants in our steam torpedo boats was about twenty pounds per horsepower and these were the lightest power plants of their time. But today the weight of some of the large aviation motors is less than one pound per horsepower. As for cost per horsepower, well — although the value of the dollar has decreased, still the horsepower per dollar of the motors has steadily increased. The modern motor is a wonderful thing — reliable, compact and efficient. Not so with the modern motor boat, however, for they have gone from the sublime to the ridiculous in rapid succession, and seem at present to be designed for no other purpose than to use round corners where sharp corners would have been better, and sharp corners where round edges are best. They have about as much sense to them as women's hats and will prove just as useful. Of course there are exceptions and one of them is the 'New 18 foot Deluxe Utility' model built by the Chris-Craft Corporation. This launch looks sensible all over; her windshield is low enough so you can see over it when it is covered with salt; you can walk all around her engine and get at it without having it hoisted out of the hull. She looks like a model that could be built reasonably, so the purchaser would always remain satisfied. And that is a very important matter, for every time a customer gets a shellacking there is danger he will be lost to yachting or boating, and THE RUDDER may even lose a subscriber."

"Well," said the Editor, "do you think yachts and boats used to be more sensible than at present?"

"Yes, I do," I said, "for in the old days people used to sail and cruise in masterpieces, for there was not much else to cruise and sail in but masterpieces, as no one then thought of having a boat built by anyone but a boat builder, and no one thought of having a yacht designed by anyone but a yacht designer. But now that the boat builder has been superseded by the carpenter, the cabinet maker and the automobile body builder (who pass from one trade to another without any other credentials than a union card), the art of boat building is lost and perhaps forever. Now that the yacht designer has been replaced by the naval architect, the advertiser and the airbrush artist, there is no one left to either plan or build masterpieces. And perhaps all this is well, for few indeed are left who can read the poetry of the boat builder or in any way understand the perfection in the work of the designer. But in years gone by most boats, from the fisherman's dory to the square-rigged steam yacht, had character, grace and perfection."

"But I can feel a change coming," said the Editor, "a movement toward simplicity and the truth. People are tired of all this confusion and contradiction. I can see it in art, literature and even politics."

"The truth," I said, "is a rare thing; it would be nice to see it appreciated or again become stylish. I suppose this change is possible now that we have a true man for president. Do you think," I continued, "that this change will also affect advertising?"

"Let's skip the advertising," said the Editor, "for it is one of our necessary evils."

"That is all right by me," I said, "but when I think of the rapidly increasing circulation of THE RUDDER, and think of the serious minded people who read it, it seems too bad that the advertisers do not take advantage of this opportunity."

"What do you mean?" asked the Editor.

"Well," I replied, "as it is now, some of the ads are so queerly illustrated and trickily worded that few can even guess what the product is that they are trying to sell. Of course all this bunk means nothing to people in foreign countries, or even to boatmen and fishermen who in many cases are the biggest buyers. What they want to know are some dimensions, the weight, cost and where the product can be obtained."

"You are dead right," said the Editor, "and you would be surprised how many letters we get from abroad asking just these questions."

"Then," I said, "I also think the advertisers are making a mistake in trying to force queer, freakish things on the people, for all the time the people want something sensible, useful and economical. As it is now, the advertisers make all the styles regardless of the customers, but if it is the customer who pays the money he should have some say in the matter."

"Well, he has," said the Editor, "for he doesn't have to buy unless he wants to."

"Now that is just the point," said I, "and it may sound simple, but if they would only make things which are wanted they would do much more business. The only way to keep the business ball rolling is to play the game so both sides can have a crack at it."

"Yes," agreed the Editor. "The ball no question makes of aye's and no's but right and left, as strikes the player, goes."

"What is that from?" I asked.

"That," said the Editor, "is an excerpt from the Rubaiyat

of Omar Khayyam."

"What might all that mean?" I asked.

"It is something written long ago and far away," he said.

"Well," I said, "is that so? Do you remember any more of it?"

"It is some time now since I read it," he said, "but if I remember correctly it went something like this —

> 'Tis all a Chequer-board of Nights and Days, where Destiny with Men for Pieces plays. Hither and thither moves and mates, and slays. And one by one back in the Closet lays. For in and out, above, about, below, 'Tis nothing but a Magic Shadow-show. Played in a Box whose Candle is the Sun Round which we Phantom Figures come and go. The Ball no Question makes of Aye's and No's. But Right or Left as strikes the player goes. And He that toss'd Thee down into the Field — He knows about it all. He knows — He knows.

"It's hard to tell sometimes what to do," I said. "Now you have come way up here to ask me how to advertise the Prudence and I am going to suggest an experiment. Suppose we try telling them the truth."

"That is what I want to do," said the Editor, "but how would you do it?"

"Well," I said, "I wouldn't tell them she was the biggest boat in the world, but rather that she was small enough so when they got through taking care of her they would have some time left over for sailing. I wouldn't tell them she was the fastest boat in the world, but that she would sail with her original two sails and those who want to can keep the sails bent ready for hoisting. You might tell them that if they wanted to get away from the telephone, the radio and all the other strains of modern civilization, that perhaps they can do it in the Prudence as cheaply as any way that you know of. Tell them that if they build her without a motor they can sail thousands of miles with little expense and without using any fuel. But I would warn them that a boat like the Prudence has two disadvantages, for people will constantly want to borrow her and she is apt to be stolen."

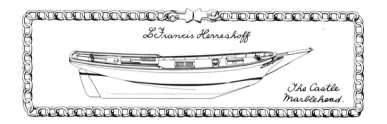

L. Francis Herreshoff

The Castle Marblehead.

The Prudence *of L. Francis Herreshoff's Introduction bustling along on the wind. The picture was made in 1939.*

DESIGN NO 71.

SMALL CRUISER

L.O.A. 22'9". L.W.L.19'9". BEAM 8'. DRAFT 3'.

Station Numbers	Hights: Top of Deck at Side	Buttock #1	Buttock #2	Buttock #3	Rabbet	Profile	At Deck	WL+2'	WL+1'	WL+6"	L.W.L.	WL-6'	WL-1'	WL-18"	WL-2'	WL-2'6"	Rabbet	Face	Diag. 1	Diag. 2	Diag. 3	Station Numbers
0	3-2-6					3-2-6	0-1-0										0-1-4	0-1-4				0
2	2-11-2	1-10-6			0-2-4	-0-0-6	1-7-0	1-0-6	0-6-4	0-3-0	0-0-4						0-1-4	0-0-2	1-4-7	0-11-3	0-0-3	2
4	2-8-2	0-1-6	1-7-4		-1-1-1	-1-2-6	2-7-0	2-3-0	1-7-4	1-3-2	0-10-4	0-5-3	0-2-0				0-1-4	0-0-6	2-5-4	1-11-3	0-8-1	4
6	2-5-4	-0-8-6	0-2-6	1-10-4	-1-6-0	-1-11-0	3-3-0	3-0-6	2-6-5	2-2-4	1-9-?	1-2-7	0-8-6	0-3-0			0-2-6	0-1-4	3-2-4	2-8-3	1-2-4	6
8	2-3-1	-1-2-6	-0-6-0	0-7-2	-1-7-6	-2-4-2	3-7-7	3-7-2	3-2-4	2-11-3	2-6-5	2-0-0	1-3-6	0-7-6	0-3-3		0-4-2	0-2-3	3-9-1	3-3-1	1-7-2	8
10	2-1-1	-1-6-1	-0-10-5	-0-1-2	-1-9-3	-2-7-2	3-10-6	3-2-4	3-7-2	3-5-2	3-0-7	2-6-3	1-9-1	1-0-0	0-4-6	0-3-4	0-5-2	0-3-0	4-1-5	3-7-6	1-10-1	10
12	1-11-4	-1-7-0	-1-0-0	-0-4-4	-1-11-2	-2-9-2	4-0-0	3-7-2	3-9-6	3-10-0	3-4-3	2-9-5	2-0-0	1-1-3	0-5-0	0-4-0	0-5-0	0-3-2	4-3-6	3-10-5	1-11-1	12
14	1-10-3	-1-5-5	-0-11-6	-0-4-4	-2-0-7	-2-10-3	4-0-0		3-10-6	3-8-5	3-5-1	2-10-2	1-10-7	0-11-3	0-5-3	0-3-7	0-4-2	0-3-0	4-4-4	3-10-7	1-10-1	14
16	1-9-6	-1-2-3	-0-9-2	-0-2-4	-2-2-4	-2-11-1	3-11-0		3-9-7	3-7-2	3-3-2	2-6-5	1-4-1	0-7-5	0-4-0	0-2-7	0-2-7	0-2-2	4-3-3	3-9-2	1-7-0	16
18	1-9-5	-0-3-0	-0-4-3	+0-2-1	-2-4-2	-2-11-6	3-8-4		3-7-0	3-3-6	2-8-7	1-8-1	0-7-2	0-3-5	0-2-4	0-1-7	0-2-0	0-1-3	4-1-0	3-5-2	1-2-2	18
20	1-10-1	-0-2-0	+0-2-4	+0-9-6	-1-0-0	-3-0-0	3-4-4		3-1-6	2-7-1	1-4-7	0-5-2	0-2-6	0-1-1	0-1-5	0-1-1	0-2-0	0-0-6	3-8-2	2-10-4	0-8-0	20
22	1-11-4	0-7-2	0-10-6				2-11-0		0-7-0								0-2-0		3-2-6	2-1-2	0-0-6	22
22'-9"	2-0-2						2-8-4															22'-9"

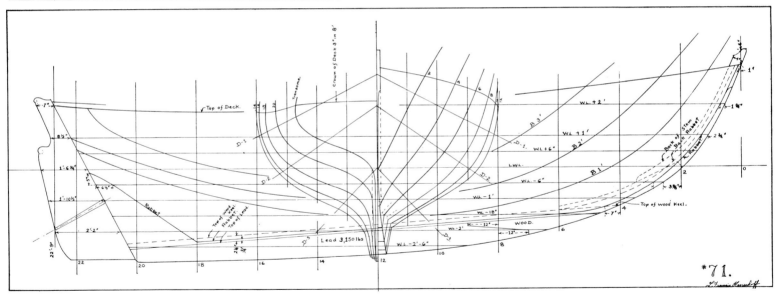

#71.

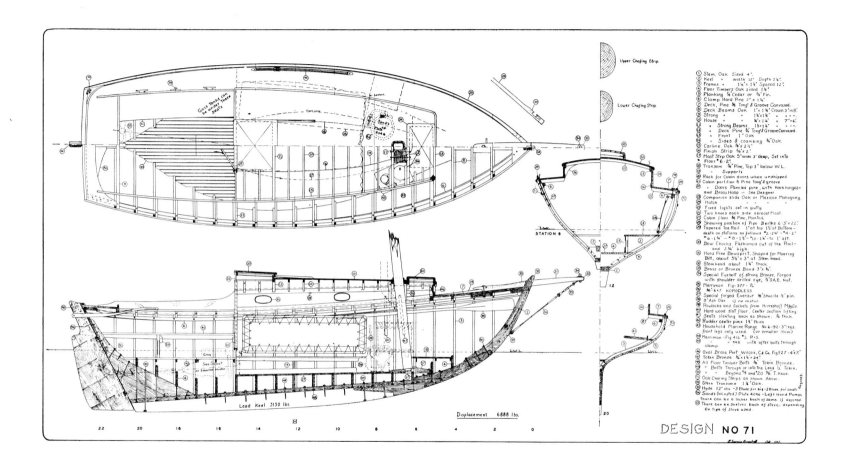

Upper Chafing Strip.

Lower Chafing Strip.

STATION 6

Displacement 6888 lbs.

Lead Keel 3150 lbs.

DESIGN NO 71

22   20   18   16   14   12   10   8   6   4   2   0

1   HOW TO BUILD THE DOUBLE-PADDLE CANOE

The double-paddle canoe, or the canoe which uses a paddle with two blades, never has been popularly adopted in this country, although in Europe it has been by far the most common type of canoe for more than half a century. Perhaps we have stuck to the single-bladed paddle because this was the type of propulsion used by the Indians when we first settled this country. It is true enough that the single-bladed paddle is the best for navigating narrow streams and thickly overgrown rivers; but when one ventures out in open water, particularly if there is a breeze, the single-bladed paddle is a poor arrangement, especially if only one person is paddling.

The kayak, as developed by the Eskimos and northern Indians, consists of walrus hide or other tough skin stretched over a framework of wood and, while this arrangement is satisfactory for cold water where the hide does not soften up or rot, it is useless in warm water. I class as kayaks all the various double-paddle canoes which have skin or fabric stretched over a framework, and my experience is that they are not easy to paddle on a long trip, and are not safe. The reason they are not easy to paddle is because their underwater shape is not good when the fabric has bulged in between the framework. The bottom then has become a series

of concave curves — the worst possible shape for low speed where the amount of surface resistance is so important. As for safety, the fabric-covered canoe can be punctured or ruptured, and sometimes quite easily, on sharp rocks which cannot always be avoided in landing on certain types of shores. However, some of these kayaks with fabric stretched over a framework are surprisingly light, so that for paddling close to shore, up small rivers, and landing on sandy beaches they have certain advantages.

For real usefulness and safety, a double-paddle canoe should be planked up nearly as thick as a light rowboat; then, with care, it will last many years. Such a boat will have quite a lot of flotation even if completely filled with water, but most of the double-paddle canoes that I have designed and used in the last twenty-five years have had watertight bulkheads at both ends. In such a craft, if one is upset, it is quite easy to get aboard again and bail her out. The procedure in getting aboard is as follows: after one has righted the canoe, he swims to her stern and then, facing forward, presses the stern under water until he can sit astride on the after deck. Next he moves forward in short stages by throwing his weight on his hands, which are at the gunwale,

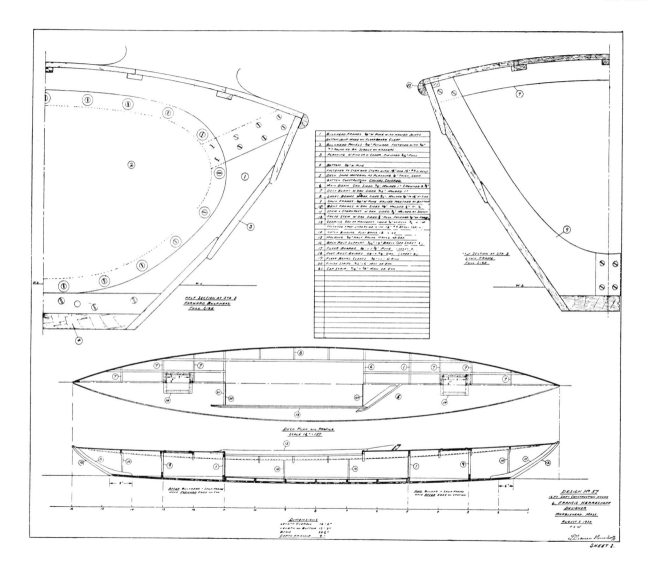

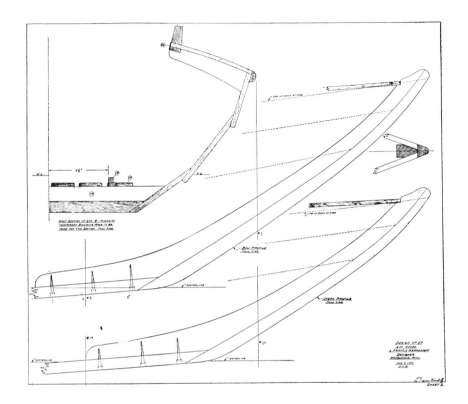

until he has come to the cockpit. Then by throwing both legs forward he can slide into his seat. All during this operation he is balancing the little craft with his feet in the water, which seems to keep her from capsizing again.

While I must say that I have never been capsized in a double-paddle canoe when far from shore, still every time I get a new or different canoe I practice getting into her in the way described above. I do it when swimming in warm water, and this gives me more confidence in the little ship. However, when one is seated in a double-paddle canoe, it is difficult to capsize, and several times I have had swimmers try to do this to me but they have not succeeded. If, however, a swimmer should grab the paddle or interfere with your use of the paddle, he can easily capsize you. But, to resist capsizing under any conditions, the footrests, seat, backrest, and knee braces must all be very strong, and, for fast paddling or comfortable long distance paddling, all these things must be arranged and adjusted just right or the work will be as arduous as pedaling a bicycle that is incorrectly adjusted for its rider.

It is my opinion that the double-paddle canoe gives the most fun for the money of any type of boat a person can possess, and I must say that it is my favorite form of aquatic sport. I have paddled them in the summer, spring, and fall, as well as two or three winters when there was pleasant weather, and I can say from experience that this form of sport is so vastly superior to frostbite dinghy sailing that there is no comparison. In the frostbite dinghy, you are apt to have wet backsides and sit around in most uncomfortable positions with so little exercise that you spend most of your time shivering. Not so in the double-paddle canoe, for after you have paddled far enough to set up a circulation of the blood, you can keep comfortably warm much easier than when walking, and this is because much of your body is shielded from the wind. Also, you can have a canvas or blanket around you from the waist down.

However, I do not recommend canoeing or going on the water in any small craft in the winter except by those who are weatherwise, but I must say that paddling in a safe boat with the thermometer around forty is most exhilarating. After you have gotten your second wind, so to say, and the heart and lungs are adjusted to the exercise, the whole body sings a happy tune and the world is a delightful place to be in. While the double-paddle canoe is at its best as a solo craft, still I must say I have had fun with passengers of both sexes, but, if two are to paddle, it takes more skill, or else the paddles may interfere. The most fun of all, in my opinion, is to make a trip with two canoes (which are very much alike as to speed) with one person in each. If you take the canoes on the top of an automobile and go upstream and paddle downstream with two canoes, while someone drives the car to some prearranged good landing place down-stream, you will have about the most fun I know of in the spring and fall.

The double-paddle canoe is one of the most seaworthy boats of its size ever built, and after you have paddled one on a trip of twenty or thirty miles you will not think them very sissy. Almost nothing will stop them, for they can go over very shallow water and between rocks, or cross rough stretches which would swamp or capsize all other small craft. In fact almost nothing but ice will stop them.

I have designed quite a variety of double-paddle canoes, ranging from racers for European builders (which were built about like a shell) to quite heavy ones, which weighed in the neighborhood of an hundred pounds; but perhaps the strongest, safest, and easiest to construct have been similar to a small lengthened-out dory. The drawings for one of these are shown herewith. It is a design from which several

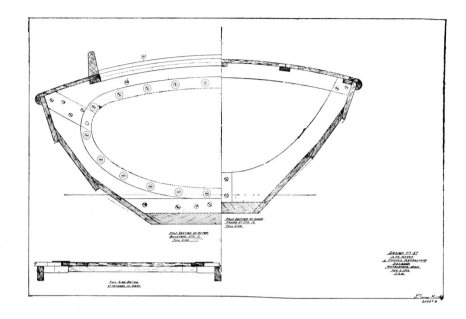

canoes have been built.

You will notice on the design that the bottom is about 3/4-inch thick, and I do not recommend reducing this very much, principally because the planking fastenings, which are on an angle, will have little to hold to if the bottom is thinner. Also, the thick bottom allows the canoe to be used really hard. You will find a little weight, if used in good construction, is not much of a disadvantage in such a craft, and in the end it will save you much work and worry. A canoe that weighs around seventy-five pounds is just about as easy for two people to lift onto the top of an automobile as a lighter one, and, in paddling to windward in a good breeze and sea, a little weight even seems to be a help. The nicely shaped canoe, although heavy, will paddle much easier on a long trip than a light, poorly shaped one.

Those who are unfamiliar with the double-paddle canoe might be interested in a little history. The double-paddle canoe was first perfected in about 1865 by J. Macgregor, M.A., who was a barrister-at-law of Cambridge, England. He paddled several thousand miles in his various canoes named *Rob Roy* and wrote the books *A Thousand Miles in the Rob Roy Canoe*, *The Rob Roy on the Jordan*, and *The Rob Roy on the Baltic*. In fact, Macgregor made the double-paddle canoe so popular in England that since that time there have been many clubs for that type of craft, and in England they are generally spoken of as Rob Roy canoes.

Of late years this sport has become very popular in central Europe and in the Scandinavian countries, so that thousands of people use them not only for short trips but also for long cruises, and spend their whole vacations in them. Some of the European canoes of this class are very beautifully made and of course rather expensive, but with good care they last a long time. These canoes have varied in length between twelve and eighteen feet, and twenty-eight inches has been the width of most of them.

The great problem with the double-paddle canoe is to build a really serviceable one cheaply. One that is safe and strong and will really paddle easily is quite a thing, and I am sure if someone built double-paddle canoes similar to this design they would sell like hot cakes, for there are a great many now who are ready to graduate from the fabric-covered kayak.

As for the exercise of paddling — well, in the double-paddle canoe you can usually make it either as strenuous or as light as you like, and, for this reason, this sort of paddling is ideal for the semi-invalid or the elderly person. I say this because the canoeist is in a comfortable seat with a good backrest, so that if he feels tired or faint he can just sit and relax. Of course none but the strong should venture into open water or swift streams. I have paddled quite a little with a gentleman who is about eighty-four years old and the only complaint he had about the sport was that I had not introduced him to it sixty years before, to which I had to reply that that would have been difficult, for it would have been some ten years before I was born. The only difficulty that people after middle age experience is in getting in and out of the canoe, and this can be obviated by having someone hold the canoe for them.

Paddling with the double paddle is one of the best ways to reduce the waistline, and one of my acquaintances who has paddled this way for some fifty years swears that it will add twenty years to one's life. One of our great national mistakes is that we do not indulge in the sports that are light and healthy exercise, like walking and paddling, for these sports can safely be kept up in later life and are by far the most conducive to health and happiness assets that we can all use.

I would like to emphasize the point that the double-paddle canoe is a failure if it does not paddle easily, and that, if the footrest, seat, and backrest are not just right, it is a very uncomfortable contraption. The design of the paddle is also very important.

Paddles

Few people realize the extreme importance of lightness in a double paddle, but in two or three hours, when the paddle is held out before you at least the length of the forearm, a very little increase in weight becomes tiring. The muscles that first become annoying on a long paddle are those that are between the back of the neck and the shoulder blades, the same muscles which become tired first in driving an automobile, when the arms are in a similar position. A lighter paddle will help these muscles much, and one of the principal ways to lighten the paddle is to make it shorter, for the shorter paddle can have a smaller diameter of loom (the part between the blades). A 7-foot paddle need not be much more than 1-inch in diameter at the loom, while an 8-foot paddle should be nearly $1\frac{1}{4}$ inches, and a 9-foot one at least $1\frac{3}{8}$ inches. However, I find too small a loom tiring on the finger muscles, and think that one of $1\frac{1}{4}$-inch diameter is about right.

As for the length of paddles, it is a common mistake in America to use them too long, often over nine feet. Apparently, some people have thought the longer paddle is conducive to speed, but this is definitely not so. The European racers use paddles on their narrow canoes of only about seven feet in length, and these are very easily driven craft indeed. It would seem that one can develop more power with more strokes with the short paddle than with fewer strokes with the long paddle. All of which is very much the same with the gear of a bicycle, where most people can get along best with a gear of under 70, but the uninformed amateur is apt to use a gear of over 80. The long paddle is not only tiresome from its necessary weight, but also it is unwieldy in a breeze, bothersome in brook paddling, and, worst of all, discouraging. By that I mean the long paddle will always make the canoe seem as if she were going hard.

Too short a paddle also has its disadvantages in anything but the very narrow and low-sided racing canoe, for the short paddle must be tilted up on quite an angle to be effective, so that with canoes of 28-inch beam, a suitable coaming, etc., a paddle around 8 feet long is best. One of the disagreeable features of a short double paddle is that it wets the hands, or, in other words, the drip from the blades runs in to the hands quicker, for it has to be tilted up more. With a paddle $8\frac{1}{2}$ feet long or more, there only has to be a seizing of string around the loom just beyond the hands to stop the drip from coming inboard, and rubber drip cups can be entirely done away with. It is most important to keep the hands dry when paddling, for that facilitates the grip of the fingers. I will note, though, that when paddling with gloves on, a slight dampness on the loom seems a help, as perfectly dry gloves or mittens slip and become tiresome. However, it is only the right hand on a right-hand-control paddle that holds the loom from revolving. While I do not intend to go into the technicalities of using the paddle, I suppose I must say something about right- and left-hand-control paddles.

It has been pretty definitely proved that the paddles which have their blades at right angles to each other work best. This was found out with two-piece paddles whose blades were joined at the middle with a brass ferrule, and which were arranged so the blades could be oscillated so that both

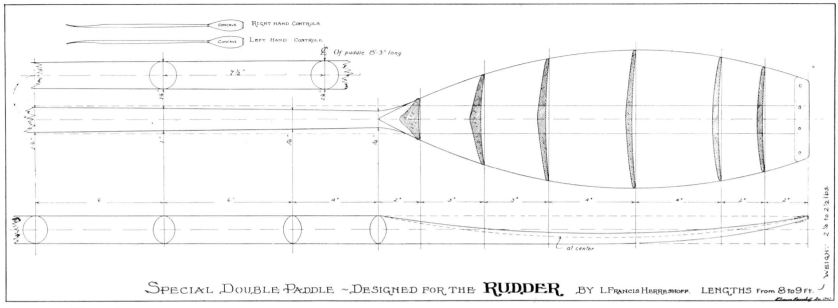

Figure 1.

blades were on the same plane, or at right angles to each other. When the blades are at right angles, the paddle is called a feathering paddle, and not only is it the most convenient in head winds, but the natural position of the palm of the hand when paddling is such that it wants to revolve the paddle just the right amount for blades at 90 degrees. You see, when the right-hand blade is in the water, the right hand will be pulling aft on it so the wrist is straight, but when the right hand has been raised for the left-hand paddle to take its stroke, then the position of the right hand is such

that only a slight bending backward of the wrists is sufficient to make the feathering-blade paddle oscillate properly. A right-hand-control paddle is one which is held from revolving by the right hand but allowed to revolve in the loosely held left hand; and a left-hand-control paddle is one held from revolving by the left hand. While it is true that the flat-bladed paddles (those not spooned) can be used as either right- or left-hand controlled, the spoon-bladed ones must be arranged as follows:

1.   For right-hand control, the right-hand blade will have

its concave side aft, while the left blade has its concave side upward.

2. With the left-hand-controlled paddle, the right-hand blade will have its concave side aft, while the left blade has its convex side upwards.

Most of the paddlers I have known prefer the right-hand-controlled paddle, and, if anyone starts his paddling with the blades arranged that way, it is difficult to change over. I only speak at some length about the right- and left-hand paddles because it is very important in making the paddle to have the blades turned the correct way, and that is where many amateur paddle makers fall down.

As for the shape and size of the blade, I must say I prefer rather less area than is customary in America, and will cite that the Eskimos use very small blades in their kayaks. While the small-area blade has more slip in the water, it certainly makes the canoe seem as if it were going easier, and after the canoe has acquired speed the slip will be very little. I like a short blade that is of about the same width as the usual paddle. In Figure 2, *A* shows the usual blade, *B* shows the shape I like, and *C* shows a common Eskimo type.

When a blade is small at both ends, like the Eskimo one shown, there is less power absorbed in rocking it from the angle it enters the water to the angle it leaves the water. (This change in angle is often 90 degrees.) Some of the Eskimo blades are sharp at the end to be used in poling offshore, but I believe the usual folded-over sheet of copper at the end is the best, as long as the blade is not too wide at its tip.

As for the amount of spoon, or concavity, in the blades,

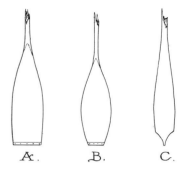

Figure 2.

after considerable experience with broken and split blades, I prefer only a small amount of spoon, as the blade is much less apt to be damaged if the grain of the wood runs with the blade. However, some spoon shape or concavity allows the blade to rock so much easier that the difference between a straight paddle and a properly curved one is quite perceptible. I also like some concavity crossways in the blade, believing it allows the blade to take a better hold on the water.

Figure 1 shows a paddle which I have designed that incorporates the features we have spoken of. Not only does it represent considerable experience on my part in using this sort of paddle, but it is also derived from full-sized drawings I have of the paddles used by European racers. This sort of paddle is best if made of northern white spruce (*Picea glauca*), sometimes called Canadian silver spruce. In making the paddle up, you will only need a piece 1¼-inch square for the shaft or loom, and the side pieces of the blade may be

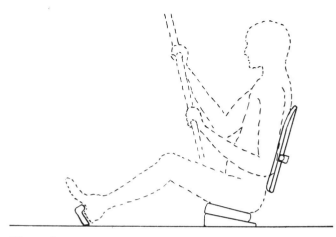

Figure 3.

glued on before shaping up. When the paddle is all done, it should weigh about two and a quarter pounds.

The paddles that have a joint in the middle are convenient, because they can be taken apart for storing either in the canoe or inside an automobile. They have never been accepted by the experienced canoeist as entirely satisfactory. Perhaps this is because they are slightly heavier and at times develop a little shake in the joint. However, they have the theoretical, if doubtful, advantage that they can be changed from right-hand to left-hand control, but a paddler never wants to change after he has adopted one style of paddling. I have used folding paddles more than solid ones during the last thirty years and believe they are less apt to get damaged during transportation or when not in use, but I advise the amateur paddle maker to make the solid paddle rather than

the folding one. There is no reason why a folding paddle, like the drawing shown, should not be ordered from the professional oar and paddle maker.

Back Rests

If one must sit in a position for a long time it is very uncomfortable unless the seat and back rest are exactly right. In the double-paddle canoe, the paddler must be braced or held in place so that his body does not twist or slide around when he throws his weight or strength into one blade and then the other. In fact, if his body is not firmly braced in the canoe, it is impossible for him to take a powerful stroke. For this reason, the back rest, seat, knee rest, and foot rest must all be in their right places and must be much stronger than one would suppose.

The position of the paddler is generally something like Figure 3, with the knees at about the level of the coaming and the feet spread well apart. If the foot rest is too far away and the legs nearly straight, the canoeist cannot push on one foot, then on the other, in preventing his body from twisting on the seat. But when the body is held in place by the back rest, the seat, the knee rest, and the foot rest, the canoeist has, so to say, become a part of the canoe and can take a powerful stroke when necessary. While this is the position you should adopt most of the time (and always in a seaway or when making quick maneuvers), it is necessary for comfort on long trips to change position occasionally. One of the alternate positions that can be used for a change of a few minutes is to cross the legs and draw them up close to the body as the Hindus often sit. Then, if the canoe is of about

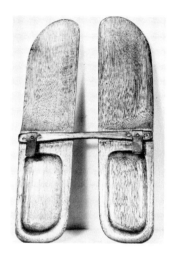

*Figure 4.   After view of
a simple back rest.*

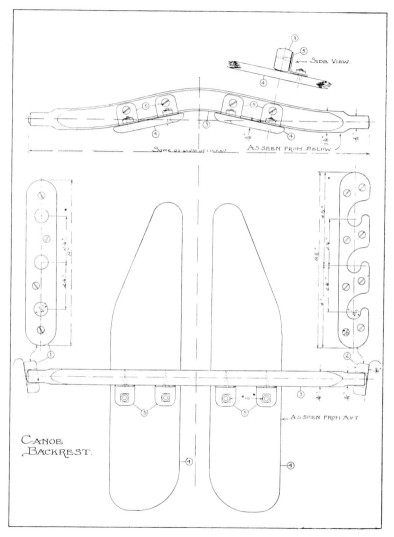

Figure 5.

28 inches beam, the soles of the feet will press on the sides
of the canoe and prevent the body from twisting.

What I am driving at is that the back rest must allow
various changes in position without discomfort. It is necessary that the slats of the back rest be arranged to pivot separately, or else bend, for in paddling, the back at the shoulder
blades twists from side to side with the strokes. Figure 4
shows a back rest that has been used a lot in a canoe which
has but one position for the paddler so that the back rest
simply hooks over the after coaming. The two slats are
fastened together with a small strip of oak that allows the
slats to spring back independently. Figure 5 shows a drawing
of a back rest that can be put in different positions to best
accommodate the paddler. On this drawing the numbered
parts are as follows:

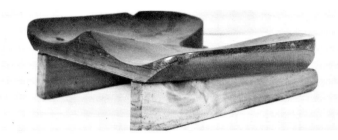

Figure 6.   Seat on skids.

Figure 7.   An adjustable foot rest.

1.   Hardwood block, with 11/16-inch holes fastened to coaming with No. 8 screws. If the coaming is thin, the screws can go through the coaming into the block. Make three of these blocks if three general positions of back rests are required.

2.   Block, similar to 1, but longer and with curved notches, as shown for removing back rest.

3.   Hardwood athwartships piece, curved about as shown. Ends ⅝ inch cylindrical. Middle section about 1⅛ by ¾ inch.

4.   Back rest slats, or staves. ⅜ inch thick, firm wood, edges well beveled.

5.   Clips of 1/16 inch or less phosphor bronze to allow the staves to spring back independently. These clips are about 1 13/16 inches long before bending, by 1 inch or less wide, and fastened to 3 with ¾ inch No. 10 wood screws; fastened to 4 with flat-headed No. 10 brass stove bolts, as shown.

This back rest is particularly adapted to canoes that have strong parallel coamings, such as the canoe shown here.

Seats

I have found that much the best seat for the double-paddle canoe is the regular-shaped wooden seat as used on the sliding seat of the rowing shell, such as the one shown in Figure 6. While it would not be difficult to make such a seat, I have always bought them from one of the shell builders. I usually raise the seat one or two inches above the floor boards and slant it back a few degrees by screwing tapered skids under the seat, as shown in the illustration. Then the seat can be slid fore and aft until the most comfortable posture is obtained, the seat being held amidships and parallel with the centerline by two small strips of wood secured to the floor boards as shown on the construction plan of the canoe.

Foot Rests

The foot rests (or what are called braces in a rowing boat) must be quite strong, for in excitement the legs are capable of pushing very hard on them. Figure 7 shows a type of foot rest that I have used in several canoes. It has a central

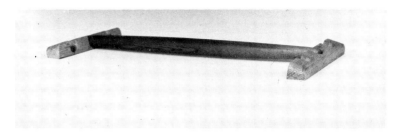

Figure 8.   Simple foot rest.

member which runs aft to a point easily reached by the hands when in a sitting position, at which point there is a brass toggle arrangement that runs in the slot between the floor boards. This foot rest can be strongly clamped in the desired position. But Figure 8 shows a foot rest which has proved quite as satisfactory and consists of only a stout tapered stick that sets in notched blocks at each end. This foot rest, however, should be above the floor boards enough so that the instep of the foot can brace against it.

With a proper light paddle, comfortable back rest and seat, and strong foot braces, the canoeist can be as comfortable as in an easy chair, can stop to rest without changing his position, and in fact he is able to travel in a comfortable seated position with far less energy than he would use in walking, and at a slightly higher speed.

2   HOW TO BUILD H-14

A sailing dinghy is a boat for young sailors to begin with; it is also a pretty nice thing to have on a hot summer afternoon or in the long twilight of our June evenings. There are evenings, too, when husband "homeward wends his weary way," that a cooling sail in the moonlight would seem to him far more pleasant than dressing for the country club, or trying to keep up with the Jones or Muskavitches.

Don't forget the boy, too, who will be halfway through his teens this summer. Maybe you can remember your first sail and its thrills, quite different perhaps but more pleasant than your first solo flight. Yes, the sailing dinghy is the best moving thing to start him off in — his early studies of space and time, we might say. There is nothing like a sailing dinghy to make a man of him; he will learn an appreciation of property and a sense of responsibility (for the dinghy is easily damaged). He will learn to be a good sportsman and take his lickings, wettings, and bumps perhaps more cheerfully in a dinghy than any other way. You will say, "Well, if all this is true, why haven't there been more sailing dinghies?" The answer is easy. Dinghies are very expensive. They are very easily damaged and quite expensive to re-

finish, paint, and varnish, etc. The Frostbite dinghies are too small, or too short, for two grown people to sail in.

So I decided to draw up a dinghy to be kept on a float, to be cheap to build, and to be at least as fast as the Frostbites; one that is light enough to haul out easily and lift on a trailer; one fourteen feet long, the same beam as the Frostbites, but with a little more sail.

Now it is quite easy to design a good expensive boat, but when you try to get out some plans for a boat which will stay tight, be light, and be easy or cheap to build, you have something to do. If this were not so, there would have been many of them in the last hundred years. So you see we must make some compromises, and fortunately most of them will not affect the general usefulness of the boat.

I have adopted dory construction for the framing, which means there are a few sawn frames (which will act as molds when the boat is being built), and a few bent frames between, which can be put in after the planking has been fastened, as in dory construction. The side planking (only two strakes) is also like dory construction. The bottom, which is quite flat, is batten seam construction, and, at the

An H-14 dinghy sailing in exotic surroundings with a light breeze and a fair tide.

SAIL PLAN OF H-14.   L.O.A 14', BEAM 4'6"

bow, where there is often trouble bending and twisting the planks, we have adopted a shoe piece or built-up forefoot made of layers of boards glued together and shaped out as model yachts are generally built. This piece is only about three feet long.

I have adopted the dagger type of centerboard because of its cheapness and because it gives more room in the boat. It also will save much trouble, for the usual long centerboard slot often opens and closes if a boat is kept on a float. The little boat is decked over at the sides and forward, perhaps enclosing more than one-third of her deck area, and this, besides keeping out a surprising amount of water, has a tendency to prevent the dinghy from twisting when driven hard.

As for the rig, I believe it is most important to have a sail plan that can be lowered away instantly, so I have adopted

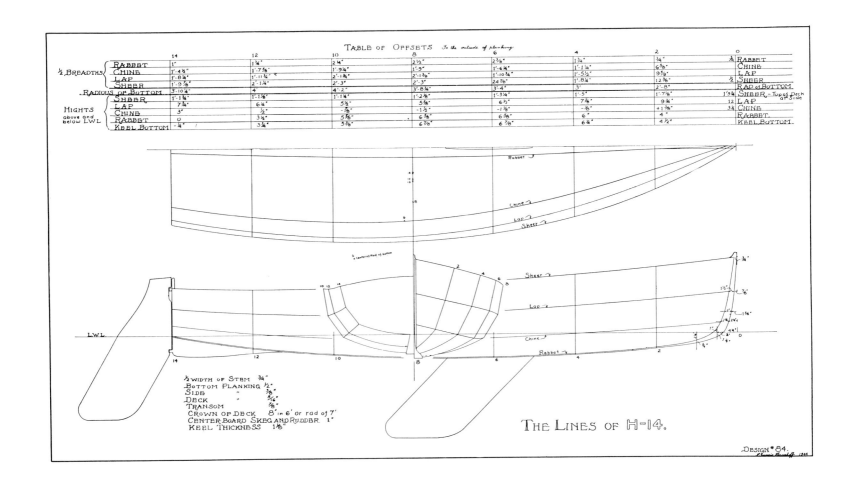

TABLE OF OFFSETS *To the outside of planking*

		14	12	10	8	6	4	2	0	
½ BREADTHS	RABBET	1"	1¾"	2¼"	2½"	2⅜"	1¾"	¾"	¾	RABBET
	CHINE	1'-4½"	1'-7⅝"	1'-9¼"	1'-9"	1'-6¼"	1'-1¼"	6⅝"		CHINE
	LAP	1'-8¼"	1'-11¾"	2'-1¾"	2'-1⅜"	1'-10¾"	1'-5½"	9⅝"		LAP
	SHEER	1'-9⅞"	2'-1¼"	2'-3"	2'-3"	24⅞"	1'-8¼"	12⅜"	½	SHEER
RADIOUS OF BOTTOM		3'-10¼"	4'	4'-2"	3'-8¾"	3'-4"	3'	2'-8"		RAD of BOTTOM
HIGHTS above and below LWL	SHEER	1'-1¾"	1'-1⅛"	1'-1¼"	1'-2⅛"	1'-3¼"	1'-5"	1'-7⅛"	1'9¾	SHEER - Top of Deck at Side
	LAP	7¾"	6¼"	5½"	5⅝"	6½"	7⅞"	9¾"	12	LAP
	CHINE	3"	½"	-⅞"	-1½"	-1⅛"	-⅛"	+1⅜"	3¼	CHINE
	RABBET	0	3½"	5⅜"	6⅜"	6⅝"	6"	4"		RABBET
	KEEL BOTTOM	-¼"	3¾"	5⅞"	6⅞"	6⅞"	6¼"	4½"		KEEL BOTTOM

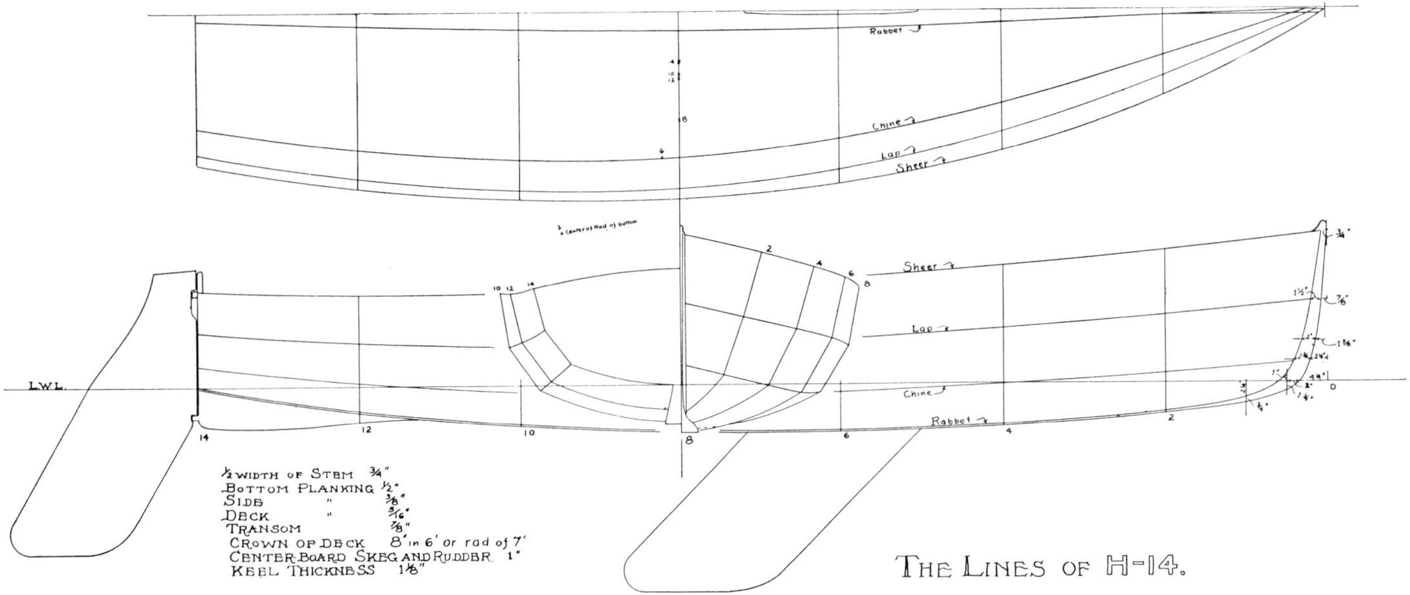

½ WIDTH OF STEM ¾"
BOTTOM PLANKING ½"
SIDE " ⅜"
DECK " 5/16"
TRANSOM ⅞"
CROWN OF DECK 8" in 6' or rad of 7'
CENTER-BOARD SKEG AND RUDDER 1"
KEEL THICKNESS 1⅛"

THE LINES OF H-14.

DESIGN # 84.
1944

an improved sliding gunter rig. With this rig, the dinghy can be rigged or unrigged very rapidly, and when reefed there will not be a long masthead above the sail which is often detrimental in a sailing dinghy.

In short, the dinghy is intended to be easy and quick to get under way, robust enough to leave in the sun and rain on a float, and lively enough for real sport in racing. If you prefer, you can have interchangeable centerboards, one ballasted with, say, forty pounds of lead for light crews in heavy weather. But for Junior or the ladies, when she is reefed down, she should be quite stable.

Of course you must understand this kind of boat cannot be built very lightly and have her cheap. The stripped hull will weigh over three hundred pounds, but you must remember this has an advantage, in that this amount of wood will make her quite buoyant when swamped and a safe life raft to cling to.

I believe this little craft will fill a long-felt want and furnish the sort of informal racing which is the most fun of all. She also would be a most excellent training boat at summer camps. She will not be too good to use on a picnic or attach the outboard to.

CONSTRUCTION PLAN

1. Special cast bronze stem-head to take shackle of halliard block (see detail).

2. The stem band and shoe are of ¾″ x ¼″ half-oval brass rod. Where the stem is narrow near the waterline, it will have to be reduced sideways. The forward strip is 5′9″ long. The two strips amidships are 6′6″ each. The after strip is 4′4″.

3. The stem is 1½″ thick full length and can be hackmatack, oak, or mahogany.

4. The breasthook should be about 1″ thick oak and well secured to the stem and clamp. Crowned to fit the deck.

5. The clamp can be oak ¾″ x 1⅛″, or spruce 1″ x 1¼″.

6. The chine piece can be oak 2″ x 5″, or larger, softer wood.

7. The frame on station 2 can be water-resisting laminated wood from ½″ to ⅝″ thick.

8. The battens can be oak, spruce, or fir, 1½″ x ⅝″.

9. The keel can be oak 1⅛″ thick, or mahogany 1¼″ thick. It is about 6¼″ wide and about 13′1″ long.

10. The lower section of the frames can be mahogany ¾″ thick, or oak ⅝″ thick.

11. The side section of the frames can be mahogany or oak ⅝″ thick.

12. The intermediate frames run only from the clamp to the chine piece and can be sprung in after planking. These can be oak about ½″ square.

13. The deck beams can be mahogany ⅝″ thick, or oak ½″ thick.

14. The transom can be ⅞″ oak or 1″ mahogany, or lighter and thinner if an outboard motor is not used.

15. The stem knee should be about 1″ thick of any wood that is preferred.

16. The centerboard logs should be oak, about 1¼″ thick and maybe 5″ wide.

17. The upper panel of the centerboard case can be most any variety of wood about ⅜″ thick, or laminated wood 5/16″ thick.

18. The forward and after pieces of the case should be oak 1¼″ thick; the after one is shaped to take the foot brace and support the thwart.

19. Clips of brass angle, about 1″ x 1″ x 14 gauge, or blocks

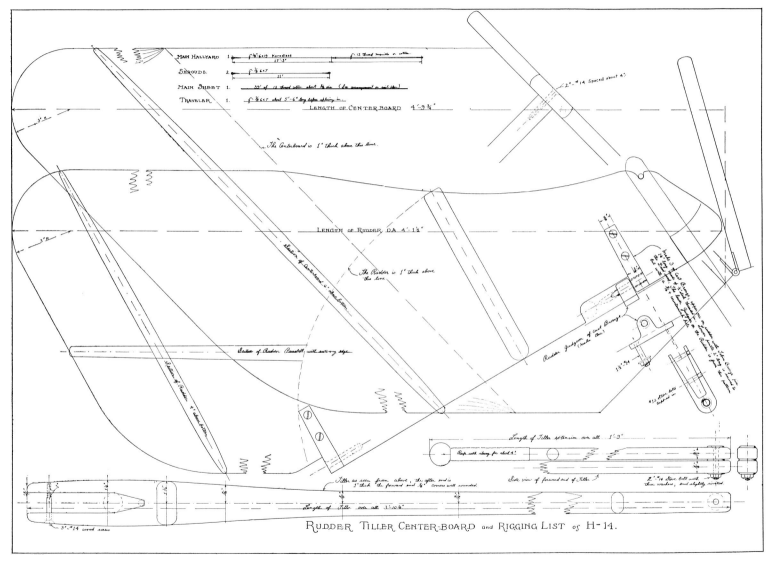

RUDDER TILLER CENTER-BOARD and RIGGING LIST of H-14.

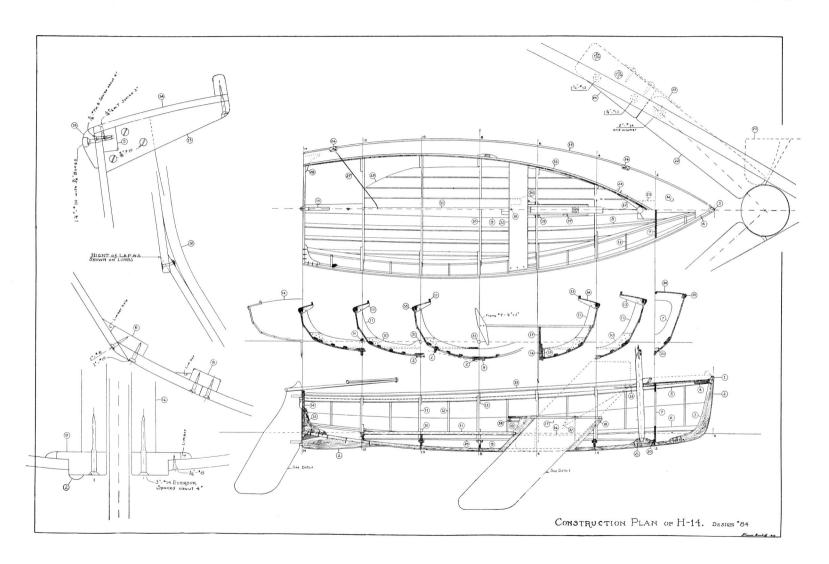

CONSTRUCTION PLAN OF H-14.   DESIGN "84

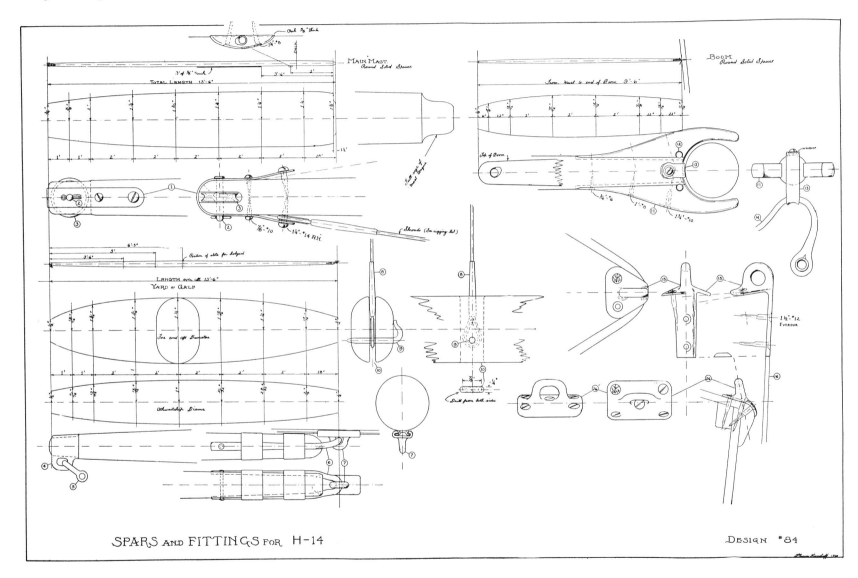

SPARS AND FITTINGS FOR H-14

DESIGN #84

① Mast head strap and shroud attachment, Phosphor Bronze 1/16" x 7/8" x 10".
② Sheave Pin, Of 7/16" Bronze Rod 2" long ~ dia 7/16 with cotter pin
③ Bronze Sheave with deep groove
④ If many dinghys are built it will pay to have a cast Bronze ferrule for the upper end of the yard for attaching the head of the sail
⑤ Merriman Fig-306-1/4" to shackle into head of sail.
⑥ 1/4" Tobin Bronze rod 12 1/2" long bent to make gooseneck for lower end of yard, secured with a through rivet and wire seizings
⑦ Special cast Bronze slide for foot of yard
⑧ Main Halyard (see rigging list).
⑨ 1/4" Tobin Bronze pin to secure main halyard; end bent over as desired for drawing
⑩ Slot through yard for eye of halyard 1/4" x 1 1/8"
⑪ Jaws of Boom 5/8 thick hard wood
⑫ Hole for tack lashing
⑬ Leather strip doubled and screwed to top of boom, for securing tack strap.
⑭ Tack Strap, 6 thread cotton or manila about 3' long thimble spliced in end
⑮ Stem Head fitting of cast Bronze
⑯ The upper end of the stem band can be flattened by hammering so it is about as shown
㉖ Special lashing eyes for shrouds and wire rope traveler (make 4) of cast Bronze.
   secured with five 1 1/2"-#14 Everdur screws

of square oak to secure frames to centerboard logs. They must be strongly secured to stand the strain of the bottom swelling.

20.   Angle clip of 1 1/4" x 1 1/4" brass to transfer thrust of mast to frame 2.

21.   Mast step of oak 2" deep, 3" wide, 9 1/2" long, with drain hole. Tongue of mast is 1 1/2" cylinder.

22.   Ratchet action mast partners of oak 7 1/16" x 1 3/4" x 3/4". Pivots on round-headed 2" No. 14 screw going up into coaming.

23.   Mainmast partner of oak 7" x 7" x 1". After end cut away as shown to 1/4" thickness to support No. 22.

24.   Oak backing piece for No. 22, 4" x 1 3/4" x 3/4", screwed up into coaming and down through deck.

25.   Phosphor bronze or hard-rolled brass spring 1/16" x 3 1/2" x 5/8".

26.   Special lashing eyes for shrouds (see detail on spar drawing). The same fitting is used for the wire rope traveler attachment, for it is found dinghies are often lifted by the traveler.

27.   Wire rope traveler of 1/4" 6 x 19 Korodless wire, spliced in so length from eye to eye is 5' in order that the same can be swung aft when rowing or using outboard motor.

28.   It would be a good thing to have oak quarter knees about 5/8" or 3/4" thick to support the stern for an outboard motor and for a place to lift when handling the boat.

29.   There are a number of ways to arrange floor boards or grating, but if they are permanently fastened down, they will act as buoyancy if the dinghy is swamped or will not float away in case of a capsize. The two central boards running between frames 6 and 10 should lift out easily for cleaning the bilge. The floor boards should be about 1/2" thick and have cleats underneath similar to a dory's floor boards.

30.   There should be a sponge hole both sides of the centerboard case, and this is a convenient place to have drain plugs each side.

31.   Removable foot brace to brace against when sailing. This must be very strong if two or three people push against it. Should be oak or hard wood 1 1/4" diameter, 5'3" long. The teats at the ends about 3/4" diameter. The foot brace fits into a hole forward and into a notch in frame 12 aft where it is tied down by a stout cord. Note the support on frame 10.

32.   The thwart should be well secured to oak lodging pieces about 3/4" x 1 1/2" x 11 1/2" and screwed to the centerboard case. This thwart is the principal support to the case and the only athwartship stay, so the auxiliary frame at 7 can be made to act as a knee as shown on the drawing. The thwart can be about 3/4" x 8" x 4'.

33.   Coaming oak or mahogany 5/8" thick and 1 3/4" deep forward, 1" amidships, 3/4" aft. Fastened with 3/4" No. 8 screws up through deck, spaced about 4", and 1 3/4" No. 10 up through deck beams.

34.   No doubt the easiest way to make the deck is to use two

strips of laminated wood about 20″ or more wide, joined over a batten on the centerline forward. If a good grade of laminated wood is used, the deck can be as thin as ¼″. However, if the deck is made of strips of cedar, it must be 5/16″ thick, with a batten under each seam.

35. The chafing strip should be oak or hard wood at least ⅝″ x 2″ amidships and tapered to smaller dimensions at the ends. It must be well secured between stations 2 and 4 because the shroud attachment, 26, is attached to it.

36. If the dinghy is to be hauled out on a float often, there should be chafing strips or bilge keels running from about station 6 to 8. They can be under the outer batten and well secured. The side next to the planking should be 1″ thick. If the chafing strips are capped with the same brass strip as the keel, they can be nicely tapered off at the ends.

37. Merriman Fig. 522, size 4″, on starboard side of centerboard case to belay main halliard.

38. Small wooden pin to secure mainsheet occasionally.

3   HOW TO BUILD H-28

All designs are a compromise in that the designer attempts to combine certain desirable features without sacrificing too much safety, comfort, and cost. H-28 was designed for the man who has only a limited time to sail but would like to go somewhere and back in that time. It was designed to be a boat that could be quickly gotten underway for a sail on a summer evening — a boat that could coast along in light breezes as well as stand up to anything. She is wider on deck than an ideal sea boat should be (particularly aft), but that is to secure maximum deck space and to make her dryer in a chop. A lively sea boat is no disadvantage on short trips such as H-28 would take.

Some of the principal objects of the design were to secure the maximum usable room for the cost without sacrificing looks and speed, and to make the boat as simple to build as is consistent with strength and long life. Whereas it is often said that a V-bottom boat is easy to build because the frames are straight and don't have to be steam bent, still, in the end, the work amounts to nearly the same, for a V-bottom practically has to have three keels (two chines and a keel) and many more joints to make watertight or they are apt to give trouble. A boat shaped like H-28, if half carefully built,

should stay entirely tight even if exposed to considerable strain or twisting.

The ballast, or lead keel, of H-28 is nearly all on the outside with a small amount inside to allow for differences in the weight of various power plants. A boat of this moderate draft, 3′6″, should have her ballast all outside if she should have to lay off a lee shore in a gale, when stability to carry some sail is much more desirable than the easier motion of a less-stiff boat. Besides, if she should take bottom in a seaway with the ballast all outside to take the shock without transmitting the strain through the wooden parts of the hull, she can pound a long time without starting a leak. But when much of the ballast is inside, the stoutest keel will soon come to grief when pounding on a rock or hard bottom. The first crack or shock usually starts a serious leak in the garboard, and if she should pound long or hard she would open up like a dump scow and let her load out. All boats run aground or take the bottom sooner or later, and an inside-ballasted boat is hardly trustworthy after that occasion. Besides that, inside ballast is one of the greatest nuisances in a boat of this size, for the bilge is always a mess and all the ballast should be removed when the boat is layed up in

the winter, or serious damage from frost and rot will result.

As for the proportion of beam and draft, we cannot suit all unless we design a rubber boat. I have no prejudices in these proportions, but to one who has become enamored of the craft used for cruising in England and Scotland, she will seem wide and shallow. I must admit, though, that the deep, narrow boats give a sense of security in night sailing and have greater head room. But for the man who lives in a shallow-water district, light draft is not only a virtue but an absolute necessity, so that to some Floridians, H-28 would seem too deep for navigating the swamps of their native state. H-28 is about as shallow as is practical for good windward performance without a centerboard, and deep enough to be really non-capsizable.

The Motor

I enjoy the interesting game of pitting my wits against the weather gods, and they always show their hand before they strike. Yes, I even take delight in using their energy to sail in the direction they have shown is to be the most advantageous, but unless one likes to think of tides and winds and clouds and has so arranged his life that he can go where and when he likes, he cannot indulge in this delightful game of cruising in the old-fashioned manner, where one discon-

The first H-28 was built with an extra large companionway hatch and a big hatch in the foredeck. Her designer would have approved of the former in a hot climate, but it is doubtful that the latter would have won his praise under any circumstances.

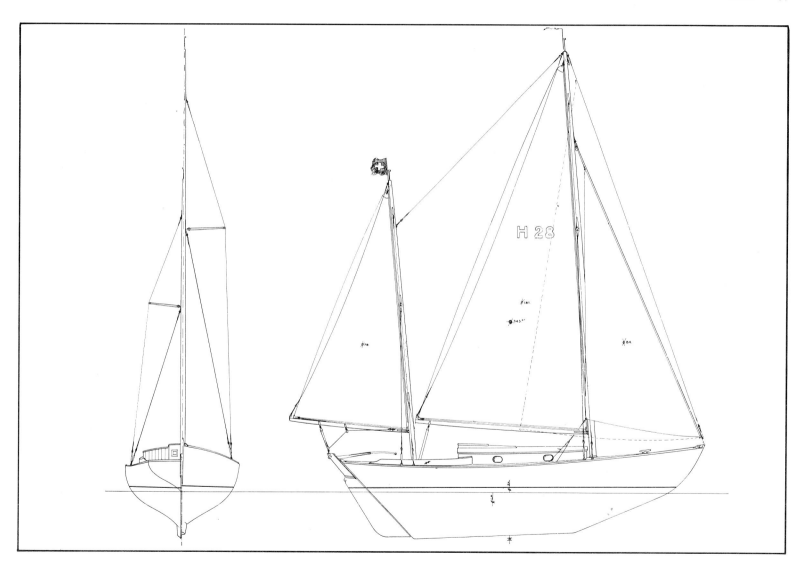

This H-28 was beautifully built on the Mediterranean coast of Spain.

nected oneself from business and family ties and went to worship in temples not made by human hands.

I fear most of the owners of H-28's will have to report to the office without fail on a Monday morning and even telephone Mother or Aunt Susie on Saturday night, and so had best have a motor. Now, motors like women are not all bad, but it must be admitted there is a great difference among them. I prefer the simple, clean, reliable ones, and admire the economical ones, and almost love the quiet ones that are small and don't smell, but here again we must make a compromise, as all through a yacht's design, for whereas the

small ones are economical, they are apt to be hot and smelly, while the big ones keep quiet and cool.

It would be far the best to have each owner choose his own engine, but for me the choice would be a small one with magneto ignition and impulse starter, as there would be no batteries and a very small amount of wiring. I might lay, for instance, in Menemsha Bight on a foggy night when the dampness penetrates everything, but would want an engine that would start positively early in the morning and carry me safely by the graveyard reefs of Cuttyhunk if there was a cross tide and no wind. On the design I show a bob-tailed Sea Scout made by the Gray Marine Motor Company, equipped with a magneto and impulse starter. Very few owners today realize how much noise and vibration comes from the reverse gear and how unnecessary that gear is to maneuver this kind of a boat, which will generally be brought up to a float under sail.

This brings up the matter of reduction gears. To me the only real important advantage of the reduction gear in a boat of this size is that it will allow a large and slow-turning propeller that will not be hopelessly ruined on its first contact with a lobster pot buoy or some other floating object.

The Sails and Rigging
The real driving power of a boat of this type is the sails and they should be judged by their nautical miles per hour per dollar, and by their reliability. Most of all to be considered is the joy of being noiselessly propelled over the ever-changing magic carpet of the sea and to contemplate the nights of relaxed slumber that follow an all-day sail.

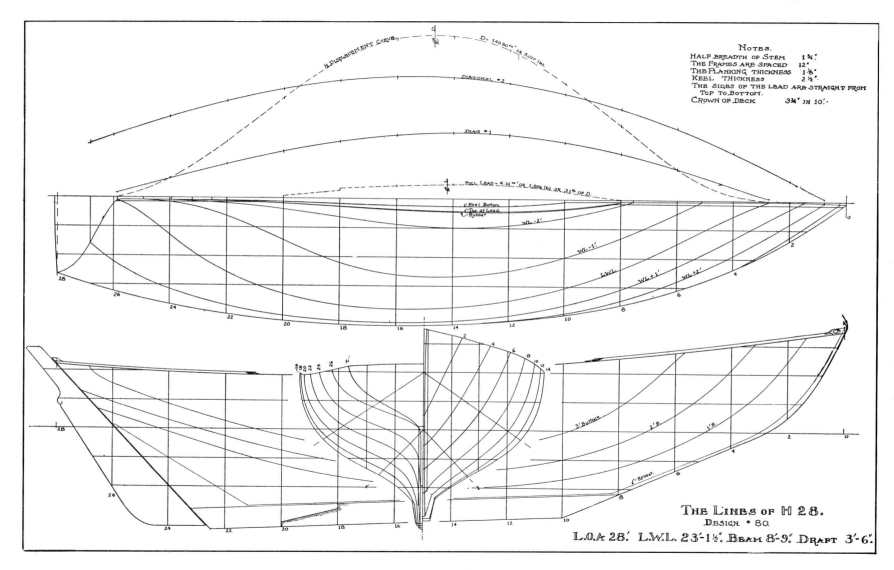

NOTES.
HALF BREADTH OF STEM   1¾".
THE FRAMES ARE SPACED   12".
THE PLANKING THICKNESS   1⅛".
KEEL THICKNESS   2½".
THE SIDES OF THE LEAD ARE STRAIGHT FROM
    TOP TO BOTTOM.
CROWN OF DECK   3¼" IN 10'.

THE LINES OF H 28.
DESIGN * 80.
L.O.A 28'. L.W.L. 23'-1½". BEAM 8'-9". DRAFT 3'-6".

TABLE OF OFFSETS FOR H-28
GIVEN IN FEET ~ INCHES ~ AND EIGHTS OF INCHES.

Station	Top of Deck at Side	Buttock 3'	Buttock 2'	Buttock 1'	Rabbet	Top of Lead	Profile	AT Deck	WL+3'	WL+2'	WL+1'	LWL	WL-1'	WL-2'	WL-3'	Rabbet	Top of Lead	Face	#1	#2	Station
0	3-6-0				3-8-2		3-6-0	0-1-0								0-1-6		0-1-0			0
2	3-2-5			2-6-0	0-9-0		0-5-6	1-4-3	1-3-0	0-9-2	0-3-3					0-1-6		0-0-4		0-8-4	2
4	2-11-4		2-2-6	0-6-7	-0-5-3		-0-6-3	2-4-4	1-10-4	1-3-4	0-6-6					0-1-6		0-0-4	0-5-0	1-7-1	4
6	2-8-6	2-5-6	0-6-7	-0-6-1	-1-3-1		-1-4-2	3-1-2	2-9-5	2-3-2	1-6-1	0-5-3				0-1-6		0-0-5	1-0-6	2-5-3	6
8	2-6-2	0-10-0	-0-4-6	-1-2-7	-2-0-5	-2-2-2	-2-2-1	3-7-5	3-5-7	3-1-1	2-4-7	1-3-3	0-2-2			0-1-6	0-0-6	0-0-6	1-7-1	3-1-7	8
10	2-4-0	-0-0-6	-0-11-7	-1-8-2	2-2-4	2-3-1	-3-0-0	3-11-7	3-11-3	3-7-7	3-0-6	1-11-1	0-7-4			0-4-3	0-3-6	0-1-0	1-11-5	3-7-7	10
12	2-2-1	-0-6-4	-1-3-7	-1-11-2	2-3-4	2-4-0	-3-1-0	4-2-5	4-2-4	4-0-0	3-6-1	2-5-4	0-10-7			0-6-0	0-5-1	0-2-7	2-2-6	4-0-1	12
14	2-0-1	-0-9-1	-1-4-7	-2-0-0	2-4-4	2-5-0	-3-2-0	4-4-0	4-4-0	4-2-2	3-9-2	2-8-1	0-11-6			0-5-7	0-5-1	0-3-1	2-3-4	4-2-4	14
16	1-11-5	-0-9-3	-1-4-2	-1-10-7	2-5-4	2-6-0	-3-2-7	4-4-3		4-3-3	3-9-6	2-7-7	0-10-5			0-4-6	0-4-4	0-2-6	2-2-4	4-2-6	16
18	1-10-7	-0-6-7	-1-1-1	-1-7-5	2-6-3	2-6-7	-3-3-7	4-2-6		4-2-4	4-0-5	2-2-4	0-7-5			0-3-5	0-3-3	0-2-2	1-11-5	4-0-7	18
20	1-10-4	-0-2-6	-0-8-7	-1-3-0	2-7-3	2-7-7	-3-4-6	4-2-6		4-0-5	3-3-5	1-5-0	0-4-5			0-2-3	0-2-2	0-1-4	1-7-4	3-9-4	20
22	1-10-7	+0-3-0	-0-3-0	0-8-4	2-2-4	2-8-7	-3-5-6	4-4-0		3-8-4	2-6-5	1-7-2	0-2-0			0-1-6	0-1-2	0-1-2	1-1-7	3-4-2	22
24	1-11-5	0-10-2	+0-3-3	-0-1-2	-1-0-1		-1-11-3 / 3-4-4	3-8-1		3-2-0	1-3-1	0-1-7				0-1-6		0-1-0	0-8-0	2-9-6	24
26	2-0-6	1-6-6	0-10-7	+0-6-0	+0-1-4		+0-1-5 / -2-0-4	3-2-5	3-2-3	2-3-0						0-1-6		0-2-6		2-1-6	26
28	2-2-3		+1-7-2	+1-1-5			+2-2-3 / +1-5-2	2-8-0	~												28
Transom			+1-3-2	+0-8-0				2-8-0	2-7-1	1-6-7	0-1-2	0-1-0	0-1-0					0-2-6	0-1-6	1-10-0	Transom

Altering the Design

If H-28's design is only slightly changed, the whole balance may be thrown out. If you equip her with deadeyes, build her with sawn frames, or fill her virgin bilge with ballast, the birds will no longer carol over her, nor will the odors arising from the cabin make poetry, nor will your soul be fortified against a world of warlords, politicians, and fakers.

You may not think this description of H-28 very helpful to a builder, and it may not be so, but first of all you builders or owners must be charged with sufficient ambition and desire to carry you through the disappointments of delay and expense. For the practical-minded, the exact description of each piece and part is shown on the construction plan, where they can be readily found without referring to some index of specifications.

I have now had enough years of experience in observing and inspecting the construction of small wooden yachts to know that the equipment, or lack of it, has such an influence on the technique of building that it is best for each builder to work the things out according to his likes and prejudices, and the final results may be quite equal. For instance, two quite good violins might be made in distant countries and a century apart, and the procedure of each step of manufacture be quite different, but if each of the builders had exactly the same picture in his mind of the finished article, in all probability the instruments would be very nearly alike. If either of these instruments came into the hands of one who loved and cherished it and studied its peculiarities, even if the owner were a Canadian woodchopper or a Baltimore belle, he could finally make it respond to all his moods and draw from it delightful melodies even when playing in the dark. But if, dear reader, either violin maker had listened to someone who could not design a violin or had changed it or mutilated it with parts belonging to some other type of music box (deadeyes and inside ballast) it could never be tuned again.

So, too, with H-28. If you love and cherish her, you can learn to draw sweet melodies from her and she will carry you through all gales and calms, for she is based on well-proven principles. She will lay-to well into the wind, under the mizzen, or steer well in a following sea and coast along in light weather.

In a great many ways H-28, I suppose, will be a successor to the Sea Bird, designed by the late C. D. Mower for the editor of *The Rudder*, Mr. Thomas Fleming Day, who was familiarly known as the Old Man (this being the term used on shipboard to designate the captain), and no doubt because he had some strong opinions. However, the Old Man took an unusual interest in Sea Bird and Mr. Mower made some nice drawings of her which have been hard for me to equal in draftsmanship.

Sea Bird's drawings were published in *The Rudder* in the year 1901, and I would recommend that those interested in building look them up and read the very fine description of building on page 429, November, 1901, for the boats are very much the same size.

As for speed in sailing, H-28 has the advantages of greater length of entering edge of sails (modern, high, narrow, sail plan); more stability and lateral resistance with an easier form to drive through the water.

	Sea Bird	H-28
L.O.A.	25' 9"	28'
L.W.L.	20'	23' 1½"
Beam	8'	8' 9"
Draft	2'	3' 6"
Sail area	340 sq. ft.	343 sq. ft.
Headroom	4'	4' 8"
Length of cabin house	8' 9"	10'
Cockpit area	18 sq. ft.	36 sq. ft.
Frame spacing	12"	12"
Size of frames	1¼"x2½"	1⅝"x1⅝"
Deck beams	1½"x2½"	1⅜"x2"
House beams	1"x1½"	¾"x1½"
Planking	1"	1"
Deck	⅞"	¾"
House deck	½"	⅝"

The greatest difference is in the amount of displacement — about 50 percent more on H-28 — and usable cabin room, maybe 100 percent more.

Getting Started

First of all it is usual to lay the lines of the yacht down on the floor, full size, and, if you want to do this, the most satisfactory way in most cases is to get some building paper (enough to cover a space about twenty feet by eleven feet). The building paper is what is generally used on a house under clapboards or between flooring. It comes in colors of light green and brownish pink. Get a grade which has a surface hard enough to draw on. Of course if your floor is smooth enough to draw on, the paper will be unnecessary, but the floor will have to be either painted black to be drawn on with soapstone chalk, or painted white if you are to use a lead pencil, so that the paper is often the best in the end, for it can be rolled up for future use if the yacht is set up on the floor where the lines would have been laid down.

Before tacking down the strips of paper, be sure the floor is swept well and the heads of protruding nails are driven down. On this design, the waterline length is the base line and all elevations are given in distances above and below it. After snapping the chalk line for the waterline, you can tack a batten along the line for temporary use of a large square for laying off the stations. It will probably be best for you to make up a light but stiff wooden square with one limb about six feet and the other about four feet because there will be many other uses for this square as the work goes on.

Of course I cannot here give full instructions for laying down a yacht, but be sure you have many battens, some very stiff for such lines as the sheer and some very light and flexible for the sections. Many yachts that I have designed were built without being laid down, as the builders had confidence in the table of offsets and simply laid off the sections for making the molds, keel, etc., full size. I would recommend this if you are familiar with every step of what you are doing. For most people, however, it is safer to lay the whole of the lines down full size.

Lead Keel

Lead is a wonderful material to make a keel from for it gets along well with the bronze keel bolts. It is ductile enough to absorb shocks when running aground. It can be melted at low temperature and is heavy. It also can be planed with a carpenter's plane. But I advise you to have your local foundry cast the keel for you, or you may find yourself in the same predicament that Cellini was in when he was casting the statue of Perseus, and have to tear down your neighbor's houses and fences to keep the pot boiling at the last minute.

The lead for H-28 is purposely shaped so it will be easy to make a pattern, or a wooden mold, to flow it into. In the latter case, flat boards about one-inch thick can form the sides, but the frame outside must be very strong, for the melted lead will press down and outward about 700 pounds for each square foot. So, besides strong cross pieces above and below the mold, it is well to have a few iron rods passing right through where the lead will be to hold the two sides from spreading. These rods, if heavily painted with graphite paint, will drive out easily when the mold is removed.

The mold should be backed up with tightly tamped earth on the outside to help support it between braces and to prevent the lead from running far if a leak is started when the side boards shrink or crack under the heat of casting. If the lead is cast for you by a professional foundryman, he will mold it right in the earth (probably dig a hole in his foundry floor) so he will require a pattern to cast from just as if it were to be of iron. And, by the way, for those who prefer an iron keel, it can be made the same size and shape as the lead one and the difference in weight simply made up by inside ballast. At any rate, in casting the lead keel be sure that at least one percent of antimony is added to it, for this stiffens up the lead enough so that it drills well and even planes better. On this design, the keel bolts are tapped into the top of the lead and it is almost impossible to tap pure lead, for it balls up the tap so that a clear thread is unlikely. When antimony is added to the lead, or junk lead is used, which has some tin, solder, or pewter in it, it seems to tap O.K. Be sure to drill a hole larger than is called for when tapping bronze or iron, because some of the lead will squeeze out and make a full thread, and remember that, as these bolts go into the lead about six times their diameter, a perfect thread will not be necessary. In drilling and tapping, use kerosene for lubricant; in screwing down the bolts use heavy oil.

Setting Up

There are many different methods of setting up the framing of a yacht and they all have their advantages and disadvantages, but it is likely that most amateurs would prefer to build her right-side-up and bend the frames inside ribbands or battens bent over the molds. This is the most common way in most places. A perfectly good job can be done on a yacht of this size and shape by simply planking her up over the molds. As each mold is removed one by one, frames are steam bent over the mold to approximate shape and fastened in place by fastenings in the same holes that held the planks on the molds. Be sure to keep battens or temporary deck beams across the yacht so she will not spread at the deck line when the molds are removed. This is the simplest and cheapest method I know of and perfectly satisfactory. It is the method that was used by the late John Harvey, who for

many years had charge of the small boat building department of the George Lawley and Sons Corporation.

No matter what system is used for setting up or bending the frames, it is well to have the floor timbers bolted in place on the keel first so they can have their outer faces correctly lined up and beveled to receive the planks, for much of the strength of the yacht will depend on a good wood fit between the planking and the floor timbers. The first few frames at the bow can be sawn frames, as they are so straight that the grain can run a long distance on them. They will be as strong as steam-bent frames and they can be beveled so their lower ends will fit on the floor timbers and their upper ends on the clamp. This is not so with the usual bent frames near the ends of a yacht, where the planking is not very parallel with the center line.

The clamp of H-28 is made in two pieces as is done on larger yachts and sometimes is referred to as a shelf and clamp. It is done on this design as it is much easier for the amateur to bend in two light pieces than one stiff, square one and, as this boat has such a long cockpit and cabin house, the deck beams need the additional support this arrangement gives.

Materials

There are a great many varieties of oak and most of them are very poor indeed, for they soon rot. The true white oak is one of the best things God gave us here in New England, and I will try to describe it because every lumberman will attempt to palm something else off on you. He (for the white oak is very masculine) is not called white oak because

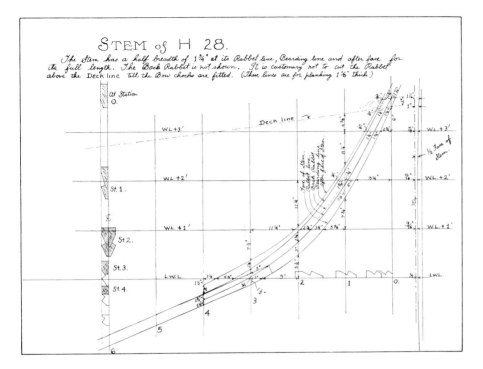

STEM of H 28.

The Stem has a half breadth of 1¾" at its Rabbet line, Bearding line and after face for its full length. The Back Rabbet is not shown. It is customary not to cut the Rabbet above the Deck line till the Bow chocks are fitted. (These lines are for planking 1⅛" thick.)

the wood is white or light color, but because as you walk through the woods his bark has quite a light shade in contrast with the rest of the forest, and when the breeze lifts or turns the leaves, their undersides are quite light. His botanical name is *Quercus alba* and I would call him *Quercus alba connecticus,* because the best ones grow in Connecticut, though there are many in Rhode Island and Massachusetts, and he is found all the way from Canada to Cape Hatteras. The farmers sometimes call him a pasture oak, and the small

trees are called basket oaks, as the old-time bushel baskets and many articles for hard use were made of him. White oak is without doubt the best wood in the world for the frames of small boats.

The wood itself is a brownish-green color and I cannot describe it better than to say it resembles laminations of cat gut and horn in thin, alternate layers, and it acts like it. Patient readers, I apologize for taking so much space for *Quercus alba,* but he is an acquaintance worth making, for he can be bent into frames without breaking and will last indefinitely. You will practically have to use white oak for the frames and, if you can, use it for the stem, keel, floor timbers, and stern post; it would also be good for the deck beams and transom, but here yellow bark oak will do.

The so-called hurricane pine — that is, our native soft pine — is a little different from the regular large forest white pine named *Pinus strombus,* but as no two botanists agree as to the exact number of varieties in any region, we shall have to go by local names. The hurricane pine around here (Massachusetts) is the variety the old-fashioned cabinetmakers and boatbuilders called punkin' pine. It is of a pinkish, yellow color and one of the nicest woods to work. It does not swell or shrink much, or rot easily, but do not confuse it with some of the western and California pines which rot very quickly. If you can get some of this hurricane pine, even if it has some knots in it, it will make most excellent decking, very good planking, and the very best interior trim.

For planking, if you use fir, which is called for on the construction plan (because it is the cheapest satisfactory wood for the purpose), be sure that it is all rift-grain and of fine texture and has been kiln-dried down to the same moisture content that commercial flooring is. Of course there are a number of very good woods for planking, but in most cases they are expensive.

As for the metals, you will do well if you stick to Tobin bronze for everything, except the screws which we will speak of later. Tobin bronze is like white oak — it will bend without breaking and last indefinitely. It also is a pleasure to work. Almost all boatbuilders today agree that Everdur screws are the cheapest in the end, for so few of them break in driving even if the hole is not exactly the right size; and, of course, Monel screws are very fine, also. But no matter what sort of screws you use, do not rub them on soap, as so many writers advise, but use a heavy grease to lubricate them. Soaps nearly all have strong chemicals in them which shorten the life of screws while grease preserves them.

The canvas for the deck and deckhouse is another material on which many builders go wrong. The proper thing to use is loosely woven light cotton sheeting, and if this material is set on a deck well coated with white lead and oil paint, the paint will penetrate up through the sheeting and meet, or amalgamate, with the later coats of paint on top so that a solid, long wearing and watertight cover is made. Strange to say, this is the place where the cheapest material is the best and, besides, the cotton sheeting can be bought in very wide strips.

Paints

A whole lot could be said about paint, for on this subject in particular, there is a lot of misinformation. You hear some people say, "Save the surface and you save all," but this is far from the truth in boat construction. Many of the modern paints and lacquers are quick and easy to apply, but they do not penetrate. They make a hard shell on the surface so that at the seams, and particularly at the fastenings, the water gets below the surface and causes the wood to swell and gives a chance for rot to start. No doubt you have noticed how the fastenings will stain and corrode under these hard surface lacquers. When a penetrating paint like linseed oil, lead, and turpentine is used, the texture of the wood for some distance in is sealed or filled with a water-repelling substance.

It is very easy to mix your own paints and you can vary them to meet your own needs by using only a little common sense. If you are bound to use the more modern paints with a cellulose base, or the varnishes used today, be sure to first put on a filler coat of a mixture the paint-makers recommend and sell for this particular purpose, and that will, to a certain extent, seal or fill the wood underneath.

Engine Installation

The propeller is set off center for the six following good reasons:

1. The propeller shaft does not interfere with the normal keel bolts, which are very important in this region.
2. The yacht is faster and more economical under power.
3. The yacht is faster under sail.
4. The yacht steers better under power.
5. The yacht steers better under sail.
6. If it is decided to remove the motor to make a straight

sailer, or to set up a different shaft line for a different motor, the matter is much simplified with the off-center screw.

As to number 2, actual experience has proven that the off-center propeller increases the speed or economy from ten to twenty percent over a center-line propeller. The reason for this is that, as a vessel passes through the water, she gathers up a swirl of eddies caused by skin resistance, and under the stern at the center line considerable water is following along with the vessel. Now, if you place your propeller in this wake and upset its natural eddies which are decreasing surface resistance, and put in its place a propeller slip stream going thirty percent faster than the vessel, then you will probably increase the total resistance some fifteen percent. To check on this, ask some ex-skipper of one of the World War II 110-footers how his center engine compared with his wing engines for power.

Engine Bed

I should prefer to have the engine bed made of angle iron or pipe properly folded, forged, or welded at the engine lugs, etc. The ordinary wooden engine logs prevent one from reaching around and wiping off the crankcase and are a fire menace, as they are often saturated with oil and gas. On H-28 the after, outer engine lug or support comes right out to the planking, so that a properly shaped block at this point will hold the engine from fore and aft and sidewise motion, if there is a diagonal brace to one of the other supports, so that the other supports can be run directly to a floor timber. With a little ingenuity a quite simple metal engine bed can be made, and sometimes it is advisable to do away

entirely with the shoe the engine maker has furnished for a wooden log.

Other Metal Fittings

Throughout the design I have tried to use stock fittings, but in the case of the rudder pintles and gudgeons I am unable to find a suitable pattern, so that these and the spar fittings I have designed will require three quite simple patterns and a little machine work.

Spars

All the spars are of rectangular section and so are about as easy to make as a long box. Their flat sides make the attachment of the shrouds more efficient. These reasons are why I invented the rectangular spar construction some twenty years ago, and their use is now quite universal. On H-28, the forward and after staves of the masts, and upper and lower staves of the boom, have a slight rabbet cut in them which you can easily do with a rabbet plane by tacking a batten along to guide the plane. This is done to hold the side pieces in place when gluing up. The principal trick in making this sort of spar is to hold it straight and stop it from twisting when gluing up, and this can often be done along the side of a building by nailing pieces of wood out at right angles to the studding so the building and the strips hold the staves straight in two directions with room for clamps between.

Rigging and Ground Tackle

The sizes of rigging given are the minimum that would be practical. For hard use the next larger size could be used if

RIGGING AND BLOCK LIST FOR H 28
DESIGN #80.
9,000 lbs Displacement.

STANDING RIGGING

NAME of PART.	NUMBER REQUIRED	ARRANGEMENT.	SIZE	MATERIAL	FITTINGS.	BLOCKS ETC.	RIGGERS NOTES.
HEAD STAY.	1	about 30'-11"	3/16"	6×7 Korodless.	2 meriman Thimble Fig 383-#3	1 meriman Turnbuckle Fig 377 - 1/4"	
FORE STAY.	1	Exactly 24'-9"	1/4"	6×7 Korodless.	2 meriman Thimble Fig 383-#4		
MAIN UPPER SHROUDS	2	about 27'-3"	3/16"	6×7 galv Cast steel	4 meriman Thimble Fig 383-#3	2 meriman Turnbuckles Fig 377-1/4"	
MAIN LOWER "	2	about 17'	5/16"	6×7 galv Cast steel.	4 meriman Thimble Fig 383-#5	2 meriman Turnbuckle Fig 377-3/8"	
MAIN STANDING BACKSTAYS if used	2	about 33'-9"	1/8"	6×7 Korodless.	2 meriman Thimble Fig 383-#1 / 2 open " 1/8"	2 meriman Turnbuckle Fig 377-1/4" / 2-3/16" galv Steel Chain Shackle	
SPRING STAY.	1	Seizing wire about 17'-3"	1/8"	6×7 Korodless.	2 open Thimble 1/8"	1-3/16" galv Steel chain Shackle	
MAIN BOOM LIFT.	1	Cotton line about 27'-9"	1/8"	6×7 galv Cast Steel.	2 open Thimble 1/8"	1-3/16" galv Steel chain Shackle	
MAIN BOOM CROTCH Attached to mizzen mast	1	3'-6" see detail on boom drawing	1/4"	6×7 Korodless	2 open Thimble 1/4"	Attachments shown on boom drawing	
MIZZEN UPPER SHROUDS.	2	about 19'-1"	3/16"	6×7 galv Cast steel	4 meriman Thimble Fig 383 #3	2 meriman Turnbuckle Fig 377-1/4"	
MIZZEN LOWER SHROUDS.	2	about 12'	1/4"	6×7 galv Cast steel	4 meriman Thimble Fig 383 #4	2 meriman Turnbuckle Fig 377-5/16"	
MIZZEN BOOM LIFT.	1	Cotton line about 18'	1/8"	6×7 galv Cast steel	2 open Thimble 1/8"	One galv Steel Chain Shackle 3/16" or larger	
MIZZEN BACK STAY.	1	3'-9"	5/16"	6×7 galv Cast steel.	1 meriman Thimble Fig 383-#5 / 1 open Thimble 3/16"	1-meriman Turnbuckle Fig 377-3/8" Short	

RUNNING RIGGING.

NAME of PART.	NUMBER REQUIRED	ARRANGEMENT.	SIZE	MATERIAL	FITTINGS.	BLOCKS ETC.	RIGGERS NOTES.
BALLOON JIB HALLYARD if used	1	63'	1-1/8" Cir or 3/8" Dia	Cotton Linnen or manila	1 meriman Snap Shackle Fig 391-#1	One meriman Fig 363 #1 Front Shackle	
JIB HALLYARD	1	22' wire 26' rope	1/8" wire / 5/16" Dia	6×19 Korodless / Cotton	1 meriman Snap Shackle Fig 391-#1	One meriman Fig 363 #1 Front Shackle / One " " 370-A #0	
MAIN HALLYARD	1	Sheave in mast head 28' wire 32' rope	3/16" wire / 3/8" Dia	6×19 KORODLESS / Cotton or Manila	2 Open thimbles 3/16"	One galv Steel Chain Shackle 3/16" / One meriman Fig 370-A #1	
MIZZEN HALLYARD	1	Sheave in mast head 21' wire 23' rope	1/8" wire / 5/16" Dia	6×19 Korodless / Cotton or manila	2 Open thimbles 1/8"	One galv Steel Chain shackle 1/4" / One meriman Fig 370-A-#0	
BALLOON JIB SHEETS.	1 Pair	Each 22'	1-1/8" cir or 3/8" Dia	Cotton Linnen or manila	2 open thimbles 3/8"	One galv Steel Anchor shackle 5/16" / 6-meriman Fig 422-#1 (for jibs)	
JIB SHEETS.	1 Pair	2' wire 35' rope	3/16" / 3/8" Dia	6×19 Korodless / Manila	2 open thimbles 3/16"	2-meriman Blocks Fig 364-#1 / 1-galv Steel anchor shackle 1/4"	
MAIN SHEET.	1	On boom 60' on mizzen mast 1'-9" above cockpit floor	1-1/8" Cir or 3/8" Dia	Cotton Linnen or manila	none	1 meriman 352-#2 front Shackle and becket / 1 " 440-A-2-1/4" on main boom / 1 " 3-1/8" mizzen mast	
MIZZEN SHEET	1	On boom 35' on rudder	1-1/8" Cir or 3/8" Dia	Cotton Linnen or manila	none	1 meriman 352-#1 front Shackle and becket / 1 " 440-A-1-3/4" on mizzen boom / Special fitting on rudder head	
ANCHOR WARP.	1	about 20 Fathoms	2" Cir or 5/8" Dia	MANILA	none	30 lbs-three piece Herreshoff type anchor	
TOW ROPE	1	about 15 Fathoms	2-1/2" Cir or 13/16" Dia	MANILA	none		
DOCKING LINES	2	about 10 Fathoms	2" Cir or 5/8" Dia	MANILA	none		
CLEW OUTHAUL TACKLES.	2	For main and mizzen (see boom drawings for arrangement)				1-meriman Fig 409-B #1 - main / 1 " " - " #0 - mizzen.	

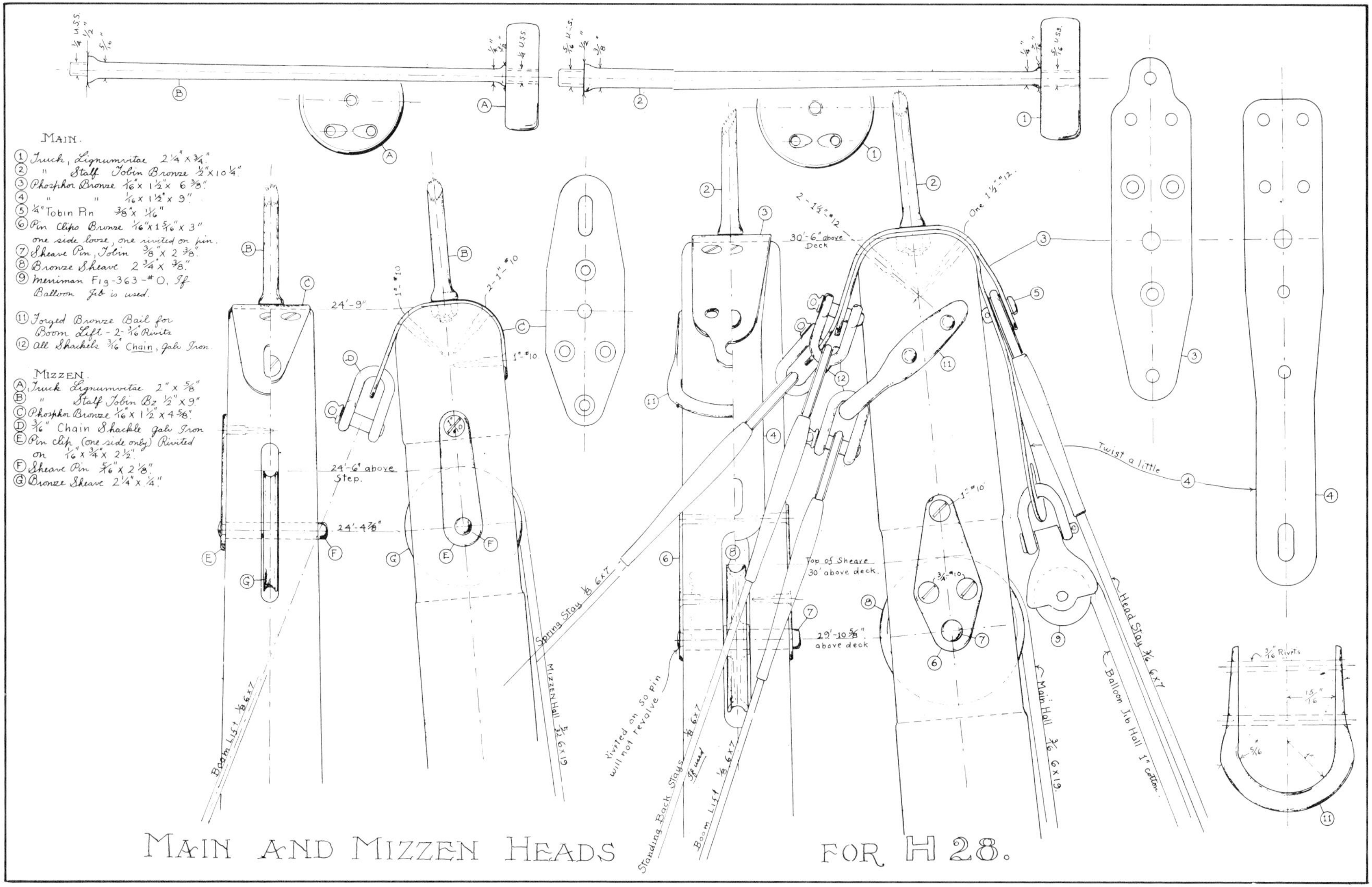
MAIN.
(1) Truck, Lignumvitae 2¼" x ¾".
(2) " Staff Tobin Bronze ½" x 10¼".
(3) Phosphor Bronze 1/16" x 1½" x 6⅜".
(4) " " 1/16 x 1½" x 9".
(5) ¼" Tobin Pin ⅜" x 1/16"
(6) Pin Clips Bronze 1/16" x 1 5/16" x 3" one side loose, one riveted on pin.
(7) Sheave Pin, Tobin ⅜" x 2⅜".
(8) Bronze Sheave 2¾" x ⅜".
(9) Merriman Fig-363-#0. If Balloon Jib is used.
(11) Forged Bronze Bail for Boom Lift - 2-3/16" Rivets
(12) All Shackels 3/16" Chain, Galv Iron.
MIZZEN.
(A) Truck Lignumvitae 2" x ⅝"
(B) " Staff Tobin Bz ½" x 9"
(C) Phosphor Bronze 1/16" x 1½" x 4⅝".
(D) 3/16" Chain Shackle Galv Iron
(E) Pin clip (one side only) Riveted on 1/16" x ¾" x 2½".
(F) Sheave Pin 5/16" x 2⅛".
(G) Bronze Sheave 2¼" x ¼".
24'-9"
24'-6" above Step.
24'-4⅞"
30'-6" above Deck
Top of Sheave 30' above deck.
29'-10⅝" above deck
One 1½"-#12
2-1½"-#12
2-1"-#10
Twist a little
Spring Stay ⅛ 6x7
Boom Lift ⅛ 6x7
Mizzen Hall 5/32 6x19
Riveted on so pin will not revolve
Standing Back Stays ⅛ 6x7
Boom Lift ⅛ 6x7
Main Hall 3/16 6x19
Balloon Jib Hall 1" cotton
Head Stay 3/16 6x7
3/16 Rivets

MAIN AND MIZZEN HEADS FOR H 28.

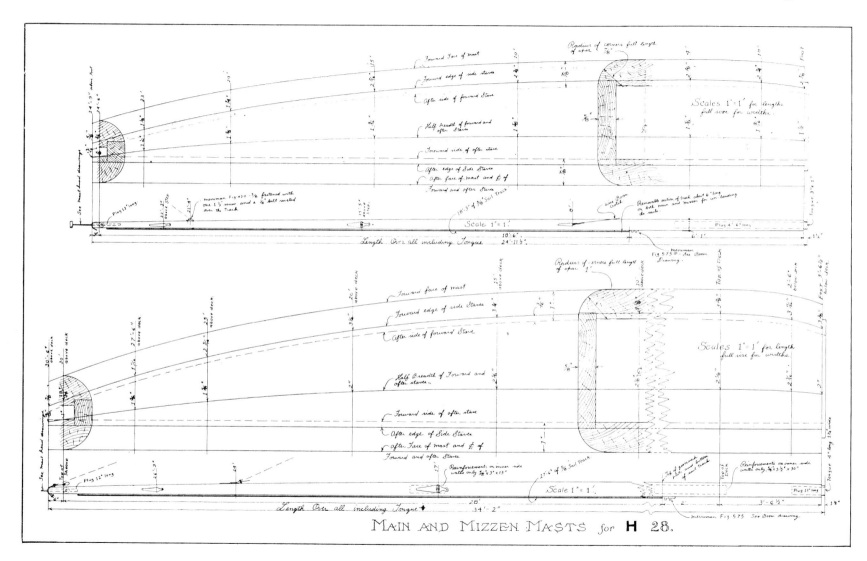

MAIN AND MIZZEN MASTS for **H** 28.

desired, of course with a suitable increase of sizes of blocks, etc. On account of cost, Korodless or rustless steel wire is only specified where wear or strain make it advisable, but rustless steel wire would be best throughout and possibly the cheapest in the end.

As for the ground tackle, if two anchors are preferred, then one of twenty-five pounds and one of fifteen pounds would be about right. For the second anchor, the docking lines or tow rope could be used. The weights of anchors specified only apply to the Herreshoff type. An increase of ten or fifteen percent in weight would be necessary for all other types. For cleats see the list on the boom drawing.

The Cabin
What a joy is a sweet-smelling, spotless cabin, with all clothes neatly stowed high and dry. What a joy to sit in such a cabin under the soft glow of a kerosene lamp and study the chart for an even more snug and romantic cove than the one you are anchored in and lay a course to regions even farther from the maddening crowds: places where men are sailors or farmers and can converse directly with the gods and can feel the pulse of nature and tell what the weather is going to be without benefit of radio. I can, or think I can, design a cabin plan for H-28 for those who want to go to where the water is clean, the pine trees are green, and the offshore breeze is laden with ozone, and where breathing, living, and sailing are joys.

It is much easier for me to write about cabin plans of a boat of this size than to draw them up. Also, if I drew two hundred different plans, none of them would be ideal for each family, climate, or purse. An old bachelor like myself, living north of Cape Cod, could start out on a cruise with remarkably simple equipment. It could be divided up into two categories:

1. Those things normally kept on board.
2. Those things jammed into a duffle bag or two which might be called expendable supplies.

The things kept on board might be the stove, pressure cooker, pipe berths, Hudson Bay blankets, oilskins, a clam hoe, and, because a cabin does not look homelike without it, also a gun. Oh, yes; and the cedar bucket. The expendable supplies would be clothes, shoes, food, some reading material, and a camera.

I will take most of these items of equipment up later and describe their particular functions. But first, if you can bear with it, I will tell you some of the reasons how and why I have made their selection. If I appear egotistical and use the word *I* rather often, this is not intended to give the impression of self-appointed authority but rather because it is nearly unavoidable in describing the experiences of the first person singular.

It has so happened that I have made short trips or cruises in about fifty different small craft that ranged from open boats to steam yachts, and lived two whole winters on them in New England waters. Several of these craft were of my design. My first cruises were all on steam yachts, and it is told that the first time I boarded ship was in a baby carriage. This was in the eighteen-nineties. I can't say I gained much nautical knowledge then, being under the watchful eye of a nurse and a mother. Life on board was very much as on

LIST OF CLEATS FOR H 28				
WHERE USED	NUMBER REQUIRED	LENGTH	LOCATION	"Notes"
mooring cleat	1	10"	See construction plan	The cleats here specified
main halyard	1	5½"	Starboard side mast 15" above deck	are Wilcox, Crittenden Fig 4020
jib halyard	1	4½"	Port side mast 15" above deck	But any of the other makes of
Balloon jib halyard	1	4½"	under gooseneck 15" above deck	the so called hollow cleats
jib sheets	2	4½"	on cockpit combing	might do. — Also wooden cleats like the attached sketch
mizzen halyard	1	4½"	Starboard side mizzen mast 5' above step	could be used in all cases
main sheet	1	5½"	lee side mizzen mast 4' above deck	except the mooring cleat which
mizzen sheet	1	4½"	on starboard side mizzen from 18" aft of mast	should be strong and well
main clew outhaul	1	3½" Fig 408	starboard side of Boom 11'-6" aft of mast	fastened.
mizzen clew "	1	2¾" Fig 408	starboard side of mizzen 6' aft of mast	

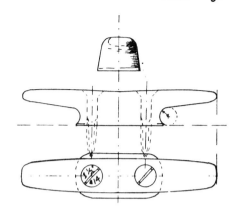

shore. Since then I have gradually descended 'till my last cruises were in kayaks, which have had the advantage of bringing me much closer to the water — in fact I could sit right in them without having my diapers changed, the thing I wanted to do from the very beginning. I have never made any long ocean voyages in small craft or had the least desire to do so, preferring rather to anchor each night in a well-sheltered cove, walk along the waterfront of its picturesque village, and pass the time of day with some waterside character who was whittling a plug for a bunghole that never existed.

I was first initiated into the virtues of simplicity as a lad of about sixteen, when I went on a couple of trips on the Q-boat *Dorothy Q*, owned by Hollis Burgess. *Dorothy Q* had about the same cubic feet of cabin as H-28, though twice her draft and three times her sail area, but her paid hand is our present subject (for he was my mentor). This son of the sea of about seventy winters Hollis annually took from the Old Sailor's Home at Boston. He was one of those hardy perennials who subsisted mostly on rum and tobacco. In his voyage through this life, he was not hampered by any other possessions than the few things attached to his body, which were his clothes, a glass eye, a steel hook in lieu of a right hand, a sheath knife, and a plug of tobacco. His body seemed immune to germs and the ravages of time as some copper-sheathed teak planking. Not one piece of clothes would he take off on the hottest day, or add to in a rainy nor'easter. He could make a pier head leap, arrive on board en masse, complete, ready for instant action. He lived aboard the *Dorothy Q* without benefit of heat, light, or pillow. But what I am getting at is his cabin arrangement. He had an exact place for everything; the anchor warp, ditty bag, and reefing tackle were as reverently displayed as the chalice and relics on some high priest's altar.

The chart, compass, and binoculars — those symbols of his calling — he placed and rearranged as carefully as a lady arranging a bouquet of flowers. When in port these decorations were enhanced by a tasteful addition of the marline-

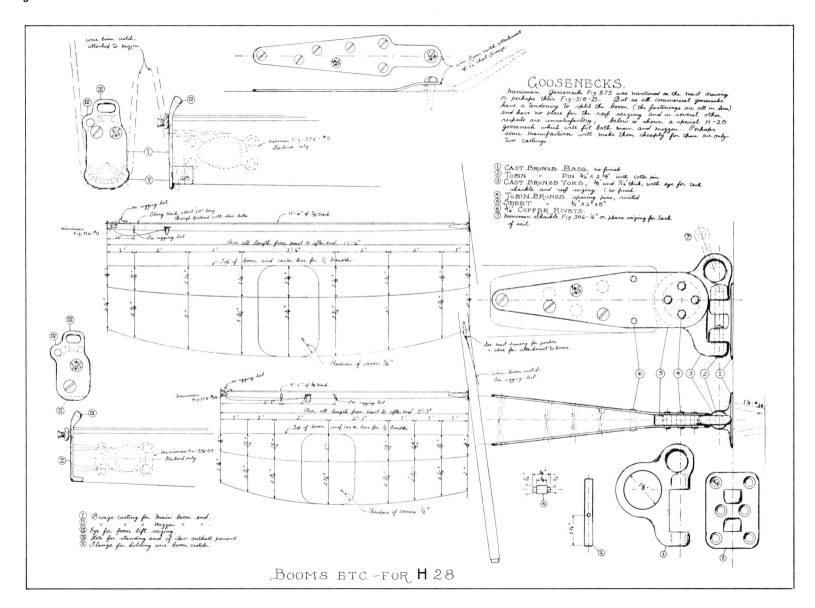

GOOSENECKS.

Merriman Gooseneck Fig 575 was mentioned on the mast drawing or perhaps their Fig-518-B. But as all commercial gooseneck have a tendency to split the boom (the fastenings are all in line) and have no place for the reef seizing and in several other respects are unsatisfactory, below is shown a special H-28 gooseneck which will fit both main and mizzen. Perhaps some manufacturer will make them cheaply for there are only two castings.

① CAST BRONZE BASE, no finish.
② TOBIN   "   PIN ⅜"×2⅜" with cotter pin.
③ CAST BRONZE YOKE, ⅜ and ¼" thick, with eye for tack shackle and reef seizing. (no finish.
④ TOBIN BRONZE spacing pins, riveted.
⑤ SHEET   "   ¼"×2"×8".
⑥ ¼" COPPER RIVETS.
⑦ Merriman Shackle Fig 386-¼" or plane seizing for tack of sail.

Ⓘ Bronze casting for main boom end.
Ⅱ   "   "   "   mizzen   "   ".
Ⅲ Eye for boom lift seizing.
Ⅳ Hole for standing end of clew outhaul pennant.
Ⅴ Flange for holding wire boom crotch.

BOOMS ETC.-FOR H 28

spike, fid, and serving mallet as he sat arming the sounding lead and rechecking the marks and deeps on the lead line. And so the olfactory nerves could share this enchantment, a ball of marline, a hank of oakum, and some tarred hemp lay on the transom. What a setting this was for the yarn which was always forthcoming, for this son of the sea was both playwright and actor. As he approached the point where the great tragedy was to be re-enacted (it might have been the fall of the mizzen as the waterspout passed over them in the Bay of Bengal), he pounded on the foghorn with his steel hook and removed his glass eye lest that orb, like the mizzen, should crash in the confusion. But as the weather cleared and a jury rudder was rigged, he snapped it back in place, for he handled this optic as if he were a Hindu magician.

Since that time I have designed many cabins, some paneled in teak, upholstered in leather; others in Chinese Chippendale style with *toile de Jouy* covered walls and blue leaded-glass cupboards, tiled bathrooms, and streamlined galleys, sometimes assisted by an interior decorator or guided by a "dry" architect, who specialized in onshore construction, but never have I equaled the pure nautical simplicity of the *Dorothy Q's* cabin or its charm, where each decoration was a sailorman's symbol, for what is there more pleasant to contemplate than the polished log and its rotor, or the folded trysail — that auxiliary motor. Well, to get back to the H-28's cabin.

Pipe Berths

So few people nowadays are acquainted with the many tricks of a pipe berth that I will give them some space. In the first place a pipe berth can be made the most comfortable of all beds, for as you use it it sags at the shoulders and hips 'till it is molded to your particular shape. It can be triced up or let down so the weather or leeward berth is level when sailing. It is cool in the summer and warm in the winter. When closed up it makes a comfortable back behind the cabin seat or transom. When in folded position it makes a convenient press which can hold all one's clothes and belongings so nothing will clutter up the cabin and one can instantly get at any of his personal gear which is wanted with a change of weather.

When a pipe berth is let down, it should be three or four inches above the transom under it so you can stow here the things normally kept back of it during the day. Some of the best features of pipe berths are that they are cheap, light, and easily removed for washing the cabin or painting. They can easily be taken on deck for a sunning or drying. But best of all, with a pipe berth you can have several cabin plans. Their only attachments to the hull are quite simple hooks, so by having these hooks at various places on the frames you can change your cabin plan on the H-28 so she has two, three, or four berths as the occasion arises (of course, leaving the unused berths ashore) — maybe the berths way aft and a coal-burning stove forward. I use seizing wire for lacing on the berth bottoms because they require less adjustment from stretching. On English yachts the berths are often made tapering so at the foot they are only about 16 inches wide.

Be sure to use a cotton rope for a lanyard to support the inboard end for the chains, as manila ropes used by some are quite disagreeable against the face when you suddenly get up in the dark. It is customary to have a plain hook at the upper end of the lanyard, so when folding the berth up in the daytime this rope is out of the way.

To me the bottom of a pipe berth is not an unpleasant sight, particularly if the lacing of the berth bottom has been neatly done and the ticking of its mattress is well covered with a good Hudson Bay blanket (one of their green ones to starboard and a bright red to port). However, the bottom of a pipe berth presents a surface adapted to decoration. The oldtime sailors could make some drawn work on the style of a gangway cloth for here, but they served their apprenticeship with palm and needle, while the present monkey-wrench sailor lacks all creative ability, so this may have to be left to some member of the fair sex. The Woman, the wife of the Man who built the Snarke, the one who had good taste and wrought wondrously well with the needle, made these covers of blue denim boxed up around the edges so they covered the mattresses. The seams were piped with a white binding. To hold them on the pipe berth frame, she had several tabs which snapped over the tubing which stretched and held the cover in place, for these attachments were quite close together along the topside. She had stitched or embroidered a design that the Man had drawn out for her showing H-28 underway, and a few aquatic objects in the corners, as is shown on the plan.

Stoves
It seems as if the pressure cooker has changed the whole galley arrangement and particularly the stove. With its use, good meals can be cooked in less than one-quarter the time

generally taken, but best of all you can cook those things like beans, lentils, salt cod, and prunes, which are easy to stow and keep indefinitely. With me almost everything that goes into the pressure cooker comes out tender and succulent, although I am no cook. Be sure to get a pressure cooker that is all stainless steel, for they are much the easiest to clean and they resist scratching. With the pressure cooker it is generally unnecessary to cook when underway for you can cook things so quickly — several good vegetables one minute, a good lamb stew twenty minutes. What is needed for a stove is a flame or heat capable of quick adjustment, for after the pressure cooker has been brought to working pressure the heat can and often must be turned down quite low.

On the cabin plan there is shown an alcohol stove which acts much as a gas stove; it can be started up and stopped quickly. This is called a Sea-Cook. It's the small one you want (which may be called the Son of a Sea Cook, for all I know), but it is Fig. 825 in Wilcox, Crittenden & Co.'s catalog. It can be bought in gimbals if desired. With a pressure cooker, the cooking can be done so quickly it will probably be done when at anchor, so gimbals are unnecessary.

Eating to a great extent is sort of a mental process. You hear one say "I feel faint," and almost falter in his tracks, but after throwing a load on his stomach he feels revived just as if the food were instantly digested and assimilated, had made its thirty-mile cruise of the circulatory system, and built up new muscle tissue, a process requiring hours if not days. We have so accustomed ourselves to eating at certain times that many are seriously upset by any change in the schedule. The salivary and digestive glands have been so used to pouring forth their juices at certain periods that if retarded the whole nervous system is affected. Even our domesticated animals have acquired our habit. I used to plow with a pair of horses (for I have plowed other things than salt water) who, as the noon hour approached, slowed down and came to a determined stop, and, while I was remonstrating with them to recommence, often faint but clear in the distance could be heard the factory whistles and the town clock summoning the townspeople to their noonday meal, but the horses knew better than I when to unhook the traces and let down the whiffletree. As I sit here writing at this moment my two dogs sit looking at me with beseeching brown eyes plainly speaking of an urgent inner need, for it is a few minutes past their eating time.

You will say, "What has this to do with the cabin plan of H-28?" Well, it is really most important for, if you can keep your nerves and your companion's nerves quieted and rested, much has been done toward the success of a cruise. As for nourishment, most of us are overfed anyway and should not hesitate to miss a meal now and then if it should interfere with a long run. One of the healthiest men in spirit and body that I ever cruised with never ate unless he was hungry. This occurred at irregular intervals, never interferring with sailing. He was a Greek, an ex-sponge diver, and I learnt much about life on small craft from him. While he never went swimming for pleasure he would think nothing of going down to visit the anchor on the bottom, if there were any question about its holding, and insert its fluke or palm in some subterranean crevice.

There are some other things about eating and, without going into too much detail or taking you for a cruise through the alimentary canal with rod and gun, so as to say, I will speak of some things near the entrance of that tortuous channel. The teeth. Teeth, like the blacksmith's arm, are only developed and kept in vigor by use. If you want to you can pour a thousand gallons of orange juice over them or plaster them with all the vitamins in the alphabet but it won't make much difference. What they want is to be used, some setting-up exercises. The best way to do this is the way the Great Designer intended: chew with them. If you throw the butter overboard (it's a nuisance to keep on board anyway), you will have accomplished a lot, for butter is a pleasant-tasting grease which lubricates the food so lazy people can swallow it without chewing. If you give the toothbrush a sea toss now and go over your teeth with a freshly whittled soft-wood peg or the chisel-shaped end of a match, life will be simplified and improved.

As for the other end of the canal, in youth the walls are surrounded with healthy muscles which, if they decided an empty house was better than a poor tenant, would cause a complete evacuation, but after thirty or forty years of idleness because their owner only ate soft, refined foods which were completely absorbed before they reached the end of the canal — well, it is just too bad. It was not so with my friend, the Greek sponge diver, who lived on hard, dry bread, cheese, salami sausage, raw onions, and figs. When he was nearing fifty one winter day, he was on Long Wharf, Newport. A careless driver who was dumping a load of snow overboard backed his team over the edge, horses, tipcart, and all.

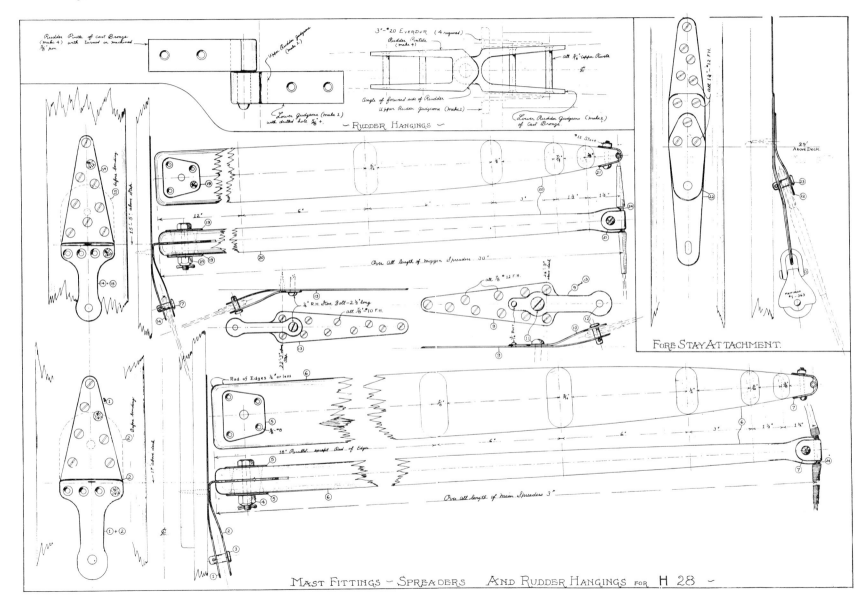

~ RUDDER HANGINGS ~

FORE STAY ATTACHMENT.

MAST FITTINGS ~ SPREADERS   AND RUDDER HANGINGS for H 28 ~

① main Lower Shroud Attachment (Phosphor Bronze) 1/16" or thicker x 3"x 9 7/16") make 2)
② " " " " " " 1/16" or thicker x 3" x 7 3/4") " make 2
   and Spreader attachment (Phosphor Bronze)
③ 3/8" Tobin pin 1 1/8" long, 1/2" dia head (make 2)
④ Spreader bolt Bronze 3/8" x 2" (make 2)
⑤ " " washers Bronze 1/16"x 2"x 2 1/2" (make 4)
⑥ main Spreaders, Ash, Oak or hard mahogany 1 1/4"x 3"x 3' (make 2)
⑦ Spreader tips, Bronze 1/16" x 1" x 3" - #12 stove bolt 1 1/2" long (make 2)

⑨ main Upper Shroud Attachment, Phosphor Bronze 1/16" x 2" x 9 1/16".
⑩ main Upper Shroud Attachment, outer layer 1/16" x 1 3/8" x 4 7/8" (make 2)
⑪ Round-headed Stove bolt, about 5/16" x 3 1/2" (1 needed)
⑫ 3/8" Bronze Pin 1" long, 1/2" head (make 2)
⑬ mizzen Upper Shroud Attachment, both layers 1/16 Bronze, 1/4" Pin and
   one R.H. Stove bolt 1/4" x 2 1/2" — layers (1/16"x 1 1/2" x 8 1/16") and (1/16" x 7/8" x 3 3/8")
⑭ mizzen Lower Shroud Attachment 1/16" x 2 1/2"x 8 3/16" (make 2)
⑮ " " " " " and Spreader Attachment 1/16"x 2 1/2" x 6 7/16"
⑰ 3/8 Tobin pin 7/8" long 1/2" head (make 2)
⑱ Spreader bolt Bronze 5/16" x 2" (make 2)
⑲ " " washers Bronze 1/16" x 1 3/4" x 2 (make 4)
⑳ mizzen Spreaders 1 1/8" x 2 1/2" x 30' (make 2)
㉑ Spreader tips Bronze 1/16"x 7/8" x 2 7/8" (make 2)
㉒ Fore Stay Attachment Phosphor Bronze
   Inner layer 1/16" x 1 3/4" x 11 1/2" (make 1)
   middle " 1/16" x 1 3/4" x 8" (" ")
   Outer " 1/16" x 1 3/4" x 4" (" ")
㉓ 3/8 Tobin pin, 1" long 1/2" head (" ")
㉔ Serve the shrouds for about 5" where the
   Spreaders bare and make a tapered stop
   above and below as shown.

Manuel, for that was his name, without hesitation dived into the icy water after them and, being a Mediterranean sailor had a strong, sharp knife with him, soon cut the harness so the struggling horses swam ashore. One of our societies, hearing of the deed, gave him a medal either for braveness or kindness to animals. It was quite a pretty thing on a ribbon but Manuel gave it to one of the girls, for the girls liked him as well as he liked them, though he was often thirty years their senior.

Patient reader, you may wonder what I am driving at — well, it is the icebox. Manuel lived many happy, healthy years aboard small craft without an icebox and so can you if you are a mind to. To me an icebox seems a terrible thing — too often have I had to clean out of them ossified lamb chops or some other concoction which resembled a pre-Cambrian custard. So on the H-28 no icebox is shown, but opposite the stove is a removable box shaped to fit the side of the yacht with a shelf or two to hold those dry foods which keep each end of the canal in working order — potatoes, onions, rice, beans, lentils, prunes, figs, salt cod, dried beef in jars, canned goods, tea, coffee, sugar, dry Italian bread, hardtack, etc. It is not difficult to keep eggs a few days, or well-cured unsliced bacon. If you can get it that hard, black salami sausage is wonderful; it will keep indefinitely. Manuel could make from it most anything from a thin soup to an Hungarian goulash. It is good fried with the eggs at breakfast, or on sandwiches for lunch, or as a last snack at night. Take my advice — eat your potatoes with their jackets on; eat your whole apple, skin, core, seeds, and all; chew everything well. Don't forget the prunes.

The Cedar Bucket

I hope you won't think I delight in these homely subjects, for it is not so. My only object is to help you to get more hours under sail out where the mackerel, gulls, and tern wheel in the sunshine. Perhaps I can best describe to you what I think of below-the-line water closets in small boats by quoting a few lines of that poem "A Sailor's Yarn" by J. J. Roche.

> They bored a hole below her line to let the
>   water out
> But more and more, with awful roar, the
>   water in did spout.

A good pump water closet represents an investment of well over a hundred dollars after it is installed with proper copper pipe, fittings, sea cocks, and all. It requires quite a lot of annual overhauling to prevent freezing and insure tightness of all valves and joints. But worst of all, no matter how much you scrub and polish up around them, they will still have a certain suggestive odor perhaps from their metal parts or rubber and leather valves and packings on which the salt water is having a chemical action. Of course, on yachts large enough to have a separate toilet room, such a closet is indispensable. But to sit, eat, and sleep beside the toilet is too much for me. Far, far rather would I have a good wooden bucket which can easily be kept clean. But best of all, the bucket can be used wherever you choose. It might be while you are at the helm when single-handed, or in the cockpit at night when you would not disturb either the tympanic or olfactory nerves of your shipmate. With the male gender it can often be used to advantage in rough weather when held quite high, and in case of *mal de mer* is much the most practical arrangement.

On the cabin plan is shown a cedar bucket with a removable, wide-rimmed top, for I know there are those who like to take their ease with their elbows on their knees. I use a bucket with brass hoops, and remove the metal bale and its ears and replace these with a rope bale, as shown on the drawing. Keep the bucket well varnished and use it when half full of water. There is a certain way to empty it which requires some skill. When the bucket is held down quite close to the surface of the water it should be suddenly turned right upside down. Ah-h, I am glad that is over; now we will take up things which are more fun to read about.

The Clam Hoe
I must confess I catch all my fish with a silver hook and like doing it that way. Sometimes I land a well-cured cod which has dried on the flakes of an offshore island far from the smoke of the city. Sometimes it is a pound of fresh cod roe which cooks to perfection in the pressure cooker. But, as some men of my age feel well dressed on Sunday morning as they saunter down the avenue with gloves and cane in hand, I too feel well dressed for the occasion as I land on the beach with the rope bale of the bucket in the crook of my left elbow, and the handle of the clam hoe in my right palm. There is something about the gritty feel of the handle which brings me close to nature, back to earth as it were, and as I stumble along the beach, making the fiddler crabs scurry for shelter, or see the squirt of a clam on ahead, a sense of contentment fills me. My dog, too, feels the joy of living as he bounds on ahead, starting up a flight of kildees or rock snipe, which wheel overhead, making a delicate pattern on the sky, coasting downwind on curved pinions. As I sit on a rock and give thanks for all these blessings which are freely given to all who will see them, the H-28 comes in view at her mooring, and as her white form is silhouetted against the opposite shore she seems beyond the realm of mere things — a mythical dream come true, the answer to a sailor's prayer.

Guns
It is not difficult to keep guns from rusting on a small boat even if they are handled occasionally. The trick is to give

them a coat of white shellac over the outside of all metal parts. This trick I learned from a Cape Cod gunner who shot over salt water. First you must clean the metal very carefully, then wipe it with alcohol; next, without touching the metal, give it a thin, even coat of shellac. In the fall, when you lay the boat up, the shellac can be easily removed by wiping the metal parts with a rag wet with alcohol. To preserve the inner parts, I find pure sperm oil much the best. The best cruising gun I ever had was a three-barreled hammerless Charles Daley. It shot four different useful charges or shells. The two upper barrels were 12 gauge. These, of course, shot the various shot loads and also the Brennecke slug, that most powerful stopping charge at close range. The lower barrel fired the popular 30-30 cartridge and, by using a cartridge adapter, fired the sweet-shooting .32 Smith & Wesson revolver cartridge.

This was an ideal gun to carry when landing on unknown country where you might get a wing shot or distant shot for a rifle. I personally enjoy shooting a revolver most and think the motion of the boat rather adds to the sport.

Shooting a revolver from a yacht can be quite safe when sensibly done, and perhaps it is the best training for coordinating the hands and eyes. I like to have a signal pistol, like the Very, always ready for, if a steamer should bear down on you in the dark or fog, this visual signal will enable them to locate you, whereas sound signals are vague and confusing.

All guns should be mounted on strong wooden brackets so they cannot fall under any circumstances, and it is best to leave all guns unloaded. Ammunition should be kept in a secret place, for almost all youth today are gun thirsty.

Cameras

As the target rifle is improved with weight, so too the camera, for the most important requisite for good picture taking is to stop the image from dancing on the negative. No matter how expensive a lens you have, it can't do good work unless kept in poise and perfect alignment at the instant of exposure. The ideal camera for a cruise has yet to be made. It should be heavy, strong, simple, and rustproof. You will not have to carry it around; it may be dropped or banged. It should be ready for instant use (on the water almost all targets are beyond infinity). It should stand handling with salty hands.

The sighting arrangement, or finder, is most important. On account of their weight and rigidity and because of the bright light on the water, the high speed lenses are unnecessary, for you will generally be stopped down to $f8$, as you must remember our modern sensitive materials are just as adapted to stopping down as to high speed, if the camera is held steady. Such a camera can have a rack for it on the H-28 as the guns do, so you can instantly reach it for that shot which may never be seen again, or if you want to take it ashore to record some scene which will be prized in the future.

If you throw the range finder and the exposure meter overboard, you will save yourself much time and worry and then may be able to get that picture before the subject has disappeared forever. Much of our modern sensitive material, like Verichrome, can stand exposures 100 percent either over or under the prescribed time or light volume. With a heavy camera the exposure can be much slower, so you can stop down 'till the range is less important. On a small boat the reflex cameras are almost useless; when you look down in their hood you may lose your balance.

Clothes

Of late years young yachtsmen are often seen dressed in a so-called swordfisherman's hat and wearing a lumberman's shirt with the tails outside, apparently endeavoring to make someone think they are much hardier or saltier than a mere yachtsman. Most of them wouldn't know swordfish from a skilagalee (skilagalee is the local Block Island fisherman's name for a fish which to an amateur resembles a swordfish in the distance) if the two were moored side by side right under the pulpit. These yachtsmen might be surprised to know that the best strikers and high liners of Block Island, Provincetown, and Gloucester wear derby hats when they walk up the streets of their native towns. Their kind of derby might not be as easy to acquire as the so-called sword-fisherman's hat (which is a commodity in most hardware shops), for they have an intriguing gradation of color from grayish black at the band to light green at the crown and brim, but you can acquire one if you really insist. The formula is this — purchase a rather cheap grade of derby, hang it in the forecastle when the ship is being fumigated for bedbugs; if it comes out too green don't hang it so close to the sulphur candles next time.

Of all the hats least adapted for sailing, a hat with a long visor is the worst, for much of the time is spent looking up at the sails. The one international peculiarity of sailormen's hats for centuries is that they are all brimless and visorless —

with the exception of the sou'wester. I happen to prefer the Breton fisherman's beret, from which probably our sailor caps are descended, with the addition of the black ribbon to commemorate the passing of Admiral Lord Nelson. If I were to sail on a Scotch Zulu or Fifie, a tam o' shanter would seem most appropriate. Most of the other nations have used some sort of a stocking hat, jersey, or watch cap. All have the peculiarity of not blowing off easily. If your old gray felt sticks on well, wear it on the H-28.

As for the other clothes, if you are going riding, golfing, or shooting, by all means use the clothes for these purposes, but don't wear them yachting unless you want to belittle the sport. The proper thing for a yacht of this size is a double-breasted blue jacket not cut too low in front, good service-able black buttons, good-size pockets, material of strong serge or, in cold weather, pilot cloth worn with gray flannel trousers. In England such clothes can be bought at almost any waterfront town. Brooks Brothers now have some tan corduroy jackets which would be nice to wear any place out of town. The salt brushes off them well and they are nearly windproof.

Of course dressing too perfectly is nearly as conspicuous as the swordfisherman's hat and almost as ridiculous, for if it is true that clothes make the man, then it is interesting to note which of our acquaintances can stand a patch or two and still be respectable. I have seen some of the high Brahma of Boston who demonstrated they could pass this test. In other words, if clothes do make the man, then the logic would seem that most of us are merely stuffed shirts.

As for shoes, be sure to use ones which are white all over,

soles and all, for the others make disagreeable marks about the yacht. I prefer plain tennis shoes in two sizes, one for thick socks, one for no socks at all; and some sort of boots for exploring the beach or clamming. I like plenty of socks, thick woolen ones.

While I think of it I want to mention the clock and cabin lamps, not that they are particularly connected, but they seem cheerful parts of the cabin. A good clock is almost necessary to get the most out of cruising. It is often quite important to know exactly when to expect a change of tide, and, even in the simplest navigation or in the fog, your time of rounding marks. In beating dead to windward you stay on each tack equal intervals of time, etc. I always use a clock with a set hand like that of a barometer to set over the minute hand at the beginning of any interval to be timed. It saves writing down or the uncertainty of remembering. The Chelsea Clock Company, I believe, can furnish any of their models so equipped. There was quite a lot said about Chelsea clocks the time the Snarke was built, but in the conversation they forgot to mention that Chelsea makes one inexpensive non-striking screw-bezel marine clock and that is the one shown on the plan.

Lamps or Cabin Lights

The lights in the cabin of a small yacht are a serious problem. All electric lights are cold and cheerless; however there are several so-called flashlights which are most useful for finding your way around in the dark, and some of them which have an adjustable or swivel reflector can be hung up back of that comfortable place you have found to read in.

One would be good over the stove for cooking. But the real cabin light, inexpensive to run, is a kerosene burner. I suppose on the H-28 it could be over the food locker on the starboard house side, as shown on the drawing, but the placing of lights can be done much better after the cabin is built, for on a small yacht they must be where you will not hit them when moving around.

Sometimes two small lamps are best. The Petite model, Wilcox, Crittenden Fig. 99, then would do, but on the plan the regular, or No. 1-99, is shown. For the benefit of those who have not been shipmates with a kerosene lamp, I will try to tell a few things. There must be a so called "smoke bell" or other arrangement to keep the heat from burning the under side of deck. Sometimes this can be arranged by tacking against the deck a piece of sheet metal over thick asbestos.

To fill a lamp the procedure is this — remove the filler screw, lay it down so both hands are free; now hold the cedar bucket or a basin under the lamp with the left hand and fill the reservoir, the neck of the can right in the filler hole, until oil runs over in the bucket. Next tilt the lamp in its gimbals till a little oil spills out, for if there is not an air space to take up expansion the flame will burn unevenly. Now replace the filler cap and wipe the whole lamp off carefully with a rag. If the lamp has been used many hours the wick must be trimmed. This is best done with the thumb and forefinger by simply rubbing off the carbonized parts, leaving the wick smooth and even across the top with the outer ends slightly lower. Pick up and clean the carbon, drippings, etc., around the burner, for a clean burner is almost odorless. Do not wash the lamp chimneys, but use a twisted newspaper in them for cleaning; sometimes breathing in them is a help. Be sure to use a high grade oil or kerosene.

Don't forget the candles, for if everything else goes wrong, these most reliable lights will work. There are running or sailing lights made today with dry batteries in them. Wilcox, Crittenden Fig. 710 would seem best for a boat like H-28 which would not often be out after sunset.

Reading Material

It is a strange thing that, though the alphabet is taught us at a tender age, still few of us learn to read until we reach forty. At school and college he is counted best scholar who names the words "most rapid." Like an express train rushing down the track, the end of the run — the last page — is the object. But he who went on foot, so to say, and bathed his feet in the cool stream under the railroad bridge and sat with the hay makers at their noonday meal beside the swamp oak at the edge of the thicket, might take longer on the trip, but at the end of the book or journey he will have absorbed some lasting good from that junket. A young lady acquaintance of mine took a train ride up-country not long ago and as the track lay through country I had paddled — lush marshes and woodland — I asked her what she saw. "Well," said she, "two drunken sailors got aboard at Centerdale and the woman right in front of me had the prettiest baby." Thus it is with most of us, sordidness, sex, and the mystery story first claim our attention, and the train curtains might just as well have been drawn as we went through those passages where poetry and painting made up the landscape or composition.

I choose books for a cruise mostly for their compactness, and for that reason count the best literature those books which can be read over and over. I have one which measures only four and one-half by seven by fifteen-sixteenths inches, though it contains nearly the whole history of art, music and drama, if you can read it. This octavo is the *Oxford Book of English Verse*. It is well of course to have some other sheet anchor, as it were, in case of a rainy day in port or if fog bound. And because some illustrations speak volumes to me, a book like *Mast and Sail in Europe and Asia* by H. Warrington Smyth will entertain me indefinitely, for its several hundred illustrations are chock full of meaning.

It is true there are still some magazines with material that will stand reading over again, like the *Atlantic* or *Blackwood's* magazine, that Scotch publication, but you will hardly want to clutter up the beach of some quaint cove with the photographic leaves of most others whose subjects are rape, murder, and arson. Even *The Rudder* (which we hope you will not give a sea toss), which once had illustrations by Fred Cozzens and Warren Sheppard and pictures of men who went down to the sea in ships, now features mostly photographs of young females who go down to the sea in slips, as the current saying is. All this, some of my younger readers will say, is some form of senile dementia, and if so, they are quite welcome to this opinion for it is a most pleasant dementia to be allowed to rest, to think, to read quietly far from the honk of horn, jingle of phone, and surge of the city. Undisturbed reading — ah, yes, this is one of the objects of the cruise.

Companions or Crew

Your companion on a cruise has a far, far greater effect on the success of the venture than any cabin arrangement. Beware of those guests who board you with portmanteaus and satchels filled with shaving gear, sunburn lotion, and sport clothes. If they do ever unpack, the H-28 will look like the combination of an apothecary shop and second-hand clothing store. They will spend most of their time on board pawing over bags looking for that gadget which, although they don't know it, was left at home on the bureau where they will find it at long last on their return. Watch out also for those females who are triced up and gasketed-in in some futile attempt to alter their model from that of a Hanseatic Cog to a Whitehead torpedo, for if called on deck early in the morning to hear the birds caroling overhead, they will be about as good natured as a hermit crab snapped out of its shell, which was built by another. Beware also of those beauties who are periodically rebuilt and refitted at the dockyard of some beautician, whose only ambition is to look "killing" and whose murderous claws are painted as if they were an accessory to the fact.

These females may be all right if you can afford a steam yacht with a French maid to assemble them in the morning and unrig them at night, but on the H-28 there will be no room for their spare gear and top hamper, and they will affect the smooth working of the H-28 like a monkey wrench in the crankcase.

But there are girls (God bless them) who can take it, are real companions and helpmates; who can stand a trick at the tiller or galley. That's the kind that's right up our alley.

If you have some kind of a life contract or agreement with such a one, you had better build a golden halo around her in your mind's eye, and let her know it once in awhile, for you and she working together can bring out all the pleasure, charm, and melody there is in a craft like the H-28.

The kind of a companion you want is one who likes either the east wind fresh from the Gulf Stream, or a west wind which has blown through the needles of ten thousand pine trees; who can enjoy the dramatic prelude of a thundersquall or, when the fog bank rolls in from the old Atlantic, will hand you the right chart and help you to make a true fix.

Don't forget the elder men, for they were educated in those halcyon days when art had beauty, music had melody, and poetry had rhyme. You will not tire of their conversation like the younger ones whose every word is a boast. These old boys also may be able to teach you some tricks of piloting and seamanship which are not printed in books, if you will only listen to them. But best of all they can entertain you with the true drama of life which has been seen through wise old eyes, so that in the future you may count your time with them the most enjoyable and profitable of any in your life.

Also don't forget the teenage boys, for, besides teaching them to sail, you must teach them to shoot (if you have the patience), as in this world those nations which can aim things best are looked on with the most respect. Sometimes nowadays a boat is the only place, outside of a shooting range, where shooting can be taught safely, and the pattern on the water is a great help.

Remember now, keep the cabin simple with everything

stowed where it won't get wet or shifted in a knockdown. Eat sensibly. Don't get sunburned, for no berth is comfortable under those circumstances. Make the whole cruise an interesting game where you have pitted your wits against the elements: try to do everything in the best and simplest way; try to improve your technique each time; rest and relax whenever you can, for there may be some occasion coming when you will need a well-rested mind and body. If you cruise this way for a week in a small sailboat you will be greatly refreshed and strengthened, and if you go for a whole month you will feel like a Clydesdale stallion in the leafy month of May.

This account has only touched on some of the highlights of the construction and has tried to help on points where many are apt to go astray. It would take a whole book to cover the complete construction of a yacht of this type, but a little common sense and Yankee ingenuity should cover the rest. And remember, the drawings are only a guide to shapes and sizes so that the owner can make variations in cabin arrangement, etc., to suit himself. For instance, someone might want a narrower cockpit, or a self-bailing cockpit, and all such things would be improvements for certain uses. So, here's wishing you luck!

CONSTRUCTION PLAN

1. Lead keel, 2,800 lbs.
2. Main keel, oak, $2\frac{1}{2}''$ x $13''$ x $16'$.
3. Fore keel, oak, $2\frac{1}{2}''$ x $4\frac{1}{2}''$ x $6'$.
4. Stem, white oak, natural crook, $4\frac{1}{2}''$ x $6'$.
5. Stern post, oak, $4\frac{1}{2}''$ x $9''$ x $7'3''$.
6. Knees, oak, $4\frac{1}{2}''$ athwartships.
7. Deadwood, hard pine, $7''$ x $9''$ x $5'3''$.
8. Scarf bolts, $\frac{3}{8}''$ Tobin, nut and washer both ends.
9. Floor bolts, all $7/16''$ Tobin, nut and washer both ends, two on floor 10 to 17.
10. Lead through bolts, $\frac{1}{2}''$ Tobin.
11. Drive bolts, $\frac{3}{8}''$ galvanized iron or Tobin (self heading or clinch ring).
12. Hanger bolts for attaching lead, $\frac{5}{8}''$ Tobin, U.S.S. thread, let into the lead $3''$ or more, staggered. See deck plan.
13. All other bolts through keel, $7/16''$ Tobin.
14. All floor timbers, oak, $1\frac{1}{2}''$ thick. Take depth from plan.
15. All frames, white oak, $1\frac{5}{8}''$ x $1\frac{5}{8}''$. Those on station 6 and forward can be sawn and beveled, the other steam bent. The frames, floors, and deck beams change at 15 where the midship section, or dead flat mark, is.
16. Planking, rift grain fir, $1''$ thick. If cedar or soft pine, $1\frac{1}{8}''$ thick. If mahogany or yellow pine, $\frac{7}{8}''$ thick. The plank above the W.L. should not be more than $4''$ wide, with the exception of the sheer strake.
17. The sheer strake should be of fairly hard wood to take the shelf bolts; hard, fine grain fir, oak, or yellow pine will do, $5''$ or more wide amidships.
18. Clamp, fire, spruce, or hard pine, $1''$ x $3\frac{1}{2}''$.
19. Shelf, fir, spruce, or hard pine, $2''$ x $2''$.

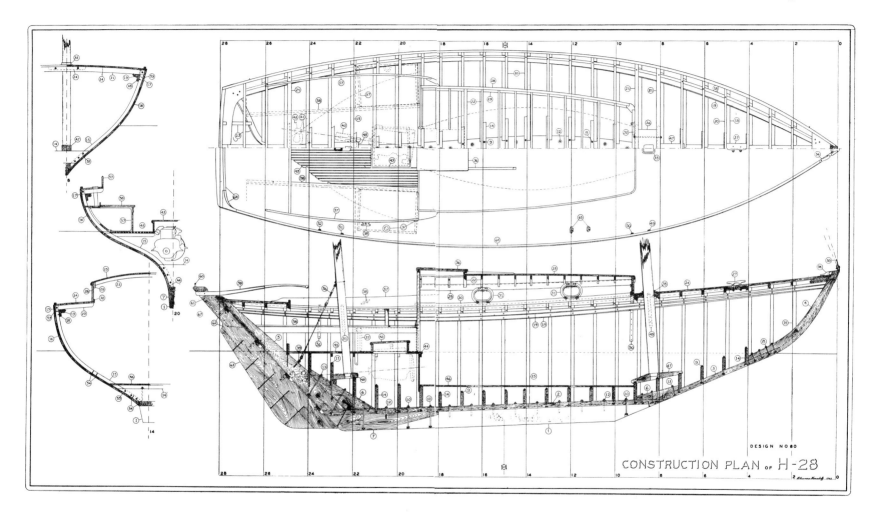

DESIGN NO 80

CONSTRUCTION PLAN of H-28

20.   Regular deck beams, 1⅜″ x 2″, crown 3¾″ in 10′.

21.   Strong beams, three, 2″ x 2″, crown 3¾″ in 10′.

22.   House beams, ¾″ x 1½″, spaced 9″, and one at hatch 1½″ x 1½″, crown 6″ in 6′, or a radius of 8′3″. All beams can be white oak, ash, elm, or yellow-bark oak, or even red oak, for they are larger than usual.

23.   The transom can be planked up of 1″ thick oak over the stern post, frames, and aprons as shown. Planks about 6″ wide fastened and caulked same as planking.

24.   Main deck, ¾″ or more, tongue-and-groove pine 3″ or less wide, canvas covered.

25.   House deck, ⅝″ or more, tongue-and-groove pine, 2½″ or less wide, canvas covered.

26.   Mast partner, oak, 1½″ x 10″ x 20″, with ⅜″ through bolts.

27.   Mooring cleat, Wilcox, Crittenden Fig. 4020 or similar. 10″ long on oak block, 1″ x 6″ x 10″.

28.   House sides and forward end, soft pine, if painted 1¼″ thick; if varnished, mahogany, oak, or teak 1″ thick.

29.   Lodging piece for deck beams about 1″ x 3″, oak or mahogany.

30.   Finish piece to cover the deck canvas where turned up — any wood to match interior trim.

31.   Wilcox, Crittenden Fig. 5252, size 5″ x 9″ or 4″ x 7″, as owner desires.

32.   Wilcox, Crittenden Fig. 523, size 4″, port and starboard.

33.   Stem band in two parts for attaching both the forestay and the headstay. Inner piece 3/16″ x 2″ x 27″; outer piece 3/16″ x 2″ x 13″. Hard Tobin or phosphor bronze 7/16″ pin for thimble of forestay. The outer layer extends up to take the clevis of the headstay turnbuckle and has a 5/16″ hole.

34.   Cast bronze bow chocks.

35.   Mast collar to take the mast coat, can be either cast bronze or shaped up of sheet copper. Mast is 4¼″ x 5½″ at deck.

36.   Hatch and slide of hard wood, opening 20″ x 26″.

37.   Gas and water tanks, alike of tin-lined copper. The size shown will hold about 23 gallons and is shaped to fit the yacht on the other sides. They have filler pipes and vents outside the coaming as shown to allow the gas to settle outboard when filling tank. If smaller capacity is sufficient, round or oval tanks can be used. It is recommended to have the water tank on the side the stove will be on (if the stove is near the cabin bulkhead), very firmly secured.

38.   Jibsheet cleats, port and starboard, Wilcox, Crittenden Fig. 4020, 5½″.

39.   Screw eye bolt for mizzen brace or backstay. Wilcox, Crittenden Fig. 2181, ½″ x 3¼″. See rigging list for other parts.

40.   Special cast bronze inside stuffing box, depending on size of motor used.

41.   Special one-legged strut of cast bronze bolted through stern post.

42.   Hyde 2-blade, feathering propeller, 12″ diameter.

43.   Removable box cover over engine, top same as house deck, canvas covered.

44.   Threshold is a removable board, ¾″ x 9″ x 21″, of hard wood to lift out when cranking motor.

45.   The best cockpit floor would be of slats about 1″ wide, ¾″ thick, spaced about ¼″, of teak, elm, or oak, with removable section near the center line.

46.   The cabin floor can be tongue-and-groove soft pine from ⅝″ to ¾″ thick, painted or varnished.

47.   Mast step, oak, 3½″ x 5″ x 2′5″, cut mortise for mast tongue way through to drain water. Tongue of mainmast is 4″ x 1¼″.

48. Mast step, oak, 2½″ x 6″ x 13½″, tongue of mizzen 3″ x 1″.

49. Main upper shroud chainplates, 3/16″ x 1¼″ x 18″.

50. Main lower shroud chainplates, 3/16″ x 1½″ x 24″.

51. Mizzen upper shroud chainplates, 3/16″ x 1″ x 15″.

52. Mizzen lower shroud chainplates, 3/16″ x 1¼″ x 18″. All chainplates of hard-rolled Tobin or Phosphor bronze and fastened through planking with ¼″ stove bolts, spaced to clear seams of planking.

53. If the shelf and clamp are well through-bolted, there will be no need of hanging or lodging knees to support the deck beams. On the drawing there is shown a 5/16″ x 6″ stove bolt which can be either galvanized iron, Everdur, or brass. The clamp can be fastened with wood screws of about 2½″ #14. The head of the frames and deck beams can be joined with ¼″ bolts or slightly smaller copper rivets. The ends of the deck beams can be secured to the clamp with 3½″ #16 Everdur wood screws, and it would be well if the ones through the strong beams were larger.

54. Planking fastenings, #14 Everdur screws 2¼″ long, into frames with a ½″ bung. The fastenings through the garboard into the back rabbet of the keel may have to be shorter. Be sure to fasten the planking to both the frames and the floor timbers as this relieves the strain on the bolts through the frames and floors #55.

55. These should be 5/16″ bronze bolts or copper rivets about ¼″ diameter.

56. I am sorry to say the mizzen will need an after brace or stay, and this will be shown on the rigging plan. If preferred, the mizzen can be supported by a stout thwart between frames 22 and 23. The springstay from the mizzen to the mainmast head will hold the mizzen forward.

57. The cockpit coaming, from ¾″ to ⅞″ thick, depending on hardness of the wood; of mahogany, oak, or teak, and would look nice if it matched the other deck trim, if varnished. The forward end is fitted to a shaped block to avoid the necessity of steaming.

58. The cockpit seats can be soft pine about 1″ x 19″ x 7′8″ with lighter sheathing back of them. The apron or skirt near the inboard edge must be quite strong unless there is more than one support as shown. The apron can be ⅞″ x 3″ if soft wood, and smaller if hard wood. Aft of the tanks there can be some athwartship cleats, if desired. Very good seats can be made like the cockpit floor, as slats let the rain or water through quickly. Also they prevent one from slipping sideways somewhat. But remember 19″ is about the minimum width to sleep on.

59. The tiller can be of ash, oak, or locust, 2″ square at rudder head, about 1⅜″ and 1½″ at fluting, ⅞″ at the neck, with 1½″ ball.

60. Cast bronze bale for attaching mizzen sheet, about ½″ diameter where round.

61. Copper rivets through the rudder to secure the cheek pieces.

62. The forward plank on the rudder, or rudder stock, is 2″ x 9″ x 8′5″ and the deck pieces ⅞″ x 5½″ x 2′10″ and well beveled off forward to allow the rudder to swing 45° each side of center line. Some kind of oak is the usual material for rudders of this size.

63. The after piece of rudder is 1½″ x 10½″ x 6′1″ and secured with 5/16″ self-heading drive bolts of either galvanized iron or bronze, the trailing edge of rudder about 1¼″ at waterline, ⅞″ at widest part of rudder.

64. Toe rail, quarter knees, and taffrail, either the same material as coaming and house sides, or teak, mahognay, oak, or

yellow pine — about 1″ wide, ¾″ deep amidships, increasing at ends to about 1″ x 1″ taffrail as shown.

65.   Jibsheet leads — Wilcox, Crittenden Fig. 5811, size #2.

66.   Don't forget the limber holes. They should be cut in the floors before they are set in place, and cut in the heels of the frames before planking. Large, smooth limber holes are a great convenience and quite worthwhile making right in the first place, and quite difficult to enlarge later.

67.   Rudder pintles. See detail. There is a way to fit an oak block in the cavity below the upper pintle and gudgeon so that the rudder cannot rise and unship. This block can be about 1¼″ x 2″ x 3″ and held in place by gravity as the cheek pieces of the rudder will hold it sideways, but it can be lifted out when the rudder is at 45° or more.

CABIN PLAN

1.   Oak stanchion, about 1¼″ x 1¼″ x 9″.

2.   Transom seats, pine about ¾″ thick, or ½″ laminated wood.

3.   Cross pieces, any wood abut ⅞″ x 2″.

4.   Upper face piece, ⅝″ x 3″.

5.   Lower face piece, ⅝″ x 3″.

6.   Combination tool box and step with hinged top. Outside of box about 18″ long, 8″ high, 11″ wide. After corners may have to be cut away for frame 19.

7.   Removable threshold for cranking motor.

8.   Removable section to raise cabin doors above motor cover. One end Wilcox, Crittenden Fig. 3600, other end two No. 14 screws with heads sawn off. Ventilation holes, if wanted.

9.   Cabin doors are best if paneled up so as to reduce shrinking and swelling. They can be about ¾″ thick. Cabin doors should be un-hung when sailing and can be stowed under the cockpit seats aft, if desired.

10.   There are no commercial unhooking hinges that have the butts covered so thieves cannot unscrew the screws, so a full size drawing of proper ones is given. They must be made up in pairs, right and left hand, with the pins or pintles of the lower hinges longest to facilitate hanging the doors. The pin is best if of 5/16″ Tobin bronze, either threaded or driven in, with well rounded upper end.

11.   Wilcox, Crittenden Fig. 3600, brass.

12.   Wilcox, Crittenden Fig. 475, polished brass.

13.   Berth stop, oak ¾″ x 1½″ x 4½″.

14.   Ratchet action clip to hold berth in folded position. Oak ¾″ x 1½″ x about 7 or more inches. No. 14 round-head screw over washer.

15.   Berth hooks of sheet brass or bronze from 1/6″ to 1/8″ thick.

16.   Merriman Fig. 431, No. 2.

17.   Food locker doors, flush for back rest when cooking, pine about ¾″ x 9″ x 18″.

18.   Wilcox, Crittenden Fig. 358.

19.   Wilcox, Crittenden stove Fig. 825.

20.   Suggested position of Wilcox, Crittenden lamp Fig. 99 — No. 1.

21.   Curtain, if wanted, can be tied back against shelf and clamp at frame No. 10, or privacy can be had by putting on the cabin doors.

22.   Wooden bucket with wide rim removable top — both to be hung normally under after deck.

23.   Suggested position of Chelsea clock with marine 4½″ dial, and set hand.

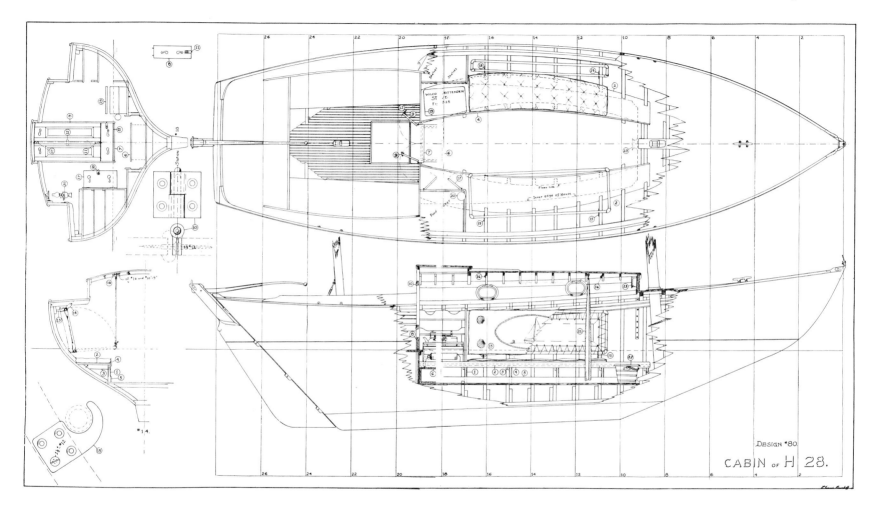

DESIGN #80

CABIN OF H 28.

4　HOW TO BUILD ROZINANTE

A few years ago *The Rudder* published a series of articles called *The Compleat Cruiser* and, although this discourse about cruisers and cruising was later printed in book form, the publishers of the book left out about one third of the original material that was printed in *The Rudder* and, rather unfortunately, omitted much that had to do with sailing and passage-making. Nevertheless, so much interest was manifested in a small cruising boat mentioned in the story, called *Rozinante,* that I have since drawn up for clients two of these boats with several of the characteristics of the original *Rozinante.*

This little yacht is a small double ender of a type that used to be called canoe yawls, and in the 1890's was a very popular type in England for cruising some of their delightful waterways like the Clyde, Firth of Forth, Humber, Mersey, and of course the Solent in days gone by. The canoe yawl is sort of a descendant of some of the sailing canoes that were used in these waters for cruising during the previous decade. The name "canoe yawl" simply means a boat with a sharp stern that is larger than the usual sailing canoe, or about the size of what was called a yawl boat in those days. Admiral Smyth in his dictionary of nautical terms, 1867, describes a yawl as "A man-of-war's boat resembling the pinnace, but rather smaller; it is carvel-built, and generally rowed with twelve oars." The term "canoe-yawl" in its day had nothing to do with the rigs these pretty vessels used, for among them there were sloops, ketches, yawls, luggers, and cat yawls, but my knowledge of the past is not sufficient for me to state definitely that the name of the yawl rig did not come from that sail plan being often used on boats that were called yawls or yawl boats. Of course, many yawl boats had no rig. I, myself, am old enough to remember when the canoe yawls were still in vogue, so I will tell you what some of their characteristics were and that will partly explain Rozinante.

A canoe yawl should be light and rather narrow so that she may be easily propelled by rowing when necessary. It should be a good sea boat and a fast sailer under a small sail plan. It should have comparatively shallow draft so that occasionally a person can land from one without a tender and, although Rozinante is quite a little deeper than is usual for a canoe yawl (many of them had a centerboard that went through a shallow ballast keel), still I think there are many places where Rozinante could be rowed close enough to shore so one could land over the bow in less than two feet of water.

The Rozinante canoe yawl Wind Song *slipping along in light going.*

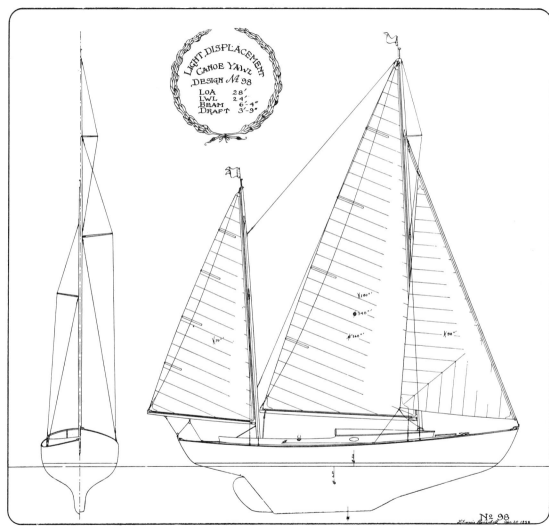

LIGHT DISPLACEMENT
CANOE YAWL
DESIGN № 98
LOA   28'
LWL   24'
BEAM   6'-4"
DRAFT 3'-9"

№ 98

A pair of Rozinantes taking shape.

A good canoe yawl should not have any combustible or noise makers aboard so that one can really relax and commune with God and Mother Nature but still use his wits in the interesting game of getting the most out of tide and wind. A good canoe yawl will give more lasting pleasure for the dollar than any other vessel except a double-paddle canoe, and while her first cost may be considerable these days, if she is treated sensibly she will not depreciate much in forty years, and her annual expense will be negligible. Best of all a canoe yawl can be about the safest vessel that can be had, since her design is based on those most seaworthy open boats ever known — whaleboats. Rozinante is a partly decked-over whale boat with a ballast keel that will make her non-capsizable. She is rigged with a sail plan which can be decreased without perceptibly affecting her balance, and she can be made to lay to in a seaway under the mizzen alone. A boat of this type can be gotten under way or laid up for the night in a few minutes, so that she is practical to use on summer evenings, often the pleasantest times of all for sailing, while evening sailing is generally out of the question with the more complicated or larger craft on account of the time factor.

I realize that most of the people on the water today are without experience and will want tail fins, aluminum masts, reverse sheers, mast head rigs, and dog houses. I hope they won't write to me about putting these things on Rozinante until they have had a few years of experience on the water. Some of them remind me of the young lad who came to call on me one day all out of breath to inquire why I did not use aluminum instead of lead on the keels of yachts.

There will be many who will want more head room than Rozinante's proportions allow, and to them I will say that most of the sailormen I have known sat down when they ate, and much preferred to lie down when they slept. Of course there will be many who will prefer other constructions than have been found best during the last thousand years of careful development in boat work, and to these people about all I can say is "Look at the prices that are asked for these makeshifts that are made up of materials two to three times the weight of wood." "Well, how about laminated wood?", they will ask. So I shall have to answer that

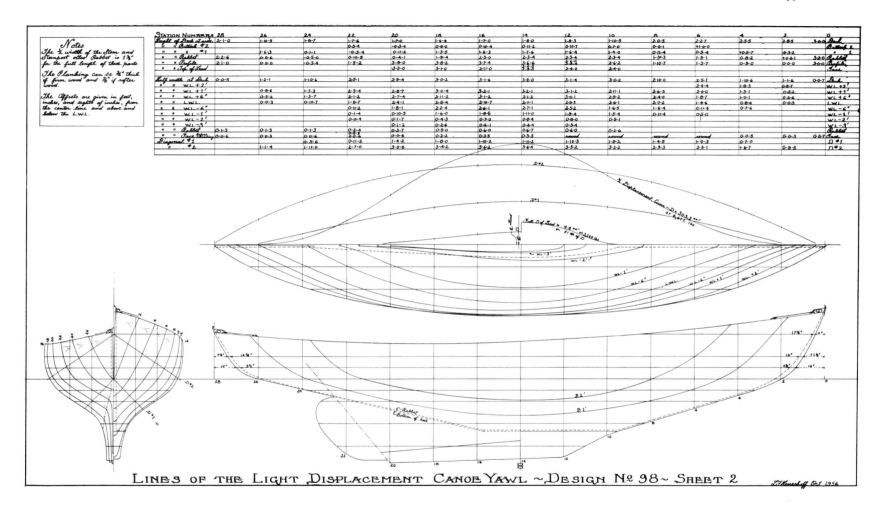

LINES OF THE LIGHT DISPLACEMENT CANOE YAWL ~ DESIGN Nº 98 ~ SHEET 2

L. Francis Herreshoff Oct. 1956

Notes

The ½ width of the Stem and Sternpost other Rabbet is 1⅜" for the full length of these parts.

The Planking can be ¾" thick if firm wood and ⅞" if softer wood.

The Offsets are given in feet, inches, and eighths of inches, from the center line and above and below the L.W.L.

Station Numbers	28	26	24	22	20	18	16	14	12	10	8	6	4	2	0	
Height of Deck at side	2-1-0	1-10-5	1-8-7	1-7-6	1-7-0	1-6-6	1-7-0	1-8-0	1-8-3	1-10-5	2-0-5	2-2-7	2-5-5	2-8-5	3-0-0	Deck
" " Buttock #2				0-3-4	0-9-0	0-8-4	0-11-2	0-10-7	0-7-0	0-0-0	+1-0-0					Buttock #2
" " #1		1-6-3	0-1-1	-0-5-4	0-11-2	1-3-5	1-6-3	1-7-6	1-6-4	1-4-0	0-5-4	10-5-7	2-5-2			Buttock #1
" " Rabbet	2-2-6	0-0-6	-0-5-0	0-10-3	0-4-1	1-9-4	2-5-0	2-3-4	2-3-4	1-10-3	1-3-1	0-8-2	+0-3-1	3-2-0	Rabbet
" " Profile	2-1-0	0-0-0	-0-5-4	1-5-2	3-8-0	3-8-2	3-7-4	3-6-6	3-6-6	2-6-2	1-10-7	1-3-7	0-9-0	0-0-0	3-0-0	Profile
" " Top of Lead					3-3-0	3-1-0	2-11-0	3-3-3	2-4-0	2-4-0						Base
Half width at Deck	0-0-5	1-2-1	1-10-6	2-5-1	2-9-4	3-0-2	3-1-6	3-2-0	3-1-4	3-0-2	2-10-0	2-5-1	1-10-6	1-1-6	0-0-7	Deck
" " WL +2'												2-4-1	1-8-3	0-8-7		WL +2'
" " WL +1'		0-8-6	1-7-3	2-3-4	2-8-7	3-0-4	3-1-2	3-2-1	2-11-1	2-6-5	2-0-0	1-3-1	0-5-2			WL +1'
" " WL +6"		0-5-2	1-3-7	2-1-2	2-7-4	2-11-2	3-1-2	3-1-2	3-0-1	2-9-2	2-4-0	1-8-7	1-0-1	0-2-6		WL +6"
" " L.W.L.		0-0-3	0-10-7	1-8-7	2-4-1	2-8-4	2-10-7	2-11-0	2-9-3	2-6-1	2-0-2	1-4-6	0-8-4	0-0-3		L.W.L.
" " WL -6"				0-1-2	1-8-1	2-2-4	2-6-1	2-7-1	2-5-2	1-6-5	1-6-4	0-11-4	0-3-6			WL -6"
" " WL -1'				0-1-4	0-10-3	1-6-0	1-8-6	1-11-0	1-5-4	1-5-4	0-11-4	0-5-0				WL -1'
" " WL -2'				0-0-4	0-1-7	0-4-3	0-7-0	0-8-4	0-8-0	0-5-1						WL -2'
" " WL -3'				0-1-2	0-2-6	0-4-1	0-4-4	0-3-4								WL -3'
" " Rabbet	0-1-3	0-1-3	0-1-3	0-2-4	0-3-7	0-5-0	0-6-0	0-6-7	0-6-0	0-2-6	round	round	round	0-0-5	0-0-7	Rabbet
" " Face Stem	0-0-6	0-0-3	0-1-0	0-0-6	0-2-2	0-3-5	0-5-5									Face
Diagonal #1				0-5-6	0-11-3	1-4-2	1-8-0	1-10-2	1-11-2	1-10-3	1-8-2	1-4-5	1-0-3	0-7-0		D #1
" #2		1-1-4	1-11-0	2-7-0	3-0-6	3-4-2	3-6-2	3-6-4	3-5-2	3-2-2	2-3-3	2-3-1	1-6-7	0-8-3		D #2

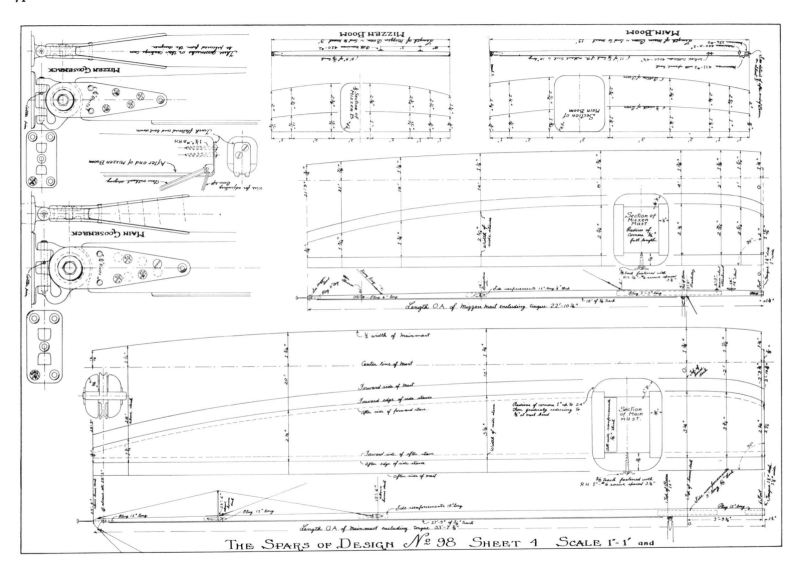

THE SPARS OF DESIGN №98 SHEET 4 SCALE 1"=1' and

it is a fine material for some specific purposes, but when you take some nice stock and slice it up into thin layers and glue it together again it will naturally cost some three times as much as it did originally. If you can't bend a material in two ways it is not suitable for nautical shapes, so if you want a nicely shaped boat that will last a long time and be a joy forever — as well as perhaps be the cheapest — my advice is to build her of a carefully thought-out construction that has proved to be good. Perhaps then you will say "But where can one have a boat like that built today?" And I will tell you that there are still some honest men who are not scared to use hand tools, who can sharpen a saw, plane, or adz: there are still some who know that a little healthy exercise will not do them any lasting harm. To be sure most of these honest men live and work in rather out-of-the-way places, but that is lucky, for in most cases they can acquire the proved boat-building materials for perhaps one-third the city prices. But, best of all, some of these honest gentlemen's boat shops are in places where nothing but the occasional honk of a wild goose will distract them from their work. While I do not know what the next election will do to reduce pride in workmanship, I do know that there are still many who can make things out of natural materials that will function as well as they used to, and it is our duty to encourage them or else it will be necessary to have most yachts and boats built outside of the United States of America.

Some people will inquire why it is that I designed this Rozinante with leg-o'-mutton sails instead of the short gaffs that were shown in *The Compleat Cruiser.* I can only say it was first done by request of the prospective owner, but also

on a small boat the gaffs interfere with standing backstays so that it is not feasible to carry a large jib in strong winds. However, the short gaffs have worked so well on my Meadow Lark design that I expect to use that sort of sail in most of the boats that I design that have tended backstays.

As for the peculiarities of Rozinante — you will find her a beautiful model that would have pleased the sailor of the past, and, as a beautiful sailboat is ageless, she will still be in style long after the abortions of the present are forgotten, for every curve of her shape is for some specific reason and not some crazy whim of her designer to create a ridiculous controversy. Rozinante is not intended for ocean racing so will rate high under most measurement rules. These rules all penalize the speed-giving qualities of a sailboat and the result is that the miserable craft now in vogue cannot get up speed enough to go places without setting dangerous and expensive rule-cheating wind bags, while Rozinante will ghost along in light weather with her regular working sails, and in a breeze and chop of a sea will reach right past an ocean racer of her size: all the while Rozinante's crew will be comfortably seated in a roomy cockpit all safe and dry. This, of course, is because her waterline length is great enough to allow her to be driven fast, whereas if she had been modeled to fit the ocean racing rules, her displacement for the length would have been so great that no amount of sail could have made her fast.

A boat like Rozinante is an ideal single hander yet she can accommodate a party of six very comfortably for day sailing. One of the reasons she will slip along easily in light or medium weather is that she has no propeller strut and shaft, or propeller aperture, together with the great blessing of nothing to catch the lobster pot buoys that make navigation difficult these days.

As for her below-deck arrangement, the principal item is a very comfortable double berth and that is a very unusual thing in a boat of this size. As one of my friends says, most small boats have berths that can't be slept in unless you are either exhausted or partly drunk, and perhaps few things spoil a happy ship as much as sleeping arrangements that prevent the relaxation of sound sleep. Rozinante's berth will comfortably accommodate two adults, or two grownups and a child, or other combinations, such as a large person and two children. Of course, if a tent or weather cloth were rigged over the boom and cockpit so that one could spread an air mattress on the cockpit floor, then Rozinante might accommodate two grownups and two children, but I do not approve of packing Christians in as small a vessel as will hold dead sardines, although that may be the present style.

On the drawings of Rozinante, the space aft of the double berth is intended for a galley, and I have not drawn in any cooking arrangements for no fixed arrangement in this department is best for various climates and family combinations. Certainly an old bachelor like myself can get along well without making a mess at meal times, for about all I would require would be a can opener and the means of heating a little hot water for tea. While at home perhaps I consume less canned goods than the average person. I don't believe it is harmful to exist a few days at a time on a three-quarter canned food diet, for there certainly are fine, appetizing varieties of canned goods these days. Of course, on a

ship of this size, it is nice to have a frying pan and a pressure cooker, and one must learn to sit down on either the foot of the berth or a camp stool when cooking.

Now, Gentle Reader, while on the subject of cooking in small craft I am apt to get a little excited, so if I cast loose a broadside or two don't be alarmed, for I only hope to rake some of the devils, both male and female, who are spoiling much fun on the water and shortening people's lives, as well as prostrating good sailormen for a couple of hours a day in the best sailing weather. Some of these gluttons and show-offs want a galley with great head room to carry off the steam of four or five pots, kettles, and pans stewing at once, and, while I pity them as galley slaves, their egotism is driving them to the hardest kind of work just to show off. These are invariably the ones who serve up meals one or even two hours later than one is used to eating. It is said they do it on purpose so the poor guest has acquired an unnatural appe-

---

1. Lignumvitae Truck with 5/32" hole for Flag halyard
2. Tobin Bronze 5/8" x 10"
3. Spring Phosphor Bronze 1/16" x 1" x 4".
4. " " " 1/16" x 1" x 8 1/2"
   Clips of same material rivetted on ends
5. Special Tobin Bronze shackle for Boom-lift.
6. 1/4" Tobin Bronze pins 1/2" long 3/8" head
7. Main halyard Sheave of cast Bronze
8. Sheave pin 3/8" Tobin Bronze, One end rivetted to clip to prevent it from revolving clips can be strong Bronze 1/16" x 3/8" x 1 3/8"
9. Inner plate of Upper shroud attachment spring Phosphor Bronze 1/16" x 1 3/4" x 8"
10. Outer plate and Span stay attachment Spring Phosphor Bronze 1/16" x 1 3/4" x 5 1/2"
11. Fore Stay inner plate Spring Phosphor Bronze 1/16" x 1 1/2" x 8 1/2"
12. Outer plate 1/16" x 1 1/2" x 4 1/2"
13. All pins 3/8" Tobin Bronze 7/8" long 1/2" heads
14. Jib halyard strap Phosphor Bronze 1/16" x 1" x 3 5/8"
15. Spinnaker Halyard Lizard of fine grained wood 7/8" x 1 3/4" x 4".
16. Lower Shroud Inner plate Spring Phosphor Bronze 1/16" x 2 3/4" x 10"
17. Outer Plate P B 1/16" x 2 1/2" x 8"
18. Clip for Span stays P B 1/16" x 7/8" x 2 3/8"
19. Bushings of Tobin Bronze to increase the bearing area of the pins
20. Adjustable friction plate of Bronze 1/16" x 2" x 2 1/2"
21. 3/8" Bolt 1 5/16" long, head 3/8", thread 16, - Bronze
22. Spreader tips Bronze 1/16" x 3/4" x 3".
23. Strut 1/16" x 3/4" x 2 1/2"
24. Strap on end of main Boom to take the boom lift, clew outhal pendant and button for Boom crotch, of Phosphor Bz. 1/16" x 2 3/8" x 3 1/2"
25. Made of two parts of Tobin Bronze.
26. Jaw band of Tobin Bronze.
27. Button hole Bronze 1/16" x 1 3/4" x 2 1/2"
28. Spring Phosphor Bz 1/32" x 1" x 11 1/4"
29. Bronze 1/16" x 1" x 2 3/8" ~ 3/8" Bolt.

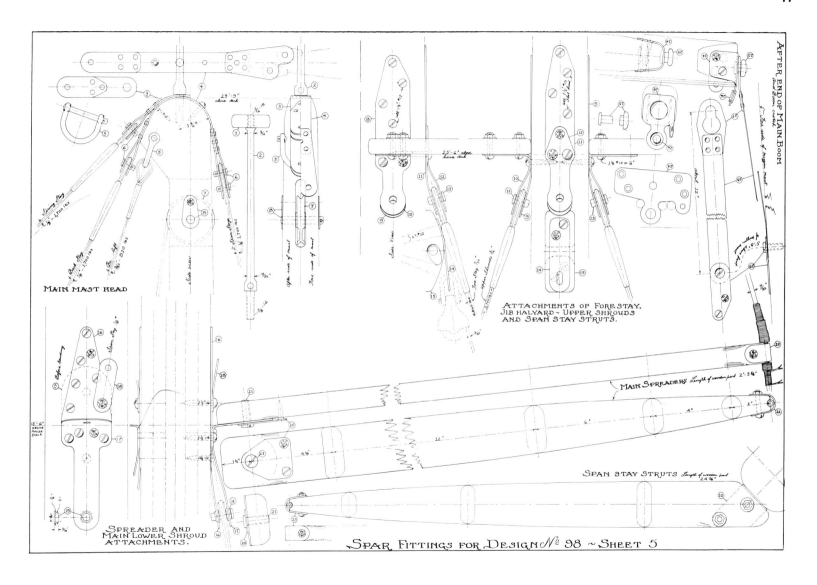

MAIN MAST HEAD

ATTACHMENTS OF FORE STAY.
JIB HALYARD ~ UPPER SHROUDS
AND SPAN STAY STRUTS.

AFTER END OF MAIN BOOM

MAIN SPREADERS

SPAN STAY STRUTS

SPREADER AND
MAIN LOWER SHROUD
ATTACHMENTS.

SPAR FITTINGS FOR DESIGN № 98 ~ SHEET 5

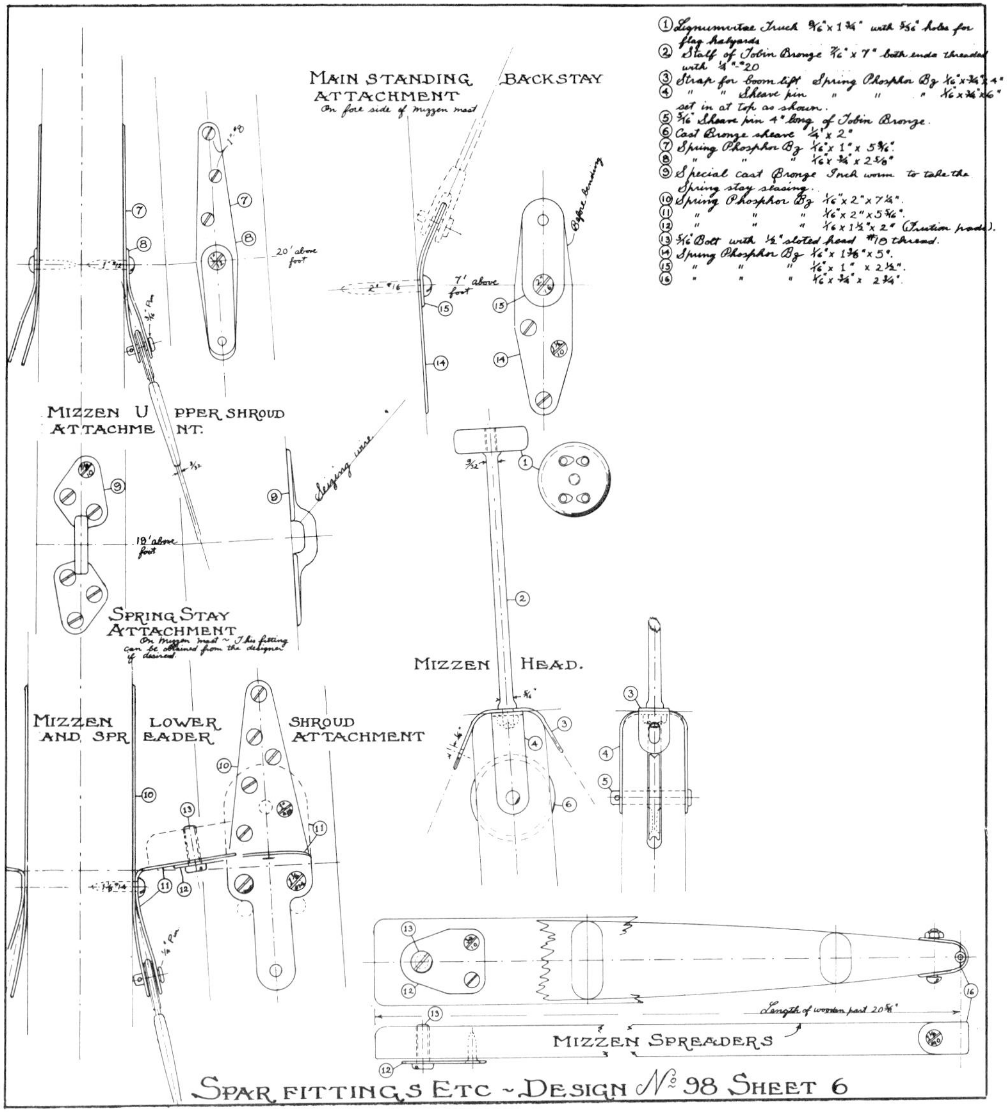

① Lignumvitae Truck 9/16" x 1 3/4" with 5/32" holes for flag halyards
② Staff of Tobin Bronze 7/16" x 7" both ends threaded with 1/4"-#20
③ Strap for boom lift Spring Phosphor Bz 1/16" x 3/4" x 4"
④ " " Sheave pin " " " 1/16" x 3/4" x 6" set in at top as shown.
⑤ 5/16" Sheave pin 4" long of Tobin Bronze.
⑥ Cast Bronze sheave 1/4" x 2"
⑦ Spring Phosphor Bz 1/16" x 1" x 5 9/16".
⑧ " " " 1/16" x 3/4" x 2 5/8"
⑨ Special cast Bronze Inch worm to take the Spring stay seizing.
⑩ Spring Phosphor Bz 1/16" x 2" x 7 1/4".
⑪ " " " 1/16" x 2" x 5 5/16".
⑫ " " " 1/16 x 1 1/2" x 2" (Friction pads).
⑬ 5/16" Bolt with 1/2" sloted head #10 thread.
⑭ Spring Phosphor Bz 1/16" x 1 7/8" x 5".
⑮ " " " 1/16" x 1" x 2 1/2".
⑯ " " " 1/16" x 3/4" x 2 3/4".
MAIN STANDING BACKSTAY ATTACHMENT
On fore side of mizzen mast
20' above foot
7' above foot
MIZZEN UPPER SHROUD ATTACHMENT
19' above foot
Seizing wire
SPRING STAY ATTACHMENT
On mizzen mast ~ This fitting can be obtained from the designer if desired
MIZZEN HEAD.
MIZZEN AND SPREADER LOWER SHROUD ATTACHMENT
Length of wooden part 20 1/8"
MIZZEN SPREADERS
SPAR FITTINGS ETC ~ DESIGN No 98 SHEET 6

Block and Fittings List

Item	Number Required	Size	General Description	Size of rope or wire used with fitting
Main Lower Shroud Turnbuckles	2	3/8"	Merriman Fig 377	7/32 wire
Main Upper Shroud Turnbuckles	2	5/16"	" " "	3/16 "
Main Standing Backstay Turnbuckle	1	1/4"	" " "	1/8 "
Main Span Stays Turnbuckles	2	1/4"	" " "	1/8 "
Mizzen Lower Shrouds Turnbuckles	2	1/4"	" " "	1/8 "
Mizzen Upper Shrouds Turnbuckles	2	1/4"	" " "	3/32 "
Special Mizzen Backstay See ㊻ on Construction Plan	1	5/16"	377-S / 525-R	2' of 5/16" Tobin Rod
Jib Halyard lead Block (Port side of mast)	1	#1	Merriman Fig 356 #1	3/8 Dia rope
Jib halyard blocks " " "	1 1	#1 #1	Merriman Fig 352 with Becket " " 358-S-#1	3/8 Dia rope
Main Halyard Jig Block	1	#1	Merriman " 370 #1 with Becket	3/8 Dia rope
Jib Sheet (Shackle)	1	5/16"	" " 388-J	7/16 Dia rope
Main Sheet Blocks	1 1	#1 #1	M-Fig 352 Becket and Fig 416 size 1 " " 353 Double and # 440-A-2"	
Mizzen Sheet Blocks	1 1	#0 #0	" " 352 " " 353 and 420-#2	5/16 rope " "
Main Clew Outhaul " " " Block	1 1	2 0	Merriman 411-#2 with track " 356-#0	
Main Mast Track		5/8	M-Fig 406 ~ 28' long	
" Boom "		"	" " " ~ 11' "	
Mizzen Mast "		"	" " " ~ 18' "	
" Boom "		"	" " " ~ 8'-8" "	

Cleats

All Wilcox-Crittenden Fig 4020

Mooring cleat ㊼ on construction plan 10" long
2 - Jib sheet on outside of coaming ㊾ on construction plan 5 1/2 long
1 Main Halyard on Starbord side mast 6" above house deck 6 1/2" long
1 Jib halyard ㊽ on construction plan 5 1/2" long 1 Spare cleat ㊽ " " " " "
1 Spinnaker halyard cleat 5 1/2" long on after side of mast under goose neck.
1 Mizzen Halyard cleat 4 1/2" long on starboard side of mizzen mast about 8" above foot
1 Mizzen sheet cleat ㊿ on construction plan 5 1/2" long (This cleat is big because it will be used for other things)
1 Main Sheet cleat on Port side of mizzen mast about 12" above foot 5 1/2" long.

tite and will think the devilish cook a wizard, but during this two hours' wait with the guests' stomachs rumbling and grumbling, only fed with cocktails, the men folks up in the cockpit are getting fighting mad, so quite likely someone will say something that was intended as a joke but will be taken by the other empty stomach as an insult. Well, when the rich over-seasoned food is served up everyone will gobble it down so quickly that they are beyond their plimsoll marks before they know it and have to spend the afternoon in gradually overcoming this tax on the system. More than one will resort to pills or effervescent medicine for relief while they sit or lie sweltering in their blubber. Of course the whole day has been wasted and it is doubtful if the galley can be straightened out before the next weekend.

So, Gentle Reader, please don't write in to me about the wonderful idea you have of spoiling Rozinante with a dog house for a galley, for if you like eating better than sailing, you should stay home and have a barbecue in the back yard. Then you can turn in and sleep off your gastronomical jag. There is no reason why good meals for two or four cannot be served up on time in rain or shine from the space allowed for a galley on Rozinante, and the cleaning up will be a matter of minutes. If the steward happens to be an egotist or exhibitionist, he will get much more credit and satisfaction from serving good meals on time from a small space, for that really calls for a dexterity not described in cook books, while somehow or other those light meals taken while under way taste much better than the kind previously described which sink the captain and crew beyond the ability to enjoy sailing.

If a boat like Rozinante is to be used in the spring and fall north of Cape Cod, then she should have a small coal-burning stove, for perhaps few sensations are pleasanter than entering a warm, dry cabin after a sail in cool and overcast weather. But, for summer sailing south of the Cape, any of the safe, light stoves are quite adequate. Around 1890 and before, there were some small folding aluminum stoves made for canoe cruisers. These outfits with several cooking utensils fitted into a small box that could be used as a stand to mount the stove on, and I cruised with one of them many years ago, and, strange to relate, this little cruiser had a mid-ship section nearly the same size and shape as Rozinante. There are some very small, compact stoves now made in Europe for campers, but you will have to get them from one of the camping supply companies.

In some ways Rozinante would be better with a sliding hatch over the after end of the deck house, for it is very pleasant to stand in this place some of the time on a self-steering boat of this type, but the expense of a well-made hatch would be perhaps $150 these days, and I would duck my head many times for that sum. The modern tendency to make boats higher and higher, and automobiles lower and lower for looks doesn't make much sense. Certainly the cabin of Rozinante would be easier to enter than all present sport cars with the top up, but in both cases a little practice makes the maneuver quite easy. It is the combination of many things like this hatchway that makes the expense of the modern yachts more than they are worth, so we will consider the cost of complications.

When H-28 was designed I wrote an article or two in praise of simplicity and tried to tell how much first cost and

STANDING RIGGING

Name of Part	Number Required	Dimensions	Diameter and construction of wire	Approximate stay weight in lbs	Total breaking strength in lbs	Length of stay	Fittings	Rigging notes
Fore Stay	1	24'-6" — 7/32	7x7	1/4	4,800 lbs	29'	1-1/8 solid thimble; 1-1/8 open thimble; 1-1/8 closed shackle	
Main Standing Back Stay	1	20' — 1/8 ... 1/4	7x7	1/8	1,700 lbs	32'	2-1/8 solid thimbles	
Main Upper Shrouds	2	24'-3" — 3/16 ... 3/16	7x7	3/16	3,700 lbs	55'	4-3/16 solid thimble	
Main Lower Shrouds	2	16'-2" — 7/32 ... 3/16	7x7	7/32	4,800 lbs	97'	4-1/8 solid thimble	
Span Stays	2	13'-5" — 1/8 ... 1/4	7x7	1/8	1,700 lbs	30'	4-1/8 solid thimble	
Spring Stay	1	17'-9" — 1/8	7x7	1/8	1,700 lbs	21'	1-1/8 solid thimble; 1-1/8 open thimble	one seizing
Mizzen Upper Shrouds	2	17'-10" — 3/32 ... 1/4	7x7	3/32	920 lbs	40'	4-3/32 solid thimble	
Mizzen Lower Shrouds	2	11'-10" — 1/8	7x7	1/8	1,700 lbs	30'	4-1/8 solid thimble	
Main Boom Lift	1	29' — 3/32	7x7	3/32	920 lbs	31'	2-3/32 open thimble	
Mizzen Boom Lift	1	18'-3" — 3/32	7x7	3/32	920 lbs	20'	2-3/32 open thimble; 1-shackle with M-Fig 306	

RUNNING RIGGING

Name of Part	Number Required	Dimensions	Size and construction of rope	Approximate weight in lbs	Approximate length of rope	Fittings	Copper notes
Jib Halyard	1	78' — 1-1/8 cir	7x19	1,900		79'	No fittings on slack list
Main Halyard	1	27' / 31' — 1/8 Korotless; 1-1/8 cir Manila		30'	32'	1-1/8 open thimble; 1-shackle M-Fig 306; etc.	
Mizzen Halyard	1	42' — 1/8 dia Dacron			33'	1-1/8 open thimble; 1-1/8 solid thimble	
Spinnaker Halyard	1	48' — 12 Thread or 1/8 cir manila			48'	No fittings	Head of spinnaker
Jib Sheets	1 pair	25' — 1-1/8 cir manila			52'	2-1/8 open thimble; 1-shackle M-Fig 306-J; 3/16 rope	
Main Sheet	1	60' — 1-1/8 cir Linen			61'	No fittings on slack list	
Mizzen Sheet	1	24' — 1 cir Linen			25'	1-1/8 open thimble; 1-smallest size shackle	
Main Flag Halyards	1	65' — 1/8 or less fish line					
Mizzen Flag Halyards	1	43' — 1/8 or less fish line					
Anchor Warp	1	125' — 1/2 dia 1-1/2 cir NYLON					
Dock Lines	2	35' — 1/2 dia 1-1/8 cir manila					

annual expense could be saved by sticking to simplicity. Well, the first few H-28's were built something like the drawings and cost about one third of what several builders quote for them today. Most of this increase in cost is because the builders and owners have added complications and made changes from the original design. I hate to say it, but most of these changes have been made simply to show how much smarter the builder and the owner are than the designer, and, while I grant that that is so, still I sometimes wonder if they had spent fifty years designing, building, and

sailing yachts, they, too, might not want to do things in the simplest and best way. If many of them knew that when you alter the design of a well-proportioned object, say a fine English shotgun or a violin, it is necessary to make a complete new design or the proportions will not be correct to work well or look well, perhaps they would hesitate. This is also true with the design of a small sailboat that has been carefully worked out by anyone who has a sense of proportion developed from long years of experience. I don't know why so many young sailors think a boat is modern if she is homely, slow, and dangerous, but it has been said that art, music, and poetry went democratic or bolshevistic because the modern youth was not willing to take the time to study these arts and develop a sense of proportion. I, myself, think most modern things are pretty rotten, so my advice to you, Gentle Reader, is, if you want to make changes, by all means get a modern boat for your changes cannot make her any worse.

The cost of modern yachts seems to be fifteen times greater than those built before World War I, while the cost of real estate, clothes and food is only about three times greater. Much of the increase in the modern yacht costs comes from complications and changes in design where the details are not properly drawn out in scale drawings for the workmen. It used to be that the cost of a small sailing yacht was divided about as follows: one third for the hull; one third for the interior; one third for sails, spars, rigging, and deck hardware. If she were an auxiliary, the engine and its installation was figured another third; in other words an auxiliary usually cost one third more than a straight sailer, so the Rozinante, with her very simple interior and no engine, should cost something like five eighths of the usual auxiliary of this size and grade. If these little ships become popular, don't let the builders jack their prices up because they are popular, as they have been doing of late with H-28's. In getting estimates on a boat of this kind, it is well to let the builder know you are getting estimates from several builders. Perhaps a boat like Rozinante is the only type that

many of us can really afford today for, although her first cost will be quite a little, she will hold a high resale value for many years to come and that is the cheapest or most economical kind of boat you can have.

And remember that a thing of beauty is a joy forever.

CONSTRUCTION PLAN

1. Lead keel, 3,360 pounds. It would be best if the keel were cast of junk lead for this often contains some tin, etc., which stiffens it. Also, it will plane, drill, and tap best if about 2% of its weight in antimony is added to the last of the pouring to stiffen the top.

2. Wood keel, 2" thick, about 14" wide, and 12'4" long. It may be white oak, yellow pine, or Philippine mahogany.

3. Fore keel, 2" thick, 2¾" wide forward of station 8. Aft of this the width can increase to the width found necessary on the lines. Length 7'2". The fore keel should be of white oak to hold the planking fastenings well .

4. After keel, 2" thick, 2¾" wide aft, and about 11½" wide forward at station 16; 11'1" long. It would be best if made of white oak or other firm, rot-resisting wood, such as yellow pine or Philippine mahogany.

5. Stem, 2¾" wide full length at both the rabbet, back rabbet, and after face. It may be white oak or hackmatack if a natural crook; or if steam-bent it may be two layers of 2" white oak, and if glued up in layers it may be fabricated from 5/16" strips of Philippine mahogany.

6. Stern post, is the same in all respects as the stem except length and shape.

7. Deadwood, hard pine, ball pine, yellow pine, or Philip-

pine mahogany. The piece between the main keel and the after keel will be about 10″ wide forward and approximately 13″ deep aft, and 6′1″ long. If desired it may be made up of layers.

The *lower* deadwood may be of the same materials but about 13″ wide forward, 11″ deep aft, and 7′1″ long. May be made up of layers if desired.

8. Floor timbers, white oak, their thickness and depth are given on the drawing.

9. Floor timber bolts, all of Tobin bronze, and all of the hanger bolt type, except the one on station 20. All to have washers under the nuts. If these bolts are made up special, then only the lower 2½″ need be threaded. The diameter and length of these bolts are given on the drawing in most cases, but where not they are to be 2″ longer than the floors are deep.

10. Keel bolts, all of Tobin bronze, ½″ diameter with 13 threads to the inch. They should pierce the lead from 6 to 8 times their diameter.

11. Hoisting bolts, ⅝″ diameter Tobin bronze, Everdur, or Monel. It would be well if the threads were National Fine, or 18 to the inch. There should be good washers under the lower nuts of 1½″ or more diameter. The upper end nut is shown on one of the sheets of rigging fittings. The *forward* bolt is about 9½″ long, and the *after* one about 25″ long.

12. Drive bolts, at the after end of the keel, two or more ⅜″ diameter, self-heading bronze drive bolts.

13. The deep floor timber on station 20 is to have a Tobin bronze keel bolt, ⅝″ diameter and about 2′5″ long. This bolt is the principal fastening of the after end of the keel. As the drilled hole is quite long, the auger or bit should be started with a guide to hold it plumb, or it will not stay on the center line. A bare-footed ship's auger will drill the straightest hole, for those with a spur are apt to follow the grain of the wood. After this bolt is in place the mortise hole at the lower end can be blocked off from both sides.

14. Upper deadwood: the upper part may be secured with 7/16″ bronze lag screws, 5″ long, with washers under the heads. It would be well if they were staggered as shown.

15. Frames or timbers are steam-bent white oak, 1¼″ x 1¼″. They should be secured to the floor timbers with either 3/16″ copper rivets, 2″ Monel Anchorfast boat nails, or #12 stove bolts or machine screws with washers under nut. These fastenings are not of much importance after the yacht is built if there are planking fastenings in both frames and floors.

16. Deck beams: *regular* deck beams are 1″ x 1½″. The *strong* beams on stations 5, 7 and 23 are 1½″ x 1½″. *Deck* beams of oak, ash or elm. Crown of deck is ⅜″ to the foot, or 2⅝″ in 7′.

17. Clamp, 1″ x 2¼″ or more, of spruce or Douglas fir. If possible in one length.

18. Shelf, 1″ x 1¼″ of the same material as clamp, fastened as shown on the full-sized section.

19. Planking to be about ⅞″ thick or a little less when planed up. It may be rift-grain fir of a fine texture, soft pine, Eastern cedar, or Philippine mahogany. If the last, it need not be more than ¾″ thick.

Planking is fastened with 1½″ #12 screws set in enough to properly bung the heads. The size of the bungs may be 7/16″. It is often cheapest to use Everdur or Monel planking fastenings because so few of them will break in driving.

20. Deck: fir, spruce, soft pine, cypress, or California redwood. Of tongue and groove strips ¾″ thick by 3″ wide. Several fastenings are satisfactory for the deck, among which are brass and bronze screws, galvanized steel screws, galvanized boat nails, or Monel Anchorfast boat nails, 1½″ #10. The deck

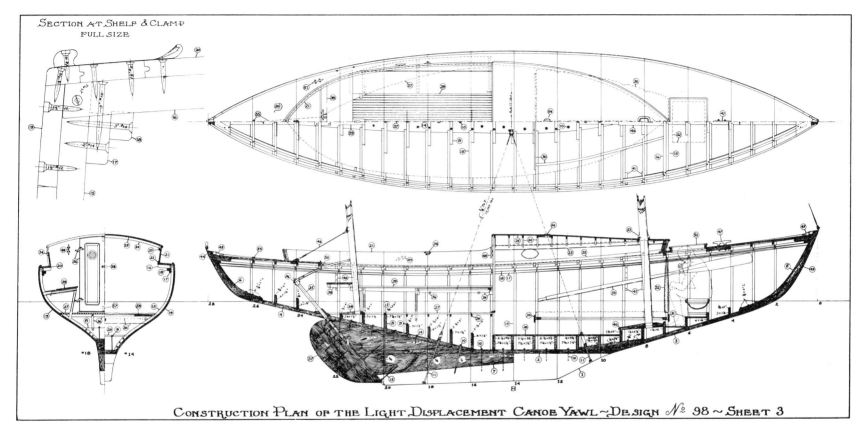

SECTION AT SHELF & CLAMP
FULL SIZE

CONSTRUCTION PLAN OF THE LIGHT DISPLACEMENT CANOE YAWL ~ DESIGN № 98 ~ SHEET 3

should be planed up carefully, puttied, cross sandpapered, and given a coat of thick white lead paint before laying the canvas cover. The latter should be loose-woven light sheeting which comes in wide widths and takes to the paint better than hard-woven canvas. Fiberglass decks are said to be very good if painted with a non-skid paint.

21. Cockpit coaming and house sides, oak or mahogany, ¾″ thick. On an angle of about 8°, and fastened up through the deck. This coaming will be about 19′ long, and, if it is not convenient to have it in one piece, it may be scarfed just forward of the house partition.

22. Inside house: the joint between the deck and house side

should be covered with a wood strip about 5/16" thick and 1¾" wide to cover the canvas decking which is turned up in this region.

23.   Lodging strip for house beams: oak about 2½" x ⅞".

24.   House beams: oak, ash, or elm, ⅝" x 1⅛" spaced 8". Crown of house deck 8" in 6', or radius of 7'.

25.   House deck: soft pine, clear spruce, or Port Orford cedar, ½" thick, tongue and groove, canvas covered.

26.   Cockpit floor supports: oak, 1½" x ⅞", with some supporting struts where necessary, as shown on section 18.

27.   Cockpit floor would be best if made of teak slats unpainted. The slats can be 1" wide and ¾" thick, spaced ¼", and bunged over the fastenings.

Other good material for the slats are oak and elm, but any fine grain strong wood will do. The central section of this floor should lift out the full length for cleaning the bilge, and there should be a short section forward for the bilge pump so the sections can be of about the following lengths, 11½", 2', 11½", and 4', as shown.

28.   Cabin sole, ¾" thick soft pine, cypress, California redwood, or other suitable wood, and painted dark brown. It should also open up the full length in two or more lengths about 9" wide.

29.   Cockpit seats, soft pine about ¾" thick and varnished or painted a light color that will not get too hot in the sun. The seats should be about 12" wide and 6' 6" long. Back of the seats there is a slat about ½" thick to hold ropes, etc. The seats are on an angle of about 8° to correspond with the coaming. The bracing under the seats should be of strong wood well secured to the hull with screws.

30.   Berth support or frame should be quite strong and arranged to use rope lacings running both athwartship and fore and aft, spaced about 6". The reason rope supports are used instead of a canvas berth bottom is that after the mattress is rolled back one can reach down between the lacings to get at objects stowed under the berth.

The mattress for this berth frame is about 4' 6" wide at its after end, so should be made in two halves. This also allows a cutout for the mast. The outboard edges of the mattress will be quite flaring, and the mattress is shown in dotted lines on the deck view.

There should be a removable wooden pole or spar amidships just under the berth lacings. This is shown on section 14 but not shown on the deck plan or side view because it would be confusing, but this spar should be round, about 1" diameter and supported at the mast and after end.

The *side pieces of the berth frame* may be oak, about 1¼" square with the outboard edges well rounded off between the frames.

The *vertical athwartship pieces* may be ¾" x 2¾" with the horizontal pieces the same dimensions but cut out for the lacing and screwed together to make a tee-shape as shown.

31.   Bays between stations 5 and 7 may be floored over as shown, and if so a bucket toilet may be used very conveniently in this region which is right under the hatch.

32.   Curtain to shut off the fore peak.

33.   Oar, 10" ash.

34.   Rowlock socket, bronze, for rowlock with ⅝" shank.

35.   Rudder stock assembly is as follows:

Rudder stock may be either Monel or bronze, 1" extra heavy iron pipe size with an O.D. of 1.315", and I.D. of .957; length 3' 5".

Rudder tube may be either Monel or bronze, 1¼" standard iron pipe size with O.D. of 1.660" and I.D. of 1.380"; length 2'.

The rudder tube is to be threaded on its lower end for about 4″ and screwed into a wooden block about as shown on the plan. It is important to bore the hole in this block quite parallel with the groove for the rudder in the deadwood. This can be done by drilling a small hole in approximately the right place and then stretching a chalk line through the hole so that it lines up correctly. The hole can then be enlarged by using a boring bar, say ¾″ diameter, 3′ long, supported by wooden guides at both the upper and lower ends. The cutter of the bar can be similar to that on an expansion bit. The hole should be about 1 9/16″ diameter, or a size that is shown by trial takes the threads well in a similar piece of wood.

When the tube is finally screwed in, the threads should be coated with thick white lead paint. The rudder blade is fastened to the stock with four 5″ #24 flathead wood screws, either silicon bronze or Monel.

At the lower end of the stock there should be a bronze plug to take the upper rudder strap. Both rudder straps may be made of bronze, about ⅛″ thick x 1½″ wide, and about 8″ long before bending, and can be held in place with either wood screws or through copper rivets.

36. Tiller socket, Merriman Fig. 483 — size 2. The *tiller* should be of hard wood such as locust, ash, or white oak, and of a length which will jam against the mizzen mast when the tiller head is depressed. This is for making a steering adjustment when rowing with one oar.

The ball at the head of the tiller can be 1⅜″ diameter; the neck of the tiller ⅞″; the depth of the tiller at the socket 1⅜″.

37. Rudder blade should be of oak of the thickness called for on the full size lines, which will be about 1½″ forward. The trailing edge should be about ¾″ thick.

On the drawing the rudder is made up of strips of the follow-ing widths, 6¾″, 6″ and 4½″. The *first* two of these strips can be fastened with four ⅜″ self-heading drive bolts about 9″ long. The *after strip* can be secured with three 5/16″ drive bolts about 7″ long. These drive bolts can be bronze, brass, or galvanized iron. There also can be some wood screws of about 3″ #14, to hold the ends together as shown.

38. Thwart: at the after end of the cockpit there may be a removable thwart notched over frame 22 and resting on cleats screwed to the planking. This thwart is about 2″ higher than the other seats. It can be 14″ wide and 1″ thick of light-colored wood if to be varnished. This thwart is made removable so one can get under the after deck for cleaning, painting, etc.

39. Mizzen mast step: oak or other rot-resisting firm wood 3″ wide, 2″ thick forward, ⅞″ aft, and 13½″ long. Set over the floor timber bolts and held down with small screws. The mortise for the tongue of the mast is 3″ x 1″.

40. Main mast step: oak, 4″ wide, 2½″ thick, 25′ long. The mortise for the tongue of the mast is 3¾″ x 1¼″. The mortise for both masts should go way through as shown so as not to hold water. The forward end of the main step should have two screws or nails to hold it to floor timber 7. Also a 1½″ oak block under its forward end. (This is not shown on the drawing.)

41. Main chain plates all of Tobin bronze, Everdur, Phosphor bronze, or Monel. All half-hard or harder; 3/16″; or more thick, 1¼″ wide, and 20″ long. Well secured with several flat-headed non-ferrous machine screws, ¼″ x 1″ or larger, heads set into planking ¼″, or enough to bung. It would be well if the holes for these bolts were layed off to clear the seams of the planking, and spaced from 2″ to 2½″.

42. Mizzen chain plates all of the same material as main chain plates, but ⅛″ thick, 1″ wide, 16″ long. Fastened same as main.

43. Stem band same material as chain plates, about ¼″ thick, as wide as the face of stem at head, and approximately 14″ long if it is desired to carry it to the LWL.

44. Sternpost band, bronze ¼″ thick, width of face of stern post at face, and about 8″ long.

45. Chocks, cast bronze, riveted through stem head.

46. Mizzen backstay made up of Merriman short-body turnbuckle, Fig. 3775 — 5/16″ with 2′ bronze rod at one end, and Merriman Fig. 525R at mast and deck. Also block under deck as shown. The upper end of this fitting is supposed to be close under the goose neck.

47. Mooring cleat, Wilcox, Crittenden Fig. 4020 — 10″, through-bolted to oak block under deck.

48. Main and jib halyard cleats on each side of deck house, W. C. Fig. 4020 — 5½″.

49. Jib sheet cleats P & S, W. C. Fig. 4020 — 5½″.

50. Mizzen sheet cleat 4″ to port, W. C. Fig. 4020 — 5½″.

51. Cleats P & S, for mooring, towing tender, etc. W. C. Fig. 4020, 6½″.

52. Hatch with opening 22″ x 18″. Top may be ⅜″ laminated wood, canvas covered.

53. Canvas mast coat on wooden grooved collar. The mast is 4½″ x 3½″ at deck, radius of corners 1″.

54. Hand-hole plate for hoisting sling. W. C. Fig. 532 — 2″ opening. Block under as shown.

55. Mizzen sheet lead W. C. Fig. 5811, #1. The mizzen sheet leads to one side and through the coaming just above the deck as shown on deck view.

56. Cabin doors can be made of a frame and panel of soft pine about ¾″ thick as shown on drawing; or of ½″ laminated wood bound around the outside with ½″ brass angle. In either case, there should be ventilators similar to W. C. Fig. 8798 — 4″ diameter.

As mentioned under 29 the cockpit seats are arranged to make a rack to hold the cabin doors when unhung, but they must be slid in their racks with the hinges downward as shown. It will be found best to carry the cabin doors unhung all the time when sailing for this gives free access to the cabin, and the doors will not bang about when rolling or tacking ship.

There should be a removable wooden plug at the forward inboard end of the rack to hold the doors from sliding out when the vessel is heeled.

57. One door can have brass flush bolts similar to Perko Fig. 1052 — #1 to top and bottom.

58. Hasp for padlock to secure the other door — W. C. Fig. 4740 — 3″.

59. Bench: there may be a bench for a stove on the starboard side between frames 13 and 15, but the height and width of this bench will be dependent on the type of stove selected by the owner. Opposite this bench or the stove there may be a comfortable seat of a type selected by the owner.

5   HOW TO BUILD MEADOW LARK

A great many people have asked for the design of a shallow-draft yacht or cruising boat. Apparently there are many who would like to cruise in some of the very shallow lagoons and bays in the Gulf of Mexico, Florida, Albemarle Sound, and the Chesapeake, and I can say from my experience that even in New England waters some of the most pleasant cruising grounds require shallow draft.

Meadow Lark is a suitable name for this craft as she could venture inland and, you might say, skim over the marshes and meadows as the joyful bird of that name does over many of our fields which border the Atlantic. The boat is somewhat reminiscent of the *Lark* of Tom Day's time.

There are many today who can visualize a different type of yachting than ocean racing, and who would like to spend their vacations in pleasure with comfortable relaxation. Some of these people have artistic tastes and know that the prettiest scenes are along shore, with the woods in the background contrasting with the marshland, beach, and river banks. They would like to anchor in sheltered places, or lie on the bottom of a sandy inlet, cook supper in comfort, and sleep without worry.

But the principal object of Meadow Lark is economy, for she should be cheap to build, easy to keep up, and could be hauled out by an amateur with a few planks and rollers.

The model of Meadow Lark is that of a modified sharpie with a slightly rounded bottom and sides, and it will be found that these slight curves are nearly as easy to plank up as straight surfaces but have greater strength. The freeboard aft is rather high compared to that forward, but this is to discourage her tacking around when at anchor, a feature somewhat annoying in sharpies. The chine forward is well below the waterline so that she should not pound either when at anchor or when sailing in a small chop, and it is believed that the slight round to the bottom forward will cause less slap than most sharpies have in a seaway.

As seen from on deck, Meadow Lark is rather more triangular than most sharpies, but this is done to give a large cockpit, and with the rounded bottom she should not drag much water at a slight heel.

At first I drew out Meadow Lark drawing only twelve inches of water, but I found that this draft did not allow a large enough propeller to be efficient, so the draft was increased to fifteen inches, and this only allows one and one-half inches of water over a twelve-inch propeller whose

Whether on the sand, waiting patiently for the tide to return while the crew plays baseball, or driving to windward in a fresh breeze, the versatile Meadow Lark *has an eminently practical look about her.*

lower blades are one and one-half inches above the skeg bottom. Of course such a high propeller will cavitate for a few seconds before the boat gets under way. The propeller also will not work very well in reverse, but these are some of the disadvantages of shallow craft.

The construction of Meadow Lark is as simple as is compatible with strength and long life. The bottom is thick, strong, and heavy in order to act as ballast and also to give adequate strength for taking the bottom in some sea. While it will be necessary to have some inside ballast on Meadow Lark, still she has an outside lead keel two inches deep and about twelve inches wide running for half of her length.

Leeboards are used on Meadow Lark instead of a centerboard for the three following good reasons:

1. They are cheaper and no great disadvantage on a boat which will do little quick tacking.

2. They take up no room in the cabin, whereas a large centerboard box sometimes quite spoils a cabin.

3. (And most important.) Having no centerboard box allows the frames to pass from side to side so the bottom can be strong enough for almost any sort of stranding.

Some Dutch boats take the bottom every tide and think

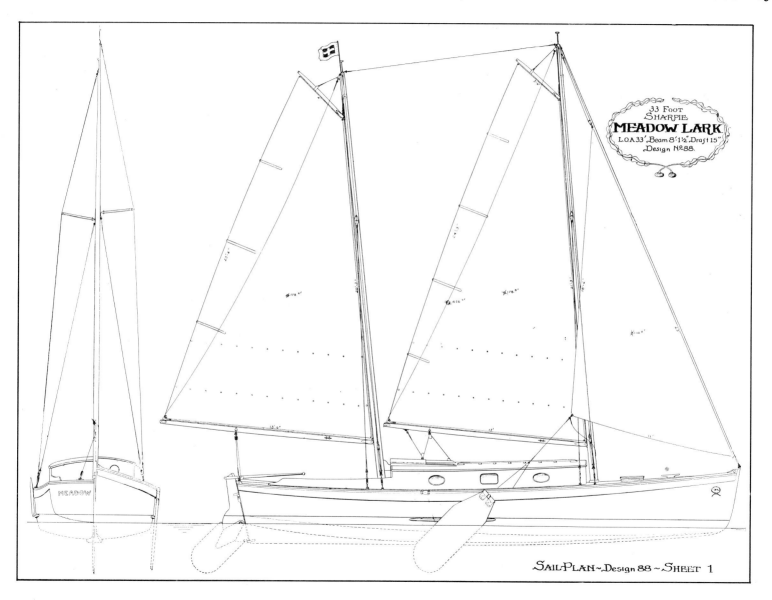

33 FOOT
SHARPIE
MEADOW LARK
L.O.A. 33', Beam 8'1½", Draft 15"
Design No. 88.

MEADOW

SAIL PLAN ~ Design 88 ~ Sheet 1

nothing of it, whereas a centerboard slot, if long, opens or closes if the bottom of the yacht is strained by stranding, and the slot is invariably jammed with mud, sand, or pebbles, so the centerboard cannot be lowered again until the mess has been cleared away.

The rudder is an improved pattern that will swing or fold backwards when striking bottom, or can be hauled up with a pennant, so that altogether Meadow Lark can be run into very shallow water. The draft amidships and aft, being only fifteen inches, would allow one to wade around her, if there were a level bottom, without getting wet above the knees. Way forward she only draws six or eight inches, so that a tender is not at all necessary.

Of course such a shallow boat will not have much head-room in the cabin, only about four feet eight inches. How-ever there is plenty of headroom when in a sitting position. Way aft near the hatch there can be a stove with plenty of room for cooking, and forward of this four berths. As the cockpit is seven feet long, by putting a tent over the mizzen boom two others could sleep aft, altogether giving sleeping accommodations for six people, which is quite remarkable in a boat of this size and cost. As more is written about the cabin in the description that accompanies the construction plan, I will say no more about the cabin now.

Sail Plan

There are several things about the sail plan that are adopted or proportioned particularly for this type of boat. First, the spacing of the masts is to give a long deckhouse and an un-obstructed cockpit. This has put both masts rather farther forward than is customary on a ketch. In fact she nearly becomes a schooner.

The second peculiarity is the use of short gaffs instead of the usual leg-o'-mutton sail, and this was done in order to get sufficient sail area without excessively high masts. Too high or long masts are a dangerous thing on such a shallow yacht. Also for inland cruising they prevent one from passing under many bridges. A gaff sail also has many advantages, the principal one being that almost any sailmaker can cut a good setting one, and the amount of draft in the sails can easily be regulated by simply peaking the gaff up more or less. This makes it possible generally to use a gaff sail longer without recutting, so that it is the most economical type of sail for cruising.

It is believed that the proportions of the sail on Meadow Lark are such that she will, for all practical purposes, be as fast as if she had higher masts and leg-o'-mutton sails. The main and mizzen sails have quite deep reefs, and with the jib down and both sails double reefed it is believed she can be sailed in a storm. Nevertheless her spars and rigging will be as light as I dare to make them simply to gain stability, which is a vital point on a boat of such shallow draft.

A loose-footed jib has been adopted because it is easy to set and take off the stay, but in some ways a self-tending jib would be an advantage where there are leeboards to handle, and I would advise the use of a self-tending jib in cases where the owner would leave the jib on the stay for long periods.

It is hoped that Meadow Lark can get along without backstays, for the masts are quite large in their fore-and-aft dimensions at the deck and will be stepped with two or three degrees more rake than shown on the sail plan, but brought up to the rake shown by tension on the forestay and springstay. (In this way fishing schooners often can get along without backstays.)

The procedure in coming about with Meadow Lark would be to first lower away the weather leeboard (and it can swing out to weather if it wants to), then put the helm down, and when she is in the wind change the jibsheets. Then when she has taken up the new tack, haul up the leeboard which has become the weather one. This last need not be done at once. In fact in short tacking both leeboards can be left down so that one person can tack ship easily after he has learned how.

Sharpies have been famous for many years for being good sea boats, but they must be handled carefully for, like many other good sea boats, it is possible to capsize them. Every effort, however, has been made on Meadow Lark to get the weights as low as possible.

Power Plant

On such a shallow boat it is almost necessary to use twin screws in order to get sufficient propeller area with small diameter, so that Meadow Lark has been designed using two of the Kermath one-cylinder engines called Model Sixteen 5. Although this is a very small engine, still when used with a two and a one-half to one reduction gear, two of them apparently will give an aggregate of ten horsepower at some 1,200 revolutions of the propeller per minute. The first cost and economy of these engines is so remarkable that they should prove a most efficient power plant for a boat of this type.

All things considered, Meadow Lark may be the most fun for the money of any boat that I have designed, for such a craft could be kept in commission the whole year 'round if her home port were a well sheltered cove or river, and in most places south of Delaware Bay could be used in pleasant winter weather. Perhaps she is in a class by herself for certain types of shallow water fishing and shooting, and perhaps at times she would make better time along the coast than larger and much more expensive yachts, for with a good breeze on the quarter and both engines going she might travel at seven or eight miles an hour and, of course, take advantage of many short cuts.

Best of all, some of the ladies would enjoy a sail in Meadow Lark who would not go out more than once on some of the deep craft which lay on their ears and have to beat through rough weather because their excessive draft keeps them offshore. Meadow Lark is also the only type of yacht some fathers with two or three children can afford.

Lines

The model of Meadow Lark is shaped principally to make construction easy, and the lines are drawn in a way that will make the laying down of the full-size lines a simple matter; in fact only the sections need be drawn, which can be done on a scrive board only about 9 by 5½ feet.

The two principal points on each section are the height and width at the sheer, or deck line, and the chine fairing line. This latter line is shown on the drawing as a dotted line and represents a point where the curve of the bottom and sides would converge if the chine were not rounded off on a radius of three inches.

The curve, or shape of the sides, is the same the full length, and this curve is shown half size at the top of the drawing. If the builder makes a wooden template this shape, he can readily draw out all sides of the sections from it by simply keeping the zero point at the chine fairing line and swinging the upper end of the template in until it comes to the deck line.

The offsets are given in feet, inches, and eighths of inches. The load waterline (LWL) is the base line for heights, and their dimensions are given above or below this point.

Meadow Lark has no keel proper, but the bottom planking, which is 1¾ inches thick, joins directly to the stem as is shown on the construction plan. The outside keel, which is lead, from 5 to 28, can be cast in sections of convenient length and fastened in place when construction is nearly completed, so need not be considered in laying down or in the first part of construction. The bottom planking is thick for weight or ballast, the topside planking 1-inch thick of lighter material, and the deck only ¾ inch thick of light material. All through the construction the weights are to be as low as possible, and upper parts as light as is safe.

If I were building Meadow Lark, she would be built upside down, for this method not only saves a great deal of bracing to hold the frames in place during construction, but it makes the work of planking the bottom (planing, caulking, etc.) vastly easier. A shallow and comparatively narrow boat like this can easily be turned over after she is planked.

Stem

The stem and developed stern, or transom, are drawn upside down for the convenience of the workman who, after he has turned the drawing around, will have these parts with their small figures close to him. The stem can be in one piece as shown, or built up if a knee of this size is not readily procurable, but it is only about six feet overall, and pieces from the butt of an oak or hackmatack tree this size are usually easy to find. After the stem has been bandsawed out to its profile then it can be run through the thickness planer, for its total sided dimension is 3½ inches for its full length. While the stem may seem too wide for the throat of some thickness planers, it can be canted around as it is going through, which most mill men know how to do.

Developed Stern

This perhaps needs no comment except that it is drawn to the outside of the planking and deck and must be beveled slightly so that its forward side is large enough to allow for proper beveling to take the side and bottom planking. On the construction plan, the stern or transom is shown of 1½ inch oak of fairly narrow planks supported by the stern knee in the middle, and cleats or frames; altogther it is of a similar construcion to the side planking (beveled, caulked, etc.), which I have found stands up much better than transoms of other construction.

The frames are to be spaced two feet, and sawn as shown on the construction plan. If she is to be built upside down, then the frames should have legs attached to them which will come exactly to some base line, say 4 feet above the LWL,

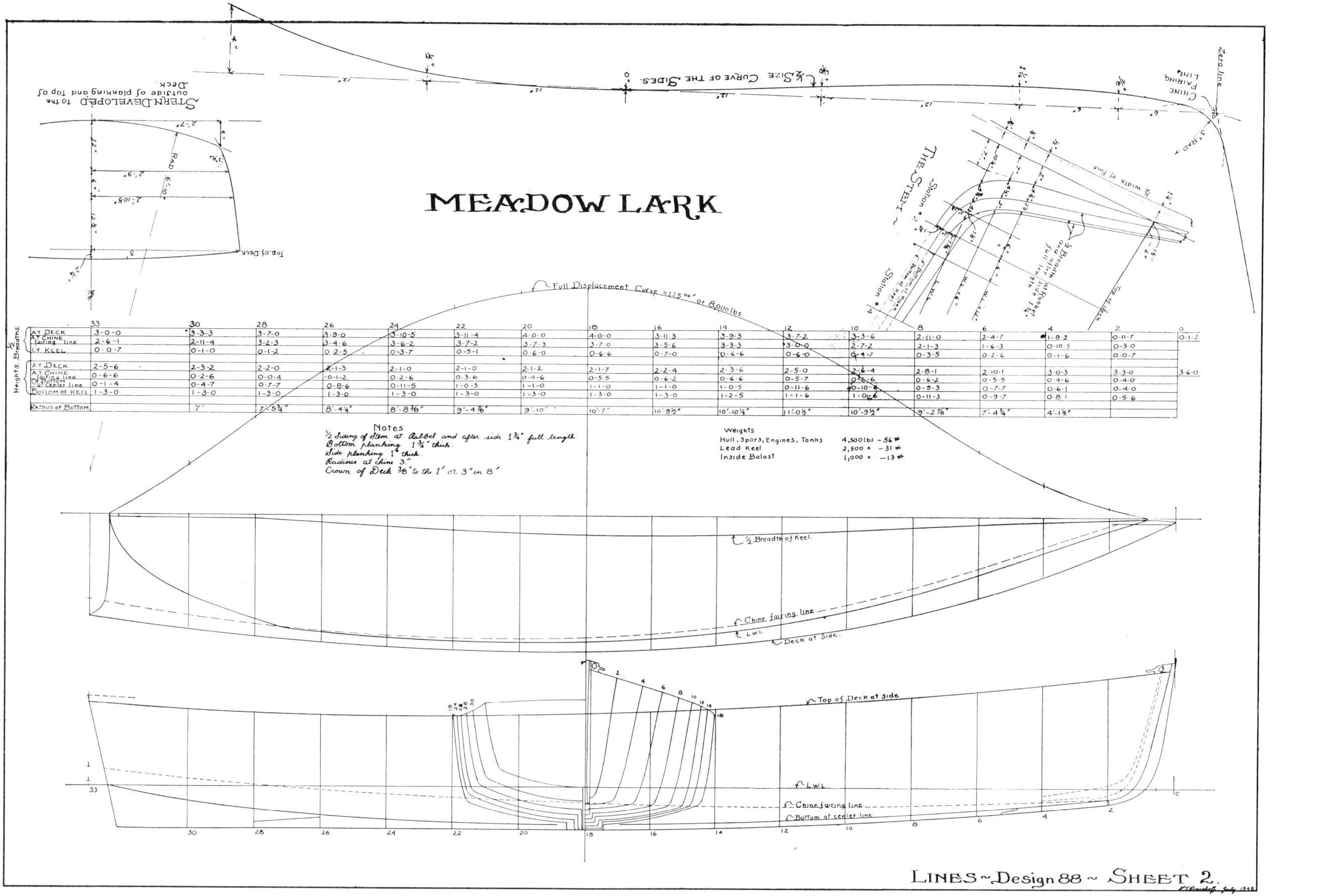
MEADOW LARK
STERN DEVELOPED to the outside of planking and top of Deck.
Top of Deck
RAD. 6'-10"
½ Size Curve of the Sides.
Chine Fairing Line
Zero line
3" RAD.
The Stem ~ Station #2
½ width of Fore
Top of deck
½ Breadth at Rabbet and after side full length 1¾"
L.W.L.
W.L. + 6"
W.L. + 12"
Bottom of Plank
Bottom of Keel
Station #4
Full Displacement Curve = 125.00' or 8,000 lbs.
½ Breadth of Keel.
Chine fairing line
L.W.L.
Deck at Side.
Top of Deck at Side
L.W.L.
Chine fairing line
Bottom at center line
LINES ~ Design 88 ~ Sheet 2.

		33	30	28	26	24	22	20	18	16	14	12	10	8	6	4	2	0
½ Breadths	At Deck	3-0-0	3-3-3	3-7-0	3-9-0	3-10-5	3-11-4	4-0-0	4-0-0	3-11-3	3-9-3	3-7-2	3-3-6	2-11-0	2-4-7	1-9-2	0-11-7	0-1-2
	At Chine fairing line	2-6-1	2-11-4	3-2-3	3-4-6	3-6-2	3-7-2	3-7-3	3-7-0	3-5-6	3-3-3	3-0-0	2-7-2	2-1-3	1-6-3	0-10-5	0-3-0	
	Of Keel	0-0-7	0-1-0	0-1-2	0-2-5	0-3-7	0-5-1	0-6-0	0-6-6	0-7-0	0-6-6	0-6-0	0-4-7	0-3-5	0-2-6	0-1-6	0-0-7	
Heights	At Deck	2-5-6	2-3-2	2-2-0	2-1-3	2-1-0	2-1-0	2-1-2	2-1-7	2-2-4	2-3-6	2-5-0	2-6-4	2-8-1	2-10-1	3-0-3	3-3-0	3-6-0
	At Chine fairing line	0-6-6	0-2-6	0-0-4	-0-1-2	0-2-6	0-3-6	0-4-6	0-5-5	0-6-2	0-6-6	0-5-7	0-6-6	0-6-2	0-5-5	0-4-6	0-4-0	
	Of Bottom at center line	0-1-4	0-4-7	0-7-7	0-8-6	0-11-5	1-0-5	1-1-0	1-1-0	1-1-0	1-0-5	0-11-6	0-10-6	0-9-3	0-7-7	0-6-1	0-4-0	
	Bottom of Keel	1-3-0	1-3-0	1-3-0	1-3-0	1-3-0	1-3-0	1-3-0	1-3-0	1-3-0	1-2-5	1-1-6	1-0-6	0-11-3	0-9-7	0-8-1	0-5-6	
Radius of Bottom			7'	7'-5¾"	8'-4¼"	8'-8⅜"	9'-4⅞"	9'-10"	10'-7"	10'-9½"	10'-10¼"	11'-0½"	10'-9½"	9'-2⅞"	7'-4¾"	4'-1½"		

Notes

½ Siding of Stem at Rabbet and after side 1¾" full length.
Bottom planking 1¾" thick.
Side planking 1" thick.
Radious at chine 3."
Crown of Deck ⅜" to the 1' or 3" in 8'

Weights		
Hull, Spars, Engines, Tanks	4,500 lbs.	-56 %
Lead Keel	2,500 "	-31 %
Inside Balast	1,000 "	-13 %

and the stem head should be left long enough to come to this same base line. It is quite easy to set up a boat that is to be built upside down even if the floor is uneven. The procedure is as follows:

Snap a chalk line on the floor where you want the center line of the vessel to be, then along the edge of that line nail down a strip of wood; say one inch or more square, the nails well set. Now with a joiner plane and a straightedge, plane off the high spots on the strip so that the top is straight and level. Lay off your frame stations with pencil on this strip. Then with a large wooden square, with one limb as long as half the beam of the vessel, carry the frame stations out sideways on the floor and mark with a pencil the approximate beam at that station. Now nail on the floor at these points some small strips of wood, say 6 by 9 inches by a lesser thickness than the central battens. On top of these strips place two shingles, or parts of shingles, with the wide ends apart so that the shingles may be slid together or apart, until a straightedge resting on the central batten brings the bubble in a level just right. Then nail the shingles down and mark with pencil the frame stations. The procedure thus far is to procure an absolutely straight and level base for setting up, which most floors in sheds used for boatbuilding do not afford.

The central or midship frame or mold should next be set up, using a plumb bob to bring it vertical. This frame should be held in place with diagonal braces, but the other frames as they are set up are simply held vertical by a strip run along the bottom, which later can be removed after the first bottom plank is fastened in place. In this method of setting up there are no braces, battens, or ribbands in the way during construction and much material is saved, which is not the case in other methods of setting up.

If the yacht is to be built outdoors, which is desirable in some warm, pleasant climates, because the light is much better than in sheds not planned for boatbuilding, then some posts could be driven into the ground for the central batten, which in that case had better be a good-size joist — say 2 by 6 inches, and used on edge with posts about 6 or 8 feet apart. Then posts of about the same spacing could be put in the ground in a curve approximately where the deck line would come, and a plank on edge sprung around them which, after being leveled up by dressing down or shimming up with shingles, could hold the frames in place quite well. It is believed the posts for this crib could be driven in some ground with a sledge hammer, the posts being from 2 to 3 inches diameter, but whatever method of setting up is used, the stem, transom, and first and last frames must be well held down, for in springing heavy planking there are at times great strains developed.

Cabin

The general construction of Meadow Lark is simplified to reduce cost and make the work easier for amateurs, and some of this simplification includes leaving out the keel proper, doing away with a chine piece, and leaving out the clamps. The cabin also is kept as simple as possible to make her easy to take care of as well as cheap to construct. The cabin might be described as follows:

At the after end of the deckhouse there is a sliding hatch

with an opening 20 inches wide and 24 inches long where one can stand when cooking in fair weather. On the starboard side of this hatch is hanging space for oilskins, etc. To port is a Shipmate coal-burning stove over a box of coal. Forward of this on both sides of the yacht are two fixed berths rigged with canvas bottoms like a pipe berth and intended to serve as comfortable transom seats in the daytime. This after compartment, which is separated from the forward by a curtain, has opening marine windows on both sides to facilitate cooking in warm water. Forward of the curtain there are two similar berths, but this forward compartment is intended to be used in the daytime as a toilet room where the cedar bucket can be used in the place most convenient, depending on which tack the vessel is on, etc.

On the forward deck is a hatch with an opening of 18 by 18 inches for ventilation, and a place to pass the anchor and anchor warp below deck. When all things are considered it will be found that Meadow Lark's cabin affords remarkably comfortable quarters at low cost and, if the curtain is properly rigged and used, more privacy than usual on such a small craft is obtained.

CONSTRUCTION PLAN

1. The lower section of the frames, or what might be called the floor timbers, are oak, 2″ in their fore and aft dimensions, and 3″ up and down. These pieces can be sawn to shape and most of them can be cut out of a plank less than a foot wide. These lower frames are spaced 24″ and should be planed all over to discourage rot, for there is quite a difference between a planed and a sawn piece of wood in its resistance to rot. Remember, the frames must be bolted together so that forward of station 18 (the midship section) the lower frames have their forward faces on the frame station. The side frames have their after faces on the station. Aft of the midship section the reverse arrangement is used (see drawing). If this frame spacing is not adhered to, many things, such as the mast steps, hatches, etc., will come in a different location. I only speak of this matter of frame spacing for the amateur, as the professional is used to it, and this arrangement is universal on wooden construction.

2. The side pieces of the frames are sawn out of oak planks, 1½″ thick and about 6″ wide, shaped to include a partial knee at the top and bottom as shown on the sections. Make them about 2″ wide below the upper knee, and 3″ wide above the lower knee. These main side frames, like the lower frames, are spaced 24″, and when they are made up together with their deck beams will be the molds or frames that the vessel will be planked upon, but because the side planking is much thinner than the bottom planking, it will be necessary to have intermediate frames at the side, which are described next.

3. The intermediate frames can be of oak about 1¼″ square, and they should be sawn out to fit the curve of the inside of the planking. The principal function of these intermediate frames is to hold the seams of the planking in place. These frames can be put in place after the vessel is planked up.

4. The deck beams, which should be of good dry oak or other suitable semi-hard wood, are all 2″ deep in what is called their molded dimension, and 1¼″ fore and aft, or what is called their sided dimension. But there are two strong beams, one on station 10 and one on station 30. These are 2″ x 2″. The crown of the main deck is ⅜″ to the foot, or 3″ in 8′.

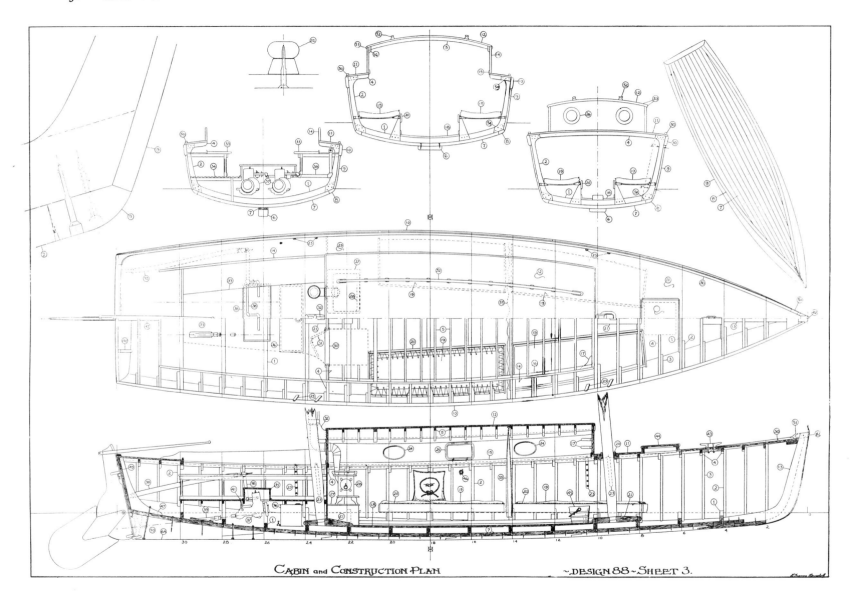

CABIN and CONSTRUCTION PLAN   ~DESIGN 88~ SHEET 3.

5. The house beams should be of good grade white oak, ash, or elm, molded 1½″, sided 1″. There is a strong house beam on station 20′ 9″, which is molded 1½″ and sided 2″. The crown of the house deck is 6″ in 6′.

6. While Meadow Lark has no keel proper, she does have a lead ballast keel about 24′ long, which can be cast in sections about 6′ long as shown on the drawing, and secured in place after planking up with bronze wood screws fastened from inside. The screws should be 3″ or 3½″ long, and size 18 or 20 flat head. Forward of the ballast keel is a short wooden piece to fair into the stem, while aft the lead is scarphed into the deadwood, and the two fastened with ⅜″ or larger through-bolts of bronze.

6A. The deadwood or skeg at the after end of the keel should be made of semi-hard wood, such as oak or yellow pine, and will be a little difficult to get out as it is tapered both ways. Its forward end is about 5¼″ athwartships, and after end 1¾″, but as it is not much over 14″ deep it can be sawn out both ways on a bandsaw and planed up by hand. The deadwood can be fastened principally by two galvanized-iron drive bolts about 5/16″ diameter, and one ½″ through-bolt at its after end, all as shown on the drawing.

7. The bottom planking should be as heavy as possible for ballast, and while any heavy wood that lasts well will be suitable, perhaps extra heavy longleaf yellow pine would be the best. This planking is 1¾″ thick. At the upper right-hand corner of the drawing is a sketch showing how the planking might be laid or lined off, the planks having a slight taper so that they are each approximately 5″ wide on station 8, 7″ wide on station 20, and 6″ wide at the stern. The bottom planking can be fastened with galvanized boat nails about 3″ long, heads well set and puttied, but the central plank and the edge of the adjoining planks, which will come in contact with the lead keel, should be fastened with bronze screws about 3″ or 3½″ long, and with #18 wire.

8. The outside or border planks of the bottom can be sprung into place and must be very securely fastened, for when the planking swells it will have a tendency to start this plank, so this plank should be fastened at each main frame with two 3″ or 3½″ #18 Everdur screws, somewhat staggered so that one screw comes on the bottom frame and one into the side frame. This outer plank is rounded off on its outer edge to the thickness of the side planking, all of which is shown full size on the upper lefthand corner of the drawing. Perhaps this border plank should be put in place before the bottom planking is commenced, as then a better fit can be secured at the nib ends forward and aft.

9. The side planking, which can be about 1″ thick, should be of cedar, cypress, soft pine, yellow pine, or any other suitable durable wood that is not too heavy, and fastened either with boat nails about 2″ long, or wood screws of that length and #14 or #16 wire.

10. The sheer strake of Meadow Lark is made 1¾″ thick to make a strong fastening for the upper end of the leeboard, and because this yacht does not have a clamp at the sheer line the sheer strake is intended also to act as a chafing strip. It can be yellow pine or white oak (if oak is 1½″ thick), and for looks tapered to the same thickness as the planking at the ends, while its depth might be about 4″ at the bow, 6″ amidships, and 3″ at the stern (see the sail plan).

11. The main deck can be of ¾″ thick tongue and groove soft pine, fir, cypress, or redwood, or any other light, strong wood that does not shrink much, canvas covered.

12. The house deck can be of many light, strong wood from ⅝″ to ¾″ thick, canvas covered.

13. The stem can be either a natural crook as shown, or built

up of hackmatack or oak, and $3\frac{1}{2}''$ thick in its athwartships dimension for its full length.

14.   The deckhouse sides and forward end, as well as the cockpit coaming, should be $1\frac{1}{4}''$ thick if oak or mahogany, but slightly thicker if softer wood is used, and fastened to the deck with wood screws passing up through the deck.

15.   After the deckhouse has been fastened down the canvas deck covering should be folded up along the inside of the deckhouse and, after being tacked in place, covered with a finishing strip about $5/16''$ thick by $2''$ wide.

16.   At the upper inside edge of the house sides there should be a strip of oak about $1\frac{1}{4}''$ x $2\frac{1}{4}''$, notched out for the deck beams to lodge in.

17.   If two small knees are used in the forward ends of the deckhouse, this point will be less apt to leak than if secured with the usual corner piece, which will not allow the house sides to shrink and swell without starting the seam, or splitting.

18.   The cabin sole or floor can be of $3/4''$ soft wood, and would be best if it had sections in the middle which could lift out. These sections could be about $9''$ wide and run for the full length.

19.   The berths are constructed by having canvas berth bottoms (like a pipe berth) permanently laced in place, with seizing wire running over oak strips between the frames and along the berth frame. These oak strips can be about one inch square and rounded off on their outside corners where the lacing will come, and of course held about $\frac{1}{4}''$ away from the berth frame and the planking. The after starboard berth is 6' 6" long, the forward one about 6' 3", the after port one 6', and forward port one 6' 3", with widths about as shown on the plan. The mattresses will have to be shaped, but need not be more than $3''$ thick if they have some real curled hair in them.

20.   The berth frames can be of semi-hard wood $1''$ x $5''$, and supported by triangular oak brackets well secured to each main frame, or spaced $24''$ apart as shown on the drawing.

21.   The mast steps should be of hard wood about $28''$ long and $6''$ wide. If the forward one is made $2\frac{1}{2}''$ thick at the ends and $3\frac{1}{4}''$ in the middle, and the after one $2''$ thick at the ends and $4''$ in the middle, they will be tapered correctly to take the foot of the mast. The tongs of the mast are both $4''$ long and $1\frac{1}{2}''$ wide. The after ends of both tongs are $7''$ forward of the nearest frame station. The mast steps can be held down on the frames with two $15/16''$ iron drive bolts at each end.

22.   The foremast is $4\frac{1}{2}''$ x $6''$ at the deck, and should have a collar for a mast coat.

23.   The chainplates, eight in all, are alike and of semi-hard rolled phosphor or Tobin bronze, $3/16''$ x $1\frac{1}{2}''$ x $18''$, and fastened with several bronze stove bolts about $5/16''$ diameter.

24.   The forward and after cabin side lights can be oval, about $12''$ long and $7''$ high, set in putty.

25.   The central cabin side lights can be Wilcox, Crittenden Fig. 5258, size 7 by 14. Or if you want to save a little money, use some of the smaller round ports.

26.   It would be nice to have opening ports in the forward end of the house, and if so Wilcox, Crittenden Fig. 525 with a $6''$ opening would be suitable.

27.   Coal or wood box under stove about $24''$ athwartships, $18''$ fore and aft, and top approximately $12''$ above cabin sole (part of the top should lift off for filling).

28.   Shipmate stove, No. 211, for coal or wood with stack through after side of house, and Liverpool head as shown.

29.   Space for shelves, or food locker, etc.

30.   Oak threshold at about the level of the cockpit floor.

31.   If the cabin door is made in two leaves, hinged as shown,

it can be swung back and hooked to the mast, or unhung and stowed under the afterdeck.

32. Shoe-shaped block of wood about 2″ thick, to hold mast back in position, can be fastened to after end of deckhouse with screws from inside.

33. The cockpit seats can be soft wood, ¾″ or ⅞″ thick, supported by oak stanchions as shown. The seats need not be more than 15 inches wide, but back of them under the deck it would be well if there were a thin wood tray to hold deck gear, etc. The tops of the seats can be 14″ above the cockpit floor.

34. Cockpit floor of slats about ¾″ by 1½″ hard wood supported by oak beams 1¼″ x 1½″ and supported by uprights where necessary. Middle section of flooring should lift out.

35. Canvas covered box over engine about 2′ 7″ by 14″ inside, and 6″ or more high.

36. Tin-lined copper gasoline tank, 12″ x 12″ x 3′, capacity 22 gallons. Large filler hole at central forward edge. It would be well if the tank had an outboard vent, but that is not so necessary with a well-ventilated slat cockpit floor.

37. Two Kermath Sixteen 5 engines with reverse and reduction gears, also fuel pump and kits 2 and 4.

38. The exhaust line of the engines can consist of the following parts:

2 pieces of 1″ iron pipe, 8″ long.
1 piece of 1″ iron pipe, 5″ long.
1 piece of 1″ iron pipe, 17″ long.
2 nipples of 1″ iron pipe.
1 union for 1″ iron pipe.
3 elbows for 1″ iron pipe.
1 reducing T for 1″, 1″, and 1¼″ iron pipe.
1 piece of 1¼″ iron pipe, 17″ long.
1 piece of 1¼″ iron pipe, 12″ long.

1 elbow for 1¼″ iron pipe.
1 reducing elbow for 1¼″ iron pipe and smallest size pipe.
1 piece of 1¼″ iron pipe, 5″ long.
1 piece Edson exhaust hose for 1¼″ iron pipe about 5′ 3″ long.
1 piece brass pipe, I.P.S. 6″ long to go through stern.

In the small end of the upper reducing elbow there should be a gas plug which has been drilled and tapped out with a straight thread to take a small pipe or tube to lead the circulating water from both engines into the exhaust line (see drawing). The water can be taken from the engine to this induction pipe with rubber hose. If the water has been properly introduced beyond the highest point of the exhaust line, there will be no need of a muffler.

39. The stuffing boxes can be either those furnished by the engine builders, or Columbian Bronze Corporation Fig. 177 for a ¾″ shaft.

40. The struts can be either those furnished by the engine builders or Columbian Bronze Corporation Fig. 131, but in that case the drop and angle of shaft must be taken from the yacht. Either rubber babbit or bearing bronze should be satisfactory on this size and speed of shaft.

41. It is believed that the top of the reverse levers will come just above the floor, and if so they can be shifted with the foot without any other extension. These engines can be furnished with a governor which might be very convenient together with this foot operated reverse lever.

42. Bronze stem band about ¼″ thick, upper end about 3⅜″ wide tapered below this to fit face of stem. Total length of stem band 6′, but can be in two lengths if desired with upper end not less than 12″ long. Upper end is bent back and drilled with 7/15″ hole for forestay shackles.

43. Hardwood mooring cleat about 12″ long, secured with

two ⅜″ or larger bronze bolts passing through oak reinforcing block under deck. 6″ wide.

44. Forward hatch opening 18″ x 18″. Top canvas covered.

45. The famous cedar bucket, which can be used in several places and for several purposes.

46. Bolt for attaching the leeboards.

47. Stem knee can be oak or hackmatack about 2″ thick.

48. Stern frames about 1¼″ x 1¼″ oak, spaced 18″.

49. Stern or transom planking can be oak or yellow pine, about 1½″ thick, planked up the same as topside planking in strips about 6″ wide, and caulked.

50. Toe rail around edge of deck, hard wood about ⅞″ x ⅞″ but increased forward to fit the bow chocks.

51. Bow chocks of cast bronze, pattern made from yacht. Chocks well secured with ⅜″ copper rod rivet through stem head, and screws aft.

52. Hand rail on both sides of deckhouse made from hard wood strip with blocks under it. See full size section.

53. Hardwood finishing strip, about ½″ x 1¼″ over turned-down canvas of deckhouse.

54. The fastenings between the lower frames and side frames can be either 5/16″ galvanized-iron stove or carriage bolts, 3½″ long, or #18 bronze wood screws 3″ long, heads on side frame side, or ¼″ copper rivets. In either case use four fastenings at this point. The fastenings between the side frames and the deck beams can be 5/16″ galvanized-iron bolts or #18 wood screws, or ¼″ copper rivets. Three on each joint as shown on the drawing.

55. The curtain between the forward and after cabin can be tacked to the side of the yacht under the main deck, and that part of the curtain under the deckhouse attached to sail slides running on sail track. The curtains can then be either brought together at the middle and hooked with several hooks, or slid and pushed all the way back, making the cabin all one long run.

Altogether the construction of Meadow Lark is very strong, and she should last a great many years and stand lying on any bottom except sharp rocks.

RUDDER AND LEEBOARDS

1. Rudder blade, main parts of oak 1½″ thick, length overall 4′ 6″, width 18″. If this cannot be secured in one width then it may be made up as shown on the drawing with ⅜″ drive bolts, either galvanized iron or Tobin bronze.

2. Rudder pintle, Wilcox, Crittenden Fig. 460. Either galvanized iron or brass. Note: there is a hole drilled up in the rudder for the end of this long pintle.

3. Wilcox, Crittenden Fig. 463.

4. Wilcox, Crittenden Fig. 460, but with long pintle cut off as shown.

5. Piece of hardwood to prevent rudder from lifting. This piece may be removed or put in place when the rudder is hard over.

6. Wilcox, Crittenden Fig. 462.

7. Wooden shim. It may be necesary to use a wooden shim here to bring the center line of the pintles far enough aft so the swinging rudder fitting will not come against the transom when the rudder is hard over.

8. Rudder blade. This may be made up of two pieces of oak, 1½″ x 12″ x 3′ 2″, fastened together with blind drive bolts about ¾″ x 12″, either galvanized iron or Tobin bronze. If preferred these bolts may be driven in from the forward edge instead of being blind. The blade should be carefully tapered as shown

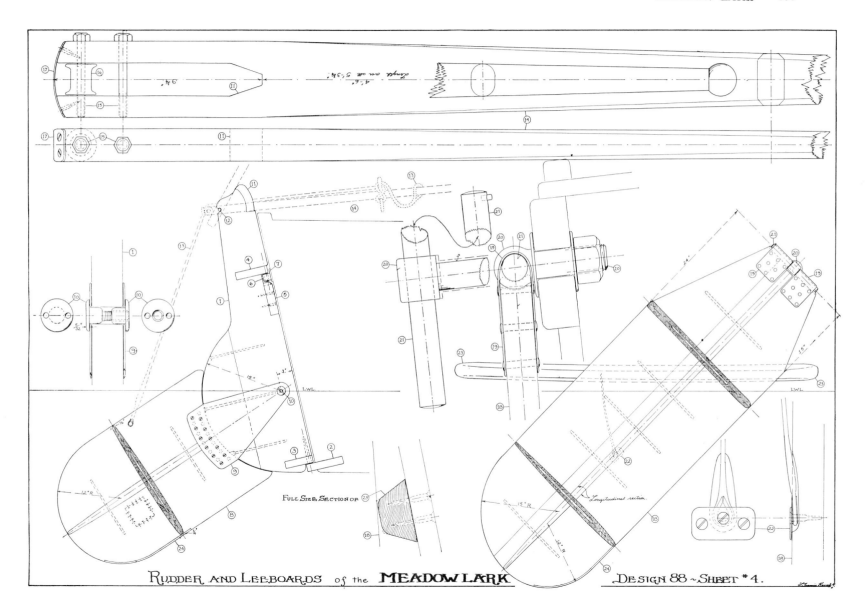

RUDDER AND LEEBOARDS of the **MEADOW LARK**

FULL SIZE SECTION OF

DESIGN 88 ~ SHEET #4.

so the leading edge is about ¾″ thick and the after and upper edges about ½″.

9. Swinging hinge straps on both sides of the rudder of strong bronze plates, either half hard or hard rolled, 1/16″ or more thick by 12″ by 1′ 8″. Lower ends drilled and countersunk for eleven 1½″ #14 flat-head Everdur screws so spaced that the screws from each side will clear as is shown in dotted lines.

10. Hinge pin, made up of Tobin bronze in two pieces, as shown, with heads not much over 5/32″ thick.

11. Rudder. The upper end is shaped in such a way that the tiller may be unshipped by simply rocking it upwards, as shown in dotted lines. The forward side is beveled off to make a shoulder each side to support the tiller when it is in its normal position.

12. After side of rudder head is notched to take the ⅜″ bolt on which the tiller pivots.

13. Pennant for hoisting and lowering the rudder blade may simply be a piece of manila rope of ⅞″ or ½″ diameter, spliced into a ½″ hole in the rudder and passing over the roller in the tiller, then running forward to a belaying pin in the tiller. If desired, the forward end of the pennant may be spliced around the tiller so it will not be lost.

14. Tiller, 5′ 3¾″ x 3½″ x 1½″, may be white oak or other suitable hardwood.

15. Bronze bolts. Two ⅜″ bronze bolts 3½″ long through after end of tiller, threaded directly into the wood one side, so that a slight adjustment may be made in the slot to compensate for wear and shrinkage. If the tiller is a hard piece of wood you may have to tap the hole with a standard tap.

16. Roller for rudder pennant, of either hardwood or bronze.

17. Strap to hold rudder pennant in place, bronze 1/16″ x 1½″ x 3¾″ with four 1″ #12 flat-head screws.

18. Leeboards should be of white oak or other suitable hardwood. They are 6′ 6″ long overall, 2′ 3″ wide, and 1½″ thick. They may be made up of two 12″ wide boards and a 3″ board, as shown on the drawing, or other widths as convenient.

If held together with blind drive bolts as shown on the drawing, the bolts should pierce the first and last layers at least 6″. The technique of driving blind drive bolts is somewhat as follows: Drill the holes in the central plank very square by using a guide for the auger. Clamp the central piece on one and then the other of the planks, using the central piece to guide the auger, when you will find all the holes will line up exactly. Remember, the holes for the bolts must be almost exactly the same size as the bolts for an easy driving fit.

Now drive the bolts through the central layer into an outside piece and file up the heads of the bolts until they are somewhat conical. Grease the bolts and drive the last outside piece down into place, using strong clamps and a sledgehammer over a piece of wood so as not to damage the leeboard. The bolts should be ⅜″ or larger in diameter, either black iron or galvanized, and if they rust and expand they will hold all the better.

The leeboards may be beveled off so the trailing edges below the water are about ½″ wide, the lower and leading edges about ¾″. The longitudinal and cross section on the drawing give the approximate shape but above the water the leeboards should be 1½″ thick all over. Their upper ends must be very securely attached to the hull, but still so they can swing in two ways. This is arranged with the following parts.

19. At the head of each leeboard there are two straps of half-hard strong bronze (preferably phosphor) 1/16″ or more thick x 4½″ x 12″. You may think 1/16″ is thin for these straps, but their width gives them considerable strength, while thicker ones would be more difficult to bend properly. These straps are

secured in place by six 5/16″ copper rivets, well headed up over countersunk holes in the straps.

20. The king pin may be a cast bronze eye bolt of about the size shown in the full size detail, and only machined or finished on the shank. Two washers as shown are to be used with each of these bolts to bear against the sheer strake.

21. Bronze rod 1¼″ diameter by 12″ long. The upper end is to have a short pin to prevent this rod from dropping or sliding out of place. Some of the parts of these leeboard attachments may appear heavy, but besides the strains of a seaway they must stand the heavy strains which sometimes occur in lying beside a wharf. All things considered, this attachment is simple and strong.

22. Wire pennant to hoist leeboards. The attachment of this is somewhat of a problem, for when the leeboards are hoisted clear of the water, their after or upper edges will come well above the sheer line where the hoisting sheave is located, so the point of attachment must be down on the side of the boards. However, this may be arranged by cutting a depression or shallow cavity in the inboard surface of the leeboards and allowing the thimble of the pennant to lodge there while it is held in place by a 1½″ #16 F.H. wood screw. The head of this screw is supported by a bronze plate 1/16″ x 1½″ x 3″, as shown in the full size detail. As the hoisting pennant is only 3/16″ diameter wire, it will not have much resistance when under water.

23. Chafing strips or guards for the leeboards may be oak about 5′ 9″ long with the forward end starting at station 16. Shaped like the full size section, which is 3″ wide and 1½″ thick, the upper edge is about 5″ above the waterline. These strips would be best if fastened with screws with their heads on the inside of the planking (see section), for if the strips should wear down the screw heads will not dig the leeboards. The screws may be 2″ #16 spaced about 12″, and slightly staggered.

24. Bronze bands. If a Meadow Lark is to be used much in shallow water where there is a rough bottom it would be nice if the leeboards and rudder had bronze bands at their lower forward edges to prevent splintering. These bands could be about ¼″ x ¾″ x 18″.

Note: It is thought the leeboards and rudder should be about neutral buoyancy (or about the weight of water), which their metal fittings may make them, but if they do not sink well enough to be effective, then lead weights may be added (see dotted lines on rudder). This is usually accomplished by cutting out a square of the desired size, driving in a few copper nails around the aperture, then nailing a nice fitting piece of plank on both sides.

One of these planks should have a hole about 1″ diameter at its center for pouring in the lead, and small vent holes for the escaping gas and smoke at each corner.

After the lead has been poured, the surface and the wood around it will have to be planed down slightly, but if done properly and the lead is not too hot or the wood around it too wet, it will make a neat job.

It will be best not to weight the leeboards and rudder until after they have been tried, for they should be as light as is practicable for ease of hoisting.

SPARS

Masts. Both of the masts are alike in construction and only very slightly in length and taper.

The masts are box section with the after side straight for the full length. The forward and after staves are 1⅛″ thick with a

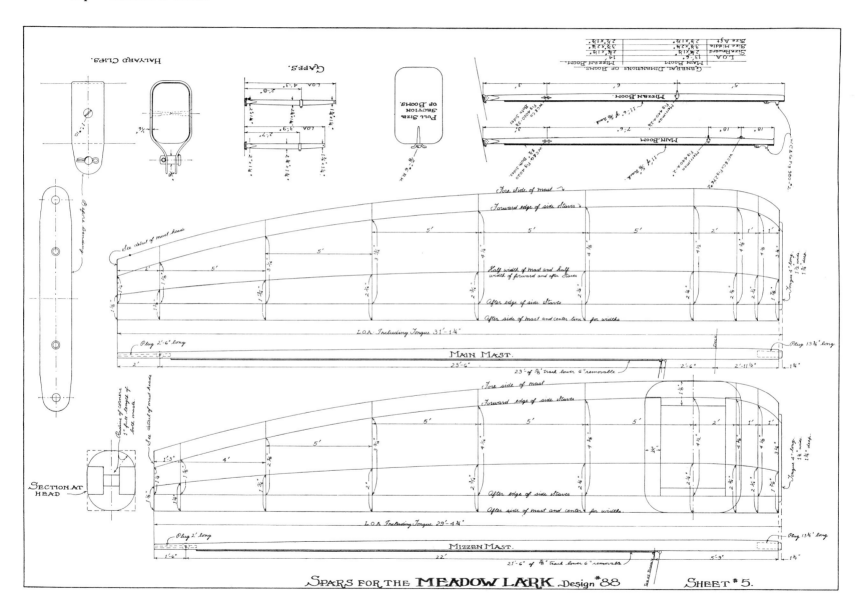

SPARS FOR THE **MEADOW LARK** Design #88   SHEET #5.

⅜" deep rabbet cut in them to make gluing up more simple. The side staves are ¾" thick.

There are to be plugs at each end of both spars of the length shown in the drawing, but no other internal reinforcement.

The corners of the masts are rounded off on a radius of 1" for their full length.

The best material for the spars is Sitka spruce, but rift grain Douglas fir of fine texture is satisfactory. See detail for mast-heads and goosenecks.

Booms. Both booms are solid of Sitka spruce or fir, of rectangular section as shown on the drawing. Both 3½" x 2½" in the middle, 2¾" x 1½" at forward end, and both 2½" x 1½" at after end. The forward and after end are shown on a separate detail. The booms are straight on their upper sides.

Gaffs. The gaffs may be eastern white spruce, Sitka spruce, or fir of rectangular section, with corners rounded off on a radius of ½", and straight on their lower sides.

The clip for attaching the peak halliards to the gaff is shown full size and should be made of 1/16" or thicker half-hard strong bronze, preferably phosphor.

MAST FITTINGS

1. Half-hard phosphor bronze, 1/16" x 1¼" x 10⅞", with 2" long reinforcements riveted to each end as shown.
2. Half-hard phosphor bronze, 1/16" x 1¼" x 7⅛".
3. Half-hard phospher bronze, 1/16" x 1¼" x 3½".
4. Half-hard phosphor bronze, 1/16" x 1¼" x 11¼".
5. Half-hard phosphor bronze, 1/16" x 1¼" x 11¼".
6. Flagstaff and trucks. Make two alike. Staff of Tobin bronze rod ⅝" x 11". Lower end threaded with standard ⅜"

threads. Upper end threaded with 5/16" standard threads. ¼" tommy hole for screwing in. Truck of lignum vitae, ⅞" x 2¼". Four ¼" halliard holes.

7. Tobin bronze pin, ½" at head, ⅜" at shank, 1" long O.A.
8. Tobin bronze pin, ½" at head, 5/16" at shank, ⅞" long O.A.
9. Tobin bronze pin, ½" at head, ⅜" at shank, ⅞" long O. A. Make four.
10. Half-hard phosphor bronze, 1/16" x 1¼" x 5¾".
11. Half-hard phosphor bronze, 1/16" x 1¼" x 5⅞".
12. Same as 5.
13. Same as 4.
14. Tobin bronze pin, ½" at head, 5/16" at shank, ⅞" long.
15. Merriman Fig. 363WF No. 3 and becket for single parted wire peak halliards; the becket is for boom lift. One for mainmast, one for mizzenmast (see block list).
16. Merriman Fig. 509B No. 2 for manila fore staysail halliards (see block list).
17. Merriman halliard sheave pins for throat halliards. Figure 504-P, ⅜" diameter, 3" long. Two with cotter pins.
18. Merriman Fig. 504, 3½", two for wire throat halliards.
19. Lower shroud attachment inner plate, phospher bronze plate, 1/16" x 3" x 10½". Make four, two for mainmast, two for mizzen.
20. Outer plate of shroud attachment bent to form spreader attachment. Phosphor bronze plate 1/16" x 3" x 7¾". Make four.
21. The two layers are fastened together with countersunk copper or bronze rivets, as shown.
22. The lower four screws are 1" #14 R. H. bronze. All the upper screws can be either ⅞" or 1" #12 F. H. bronze.
23. Pins. Tobin bronze ½" at heads, ⅜" at shanks, 15/16" long. Make four.

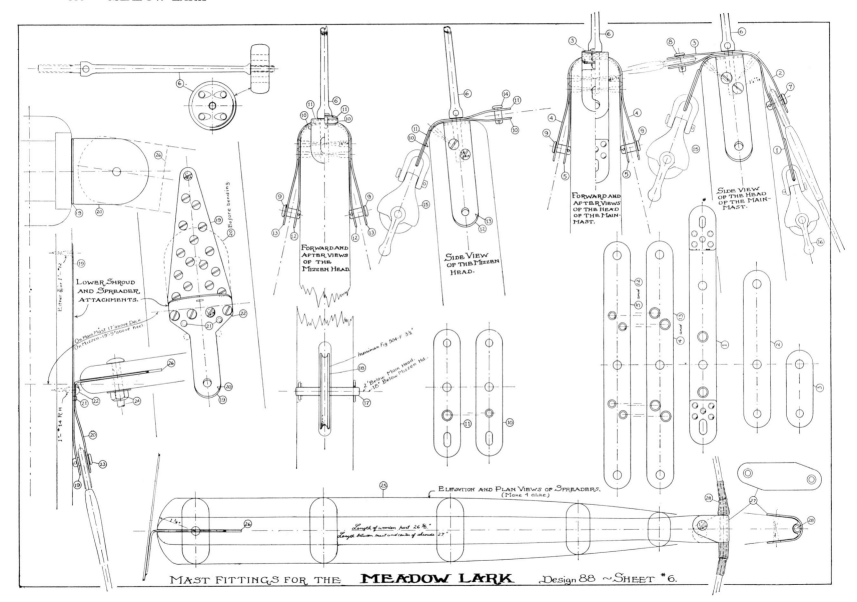

LOWER SHROUD
AND SPREADER
ATTACHMENTS.

FORWARD AND
AFTER VIEWS
OF THE
MIZZEN HEAD.

SIDE VIEW
OF THE MIZZEN
HEAD.

FORWARD AND
AFTER VIEWS
OF THE HEAD
OF THE MAIN-
MAST.

SIDE VIEW
OF THE HEAD
OF THE MAIN-
MAST.

ELEVATION AND PLAN VIEWS OF SPREADERS.
(Make 4 alike.)

MAST FITTINGS FOR THE   MEADOW LARK   Design 88 ~ Sheet #6.

24. ⅜″ bronze carriage bolts, 2″ long with nuts and washers. Four required.

25. Spreaders of spruce, ash, mahogany, or fir. Make four.

26. Saw slot at inner end of spreaders, 1/16″ wide and about 4″ deep.

27. Spreader tips made of bronze sheet, 1/16″ x 1¼″ x 4″. Countersink for #12 screws. Make four.

28. Serve shrouds with marline for about 4″ where spreader bears, and make marline seizings above and below tips.

GOOSENECKS

I have tried to make the goosenecks for the booms as simple as possible, and they consist of only three castings that require two patterns. All finishing can be done with a file and drills. This gooseneck will allow the boom to swing off to more than ninety degrees, and rise considerably without jamming. It does not have a tendency to split the boom, and allows the tack of the sail to be lashed so the foot and luff are in line. To remove the boom it will be necessary to take out the screws and remove one of the pieces (see drawing).

The goosenecks for the gaffs are a little more complicated, but like the boom gooseneck they only consist of three simple castings made from two patterns. It is likely that short gaffs or headboards fastened to a track have not been in use lately because no one has taken the trouble to work out an arrangement that allows the gaff to swing more than ninety degrees without straining the track. These fittings can also be made with simple hand tools, and the only difficult work is cutting the slot for the track in the slides, but with care these slots can be cut by using a hacksaw with two blades side by side in the frame. If the slides are properly fitted, the fitting will give trouble-free service for years.

Following is the numbered description:

1. Sockets for boom goosenecks, cast bronze, no finish. Drill for ⅜″ pintles of 2 (see drawing). Drill and countersink for 1½″ #14 F.H. screws. Make four.

2. Gooseneck center link, cast bronze ¾″ thick all over. No finish except filing pintles round. Make two.

3. Hardwood disk to act as spreader for the sheets 4 (see drawing) when they are riveted together. About 13/16″ thick. Make two.

4. Sheets of hard or half-hard bronze plates, 1/16″ x 2½″ x 9″. Shaped as shown. Make four.

5. ¼″ bronze or copper rivets well headed over countersunk holes in 4 (see drawing).

6. ¼″ copper rivets through boom.

7. 1″ #12 F.H. screws so spaced that port and starboard screws clear each other. End screw can be ¾″ long if desired.

8. Slides, cast bronze, no finish except cutting slots for track. Slides should fit loose. Make four.

9. ¼″ bronze pin, one end slightly headed over, other end with cotter pin.

10. Gooseneck center link cast bronze, ½″ thick all over. Eye at lower end for thoat lashing. Lug at upper end for throat halliard shackle.

11. Hardwood disk to act as spreader for the sheets 12 (see drawing) when they are riveted together. About 9/16″ thick. Make two.

12. Sheets of hard or half-hard bronze plate, 1/16″ x 2″ x 6½″. Shaped as shown. Make four.

13. 3/16″ bronze or copper rivets well headed over countersunk holes.

14. 3/16″ copper rivets through gaffs.

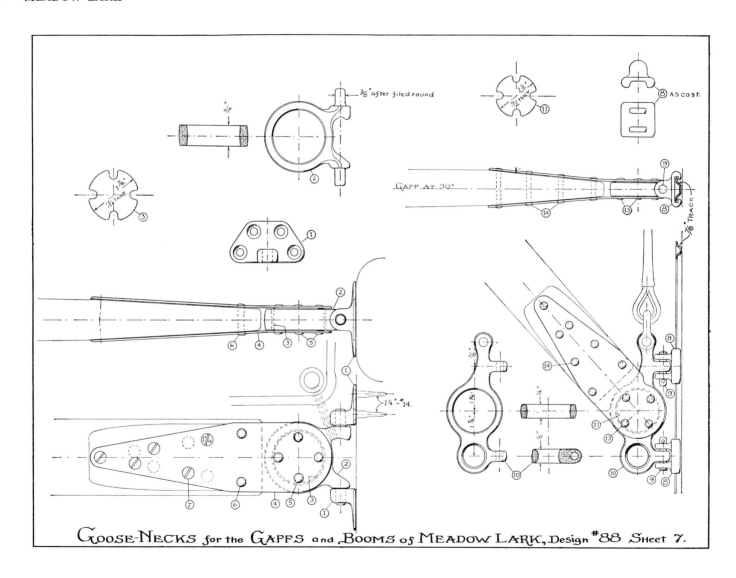

GOOSE-NECKS for the GAFFS and BOOMS of MEADOW LARK, Design #88 SHEET 7.

Rigging List.

Name of Part	Number Required.		Dia and construction of wire	Length required with allowance for splicing.	Dia. rope	Length of rope required.	Fittings.
Fore Stay	1	29'-3"; 1/4" stainless or 5/16" Galv steel.	1/4 Stainless 6x7 or 7x7	33'			2-Open Thimbles; 1-5/16" Chain Shackle
Spring Stay.	1	13'-10"; 3/16"	3/16" 6x7	17'			2-3/16 Open Thimbles
Upper Shrouds.	4	2-main upper 27'-11"; 2-mizzen upper 26'-7"; 1/4"	1/4"-6x7	120'			8-1/4" Solid Thimbles; 4-3/8" Turnbuckles
Lower Shrouds	4	2-main Lower 16'-10"; 2-mizzen Lower 16'-10"; 1/4"	1/4"-6x7	76'			8-1/4" Solid Thimbles; 4-3/8" Turnbuckles
Boom Lifts (See Sail Plan)	2	33'; 1/8"; 3/8"; 8'; Spliced into becket of Peak halyard blocks.	1/8" 7x19 Stainless	72'	3/8 or 7/16	20'	none
Peak Halyards	2	main 27', 24'; mizzen 25', 24'; 1/8" Merriman 363-W.F.; Merriman 370; 7/16" Dia	1/8" 7x19 Stainless	58'	3/8" or 7/16	60'	2-1/8" Open Thimbles
Throat Halyards	2	main 24', 22'; mizzen 23', 22'; 1/8"; 7/16"	1/8" 7x19 Stainless	53'	3/8" or 7/16	60'	2-1/8" open thimbles; 2-1/4" Chain Shackles
Clew Outhauls	2	10'; 5'; 1/8"; 3/8"	1/8" 7x19 Stainless	26'	3/8"	10'	2-Open Thimbles
Lee Board Pendants and tackles	2	4'; 3/16"; 25'; 7/16"	3/16" 7x19 Stainless	14'	7/16"	52'	4-3/16 Open Thimbles
Jib Halyards	1	90'; 3/8"			3/8"	90'	
Jib Sheets	2	4'; 1/8"; 35'; 7/16"	1/8"-6x7 Stainless	12'	7/16"	70'	1-5/16 Anchor Shackle; 2-1/8" Open Thimbles.
Main Sheet	1	50'; 7/16"			7/16"	51'	1-3/8" Sister Hook or 5/16" Shackle
Mizzen Sheet	1	60'; 5/16"			7/16"	61'	1-3/8" Sister Hook or 5/16" Shackle

Block List Etc.

Name of Part	Number Required.	Size.		Size of Wire or Rope.
Turnbuckles For the Main and Mizzen Upper and Lower Shrouds.	8	3/8"	Either W.C.&.Co. Fig 3162. or Merriman Fig 377.	1/4"
Jib Halyard Blocks	1 1		Merriman Fig 509-B-#2. or W.C.&Co. Fig 9520-#1 Merriman Fig 509-#2. – or W.C.&Co Fig 967-#1	3/8"
Peak Halyard Blocks One for Main, One for Mizzen.	2 2	#1	Merriman Fig 363-W.F. #1 with becket. " " 370 #2 with becket.	1/8"
Sheaves for main and mizzen throat halyards, (See Sheet #6) and snatch blocks for throat halyard.	2 2 2		Merriman Fig 504-F-3½" and sheave pins 3" long like Fig 504-9 Merriman Fig 370 #2 with becket.	1/8"
Clew Outhauls with tracks and blocks for both main and mizzen.	2 2		W.C.&Co Fig 980-#2 with tracks " " " Fig 580-#2	1/8"
Lee Board Pendant Blocks	2 2 2 2		W.C.&Co. Fig 380 #2 either galv. I. or brass, or Merriman 410-#3 or #4. " " " Fig 9510 #1 or Merriman 352-#2-D " " " Fig 950 #1 with becket " " 352 #2-B " " " Fig 202 #1 or Merriman 416 #2.	3/16 and 7/16
Jib Sheet Blocks and Fair leads	2 4		Merriman Fig 364-#2 W.C.&Co Fig 5811-#1 or Merriman Fig 422-#1	7/16"
Main Sheet Blocks	3 2		W.C.&Co Fig 951-#1 or Merriman 352-#2 " " " Fig 902-#1 or " 416-#2	7/16"
Mizzen Sheet Blocks	2 1 2		W.C.&Co Fig 951-#1 or Merriman 352-#2 " " " Fig 9530-#1 or " 353-#2 double. " " " Fig 902 #1 or " 416-#2	7/16"
Boom Lift Blocks Near after end of booms	2		W.C.&Co Fig 5800-#2 or Merriman 410 #1 or #2	1/8"
	Cleats all W.C.&Co Fig 4020		Jib Halyard 1-5½" on after side of mast under gooseneck. Throat halyards 2-6½" on port side of masts 12" above deck. Peak halyards 2-6½" " starboard " " " " " " Jib sheets 2-6½" on outside of cockpit coming. Lee Board 2-6½" " " " " ". Main sheet 1-6½" on after side of deck house. Mizzen sheet 1-6½" on after face of cockpit, amidships Boom lifts and Clew Outhauls-4-5½ on booms as shown.	

Rigging and Block List for the MEADOW LARK Design #88-Sheet 8.

RIGGING AND BLOCK LIST

The rigging and block list is only intended to be a guide. Each owner or builder should change things to suit best his conditions (such as what wires, ropes and hardware he can most easily acquire), only using this list as a guide to strength or approximate sizes. In the list I have not gone into as much detail as I usually do, and have not mentioned flag halliards, anchor warps, docking lines, etc., or anchors.

As to this last, I would recommend two anchors of the Wilcox, Crittenden Company's Figure 2002 type — one 42 pounds and the other 30 pounds. I would recommend one anchor warp of 2¼″ circumference, 25 fathoms long, and use the two docking lines bent together for the other anchor.

Of course this boat or yacht, or any other one with an open cockpit, should have a good portable bilge pump, and I recommend Wilcox, Crittenden 539, No. 4. Also a tent which could use the mizzen boom for a ridgepole would be convenient. Not only would it keep rain out of the cockpit, but it would allow the cockpit to be used as sleeping quarters when wanted. At times it could be used as an awning for those who prefer the shade.

I believe Meadow Lark is a type that will give much pleasure, and perhaps is the cheapest small moving home which combines safety and some speed. I believe one can live aboard her the whole year around anywhere south of the Mason-Dixon line, and always find a sheltered creek or cove that would float her at the end of a day's run.

I am sure she would be cheap to service and keep up, and with her strong hull might last fifty years and retain a good sales price to the end, which is the only thing that makes yachting cheap, for if you can use a boat for ten or twenty years and sell her for as much as she cost, you have done your yachting very cheaply.

6   HOW TO BUILD GOLDEN BALL

In the *Compleat Cruiser,* I described a shallow draft cruising ketch named *Tranquillo.* That design aroused considerable interest, even though the boat at the time was only a figment of my imagination. The owner of one of my thirty-three-foot Meadow Larks decided he wanted a larger boat to take out parties on the western coast of Florida, where the waters are quite shallow. I finished the design, the boat was built in Buzzards Bay, she was named *Golden Ball,* and the owner sailed her south, part of the way singlehanded. Her cost in 1962 was $30,000, quite a little less than other ketches of her size being built then. If I could have afforded her when I was younger, I would have had a boat to this design, because I think she is one of my best.

Golden Ball's statistics are: LOA forty-six feet six inches; LWL forty feet nine inches; beam eleven feet; draft two feet; outside ballast 4,200 pounds; inside ballast 4,920; sail area 874 square feet; 2 motors, 25 h.p. each; weight of hull and engine 12,000 pounds; displacement 21,120 pounds.

She can sleep eight people and her below-deck arrangement is: forward, a fo'castle with two berths and a W. C. — there is full headroom in the after part of the fo'castle. The fo'castle has its own hatch and is separated from the rest of the cabin by a watertight bulkhead. Next aft is a double stateroom. Then further aft is a large toilet room and dressing room, which by the use of doors can be turned into one room or two rooms. Next aft is the combination main saloon and galley — the galley being on both sides of the companionway so the one cooking can occasionally run up on deck or be constantly in conversation with the helmsman. At the stern under a raised deck is a double stateroom, originally designed for boys about 15 years old, but when one stands in the hatchway for such things as pulling up the trousers, this whole after part is usable for grownups.

The hull of this shallow design must be very light because she does not have much reserve stability — the result of her small draft. Her deck and topsides must be extra light and her hull quite light in order to have enough outside ballast to make her non-capsizable. A shallow boat such as this should never be taken to sea except by an experienced crew, but don't let that statement scare you: *Golden Ball* is as self-righting as Captain Slocum's *Spray* or Captain Voss's *Tillicum.*

I think this is a rather large boat for one to build in his backyard. I would suggest that before you start this project,

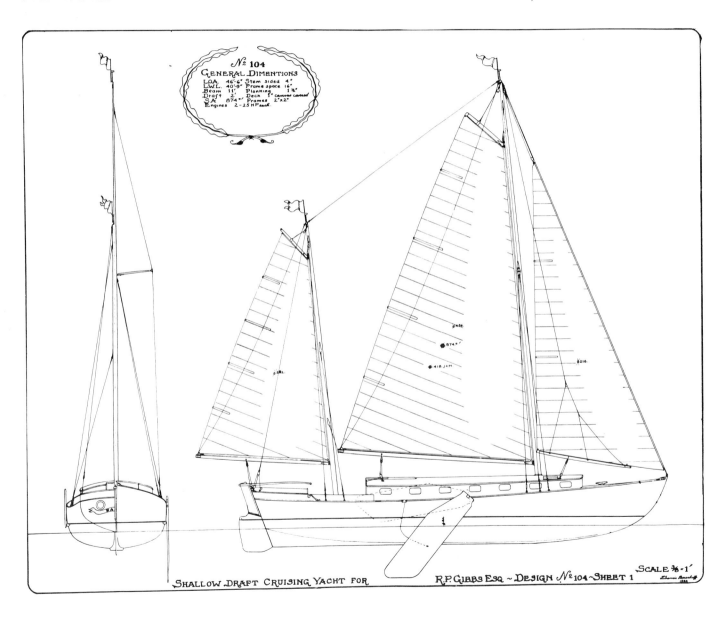

Nº 104
GENERAL DIMENTIONS
L.O.A.   46'-6"   Stem sided   4"
L.W.L.   40'-9"   Frame space 16"
Beam   11'   Planking   1½"
Draft   2'   Deck ⅞" canvas covered
S.A.   874□'   Frames   2"x2"
Engines 2–25 H.P each.

SHALLOW DRAFT CRUISING YACHT FOR   R.P. GIBBS ESQ ~ DESIGN Nº 104 ~ SHEET 1   SCALE ⅜ -1'

	Transom	44	40	36	32	28	24	20	16	12	8	4	
Deck at side	3-2-4	3-1-0	2-10-4		2-8-7	2-9-4	2-11-1	3-1-6	3-5-0	3-8-4		4-6-2	Height of Deck at Side
B-5				1-1-1	0-0-0	0-0-0		2-6-0					" Buttock 5
B-4		1-10-4	0-7-4	-0-2-1	-0-8-2	0-11-0	0-8-2	0-1-0		4-5-6			" " 4
B-3	1-2-6	1-0-7	0-0-0	-0-8-1	-1-1-3	1-4-1	1-2-7	0-11-0	-0-1-4	12-1-4			" " 3
B-2	0-8-4	0-5-3	-0-5-4	1-0-3	1-4-6	1-7-1	1-6-4	1-4-0	0-10-4	10-0-5	3-8-0		" " 2
B-1	0-4-0	0-1-0	-0-10-0	-1-3-7	1-9-0	1-9-1	1-8-7	1-7-5	1-4-2	0-7-4	1-5-4		" " 1
Rabbet	0-0-0	0-2-4	1-0-4	1-6-0	1-8-5	1-9-4	1-9-4	1-9-1	1-7-0	1-1-0	10-2-2		" Rabbet
Keel Bottom		2-0-0	2-0-0	2-0-0	2-0-0	2-0-0	2-0-0	2-0-0	1-3-0				" Keel Bottom
½ Width of Deck	3-11-0	4-3-0	4-9-4	5-2-0	5-4-5	5-6-0	5-6-0	5-4-6	5-1-7	4-8-1	3-9-7	2-5-0	½ width at Deck
WL+4'											3-9-4	2-1-4	WL+4
WL+3'	3-8-5	4-0-3	4-8-6	5-2-1	5-5-1	5-6-2	5-5-4	5-1-0	4-5-5	3-4-4	1-8-4		WL+3
WL+2'	2-7-0	2-1-3	4-3-3	4-11-4	5-3-6	5-5-0	5-3-7	5-0-7	4-7-2	4-2-1	2-11-2	1-3-3	WL+2
WL+1'		0-9-4	3-0-0	4-9-6	5-0-0	4-11-3	4-8-0	4-1-2	3-9-2	1-8-0	0-9-0		WL+1
LWL	0-2-0		0-5-0	2-0-5	3-3-1	3-9-4	3-6-2	2-10-2	1-8-0-0	0-0-7		LWL
WL-1'		0-2-1	0-2-7	0-4-1	0-5-5	0-7-0	0-6-0	0-4-2	1-9-3	0-4-6		WL-1
Rabbet	0-2-0	0-3-4	1-2-5	1-3-1	2-1-4	0-7-3	0-2-1	1-1-2	0-2-5	0-2-2		Rabbet
D-1	1-3-4	1-7-4	2-9-2	1-9-4	2-4-7	2-3-6	2-3-4	2-1-4	1-9-2	0-7-4		Diagonal 1
D-2			2-9-2	2-9-2	4-0-7	4-4-3	3-9-2	1-11-6				" 2
D-3	3-5-2	4-4-4	5-0-0	5-4-5	5-5-4	5-4-7	5-1-7	4-8-3	3-10-7	2-8-4	1-2-0		" 3

Offsets in feet, inches, and eighths of inches to the outside of planking.
Average thickness of planking 1½ garboard thicker, topsides thinner.
See details of Stem Stern Etc. Sheet #3
Crown of main deck 4½" in 12'

Half width of the face of Stem at WL 5'-3" 1½"
" 5 1½"
" 4 1⅜"
" 3 1¼"
" 2 ⅞"
" 1 ⅝"
" LWL ⅝"

Weight of Hull Engines Etc. 12,000 lbs
" " Outside Balast 4,200 "
" " Inside 4,920 "
Displacement 21,120 "

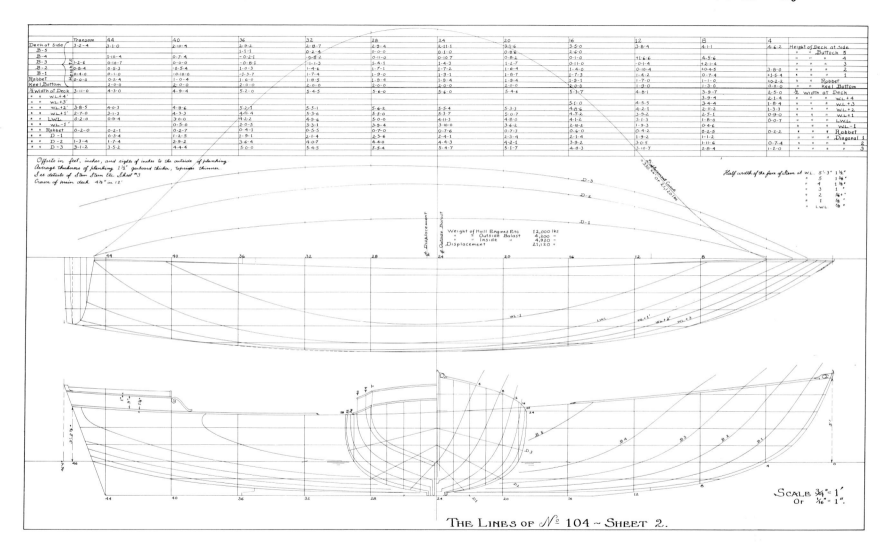

THE LINES OF № 104 ~ SHEET 2.

Scale ⅜"=1'
Or 1/16"=1"

try to get someone to build the hull, even if the builder were some distance off, because this hull without a deep keel can be easily shipped by truck long distances.

A few words about leeboards: Leeboards give very little trouble if properly and strongly attached to the hull and they have been successfully used in both England and Holland for over 200 years. They are not easily damaged alongside wharfs or by striking bottom. Some wonder about the possibility of leeboards banging against the side of the boat in a seaway. They don't bang disagreeably or often and I should say there is no problem this way or has been on the English Thames barges and the several types of Dutch boats.

When steering a leeboard boat like the *Golden Ball,* one must get used to handling her, and in very shallow water, even under bare poles, she will make considerable leeway with the leeboards up, as they have to be in the shallows. I never heard that she steered badly off the wind, and generally shallow draft boats with either leeboards or a centerboard have no trouble running.

CONSTRUCTION PLAN

1. Lead keel made in four sections as shown, and secured with bronze lag screws, 5/6" x 5", on bronze washers. These bolts are about 3" in from the top or keel, and staggered so there is only one in a bay; 20 required.

2. Deadwood may be made up of layers about 4" deep as shown. It may be of hard pine, bull pine, or other cheap rot-resisting wood. Deadwood fastenings are shown on Sheet #4.

3. Main keel is in two layers so it can be made up of several planks if desired with seams both crossways and fore and aft. The inner keel is nearly 18" wide at station 24. In bays 26 and 27 are shown crossways joints in the keel, with the joints or butts in these positions:

Forward upper keel plank would be 17' 3" long.
After upper keel plank would be 17' 9" long.
Forward lower keel plank would be 17' long.
After lower keel plank would be 19' long.

There is a butt block shown over the inner seam; but the lead keel should do to cover the seam in the lower keel.

One of the important things in this sort of a joint is to have it well stopwatered, and I sometimes think cedar makes a good stopwater.

The horizontal seam between the keel planks comes at the bearding line, or inner rabbet, so that both layers can be sawn out on the bandsaw and then beveled so that if the lower planking is 1⅜" thick the lower keel should be that thickness, but the upper keel need not be more than 1½", or less than 1¼" thick.

The two layers of the keel do not have to be the same variety of wood, but yellow pine, oak, or any of the varieties of mahogany may be used (see the construction sections). It would be good if there were a thick coat of white lead paint between the layers.

4. Fairing piece — between the lead keel and the stem there is a scarfed fairing piece which could be made of oak or locust, and fastened from the outside as desired.

5. Fore keel should be oak, yellow pine, or mahogany, and can be gotten out of timber 6" thick, 9" wide, and 7' 4" long. *Note:* the width of this piece is given on Sheet #4.

6. Anchor stock may be made of oak or locust. Its dimensions and fastenings are shown on Sheet #3. It can be gotten out of a piece 4½" thick, 4¾" wide, and 2' 9" long.

7. Stem should be white oak, and is 4½" sided its full length

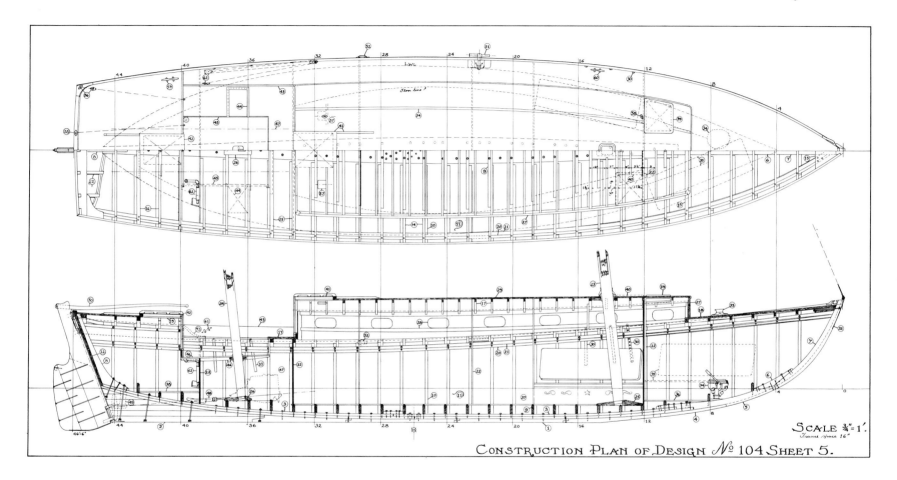

SCALE ¾"= 1'.
Frame space 16"

CONSTRUCTION PLAN OF DESIGN № 104 SHEET 5.

at both rabbet and back rabbet, and 6′ 8″ long when finished, but is a good plan to have it a few inches longer during construction.

It would be best if this piece were gotten out of a natural crook, but otherwise it may be made from a timber about 11½″ wide. As soon as the stem is planed up, and even before cutting the rabbet, it is well to keep it well slushed down with a mixture of half linseed oil and kerosene, for this mixture will have the three advantages of making the cutting easier, stopping the outside from shrinking and checking, and preventing rot later.

8. Stern knee may be of oak or hackmatack or other firm wood and would be best if a natural crook. This knee is to be sided between 2½″ and 3″, and is about 5½′ long. It is fastened down as follows: 2 large wood screws at forward end; ¾″ deadwood bolt in bay 43; ½″ x 7″ lag screw and a ⅝″ through-bolt at station 44.

9. Floor timbers are all 1¾″ in their fore-and-aft dimensions, and their depth and approximate half-width (½ w.) are as follows:

Frame, 5′ 4″ — 6″ deep, ½ w. 9″.
Station 8 — 6″ deep, ½ w. 1′ 1″.
Frame, 9′ 4″ — 4½″ deep, ½ w. 1″.
Frame 10′ 8″ — 6½″ deep, ½ w. 2′ 5″.
Station 12 — 4″ deep, ½ w. 18″.
Frame 13′ 4″ — 5½″ deep, ½ w. 22½″.
Frame 14′ 8″ — 6¼″ deep, ½ w. 2′ 2½″.
Station 16 — 7″ deep, ½ w. 3′ 6″.
Frame 17′ 4″ — 7¼″ deep, ½ w. 2′ 9″.
Frame 18′ 8″ — 7⅜″ deep, ½ w. 3′.
Station 20 — 7⅜″ deep, ½ w. 3′ 2″.
Frame 21′ 4″ — 7⅜″ deep, ½ w. 3′ 4″.
Frame 22′ 8″ — 7⅜″ deep, ½ w. 3′ 5½″.
Station 24 — 7⅜″ deep, ½ w. 3′ 6″.

Frame 25′ 4″ — 7⅜″ deep, ½ w. 3′ 6″.
Frame 26′ 8″ — 7⅜″ deep, ½ w. 3′ 6″.
Station 28 — 7⅜″ deep, ½ w. 3′ 5″.
Frame 29′ 4″ — 7″ deep, ½ w. 3′ 3″.
Frame 30′ 8″ — 6⅞″ deep, ½ w. 3′ ½″.
Station 32 — 6½″ deep, ½ w. 3′ 10″.
Frame 33′ 4″ — 5¾″ deep, ½ w. 2′ 6″.
Frame 34′ 8″ — 8½″ deep, ½ w. 2′ 7″.
Station 36 — 6¾″ deep, ½ w. 2′ 4″.
Frame 37′ 4″ — 5½″ deep, ½ w. 2′.
Frame 38′ 8″, no floor.
Station 40 — 7″ deep, ½ w. 2′ 1½″.
Frame 41′ 4″ — 4½″ deep, ½ w. 18″.
Frame 42′ 8″ — 7″ deep, ½ w. 20″.

The floor timbers can all be held down by ½″ galvanized lags with washers under heads. Two on a timber from stations 16 to 32. These lags should pierce the keel from 2″ to 3″, so in most cases 8″ long lags will do, but on 9′ 4″ there is a good size wood screw.

Frame 34′ 8″ can have a 9″ or 10″ lag, so there should be about thirty eight (38) ½″ x 8″ lags. See sheet 3 for limber holes, but there should be no limber holes at station 12, Frame 31′ 4″.

The floor timbers can be of various woods, but oak and locust are excellent, and yellow pine good if the fastenings are not too close to the edges. It would be a good thing if floors under the main mast step were locust.

10. Frames or timbers are 2″ x 2″. It would be well if the frames from 8 forward were sawn and beveled, the others all should be steam bent. They may be bent in two layers if desired, in which case the planking fastenings should enter partly into the inner layer.

New England white oak is the best bending wood for frames. Frames may be fastened to the floor timbers with either 5/16″

copper rivets or galvanized carriage bolts, about ⅜″ x 4″, but probably it will be cheapest to cut up 5/16″ copper rod in lengths of a little over 4″ and rivet both ends over a burr in the old fashioned way.

If the frames are bent in two 1″ layers, perhaps staggered 5/16″ copper rivets will be best, for they can be staggered to clear the seam between the layers. These frame-to-floor fastenings are not so important after the vessel is built for if some of the planking fastenings are put into the frames and floors they take the place of those fastenings.

11. Planking — in a yacht of this type it is important to make the lower parts heavy and the upper parts light, so the planking would be best if about 1¾″ thick at the garboard, and 1¼″ thick at the sheer strake. Perhaps the first three or four planks can be 1¾″ thick, and each 1/32″ thinner to the succeeding strake until 1¼″ is arrived at.

As for material — long leaf yellow pine would be the best for the lower planking, perhaps up to the LWL amidships, then soft pine, cypress or mahogany, or rift-grain fir, above that. In spite of its weight the sheer strake should be of oak or yellow pine.

Planking fastenings are bound to be an expense, and while I think the fastenings into the stem, transom and sheer strake should be bronze screws, say 3″ #20 where the planking is thick, and 2¾″ #20 where it is thinner, I think the rest of the planking could be fastened with 3″ hot galvanized boat nails. The nails have the advantage of not requiring a bung if they are carefully covered with plastic wood applied with a putty knife which can be quickly done. Cast bronze nails would also be very good.

12. Transom may be planked up the same as the topsides, or approximately 1½″ thick. Besides the stern knee there are two oak frames each side, about 2″ x 2″, and an apron about 1½″ x 4″. The planks of the transom are to be beveled and caulked the same as the topsides. The transom is flat so two circular windows, similar to Wilcox, Crittendon Fig. 524, or a glass set in putty, or an opening portlight like W. C. Fig. 525, may be used. This might be nice in rainy weather if the companion slide were kept closed.

Across the top of the transom there is a special heavy deck beam, 2¼″ deep and about 7″ fore and aft. This beam is tailed out with lodging knees, which should be well secured to the shelf and clamp.

13. Breast-hook forward should also be well secured to the shelf and clamp, and have about a ½″ bronze bolt securing it to the stem head as shown.

14. Deck Beams — the regular deck beams are 1½″ x 2½″ with a crown of 4½″ in 12′. The deck beams may be white oak, yellow bark oak, white ash, elm, or locust.

15. Strong Beams — 2½″ x 2½″, and are on frames 9′ 4″, 33′ 4″, and 35′ 8″. If desired one may also be on station #8.

16. After Deck Beams — 1½″ x 2¼″, crowned 6″ in 10′, with a strong beam 2¼″ x 2¼″ on frame 42′ 8″.

17. House Deck Beams — 1¼″ x 1¾″, spaced 12″, with a crown of 10½″ in 9′.

The strong house beams are 1¾″ x 1¾″ on 13′ 7″, 16′ ½″, and 30′ 3½″. *Note* that the beams at the main mast have uneven spacing for hatchways, etc.

18. Main Deck — 1¼″ thick, covered with canvas or fiberglass. It can be soft pine, cedar, California redwood, cypress, spruce, or rift-grain fir.

19. After Deck — 1″ thick of same material as main deck.

20. Clamp — 4″ deep and 1½″ athwartships, and may be of hard pine, Oregon pine, fir, or other firm wood that can be secured in long lengths. The scarf in this member should be away from amidships and made the same as the scarfs in the staves of a mast. The clamp is secured to the frames with 3″ #20 screws.

21.   Shelf — $2\frac{1}{4}''$ x $2\frac{1}{4}''$, same material as clamp but scarf at other end of vessel. The shelf is fastened with galvanized iron lag screws, $\frac{3}{8}''$ x $6''$, with washers under heads.

22.   Bulkheads run from side to side and may be made of panels of laminated wood about $\frac{5}{8}''$ thick. It will be best to have the seams run up and down with a stiffener of oak about $1\frac{1}{4}''$ x $2''$ over the seams as shown on the bulkhead at station 12.

23.   Mainmast at deck is $6''$ x $8''$, corner radius $1\frac{1}{4}''$. Make allowance for wedges, etc. After side of mainmast is straight and raked $6\frac{1}{2}°$ below deck.

24.   Mizzen mast at cockpit floor is $5''$ x $6\frac{1}{2}''$, and the after side rakes $7\frac{1}{2}°$.

25.   Main mast step may be oak or locust, $4''$ deep, $7''$ wide, $23''$ long. The forward and after ends are $1\frac{1}{2}''$ deep, and upper after side beveled to be at $90°$ from after side of mast. The main mast's tongue is $6''$ fore and aft and $1\frac{1}{2}''$ sideways.

26.   Mizzen mast step may be oak or locust, $3\frac{1}{2}''$ deep, $6''$ wide, $20''$ long. The forward and after ends are $1\frac{1}{2}''$ deep with the upper surface beveled to be at right angles to the after side of mast. The mast tongue is $4\frac{1}{2}''$ fore and aft, and $1\frac{1}{4}''$ sideways.

27.   Deck house — side and ends may be soft pine, mahogany, California redwood, cypress, or fir of fine grain. It is $1\frac{1}{4}''$ thick. After end will require a board about $19\frac{1}{2}''$ wide but only $13''$ forward. At the four corners there are posts of oak with the outer corner rounded to a radius of $2''$.

28.   Window openings in house sides are $7''$ x $15''$ with corners rounded on $3''$ radius. The windows are spaced $3'\ 5''$, with the center of the forward window about $18''$ aft of the rabbet line of forward port.

29.   House deck — $\frac{7}{8}''$ tongue and groove, matched boards of cedar, soft pine, spruce, redwood, cypress, or fine texture rift grain fir. It should be well-dried stock and covered with either canvas or fiberglass.

30.   Chainplate for mainmast — all $3/16''$ x $1\frac{3}{4}''$ x $27''$. Tobin bronze, Everdur, phosphor bronze, or Monel, and each secured with about eight (8) $\frac{3}{8}''$ x $1\frac{1}{2}''$ silicon bronze stove bolts, 48 required.

The chain plates are to be drilled so the lag will clear the seams of the planking and the clamp, when the top of the chain plate is about $1\frac{1}{2}''$ above the top of toe rail and $2\frac{1}{2}''$ above top of deck, as shown.

31.   Mizzen chainplates — $3/16''$ x $1\frac{1}{2}''$ x $24''$, same material as main, but secured with about six $\frac{3}{8}''$ x $1\frac{1}{2}''$ stove bolts. Number required: 24.

32.   Stem band — $\frac{1}{4}''$ x $3\frac{1}{8}''$ x $24''$, fastened with several large flat-head wood screws, #18 or more, spaced about $3''$. The stem band should be nicely beveled off to conform with the face of the stem. Its lower end will be about $2\frac{1}{4}''$ wide.

33.   Mooring bitt. Upper half, bronze casting from pattern kept by designer. Lower half, oak, locust or teak block, $2''$ x $6''$ x $12''$.

34.   Forecastle water closet — W. C. Fig. 1591, also vented loop W. C. Fig. 1548, and sea cocks, W. C. Fig. 1511, $1\frac{1}{2}''$ size, and one Fig. 1507, $\frac{3}{4}''$ size.

35.   Pipe berth and transom seat to starboard.

36.   Forecastle soles — underside $9''$ below LWL. May be made of $\frac{7}{8}''$ fir flooring and should have a central opening section.

37.   Main cabin soles — underside is $12''$ below LWL. May be $\frac{7}{8}''$ fir flooring with an opening section about $9''$ wide the full length.

38.   After cabin soles — underside is $3''$ below the LWL, and may be the same construction as others.

39.   Forecastle hatch — see detail. I suppose there will be

steps on the bulkhead, but this may be arranged best after yacht is partly built. Hatch opening 18″ fore and aft.

40. Forward cabin escape — same construction as #39, but fore and aft opening 17¾″.

41. Main hatch has opening of 2′ 3″ x 2′. Top is made of sheet brass. See detail.

42. After hatch has an opening of 2′ 4″ x 20″. Same construction as main hatch.

43. Cockpit coaming is straight and so must be a little thicker than usual and well fastened down. It can be 9″ high and 1″ thick. If it is to be bright, it should be the same as the rest of the trim, but if painted oak would be good.

44. Engine room hatches are on both sides of the cockpit with openings of 14½″ x 19″. They may be made of ½″ laminated wood and covered with canvas or fiberglass to match rest of deck. Around three sides of the border there are strips of brass about 1/16″ x 1¼″; inboard there will be the same finish strip as rest of cockpit.

45. Cockpit sides and forward end may be oak or cypress, 1″ or more thick. After end may be the same but must run out to lodge on the shelf and clamp as shown on construction section 40. This is to support the main deck at that point. Above the deck there may be a panel to make the forward end of the after cabin.

46. Cockpit floor pitched aft for the following reasons —
    1. to get more room in the engine room,
    2. to make the entrance to after cabin easier, and
    3. to accommodate short and long legs.

The floor of the cockpit may be either a ¾″ laminated wood panel or planked up crossways of ⅞″ pine, cypress, or fir; in any case it is to be covered with canvas or fiberglass.

Cockpit floor has two fore-and-aft oak frames about 1½″ x 2″, spaced about 16½″ center to center. Between these is the mizzen mast partner, which is oak, 1½″ thick, 15″ athwartships, and 12″ or more fore and aft, as shown. There may be quite a fore-and-aft strain on this partner at times so it must be well fastened to both the frames and flooring.

A tub cockpit of this type is usually built separately from the yacht and the procedure is as follows: plank the floor up on the frames then canvas cover it; then fasten the floor to the box making the ends and sides. Some people lap the corners as is shown, but remember the after end piece is about 9′ 4½″ long and 14″ deep and curved up as shown on the construction section. The whole tub cockpit must be put in place before the deck is laid.

47. Engine — the one shown in dotted lines is the Gray Marine Model Four 112 with 2:1 reduction gear. The shaft line is 15″ out from center line, about 2½″ below LWL on station #32, and 13½″ below at station 40.

Propellers for this engine will be 19″ diameter 14″ pitch.

48. Stuffing boxes — Wilcox, Crittenden Fig. 8654, or Columbian Fig. 177, but if the latter is used the after end of the base may have to be cut off to clear station #40 floor timber. (There is no timber on 38′ 8″.) It is assumed that the shaft will be 1⅛″ Tobin bronze and be about 7′ 2″ OA with Gray Marine Four 112.

49. Struts — Columbian Fig. 131, well secured by Columbian strut bolts passing through an oak block inside the planking.

50. Rudder and tiller are on a separate drawing.

51. Upper attachment of leeboards.

52. Leeboard pendant blocks — Merriman Fig. 410 with 4″ sheave.

53. Moulded decoration to cover forward end of after raised topsides. See construction, and do not forget to make the four after frames long enough.

54. Hand rails — full length of deck house.

55. Mizzen sheet deck plates — P and S. See block list.

56. Backstay deck plates — P and S. See block list.

57. Main sheet deck plates — on oak block. P and S. See block list.

58. Jib sheet deck plates — on oak block. P and S. See list.

59. Combination towing and docking cleat — W. C. Fig. 4020 — 12″. P and S.

60. Docking cleat. W. C. Fig. 4020 — 10″. P and S.

61. Special cheek block and cleat. W. C. Fig. 4020 — 8″, for leeboard tackle. P and S.

62. Cockpit scuppers have to lead forward a way to clear the after cabin berths and consist of the following parts;

    1—strainer in cockpit floor made of 1/16″ bronze with several 3/16″ holes.

    2—close nipple screwed into cockpit floor.

    3—elbow

    4—length of pipe, about 6″

    5—elbow

    6—length of pipe, about 5″

    7—length of rubber hose to fit pipe

    8—length of pipe to screw into oak block just above waterline. See sheet 4. P and S.

CONSTRUCTION SECTIONS

A. On the construction plan it was noted that the scuttle in the cabin sole could be 9″ wide, but as the table and other parts clear the scuttle it will be better to make it 12″ wide for the convenience of stowing inside ballast.

B. The top of the house deck is straight at the center line, and about 5′ 6″ above the LWL at forward end, and 5′ 3″ at after end.

C. The height of the house sides from the top of the main deck to the top of the house deck is about as follows:

Stations	9′ 4″	16	20	24	32	33′ 4″
Heights	13″	15¼″	16½″	17¾″	19⅜″	19⅜″

D. The lodging piece for the house deck beams can be oak about 3½″ x 1¼″. Note that the elevation of this piece, as well as the cabin windows, are drawn in correctly. They should all be about 1¼″ higher forward, and 2″ higher aft, so don't take elevation dimensions from the lines marked with a cross.

E. For details of windows and draining gutters see Sheet 11.

F. For details of the hatchways see Sheet 11.

G. The fuel tanks should be of tin-lined copper or Monel metal, about 1/16″ thick. They hold approximately fifty gallons apiece and, if the engines are used little, perhaps one tank will be sufficient. The filler pipes and vents should be outside the cockpit coaming.

These tanks are supposed to rest on frames 37′ 4″ and 39′ 8″ so it will be necessary to make a wood pattern for the frames. The tanks should be securely held in place, particularly on their forward sides so they will not shift in case of collision or grounding. The fuel line should definitely enter from the top.

H. Forward engine room ventilators made of wood. The ventilator for incoming air will have to be arranged after the yacht is partly completed.

I. If all of the circulating water is introduced to the center of the exhaust pipe, there will be no need of mufflers, and this can be done by using the right type of reducing elbow that allows the water ejection pipe to go beyond the elbow as shown. The latter part of the exhaust pipe may be Edson hose, and the pipe which pierces the planking should be brass or bronze.

J. The water tank rests on some strips of wood to raise its level where frame 32 comes above the cabin sole. These strips of wood should be cypress arranged so the air can circulate between the tank and sole. The tank must be well secured.

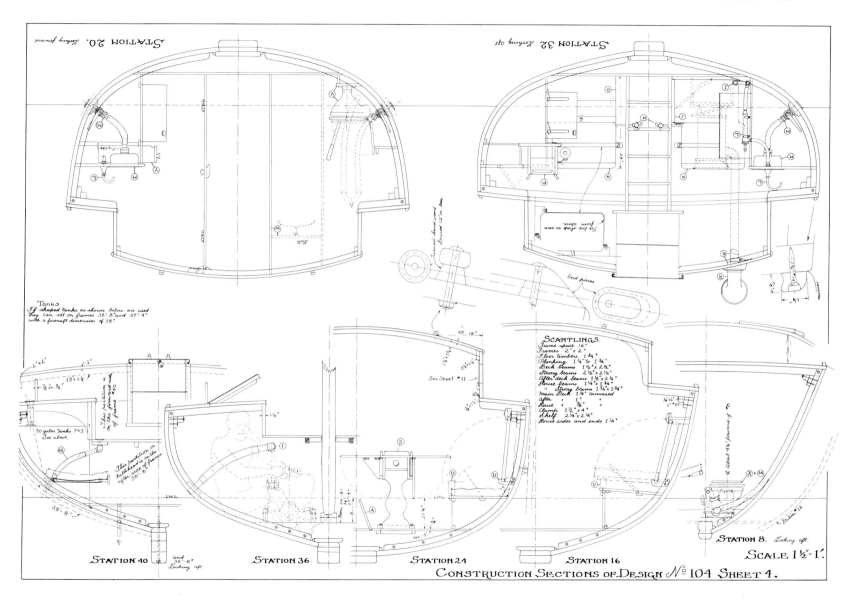

STATION 20. *Looking forward*

STATION 32. *Looking aft*

Tanks
If shaped tanks as shown below are used
they can set on frames 38'-8" and 37'-4"
with a foreaft dimension of 18"

SCANTLINGS.
Frame space 16"
Frames 2" x 2"
Floor timbers " 1¾"
Planking 1¼" to 1¾"
Deck beams 1½" x 2¼"
Strong beams 2½" x 2½"
After deck beams 1½" x 2¼"
House beams 1¼" x 1¾"
Strong beams 1¾" x 1¾"
Main Deck 1¼" canvased
after " 1"
House " ⅞"
Clamp 1½" x 4"
Shelf 2¼" x 2¼"
House sides and ends 1¼"

See Sheet #11

50 galon tanks P+S
See above

This partition or
bulkhead is on the
forward side
of frame 40

This partition is on the
after side of frame
38'-8"

See Sheet #11

STATION 40   *and 38'-8" Looking aft.*

STATION 36

STATION 24

STATION 16

STATION 8. *Looking aft.*

SCALE 1½"=1'.

CONSTRUCTION SECTIONS OF DESIGN № 104 SHEET 4.

The inside dimensions of the tank may be about 15″ fore and aft, 16″ high, and 24″ athwartships. The tank should be of tin-lined copper or Monel of the thickness recommended by the tank maker. This tank would be better and stronger if it had one swash plate running fore and aft. It should have a good size filler pipe near the companionway steps, and a flange for the water pipe as shown. The center of the water pipe has to be two or more inches above the floor to clear the frames, and it should have a drain plug for winter drainage.

K.   Omitted.

L.   The water pumps may be Wilcox, Crittenden Fig. R-6542-B, and the swinging spouts Fig. 8283, but the galley spout has a longer and higher spout for filling receptacles, 9″ or so high, and will have to be made special.

M.   Both sinks are Perko Fig. 402, and have drain fittings Fig. 586. The drawing shows these sinks draining out through sea-cocks, for there may be times when the yacht is heeled that water will come up into the sinks momentarily, but, if the owner wants to economize, through-hull connections alone can be used, so either W. C. seacocks Fig. 1507 — 1½″, or W. C. Thru-hull Fig. 8569 — 1½″ may be used.

N.   The ice boxes shown measure on the outside 24″ x 14″, x 17″. They would be much cheaper than a built-in ice box. The starboard ice box sets on the water tank, while the port box rests on a food storage box.

The ice boxes are secured in place by shaped wooden pieces on two sides, and bronze straps 1/16″ x 1¼″ on two sides as shown. These ice boxes have a drain pipe in back which can be connected by pipe or hose to cocks under the companion ladder for drainage.

O.   On the port side, the ice box is supported by a wooden box about 16″ fore and aft, 17″ high, and 26″ athwartships. This box has a removable shutter across its forward side about 6″ wide. The box can be made of any material and painted. It is principally for storing canned goods, potatoes, etc.

P.   The cooking stove is W. C. Fig. 8255. This rests on a shelf or counter about 26″ above the cabin sole so that its cooking grate is 34″ above the sole. The top of the counters, the ice boxes, and the heating stove are all the same, 34″. Back of this stove the counter top can be lifted up to give access to a storage space about 7½″ deep, as shown on section 32.

Q.   The heating stove is the Concordia Cabin Heater and should be mounted on a strong box about 10½″ high, 17″ fore and aft, 16″ athwartships. This box must be well secured in place and the top should be strong enough to hold the stove in place in rough weather. Perhaps it would be best if most of this box were made of 1″ oak.

The box is intended to hold stove fuel, so a section of the inboard side about 3″ deep and 7″ wide can be cut out as shown in dotted lines. Also the middle section of the top, about 10″ wide, should lift out for the convenience of filling the box.

R.   The stove pipe is 3″ diameter and arranged to exhaust into a 5″ cowl ventilator like Perko Fig. 510, which has a screw plate to replace the ventilator in hot weather. There will also have to be a piece of 5″ diameter stove pipe, (preferably brass), about 3″ deep to extend downward to surround the stove pipe, making a 1″ air space between the two as shown on Section #32.

S.   The dining table should be of firm wood such as mahogany, ash, oak, or butternut, but if the top is to be kept scrubbed then elm is the best for that part. The table top when open measures 4′ x 3′ 6″. The central leaf is 12″ wide. The box under the central part of the table is 10″ wide and contains a drawer about 8¼″ wide and 4″ deep which slides out either fore or aft, and is intended to hold the silverware, etc. The table side leaves are supported by triangular pieces of wood hinged at their upper end which drop down when the leaves are raised.

The table is shown with removable racks only on the center section, which experience has shown to be a good arrangement for these racks are left on most of the time, in fact all of the time when the table is not used for chart work or card playing.

The table must be very strongly secured to the floor, for people may brace against it in a seaway, so it would be well if it were fastened with ⅜″ x 3″ lag screws going to a reinforcement under the floor, as shown.

T. There are ventilation holes for the lockers under the transom seats. The star can be cut out by first cutting through the outer layer of laminated wood with a chisel or knife, and then drill a good size hole in the center when the lines of the star can be cut out with a keyhole saw. The other curved openings are made by cutting two holes about 5″ apart with a hole saw, then connecting these holes with two curved saw clefts cut with a keyhole saw. The large holes are 2″, the small ones 1″ or more. If this work is done right it makes an attractive appearance even in laminated wood.

U. Berth hooks on the frames can be either cut out of sheet brass or cast from a pattern. The berths are supported when open by small removable blocks of wood, as shown, and the berths are held in their closed position by wooden turn battens properly mounted on blocks. There will have to be some small blocks also for backstops.

V. The W C is made by Wilcox, Crittenden and is their Fig. 1593. It will have to be mounted on a riser about 4″ high to bring it to a useful height and allow it to be placed further outboard. There must be a shelf or other support to hold the seat cover in place when it is open, as shown.

The other accessories to the W C are a 1½″ seacock, W. C. Fig. 1507; and a ¾″ seacock, W. C. Fig. 1507, which is supposed to pierce the hull below and ahead of the waste pipe; and a vented loop W. C. Fig. 1548.

W. Clothes closet for the forward stateroom with a shelf above for hats; shoes go on the floor.

X. The forecastle W C, as shown on section 8, is Wilcox, Crittenden Fig. 1591, and while it should have a ¾″ seacock for the waterpipe, the waste pipe could get along without a seacock for this outlet is so near the centerline that heeling won't affect it much. However, the waste pipe should be slightly above the LWL. In this case, a through-hull connection, Wilcox-C. Fig. 857 — 1½″, could be used, together with a curved tailpiece like W. C. Fig. 1510 — 1 ½″

Y. Beside the sink in the dressing room, there could be a large drawer, about 23″ x 21½″ x 6″ outside. If this drawer has a central runner for the notched guide on the back of the drawer, there will be no need for the complicated framing usually required, and as this arrangement gives the drawer a three-point support, the drawer will always run well even if it gets out of square. If the side runners are notched in front, as shown on section #20, the drawer will stay closed with the vessel heeled.

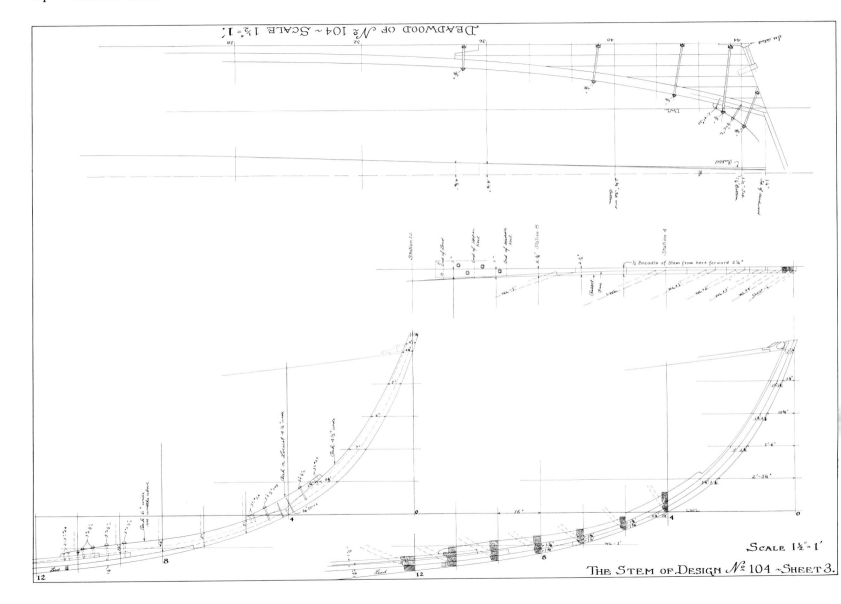

DEADWOOD OF N⁰ 104 ~ SCALE 1½"=1'.

Scale 1½"-1'

The Stem of Design N⁰ 104 ~ Sheet 3.

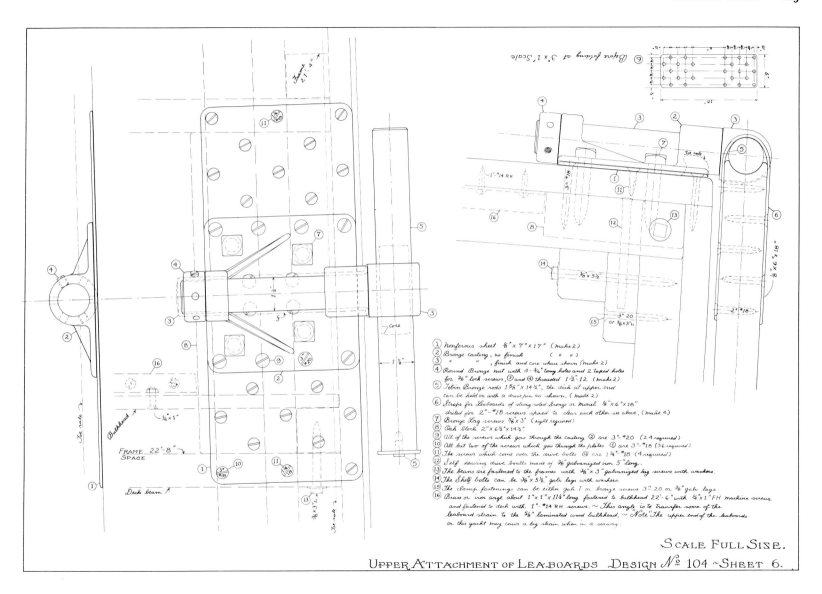

⑥ *Before fastening at 3"x 1" Scale*

Frame 21'-4"

Tot rate

1"-#14 RH

3/8"#18

7/8 x 5 1/2

3" 20 or 3/8"x 3" L

8"x 6"x 18"

2"-#18

Core

Frame 22'-8"
Space

Deck beam

Bulkhead

Toe rails

1/4" x 1"

① Nonferous sheet 1/8"x 7"x 17" (make 2)
② Bronze casting , no finish   (" ")
③   "   " , finish and core where shown (make 2)
④ Round Bronze nut with 4 - 3/16" tommy holes and 2 taped holes
   for 3/8" lock screws ③ and ④ threaded 1 1/2"-12. (make 2)
⑤ Tobin Bronze rods 1 5/8"x 14 1/2", the disk at upper end
   can be held on with a drive pin as shown. (make 2)
⑥ Straps for Leaboards of strong rolled Bronze or monel 1/8"x 6"x 18"
   drilled for 2"-#18 screws spaced to clear each other see above, (make 4)
⑦ Bronze Lag screws 5/8"x 3" (eight required)
⑧ Oak block 2"x 6 1/2"x 14 1/2".
⑨ All of the screws which go through the casting ② are 3"-#20 (24 required)
⑩ All but two of the screws which go through the plates ① are 3"-#18 (36 required)
⑪ The screws which come over the drive bolts ⑫ are 1 1/4"-#18 (4 required)
⑫ Self heading drive bolts made of 3/8" galvanized iron 5" long.
⑬ The beams are fastened to the frames with 3/8"x 3" galvanized lag screws with washers.
⑭ The Shelf bolts can be 3/8"x 5 1/2" galv lags with washers.
⑮ The clamp fastenings can be either galv. I or bronze screws 3"-20 or 3/8" galv lags.
⑯ Brass or iron angle about 1"x 1"x 11 1/2" long fastened to bulkhead 22'-6" with 1/4"x 1" FH machine screws
   and fastened to deck with 1"-#14 RH screws. ~ This angle is to transfer some of the
   leaboard strain to the 5/8" laminated wood bulkhead. ~ Note" The upper end of the leaboards
   on this yacht may caus a big strain when in a seaway.

SCALE FULL SIZE.

UPPER ATTACHMENT OF LEABOARDS DESIGN № 104 ~ SHEET 6.

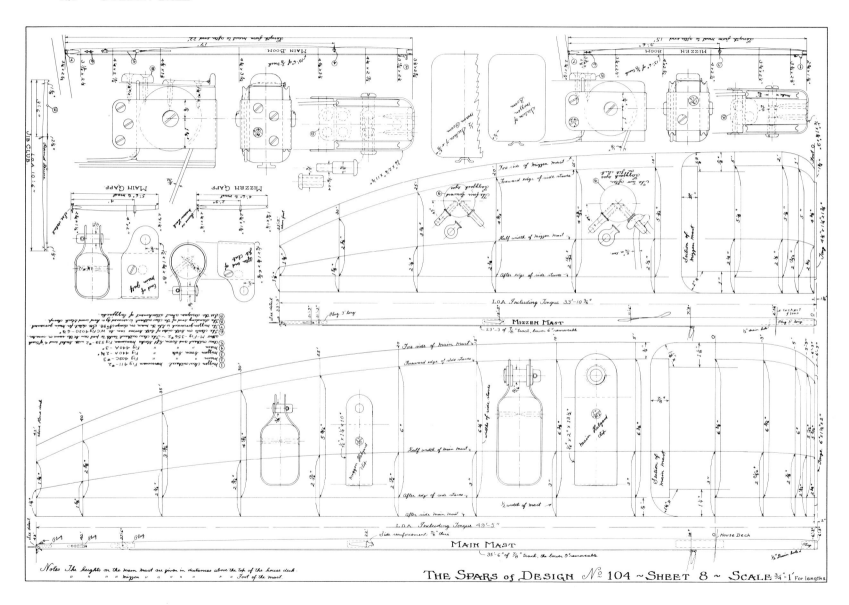

THE SPARS of DESIGN № 104 ~ SHEET 8 ~ SCALE ¾"=1' For lengths.

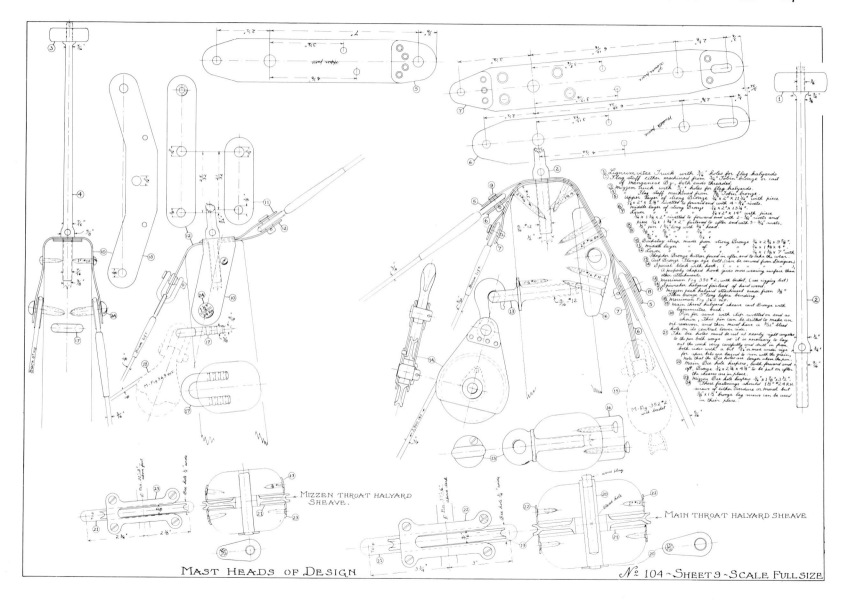

MAST HEADS OF DESIGN

Nº 104 ~ SHEET 9 ~ SCALE FULLSIZE

MIZZEN THROAT HALYARD SHEAVE.

MAIN THROAT HALYARD SHEAVE

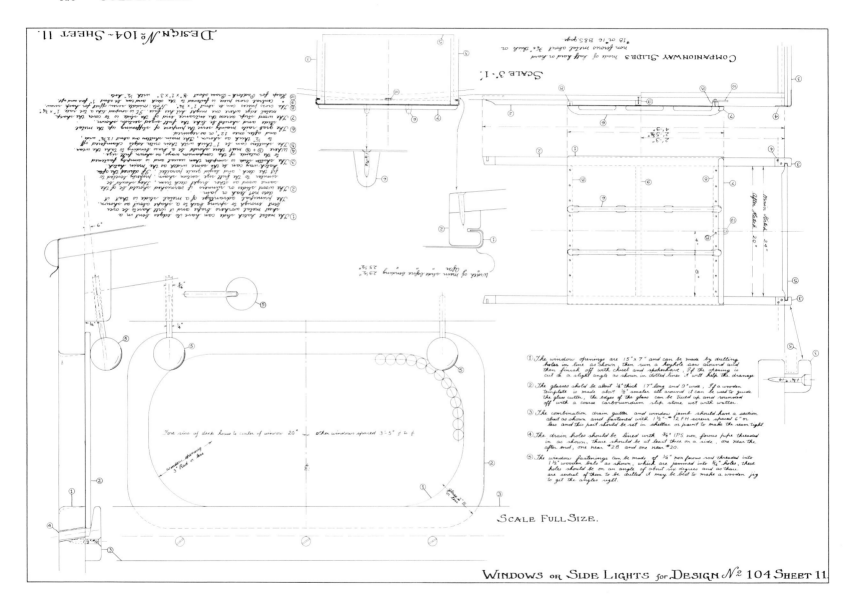

SCALE FULL SIZE.

① The window openings are 15" x 7" and can be made by drilling holes in line as shown, then run a keyhole saw around and then finish off with chisel and spokeshave. If the opening is cut on a slight angle as shown in dotted lines it will help the drainage

② The glasses should be about ¼" thick 17" long and 9" wide. If a wooden template is made about ⅛" smaller all around it can be used to guide the glass cutter, the edges of the glass can be trued up and rounded off with a coarse carborundum slip stone wet with water.

③ The combination drain gutter and window jamb should have a section about as shown and fastened with 1½"—#12 F.H. screws spaced 6" or less and this part should be set in shellac or paint to make the seam tight.

④ The drain holes should be lined with ¾" IPS non ferous pipe threaded in as shown, there should be at least three on a side, one near the after end, one near #28 and one near #20.

⑤ The window fastenings can be made of ¼" non ferous rod threaded into 1½" wooden balls as shown, which are jammed into ¾" holes, these holes should be on an angle of about six degrees and as there are several of them to be drilled it may be best to make a wooden jig to get the angles right.

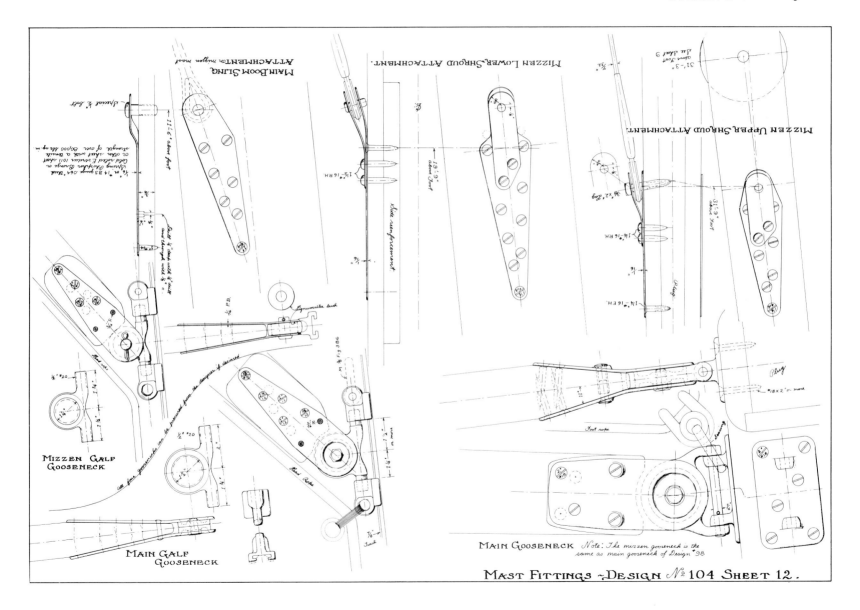

MAST FITTINGS ~ DESIGN №104 SHEET 12.

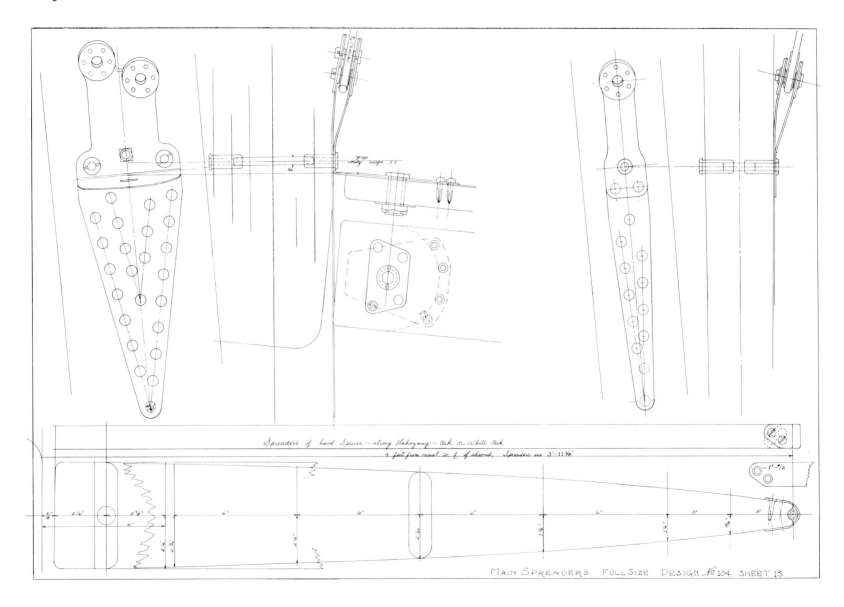

Spreaders of hard Spruce ~ strong Mahogany ~ Ash or White Oak

4 feet from mast to ℄ of shroud, Spreaders are 3'-11¾"

MAIN SPREADERS   FULL SIZE   DESIGN № 104 SHEET 13

STANDING RIGGING

Name of Part	Number required	Description / Length	Fittings
FORE STAY	1	Exactly 46'	
MAIN LOWER SHROUDS	4	about 22'-8"	
MAIN UPPER SHROUDS	2	about 41'-6"	
SPRING STAY	1	Exactly 26'	
MIZZEN UPPER SHROUDS	2	about 28'	
MIZZEN LOWER SHROUDS	2	about 16'-6"	
MIZZEN BACK STAYS	2	27'	
MAIN BOOM SLING	1	6'2"	
MAIN BOOM LIFT	1	61'	
MIZZEN BOOM LIFT	1	37' / 12	
FORESTAYSAIL LAZY JACK PENDANTS	2	32'	
MAIN CLEW-OUTHAUL PENDANT	1	18'-6"	
MIZZEN CLEWOUTHAUL PENDANT	1	13' / 8'	
LEE BOARD PENDANTS	2	7'	

RUNNING RIGGING

Name of Part		Description / Length	Fittings
FORESTAYSAIL HALYARD	1		
MAIN PEAK HALYARD	1	42' / 47'	
MAIN THROAT HALYARD	1	35' / 44'	
MIZZEN PEAK HALYARD	1	27' / 32'	
MIZZEN THROAT HALYARD	1	28' / 29'	
FORESTAYSAIL LAZYJACKS	2	12' / 13'	
FORESTAYSAIL SHEET	1	7/16 DIA — 1¼ CIR	
MAIN SHEET	1	105' — ½ DIA — 1½ CIR	
MIZZEN SHEET	1	65' — 7/16 DIA — 1¼ CIR	
MIZZEN BACKSTAY TACKLES	2	36' — 7/16 DIA — 1¼ CIR	
LEE BOARD TACKLES	2	34' — 7/16 DIA — 1¼ CIR	
FIRST BOWER ANCHOR WARP		35 Fathoms	
SECOND BOWER ANCHOR WARP		30 Fathoms	
DOCKING LINES	2	50' — 2" CIR — 5/8 DIA	
MAIN BOOM LIFT TACKLE		14' of 7/16 DIA	

BLOCK LIST

Block List		Size	General Description
MAIN LOWER SHROUD TURNBUCKLES	4	7/16	MERRIMAN FIG 377
MAIN UPPER SHROUD TURNBUCKLES	2	7/16	"
MIZZEN LOWER SHROUD TURNBUCKLES	2	3/8	"
MIZZEN UPPER SHROUD TURNBUCKLES	2	3/8	"
FORESTAYSAIL HALYARD BLOCKS	1	#2	Merriman Fig 362 #2 with becket
	1	#2	" 355 #2
MAIN PEAK HALYARD BLOCKS	1	#2	Special block see sheet #9
	1	#2	Merriman Fig 370 #2 with becket
MAIN THROAT HALYARD BLOCK	1	#2	" " "
MIZZEN PEAK HALYARD BLOCKS	1		" 363 W.E.
	1		" 370 with becket
LAZYJACK BLOCKS	2	O	" 304
FORESTAYSAIL SHEET BLOCKS			
MAIN SHEET BLOCKS			
MIZZEN SHEET BLOCKS			
MIZZEN BACKSTAY BLOCKS			
MIZZEN THROAT HALYARD BLOCK	1	#1	" 370 with becket

CLEAT LIST
All cleats are WILCOX CRITTENDEN FIG 4020

Forestaysail halyard   One 6½" under gooseneck

Main Peak halyard   One 8" on Starboard side of mast 1' above house deck

Main Throat halyard   One 8" on Port side of mast 1' above house deck

Mizzen Peak halyard   One 6½" on Starboard side of mizzen mast

Mizzen Throat halyard   One 6½" on Port side of mizzen mast

Fore Staysail sheet   One 6½" on after side of deck house to port

Main Sheet   One 8" on after side of deck house to starboard

Mizzen Sheet   One 6½" as shown on sheet #5

Backstay tackle   Two 8" as shown on sheet #5

Lee board tackle   Two 8" as shown on sheet #5

Towing cleats   Two 12" on sheet #5

Docking cleats   Two 10" on sheet #5

DESIGN # 104
SHT. 14

7 HOW TO BUILD NEREIA

This yacht is named Nereia instead of having a number and letter like the H-28, for after the H-28 came out there appeared a whole flock of H numbers ranging from motor boats to racing freaks. Nereia was one of the many daughters of Nereus, the sea god, and because she had several sisters we thought it would be a good name for a yacht in a one-design class. Nereia and her sisters were called the Nereids. One of Nereia's sisters was the famous Amphitrite who became the wife of Neptune and subsequently the mother of Triton. Two of her other sisters were Thetis, the mother of Achilles, and Galatea who was loved by the cyclops Polyphemus. In fact some say all the various naiads, mermaids, water sprites, and sirens are descended from the Nereids. At any rate it would appear that Nereia's brother-in-law was no less than Neptune himself. However I have no intention of talking to you about Greek mythology, for I am not much of a scholar with the ancient languages but prefer rather to give you some myths in our present languages which no doubt you have noticed in my previous writings.

Nereia is a real little ship, one that can carry a figurehead gracefully, and while that isn't the easiest thing in the world to do on thirty-six feet overall length, still I believe she will prove to be very able and comfortable as well as quite a little faster than one would suppose in a boat of her accommodations and sail area. I have now had quite a little experience in designing yachts of a somewhat similar model, and one of them, Mobjack, is shown in another part of this book. Strange to say, some of these clipper-bowed yachts have won ocean races, and all of them turned out cheaper to build than others I have designed of like size. As compared with the H-28, Nereia is deeper in proportion and has quite a little more comparative sail area, so she should be even a better performer to windward. While some may not like the increase in draft, still it is almost necessary in getting full headroom in a boat of this size.

Nereia has bulwarks all around her which some people like very much, and I must say this gives a sense of security on board, but if she were to have high freeboard (high deck level) and bulwarks she would look very high sided, so that altogether the problem of securing headroom and good looks was rather difficult. But I am glad to say it seems to have worked out all right.

One of the great problems on a yacht of this size is to find a place where a tender can be carried on deck. This has been

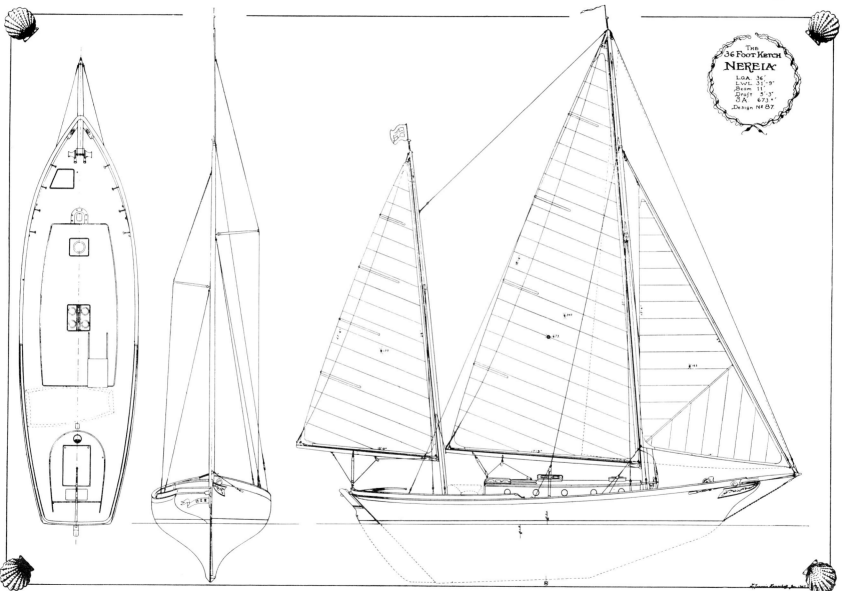

THE
36 FOOT KETCH
NEREIA
L.O.A. 36'
L.W.L. 31'-9"
Beam 11'
Draft 5'-3"
S.A. 673 '
Design No 87

arranged on Nereia by having a rather large bridge deck over the engine space, which is just forward of the mizzen. Of course the tender will only be carried on deck when making long passages in broken water, and this large bridge deck at other times will be a favorite place for the ladies and children to lounge, for it is sheltered by the deckhouse ahead and the bulwarks in this region are about eleven inches high. There is no doubt that a tender on a yacht of this size is almost a necessity, and there is no doubt that there are times when the tender is best on deck. The stern of the Nereia is quite similar to the H-28 in shape and construction below deck, and this has been done because that type of stern is much the cheapest to construct.

Below deck, way forward, Nereia has a forepeak which on a yacht of her size is a great convenience, for the anchor warp and other things, which may at times be damp and salty, can be kept out of the living quarters. Next aft comes a double stateroom with built-in berths and full headroom in its after part. Then there is a toilet room, or dressing room, with a water closet to port (for Nereia is large enough to have graduated out of the cedar bucket class), and to starboard are a lavatory and clothes closet. This dressing room will separate the forward stateroom from the rest of the cabin enough to secure quietness. Next aft comes the main cabin with two folding pipe berths which, when closed up, make back rests for the transom seats. Amidships in this room is a folding table for eating and card playing. Next aft comes the galley with coal-burning stove on one side, sink and dish racks on the other. This brings us to the after end of the deckhouse. Under the bridge deck is a four-cylinder Lathrop LH-4 motor, an icebox, and the water tank. The gasoline tanks are abreast the cockpit.

Although this is a rough description of Nereia's interior, the cabin plan drawing and its descriptions go into much detail. There is no doubt that some will prefer a different cabin layout, and in most cases they will be right, for no one cabin arrangement is best for various families, all depending on the age, sex, and experience of the crew. The inexperienced will invariably want a cabin all filled up with drawers, closets, chart tables, radio cabinets, etc., but, if you consider that the cabinet work or interior of a yacht of this size often runs into one-third of her total cost, you can see the principal reasons for extreme simplicity. The complicated interior is also a continual expense and nuisance throughout the life of the yacht. However, the cabin of Nereia is planned so that four adults can live comfortably and decently for quite a long cruise without continually stepping on one another's toes at every turn.

Sail Plan

There is little to describe about Nereia's rig and rigging which is not clearly shown on the sail plan, but a loose-footed jib has been adopted because many people nowadays prefer to take the jib off at night and store it in a bag, and while a loose-footed jib cannot be arranged to be self tending, it is on the whole the easiest rig to take care of, particularly on yachts used only on weekends. When not in use, the jib, if not all the sails, is best off below decks. While some people dislike a bowsprit, it is a fact that those who were brought up with them are very fond of them, and I

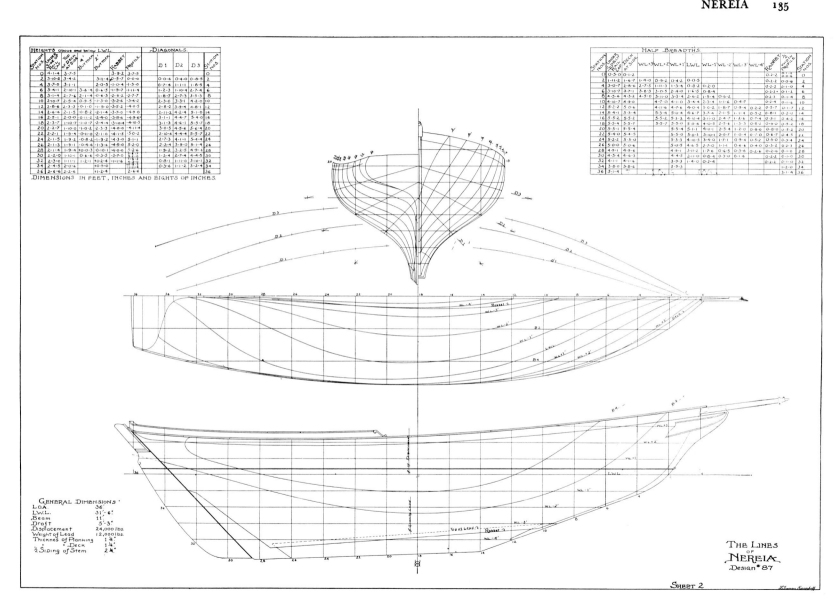

GENERAL DIMENSIONS
L.O.A.   36'
L.W.L.   31' 6"
Beam   11'
Draft   5' 3"
Displacement   24,000 lbs.
Weight of Lead   12,000 lbs.
Thickness of Planking   1 ¾"
            " " Deck   1 ½"
½ Siding of Stem   2 ¾"

THE LINES
OF
NEREIA
Design #87

SHEET 2

DIMENSIONS IN FEET, INCHES AND EIGHTS OF INCHES.

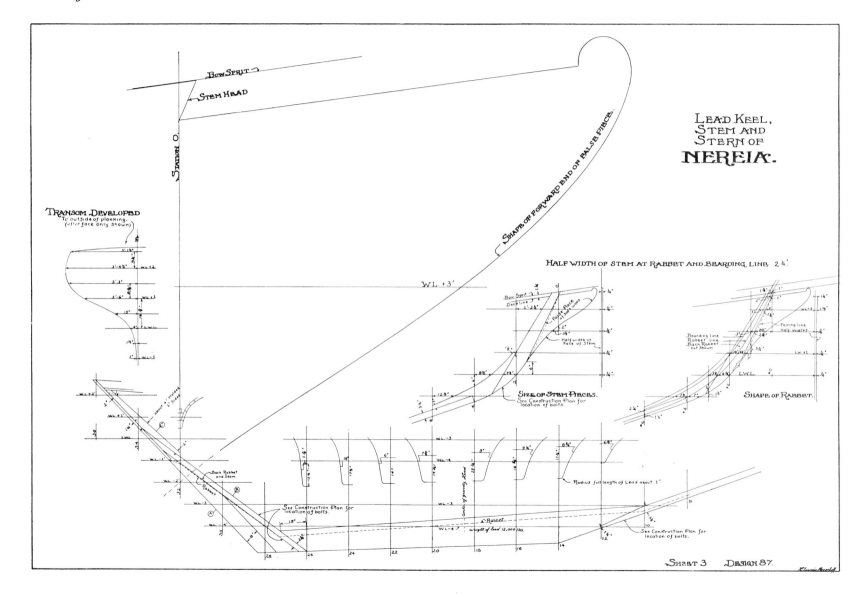

LEAD KEEL,
STEM AND
STERN OF
NEREIA.

TRANSOM DEVELOPED
To outside of planking.
(after face only shown)

SHAPE OF FORWARD END OF FALSE PIECE.

HALF WIDTH OF STEM AT RABBET AND BEARDING LINE 2¼"

SIZE OF STEM PIECES.
See Construction Plan for
location of bolts.

SHAPE OF RABBET.

SHEET 3   DESIGN 87.

must say that when you get accustomed to riding the nose pole with your toes hooked around the bobstay you are very securely attached to the vessel and much better off than teetering around on the foredeck at night.

There is a balloon jib shown in dotted lines on the sail plan, and, as this sail hoists on the headstay, the working jib can be left on the forestay. A balloon jib is a very useful sail on a cruiser to carry in reaching and running as well as in very light airs when close hauled, but the designer of Nereia does not think a regular genoa jib, as used on a racer, anywhere near worth its cost, for it must be made of about the same weight of cloth as the mainsail and requires much complication in its sheets, etc.

My experience is that it is not necessary to have reefs in the sails of an outside-ballasted ketch of this size, for in squalls or heavy weather they will handle all right with some one or two combinations of her three sails. I favor this arrangement principally because a sail which has once been reefed never sets as well again. Also you will find that Nereia with her draft and displacement will carry full sail in any ordinary summer weather. But those who want reefs in their sails should have them by all means if it will make them feel any better; in fact Nereia is designed so that many changes can be made without complications. For instance, the mainmast head is stayed well enough for a lapping jib for those who want one; or if a self-tending jib, on a club or boom, is preferred, the deck layout allows this. As for different cabin arrangements or even different figureheads and trailboards, well, these things will be lots of fun for prospective owners to work out.

The Nereia is no chichi imitation of foreign yachts or a copy of those vessels which were developed to carry dead fish to market, but is a descendant of the purely American type of yacht that was developed for ladies and gentlemen to sail on before racing measurements spoiled the cruising yacht.

Lines

I believe that the lines of Nereia need little explanation. Nereia is deeper bodied than other yachts of this type that I have designed, and that was necessary in getting headroom on a boat of her length. This has made the displacement rather large and consequently the amount of lead also great, but this cannot very well be avoided where full headroom and room in general are required with short length, although it is thought that if someone makes a half model from these lines it will turn out surprisingly handsome.

Lead Keel

Generally the lead keel is the first member put in place when building a yacht, and on Nereia the lead is a structural member as well as ballast, so that it must be set up carefully and leveled properly. The fore and aft incline of the bottom is $4\frac{3}{4}$ inches in 12 feet, or about 2 degrees; the incline of the top of the lead, also the rabbet line, is $13\frac{5}{8}$ inches in 16 feet, or about 4 degrees. Perhaps I should say something about this modern keel construction where the planking is rabbeted right into the lead, as it has been adopted on Nereia for the following reasons:

1. It is nearly impossible today to secure a suitable piece of wood as large as the wooden keel should be, 20 feet long

and 20 inches wide. Of course it is easy to secure unseasoned pieces of this size that will develop shakes and soft spots after they are seasoned.

2. A wood keel always shrinks and swells sideways and invariably strains or starts the garboard planks, a condition that is shown in *The Common Sense of Yacht Design*.

3. There is a great saving in cost by leaving out the wood keel and its consequent bolts.

4. The life of the yacht is much increased by leaving out that part which is most apt to rot.

It is just about as easy to cast the lead with the rabbet in it, and it usually only needs a little cleaning up with a rabbet plane to make a strong permanent landing for the garboard strake, which is almost never the case with a wood keel after it either shrinks or swells. It might be mentioned that I have designed seven different yachts that were built without the wooden keel and they have proved this construction to be most excellent. Some of them are twenty years old now. But if one should prefer a wood keel, the same can be laid in the space where the rabbet is shown on the lead and the difference in weight simply made up with inside ballast. However, the wood keel would require a different arrangement of keel bolts, which could be worked out by the builder. Of course, where an iron ballast keel is used, it will be necessary to have a wood keel, but, as there is little saving in the end with an iron keel, it is not recommended.

Stem

The stem and its knee (which is usually called an anchor stock) should be of white oak. Locust is also good. Both of these parts are 4½ inches thick for their full length so they can be run through the thickness planer. The stem itself should be gotten out with a curved forward side, which I have called a fairing line, as this will assist in getting the proper bevels, but after the yacht is set up this forward side can be dressed down to a straight line, as shown, to take the false piece. The false piece itself may be made of any variety of wood and can be soft, as it is protected by both the bowsprit and the bobstay. It may be made up of several pieces if desired. The lower end of the false piece will butt against the bobstay anchor plate so there will not be a feather edge.

Stern Post

The stern post (see drawing) is made up of three members as follows:

A. The deadwood can be made of two layers as shown, or in one piece if it can be secured. It should be of hard pine or similar wood. Its forward or upper edge makes the rabbet line. The thickest part of this piece is at station 32 where it is about 4 inches thick athwartships.

B. This piece should be of white oak about 2¾ inches deep and 4 inches or more wide, for, at its lower end below the rabbet line, it is as wide as the lead.

C. This piece, which acts as the upper end of the stern post, should be of oak about 4 by 2 inches.

The bolting for all these parts is shown on the construction plan. It might be mentioned that there is no knee at the joint of the lead and stern post since the planking, which is quite vertical at this point, makes a deep double panel which is much stronger than any knee.

Transom

On the drawing, the dimensions give the width of the transom to the outside of the planking. At the angle of the face of the stern the waterlines come about 16¾ inches apart, so that the half intervals shown are 8¾ inches apart. The transom should be planked up of 1¼-inch-thick well-seasoned oak planks not over 6 inches wide running athwartships with an apron around its border to take the planking fastenings. Besides the center stern post C, there should be oak frames about 1¾ inches square spaced 12 inches, for the transom will be built, fastened, and caulked the same as the planking.

All of these things are shown more clearly on the construction plan. The transom drawing is merely to give more dimensions than is feasible on either the lines or the construction plan for the aid of the loftsman.

CONSTRUCTION SECTION

1. Fore keel. Oak, 3½" deep, 5" wide, 8' 6" long.
2. Lead keel. 12,000 pounds cast with one percent antimony so it may be drilled and tapped easily for the lead bolts.
3. Deadwood and sternposts. See sheet No. 3.
4. Rudder. See later detail.
5. Floor timbers. All 1¾" thick, white oak, depths and widths according to longtitudinal construction plan sheet No. 5.
6. Frames. It is recommended that all the frames be of white oak and 1¾" in their sided and fore-and-aft dimensions, 2" in their molded or athwartships dimensions.

Frames forward of station 8 may be sawn and beveled so they will fit on both the floor timbers and the clamp.

Frames between stations 8 and 24 may be steam bent of two layers, each layer being one inch thick. The frames aft of No. 24 may be sawn and beveled, made up of sections as shown on the plan, or of other lengths as found convenient, but the juncture of the sections must be well bolted to a butt block. Their lower ends need not be carried down on the floor timbers farther than is necessary for proper attachment.

Frames are spaced 12". If one should prefer to build the yacht with sawn frames throughout, then the frames should be about 2¼ by 3" and spaced perhaps 15" or more, in which case the longtiudinal construction sheet No. 5 would have to be considerably altered.

7. Deck beams. There are only two sizes of deck beams on Nereia. The regular ones are 1½ by 2½"; the strong beams, which are at the masts and deck openings, are 2½ by 2½". All beams should be of white oak and crowned ⅜" to the foot or 4½" in 12'.
8. House beams. The regular house beams are to be 1" by 2" and the strong house beams 2 by 2", all white oak, crowned about 5" in 7'.
9. Mast partners. Hard wood, 2" by 9" by 2'.
10. Mast partner fastening. Four ⅜" bolts, nuts both ends, either galvanized iron or strong bronze.
11. Planking. May be rift grain fir of fine texture or any other suitable wood. If fir, about 1¼" thick; if other wood, then in proportion to its weight as compared to fir, but never less than 1" thick. The narrower the planking is the better. It would be well if the lower few planks were of yellow pine to resist rot.
12. Sheer strake. Oak, yellow pine, or other firm wood to best hold the shelf bolts. The sheer strake may be in two or three lengths if desired. The butts should be well bolted to a butt block. It will probably be necessary to make the sheer strake quite wide, perhaps 8" forward, to take the shelf bolts so

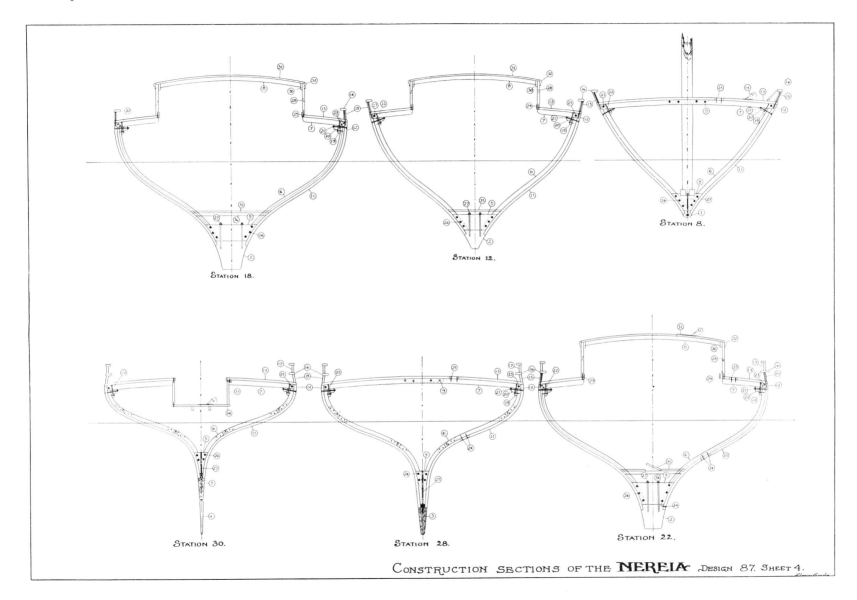

Station 18.

Station 12.

Station 8.

Station 30.

Station 28.

Station 22.

CONSTRUCTION SECTIONS OF THE **NEREIA** DESIGN 87. SHEET 4.

the planking may be lined off for a sheer strake which is wide forward and narrower aft.

13. Main deck. Soft wood like soft pine, California redwood, or any other wood that does not shrink much. It will be canvas covered, so can be square seam and laid straight for cheapness. However, the planks should not be too wide, never over 4", and the hood ends edge nailed and caulked where they extend beyond the deck covering.

The deck may be from 1 to 1¼" thick. Of course a sprung deck, running parallel with the waterways and lodging on a king plank, is the best but also the most expensive.

I might also note that any deck which is caulked increases the rigidity of the vessel, but a properly laid canvas will also add rigidity.

14. Canvas covering for the deck should be soft-woven sheeting, not very thick and in as wide a width as procurable. After the deck has been planed and the fastening holes puttied (or filled with plastic wood) the deck should be lightly wet down or sponged to raise the grain of the wood. After it has dried it should be well cross-sandpapered with medium sandpaper, then given a heavy coat of white lead paint, when the canvas or sheeting may be stretched into place and tacked down around the edges. It is just as well if the sheeting is now given a light coat of paint on top. This top coat, of course, should be about the color that is desired when finished. If it is mixed with a little dryer and applied light, it should harden up overnight and not hold up the work unduly.

15. Bulwarks or gunwales are set on top of the deck sheeting and fastened down with 5/16" galvanized iron drive bolts which pierce the deck and enter the sheer strake as shown. Forward, the bulwarks are supported by bulwark stays. The bulwark plank should be an inch or more thick, of rift grain fir, and conform somewhat to the lines of the yacht.

16. Main rail cap. Can be about 1⅛" thick by 3¼" wide and if of oak should be of extra selected pieces free from shakes, large knots, or seasoning cracks. It may be in short lengths if well scarphed.

If the rail caps are to be bright finished, mahogany or teak are very nice, but oak is harder and looks more American.

The rail caps can be fastened to the bulwark planks with bronze, brass, or galvanized screws and carefully bunged.

17. Upper bulwarks or top gallant rail. 1 by 4" of any suitable wood, sprung in vertically as shown, and may be fastened with ½" galvanized iron drive bolts.

18. Upper rail cap. 1 by 2¾". Same material as main rail cap.

19. Clamp. 1½" by 4" fir, fastened to the frames with 5/16" lag screws or No. 18 wood screws, galvanized iron. One on each frame.

20. Shelf. 2¼ by 2½" fir.

21. Shelf bolts. Either bronze or galvanized iron, ⅜" diameter, 7½" long. On account of their length these bolts will have to be made up special, so it is best to have fin-headed bolts. There should be a washer under the nut on the inboard side.

22. Deck beams are fastened to the clamp with galvanized iron drive bolts, large galvanized nails, or ship spikes. 5/16" diameter by 5 or 6" long.

23. Deck beams are fastened to the frames as follows: On the sawn frames forward of 12 and aft of 28, use 5/16" galvanized carriage bolts, 4" long, except on the strong beams where the bolts should be ⅜" diameter by 5" long. On the frames between 12 and 28, if they are bent in two layers, use two wood screws or two stove bolts about No. 18, or two copper rivets ¼" diameter or larger.

If the frames amidships are in one layer, then use the same single fastening used on the forward and after frames.

24. Planking fastenings would be best if Everdur screws 2¾" long, No. 16. While 2¾" is not a standard length, still as planking fastenings are usually ordered direct from the factory, the manufacturer will usually make up these bastard lengths very readily. However, anything from 2½" to 3" will do. If brass or galvanized screws are used, they should be at least No. 18.

Properly set boat nails of about ¼" diameter will do but are perhaps little cheaper in the end.

Where the planking rabbets into the lead, No. 16 or larger Everdur screws should be used.

25. Deck fastenings may be galvanized boat nails between 3/16 and ¼" diameter.

26. Fastenings between frames and floors should be 5/16" bronze stove bolts or ¼ to 5/16" copper rivets. Use three fastenings on each frame forward and over the lead. Two fastenings will be sufficient aft of the lead.

27. Keel bolts and lead bolts forward of station 26 are all ⅝" diameter Tobin bronze and their length can be taken from the longitudinal construction plan.

Where the bolts are threaded into the lead, they should be set in from six to eight times their diameter and the lead tapped out with a special long-shanked tap well lubricated with kerosene during the tapping. The bolts should be lubricated with grease during their setting. In all cases there should be washers under the upper nuts.

Aft of 26 the keel bolts can be galvanized iron drive bolts of about 7/16" diameter.

28. House sides and ends may be of soft pine 1¼" thick; mahogany or teak 1⅛" thick; or oak 1" thick. As the house sides are about 19" high in some places, the after end will require a board some 23" wide. It may be necessary to make them up of two planks, in which case make the seam a ship lap, with the lap outboard and the joint secured with both screws and glue.

The house is set right on top of the canvas deck covering and fastened down with screws up through the decking as shown. If the deck covering is turned up and tacked and then covered with a finishing strip (29), it will never leak and, on account of the curvature of the house sides, the house will be very strong and rigid in spite of its apparently weak deck attachment.

29. Finishing strip. Oak, mahogany, teak, about 2½ by ⅜".

30. Stringer for house beams. Oak about 1¼ by 3½" notched out full size of beams. Do not fasten beams to the stringer. The decking will do that.

31. House decking. Tongue and groove soft pine about ¾" thick. Canvas covered.

32. Finishing strip over the turned down deck covering, of the same variety of wood as other deck trim. About 1 by 3".

33. The forward, after, and side pieces of the cockpit can be oak, about 1" thick and fastened to the deck with cleats between the deck beams, but if the cockpit tub is put in place before the deck is canvas covered, then there will be no need of other fastenings than those down through the deck. (Both cases are shown on the drawing.)

34. Cockpit floor. May be ⅞" tongue and groove soft pine, planked crossways and supported by two fore and aft oak beams about 1 by 2". It is well to make this panel up and canvas cover it before attaching it to the side pieces with screws up from underneath.

35. Cabin sole. Fir, ¾ or ⅞", with an opening hatchway about 9" wide for its full length. It is best if the sole does not extend way out to the planking except where necessary for looks, since if there is no ventilation under the sole, the planking is apt to rot on the inside at this point.

36. Cabin sole beams. Oak, about 1 by 1½" and fastened to the frames. Perhaps one or two vertical supports will be required amidships.

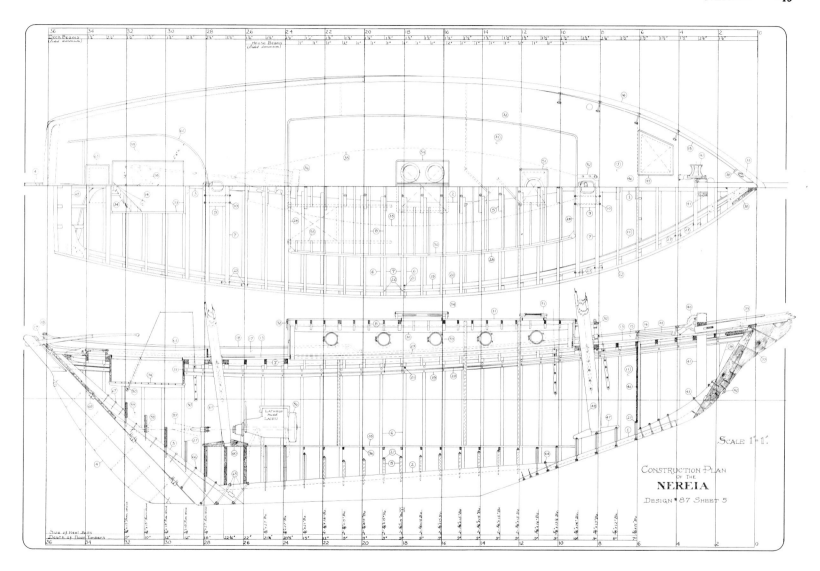

SCALE 1"-1'.

CONSTRUCTION PLAN
OF THE
NEREIA
DESIGN #87 SHEET 5

CONSTRUCTION PLAN

The reader may think that this is quite a fancy drawing for a vessel the size of Nereia, but a construction plan can never be too explicit as long as it is not confusing, and the nicely executed drawing very much encourages the boat builder to do his work well, while he is inclined to be sloppy when working from sketchy plans. I have tried to leave out all parts, such as the cabinet work, engine bed, exhaust pipe, etc., etc., so as not to confuse the boatbuilder when setting up the main frame of the vessel, and I believe the drawing will answer almost all questions the builder will want to know, which is not always the case on construction plans. The cabin plan and other drawings show various parts in detail.

The numbers on this plan below 36 are given with the Construction Section.

37.   The false piece can be secured with three $\frac{3}{8}''$ galvanized iron drive bolts and two wood screws at its lower end. The false piece does not have to be strongly attached because it is protected by the bobstay and supported by the trailboards.

38.   Knight heads, to support the bowsprit and hawser holes. Oak, about $1\frac{1}{2}$ by $12''$. There may be some twist to the knight heads, so probably they must be adzed out of a plank some $2\frac{1}{2}''$ thick.

39.   Hawser pipe or hawser hole. Although there are many stock hawser holes made, it may be the easiest in the end to make port and starboard patterns and have the hawser holes cast of bronze. The inside diameter should be more than $1\frac{3}{4}''$ with a nicely shaped outer flange about 7 by $5''$ to take the fastenings.

40.   Windlass. Torrey Roller Bushing Works, Yacht Gypsy windlass. Figure 194, size C.

41.   Oak bitts, each 2 by $6''$ and spaced for $6''$ wide bowsprit.

42.   Bobstay anchor plate. See detail.

43.   Fastenings of anchor stock knee can be as follows: forward, a $\frac{1}{2}''$ by $5''$ galvanized iron lag screw; next bolt to forty-two at station 1 a T-headed bronze bolt $\frac{5}{8}''$ by $10''$; between stations 4 and 6, four $\frac{5}{8}''$ bronze bolts, preferably fin-head. Lengths 8, $7\frac{1}{2}$, $6\frac{1}{2}$, and $6''$.

44.   Cast bronze bulwark stays. Four on a side with ends well fastened. All cast from same pattern with ends bent to fit deck. Shank about $\frac{5}{8}''$ diameter.

45.   Forward hatch opening. Canvas covered, $18''$ fore and aft by about 15 and $22''$ athwartships.

46.   Watertight bulkhead on after side of frame 6, either double planked of $\frac{3}{8}''$ stock or $\frac{3}{4}''$ ship lap and supported with oak stanchions about 1 by $1\frac{1}{2}''$, as shown.

47.   Mainmast step. Oak, $4''$ by $6''$ by $2'$ $5''$. If tapered about as shown the mast will set square in it. The step can be beveled and notched to fit the forward and after floor timbers, but the timber on No. 8 should be notched for the step as shown on sheet 4. If so fitted, the step will not move either athwartships or fore and aft, but it should be further fastened with a couple of drive bolts in the forward and after floors. The mortise for the mast tongue should be cut clean through for drainage. The mortise is $1\frac{1}{2}$ by $6''$.

48.   After side of mast is straight and should be raked about $6\frac{1}{2}$ degrees below deck, so when the mast is brought up to the rake shown on the sail plan there will be a tension on the fore and headstays. The size of the mast at the deck is $5\frac{3}{4}$ by $7\frac{1}{2}''$.

49.   Forward chainplates, six in all, can be made of three layers of hard-rolled Phosphor bronze, $1/16''$ or more thick, in which case each of the inner layers can be one fastening shorter as shown on the drawing. Or the chainplates can be of one layer of phosphor bronze, Tobin bronze, or hard Monel metal between $3/16''$ and $\frac{1}{4}''$ thick. In all cases the chainplates should be about $1\frac{3}{4}''$ wide and $2'$ $3''$ long, fastened with at least five

⅜" strong bronze stove bolts, clearing the seams of the planking. The holes at the upper ends are also ⅜".

50.   After chainplates and the main topmast backstay chainplates, six in all, can be of three layers of 1/16" phosphor bronze, or one thickness of 3/16" strong nonferrous metal, 1½" wide, 2′ long. Fastened with 5/16" stove bolts.

51.   Stateroom hatch. See detail. Deck opening 18 by 13".

52.   Fife rail. Oak, 1¼ by 2¼" on turned stanchion 10" high, held down with ⅜" bronze rods. Flange eye above nuts and washers below. After end secured to house with bent brass brackets, 1½" wide, ⅛" thick.

53.   Port lights. While the drawing shows five port lights on a side, in regions of cool water three on a side might do, but in warm climates even more than the ten shown might be nice. There could be two on the fore side of the house and one aft. However port lights are always expensive and leak more or less. The ones shown on the drawings are made by the Torrey Roller Bushing Works of Bath, Maine, and are their Figure 127. Diameter of opening 7 inches.

54.   Cabin skylight. See detail. Deck opening 24 by 25".

55.   Cabin sliding hatch. See detail. Deck opening 20 by 28".

56.   Engine. The most suitable engine that I know for the Nereia is the Lathrop Model LH-4 with a 2 to 1 reduction gear. The code word of this engine is LAIRU. This engine will develop 27 horsepower at 1,600 revolutions a minute and a shaft speed of 800, but as many people will be compelled to use other motors I have not drawn in the engine bed. However I recommend a metal engine bed made up of angle iron, somewhat as shown in dotted lines, simply because the engine can be gotten at and wiped off all over and thus smells and fire hazards can be reduced. The shaft line is horizontal, 18" below the waterline, and toes out so that it is 12" outboard at station 32 and on the center line at station 22.

57.   Stuffing box. Can be Columbian Bronze Corporation Figure 171 for 1¼" shaft. This stuffing box has its flange on the outside, which usually does away with the necessity of cutting the frames. Although the gland of this stuffing box is somewhat self aligning, the exact angle of the shaft with the planking should be taken from the yacht.

58.   Strut. The strut can be Columbian Bronze Corporation Figure 131 for 1¼" shaft, the bearing either of rubber, babbitt, or bearing bronze. Like the stuffing box, the exact angle of the yacht's skin and the length of arm must be taken from the yacht, but it is likely that the strut bearing will be about 9½" from the planking. The strut must be very strongly bolted in place to take the stresses that it will receive.

59.   Shaft line is laid out for a propeller of 20" or less diameter. I recommend a three-bladed feathering wheel, and the exact diameter and pitch should be obtained from the engine builder. However if an engine without a reduction gear is used it will allow a much smaller propeller, and perhaps the shaft line can be swung in to about 9" on station 32 depending on the speed and horsepower of the engine.

60.   Mizzenmast step. Oak, 4" by 5" by 2′ 3". If tapered about as shown, the mast will set square in it. The step sets on the top of the floors, which here are 2′ 4" below the waterline. The step should be held in place with drive bolts. The size of the mortise for the mast tongue is 1½ by 4" cut clean through.

61.   The after side of the mizzenmast is straight and raked 8 degrees. The size of the mizzenmast at the deck is 4¾ by 6".

62.   Cockpit coaming. While this is not a necessity on a yacht like Nereia, still it will keep one's seat dry when the spray forward starts to fly and runs aft on the deck. The coaming can be of the same wood as the other deck trim, from ¾ to ⅞" thick; 5" high forward, 4" aft. Fastened from below. The strip across the after side is about 1¼ by 1¾".

63. Lazarette hatch. Canvas covered with a deck opening of 10½″ by 21″.

64. Bolts attaching the fore keel to the lead can be as follows: one, ⅝ by 6¼″ Tobin bronze, nuts and washers both ends; and two, ½ by 5″ Everdur lag screws with washers. The principal tie in this region is the two garboard planks which distribute the strains over a long space.

65. Lead is secured to the sternpost with two ¾″ diameter Tobin bronze bolts, one 15″ and the other 16″ long, nuts and washers both ends. There should also be a good hardwood key as shown.

66. Deadwood is secured to the sternpost with two ½″ Tobin bronze through-bolts and three ½ by 6″ Everdur lag screws.

67. Tail feather is secured to the sternpost with three ½ by 5″ Everdur lag screws.

68. Rudder pintles and gudgeons are shown on the detail of the rudder.

69. Stern beam should be quite large so as to not be unduly weakened by the mortise for the tail feather and stem framing. It should be well-dried oak and kneed out on the quarters to take the fastenings into the shelf and clamp. This is a part of the yacht that is apt to rot out unless ventilated occasionally by opening the hatch, 63.

CABIN PLAN

1. Shelf. From side to side, about 18″ above L.W.L. with strong partitions as shown, about 24″ apart. Battens, across front, oak, 2 by ¾″.

2. Berth sides. Laminated wood from ⅝ to ¾″ thick, erected about on the floor line. One of these sheets of laminated wood extends from bulkhead to bulkhead and measures 6′ 1½″ long by 2′ 10″ wide. The other one is about 5′ 6″ by 2′ 10″.

These berth sides should have a rail cap about 1 by 1½″ which is curved upward at the after end to hold the pillow in place when the yacht heels.

3. Canvas berth bottoms, laced in place with seizing wire.

4. Oak strips, about 1″ by 1″, for berth bottom seizing. These strips should have their corners rounded off. The top edge of the strips is right on the L.W.L. level. Strips should be strongly secured in place with screws spaced 4 or 5″. The back side of the strip can either be cut away between the fastenings, or the strip can be mounted on shims about 1/16″ thick at the fastenings so the lace line can rove freely. On the outboard side the strips are intercostal between the frames.

5. Mattresses. These will have to be shaped ones, tapering both fore and aft and flared out on the outboard side as well as having the ends at an angle. An all-curled-hair mattress can be as thin as 3″ on a proper berth bottom, but due to the cost of curled hair, the mattresses shown are about 5″ thick, and the lower 3″ can be of the cheaper types of filling, but it would be well if the upper 2″ were curled hair.

6. Brace for berth sides, about 1¼ by 1¼″ oak.

7. Removable panel in berth sides, with thin hardwood lapping border pieces. This panel can be held in place with two wooden fingers below and a turnbutton above.

8. Sands toilet, called the Sanette. Figure R-4049, or some smaller, cheaper, and lighter model. One called the Seaman made by the Columbian Bronze Corp., Figure 2027, would also fit in this space nicely. The toilet can be mounted on an oak block about 1 by 4 by 15″ and strongly fastened in place as far outboard as possible. Perhaps the feet will fit in between the frames if trimmed off slightly.

9. Rubber tube, of the size and kind recommended by the toilet manufacturers, looped to at least 18″ above L.W.L. and fastened to the forward bulkhead.

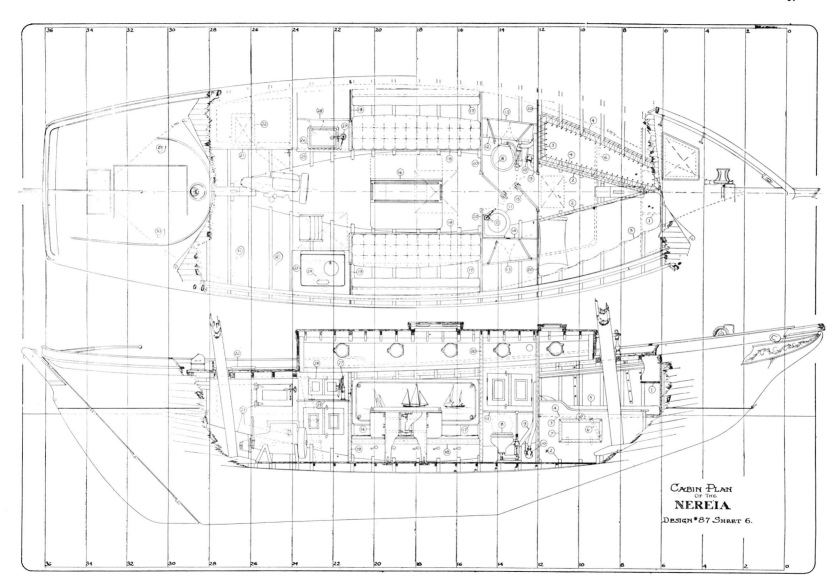

CABIN PLAN
OF THE
NEREIA
DESIGN #87 SHEET 6.

10.   Seacock, 1½″, similar to Wilcox, Crittenden Figure 1057 or Columbian Figure 1095 or 1096. There must also be a seacock or valve for the water supply pipe.

11.   Lavatory, Columbian Figure 2051, and basin pump Figure 1556. Top of basin 32″ above floor.

12.   Panel to support the toilet cover, back of toilet and about 28″ above floor. This panel can have a removable top so the space back of it can be used for laundry, etc.

13.   Partition. Right under the edge of the deckhouse there may be a partition running down to the planking or framing. May be made of laminated wood or soft pine and painted. In its upper part, as shown, there are two hinged paneled cupboard doors making an opening about 2′ 3″ by 18″. These doors are held closed with turnbuttons top and bottom. These lockers are the same port and starboard and are intended for hanging clothes lockers.

14.   Shelf. On the starboard side in front of partition thirteen there can be a shelf about 30″ above the floor, and this shelf has a raised rim which on its after side is high enough to take the back of the lavatory, but forward it can be cut down to about 1½″ above the shelf. There should be another light rimmed shelf under this shelf for linen.

15.   Paneled doors, about 20″ wide and 5′ 11½″ high, 7/8″ thick. Brass butt hinges and suitable locking latches similar to Perko Figure 1087. These doors must have a good stop at their upper ends and brass hooks to hold them from swinging when sailing.

16.   Folding table, mostly made of hard 7/8″ thick wood. Top when open 42 by 42″. Middle section of top 12″ wide. Body of table 10″ wide with two drawers to pull out either end. Below the drawers there is a filler piece about 12 inches deep to give the table diagonal strength. The butterfly leaf supports may be of wood as on some antique tables, but it would be well if the upper end hinged on a rudder pintle and gudgeon like Wilcox, Crittenden Figure 460 and 462, size 7/8″. The table must be firmly secured to the floor, for while it is 3½′ wide on top, the legs are only spaced 10″. One way to secure the table would be to use strap hinges like Wilcox, Crittenden Figure 471 at each leg, as shown on the drawing, and they should have fastenings going into strips under the floor which can be 1 by 6 by 18″ each. Don't forget the hooks to hold the table leaves from swinging and banging all night.

As for the racks on the table top, experience on yachts of this size leads me to believe the racks on the center section will be left in place all of the time except when the table is used as a chart table and for card playing. These racks should be at least 2″ high. It is doubtful if it is necessary to make racks for the leaves, as when a yacht of this size is under way the table most likely will not be set and the crew will be thankful for a picnic lunch consisting of sandwiches and hot soup served up in a pannikin. On the other hand, when the yacht is at anchor and the table set, the racks are not necessary. However, a good cabin table is a great convenience.

17.   Folding berths, either with a pipe or wood frame. They should be about 26″ wide and 6′ 2″ long with a canvas berth bottom laced in with seizing wire. This seems to be the best all-around arrangement, as the berth bottom makes a comfortable back rest when the berth is closed up.

The berth bottoms can be covered with some figured material or decorated somewhat as shown on the drawing. The lower sides of these berths can be hinged 21″ above the floor and 4′ 1½″ out from the center line. The hinge supports or hooks can be on frames 16 and 20.

The mattresses for these berths need not be over 4″ thick if they have some curled hair in their stuffing.

18.   Transom seats, about 2′ out from center line. The front

can simply be a $7/8''$ pine board with some ventilating holes near its upper edge. The top of the transom should be about $12''$ above the cabin sole, so that if it has a cushion some $3''$ thick it will give a comfortable seating level. The wood top should have some lifting-out sections for access to the storage place below.

19. Partial bulkheads between the galley and the cabin can be of laminated wood. Their lower face is $2'$ out from the center line for a height of $3'$ $3''$. From there up they are cut back to the underside of house. This bulkhead must be banded with a substantial finishing piece about $13/4''$ wide.

20. Bulkheads at each end of the toilet room can be laminated wood about $3/4''$ thick and banded on their inner edges by the door jambs.

21. Icebox. I should very much prefer not to have an icebox on a yacht of this size. This is principally on account of its cost, which will be several hundred dollars. When an icebox is made especially to fit the yacht, well insulated and lined with Monel metal, it is altogether very expensive, but for those who must have one I would recommend the following:

Have a good space for ventilation all around the icebox so that the deck, frame, and planking back of it will not rot. The lower part of the icebox should be watertight, with a draincock for draining the same. The walls, including the insulation, should be about $4''$ thick all around. There should be a good-size door at least 12 by $18''$ so one can reach in for scrubbing.

I have shown the rough outline of an icebox which has a hatch for the ice up through the deck and is divided into two compartments, the after one for ice and the forward one for food. The division plate should not extend nearer the top and bottom than about $4''$ so as to give room for the circulation of cold air.

My advice is to build the icebox complete out on the bench from templates from the yacht's frames. The inner walls should be completely sheathed with Monel metal and all the lower seams soldered.

Cypress is a good wood for the inner and outer frames, and packed ground cork makes a good insulation. I advise the builder to build the icebox complete and install it in place before the motor is put in or the deckhouse built.

22. Ice hatch should be in two thicknesses, the upper section simply a weather hatch and the lower section, which can hang on metal hooks, an insulated block about $8''$ thick. The hatch opening should be 9 by $14''$.

23. Shipmate stove, No. 1012, top $36''$ above cabin sole, with legs removed and set on top of coal bin with sheet metal top set on asbestos sheeting. Top of coal bin $22''$ above cabin sole. The bulkhead beside the stove must also be covered with the same insulation.

24. Water iron. Wilcox, Crittenden Figure 668, either $41/2$ or $5''$ directly over stove smoke vent. It would be well if the smoke head were removable, and this can be replaced by a metal cover when stove is out. A Liverpool Head, similar to Wilcox, Crittenden No. 669 about $2'$ $6''$ above deck should do, and when it is removed it can be kept in a box in the after lazarette, for Liverpool Heads are generally full of soot.

25. Sink top, about $35''$ above cabin sole with cupboard underneath for pans, as shown.

26. Sink, similar to Columbian No. 1515. $12''$ by $18''$ by $6''$ or more deep. As the bottom of this sink is practically at the waterline level, it is suggested that it be arranged to drain into a receptacle under the sink. This receptacle can simply be a galvanized pail set into a rack. The other alternative is to have a pump, which entails some expense and complications.

The hand basin in the toilet room must also have a drain basin or an exhaust pump.

27. Galley pump, similar to Columbian Figure 1566.

28. Cupboard, back of the sink with a shelf for dishes, etc.

29. Gasoline tank, of shaped tin-lined copper, and shown on another drawing, is located abreast of the cockpit aft of the ice-box.

30. Water tank, which is of tin-lined copper and shown on another drawing, is abreast the cockpit to starboard.

31. Space for rack for canned goods and dry food arranged according to the wishes of the owner.

32. Space for hanging clothes, and particularly for drying out clothes.

No doubt many prospective owners of Nereia can work out a better cabin plan than the one shown, but it is rather doubtful if they can work out one cheaper to build, and in making changes they should keep in mind that the interior of a yacht is often one of her most expensive parts, but simplification is a sure way of reducing cost, so that if anyone can simplify this cabin arrangement, he will please no one more than this designer.

TANKS, COCKPIT SCUPPERS, EXHAUST PIPE, AND ENGINE CONTROLS

The gasoline and water tanks are both alike, or port and starboard pairs. They can be made of 16-gauge tin-lined copper or Monel metal. Their capacity is about 67 gallons each. The seams of the tanks should be both riveted and soldered with a lap of approximately ¾". It should be noted that the inboard upper seams of both tanks are flanged upward so the body of the tank can bear against the cockpit. It is recommended that the tanks be put in place before the deck beams are laid, but it will be possible to slide them in from forward. Numbered description is as follows:

1. The filler pipes can be Wilcox, Crittenden Figure 536. Pipe size 1½", and best if set over the canvas of the deck with the upper edge of the flange rounded off. It is best if the caps of the deck plates are marked "gas" and "water" and I would suggest that the port tank be used for gasoline, for it is farthest from the stove.

2. Neck of filler pipes can be standard 1½" brass pipe threaded into a suitable flange, soldered and riveted to the top of the tank, and the top of the tank should be bent slightly to make up for the crown of the deck, so the filler pipe should screw in easily if well greased. However, getting a tight filler pipe is one of the tricky jobs of boatbuilding.

3. Swash plate. There need not be more than one diaphragm or swash plate in the tank, but it should be of about the same thickness as the tank walls, for it is also a structural member and so should be both riveted and soldered in.

4. Vent pipes. It is well to have a good size vent pipe if the tanks are filled rapidly. The ones shown are about ⅜" I.D. and made up with soldered unions. The final loop of the vents should be just outside of the cockpit coaming as shown. It will be best if the tanks are installed and all connections made before the cockpit tub is put in place.

5. Drain plugs. The tanks should both have a drain plug from their lowest part. About 1½" pipe size.

6. Stop valves. Both tanks should have good main stop valves so the pipelines can be disconnected for cleaning. The valve on the gasoline line should be one of the modern approved valves for gasoline. Both valves can be straight or right angle depending on the piping.

7. The tanks can rest on soft pine chocks about 1½" thick.

8. Brass clips about ⅛ by 1½ by 3" bent to clamp over flange of tank.

9. The tanks must be firmly secured on their forward sides

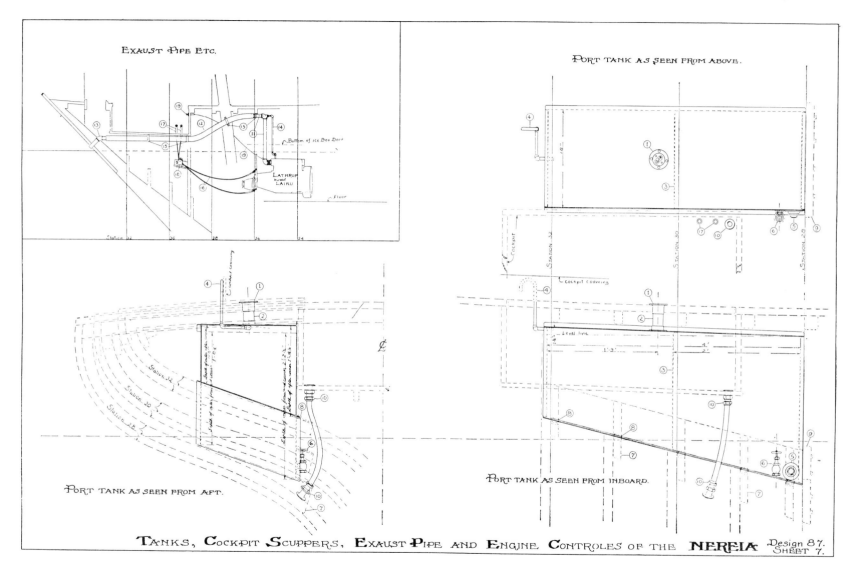

EXAUST PIPE ETC.

PORT TANK AS SEEN FROM ABOVE.

PORT TANK AS SEEN FROM AFT.

PORT TANK AS SEEN FROM INBOARD.

TANKS, COCKPIT SCUPPERS, EXAUST PIPE AND ENGINE CONTROLES OF THE NEREIA   Design 87. Sheet 7.

so they will not shift readily in a collision. Perhaps this can be done by securing an oak block to the frames with lag screws, as shown, or any other strong blocking. On the port side maybe the tanks can partly butt up against the icebox.

10. Cockpit scuppers. If desired these can connect to Wilcox, Crittenden "Through-Hull" connections, Figure 857, pipe size ¾", with a copper tube between, but I have seen lead and also rubber scupper pipes that were satisfactory, so if the builder can install a cheaper arrangement that is safe he should do so.

11. Exhaust pipe. There are a number of ways to arrange an exhaust pipe on a yacht of this size, and while a copper water-jacketed exhaust is both best and most expensive, still a plain iron one that is asbestos covered is quite satisfactory. Also, if the circulating water is introduced to the exhaust line in the proper way it will do away with the necessity of a muffler.

The exhaust pipe and the water discharge pipe on Nereia must be carried sideways to slightly beyond the center line of the yacht so the icebox door can swing over the after end of the engine. The exhaust pipe can be made up of the following:

One 1½" nipple to screw into the exhaust manifold.
One 1½" right angle elbow.
One length of 1½" pipe about 13" long.
One 1½" right angle elbow.
One length of 1½" pipe 23" long for riser.
One so-called 1½" heel outlet elbow.
One length of 1½" pipe about 7" long.

12. Exhaust hose. About 7' 3" of Edson exhaust hose of the right I.D. at ends to fit on standard 1½" iron pipe which is approximately 1 15/16". This pipe runs aft close to starboard of the mizzenmast.

13. Tail pipe can be either galvanized iron or brass and consists of two 6" lengths of 1½" pipe and a 45-degree elbow. The final pipe should pierce the transom as near to the starboard side of the sternpost as is convenient and can simply be screwed into the oak transom planking.

14. All of the circulating water should empty into the exhaust line so a ⅜" pipe or hose should lead up to the heel outlet elbow in the exhaust pipe. This point is the most important part of the exhaust line, for if the water is introduced so that it sprays into the center of the exhaust pipe then the exhaust will be quiet and comparatively cool from there on.

To do this, get a gas plug that fits the heel outlet of the elbow, drill and tap the plug with a straight thread (not a pipe thread) that is the right size for the water pipe; thread the last section of the water pipe for about 5" so that when it is screwed in it will be beyond the elbow. Sometimes this water pipe has to be screwed in and out to get the best results, so it should have a lock nut on it. This whole arrangement makes a sort of injector in which the high velocity of the exhaust gases atomizes the circulating water.

15. The exhaust pipe should be supported in several places with brass straps so it will not take up undue vibration.

16. Engine controls. The simplest, cheapest, and quietest engine controls I have found from experience are those made of manila rope. Not only do they appeal to a sailorman, but they can be instantly taken out of the way when working on the engine. They should be of rope, at least ½" diameter or larger to afford a good grip, and the ends which are up in the cockpit finished off with a rose knot or some other stopper knot. The forward ends are spliced into shackles which fit the engine reverse gear lever.

The lines should be carried quite loose so that the knots can be pulled up to the deck level before the clutch or reverse takes hold. I find that the clutch or reverse can be controlled in this way better than with some of the arrangements which have rods, levers, and cranks.

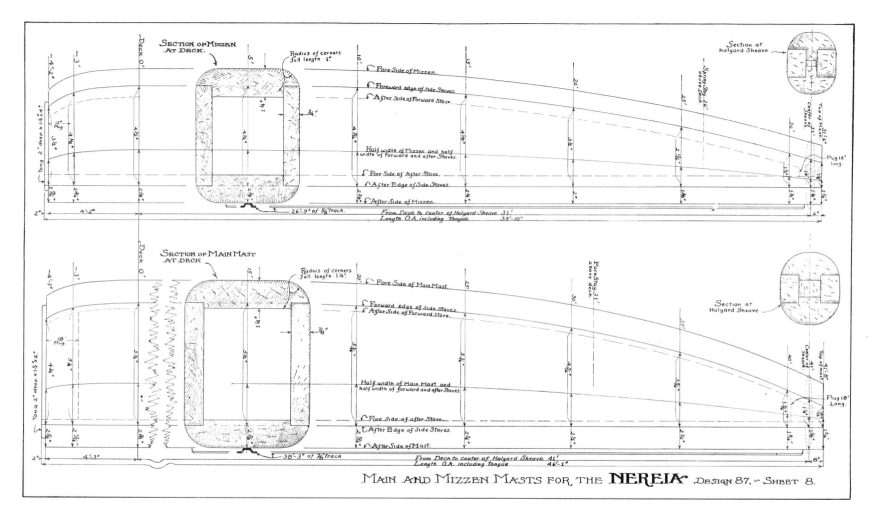

MAIN AND MIZZEN MASTS FOR THE **NEREIA** DESIGN 87, SHEET 8.

17. Two brass tubes or pipes about 6″ long threaded into the cockpit floor about ¾″ from the port cockpit side walls and respectively 4 and 7″ aft of the forward end of the cockpit. The I.D. of the tubes should be such that the ropes run easily and they should extend above the cockpit floor 4 or 5″.

18. Double deck block, Wilcox, Crittenden Figure 386, No. 4, brass.

19. Throttle control. Bowden wire throttle control from forward port side of cockpit; wire handle, Perko, Figure 692, polished brass.

MASTS

The masts for Nereia require little description, for they can be built by anyone who is capable of building a long box. Of course the seams are glued with waterproof glue, and during the gluing up operation the spars must not only be kept absolutely straight but they must not be allowed to twist. If the builder does not have many clamps of the proper size, he can hold the staves in place by twisting a rope spirally around the assembled mast and then driving wooden tightening wedges where required, always remembering that with most modern glues the seams should not be pressed together too hard, for this will make a weaker joint than if only a moderate pressure is applied. Excessive pressure squeezes the glue all out of the joint, making a wood-to-wood contact that has little strength. The thing to do is to have the seams all evenly pressed together with no more pressure than is necessary.

As for material, any of the spruces or rift-grain firs of fine texture would be good, and if the staves cannot be secured in one length, then the pieces should be scarphed together with glued joints about eight or ten times as long as the thickness of the plank. The forward and after staves of both masts are 1¼″ thick. The mainmast staves are rabbeted out ¼″, the mizzen ½″. The side staves of the mainmast are ⅞″ thick and the mizzen ¾″.

There are no reinforcements on the inner walls of the spars anywhere, but the mainmast has plugs at each end 18″ long, while the mizzen plugs are 12″ or more long.

The corners are rounded off at the same radius full length; mainmast 1¼″, mizzen 1″.

Details of the mastheads, as well as other rigging attachments and their elevations, are given on separate drawings.

The foot of the masts are at 90 degrees, or right angles to the after side of masts. See forty-seven and sixty on construction plan. The tongues of both masts are 2″ deep, 1½″ wide. The main is 6″ and mizzen 4″ in its fore-and-aft dimension.

BOOMS AND THEIR FITTINGS

The booms are made solid, so that their weight will hold the sails more on one plane when reaching and running. It is also thought that solid booms of this size are slightly easier to make than hollow ones. Nevertheless if one prefers hollow booms, they can be made the same size as shown with a wall thickness of from ¾ to 1″. The booms are straight on top and the radius of the corners full length is ¾″.

Spruce or fine grain fir would be good materials for the booms, and, if it is desired to make them up of several pieces glued together, it will be entirely satisfactory from every point but looks.

Special goosenecks are shown, as there are no suitable commercial ones of this size which go well on a square mast and boom.

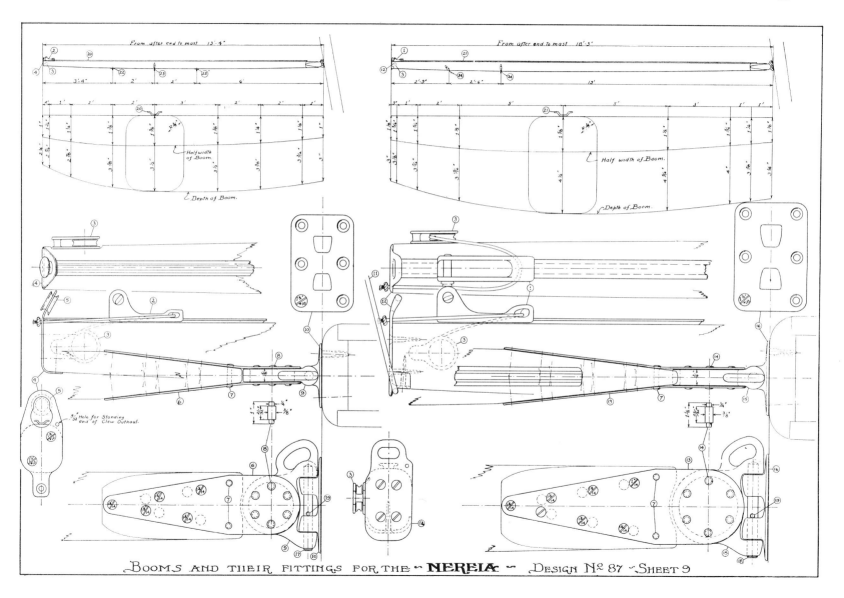

BOOMS AND THEIR FITTINGS FOR THE ~ **NEREIA** ~ DESIGN Nº 87 ~ SHEET 9

I purposely have not given many dimensions on the drawings so that each builder may vary the parts to suit his tools, etc. The drawings are intended only to be a guide to give the idea and to suggest approximate sizes, shapes, and materials.

1. Clew outhaul. Wilcox, Crittenden Figure 980, No. 2.

2. Clew outhaul. Wilcox, Crittenden Figure 980, No. 1. This clew outhaul slide moves on standard 5/8″ track, so be sure to put the screws in the track close together to stand the strain, or if the yacht is to lay-to in heavy weather it may be best to use the same size outhaul as on the main boom.

3. Outhaul cheek blocks. Wilcox, Crittenden Figure 5800, No. 2 on port side of each boom.

4. Mizzen boom lift attachment. Phosphor bronze 1/16 by 2 by 5″. Upper end drilled to take 5. Lower end bent as shown.

5. Brass sail thimble, similar to Wilcox, Crittenden Figure 785, size No. 1.

6. Side pieces of mizzen gooseneck. Phosphor bronze, 1/16 by 2¾ by 9½″.

7. ¼″ copper rivets.

8. Mizzen gooseneck spacers. Make six. Tobin bronze of the dimensions shown. Both ends riveted over countersunk holes in 6.

9. Bronze casting, as shown, with large lashing eye at top for tack lacing and reef pennant.

10. Bronze casting, as shown.

11. Wire rope, main boom crotch. Attached to mizzen.

12. Cap on after end of main boom, bronze casting, as shown. This acts as an attachment for the boom lift, standing end of clew outhaul, and boom crotch.

13. Side pieces for main gooseneck. Phosphor bronze, 1/16 by 3½ by 11¾″.

14. Main gooseneck spacers. Make six. Tobin bronze with both ends riveted over countersunk holes in 13.

15. Bronze casting, as shown, with large lashing eye at top for tack lacing and reef pennant.

16. Bronze casting, as shown.

17. Tobin bronze rod, 7/16″ by 3⅞″.

18. Tobin bronze rod, ½″ by 4⅜″.

19. Hole for cotter pin.

20. 12′ 6″ of 5/8″ track.

21. 16′ of ⅞″ track.

22. Wilcox, Crittenden Figure 275, size No. 2.

23. Merriman, Figure 440A, 2¾″.

24. Merriman, Figure 440A, 3″.

RUDDER AND TILLER

1. Rudder. Two inches thick for its full length on the forward side, and the forward side semi-cylindrical the full length. Hard rift-grain oak is the best material, but any hard wood that resists rot and does not have a tendency to warp will do.

On this drawing I have not shown the widths of the planks, for it is usually most convenient to use planks of a width that may be on hand, but the construction plan (sheet 5) shows how the drive bolts may be arranged if the forward plank is 10″ wide. The drive bolts should be from 5/16 to ⅜″ diameter, either galvanized iron or bronze. The after edge of the rudder should be about ¾″ thick.

2. Cheeks. The cheeks of the rudder should be of white oak or other hard wood, 1″ thick by about 6½″ wide, with forward edges beveled off as shown so rudder may swing to at least 45 degrees from amidships. These cheek pieces may be fastened to the rudder with either 5/16″ copper rivets or with 3″ No. 18 flathead bronze screws.

3. Rudder pintles. All alike and of cast strong bronze. The

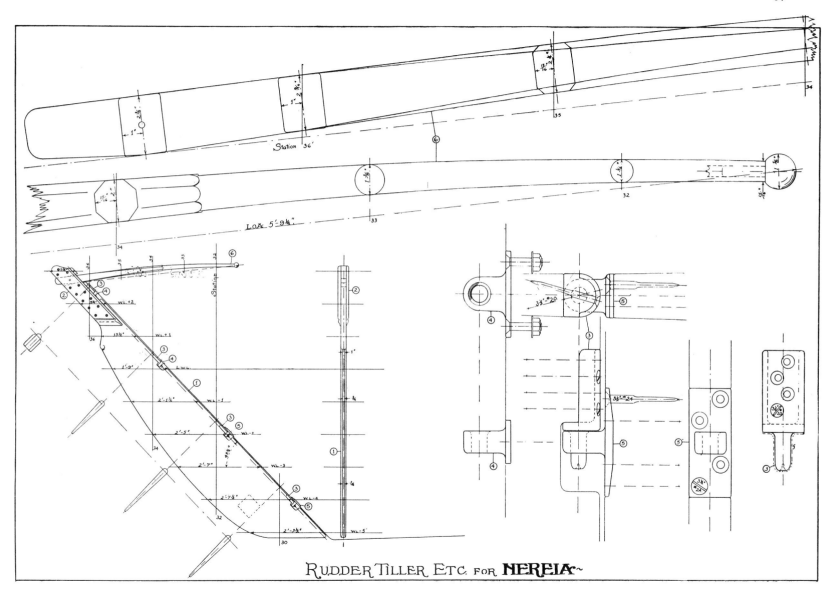

RUDDER TILLER ETC. FOR **NEREIA** ~

reason this type of pintle is recommended is because it can easily be held in any small lathe while the pintles are machined, and because this type of pintle is easiest to line up. The lining up of close fitting pintles is sometimes difficult.

4. Gudgeons. The two upper gudgeons of cast bronze are about 4″ wide at the base and secured with Everdur stove bolts ⅜ by 1¾″, washers under nuts. The base is set in flush with the transom as shown.

5. Gudgeons. The two lower gudgeons of cast bronze are about 2″ wide at the base and secured with four 3½″ or more No. 24 Everdur flathead wood screws.

Neither of the gudgeons will require finish for machining, for outside of drilling and chamfering off the ¾″ hole for the pintles, and drilling and countersinking for the screws, there is no machine work.

6. Tiller. The best wood for a tiller is locust, the next choice ash, but oak or any other nice looking strong wood is all right. Sometimes the knob for the end is turned on the lathe with a pin on it which is driven onto the tiller, as shown in dotted lines.

There is nothing much more to say about these parts except to remark that a nicely hung rudder with good pintles generally will stay quiet for many years, but a loosely hung outboard rudder is a continual annoyance, for it will chatter and chug all night long. Sometimes a rudder of this type will try to float up and swing around, in which case a lead insert, as shown in dotted lines, will hold it amidships when at anchor. At any rate it is well to have the rudder made of heavy wood and use several good drive bolts in its after edge, then if the head of the tiller is small and light the rudder will stay in line.

HATCHES AND SKYLIGHT

1. Sill. Oak, mahogany, or other firm wood; 1½ by 1½″ or smaller if desired. The corners may be half-lapped, or consist of one dovetail. Where possible the sills should be fastened to the deck from underneath.

2. Hatch frame. 1 or 3″, corners mitred. Same material as 1.

3. Half round finishing strip over edge of canvas cover, about ½ by 1″.

4. Top of hatches may be ¾″ tongue and groove soft pine, or ½″ laminated wood, canvas covered.

5. Finishing strip to cover canvas of house deck or main deck. About 5/16″ thick, as wide as necessary.

6. Glazing. If it is desired to have a glass in the stateroom hatch, the glass may be held down with Wilcox, Crittenden round frame, Figure 5260, size 8 or any of the smaller ones, but it must be remembered that these glasses, which are nearly on a level, are apt to leak unless very carefully set. In most cases it is necessary to put extra screws in the flange. The glass in this hatch is not necessary unless one wants to read when in bed, which is nice at times.

7. Companionway slide is made of half-hard brass or bronze sheet, 30¾″ long, and about 24½″ wide before bending. It should be nearly 1/16″ thick but may be one or two gauges less if stiff and springy material. The side edges must be flanged over quite evenly, which can usually be done in what is called a sheet metal brake. I have found that these metal hatch slides are most satisfactory. They do not leak, shrink, or swell.

8. Fore and aft sills of sliding hatch may be of any hard wood about 1½ by 1½″, fastened from below and grooved about as shown on the full size section.

9. Crosspiece of sill, hard wood, ¾ by 1¾″, crowned to fit the deck.

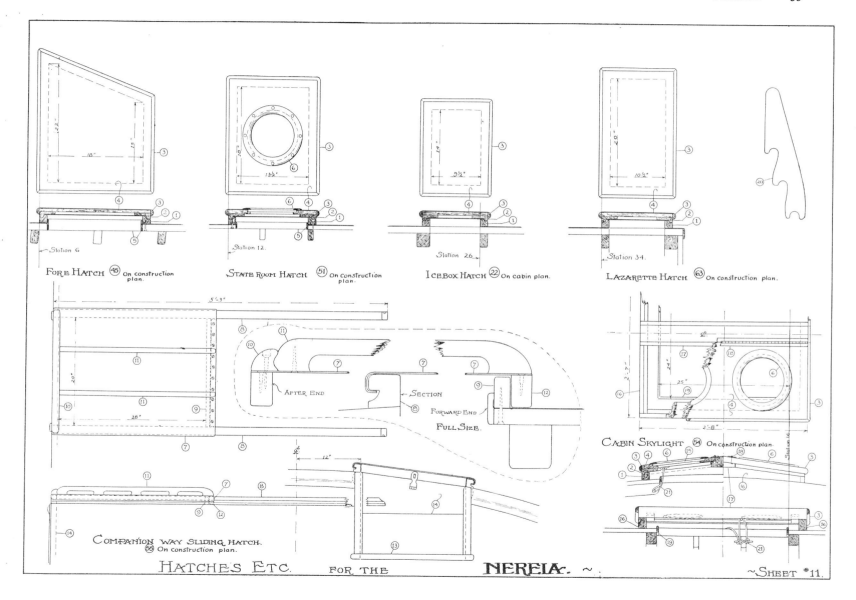

FORE HATCH ④⑤ On construction plan.

STATE ROOM HATCH ⑤① On construction plan.

ICE BOX HATCH ㉒ On cabin plan.

LAZARETTE HATCH ㊌ On construction plan.

AFTER END

SECTION

FORWARD END

FULL SIZE.

CABIN SKYLIGHT ㊌ On construction plan.

COMPANION WAY SLIDING HATCH. ⑤⑤ On construction plan.

HATCHES ETC.   FOR THE   NEREIA. ~.

10. Crosspiece on top of slide, shaped to act as grip in sliding hatch fore and aft.

11. Hand rails, as shown, of hard wood. The principal function of these hand rails is to prevent the sheet metal slide from bending.

12. Forward crosspiece of slide, 1 by 1½″ crowned to fit deck. This piece is screwed on after slide is in place.

13. Threshold, about 1 by 2″, oak.

14. Companionway slides. Hard wood, 1 inch or less thick. Upper slide may have either a hasp for a padlock or brass flush dead lock.

The cabin skylight, 54 on the construction plan, is made up of many pieces similar to the simple hatches, but, no matter how these small skylights are made, they are apt to leak, so that a drip ring about 2″ wide is made by leaving the deck opening smaller than the hatch, and having the finishing strip extend up about ½″. Some yachts have a small copper tube draining this drip ring into the bilge.

As for skylight lifters, I find nothing better than a properly notched piece of wood, and nothing much better than a stout cord for holding the skylight closed. The standing end of this cord may be tied to a pin through one of the deck beams and then rove through a bronze eye strip like Merriman Figure 420, or even a small block of wood with a hole through it. Belay the cord over the pin and tuck the end into the drain gutter.

The skylight, like the hatches, is canvas covered, for this makes it much less apt to leak, shrink, or swell and warp. It might be well if the leaves, or swinging parts, were made of one width of well-seasoned soft pine or mahogany, for they are only 14″ wide.

15. Circular glasses, about 5/16″ or more thick, set in putty.

16. Forward and after ends of the skylight may be 1½″ thick, like the side pieces, but about 3″ high before the crown of deck is cut.

17. Central pieces, or backbone, of the skylight will require a piece of wood 2 by 4½ by 32″ and need not be canvas covered.

18. Continuous hinges (sometimes called piano hinges) of wrought brass with brass pin, 32″ long and about 1½″ wide when open. Two required.

19. Finishing strips for drip ring, about 1 5/16″ or more thick. Lips to extend above deck about ½″.

20. Skylight lifter, ½″ thick mahogany. Make three.

21. Pin lanyard, etc., for closing hatch.

HEAD GEAR

1. Bowsprit, of Oregon pine or spruce. Rectangular at butt, 4 by 6″; octagonal central section; then oval, and round, as shown.

2. Two oak wedges, about 1¼″ thick by 3½ by 12″ for adjusting length of bowsprit. After wedge which bears against bitts slightly beveled. Make holes in wedges, as shown, for oak plug keepers about ½″ diameter.

3. Bowsprit cone. Cast bronze, as shown. No finish or machining except drilling holes.

4. Bobstay anchor plate. Either cast strong bronze, or cast-iron galvanized. The former will be the cheaper, for it will not have to be galvanized. Fastened at ends with 4″ No. 24 Everdur flathead screws.

5. Bolt, 5/8″ or larger, of Tobin bronze, threaded both ends. Lower end can pass through if preferred, in which case it should be slightly riveted over the threads.

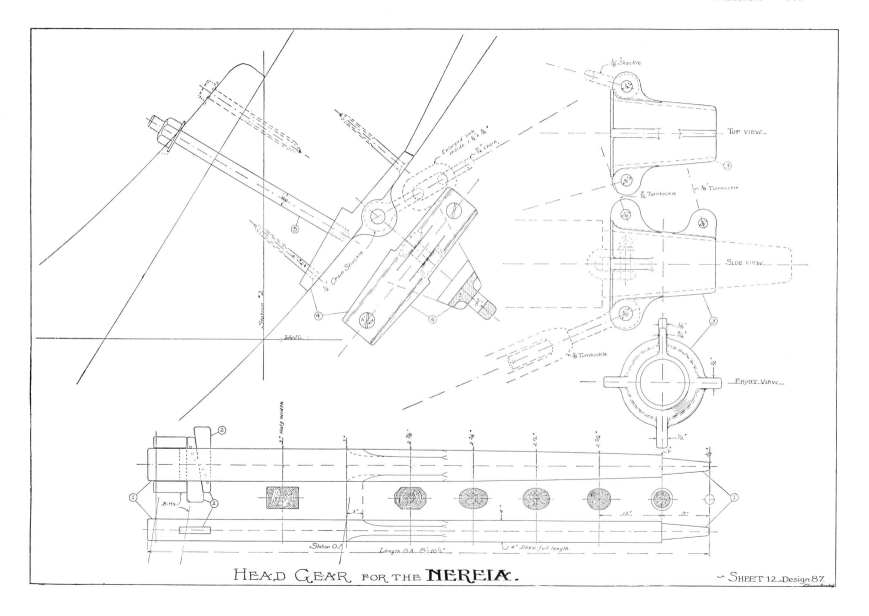

HEAD GEAR FOR THE NEREIA.

Date Material was Ordered	NAME of PART	Number Required	STANDING RIGGING	Dia and Construction of wire	Approximate Strength in lbs.	Total length required with allowance for splicing	FITTINGS	RIGGERS Notes
	BOB STAY	1	Total length 7'-8"; Length of chain 6'-3½"; ½" chain Shackle; enlarged links inside 1¾" x ¾"; 7/16" BB chain; W.C. & Co Fig 3162-5/8"	7/16" chain	12,000		1-½ chain Shackle	
	BOWSPRIT SHROUDS	2	9'-3"; 3/8" Turnbuckle; 5/16"; Shackle to cone	5/16" 6x7	7,380	23'	4-5/16" Open Thimbles 2-3/8" chain Shackles	
	HEAD STAY	1	43'-1"; 5/16"; 3/8" T.B.	5/16" 6x7	7,380	46'	2-5/16" Solid Thimbles	
	FORE STAY	1	33'; 3/8"; 7/16" T.B.	3/8" 6x7	10,540	36'	2-3/8" Solid Thimbles	
	MAIN LOWER SHROUDS	4	2-22'-11"; 2-23'-2"; 3/8"; 7/16" T.B.	3/8" 6x7	10,540	100'	8-3/8" Solid Thimbles	
	MAIN UPPER SHROUDS	2	39'-3"; 3/8"; 7/16" T.B.	3/8" 6x7	10,540	82'	4-3/8" Solid Thimbles	
	MAIN LOWER BACK STAYS	2	29'; 5/16"	5/16" 6x19	7,660	65'	4-5/16" Open Thimbles	
	MAIN UPPER BACK STAYS	2	45'-10"; ¼"; 5/16" T.B.	¼" 6x7	4,740	96'	2-¼" Open Thimbles 2-¼" Solid Thimbles 2-5/16" chain Shackles	
	SPRING STAY	1	22'-6"; Seizing wire; ¼"	¼" 6x7	4,740	26'	2-¼" Open Thimbles	
	MAIN BOOM LIFT.	1	38'-3"; 3/16"; Cotton cord	3/16" 6x7 Stainless	3,000	42'	2-¼" Open Thimbles 1-¼" chain Shackle	
	MAIN BOOM CROTCH SLING On mizzen mast	1	5'-2"; ¼"	¼" 6x7 Stainless	5,200	9'	2-¼" Open Thimbles	
	MIZZEN LOWER SHROUDS	2	19'-5"; 5/16"; 3/8" T.B.	5/16" 6x7	7,380	46'	2-5/16" Solid Thimbles	
	MIZZEN UPPER SHROUDS	2	29'-10"; ¼"; 5/16" TB	¼" 6x7	4,740	67'	2-¼" Solid Thimbles	
	MIZZEN BOOM LIFT.	1	27'; 3/16"; Cotton cord	3/16"-6x7 Stainless	3,000	33'	2-¼" Open Thimbles 1-¼" chain Shackle	

Date Material was Ordered	NAME of PART	Number Required	RUNNING RIGGING	Dia. and construction of wire	Approximate Strength	Length required with allowance for Splicing		Circumference of rope	Length required with allowance for Splicing	Fittings	RIGGERS Notes
	JIB TOPSAIL HALLIARD	1	Fig 952 #3; 40'; 45'; ¼" Dia; 1¼" cir.	¼"-7x19 Stainless	6,600	46'		1¼" manila	47'	1-¼" Open Thimble 1-5/16" chain Shackle 1-Snatch block	
	FORE STAYSAIL HALLIARD	1	Fig 952 #3; 30'; 35'; ¼" Dia; 1¼" cir	¼"-7x19 Stainless	6,600	36'		1¼" manila	37'	1-¼" open Thimble 1-5/16" chain Shackle 1-Snatch block	
	MAIN HALLIARD	1	Sheave in mast head (see detail); 39'; 45'; 5/16" Dia.; 1¼" cir.	5/16"-7x19 Stainless	8,200	42'		1¼" manila	47'	1-5/16" Open Thimble 1-7/16" chain Shackle 1-Snatch block	
	MIZZEN HALLIARD	1	Sheave in mast head (see detail); 30'; 35'; ¼" Dia.; 1¼" cir.	¼"-7x19 Stainless	6,600	33'		1¼" manila	37'	1-¼" Open Thimble 1-3/8" chain Shackle 1-Snatch block	
	FORE STAYSAIL SHEETS	1 Pair	Merriman Fig-364-#3; Stopper Knot; 3'; ¼"; 45'; 1½" cir	¼"-7x19	6,600	12'		1½" manila	91'	2-¼" open Thimbles 1-3/8" anchor Shackle	
	BACK STAY TACKLES	2	40'; 1½" cir.					1½" manila	81'	2-½" Round Thimbles	
	MAIN SHEET	1	80'; 1½" cir.					1½" manila	81'	1-½" Round Thimble	
	MIZZEN SHEET	1	55'; 1¼" cir					1¼" manila	56'	1-3/8" Sister hook with ½" round thimble	
	MAIN CLEW OUTHAUL TACKLE	1	Cleat on Port side of boom 4' from after end; 3' long; 5/32" Dia; #1; 7'; 12 thread; Standing end ties to boom bale	5/32"-7x19 Stainless	2,600	5'		12 thread manila	7'	1-5/32" Open Thimble	
	MIZZEN CLEW OUTHAUL TACKLE	1	Cleat on Port side of boom 5' from after end; #0; 4'; 6'; 1/8"; 9 thread; Standing end ties to boom bale	1/8"-7x19 Stainless	1,800	6'		9 thread manila	6'	1-1/8" Open Thimble	
	FIRST BOWER ANCHOR WARP	1	10' of lower end wire wormed and bent over open thimble; 35 Fathoms; 2¾" cir					2¾" Manila	210'	1-7/8" Open Thimble	
	SECOND BOWER ANCHOR WARP.	1	10' of lower end wire wormed and bent over open thimble; 30 Fathoms; 2½" cir					2½" Manila	180'	1-13/16" Open Thimble	
	DOCKING LINES	2	50'; 2" cir					2" Manila	100'		

RIGGING AND BLOCK LIST FOR THE **NERELA** DESIGN #87 SHEET 13

Block List.	Number Required	Size		General Description	Size of Wire or Rope.
Bob Stay Turnbuckle.	1	5/8"		W.C.&Co. Fig 3162	7/16" chain
Bowsprit Shroud Turnbuckles	2	3/8"		" " "	5/16"
Headstay Turnbuckle	1	3/8"		" " "	5/16"
Fore Stay "	1	7/16"		" " "	3/8"
Main Lower Shroud Turnbuckles	4	7/16"		" " "	3/8"
Main Upper Shroud Turnbuckles	2	7/16"		" " "	3/8"
Main Lower Back Stay Tackle Blocks.	2	4"		merriman Single front Shackle with becket	1/2" Dia
	4	4"		" " " " no becket	
Main Upper Back Stay Turnbuckles.	2	5/16"		W.C.&Co Fig 3162	1/4"
Mizzen Lower Shroud Turnbuckles.	2	3/8"		" " "	5/16"
Mizzen Upper Shroud Turnbuckles	2	5/16"		" " "	1/4"
Jib Topsail Halliard Blocks.	1	7/16"		merriman Fig 370 A and B.	1/4" wire
	1	1/4"		W.C.&Co. Fig 592 - #13	1 1/4" rope
Fore Stay Sail Halliard Blocks.	1	7/16"		merriman Fig 370-A and B.	1/4" wire
	1	1/4"		W.C.&Co. Fig 592 - #13	1 1/4" rope
Main Halliard Block.	1	7/16"		merriman Fig 370-A and B	1 1/4" rope
Fore Stay Sail Sheet Blocks	2	#3		merriman Fig 364 - #3	1/2 Dia
	4	#2		W.C.&Co. Fig 5811 #2	
Main Sheet Bloks	3	4"		merriman Single front Shackle	1/2" Dia
	1	4"		" " " " with becket	
" " "				and 2 Eye plates Fig 416 - #4 and 2 Boom Bails Fig 440-A #3"	
Mizzen Sheet Blocks	2	3½"		merriman Single Front Shackle	7/16" Dia
	1	3½"		" Double " "	
" " "				and 1 Eye plate Fig 416 - #4 and 2 " " " #3 and 1 Boom Bail " 440-A-2 3/4"	
Main Clew Outhaul Slide and block	1	#2		W.C.&Co Fig 980 - #2	
	1	#2		" " 5800 - #2	
	1	#1		" " 952 - #1	
Mizzen Clew Outhaul Slide and block	1	#1		" " 980 - #1	
	1	#1		" " 5800 - #1	
	1	#0		" " 980 - #0	
Mizzen Halliard Block	1	7/16"		merriman Fig 370-A and B	1 1/4 rope
Sail Track for main mast and main boom.	1			38'-3" of 7/8" track	
	1			16' " " "	
Sail Track for mizzen mast and mizzen boom.	1			26'-9" " 5/8" "	
	1			12'-6" " " "	
Anchors - First Bower	1			W.C.&Co "Yachtsman" Fig 2002 - 60 lbs	
Secont "	1			" " " " 50 "	

Cleats all W.C.&Co Fig 4020.			
	Jib topsail hall	1 - 6½"	on after side of main mast under gooseneck
	Fore Staysail hall	1 - 6½"	on Port side of mast 12" above deck
	main Halliard	1 - 6½"	on Starboard " " " " "
	mizzen "	1 - 6½"	" " " " mizzen " " "
	Jib sheets	2 - 8"	on outside of cockpit coambing.
	Backstay tackle	2 - 8"	on " " " "
	main Sheet	1 - 8"	on After side of Deck house amidships
	mizzen Sheet	1 - 6½"	on Starboard side of mizzen boom.
	Clew out hauls	2 - 5½"	On Port side of booms, main 4' from end, mizzen 5'.

RIGGING

This rigging list need not be adhered to very exactly, but one column gives the approximate strength of the wires, and it is expected that, if other wires are used, they will be equal in strength to those shown.

Of course stainless rigging is better than galvanized, but, on account of the cost of the former, I have taken it for granted that the galvanized will be used. In case of the more flexible pieces of rigging, however, the stainless is so much superior in its lasting quality that I have called for stainless wires where they will be the cheapest in the end.

There is no case in this rigging where wire is spliced into manila, for you will notice the halliards are arranged with a snatch block at the juncture of the wire and manila so that each part terminates with an eye splice in this block. The snatch blocks also do away with the necessity of halliard winches which, besides pleasing the sailorman, saves quite an expense.

When the sail is lowered, the hauling part of the halliard consists of a single part of manila running up to the snatch block (which, of course, is at the masthead then). The sail is hoisted by this single part until the luff rope is nearly tight, then by taking a turn around the open sheave near the deck and over the snatch block, there is at once a three-part tackle to haul with. This is by far the cheapest, quickest, and neatest way to hoist sail on a yacht of this size.

I think every small detail and fitting is accounted for on the rigging and block list except spinnaker halliards and sheets, and balloon jibsheets, but it is taken for granted that few owners of an auxiliary of this size will want these complications in these expensive times when the best way to reduce costs is to eliminate unnecessary parts.

MAST HEADS

Few dimensions are given on this drawing because all parts are shown full size (on the original tracing) and drawn accurately enough to be scaled off. The drawing is intended to be a guide giving the arrangement and proportions of the parts, and slight variations can be made in many cases. The fitting at the main masthead may at first seem complicated and difficult to make, but when it is considered that this attachment secures seven different parts, it is realized that it may be easier to make than seven separate attachments, which no doubt would not be as light and neat.

1. Main flagstaff. Tobin bronze ¾" by 15½". Both ends threaded and upper end cut off when completed.

2. Mizzen flagstaff. Tobin bronze ⅝" by 13½". Both ends threaded and upper end cut off when completed.

3. Main truck. Lignum vitae, 1 by 2½" with ¼" holes for flag halliards, and central hole tapped for 1.

4. Mizzen truck. Same as 3 but 1 by 2¼".

5. Main masthead fitting. The two upper layers are alike and of semihard rolled phosphor bronze, 1/16 by 2 by 8 5/16". Only the upper layer completely countersunk for the No. 14 wood screws.

6. Main masthead fitting. The lower layer of the masthead fitting is semihard rolled phosphor bronze, 1/16 by 2½ by 13⅛",

with the forward end reinforced with another layer of the same material, 1/16 by 1⅞ by 6¾", fastened with six 3/16" rivets slightly countersunk. The after end is reinforced with two additional layers of the same material, 1/16 by 2½ by 2⅝", also fastened with six 3/16" rivets. All as shown.

7. Mizzen head fitting. This consists of one layer of semihard rolled phosphor bronze, 1/16 by 1½ by 7", drilled and countersunk for two 1½" No. 14 flathead wood screws.

8. Main halliard sheave. Cast bronze finished all over. 3½" diameter at periphery, 3 3/16" at score, and 7/16" thick.

9. Mizzen halliard sheave. Cast bronze finished all over, 3" diameter at periphery, 2¾" at score, and ⅜" thick.

10. Main halliard sheave pin. Tobin bronze, ⅝" diameter by 3¼" long. One end turned down to ⅜" and riveted to 11. Other end drilled out as shown for grease cavity and 3/32" hole at sheave. End of cavity stopped with wooden or caulk plug.

11. Mizzen halliard sheave pin. Similar to 10 but ½" by 2⅝".

12. Phosphor bronze clips. Two 1/16" to support sheave pin. One drilled ⅜" to rivet to 10. Other clip drilled ⅝" and loose on pin. Size as shown.

13. Phosphor bronze clips. Two 1/16" to support sheave pin. One drilled 5/16" to rivet to 11. Other clip drilled ½", and loose on pin. Size as shown.

14. Jib topsail halliard block. See block list.

15. Tobin bronze pin. 1 3/16" long, ⅝" diameter at head, 7/16" diameter shank. Drilled for cotter pin.

16. Tobin bronze pin. ⅞" long. ½" diameter at head, ⅜" diameter shank. Drilled for cotter pin.

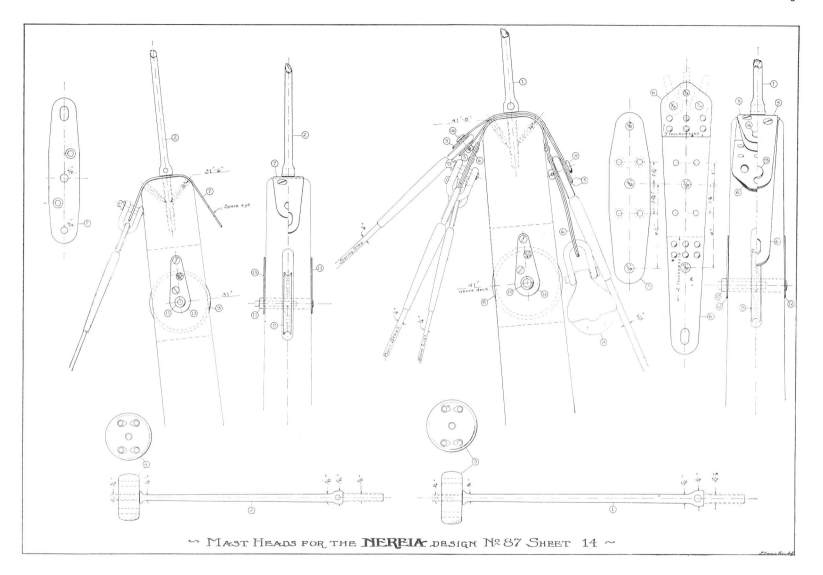

~ MAST HEADS FOR THE **NEREIA** DESIGN Nº 87 SHEET 14 ~

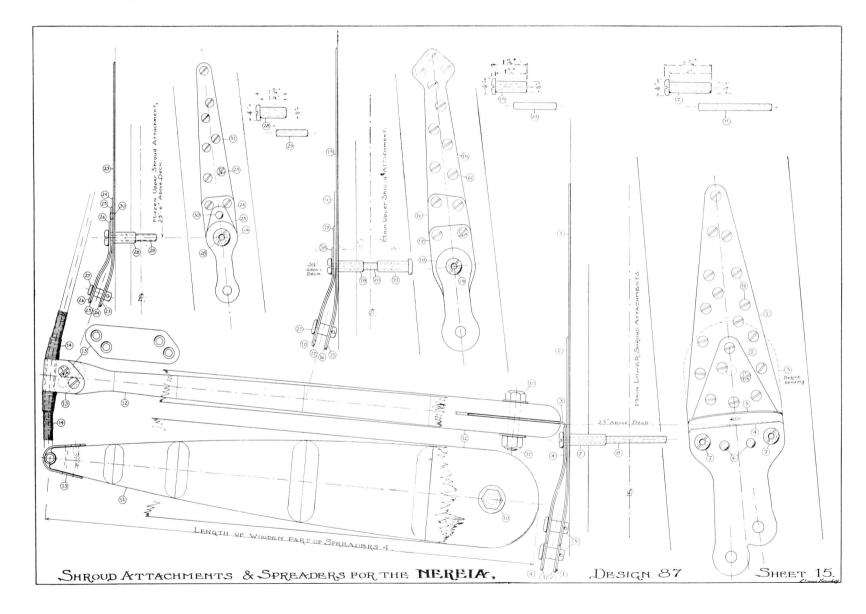

SHROUD ATTACHMENTS & SPREADERS FOR THE **NEREIA.** DESIGN 87 SHEET 15.

SHROUD ATTACHMENTS AND SPREADERS

The main lower shroud attachment is composed of the following parts:

1. Sheet of half-hard phosphor bronze, 1/16 by 4½ by 18″. Make two.

2. Sheet of half-hard phosphor bronze, 1/16 by 4½ by 11″. Make two.

3. Sheet of half-hard phosphor bronze, 1/16 by 4½ by 11½″. Make two.

4. Sheet of half-hard phosphor bronze, 1/16 by 4½ by 6⅞″. Make two.

5. Tobin bronze pins, ½″ diameter at body, ¾″ at head, 1 3/16″ long. Make four.

6. ¼″ bronze rivets through all four layers.

7. Tobin bronze gun-stock bolts. Inside tapped with 5/16″, 24 threads; head slotted. Dimensions as at top of drawing. Make four.

8. Tobin or Everdur bronze rod, 5/16″ diameter, 3½″ long, threaded full length with 5/16″, 24 thread, full length. Make two.

9. Flathead No. 14 wood screws, 1″ long. On account of these screws being very short, their holes must be most carefully drilled or they will not hold well. When countersinking the plates 1 and 2, the burr of the countersink should be left on the inner surface as this will increase their holding power on the mast.

10. Spreader bolts of bronze, ½″ diameter, length 4¼″. Two required, and four large brass washers.

11. After adjustment so the spreaders swing quite hard, the thread of 10 should be nicked with a hammer so that the nut will not unscrew.

12. The main spreaders, which can be made of hard spruce, mahogany, or ash, 1½″ by 4½″ by 4′, and tapered and shaped as shown, are to have slot or saw cleft cut at their inner ends. This slot should be very nearly 1/16″ thick, which can be done by trying the saw, end grain, in a sample of wood, and, if the cleft is too narrow, give the saw teeth more set. If the cleft is too wide, then remove some of the set in the teeth by rubbing an oil stone along the sides of the teeth. Many ripsaws will cut a slot just 1/16″ wide.

13. The spreader tips are made out of strips of half-hard phosphor bronze, 1/16 by 1½ by 2½″, with countersunk holes for four 1″ No. 14 flathead bronze wood screws, as shown. Make two.

14. The upper shrouds should be served with marline for about 6″ in the region the spreader tips will bear, and after the clips of the tips are in place, tapered seizing of marline should be slapped on to hold the spreaders in place. This arrangement will not chafe the sails.

The parts of the main upper shroud attachments are as follows:

15. Sheet of half-hard phosphor bronze, 1/16 by 2 by 14″. Make two.

16. Sheet of half-hard phosphor bronze, 1/16 by 2 by 7¼″. Make two.

17. Sheet of half-hard phosphor bronze, 1/16 by 2 by 5⅞″. Make two.

18. Sheet of half-hard phosphor bronze, 1/16 by 1¾ by 4¾″. Make two.

19. Tobin bronze gun-stock bolts. Inside tapped with 5/16″, 24 threads, heads slotted, dimensions as at top of drawing. Make two.

20. Tobin bronze rod, threaded full length, with 5/16″, 24 threads.

21. Pins same as 5. Make two.

22. All wood screws flathead 1″, No. 14.

The parts of the mizzen upper shroud attachments are as follows:

23. Sheet of half-hard phosphor bronze, 1/16 by 1½ by 11″. Make two.

24. Sheet of half-hard phosphor bronze, 1/16 by 1½ by 4⅞″. Make two.

25. Sheet of half-hard phosphor bronze, 1/16 by 1½ by 4½″. Make two.

26. Sheet of half-hard phosphor bronze, 1/16 by 1½ by 3¾″. Make two.

27. Tobin bronze pins, ⅜″ diameter at body, ½″ at head. Length 1⅛″. Make two.

28. Tobin bronze gun-stock bolts, inside tapped for 5/16″, 24 thread, heads slotted. Dimensions as at top of drawing. Make two.

29. Tobin bronze rod, 5/16″ diameter, threaded full length. Make one.

30. ½″ bronze rivet through three layers, as shown.

31. All wood screws flathead bronze, 1 or ⅞″ No. 12.

Although some variation can be made in the parts shown on the drawing, it would be best if dimensions were increased rather than decreased. The sheet metal parts are proportioned for a metal of high tensile strength and considerable hardness; if a softer metal is used, each layer should be a gauge or two thicker.

ATTACHMENTS FOR THE FORESTAY, BACKSTAYS, MIZZEN LOWER SHROUDS, ETC.

1. Sheet of half-hard phosphor bronze, 1/16 by 2½ by 19¼″. Make one.

2. Sheet of half-hard phosphor bronze, 1/16 by 1¾ by 11¾″. Make one.

3. Sheet of half-hard phosphor bronze, 1/16 by 1¾ by 7½″. Make one.

4. Sheet of half-hard phosphor bronze, 1/16 by 1¾ by 6½″. Make one.

5. Sheet of half-hard phosphor bronze, 1/16 by 1½ by 11¾″. Make one.

6. Everdur cap screws. ½ by 2″. Drill hole in wood about 7/16″. Two required.

7. Tobin bronze pin. ½″, with cotter, about 1″ long under head.

8. Sheet of half-hard phosphor bronze, 1/16 by 3 by 12⅛″. Make two.

9. Sheet of half-hard phosphor bronze, 1/16 by 1½ by 7¼″. Make two.

10. Bronze bolts. ⅜″ with nuts and washers. Two sets required.

11. Sheet of half-hard phosphor bronze, 1/16 by 3½ by 12⅝″. Make two, with reinforcement at lower end, 1/16 by 2¼ by 2¼″, riveted on.

12. Sheet of half-hard phosphor bronze, 1/16 by 3½ by 7⅞″. Make two.

13. Sheet of half-hard phosphor bronze, 1/16 by 3½ by 4″. Make two.

14. Tobin bronze pin, ⅜″, with cotters about 1″ long under heads. Make two.

15. Gun stock bolts, Tobin bronze, inside tapped with 5/16″ No. 24 threads. Length overall 1½″, diameter heads ¾″, diameter shanks ½″. Heads slotted as shown.

16. Bronze rod, 5/16″ diameter, 3″ long, threaded with 5/16″ No. 24 threads, full length.

17. Mizzen spreaders, of hard spruce, mahogany, or ash. 1¼″ thick full length. Tapered as shown.

18. Mizzen spreader tips, half-hard phosphor bronze, 1/16 by 1¼ by 4″. Shaped as shown.

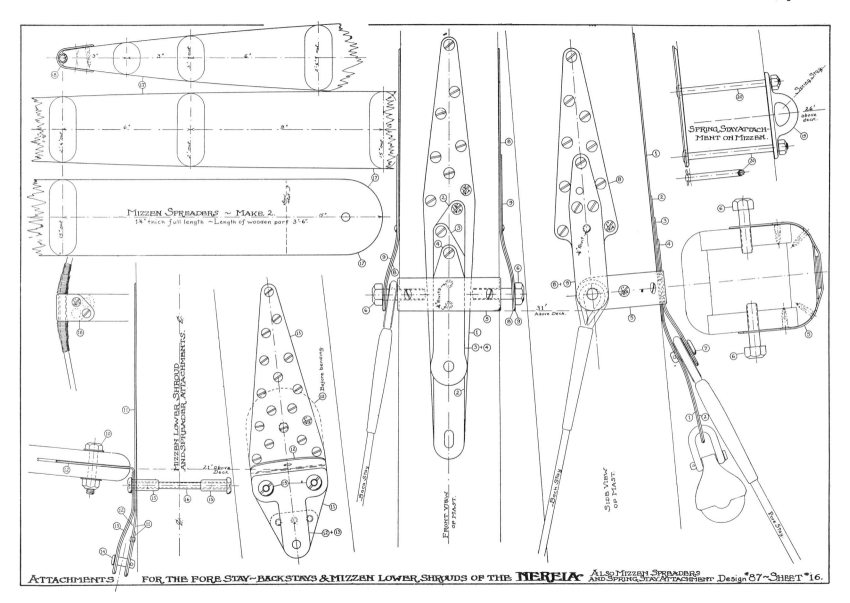

MIZZEN SPREADERS ~ MAKE 2.
1¾" thick full length ~ Length of wooden part 3'-6".

SPRING STAY ATTACH-MENT ON MIZZEN.

MIZZEN LOWER SHROUD AND SPREADER ATTACHMENTS.

FRONT VIEW OF MAST.

SIDE VIEW OF MAST.

ATTACHMENTS FOR THE FORE-STAY~ BACKSTAYS & MIZZEN LOWER SHROUDS OF THE **NEREIA** ALSO MIZZEN SPREADERS AND SPRING STAY ATTACHMENT Design #87~Sheet #16.

19.   Attachment of spring on the mizzen. Merriman Fig. 417, size 3. Seizing wire is used here instead of a turnbuckle because the weight of a turnbuckle makes the stay sag, but the seizing and the whole attachment must be strong if the yacht lies to in a gale of wind with the mizzen set.

20.   T headed Everdur bolts. 5/16″ with heads so shaped that they do not spread the sail track on the after side of mast.

While it has been my custom to draw up the scroll for the trail boards and stern decoration on similar yachts to Nereia, it has been thought that with a one-design class it would be well to have this fancy work different on each yacht. It certainly would be worthwhile to have a suitable figurehead, trail boards, and stern decoration for a yacht built like Nereia, for she will last fifty years or more with good care, and if, like her several larger sisters, she increases in value each year, she will make a good investment. However, the looks of the yacht as a whole can be very much affected by the decorations, which must be most carefully carried out and never overdone or made too large.

A TENDER FOR NEREIA

Nereia's tender is shaped mostly to fit in between the mizzen-mast and the deckhouse, as shown on the sail plan, sheet 1, and this requires that she be rather narrow on deck and have less flare to the sides than is customary in a boat of this size and type. On her bottom she is quite wide, with seats low so she may be stiff enough for general usefulness. She will undoubtedly tow well, should be easy to stow on board, and should not need lashing down except in the heaviest weather.

The little boat is of quite heavy construction so as to withstand hard use, but, if one should prefer to plank her with laminated wood, these thicknesses can be materially reduced, and I must say laminated wood is excellent for remaining tight when exposed to the sun, for it shrinks sideways very little. So for those who intend to keep the dinghy on deck most of the time, I would recommend laminated wood. However, for normal use and landing on rocky shores, the construction as shown should prove more useful.

The dory type of construction is adopted, as it is believed this is the cheapest serviceable construction. One of the reasons for its cheapness is that the frames themselves act as molds, and experience has shown that the frames do not have to be spaced as closely as with other constructions.

The numbered description is as follows:

1.   Bow piece, or bow transom, can be oak or mahogany, about 7/8″ thick with a small notch at its upper edge for the painter when towing.

2.   Bottom planking can be soft pine or cedar, 3/4″ thick. If thinner planks or laminated wood are used for the bottom, then it will be necessary to have an apron or border piece around the edges of the bottom so that there will be thickness enough for the planking fastenings. See dotted lines on section 2.

3.   Bottom frames. Oak, 5/8″ by 1″.

4.   Side frames. Oak, 5/8″ thick, shaped as shown and fastened to bottom framing with two 1¼″, No. 10 wood screws, and glued if convenient.

5.   Lower strake. Cedar or soft pine, 3/8″ thick.

6.   Upper strake. Cedar or soft pine, 5/16 inch thick.

7.   Seam battens. Oak, 3/8″ by 2″. On the drawing the bottom is planked with three planks about 12″ wide, which only calls for two battens, but narrower planks with more battens may be an advantage. If these battens are carefully fitted and fairly closely fastened they will make the seams quite watertight and act as chafing strips.

8.   Gunwale strip. Oak, ¼″ by 1″. It is customary to fasten

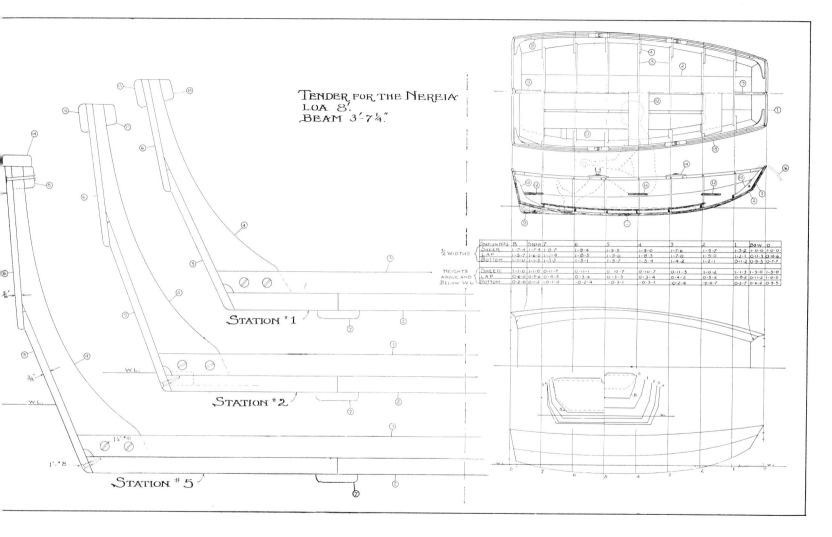

TENDER FOR THE NEREIA
LOA 8'.
BEAM 3'-7¼".

STATION #1

STATION #2

STATION #5

½ WIDTHS

HEIGHTS
ABOVE AND
BELOW W.L.

STATION Nº S	8	Stern 7	6	5	4	3	2	1	Bow 0	
SHEER	1-7-2	1-7-4	1-8-7	1-9-4	1-9-5	1-9-0	1-7-6	1-5-7	1-3-2	1-0-0	1-0-0
LAP	1-5-7	1-6-0	1-7-4	1-8-5	1-9-0	1-8-3	1-7-0	1-5-0	1-2-1	0-11-3	0-10-6
BOTTOM	1-1-0	1-1-5	1-3-3	1-5-7	1-5-1	1-5-4	1-4-2	1-2-1	0-11-2	0-9-3	0-7-7
SHEER	1-1-0	1-1-0	0-11-7	0-11-1	0-10-7	0-10-7	0-11-3	1-0-2	1-1-3	1-3-0	1-3-0
LAP	0-6-0	0-5-6	0-4-5	0-3-6	0-3-3	0-3-4	0-4-2	0-5-6	0-8-2	0-11-2	1-1-0
BOTTOM	0-2-0	0-1-2	-0-1-0	-0-2-4	-0-3-1	-0-3-1	-0-2-4	-0-0-7	0-2-7	0-6-2	0-9-5

W.L.

5/16"

3/8"

1'-8

1¼"-10

this piece with copper rivets passing through the planking and the heads of frames.

9. Skeg. Oak, ¾″ thick.

10. Forward and after knees can be of hackmatack or other suitable wood, about 1″ thick. Forward knee drilled for painter as shown.

11. Quarter knees. Oak or hackmatack, 1″ thick, with some natural crook.

12. Thwarts. ¾″ spruce, placed at least as low as shown.

13. Floor boards. ½″ spruce, pine, or fir.

14. Rowlocks, etc. Where the rowlocks come there should be pieces of oak between the planking and the gunwale strip, with a block above about 8 by 1⅜ by ½″, as shown on section 5. The oarlocks can be Wilcox, Crittenden Fig. 425 or 429.

15. Chafing strip. Oak or spruce, about ⅜ by 1¼″.

16. Painter. This dinghy should tow all right with the painter secured inside, and it is shown spliced into the bow knee. If the painter runs in a notch in the bow and is parceled at that point it should not chafe unduly. The painter should be manila, about 1¾″ circumference, and about four or five fathoms long, but when towing in a seaway, a longer rope must be bent to the painter.

8   HOW TO BUILD MOBJACK

The Mobjack was built for a gentleman who lived on Mobjack Bay, Virginia, in 1935. She has been in commission, I believe, every year since then and has cruised quite extensively, her present owner (1947), Dr. Peer P. Johnson, having taken her south one winter. Although she is of rather shallow draft for a sailing yacht without a centerboard, she has performed quite satisfactorily.

While I have only sailed on the Mobjack in smooth going, I am told that she is very dry and has an easy motion in a seaway. She is capable of making good passages, as her length on the waterline allows her to be driven faster than some other yachts of her general size, and she is very easy on the helm; in fact she steers herself much of the time.

The best feature of the Mobjack is that she turned out to be cheap to construct. She was built by George Gulliford of Saugus, Massachusetts.

Dimensions are 45 feet 3 inches overall, 38 feet 9 inches on the water, 12 feet 6 inches beam, 5 feet draft and displacement of 38,600 pounds, lead keel 10,200 pounds. Her total sail area is 1,060 square feet divided as follows: jib 295, main 490, and mizzen 275.

CONSTRUCTION

Lead keel. The lead keel is to be cast in one piece and can be second-hand lead, carefully shaped to conform with the detailed plans of the keel so as to obtain the calculated weight as used on the design. If possible, all of the lead is to be poured in one running and no pigs or cold pieces of lead are to be placed in the mold in order to avoid air pockets, blow holes, etc. It is recommended that about five percent of antimony be mixed with the lead so that the lead will be easy for drill work, etc.

Wood keel of white oak 5″ thick, sided as required. Can be made in small pieces if scarfs are over the lead and properly lapped.

Keel bolts. All bolts are to be made of Tobin bronze of size and length indicated on the construction plan. The lead keel is secured with lag screws.

Stem and stempost. The stem is to be a natural crook of hard white oak, but the upper forward part terminating in the fiddlehead can be of soft pine. A template should be made for the profile of the stem so that the exact shape of the profile will be like the lines. The stempost is to be of oak carefully shaped at the tuck.

Floor timbers. All of the floor timbers of this yacht are to be

The Mobjack *lifting along nicely, with her big, overlapping jib doing its work (from the Edwin Levick Collection, Mariner's Museum).*

of white oak of the depth and thickness shown on the construction plan and are to fit the planking.

Frames, 2¼" x 2¼", all hard white oak spaced 14" centers to centers. The frames forward of the main mast can be sawn and are to be in one length, molded and sided 2¼" x 2¼". These had best be beveled to approximate shape both inside and out before setting up, and the fore and aft sides should be square to fit the floor and deck beams. The frames from the main mast to the after end of the house are to be steam bent and can be in two layers if and where desired, their total siding to be 2¼" x 2¼". The frames aft of the house can be sawn and in lengths as required — where they are jointed a piece of the same material and size must be securely bolted on; galvanized bolts about 5/16" diameter should be used, or galvanized wood screws, size #18 or #20. It should be borne in mind that this yacht will not be sheathed up and it is important that the frames should not be crimped or dented by clamps, etc., on their inner sides, and on completion the frames are to be smoothed up and inner corners nicely rounded off where they show above the floors. Where the frames are bent in two layers they must be nicely lined up to look neat.

Deck beams, 3" x 1¼". These beams are to be made of selected well-seasoned white oak and sawn to the proper camber. There will also be one or two heavy beams 3" x 3".

Knees. There will be no lodging knees and only four hanging knees. These can be either oak or hackmatack. They are located one on each side abreast each mast, all carefully bolted as shown on the drawings, for this yacht is out for an unusually long distance by the deckhouse and cockpit so that the side decks must be supported by the deckhouse sides which, in turn, will throw the weight on these knees.

Other frame members. All other frame members, such as the mast steps, knight heads, stem knees, breast hook, quarter knees,

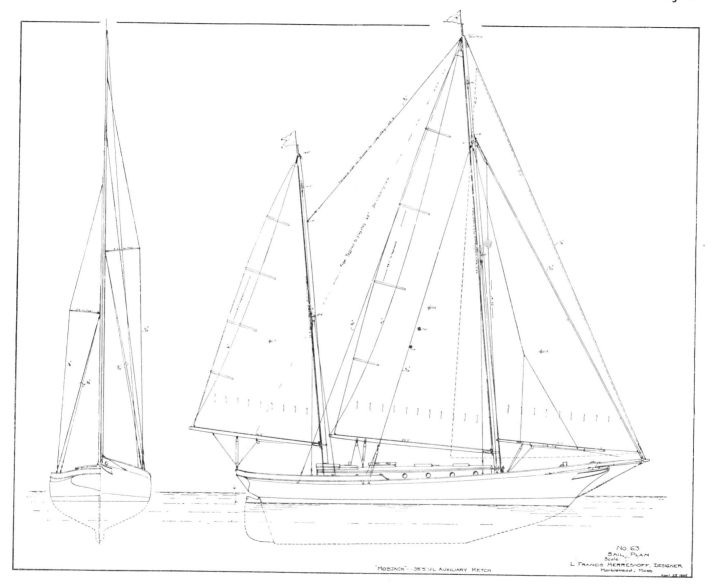

"MOBJACK"--38.5 W.L. AUXILIARY KETCH

NO. 63
SAIL PLAN
Scale
L FRANCIS HERRESHOFF, DESIGNER
Marblehead, Mass

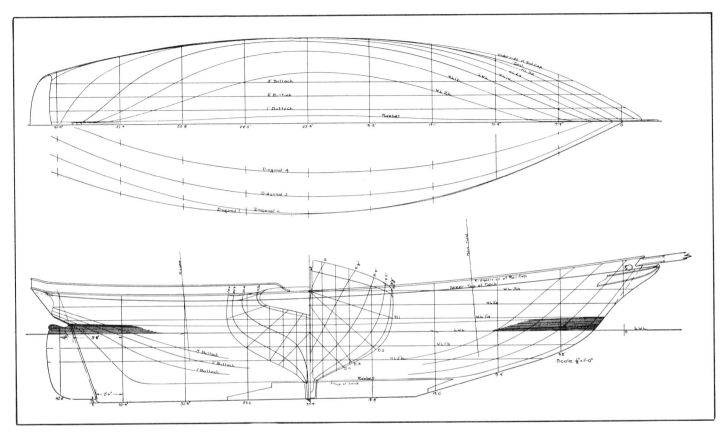

etc., are to be of well-seasoned oak or hackmatack, for these members often rot if they are in the ends of the yacht.

Plank sheer (sometimes called covering board or waterways) to be of oak 1¾″ thick, 6 or more inches wide, in lengths as convenient. A butt block one frame space long must be placed under each joint, and this should be carefully through-bolted with four ⅜″ galvanized bolts each side of the seam. This plank

sheer must be strong to take the place of the main deck, which is cut away for the deck house.

Sheer strake, oak, 1½″ x 5″ amidships. The sheer strake should be of hard white oak amidships, but at the stern aft of the deckhouse, where it will be shaped and beveled considerably, it can be of any appropriate soft wood. Although the sheer strake can be made of short lengths if desired, it must always be

No 63 38'-9" W.L. AUXILIARY KETCH
TABLE of OFFSETS
L. Francis Herreshoff · Designer, Marblehead, Mass

	Heights from L.W.L.							Half Breadths									Diagonals			
Station	Underside Rail Cap	Sheer	3'0" Buttock	2'0" Buttock	1'0" Buttock	Rabbet	Profile	Underside Rail Cap	Deck	W.L. 3'a	W.L. 2'a	W.L. 1'a	L.W.L.	W.L. 1'b	W.L. 2'b	Rabbet	1	2	3	4
1-3" Forward		4·6·0														0·2·4				
0	5·0·6	4·4·0	4·9·6			3·4·4	2·5·3	1·2·1	0·8·5							0·2·4				
4'-8"	4·5·5	3·9·4	3·9·4	2·0·6	0·1·7	1·1·2	1·5·7	3·5·2	3·0·0	2·6·2	1·11·4	1·5·1	0·10·6	0·3·4		0·2·4	2·3·0	2·2·6	1·11·0+	0·9·4
9'-4"	3·11·3	3·4·2	0·1·6	0·11·5	1·11·4	2·7·7	3·0·0	4·10·5	4·7·4	4·6·0	4·1·1	3·6·4	2·10·5	1·11·6	0·11·0	0·2·4	4·2·0	4·1·2	3·7·2	2·1·3
14'-0"	3·6·2	3·0·0	1·6·7	2·3·1	2·11·0	3·4·2	4·4·0	5·9·0	5·8·0	5·7·7	5·5·4	5·1·7	4·7·4	3·8·2	2·4·2	0·3·5	5·6·4	5·5·4	4·8·0	3·0·5
18'-8"	3·2·0	2·8·3	2·2·4	2·8·4	3·2·2	Straight	4·9·0	6·2·0	6·1·6	6·2·0	6·1·1	5·11·2	5·7·4	4·10·2	3·4·4	0·6·1	6·3·2	6·3·3	5·2·2	3·6·0
23'-4"	2·11·0	2·5·7	2·4·1	2·9·5	3·3·0		Straight	6·3·0	6·3·0		6·3·1	6·3·0	5·11·6	5·3·2	3·8·0	0·7·0	6·6·5	6·6·5	5·3·5	3·7·1
28'-0"	2·9·2	2·4·3	2·0·2	2·6·3	3·1·1			6·0·5	6·1·2		6·2·0	6·1·7	5·10·1	4·10·1	3·0·7	0·5·6	6·5·6	6·3·0	5·0·1	3·4·0
32'-8"	2·8·3	2·4·0	1·1·7	1·9·2	2·6·6	3·7·4		5·7·5	5·8·5		5·9·0	5·8·0	4·11·3	3·3·2	1·8·0	0·3·5	6·0·0+	5·5·2	4·8·0	2·7·4
37'-4"	2·9·0	2·5·3	0·3·3	0·2·0	0·10·4	2·9·0	5·0·0	4·11·0	5·0·2		5·0·0	4·3·6	2·4·7	0·11·0	0·5·1	0·3·0	5·0·3	4·1·2	2·10·7	1·4·0
42'-0"	2·11·2	2·9·0	1·9·4	1·6·2	1·3·4	1·1·3	1·0·6	3·9·6	3·10·7		3·6·3					0·3·0	3·6·6	2·4·2	1·0·0	
Stern	3·1·3	2·10·2	1·11·3	1·8·7	1·6·2	1·3·6	1·3·0	3·1·4	3·7·2		3·2·4					0·3·0	3·3·7	2·1·0	0·9·2	
Intersections of Diagonals + Centerline from L.W.L.																	3·0·0	3·0·0	2·0·0	0·0·0
Intersections of Waterlines + Diagonals out from ℄																	L.W.L. 9·4·0	W.L. 1'b 4·8·0	W.L. 2'b 3·0·0	W.L. 2'b 2·0·0

Notes
Dimensions are given in Feet, Inches and Eighths to outside of Hull
Planking 1½", Frames spaced 14" ℄-℄
See Detail for Stem and Transom

Jan 23 1935

butted two or more frame spaces away from joints in the plank sheer, and these joints must be made over an oak butt block one frame space long with five 3/8" galvanized bolts each side of the seam.

Planking. The planking is to be 1½" thick, rift-grain fir. All butts in the planking must be backed up with an oak butt block one frame space long secured with through-bolts 5/16" diameter. The garboard should be in one length. The planks above the waterline should never exceed 6" in width. The planks must fit tightly on the inside and be properly beveled on the outer edge for caulking.

Decking, 1½" thick. The decking must be made of extra selected rift-grain fir of close-grain texture and low moisture content. The planks should not exceed 1¾" in width. Great care should be used in caulking the deck, and cotton caulking is recommended. Butts to be half lapped, and, at deck beam, there should be a few edge nails in the main deck opposite the deck house. The house deck is to be of tongue-and-groove soft pine, 7/8" thick, canvas covered, butts on beams.

Fastenings. Planking to frames, either 2¾" bronze #20 with 11/16" bung or 2¾" Everdur #18 with 5/8" bung. Deck to deck beams, galvanized boat nails about 2½" x ¼". House deck to house deck beams, galvanized boat nails 1½" x ¼". Frames to floors, 5/16" galvanized stove bolts, four on each frame. Shelf and clamp to frames and deck beams, 3/8" galvanized through-bolts.

Bilge stringer. This yacht is to have no bilge stringer.

Sheathing. This yacht is only to be sheathed up where required back of bunks, stoves, etc., so that the frames and planking must be well finished off on the inside. What sheathing is required in these places can be about 5/8" country pine.

Gunwales. The gunwales or bulwarks can be either rift pine or fir, about 1¼" thick, and are secured to the waterways with 5/16" galvanized drive bolts. Forward of the mast there will be one or two stanchions on each side to support the gunwales, which are higher forward. Way aft the gunwales should be considerably thicker to allow for the tumblehome on the outside of the yacht.

Rail cap. The rail cap is to be of oak, 1¼" x 4", the section shown on the drawing, and nicely faired up and finished for varnishing. Aft there is an upper rail 1" thick and a rail cap about 1⅛" x 2⅛".

Other deck woodwork. The bowsprit bitts, hatch finish, deckhouse molding, companionway slides, skylight, etc., are all to be of white oak.

Scupper pipes. Three on each side, 1½" copper tubing emptying through the topsides between the painted and load waterline. There will also be two at the forward end of the cockpit, the same size, etc.

Deck fittings and hardware. Most of the deck fittings will be cast bronze of standard pattern finished rough or painted, and all fastened to the deck with either Everdur screws or bolts.

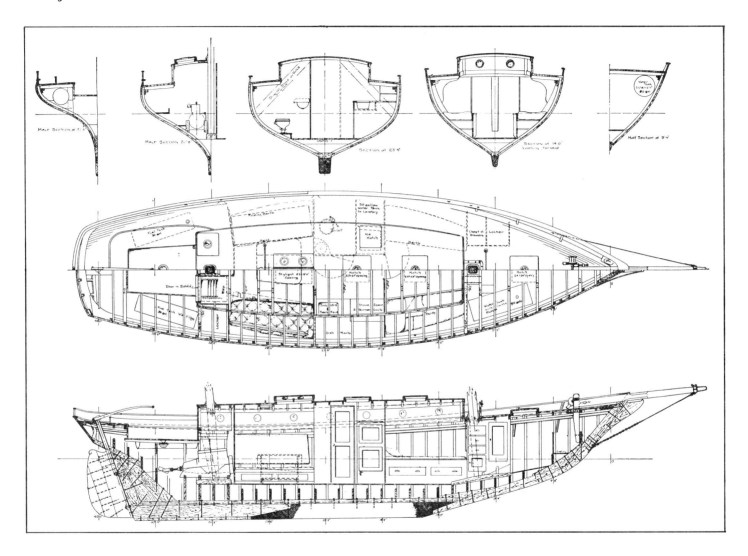

Rudder. The rudder blade is to be made of rift-grain oak fastened with galvanized drive bolts. The rudder post is to be a bronze tube, and this and the rudder pintles are shown on the detailed drawing of the same.

Rudder port, brass pipe threaded into keel as shown on construction plan.

Tanks. Both water and gasoline tanks are to be made of tin-lined copper of the size and thickness shown on the detailed drawings of the same. All joints are to be both rivetted and soldered. Tanks should be tested with a slight pressure. These tanks are to be hung as shown on the drawings and carefully fitted so that in case of a collision or heavy sea they will not easily be shifted.

Plumbing. In the toilet room there is to be a corner lavatory, Sands R-3170, draining straight down through the bottom: shut off valves, etc., as worked out during construction. This lavatory will be supplied with gravity feed water from a water tank in the bow. At the lavatory there is to be a self-closing faucet (Sands R-3205). The water closet in this room is to be Sands R-4032. The exhaust line is to loop up at least one foot above the waterline and all outboard connections are to be fitted with sea cocks. In the galley there is to be a Sands R-6015 sink, size 2 (12″ x 8″ x 6″), discharging overboard through a hand-driven Trimont rotary pump. On the water supply of this sink there are to be two self-closing faucets.

Piping to plumbing. All of the piping on supply lines is to be either brass, ¾″ iron pipe size, or copper tubing, but must be arranged with enough joints and unions so that the same can be easily taken down. Also it must be arranged for thorough draining in wintertime. The waste lines from the galley sink and lavatory should be as big as 1½″ iron pipe size.

Engine installation. The exhaust is to be iron pipe to the water-cooled muffler, and, from there to the stern, brass or copper pipe and a flexible rubber steam hose will be allowed if desired aft of the muffler. The exhaust discharges under the stern nearly abreast the rudder port. The engine controls are to be brass above deck and consist only of a throttle and folding reverse lever.

Lamps and lighting. The yacht is to be lit throughout with kerosene yacht-type gimbal lamps. The running and riding lights are also kerosene of a size specified by the pilot rules for a yacht of this class. Besides these kerosene lights there are to be the following emergency electric lights run from the engine batteries: one trouble light in the engine room, one dome light over the dining table, one light in forward cabin, one light at compass. There are also to be one or two camp-type Eveready dry battery lights, one in the galley, one in the toilet, etc.

Cabin sole. The cabin floor is to be ⅞″ thick, tongue-and-groove pine, nicely fitted at the planking. This flooring should be made of damp wood and seams loosely fitted so as to allow for swelling. Along the center line, the floor shall lift up in sections about one foot wide and three feet long. All of the floor is to be covered with battleship linoleum.

Spars. The bowsprit is to be a solid spar of heavy spruce or Oregon pine, nicely fitted and secured at the butts. The masts are to be hollow box section spars built of fir. The boom can be either hollow or solid, all the sizes and shapes shown on the detail drawings of these parts.

Cabinetwork. The partitions in general can be made of laminated wood, and all edges are to be carefully painted and covered with finish strips to protect the glued seams from dampness. Most of the other woodwork can be simple pine, painted.

9   HOW TO BUILD THE MARCO POLO

Marco Polo, a Venetian of about the year 1300, was one of the first great travelers who wrote up his adventures and told marvelous stories of foreign lands. Apparently one of the great secrets of his success was that he could travel light and could adapt himself to all conditions. Comfort and show were not the main objects of his life, but to get onward and visit strange places was more to be desired. So, like its namesake, this Marco Polo is planned to travel efficiently. It would have been easier, perhaps, to draw some wallowing tub with easy motion to lay at sea like a painted ship upon a painted ocean, with fuel gone and food and water rationed, a thousand miles ahead before next station.

The Marco Polo is designed mostly for driving under power and is shaped to accommodate a great variety of power plants, either single, twin, or triple screw. Her length, fifty-five feet, may scare some people, but the cost of a boat or vessel is nearly in proportion to her weight. Length is only one of the four factors which influence weight or displacement; the other three are width, depth, and shape. The fact is, a long, lean boat is easier to build than a short one of the same weight with full lines.

The principal objects tried for in the design are:

1.   A very long cruising radius under power.
2.   A sail plan that can be handled by one man on watch.
3.   Extreme seaworthiness (the whale boat model).
4.   Shallow draft which not only will allow her to visit unique places but often will avert serious disasters.
5.   She is cut away aft so that she will lay-to a sea anchor with her head well into the wind, and a balanced rudder designed to swing all the way around.
6.   Her wind resistance is cut to the minimum for laying at anchor in strong winds and for driving economically under power.
7.   Her construction is simplified for economy in building as much as is compatible with strength.
8.   She is arranged to sleep either four or five people, and planned to be run with one man on watch so that the watches can be four hours on and eight off. This allows a cruise to be a pleasure, but when one is not sure of eight hours' unbroken sleep, the cruise is only hard work and drudgery. Few yachts have large enough hulls and small enough sails to allow this combination.

Sail Plan

Three masts are adopted so great shifts in the center of the sail plan can be made. In running in heavy weather, the sail can be way forward and prevent broaching-to; in laying-to the storm mizzen can be well aft (where it should be). The fore mast and mizzen are very strong for heavy weather and set up-and-down-cut sails, while the mainsail is a crosscut sail on a lighter spar and easily and quickly taken in. Her spars and rigging are according to the latest scientific racing practice, but much heavier and stronger. All unnecessary top hamper is done away with to reduce chafe and wind resistance. The booms are rigged with strong forward guys to prevent them from slatting around or gybing.

On this long, narrow hull, three masts are almost necessary if each sail is to be a high, narrow airfoil. Three masts also almost entirely do away with the necessity of reefing, for one or more of her several sails can be taken in to accomplish the desired reduction of area, so that, although reefs are shown on the sail plan, they seldom would be used, thus there will be no necessity to consider roller reefing gear—that contrivance which is never entirely satisfactory and adds to expense.

In light weather with a beam wind, she sets a large balloon jib forward on a removable boom or nose pole, which is shown in dotted lines together with a light weather overlapping foresail, which goes on the fore boom and has a club sheet.

The small sail plans show various combinations of sails, but in running in heavy weather there is a bifurcated trisail hoisted on a track on the fore side of the foremast and set

like small heavy twin spinnakers, and it is believed she will be partly self steering with this rig in heavy weather.

All of the working sails are hoisted or lowered from the cockpit and have downhauls so that in a squall at night the man at the helm need not leave the cockpit. However, she is rigged with good life rails should he venture out for some other reason. She has no gunwales or bulwarks, for these only hold seas on board while the waist-high life rails will hold a person on board and let the seas pass from under.

A Marco Polo, the Talaria, *under sail. Note that her deckhouse has been extended forward of the mainmast.*

One of the features of the design is to have a place to carry a really serviceable tender, which few vessels of this displacement can do, but my experience is that an easily rowed, light tender adds to the pleasure of a cruise very greatly, for some of the most interesting places are in very shallow water. A tender that can sail, row, or go with an outboard motor is most invaluable. On this design the tender will cut off

some of the forward vision, but she is in a place where she will be out of the way and can be lashed down for the very worst weather.

The deck at both ends has a high crown like a lifeboat, and this is done to make the forward and after peaks useful for storage. The after deck, too, will protect the man at the wheel from a pooping sea, which is a matter of great importance, for it is believed this model of vessel can be driven very hard in a following sea as she has a small midship section, an easy run, and a cutaway forefoot — all of great importance in running.

No doubt you know there has never been a small auxiliary designed before that was really efficient to drive under power or really had a long steaming radius. This in itself has a great effect on the rig and rigging. The Marco Polo will use her power when going dead to windward or dead before it in calms and light weather. With wind abeam, her sail plan should be as efficient as any other of its size, but that is the point — previous long distance cruisers have nearly all had to have large sail plans for light weather or they never would have gotten anywhere, so they generally have topmasts, topsails, and all kinds of light weather gear which had to be taken in with a change of weather. With all their complicated gear there was much chafe and wear aloft and they required a large crew.

In the rigging itself we are not following any eighteenth century deep-sea myths, but are trying to make it as simple and strong as modern materials will allow. It is my belief that the only reason sail tracks, turnbuckles, and wire halliards have given trouble before is because they have not been properly proportioned, or used and rigged correctly. To be sure, the head of high, narrow sails are apt to pull away from the headboard, but the Marco Polo has oversize headboards and the sailmaker must be cautioned to reinforce the upper part of the sail and upper end of the luff ropes.

In general she is a vessel that could be built by any small boatyard.

Although the Marco Polo is designed for all-around-the-world cruising, still she would (in my opinion) be good for shorter cruising, so she is designed with built-in hoisting eyes for wire rope slings that she may be hoisted onto the deck of a steamer.

There are some almost unfrequented cruising grounds that the Marco Polo could visit, some of which have short good-weather seasons, or are shallow in places — for instance, the wild and picturesque Strait of Magellan and the Beagle Channel much farther south, while the inland waterways of southern Chile are almost unknown. There are many places in Hudson's Bay and the south coast of Alaska which the Marco Polo's cruising radius and light draft will allow her to visit which are barred to straight sailers with deep draft. There is no doubt that some of these regions would be of interest to the mineralologist and the cruise might be made a paying proposition.

Don't forget Scotland, which is said to be the prettiest cruising ground in the world but sometimes not too safe for yachts of much draft and poor power plants. Yes, the Marco Polo's draft of only 5 feet 6 inches will allow her to go up many rivers and through canals that will shorten many routes.

If stuffing the stomach is the object of the cruise, well, the Marco Polo has a good size galley with plenty of light and air, and with a few interior changes she should be as good for this purpose as some of those red-stained and chromium-plated abortions designed for the delectation of the advertisers and the profit of the agents.

Lines

The Marco Polo is shown on the lines in an unloaded condition — that is, her tanks are empty and there are no stores on board. She may float some nine or ten inches lower when loaded, and this change in draft is one of the things that influences her model. I have tried to make a form that will not change her beam-length ratio much when loaded, as a shape with flam amidships is bound to do, and this has made her rather slab-sided like many cargo vessels. However, this model has the advantages of hard bilges, which makes for slow motion in a seaway. Also her stability should not change much from the light to the loaded condition. Of course, these hard bilges will make rather sharp bends for the frames, but the frames will be bent in two layers and will make these curves without trouble.

Some people may say she rises too vertically from the water all around and therefore will be set, or throw a lot of spray, but as a matter of fact a long narrow boat is drier than a wide full one no matter how much flare the latter has.

Conor O'Brien, who perhaps has had as much experience as anyone of late years in yachts of this kind (and I believe twice won the Blue Water medal of the Royal Cruising Club), designs his yachts with practically no overhang to

Station Numbers	55	52	48	44	40	36	32	28	24	20	16	12	8	4	0 Station Numbers
At Deck	0-1-2	1-10-9	3-3-4	4-1-5	4-7-4	4-10-4	4-11-6	5-0-0	4-11-6	4-10-7	4-8-3	4-3-0	3-5-7	2-2-2	0-1-3 At Deck
WL +4'										4-10-6	4-7-5	4-1-0	3-1-7	1-7-4	-0-2-3 WL +4'
WL +3'	-0-2-6	1-4-1	3-0-6	4-1-2	4-7-4	4-10-4	4-11-7	5-0-0	4-11-5	4-10-0	4-2-0	3-9-7	2-9-6	1-3-5	-0-4-0 WL +3'
WL +2'	-0-4-4	1-0-6	2-8-1	3-11-1	4-6-7	4-10-3	4-11-7	5-0-0	4-11-5	4-8-7	4-3-7	3-6-5	2-5-0	1-0-1	-0-5-4 WL +2'
WL +1'	-0-5-6	0-5-7	2-2-0	3-6-7	4-4-5	4-9-3	4-11-3	4-11-2	4-9-7	4-7-0	4-0-6	3-3-0	2-0-5	0-8-0	-0-7-0 WL +1'
LWL	-0-8-6		1-5-3	2-10-6	3-10-5	4-5-1	4-8-3	4-7-3	4-3-2	3-8-0	2-9-1	1-6-2	0-3-2		-0-8-0 LWL
WL -1'		-0-9-4	0-4-0	1-8-4	2-10-0	3-6-4	3-11-6	4-1-0	3-11-0	3-6-1	2-10-1	1-11-0	0-9-1	-0-3-6	WL -1'
WL -2'			-0-8-2	0-5-3	2-1-4	2-7-4	2-7-5	2-7-5	2-3-2	1-7-5	0-10-3	-0-3-0			WL -2'
WL -3'				-0-2-2	0-5-3	0-11-0	1-3-4	1-5-7	1-4-7	1-1-4	0-7-7				WL -3'
Rabbet	0-2-4	0-2-4	0-2-4	0-2-7	0-3-4	0-6-1	0-6-7	0-7-0	0-5-1	0-4-8			0-2-4	0-2-4	0-2-4 Rabbet
WL -4 and Top of Lead					0-2-0	0-4-1	0-5-7	0-6-5	0-6-5	0-4-8					WL -4 and Top of Lead
Face and Keel Bottom	0-1-2	0-0-4	0-1-0	0-2-0	0-1-0	0-2-5	0-4-0	0-4-8	0-4-6	0-2-4	0-1-7	0-1-1	0-1-0	0-0-6	0-1-4 Face and Keel Bottom
Top of Deck at Sides	4-6-0	4-1-6	3-9-3	3-6-5	3-5-6	3-6-0	3-6-7	3-3-4	3-10-2	4-0-6	4-3-5	4-7-2	5-0-0	5-5-5	6-0-0 Top of Deck at Sides
B 1'	+6-11-0	2-1-5	-0-5-4	-1-6-5	-2-4-5	-2-11-2	-3-3-6	-3-5-6	-3-5-2	-3-1-4	-2-7-2	-1-10-7	+1-11-4	+7-8-0	B 1'
B 2'		4-7-0	0-8-2	-0-9-3	-1-7-2	-2-1-4	-2-5-0	-2-7-0	-2-5-4	-2-2-4	-1-8-6	-0-11-2	+0-10-4	+5-0-0	B 2'
B 3'			+2-10-3	+0-1-0	-0-10-7	-1-5-3	-1-9-4	-1-10-6	-1-9-3	-1-5-5	-0-10-4	+0-5-0	+3-6-6	+6-9-0	B 3'
Rabbet	4-11-0	0-4-0	-1-1-4	-2-2-6	-3-4-3	-3-11-2	-3-11-2	-3-11-2	-3-11-2	-3-8-6	-2-8-0	-1-7-0	-0-1-0	6-5-0	Rabbet
Profile and Keel Bottom	4-6-0	0-0-0	-1-2-6	-2-4-0	-5-6-0	-5-4-6	-5-3-5	-5-2-3	-5-1-1	-5-0-0	-3-10-6	-2-9-6	-1-8-4	-0-5-2	6-0-0 Profile and Keel Bottom
D #1				0-4-0	0-11-2	1-4-0	1-7-3	1-8-7	1-6-2	1-1-7	0-7-5				D #1
D #2			1-0-0	1-10-3	2-5-7	2-10-7	3-2-1	3-3-4	3-2-4	3-0-0	2-7-2	2-0-6	1-3-0	0-3-0	D #2
D #3		0-10-0	2-4-3	3-6-7	4-2-0	4-10-0	5-0-7	5-1-5	5-0-3	4-8-4	4-2-0	3-4-4	2-3-3	0-11-6	D #3

Disp. of Lead 20 B.³⁰ or 14,600 lbs. or 37% of D.

½ Disp.

½ Displacement Curve — Full D. = 610.⁰⁰ or 39,000 lbs.

The Lines of the
MARCO POLO.
Design #85

Scale ½=1'.

"*Notes*"

The offsets are given in feet inches and eighths of inches. from the center line and above and below the L.W.L.
The half siding of the Stem and stern post is 2½", details of the same are on a separate drawing ~ The Planking thickness
is 1½" ~ The frame spacing is 16" three to each frame station ~ Wood heel 3¾" thick ~ Crown of main
deck 3¾" in 10', crown of decks at ends various ~ The Lead weighs 14,600 lbs.

the sides or ends. And right here I should like to mention that any one interested in a vessel like the Marco Polo should by all means read the three or four books written by Conor O'Brien, particularly the books *The Small Ocean Going Yacht* and *On Going to Sea in Yachts*. I consider these books the most masterly analysis of seagoing conditions perhaps ever written, and even if he and I do not see eye to eye in all matters pertaining to rig and rigging — well, no progress would be made if we all thought alike; but under no circumstances would I contradict Conor O'Brien for he has had actual experience.

Well, to get back to the Marco Polo — you will notice the center of her displacement is rather farther forward than usual nowadays, and I believe this is very desirable for seaworthiness and steering in a following sea. Her displacement curve, however, is nearly perfect for a yacht of her averaged speed — between five and eight knots.

The Marco Polo will be extremely easy to plank up for there are no sharp bends fore and aft. The top of the lead keel is straight and level the full length, and that is a great help in casting the lead if it is poured into an open mold and also simplifies the setting up and bolting of the frames and floor timbers. The framing of a yacht of this model can and will be very simple.

As said before, the principal object of the design is to produce a yacht that is economical to drive under power, and I believe she will go farther and faster per gallon of fuel than any previously designed ocean cruiser which accommodates four or five people. With a strong steady wind on the quarter and the engine opened wide, she should maintain a speed of ten knots and should occasionally make runs of 240 miles in twenty-four hours, which, of course, can only be done with a long lean hull capable of being driven. On long distance runs of over five knots, and when this is combined with extreme seaworthiness — well, the Marco Polo can visit places seldom visited by yachts, or take unusual routes around the world without worrying about wind currents. Also, and this is very important, she could stay in regions of pleasant weather which the yacht that has to depend on sail cannot always do.

Some people will say the Marco Polo has too much weight of lead for driving under power, but it is believed most people like the feeling of a boat which is absolutely non-capsizable and some weight under a yacht of this size makes her much more comfortable. The weight is not down too low, so if a little sail is carried she will not be uncomfortable; however, she should be able to carry full sail in very strong breezes and be safe to sail at a considerable heel when necessary (as in passing through a squall). If all this can be done with only one man on deck, this weight of lead would seem worthwhile and it will be a great comfort to those below, for on many other ocean cruisers a knock-down is a serious matter and all hands must rush on deck in a half-stupified condition when they are apt to do the wrong thing.

Many people will not like the balanced rudder, but when it is considered that almost all small and medium size naval craft today use them, it is not very radical. When this sort of rudder is properly designed, it will stand as much abuse as a deadwood. On the Marco Polo, as said before, this type of rudder is adopted because it can be swung right around to athwartships or more in laying-to when it will strain itself much less than the usual rudder. Also, there will be nothing to interfere with the efficiency of a center line propeller.

Power Plants

Although some auxiliaries in the past have been called 50-50 boats, we hope and expect the Marco Polo will be better than that. She should really sail well in moderate and heavy weather with her modern scientific sails, spars, and rigging. Under power she should go farther and faster than many straight-power boats, so perhaps it would be safe to call her a 90-90 boat. Any time there is a good steady breeze, the Marco Polo would not be at all dependent on her power plant. After one has gotten used to her, he should be able to sail in and out of most any harbor, come up to wharves, etc. with confidence.

However, a power plant is absolutely necessary for making fast, scheduled, long distance runs and, as we have said before, a power plant does away with the necessity of large, light-weather sails. But if you have paid — say $2,000 — for a power plant, sacrificed some of the best space in the yacht, and have, say, a ton of fuel aboard, you will really want that engine to work, and not maybe! Well, I am going to tell you now there are some engines made today that *will* work, and not maybe. They will start almost positively and run as long as you want them to. Here is what I consider desirable qualities in an engine for a small vessel like the Marco Polo.

1. Weight. On this particular design the engine is so low down and near the fore-and-aft center that weight is an advantage and will act as ballast. This weight will absorb vibration and noise (if the moving parts are light); it will allow water jackets which will not rust through quickly.

2. The number of cylinders affects economy so that in most cases I suggest engines with only four cylinders.

3. An engine that can be throttled down or run continuously at reduced power is necessary when using sail and power together.

4. I would prefer an engine that has a piston speed of less than 1,000 feet per minute, even if this does make the engine larger than is best for good economy.

5. As a general rule, high compression is conducive to economy but takes away from flexibility, long life, and quietness. However, some of the heavy oil engines have either a pre-combustion chamber or spark ignition, which allows reduced compression without greatly affecting economy, and these engines can be built cheaper than a straight diesel, which ignites the fuel from compression alone. Generally speaking, the first cost of the diesel is about twice that of the gasoline engine, the cost of fuel to run the diesel is one-third.

6. On a long distance cruiser, a folding propeller is much

the best arrangement for it will allow the yacht to make better speed under sail in light weather. These propellers, in the sizes suitable for the Marco Polo, cannot be used for reversing so that in some cases I recommend engines without clutch or reverse gear. This will surprise some people, but on a yacht that is to make long voyages, a clutch and reverse gear are so little used that they had far better be left behind. Also, a real sailorman does not need a clutch or reverse gear (as he has never had these things in his sails), and it must be remembered that most of the early motorboats, with two-cycle engines, were direct connected. When the reverse gear and its controls are done away with, there is a great saving in cost, noise, and complication. In all cases, there should be a watertight electric switch at the steering wheel so that the helmsman can instantly and positively stop the engine the second he desires, and with this arrangement he can shoot up to a mooring or wharf as well as under sail. I hope you do not think I am recommending leaving the clutch and reverse gear off yachts used for afternoon sailing, for they use these things often.

Marine engines today are far superior to what we have had in the past and will last much longer, be cleaner, and in some cases it is safe to say the cost of upkeep will be almost negligible. Great improvements have been made of late years in the art of casting, so that today alloy iron and steel castings are made which are truly amazing. Some of the parts of these engines are actually twice as tough and trustworthy as engines of twenty years ago. The machinist has made advances equal to the foundry man, so that some of the parts of these engines are as precisely made as the finest instruments. Many of the working parts are not only exactly the right size but their working surfaces are polished so that they will show no wear if properly lubricated.

As for design, well, when I look at some of today's marine engines, I wonder if most of the brains in this country haven't gone into their design and all that was left over for architecture and politics are the dregs, for not only are we building many more internal combustion engines than any other country, but we are building the best. These engines are so highly perfected that they in themselves allow a long distance cruiser to be practical.

Heretofore, a small cruiser could not maintain a speed of, say, five miles per hour for a thousand miles at a time, but it is expected that the Marco Polo with the proper engine can generally maintain a speed of 240 miles in 24 hours. I believe these reliable, economical engines will create a new type of cruising and perhaps some new types of yachts. If so the sailorman can use the whole world as his cruising ground instead of some quite restricted zones.

CONSTRUCTION SECTIONS

1. Lead keel — 25' 6" long; weight, 14,600 pounds.
2. Wood keel — 3¼" thick or deep — white oak or other hard suitable wood. In three sections as follows:
Fore keel 12' 1" long x 5" wide.
Main keel 26' 9" long x 14" wide.
After keel 14' long x 8" wide.
3. Floor timbers — oak. All 2" thick except the ones on station 16 and 37' 4" which are 2½" thick. The depth of the floors is shown on the construction plan.

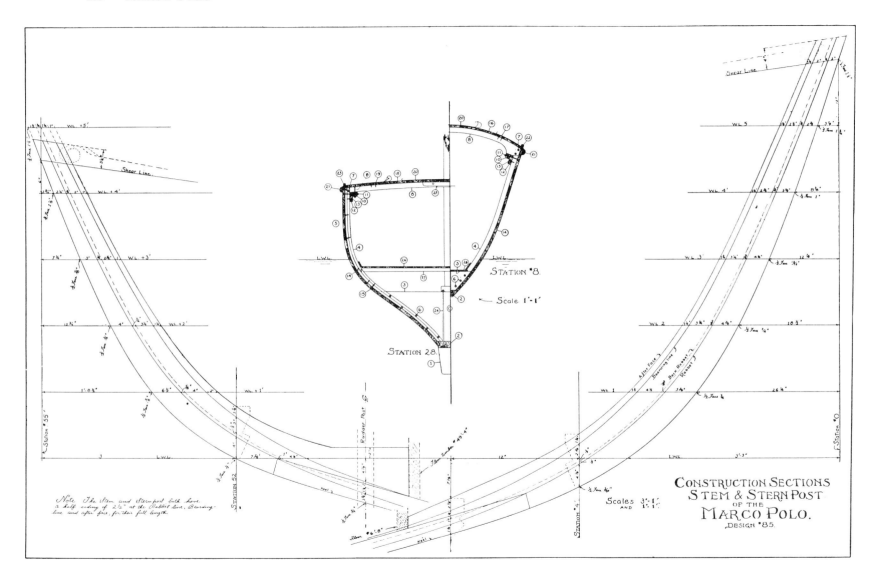

Station #8.

Scale 1'-1'

Station 28.

Station #8.

Note. The Stem and Stern post both have a half siding of 2½" at the Rabbet line. Bearding line and after face, for their full length.

CONSTRUCTION SECTIONS
STEM & STERN POST
OF THE
MARCO POLO.
DESIGN #85.

Scales 3'-1'
AND 1'-1'

4. The frames are all to be of white oak, those from 10' 8" and forward to be sawn and beveled; those from No. 12 to 44 are to be steam bent in two layers, each layer 1¼" x 2". The frames aft of 44 are to be sawn and beveled. All frames when completed are to have a molded dimension of 2½" and sided dimension of 2" for their full length.

5. Flat-head galvanized or bronze screws, 2" No. 14, spaced about 12" to hold layers of frames in line. Heads can be either in or out.

6. Fastenings between frames and floor timbers either 5/16" copper rivets or ⅜" stove bolts; the latter can be either galvanized iron or bronze with washers under nuts.

7. Fastenings between head of frames and deck beams either 5/16" copper rivets or ⅜" stove bolts. The latter can be either galvanized iron or bronze with washers under nuts. Two on each frame head.

8. Deck beams — oak. All deck beams have a molded dimension of 2¾" and are sided as follows:

At the crowned ends {
  regular beams   1⅜"
  strong beams   2"
  extra strong
  beams on 45' 4"   3"
}

On main deck {
  regular beams   1¾"
  strong beams   3"
}

9. Fastenings between deck beams and shelf, 7/16" fin-headed bolts, either galvanized iron or bronze. Washers under nuts.

10. Shelf — fir or hard pine, 2½" x 2½". (Only runs from station 8 to station 44.)

11. Shelf and clamp fastening — 7/16" fin-headed bolts of either galvanized iron or bronze. Washers under nuts.

12. Clamp — fir or hard pine. 5" x 1½".

13. Clamp fastenings — 3½" No. 18 flat-headed wood screws, either galvanized iron or bronze.

14. Planking — 1½" thick. Long leaf yellow pine below the turn of the bilge, and rift grain fir above. However, the planking can be thicker if desired or can be of other suitable woods which may be on hand at the site of building.

15. Planking fastenings — 3" No. 18 Everdur screws under bungs. (Two on each frame.)

16. Decking at ends about ⅞" thick — pine, spruce, or fir. Well dried and best if not much over 3" wide. High grade commercial tongue and groove flooring will do. (Can be thicker if desired.)

17. End deck fastenings — either galvanized boat nails 2" long or galvanized or bronze screws about 2" No. 14. (Two on a beam.)

18. Main deck — 1¼" thick. Fir, cypress, soft pine, or California redwood. Can be square seam, tongue and groove, or ship lap. Planks less than 4" wide, layed straight fore and aft.

19. Main deck fastenings — 2¾" galvanized boat nails or 2½" No. 16 screws, either hot galvanized or bronze.

20. Canvas for both decks — cotton sheeting set in white lead, then painted.

21. Chafing strip — oak, about 3" x 1¾" amidships, tapering to half that size near the ends.

22. Toe rail at ends — oak or other hard wood, tapering from size of chocks to about 1½" x 1½" at small ends.

23. Toe rail on main deck — oak or other hard wood, about 1¼" wide, 1" high. (Can be more if desired.)

24. The floor timber bolts are all Tobin bronze and mostly ⅝" diameter. Nut at both ends under washers. There is a list of keel bolts on the construction plan.

25. All three mast partners are to be oak, about 2½" thick amidship and about 2' 6" long athwartships.

26.   Cabin sole — can be regular commercial ¾″ fir flooring. It is best if it does not extend out to the planking for that will let the air circulate under the floor and reduce rot on the inner side of planking.

27.   Cabin sole beams — can be oak about 2″ x 1¼″.

CONSTRUCTION PLAN

A.   Forepeak has a hatch to port and is the usual entrance to the forward stateroom and the engine room. The forepeak is large for storage and has space enough for a pump water closet for those who are fond of this mechanical contrivance.

B.   Forward double stateroom, with two folding berths similar to pipe berths but of wood. See later detail. This room has a hatch for light and ventilation, transom lockers, and no unnecessary complications.

C.   The engine room with a large enough hatch to hoist out the largest piece of an engine. This room is about 6′ fore and aft, about 9′ athwartships, with full headroom all over. The engine room could be made much shorter for some engines, particularly if twin screws were used, but a large engine room makes a good workshop and a safe retreat away from the ladies. This engine room could have a workbench on one side and a leather covered transom seat on the other.

D.   Two 507-gallon fuel tanks side by side. There are two tanks because on a sailboat this will stop the weight of fuel from running down to leeward. There will be a detail of these tanks later.

E.   Water tanks of 172 gallons each, spaced 12″ apart so that the shaft bearings can be gotten at easily. On twin screw installations, there can be one rectangular tank amidship.

F.   Space for galley, about 4′ fore and aft by 9′ 6″ athwartships. Four windows and about 6′ 3″ headroom over all parts except stove, sink, and dresser.

G.   Combined after stateroom and dining salon, 6′ 3″ fore and aft by about 9′ athwartships, folding table and folding berths. See later detail.

H.   Storeroom under cockpit about 4′ x 9′.

J.   Navigator's room with large chart table to starboard, folding berth to port.

Numbered Description. The numbers lower than 28 were given with the construction section.

28.   Special stem band for attaching the forestay, etc. See detail.

29.   Special cast strap for attaching the mizzen sheet. See detail.

30.   14″ hollow cleat, well secured, for docking lines and to attach removable bowsprit.

31.   45 fathoms of ⅜″ BBB galvanized anchor chain with enlarged end links of 7/16″ wire to take anchor shackle. (Enlarged links both ends so chain can be reversed when worn). The chain can stow under the floor between floor timbers 9′ 4″ and 10′ 8″, and in a chain locker above the floor to starboard. The bitter end of the chain should be well secured to a strong eye bolt as shown so the whole chain can be used without danger of its loss.

32.   Marine Manufacturers & Supply Company's Brunswick windlass, Fig. 1376 for ⅜″ BBB chain. This windlass is to be mounted on a hardwood block of a thickness so that the chain will run to the wildcat clear of the forward deck. There should be a strong oak block under the deck to take the bolts. This block should be thick enough so that the bolt heads can be set in flush, for they will be right where one is apt to bump his head.

33.   The mast steps are to be oak, locust, or other hardwood, all 8″ athwartships, and 3″ or more deep. Beveled on top to

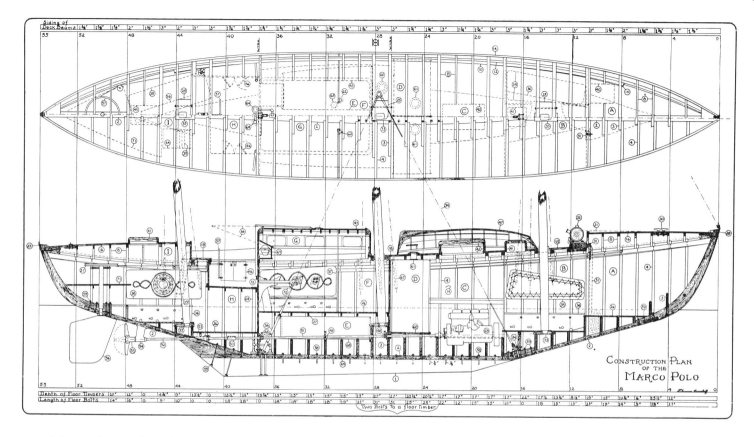

CONSTRUCTION PLAN
OF THE
MARCO POLO

come at right angles to the rake of mast. The rake of foremast is 2°, main 3½°, mizzen 5°.

34. The hoisting slings and hoisting eyes are shown on another drawing.

35. Folding berths, both port and starboard, like pipe berths but of wood with brass corners. See detail.

36. Transom locker seats under all berths; the ones in the deckhouse to have cushions 3″ or 4″ deep. All lockers well ventilated and with thin slats over frames to keep clothes off planking.

37. Folding berths both sides; the one to port may have to be tapered to clear companionway steps. These berths when closed up form backrests for the transom seats below and can have a decorated covering as shown.

38.   In the navigator's room there can be a folding berth on the port side, and the space to starboard is used by a chart table and the companionway ladder (39).

39.   Short removable companionway ladder, landing on starboard transom seat.

40.   Hatchway, 18″ by 24″ inside; hatch cover has hinge on forward side.

41.   Hatch 18″ by 18″ inside, with hinged top: the same to have deck light similar to Wilcox, Crittenden, Fig. 524, 8″.

42.   Hatch, 24″ by 41″ inside. See detail.

43.   Deckhouse, 6′ by 9′ 1″ outside, about 5′ 7″ by 8′ 8″ inside. See detail.

44.   Hatchway, 18″ by 28″ inside with sliding hatch cover.

45.   Skylight, 18″ by 26″ inside. See detail.

46.   Hinged doors to bo'sun's lockers, port and starboard. Hinges, Wilcox, Crittenden Fig. 471, 4″; catches, Fig. 358.

47.   Special tender to fit over hatches so hatches can be opened in rainy weather. The tender will be shown on a later drawing.

48.   Special steady bearings where shaft passes through watertight bulkheads. See detail.

49.   Columbia steady bearing, Fig. 512.

50.   Columbia shaft coupling, Fig. 781.

51.   About 17′ of 1¾″ shaft for larger motors. Can be steel.

52.   Tail shaft about 8′ 6″ long of 1¾″ Tobin bronze, Everdur, or Monel.

53.   Cast bronze stuffing box, special or Columbia, Fig. 175.

54.   Cast bronze strut, special.

55.   A folding propeller like the ones manufactured by the Herreshoff Manufacturing Company of Bristol, R. I., or by The Bergius Company, Ltd., of Dobbie's Loan, Glasgow, or any of the various feathering propellers. The latter is desirable if there is a reverse gear on the engine.

56.   The whole rudder assembly is shown on another drawing.

57.   The steering gear consists of a smooth bronze wheel about 28″ diameter directly connected to a winding drum about 4″ diameter, which has about eight turns of both the port and starboard steering wires. From here the wires pass outboard and aft to a complete circle of channel iron, as shown on the rudder detail drawing.

58.   Lead keel bolts which are on the centerline forward of floor 22′ 8″ and aft of floor 29′ 4″, and shown in full lines, are to be ⅝″ Tobin bronze. The bolts amidships, which are staggered and shown in dotted lines, are to be ¾″ diameter. All of these bolts can be nine inches long and threaded into the lead for five inches. The thread at both ends can be U.S.S.

59.   All bolts through keel, stem, and deadwood ⅝″ Tobin bronze.

60.   Showing position of 5″ water iron for galley stovepipe.

61.   Large filler pipes for the fuel tanks to facilitate sounding and so tanks can be steamed out to remove fuel oil deposits in later years.

62.   Filler pipes for water tanks should rise straight up from the tanks to facilitate sounding. They should be at least 1½″ diameter.

63.   Handhole plate in water tanks.

64.   There are to be two bilge pumps emptying into the cockpit and draining out through scuppers so they can be safely used in a seaway. These pumps can be similar to the Thomas Laughlin Company's Fig. B-4550, 3″ bore, 3′ 6″ stroke. The plunger, plunger rod, and handle are to be arranged to stow inside. One pump is piped to suction strainer in bilge forward of watertight bulkhead 37′ 4″; the other pump drains the after bilge. There can be an engine pump or a hand pump or both for the bilge forward of 26′ 8″.

65.   Ritchie compass, either No. 351, 352, or 340, in a binnacle

box over dining table and thus out of the way on deck.

The lower end of box is removable or can be built like a drawer for correction magnets and the underlit electric light.

66. Angle of vision when in a sitting position. These compasses when in this position are much the best for long watches, for the focus and direction of the eye will not have to be changed as much as with some other arrangements.

67. The chainplates are all alike and shown on a separate drawing. Their position and rake can be taken from drawing.

68. The sheathing under the tanks and at the sides should be some wood like cypress which resists rot. See tank detail.

69. The engine shown is the Lathrop Engineers Model, and it is thought that approximately the same elevation of shaft line could be used with other engines or for single, twin, or triple screw. Note that the floor timbers run up to the heights listed below but are cut down near the centerline for the engine and its bed; this would be different with other engines. The floors are also cut near the centerline aft for the propeller shaft.

70. Folding dining table arranged to be quickly folded up; top about 2' 6" by 4' 6" when extended. The table is a little to starboard of the centerline and shown more plainly on the cabin plan.

71. Large chart table and shelf extending around the after and starboard sides of the navigator's room as shown.

72. Oak panting girder, running athwartships from frame to frame about 1¼" by 3½", just under companionway sill.

DECK AND CABIN PLAN

The cabin plan is not drawn very fancily for it has been shown that the builder can work best from simple plans in taking dimensions. Also a great many people will prefer a different cabin arrangement, all depending on the size and sex of their family, or the type of cruising contemplated. For instance, if one were to do only coastal cruising and would make port every night (and had a large family of children) then he would not need a large, slow-turning engine or large tanks for fuel or water, so that one of the water tanks under the deckhouse could be used as a fuel tank and the engine installed under the cockpit floor. With this arrangement, the space shown for the engine room and tank could be used for a double stateroom and a toilet room.

If desired, there could be stairs or a companionway from the galley to the forward coaming out where the sink is shown on the present plan. The sink could be shifted to under the deck to starboard. With this arrangement the Marco Polo would have remarkably large accommodations for her size or cost and would comfortably sleep seven people. Still one capable man could handle her alone if he had help in cooking and cleaning up. Of course, there are innumerable other cabin arrangements that would be best for various types of cruising by the Marco Polo hull shape, with good head room from one end to the other. She seems to have an unusual amount of room for her cost.

Perhaps you have noticed that I have not shown a toilet or an ice box on the plans, but for coastal cruising both would be very useful and there are several places where they could be located with slight changes in the cabin plan. However, for ocean cruising the cedar bucket has many advantages, principally in saving space and holes through the hull. On a long cruise, nature needs every encouragement and if one can retire to the place of his choosing — bucket in hand — the whole business is simplified. And if by coincidence nature should call all of the crew at the same instant, then if there is a whole nest of buckets all can be accommodated.

As for an ice box (which, of course, is good only for coastal

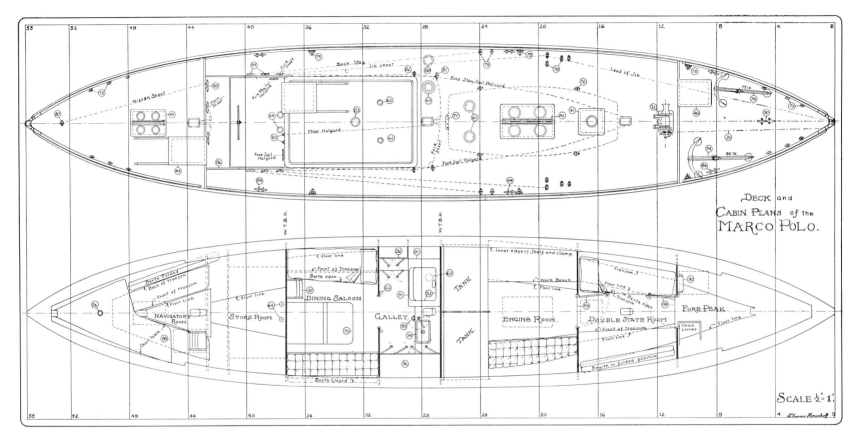

DECK and CABIN PLANS of the MARCO POLO.

Scale ½"=1'.

cruising) the space under the deck to starboard near station 28 could be used, particularly with an ice box that has the ice compartment filled from a hatch on deck by using a rectangular bronze handhole plate with an opening 10″ x 14″. Although I do not like either water closets or ice boxes, I do not want to force my peculiarities on anyone even if I do know that it will save them from much expense and disagreeable drudgery. I should like to impress on the minds of contemplated owners of Marco Polos that extreme simplicity is the only practical way to reduce the cost of a boat of this kind. On many yachts of this size the hull costs 30%, the spars, sails and rig 30%, and the interior 30%. It is very doubtful if saving in cost of the first two mentioned is economical, but, if one sticks to extreme simplicity in the cabin arrangements, he can save several thousand dollars and, strange to say, have the best time in the end for such arrangements are so much easier to take care of. In fact the principal art of cruising is to learn how to take care of yourself easily and quickly so you will have time left over for enjoyment.

As for electricity and electric wiring, my advice is to make it as simple as possible. The lead encased wires are very satisfactory and can be bent in any position and painted without any other covering. However, whatever wiring there is should be heavy enough to take 110 volts, so that when the yacht is alongside a dock or laid up in the winter she can use municipal current. When cruising I should prefer kerosene lamps, which are safe and economical if used properly. For reading charts, etc., nothing is as satisfactory as the proper varieties of battery lights or flashlights.

The folding berths, which are shown on a separate drawing, are the most satisfactory when at sea for they can be triced up to whatever angle is desired. When folded they make a comfortable back to the transom seats and a storage place for clothes behind them. This sort of berth is easily removed so will not interfere with washing or painting the interior.

The following numbers give the description of the parts shown on the drawing:

73. 12 strong flange eyes to take ends of life-rail ropes. Either Merriman Fig. 416, size 2, or Wilcox, Crittenden Fig. 902, size 1.

74. Anchors. There should be altogether four anchors of about the following weights: 100, 90, 75, 40 lbs. The 90 and 75 lb. anchors can be carried on deck as shown, setting in wood blocks secured to the deck and the anchors lashed down to stout flange eyes similar to 72.

The 90 and 75 lb. anchors should have folding stocks as shown, but the 100 and 40 lb. anchors can be either folding or two-piece and carried below deck; the 100 lb. one for a bad chance and the 40 lb. one for kedging off, etc.

The Herreshoff-type anchor is shown for so far this is the only type that combines good holding qualities without having moving parts. It is non-fouling, easy to wash off, and is free of sharp corners, except the bill of the flukes. These anchors are manufactured by the Herreshoff Manufacturing Company, the Merriman Brothers, the George Lawley Corporation, and Nevins of City Island.

If other types of anchors are used, the weight must be increased from 10% to 15% of the previously suggested weight. The anchors can be hoisted aboard or swung out on the jib halyards.

75. Shows the location of the rail sockets, which are shown on another drawing. There are only three rail stanchions on a side, for the wires of the life rail are lashed to the fore, main, and mizzen shrouds.

76. Four lashing eyes to secure tender, similar to Merriman Fig. 416, size 3.

77. Oak block about 12″ x 2″ x 1½″ well fastened to deck to hold tender in place.

78. Showing approximate position of fore staysail sheet leads, Merriman Fig. 422, size 3. There are four on a side so changes in lead can be made. The standing end of sheet is secured with a stopper knot.

79. Showing position of backstay eye plates. The same are described on the rigging list and should be secured with through bolts into oak blocks under deck.

80. 5″ opening deck plate similar to Wilcox, Crittenden Fig. 532, for filling coal bunker.

81. Showing the position of the fore sheet eye plates which are detailed on the rigging plan.

82.   Fair leads for the fore staysail halyard to port and the foresail halyard to starboard. Merriman, Fig. 422, size 4.

83.   Deck plate similar to Wilcox, Crittenden Fig. 432, opening 4″.

84.   Showing the position of the six cleats to secure the forward or running end of boom guys. All six cleats similar to Wilcox, Crittenden Fig. 4020, 10″, and well bolted to oak blocks under deck.

85.   All the cleats in and around the cockpit, of which there are 13, are to be similar to Wilcox, Crittenden Fig. 4020, 8″, well secured.

86.   The cockpit coaming should be of strong wood like oak or mahogany, more than 1⅛″ thick, and particularly well fastened in place for the combined pull of the several cleats may at times be great.

87.   Mizzen sheet eye plate as specified on rigging list.

88.   Swinging door about 5′ 2″ high.

89.   Swing door about 6′ high.

90.   Short companionway steps or ladder.

91.   Coal bunker made of sheet metal running from deck to under stove, either galvanized iron or Monel, about 18 B & S gauge.

92.   Locker for dishes and pans. Upper part running to deck, lower part as desired.

93.   Stove similar to Shipmate No. 1012 with legs removed and securely fastened down to metal top of coal bunker; top of stove about 28″ above galley sole.

94.   Dresser about 28″ high with deep sink similar to Wilcox, Crittenden Fig. 1538, size 2. Make drain large and simple.

95.   Fresh water pump, Wilcox, Crittenden Fig. 810, piped to swinging gooseneck spout to swing over sink or out in front for filling deep vessels, or out of the way against the mast.

96.   Large food compartment from cabin sole to deck with several shelves, each shelf to have high racks at inboard edge to hold heavy canned goods in place.

97.   Companionway steps.

98.   Chart table about 36″ high running around after peak with space for direction finder, etc. Charts can be rolled and stowed in rack overhead aft of station 48 and a very large number can be accommodated.

TANKS

Large tanks on a small vessel are a serious and expensive proposition and perhaps this is why small cruisers of the past have been deficient in tank capacity. If one of the Marco Polos were only to be used for coastal cruising, as I have said before the tank capacity could be very much reduced and one of the two tanks under the deck house used for fuel, thus doing away with the large fuel tanks and thereby reducing the expense and increasing the accommodations. But if one were to make a two months' cruise away from fuel stations (Hudson's Bay, for instance), he would be very glad he had large tanks, and, as a matter of fact, fuel can be bought in lots of a thousand gallons at such a reduction in price that the cost of the large tanks would be absorbed in a few years.

The weight of large tanks is enormous, as the weight increases with the cubic capacity, so the tanks must be very strongly and evenly supported. Otherwise it will be necessary to increase the gauge of the sheet metal of which they are made, for it certainly would be a serious matter if a tank should rupture and let five hundred gallons of fuel into the bilge.

The tanks of the Marco Polo are designed to be supported underneath and at their outboard sides by setting directly on sheathing. In the case of the fuel tanks (which are parallel

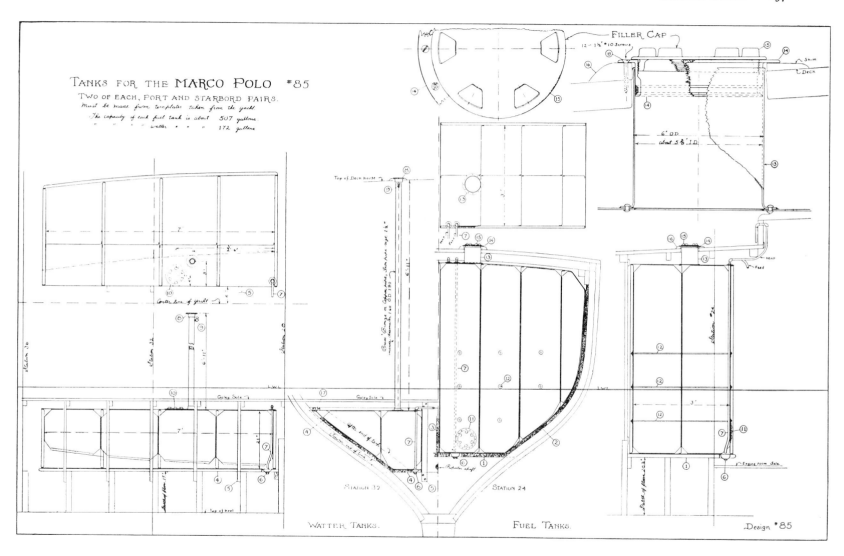

TANKS FOR THE MARCO POLO #85

TWO OF EACH, PORT AND STARBORD PAIRS.

FILLER CAP

WATTER TANKS.   FUEL TANKS.   Design #85

sided), the frames 25′ 4″ and 27′ 8″ will have to be shimmed up to make the sheathing fit the tanks, and templates must be taken from the finished sheathing for making the tanks. After the fuel tanks are slid into place there should be a space between them of an inch or more and this space filled by sliding in planks of a suitable thickness to jam these tanks in place so that they will not move in a seaway or shift if the boat gets knocked down. The sheathing under the fuel tanks should be quite thick, possibly 1½″; at the sides it can be 1″. All of the sheathing for the water tanks can be 1″. While this sheathing should not be one of the hardest woods, still it should be a variety that will resist rot; cypress would be a good choice.

In the case of the fuel tanks, it is best if they can shift slightly, or slide a little way, in case of a collision or if running aground violently for this may save them from rupturing, so it is best if the filler pipe at the top of the tanks is made of thin, soft metal which will give or collapse in case of a shift of the tanks. It is customary on seagoing vessels to have the suction pipes come out of the top of the tank, for then if someone has left a cock or valve open there will be no escape through gravity and less likelihood of leaks, for there will be a suction and not a pressure in the supply lines. But in the case of the fuel line to the engine, this will require a fuel pump and a small gravity tank, all of which is quite customary on modern power plants and desirable, for there is a constant pressure to the carburetor or fuel ejection pump in spite of the level of fuel in the main tank.

As for the material of the tanks, no doubt tin-lined copper of 16 B&S gauge, or slightly less, will be satisfactory for the outside sheets. For the inside diaphragms or swash plates, a lighter gauge, say No. 18, should do, but these plates must be tinned both sides.

For the fuel tanks, either tin-lined copper or Monel metal would be satisfactory, 16 gauge or thicker for the copper and slightly thinner than 16 gauge for Monel. All the outside seams of the fuel tanks must be carefully sweat soldered and riveted. As there are no satisfactory stock filler pipes on the market, we show one with dimensions and the same pattern can be used for the hand hole plates in the water tanks by simply turning off the collar for the packing gland. The filler caps have hexagonal castellated heads, so they can be screwed up with a bar or a stick of wood, thus doing away with the usual keys which are not satisfactory if the cap is to be screwed down hard on a packing. The packing gland on the collar of the filler pipe is to allow the deck to work up and down without straining the tank or allowing gases to escape and will compensate for slight variations in dimensions during building.

1. Sheathing under the fuel tanks about 1¼″ cypress or other durable wood.

2. Sheathing at side of fuel tanks, about 1″.

3. Boards slid in between the two fuel tanks of the thickness required to spread the tanks in place. Boards act as braces for inner tank walls; should be over 1″ thick if possible.

4. Sheathing under and at outside of water tanks about 1″ thick.

5. Braces to hold water tanks in place, oak about 1″ by 2″ securely fastened to each floor timber and cabin sole beam.

6. All tanks are to have a catch basin for sediment under the suction pipe; these depressions are made by hammering the tank bottom down in a suitable shape and then soldering in a nipple for a brass gas plug. Plug in water tanks about ⅜″, fuel tanks about 1″.

7. The suction, or feed pipes, should be fairly large — at least ⅜″ pipe size, particularly the water line to the galley pump. If the suction pipes are soldered or fastened to the tank walls their lower ends will remain central over the catch basin.

8. Torrey Roller Bushing Works, Fig. 145, for iron pipe size

1½". One for each water tank.

9. Small try cock for vents in water tanks.

10. If desired, the hand holes in the water tanks can be the same pattern as fuel tank filler caps but with the flange for packing gland cut off.

11. If one were to keep a Marco Polo for several years, or ever were to shift from fuel oil to gasoline, it would be desirable to have a hand hole plate near the bottom of tank as shown and this can be the same pattern as filler cap with a sleeve for packing gland cut off. This cap would have to be set down bar-tight on top of a packing, and the flange and packing sealed by painting with shellac after it is set down.

12. Stay rods of about 5/16" brass or bronze rod in lower part of fuel tank to prevent forward and after walls from bulging. Nuts on top of good sized washers both ends; the same to be well soldered over.

13. Neck or riser from fuel tank can be made of the same material as tank, and lower end flanged, riveted and sweat soldered in place. The upper end is belled out slightly to take the packing of 14.

14. Cast bronze deck flange of filler cap, to have neck extending down for flax packing to fit tightly in 13 to compensate for changes in angle and heights.

15. Cast bronze filler cap with hexagonal castellated head so cap can be screwed up with a bar or piece of joist.

16. Tapered wood shim to bring filler cap flange nearly parallel with top of tank.

17. Plank between top of water tank and cabin sole beams to prevent tank from shifting in a knockdown.

18. The deck flanges (No. 14) are to be drilled and countersunk for 12 No. 10 screws, but where these flanges are to be used as a hand hole plate in the tanks, then drill for 16 copper rivets about 3/16" diameter (no countersink).

HOISTING GEAR

The hoisting slings and their attachments are cut down to the minimum size that is consistent with safety, for if one should carry this gear on board for several years, weight and size would be objectionable. The ring No. 1 will be quite heavy, but this is necessary for taking various attachments.

In the case of the Marco Polos which are built without the hoisting gear, the floor timbers at station 16 and 37' 4" should have bolts the same as other floors. There also should be a 5/8" bolt through the knee near station No. 16. This bolt can be where the after hoisting bolt is shown.

On the drawing of the slings, regular wire rope splices are shown but if desired the soldered-in wire rope sockets like Wilcox, Crittenden Fig. 340 and Fig. 341 can be used, but the after sling, which passes through the hand hole plate, No. 83, on the deck house, will require a larger hand hole plate. It is also advisable to have these fittings attached by the wire rope manufacturer, or tested, or both.

1. Hand forged steel link of 1½" rod shaped about as shown. If it is larger or more circular it must be larger wire.

2. The after leg of the sling is made of 7/8" diameter galvanized cast steel or plow steel, 6 by 19 wire, or any other wire rope with a breaking strain of over 40,000 pounds. The after leg has heavy wire rope with open thimbles at both ends.

3. The forward leg also is 7/8", 6 by 19 wire, with open thimbles and 1" shackle at its lower end.

4. Metal links on after leg to span propeller shaft and to reach up to a convenient height for attaching to the wire. These links should be of strong metal about 1/4" thick. If they are of phosphor bronze or Monel metal, they will not affect the compass, which is directly above it. If desired the links can be made of two layers (each side) of 1/8" plate. In any case the completed

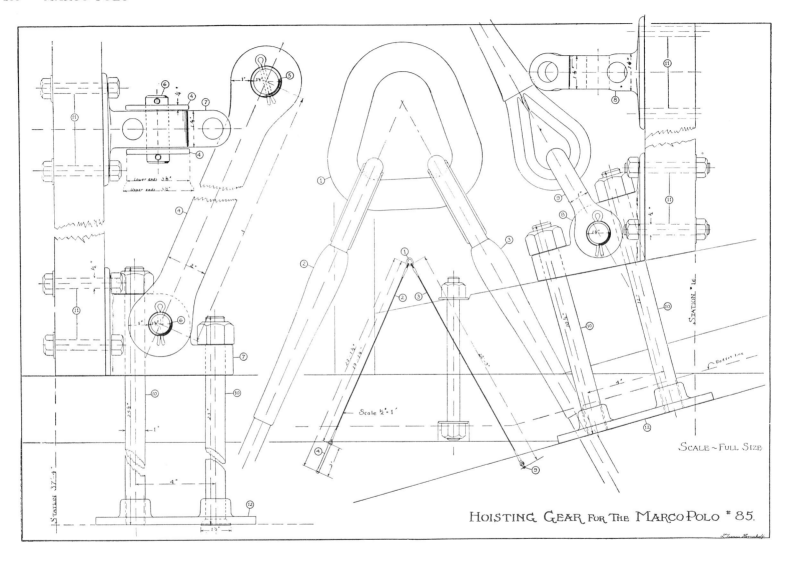

HOISTING GEAR FOR THE MARCO POLO # 85.

SCALE ~ FULL SIZE

link assembly must be good for over 40,000 pounds. Note — the upper and lower ends of the links are different diameters for different size pins.

5. Upper pin 1½″ diameter to support better the open thimble. This pin can be of Tobin bronze, Everdur, or Monel about 3¼″ long with holes for cotter pins spaced about 2¾″.

6. Lower pin same material as upper, but 1⅛″ or more diameter, 3¼″ long, drilled for cotter pins as shown. If the links, No. 4, are steel then the pins can be of steel, in which case they should all be galvanized.

7. Strong bronze casting for attaching after leg, no finish: drilled for bolts and pin.

8. Strong bronze casting for attaching forward leg: no finish. This casting is reduced to 1⅝″ between the bolts to take the shackle, No. 9.

9. One-inch round pin chain shackle (galvanized) like Wilcox, Crittenden Fig. 295. Note: be sure that it is a chain shackle and not an anchor shackle.

10. One-inch diameter Tobin bronze bolts of length shown. These bolts can be threaded both ends or have forged heads as is shown in one case. If threaded it would be well to use the American National Fine Thread Series taps of at least 12 or 14 threads to the inch.

11. One-half inch Everdur, Monel, or strong bronze bolts about 3″ long between nut and head. Washers as shown on wood side. Eight (8) bolts required.

12. Cast bronze sockets, both alike; bottom pad 8″ by 4″ by ⅜″.

This hoisting gear is planned for lifting the Marco Polo when light (on her normal water line or less, when she will weigh less than twenty tons). If she is to be lifted with full tanks or other load this gear should be stronger.

HATCHES

I have tried to make the hatches and skylights of the Marco Polo as simple and watertight as I know how; the corners and edges are rounded off so as not to catch ropes, etc. It has often been said that it is difficult to make skylights which are watertight, but this has been so because the grain of the wood often runs in the wrong direction and causes a difference in shrinking and swelling of the various parts. Also, skylights are often set on top of a deck opening which has been reinforced by carlings or reinforcements under the deck. That is a very bad arrangement, for the stiffness of the side members of the hatchway and the stiffness of the reinforced deck prevent them from springing together to make a watertight seam. The carling is also in the way of fastenings up through the deck.

The hatches and skylights, 40, 41, 42, and 45, are canvas covered with the canvas turned down inside the corner pieces, but the sliding hatch, 44, has the slide made of hard-rolled sheet brass or bronze. I have used this arrangement on some previous designs and it has proved very satisfactory, for the brass does not shrink and swell or cause binding and leaking.

Hatches 40 and 44 are shown narrower than usual, as I personally like narrow hatches and can pass through them easily by twisting the shoulders and hips, but there is no reason why each of these hatches should not be two or three inches wider, particularly for some of the ladies whose fore and aft dimension is nearly as great as their beam, so that they have difficulty with narrow hatches.

The hatch 40 and skylight 42 normally will be under the tender and can be left partly open most of the time in rain or spray. The other deck openings in most cases are over regions of the yacht that can stand a little water or leaks at times. How-

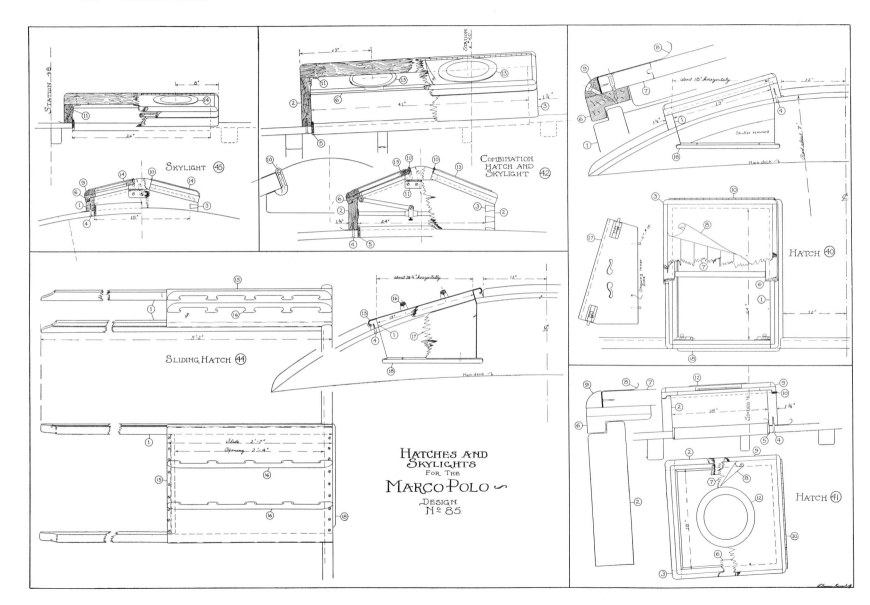

SKYLIGHT 45

COMBINATION HATCH AND SKYLIGHT 42

HATCH 40

SLIDING HATCH 44

HATCHES AND
SKYLIGHTS
FOR THE
MARCO POLO
DESIGN
Nº 85.

HATCH 41

ever, it is well to have good skylight or hatch clamps like Wilcox, Crittenden Fig. 4846 near the corners of skylights, for not only are they conducive to tightness but they make a burglar-proof lock when the yacht is left untended at anchorage, and this is of some importance in foreign ports.

I have not shown clamps on hatches 40 and 44 simply because different people will like different arrangements, but the hatch 40 might have a brass hasp with padlock, and hatch 44 could have a cast brass mortise lock like Rostrand No. 186, or a so-called cylinder-type lock if one can be secured without parts that will rust. The last mentioned lock simply prevents the slide from moving aft, which of course locks the whole opening.

A yacht like the Marco Polo seldom takes green water aboard and if she does she will soon free herself. The conditions are quite different on the heavy, deep pitching vessel which dives into a sea, or on the yacht that has high bulwarks or rails which hold solid water aboard. In these cases the skylight must be nearly as watertight as a manhole on a submarine, but if the hatches and skylights shown on this drawing are built as shown, of reasonably good workmanship, they will not drip or leak objectionably.

The numbered description is as follows:

1. The sills and slides of the hatches 40 and 44, as well as the skylight 45, are $1\frac{1}{2}''$ thick, oak, mahogany, or other suitable wood which does not shrink much and will stand wear.

2. The sills or framing of the hatches and skylights 41 and 42 are $1\frac{3}{4}''$ thick, same material as 1.

3. The joints at the corners of hatches and skylights are to be dovetailed, for if properly fitted this type of joint is the best to stand shrinking and swelling without leaking.

4. Both the hatches and skylights are to be well fastened to the deck with about No. 16 screws or larger, spaced about $3''$.

On hatches 40 and 41 and skylight 42, they can be $3''$ long; on skylight 45, $2\frac{1}{2}''$ long; on hatch 44, $2''$.

5. In all cases there should be a finishing strip about $3\frac{1}{8}''$ by $2''$ around the deck openings to seal the joint at the top of the deck, and the canvas of the deck should be turned up back of the strip. Although these strips are not shown on the drawing with hatches 40 and 44, they should be applied as well in these cases.

6. The upper parts of all skylights and hatches, except 44, are made by using a shallow rabbeted frame whose corners are half lapped together as shown on 41, or mitered if preferred. This piece is $2''$ wide on hatch 40 and skylight 45, and $3''$ wide on hatch 41 and skylight 42.

7. The top surfaces of all hatches and skylights, except 44, are to be $3\frac{}{4}''$ tongue-and-groove sheathing, well dried; or can be laminated wood if preferred, for the top surface is canvas covered and the edges bound.

8. All hatches and skylights, except 44, are canvas covered with light sheathing set in white lead and turned down at the edges and tacked as shown.

9. The exposed edges of the wooden tops are to be bound with a $3\frac{}{4}''$ quarter-round strip of hard wood well fastened with $1\frac{1}{4}''$ No. 8 or No. 9 bronze screws spaced about $3''$; and while you will think some of these hatch parts are light and flimsy, still they are scientifically arranged and, like the spokes of a bicycle wheel, with proper care they may serve better than ones much heavier. These corner pieces should be set in white lead paint, and the seams where the canvas turns down well sealed.

10. Continuous hinge (so called piano hinge) like Perko Fig. 211, size $1''$ when open. For this hinge to be watertight (or stop drips) it is important to have the canvas top covering hang down about $\frac{1}{4}''$ below the hinge as shown on the full size section of 42. This makes the drip go into the drain gutter.

11.   The central section of skylights 42 and 45 is fastened down by brass angle brackets about 1½″ by 1½″ by ¼″. This arrangement is adopted so that the upper part of the skylight can be removed if the hatchway is used in loading or unloading.

12.   Hatch 41 is to have a glass light like Wilcox, Crittenden Fig. 524, size 8; outside diameter of brass frame 11″.

13.   Skylight 42 is to have 4 glass lights like Wilcox, Crittenden Fig. 524, size 8.

14.   Skylight 45 is to have 4 glass lights like Wilcox, Crittenden Fig. 524, size 6, outside diameter 8½″. All of these deck lights to be set over the canvas, and it is well to wrap a thread of cotton caulking around them before inserting them into their holes.

15.   The slide of the hatch 44 can be made of a sheet of semi-hard rolled brass or other nonferrous metal. It should be about 1/16″ thick and the edges flanged over to run in grooves as shown. If the hatch is made the width shown on the drawing the sheet will be about 25″ wide, but wider for wider hatches; the length of the slide is 31″.

16.   Hardwood hand rails on hatch slide made of strong, hard wood, well fastened with screws from underneath. These hand rails are used for opening and closing the slide and act as reinforcements for the slide.

17.   The slides or shutters of hatchways 40 and 44 can be quite simple affairs; they can either be set in slots, as is customary, or be held in place as shown by pins and bolts. The latter arrangement is suggested, as these shutters will usually be stowed below when the yacht is under way and then simple hatchways will be appreciated. These shutters can have ventilating holes when desired, if the holes are bored slanting both outward and downward.

18.   Oak thresholds about 2½″ wide and one or more inches thick, beveled on top to slant outward.

I have given few dimensions on this drawing, for each owner will want to make variations, and the drawings are mostly to give the general scheme of things.

DECKHOUSE

The deckhouse is made as small and low as possible with no exposed sharp corners, but to get the required room on the inside it must be of scientific construction. For that reason a type of window (or porthole) is adopted which does not swing inboard, for ports take up much space when opened. The type of window shown I have used on several yachts with great success. It consists of a plain piece of glass about one-quarter inch thick with beveled edges and rounded corners. This sheet of glass can be lifted right out for washing or polishing, and in warm weather can be removed entirely and stowed in racks made for this purpose between the deck beams, as shown. When this is done the cabin will be very airy, as there will be eight clear openings 9 by 18 inches.

One of the advantages of this type of window is that the opening can easily be adjusted to any width that is desired by simply sliding the pane sideways and clamping it in place. Two types of clamps, or jambs, are shown which are quite foolproof — one kind, which we might call the light weather clamp, consists of a piece of 1/16″ spring bronze so shaped that when the end against the glass is pulled down by the thumb and forefinger it can be swung around, releasing the glass. The other clamps are simply wooden plugs of a certain size which jamb up into holes in the corner piece above. These plugs might be called heavy weather fastenings, and you can have as many as desired, but it is thought one in the middle of each upper edge will be sufficient.

Of course the secret of success of this type of window is the

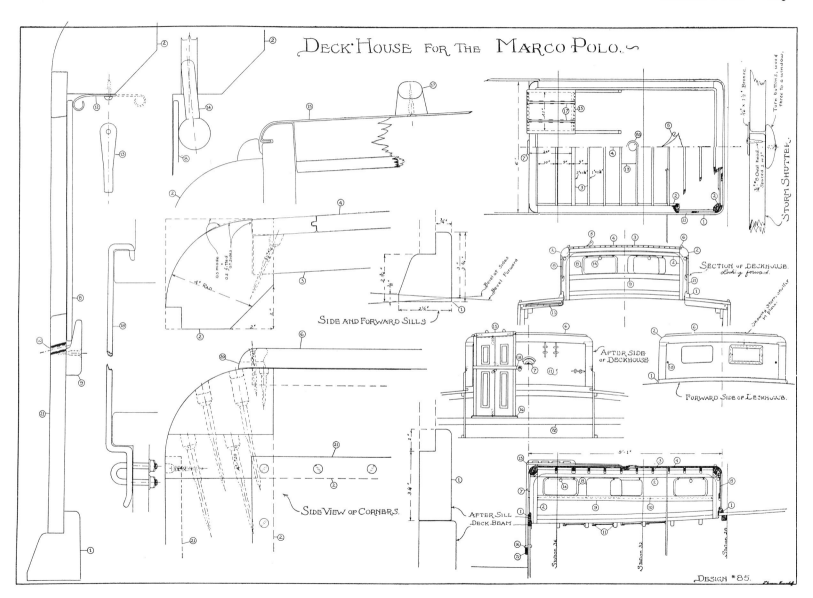

DECK·HOUSE FOR THE MARCO POLO.

STORM SHUTTER.

SECTION OF DECKHOUSE.
Looking forward.

SIDE AND FORWARD SILLS

AFTER SIDE OF DECKHOUSE

FORWARD SIDE OF DECKHOUSE.

SIDE VIEW OF CORNERS.

AFTER SILL
DECK BEAM

DESIGN #85.

gutter in which it runs, for this catches all the leaks and drips, and drains outboard, so there must be good scupper holes as shown through the deckhouse sides.

If cast bronze marine windows or portholes are to be used, the eight of them together would weigh about 240 pounds.

I have tried to find suitable places to use laminated wood on the Marco Polo, as that material is so much in vogue at present, so the four panels of the deckhouse are made of it and, because all of the edges are covered or rabbeted in, it should be entirely satisfactory, but the exposed edges at the window openings should be kept well varnished or painted. However, if the gutters drain well, all these panels should be dry much of the time, for they are set on sills which raise them above the decking.

The companionway or cabin doors are quite a problem, as most of the time they will be carried unshipped, so I have shown two narrow paneled ones only about 10½″ wide apiece, so that they can be stowed easily in some place like the navigator's room — perhaps slid into racks under the chart table. The hinges should be the unhanging type like those designed for the H 28, or the so-called loose-butt type. There can be flush bolts like Perko Fig. 1052 on one door, and wooden turnbuttons on both doors as shown. This will give the ladies privacy, when wanted, even better than the usual latch and key arrangement, but to lock the doors securely when leaving the ship, perhaps a heavy metal bar (preferably nonmagnetic) and padlock, as shown, is the best.

The numbered description will make the rest of the construction clear.

1. The house sills can be teak, oak, or other wood not inclined to rot. The side and forward sills are 2½″ wide, the after one about 1½″. If the house is built separately in the shop, the sills can be fastened with screws up through the decking. If the house is built in place, the sills can be fastened from either above or below. The forward corners can be mitered and the after corners (which are square on the outside) mortised.

2. The four upper edges of the deckhouse, as well as the four corner posts, are the same section and size and can be made of mahogany or any other fine grain wood which does not shrink much. The corners are halved together, as shown on the full size view, and set square on top of the corner posts. Between the corners, the inner edges are beveled off as shown on the full size section which shows the mortising of the end of the deck beams.

3. The deck beams should be white oak 1 by 1¾″ with the exception of the one at the hatchway, which is 2 by 1¾″. The crown is the same as the main deck, ⅜″ to the foot.

4. The house decking can be ¾″ thick cedar, pine or redwood made up of tongue-and-groove strips not over 3″ wide. It must be well-dried stock.

5. Canvas cover for deck made of soft woven cotton sheeting set in white lead paint.

6. Finish strip around border of canvas over the rabbet. This piece should be of the same material as the rest of the deck trim on the yacht if it is to be varnished, and so shaped to form a grab rail ⅞″ high and 1¼″ wide (like full-size section) and well fastened down.

7. Peep hole for compass should have drain rim over.

8. Windows of about ¼″ plate or nonshatterable glass, edges beveled and corners rounded. Size 11 by 20″. Make eight. This type of window has the great advantage that if broken it can be replaced by a spare one in a few seconds, while the bronze-framed window generally has to be sent back to the factory. The window openings can be closed by a storm shutter if desired. This can be made of laminated wood of the same thickness as the deckhouse side and held in place by bronze flanges on the outside and wooden turnbuttons inside as shown. On a long trip it would be well to have three or four storm sashes and three or

four spare windows. However, it is not likely that the Marco Polo will ship a heavy sea in the region of the deckhouse, for if she acts like the whaleboats and lifeboats which she resembles, the seas will seldom slop over her rail.

9. Gutters for windows to slide in to be made of mahogany or other fine grain wood fastened to house sides with 1¼″ No. 10 screws spaced about 3 or 4″.

10. Drain holes for gutters about four on a side and two forward. Made by screwing a section of threaded pipe into the wood. Inside diameter of pipe ¼″ or more.

11. Racks to hold windows when removed.

12. Bronze spring clips to hold windows in place. The dotted line shows position of same when swung in for removing windows. These clips should be secured with ¾″ or 1″ No. 10 round-headed screws. To release the window, the clip is grasped between the thumb and forefinger and sprung down and swung sideways.

13. Showing the shape of the window clips before bending. They should be made of 1/16″ thick hard-rolled phosphor bronze or spring brass, and may have to be rebent slightly to get the proper adjustment.

14. The heavy weather window fastenings are simply wooden plugs of a certain shape pushed up into holes in the house frame over the window. One to a window should be sufficient, but more can be used if desired. The hole should be ¾″ and the neck of the plug ⅝″. Be sure the end of the plug is well rounded.

15. The house slide can be of 1/16″ thick hard-rolled brass or stiff phosphor bronze flanged over to run in grooves about as shown. The sheet should be about 26″ wide before flanging and 27″ long. The wooden crosspiece at its forward edge can be 1″ thick and 1½″ deep. The after crosspiece 1½″ by 2½″ rabbeted for the door.

16. Hardwood sill with about ¼″ rabbet for the door. It would be well if the tread were brass lined. The sill sits on top of the panting girder (72) which takes the place of the deck beam that is cut for the companionway.

17. Hand rails on top of slide of strong wood well fastened up from underneath, as shown. These pieces, together with the crosspieces, hold the slide flat and straight.

18. Metal bar about ¼ by 1½″ for locking companionway doors. One end sets into notch in door frame; other end fits over staple made of ¼″ or larger wire with nuts on inside of cabin. If this assembly is made of bronze or Monel metal, it will not affect the compass. However, it is very doubtful if it would ever be in place when the compass is being used.

19. Oak reinforcing block about 1″ thick secured to deck beams for holding No. 83 securely.

20. Cut two or three scuppers ¼″ by ½″ in side grab rails.

21. The four panels for making the faces of the deckhouse can be made of ¾″ thick waterproof plywood. The edges should be well painted before setting in place.

I have purposely avoided giving many dimensions, so that the builder may make variations. However, where dimensions are wanted they can be scaled off the drawing.

RUDDER AND STEERING GEAR

The rudder is designed so that it can be made with the usual equipment in a yacht yard, yet it is strong enough for the strains of laying to a sea anchor, etc. While a solid cast-bronze rudder would have been much easier to design, still the amount of bronze in it would have weighed perhaps three or four times as much. The largest casting in this rudder is only 28″ long and can be machined in almost any lathe that can swing 12″. The

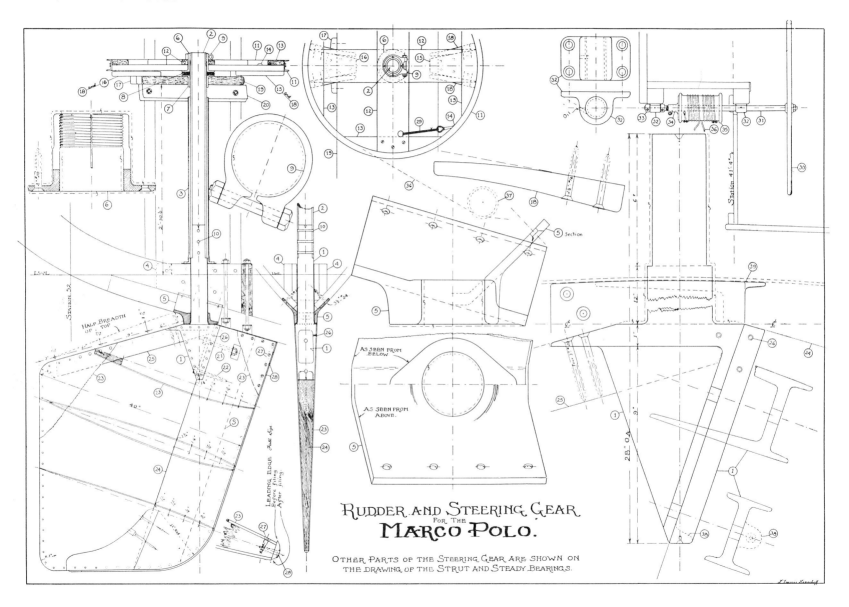

RUDDER AND STEERING GEAR
FOR THE
MARCO POLO.

OTHER PARTS OF THE STEERING GEAR ARE SHOWN ON
THE DRAWING OF THE STRUT AND STEADY BEARINGS.

principal strength in this rudder is in the ⅛″ side plates which must be carefully fastened to the rudder stock with about seventeen tapped-in Everdur flat-headed machine screws on a side.

The rudder stock goes up through the keel and sternpost neat without any lining, and this is done so as not to cut the sternpost more than necessary. If the work is done well, it will not leak and the proximity of the bronze parts will exclude worms. If kerosene is poured occasionally into the rudder port above, it will discourage rot.

The upper part of the rudder stock is a tube of ¼″ wall thickness which should be shrunk on the lower casting by having the male part exactly the same size as the female part, or possibly one-thousandth of an inch bigger. If the lower casting is chilled on some snow and ice in the winter and the tube stuck in a can of boiling water they should drive together easily, particularly if there is some oil on the casting. But the work must be done quickly!

The upper end of the tube is secured to the steering circle by a threaded split gland which will allow adjustment both axially and radially.

One of the peculiarities of this rudder and steering gear is that the rudder can swing about three hundred degrees, which is done to cut down the lateral resistance aft when laying-to in a seaway. This calls for the entire steering gear to be different from the usual type. There are spring stops on the steering circle to prevent the rudder from swinging around far enough to hit the propeller.

It is expected that this balanced rudder will swing very easily, so the steering wheel is not geared very low. One complete turn of the wheel will swing the rudder about 45 degrees, so the Marco Polo should answer her helm quickly, which is a great aid in steering to a compass and quite different from some other ocean cruisers.

It is thought that the numbered description will make all other parts clear. I have refrained from giving many dimensions so that the builder can make variations, and the drawings are mostly to give the scheme of things and, being to scale, the builder can take what dimensions are required.

1. Lower end of rudder stock — cast strong bronze or cast Monel metal. The finished diameter of the rudder stock should be the same as the diameter of the nearest 3″ O.D. tube that can be obtained which has approximately a ¼″ wall. Machine and finish where shown.

2. The upper end of rudder stock should be a strong tube of Tobin bronze, Everdur, phosphor bronze, or Monel metal, preferably hand drawn of about 3″ O.D. and about ¼″ wall thickness. This tube may have to be ordered special, but, if four or five are ordered at once, the cost will not be much more than stock size tube. The overall length of this tube is 37″, upper end threaded for 2½″ to fit No. 6.

3. The rudder port can be a copper tube of about 3½″ I.D. and from 1/16 to ⅛″ wall thickness, the lower end to be sweat soldered to a cast bronze flange set on a packing and fastened with six or eight screws. This flange can be cast from the same pattern as No. 6 but shortened up in machining.

4. There should be oak reinforcements on each side of the sternpost about 1½″ thick and 16″ long, crossbolted with about five ½″ bolts. It would be best if these reinforcements were put on before the yacht was planked.

5. Lower rudder bearing of cast bronze; the only finish is in bore and on lower surface. This fitting is set in flush so as to stay in place best. Perhaps the pattern should be made from measurements taken from the hull.

6. Threaded split gland of cast bronze for securing steering circle to upper end of rudder stock. The threaded section can have eight or more threads to the inch and should be a nice run-

ning fit on No. 2 after machining. This gland is to have four saw cuts as shown and the flange is to be drilled and countersunk for eight 2″ No. 20 screws. Machine and finish all over.

7.   Cast bronze steady bearing for upper end of rudder stock. Can be cast from the same pattern as No. 6 but shortened up to about 2¼″ long in machining. This bearing simply fits in a hole in No. 19 without fastenings.

8.   Oil-saturated hardwood disk about ½″ thick for thrust bearing.

9.   Cast bronze split clamp ring, 1″ thick to contract No. 6 with ½″ Everdur bolt and nut.

10.   Three ⅜″ inch bronze rivets to lock Nos. 1 and 2.

11.   Brass channel for steering ropes on rim of steering circle made of architectural bronze channel, 1″ by 2″ by 1″, bent to true circle and fastened to Nos. 12 and 13 with flat-headed bronze screws, size about 1″ No. 12.

12.   Steering circle crosspieces of oak, 1 by 6 by 32″, one above the other.

13.   Steering circle sectors of oak, 1 by 3 by 18½″, two up and two down.

14.   Two oval holes through No. 11 to take eye splice of steering ropes.

15.   Rudder stop, a 20-degree (or more) sector of oak, 13/16″ thick, 9″ long, 6″ wide at big end. This rudder stop must be screwed in place after the steering circle has been screwed down and adjusted.

16.   Stationary rudder stop, same as No. 15.

17.   Reinforcement to stationary rudder stop; oak, 1½″ by 2 by 10″. Make one.

18.   Rudder stop springs of oak, 13/16 by 1¼ by 9″. See full size detail. Make four.

19.   Athwartships brace for rudder stock; oak, 1½ by 19″ by about 4′, to be notched for frames and extend out to planking.

Note: this brace extends 8½″ forward of centerline of rudder and 10½″ aft.

20.   Oak cleats to support No. 19 about 1½ by 3 by 21″, well fastened to the frames and No. 19. The top of these cleats should be beveled to a level 2′ 10½″ above the waterline so the top of No. 19 will be exactly 3′ above waterline.

21.   Everdur or Monel bolt, ⅝″ by about 6″, nut on washer.

22.   Everdur or Monel lag screw, ⅝″ by 6″.

23.   Half-hard brass or bronze sheets about ⅛″ thick by 40″ wide by about 51½″ long. If these side pieces are made of cold-rolled Monel metal, they can be as thin as No. 12 gauge, or .109″; but No. 11 gauge, .125″, would be better. If the wood filler blocks, Nos. 24 and 25, are properly shaped, these side pieces will bend into shape easily. If it is impossible to obtain sheets wider than 36″, then the seam can run where the dotted line S is shown, and each edge fastened down like the forward edge of plates. The forward edge and part of the upper and lower edges are fastened down with flat-headed wood screws ¾″, No. 10, while the trailing edge and part of the top and bottom are joined with copper rivets of about 3/16″ diameter.

24.   Oak filler block, 3¾″ thick at top with straight taper to ⅝″ thick at bottom by 12″ by 47¼″. This piece should be carefully fitted to No. 1. The knee at the lower end of this piece can be of oak and is about 1⅝″ thick at its upper part tapering to ⅝″ at lower forward corner, and only about ⅛″ thick at after lower corner. See offsets on drawing of halfbreadths of No. 24. The forward and lower edge of No. 24 is ⅝″ thick the full length.

25.   Top filler block, oak 3″ deep, 3⅞″ wide and 2′ 5½″ long, beveled so the lower side is slightly wider. Forward end driven tight into No. 1.

26.   Everdur or Monel metal flat-headed machine screws, size ¼″ No. 20, ⅜″ long, spaced about 1½″.

27.   ¾″ No. 10 flathead wood screws spaced about 2″, but screws on opposite side must be spaced to clear.

28.   Half-oval brass rod, 1 by ¼″, to be filed down flush as shown in full size section in lower part of drawing; fastened with 1″ No. 10 flat-head screws spaced about 2″.

29.   Seizing wire for adjusting tightness of steering ropes.

30.   Cast bronze steering wheel about 32″ diameter, rim ⅞″ with six spokes. (Possibly Columbia Bronze Corporation has a suitable pattern.) On this type of yacht it is best not to have handles on the steering wheel.

31.   1″ diameter Tobin bronze shaft, 2′ 4″ long overall; after end reduced to ⅞″ for about 4″, then a 1″ No. 12 thread cut for 2″.

32.   Cast bronze bearings, one bored 1″, one bored ⅞″, fastened with four 1½″ No. 16 flat-head wood screws.

33.   Brass or bronze collars about ¾″ long, 1½″ O.D., ⅞″ I.D. with flush steel lock screws.

34.   Cast bronze barrel attachment. See drawing of strut and steady bearing for details.

35.   Wooden steering rope drum, 4½″ diameter. See drawing of strut and steady bearing for detail.

36.   Steering ropes of 3/16″ diameter, Korodless 6 by 19 wire. Length required for both ropes together, including splices, about 60′.

37.   Steering rope sheaves. See drawing of strut and steady bearing.

38.   Welt cast on end of No. 1 to serve as a center when machining the rudder stock. This welt is to be sawed and chiseled off after machining is completed.

39.   Halfbreadth of top of No. 1.

STRUT AND STEADY BEARINGS

1.   Propeller shaft strut of cast strong bronze. Take length and angles from this drawing, or the yacht.

2.   Cutless rubber bearing, special length. Shaft size 1¾″; bore of strut 2⅜″; length 9″.

3.   Two ¾″ diameter bronze bolts tapped in to strut.

4.   Eight 3″ No. 24 Everdur wood screws.

5.   Typical section of strut.

6.   Combination steady bearing and bulkhead stopwater. Make two of cast bronze with babbitt bearing.

7.   Wood shim to make up difference between shaft line and floor timbers.

8.   Four ½″ bronze bolts through floors, or if preferred lag screws or hanger bolts.

9.   ½″ bolts tapped in to lower half bearing.

10.   Large grease cups like Lunkenheimer Fig. 1030 No. 0. Order four, one for stuffing box, and one for each of the steady bearings.

The following numbers correspond to numbers shown on the drawing of rudder and steering gear.

31.   Shaft for steering wheel, Tobin bronze, forward end machined to fit steering wheel; after end reduced to ¾″ diameter and threaded as shown with 1″ No. 12 N.S. thread.

33.   Adjustable collars with ¾″ hole to fit after end of No. 31. Make two of either bronze or steel.

34.   Cast bronze device for attaching the steering rope drum No. 35 to No. 31. After end threaded to fit on threaded section of No. 31 and then split as shown with a saw. This split nut part to be closed with a ⅜″ cap screw, either bronze or steel.

35.   Hardwood steering rope drum to fit snugly on No. 31.

35A.   Clips to secure the ends of steering ropes.

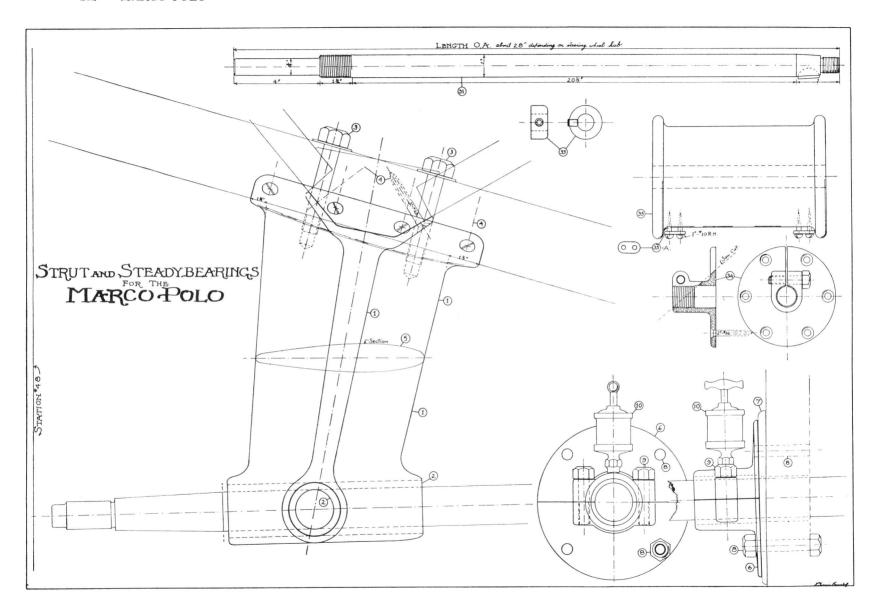

STRUT AND STEADY BEARINGS
FOR THE
MARCO POLO

The strut is designed as neat as on a racer, for reducing resistance is just as important in increasing cruising radius as it is in increasing speed. The type of steady bearing shown will be satisfactory for r.p.m.'s of less than 1,000, but the bearing must have good clearance and run easily. The grease cups should be screwed down a little for each twelve hours of running and it may be well to have a small wooden box or can under the bearings to catch the grease. Also, the floor above these bearings must be arranged to lift up to get at the grease cups, and this must be borne in mind in any galley arrangement.

STEM AND STERN BANDS, CHOCKS, AND CHAINPLATES

1.   The stem band can be of Tobin bronze or phosphor bronze, 3/16″ thick or more, 3¾″ wide, and 24⅛″ long; tapered and beveled as shown, or to fit the stem. Secure with five 3″ No. 24 Everdur flat-head wood screws.

2.   Reinforcement to stem band making shackle for forestay. Same material as stem band and 3/16″ by 2″ by 7⅝″. Fastened to stem band with three 5/16″ bronze rivets, as shown.

3.   The stem band below No. 2 can be Tobin bronze or cast bronze. If the latter, it can be thicker fore and aft at near the waterline. It would be well if this section of the stem band ran down to or beyond the scarph between the stem and fore keel.

4.   Pin for forestay ⅝″ diameter, head about ⅞″, length O.A. about 1¾″. The holes for this pin should be drilled and reamed to 11/16″ after the bands are bent.

5.   Merriman turnbuckle, size ½″; drill hole 17/32″.

6.   Stern band of cast strong bronze with eye at upper end to take shackle of mizzen sheet block; thickness about as shown. No finish.

7.   Bow chocks of cast bronze, about 2″ thick. Port and starboard patterns made to fit crown of deck, etc. The after end well fastened with 5″ No. 24 Everdur screws. The chocks can be finished all over or only made smooth where the anchor warp plays. However, the pattern-maker need not allow for finish or machining in the size of the pattern.

8.   ½″ through-rivet of bronze, well riveted into each chock, for this is the principal attachment of the chocks.

9.   Stern chocks of cast bronze about 1¾″ thick, forward ends fastened down with one 4″ No. 24 Everdur screw; otherwise similar to No. 7.

10.   The chainplates are made of layers of 1/16″ thick sheet, either phosphor bronze, Tobin, or Everdur. They should be either hard or half hard. All of the strips are 1¾″ wide. All 18 chainplates are alike and a list of the layers is as follows:

11.   18 strips 1/16″ by 1¾″ by 12″.

12.   18 strips 1/16″ by 1¾″ by 18″.

13.   18 strips 1/16″ by 1¾″ by 24″.

14.   18 strips 1/16″ by 1¾″ by 30″.

15.   It will be best if the 15/16″ hole at the upper end is not drilled and reamed until the chainplates are fastened to the hull and the upper ends bent inward to correspond to the lead of the lower shrouds.

16.   Everdur stove bolts through chafing strip ⅜″ by 3½″. It would be best if the holes for these upper bolts are not drilled until the chainplates are in place.

17.   Everdur stove bolts ⅜″ by 2½″, countersunk heads.

18.   Everdur stove bolts ⅜″ by 2¼″, countersunk heads.

The chainplates are made of layers for the following reasons:

A.   They will stand bending at the upper ends best.

B.   Thin-rolled sheet metal is stronger for its size than thicker pieces.

C.   By having the chainplates in layers they can be tapered,

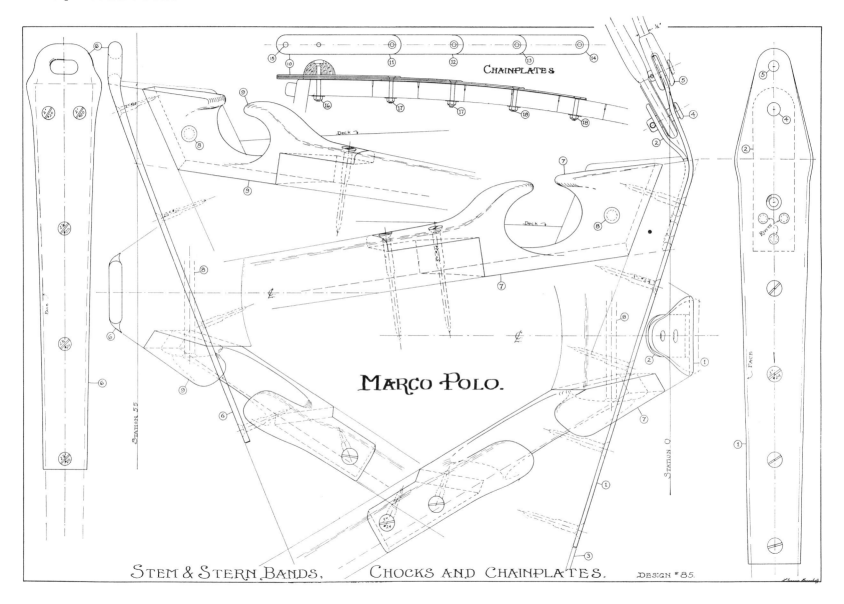

CHAINPLATES

Deck

Deck

MARCO POLO.

STEM & STERN BANDS,   CHOCKS AND CHAINPLATES.   DESIGN #85.

thus saving much weight and the cost of material.

The chainplates are outboard, so there is less damage of leaks through the deck.

BERTHS AND TABLE

The berths are made of wood because some are wider at the head than at the foot and because it is easier to secure the upholstery covering over wood. This can simply be turned over the edges and tacked on, as shown. A berth of this kind has all the good features of a pipe berth; it can easily be removed, triced up, or let down to whatever angle is required.

1. Side and end pieces of berths made of oak or other strong wood, 2″ by 1½″, shaped about as shown.

2. Jackstay of oak or strong wood, 1 by ¾″, cut out as shown for berths' bottom lacings. The jackstay should be secured about every 6″ with 2″ No. 12 flat-head Everdur screws.

3. Corner reinforcements of 1/16″ thick hard phosphor bronze or thicker weaker metal. Fastened with 1″ No. 10 screws. If the screws are spaced about as shown on the full-size detail they will come on different end grain and be less apt to split the wood parts.

4. Seizing wire lacing for berth bottom.

5. Berth bottoms of heavy canvas; grommet holes only about 3″ apart.

6. Fancy covering for bottom tacked on around edges.

7. Mattress about 3″ thick if of curled hair, but thicker if of less desirable material. Must be made special to fit taper of berth frames.

8. Special pintles or hinge pins for outboard corners of berths. Made of ¾″ bronze rod which has been forged down to ⅜″ thick after ¼″ groove has been turned in outer ends. Fastened with 2″ No. 14 screws (make 10). Can be cast, if preferred.

9. Berth hooks of ⅛″ thick sheet brass or bronze fastened to wood cleat with three round-headed No. 12 screws (make 10). The wooden cleats shaped as required to fit the frames, planking, or bulkheads.

10. Berth rope attachments or clips made of ⅛″ thick brass or bronze, 2½″ by 2½″, with ½″ slot as shown. Exposed corners and edges well rounded. If these clips are made and bent as shown, they will be quick and easy to use (make 10).

11. Berth ropes of 1¾″ circumference, 9/16″ diameter, cotton rope with thick seizings of marline sewed on as a sailorman whips the end of a rope. These seizings should be about 2″ apart with about four on each rope. The upper end of berth rope should terminate in a plain hook like Wilcox, Crittenden Fig. 227, ½″. The rope should not be spliced in but turned over and seized for later adjustment after stretching. The hook should be screwed to an eye bolt or pad eye which does not extend below the deck beams, or is not in a place which can be hit by a person's head.

12. Folding table of hard or semi-hard wood. The stationary part to have permanent built-in racks about 2½″ high and 1″ thick, well secured for a hand hold in rough weather. The table top is about 2′ 9″ wide and 4′ 6″ when open, or 2′ 6″ when folded, and about 1″ thick. The table is mounted off center as shown to give space for the companionway ladder and should be mounted on strong knees well secured to the bulkhead, for when the table is open there may be quite a strain on it at times. The table is without legs to facilitate mopping the cabin sole and to give a clear space for rigging the hoisting slings, etc.

13. Strong knees about 1¾″ thick by 18 by 18″, spaced about 1′ 11¼″ center to center, and secured as shown to the after bulkhead with 3″ by ⅜″ lag screws. Washers under heads.

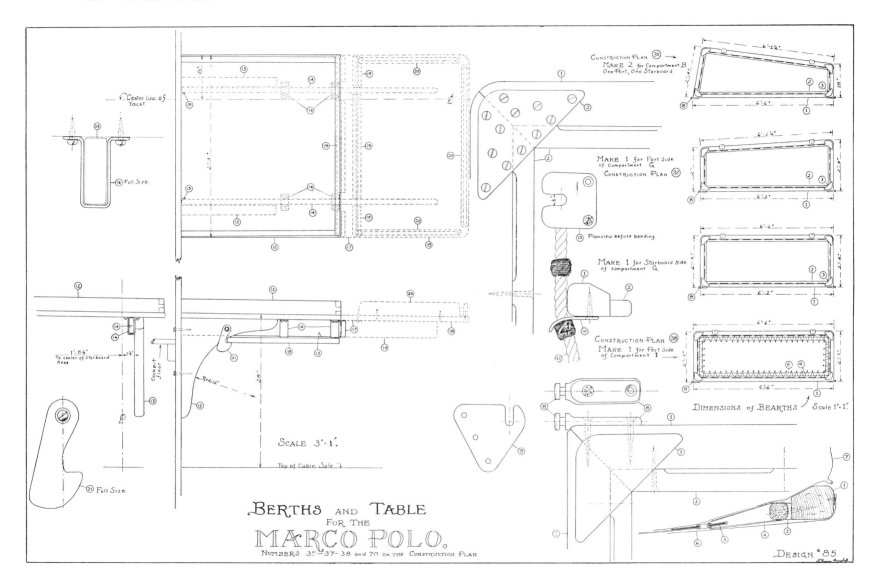

Center line of Yacht

Full Size.

Construction Plan 35 →
MAKE 2 for Compartment B
One Port, One Starboard

MAKE 1 for Port Side of Compartment G
Construction Plan 37

Planview before bending.

MAKE 1 for Starboard Side of compartment G

Construction Plan 38
MAKE 1 for Port Side of Compartment 1 →

DIMENSIONS of BEARTHS   Scale 1'-1'.

To center of Starboard Knee

Cockpit Floor

Top of Cabin Sole

SCALE 3'-1'.

Full Size.

BERTHS AND TABLE
FOR THE
MARCO POLO.
NUMBERS 35-37-38 and 70 on the Construction Plan

DESIGN #85

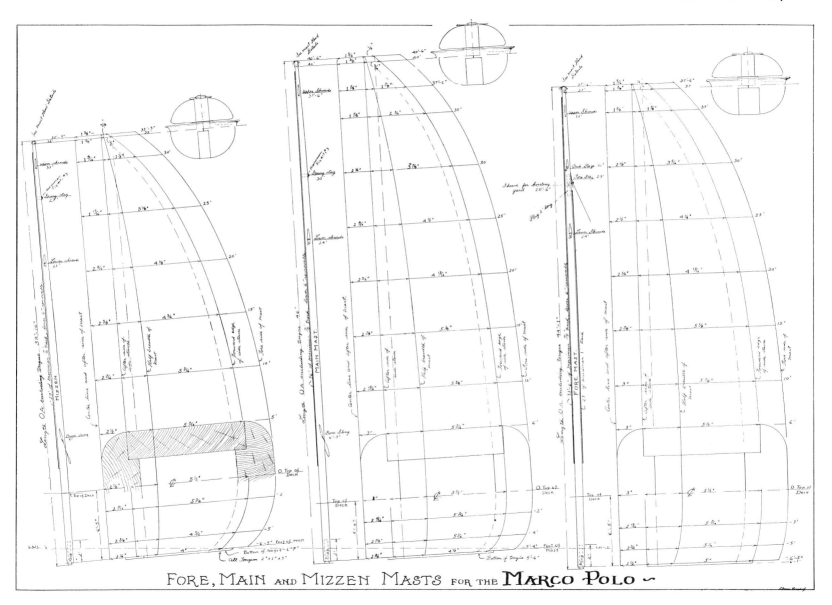

FORE, MAIN AND MIZZEN MASTS FOR THE MARCO POLO ~

14. Slides to support folding leaf of table. Oak 1″ by 3″ by 2′ 5½″.

15. Screw in end of slides for stop.

16. Four strips of brass, ⅛ by 1½ by 9″ so folded to make supports for fourteen, and each secured with four 1″ No. 14 round-head screws.

17. Short leaf of table, 1″ by 3″ by 2′ 9″.

18. Long leaf of table, 1″ by 1′ 9″ by 2′ 9″.

19. Piano hinges about 1½″ wide when open in lengths as follows: two, 4½″; one, 1′ 5″; two, 5½″; one, 1′ 7″.

20. Removable racks of hardwood.

21. Hardwood hook about ½″ thick to hold folded leaf in place. One only on starboard side. Hung on 1½″ No. 14 round-head screw.

MASTS

The masts of the Marco Polo may be of rift-grain fir of fine texture or any of the spruces, even Oregon pine. All of the side staves of the masts are 1¼″ thick, and all of the forward and after staves, except the one on the fore side of the foremast, are 1¾″. The forward stave of the foremast is 2″ thick to give a strong attachment for the track on which the squaresail and its yard are hoisted.

A mast of this section is very easy to glue up if a proper frame has been made to hold the after side of the mast straight and keep it from twisting. The rabbet in the forward and after staves makes the gluing operation simple; this rabbet should first be sawed out and then planed up with a rabbet plane.

These spars will require no plugs or reinforcements other than the plugs at their foot and at the sheave for the yard on the foremast. This latter plug should be about 24″ long. The radius of all corners full length is 1¼″. The foot of all masts is at 90 degrees from the after side of mast. The tongues are all 5″ long and 2″ wide and deep.

It would be a good plan if all masts were stepped with one or two degrees more rake than shown on the sail plan or construction plan, for then when the spars are brought up to the proper rake there will be some tension on the headstays and springstays. The rake on the sail plan is 2 degrees for the foremast, 3½ degrees for the mainmast, and 5 degrees for the mizzen. Below deck these could well be 3½, 5, and 6½ degrees.

It would be well if the upper eight feet of the sail tracks on each mast had the screw fastenings put twice as close together as the track normally comes drilled, because at sea there is a continuous jerking on this part of the track if the yacht is rolling in light weather, and you will find that the upper sail slides will have to be resized occasionally.

The lower six inches of the track is removable for sliding the sail off the track. I find it is just as convenient to have this removable section fastened to the mast with wood screws the same as the track above. In removing the sail the halliard is simply taken right around the bunt of the sail near the mast and the lot hoisted clear of the removable section while the screws are removed; or the section can be removed when the sail is set. In any case the removable section should run down to the gooseneck so that the slides cannot run off with a lowered sail.

BOOMS

The booms for the Marco Polo would be best if made of some harder wood than spruce, perhaps Oregon pine, fir, or yellow pine, for weight in such short booms would be desirable at times to hold the sail down. That is one of the reasons the booms are

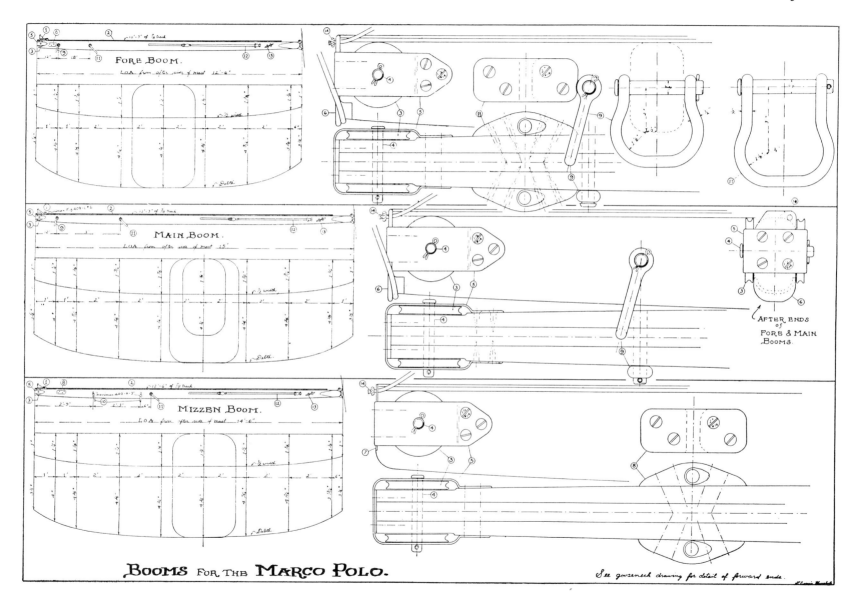

FORE BOOM.

LOA from after side of mast 12'-6"

MAIN BOOM.

LOA from after side of mast 15'

MIZZEN BOOM.

LOA from after side of mast 14'-6"

AFTER ENDS
OF
FORE & MAIN
BOOMS.

BOOMS FOR THE MARCO POLO.

See gooseneck drawing for detail of forward ends.

solid. Also a hollow boom would have to have reinforcements in several places with the type of boom fitting used on the Marco Polo, so that altogether the solid booms will be the cheapest for the Marco Polo although it is not always so on other craft. After the booms are sawn out to the proper taper and then planed up, the corners can either be rounded off in a molding machine or done with a hand plane. The radius of the corners full length on all booms is ¾". The forward ends of the booms are shown on the drawing of the goosenecks. The numbered description is as follows:

1. Clew outhauls. Three alike, either Merriman Fig. 409C No. 2 or Wilcox, Crittenden Fig. 979 No. 2, with about 15" of ⅞" track. The track can be secured with either 2" Everdur screws or bronze through-bolts.

2. Sail track. All booms have ⅞" sail track of the following lengths: fore boom, 10' 3"; main boom, 12' 9"; mizzen, 12' 6".

3. Sheaves. The two sheaves in the end of each boom are for the boom lifts and clew outhaul pennants. They can be Merriman 3" diameter, ⅜" thick, bored for ½" pin. Six required.

4. Sheave pins, made of ⅝" Tobin bronze turned down to ½" for 3⅜" cotter pins on small ends. Make three.

5. Sheave band, phosphor bronze 1/16" by 2" by 14" fastened with six 1" and four 1½" No. 14 flat-head screws. Make three.

6. Bronze casting, to take boom crotch wire strap and secure standing end of the clew outhaul pennant. Make two.

7. Plate on end of mizzen boom can be bronze about 1/16" by 2" by 3". Its only purpose is to secure clew outhaul pennant. Make one.

8. Oak blocks, for reefing pennants on fore and mizzen booms only; the same port and starboard. Well secured with 2" No. 16 flat-head screws. Make four.

9. Boom bails, for the fore and main sheets, either galvanized steel forgings or bronze castings. Make two.

10. Mizzen sheet, attached with two Merriman Fig. 440-A, 3".

11. Boom bails, for attaching forward guys. Either galvanized steel forging or bronze casting. Make three.

12. Slides for the clew outhaul pennant tackles and the boom lift tackles are alike and the parts necessary are as follows: six 5' pieces of ⅞" track; six Merriman slide blocks, Fig. 539, No. 2 with becket; six Merriman cheek blocks, Fig. 356, No. 2.

13. Cleats. Six Wilcox, Crittenden hollow cleats, Fig. 4020. 5½" long.

14. The standing ends of the clew outhaul pennants are secured by stopper knots that have been soldered neatly. The holes in Nos. 6 and 7 need not be much over 3/16".

GOOSENECKS

All three goosenecks are alike and similar in design to those that I have been using on yachts of this size the last few years. Besides being neat, they will allow the boom to swing upward and outboard without jamming, so that they do not have to be secured to the mast as securely as other types. The principal strain on the gooseneck is often from the twisting of the boom, and this type of gooseneck is less apt to split the forward end of the boom than some others. As there are only two castings and little machine work, this gooseneck is easy to make. The numbered description follows:

1. Boom attachments. Make six for three goosenecks of phosphor or Tobin bronze, 1/16" or more thick by 3½" by 12".

2. Bronze castings, ¾" thick except at pin where lugs are swelled to 1" as shown. There need be little machine work other than drilling the hole for the pin.

3. The mast attachment is a bronze casting as shown, drilled

for pin and drilled and countersunk for six 2″ No. 20 Everdur wood screws.

4. Six ⅜″ Tobin bronze pins to act as spacers and riveted in place. (See detail.) Make eighteen.

5. The eye on the top of No. 2 is for attaching tack of sail either with a shackle or a seizing and to be used when reefing.

6. Pin of Tobin bronze, ½″ by 4½″ with groove to take set screw. Make two.

7. ¼″ rivets of bronze well headed.

STANDING RIGGING

Some of the sizes of the rigging given in the accompanying list are large for the sail area of the spars they support, but it must be remembered that a vessel of the type of Marco Polo may at times only have sails set on one mast, when the size of the rigging compared to the stability is not then much oversize. The rigging list is proportioned for galvanized cast steel wire, which is economical in first cost and easy to work. However, if someone preferred the standard rigging of rustless steel, most of the sizes could be reduced one size of wire, for the rustless steels are not only stronger for their size but they last longer. This reduction in size would make a slight reduction in cost, as it must be borne in mind that rustless steel wire costs five or six times as much per running foot.

The lengths of the rigging are given with notes, either "exactly" or "about". This means that the ones marked "exactly" can be made up both ends in the rigging loft, but the ones marked "about" should have their lower ends spliced in after the masts are stepped. For instance, in the case of lower shrouds there is a difference of about six inches between the lower after and lower forward shrouds in some cases.

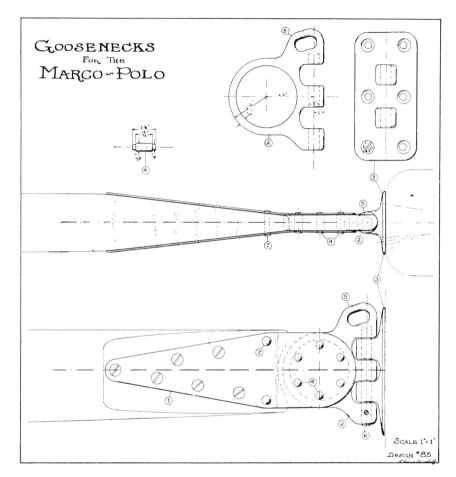

Date Material was ordered	Name of Part	Number Required	STANDING RIGGING	Dia. and Construction of wire	Approximate Strength of wire	Total length required with allowance for Splicing	Fittings	Rigger's Notes
	Head Stay	1	about 38'-6" 3/16"	7/16"-6x7	10,600	44'	2-7/8" Solid Thimbles	
	Fore Stay	1	Exactly 30'-9" 3/8"	3/8"-6x7	7,800	36'	2-7/8" Solid Thimbles	
	Main Topmast Fore Stay	1	Exactly 14'-1" 5/16"	5/16"-6x7	5,600	18'	2-7/8" Solid Thimbles	
	Main Spring Stay	1	Exactly 14'-9" 1/4" — Seising wire	1/4"-6x7	3,500	20'	1-7/8" Solid 1-7/8" Open Thimbles	
	Mizzen Spring Stay	1	Exactly 18'-9" 1/4" — Seising wire	1/4"-6x7	3,500	23'	1-7/8" Solid 1-7/8" Open Thimbles	
	Fore and Main Lower Shrouds	8	about 24'-6" 3/8"	3/8"-6x7	7,800	240'	16-7/8" Solid Thimbles	
	Mizzen Lower Shrouds	4	About 22'-6" 3/16" "Note" The forward lower shrouds are about 22'-9", the after ones about 22'-3"	3/8"-6x7	7,800	110'	8-3/8" Solid Thimbles	
	Fore Upper Shrouds	2	About 35'-9" 5/16"	5/16"-6x7	5,600	80'	4-5/16" Solid Thimbles	
	Main Upper Shrouds	2	About 38' 5/16"	5/16"-6x7	5,600	86'	4-5/16" Solid Thimbles	
	Mizzen Upper Shrouds	2	About 31'-9" 5/16"	5/16"-6x7	5,600	73'	4-5/16" Solid Thimbles	
	Fore Mast Back Stays	2	Exactly 29' 5/16" — See Running Rigging	5/16"-6x7	5,600	70'	2-5/16 Solid 2-5/16 Open Thimbles	
	Fore, Main and Mizzen Boom Lifts	1 1 1	Fore exactly 42' Main " 47' Mizzen " 41' 3/16" — See Running Rigging for tackles	3/16"-6x19 Korodless	3,200	145'	6-3/16" Open Thimbles	
	Fore, Main and Mizzen Clew Outhauls Pendants	1 1 1	Fore about 11' Main " 13' Mizzen " 12'-6" 3/16" — See Running Rigging for tackles — Slopper Knot	3/16"-6x19 Korodless	3,200	47'	3-3/16" Open Thimbles	
	Fore and Main Boom, wire Boom Crotches	1 1	Fore about 5'-3" Main " 4'-9" 1/4"	1/4"-6x19 Korodless	5,600	22'	4-1/4" Open Thimbles	

Korodless wire 6 by 19 construction is used with the running rigging, or in cases where the wire plays over a sheave as in the case of the boom lifts, etc.

The heavy black columns under "Date material was ordered" and "Rigger notes" will come out white on the blueprints of these lists and thus make a space for pencil notes which ordinarily are not plain on the usual blueprint.

If there are mistakes in spelling in this rigging list, well, you had better just forget it, for spelling certainly is not my forte.

SHROUD ATTACHMENTS

The shroud attachments of the Marco Polo are unusually strong so as to be able to resist the jerks and wear of a long ocean voyage. The general design of these attachments is similar to the type I have been using for several years, and with their use the shrouds practically never need readjustment. The numbered description is as follows:

1. Phosphor bronze, 1/16" by 4½" by 19½". Make six.
2. Phosphor bronze, 1/16" by 4½" by 13½". Make six.
3. Phosphor bronze, 1/16" by 4½" by 12¾". Make six.
4. Phosphor bronze, 1/16" by 4½" by 7½". Make six.
5. 1½" flat-headed No. 16 Everdur screws. 114 required.
6. 2" round-headed No. 18 Everdur screws. Twelve required.
7. Tobin bronze pins with cotter pins. Shank ½", head ¾", length under head 1¼". Twelve required.
8. ½" Everdur carriage bolts with bronze nuts and washers. Length under head 2". Six required.
9. End of bolt nicked so nut will not unscrew easily.
10. The ends of No. 3, which acts as a spreader attachment, should be slightly bent to cause a friction when in place so that the spreader will not swing too freely.

Date Material was Ordered	Name of Part	Number Required	RUNNING RIGGING	Dia. and construction of wire	Approximate Strength	Length required with allowance for splicing		Circumference of Rope	Length required with allowance for splicing	Fittings	Rigger's Notes
	Jib Topsail Halliard	1	37' — 40'; 7/32"; 1 1/2" cir	7/32"-6x19 Korodless	4,300	43'		1 1/2"	42'	1-1/4" Chain Shackle 1-7/16 Open Thimble.	
	Fore Stay-sail Halliard	1	90' of 1 1/2" cir manila.					1 1/2"	92'	1-1/2" Round Thimble	
	Fore Sail Halliard	1	62' of 3/16-6x19 wire; 72' of 1 1/2' cir manila.	3/16-6x19 Korodless	3,200	67'		1 1/2"	74'	1-1/4" Chain Shackle 1-3/16 Open Thimble	
	Main Halliard	1	50' of 3/16"-6x19 wire; 78' of 1 1/2" cir manila.	3/16-6x19 Korodless	3,200	55'		1 1/2"	80'	1-1/4" Chain Shackle 1-3/16 Open Thimble	
	Mizzen Halliard	1	31' of 1/4"-6x19 wire; merriman 370-A; 35' of 1 1/4" cir manila	1/4"-6x19 Korodless	5,600	36'		1 1/4"	36	1-3/16 Chain Shackle 1 merriman 370-A Block	
	Fore Stay-sail Sheets	1 Pair	1/4 wire; 3'-9"; 55' of 1 1/2" manila.	1/4"-6x19 Korodless	5,600	18'		1 1/2"	214'	1-3/16 anchor Shackle. 2-1/4" Open 2-1/2 Open Thimbles.	
	Back Stay Tackles	2	45 of 1 1/2" manila							2-Round Thimbles	
	Fore Main and Mizzen Boom Lift Tackles	3	Each 18 of 1 1/4" manila					1 1/4"	60'		
	Fore Main and Mizzen Clew Outhaul Tackles	3	Each 15' of 1 1/4 manila					1 1/4"	50'		
	Fore Sheet Main " Mizzen "	1 1 1	100' of 1 1/2" manila 88' " " 70' " "					1 1/2"	260'	1-Round Thimble	
	Forward Boom Guys.	3	Each 20 of 2" manila					2"	66'	3 Shackles Either merriman Snap #3 or Chain 5/16	
	Wire Life Rails.	2 2 2	Seizings; merriman 424; Upper about 48'; Intermediate " 46'; Lower " 43'; 1/4"	1/4"-6x19 Korodless or Phosphor Br.		330'				6-1/4" Shack. 24-1/4 Thimb. 12-Pelican hooks.	
	Watch Tackle	1	4'; Tapered braded whip; 40' of 1" cir manila					1"	42'	1-5/16 Round Thimble	
	Anchor Warps	2	10'; 40 Fathoms of 2 1/2" manila; 7/16" close linked chain with enlarged end links of 1/2" wire, one opening 5/8"x2", one 1 1/4"x2".					2 1/2"	480'	1-7/8" Open Thimble	
	Docking Lines	4	55' Each of 2 1/2" manila					2 1/2"	220'		

BLOCK LIST	Number Required	Size	Number of Sheaves	Fittings ~ Description Etc	Size of Rope or Wire.
Head Stay Turnbuckle.	1	1/2	–	merriman Fig 377 5/16" and 1/2" Jaws	7/16"
Fore Main and Mizzen Lower Shroud Turnbuckles	12	7/16	–	merriman Fig 377 5/16 and 7/16 Jaws	3/8"
Fore Main and Mizzen Upper Shroud Turnbuckles.	6	3/8	–	merriman Fig 377 regular Jaws	5/16"
Back Stay Blocks	4	4"	1	Single Front Shackle	1/2"
" " "	2	4"	1	Single Front S. and Becket	1/2".
Jib Topsail Halliard Block.	1	4 1/2"	1	Single Front Shackle	7/16 wire 1/2" Rope
Fore Stay Sail Halliard Blocks.	1	#3	1	merriman Fig 355 Upset Side Shack.	1/2 Rope
	1	#3	1	" " 352 with Becket.	
Fore and Main Halliard Blocks.	2	4"	1	merriman Fig 561 with extended straps for head boards	3/16 wire
Mizzen Halliard Block	1	#2	1	merriman Fig 370-A	7/16 Rope
Fore Staysail Sheet. Blocks.	2	3"	1	merriman Fig 344 1/4" wire strop, Bronze Sheaves.	1/2" Dia Rope
Fore Main and Mizzen Boom Lift Tackles Blocks	3	#2	1	merriman Fig 356	7/16 Rope
	3	#2	1	" " 539 with becket	
Fore Main and Mizzen Clew Outhaul Blocks.	3	#2	1	" " 356	7/16 Rope
	3	#2	1	" " 539 with becket.	
Fore Sheet Blocks	5	4"	1	merriman Front Shackle and 3-Fig 416 #3 Eye plates	1/2 Rope
Main Sheet Blocks	3	4"	1	merriman Front Shackle and 1-Fig 416 #3 Eye plate.	1/2 Rope
Mizzen Sheet Blocks	1	4"	1	Front Shackle and Becket.	1/2 Rope
	3	4"	1	" "	
Cheek Blocks on mast for Fore staysail, Foresail and Main hall.	3			Either merriman 327 or 356	1/4 wire and 1/2 Rope
Fair Leads (78) and (82) on Deck Plan.	8	#3		merriman Fig 422	1/2 Rope
	2	#4		" " "	
Flange Eyes For securing Life Rails (73) on Deck Plan.	12			Either merriman Fig 416 #2	1/4" wire
	2	For Anchors		or W.C. " 902 #1	
Cleats (30) On Construction Plan	1	14"		Wilcox Crittenden Fig 4020	
(84) " Deck "	6	10"		" " " "	
(85) " " "	15	8"		" " " "	
Mast and Boom Track		7/8		136 Running feet of 7/8" track similar to merriman 406	
Clew Outhauls	3	7/8		Either merriman Fig 409-C or W.C. Fig 979	
Watch Tackle Blocks.	1	#1	1	merriman Fig 352 with Becket.	
	1	#1	2	" " "	
Cleats on Booms	6	5 1/2"		Wilcox Crittenden Fig 4020	
Cleat For Mizzen Halliard	1	6 1/2"		" " " "	
Track For Boom lifts and Clew outhaul tackles.	6	7/8		6-5' Pieces (or 3-10' lengths) of track	
Anchor Chain For the 90 or 100 lb Anchors.	1	3/8		45 Fathoms of 3/8 BBB chain, end links of 7/16 wire, inside measurments 2"x3 1/2"	

RIGGING AND BLOCK LISTS

FOR THE

MARCO POLO

Design No 85.

L. Francis Herreshoff

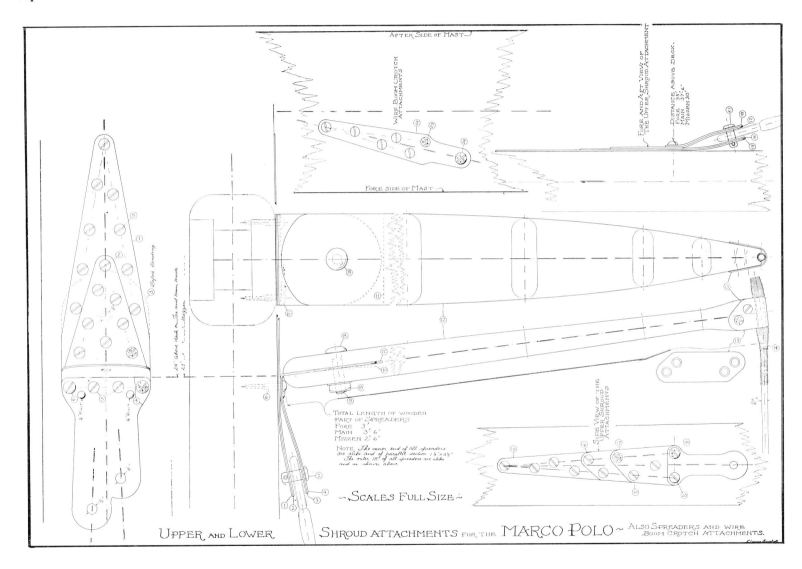

UPPER and LOWER   SHROUD ATTACHMENTS for the MARCO POLO ~ ALSO SPREADERS AND WIRE BOOM CROTCH ATTACHMENTS.

11. The slot in the inner end of the spreaders can be cut with a hand saw and should not be much over 1/16″ wide.

12. The spreaders can be of mahogany, ash, or other firm or semi-hard wood, shaped about as shown, with the outer 18″ alike on all, the difference in length to be made up at the parallel inner ends. The spreaders are shaped partly for sitting on, as a lookout may be required aloft in coral regions.

13. The outer end of the spreaders are planned to be entirely smooth so that no chafing gear will be necessary, and for this reason the spreader clips are secured with four 1″ No. 14 flatheaded screws. The spreader clips before bending are 1/16 by 1½ by 4½″. Six required.

14. The outer ends of the spreaders must be well seized in place, and this can be done by serving the shroud for six or seven inches with marline and then putting on a tapered seizing as shown above and below the spreader clip. This arrangement will have no exposed sharp corners to chafe the sail.

15. Phosphor bronze, 1/16″ by 2″ by 12¾″. Make six.

16. Phosphor bronze, 1/16″ by 2″ by 8½″. Make six.

17. Phosphor bronze, 1/16″ by 2″ by 7″. Make six.

18. Phosphor bronze, 1/16″ by 2″ by 4⅛″. Make six.

19. 1½″ No. 14 flat-head Everdur screws. Fifty-four required.

20. 2″ No. 16 round-head Everdur screws. Twelve required.

21. Tobin bronze pins with cotter pins. Shank ⅜″, head ⅝″, length under head 1″. Six required.

22. Wire boom crotch attachments on forward sides of main and mizzen masts only. Phosphor bronze, 1/16 by 1½ by 8″ (single layer). Make four.

23. 1½″ No. 14 flat-head screws. Twenty-four required.

24. 1½″ No. 18 round-head Everdur screws. Four required.

Note: The exposed corners and edges of all metal parts are to be rounded off, for sharp edges have no place on an ocean cruiser.

STAY ATTACHMENTS

1. Phosphor bronze sheet, 1/16 by 3¾ by 12″. Make 2.

2. and 3. Alike. Phosphor bronze, 1/16 by 1½ by 5⅜″. Make 4.

4. Bronze lag screws, ⅜″ by 1½″. Two required.

5. Bronze lag screws, 7/16 by 3″. Two required.

6. Phosphor bronze, 1/16 by 2 by 18⅜″. Make 1.

7. Phosphor bronze, 1/16 by 2 by 11 9/16″. Make 1.

8. Phosphor bronze, 1/16 by 2 by 8¼″. Make 1.

9. Phosphor bronze, 1/16 by 2 by 7⅛″. Make 1.

10. Phosphor bronze, 1/16 by 2 by 9½″. Make 1.

11. Tobin bronze bolt, ⅝″ diameter, 1⅜″ long under head, with large cotter pin.

12. Bronze lag screws, ⅜ by 3″. Two required.

13. Sheave for squaresail yard halliard, but this need not be included on Marco Polos which will not carry a squaresail. The sheave can be of cast bronze about ½″ thick at hub, ⅜″ thick at periphery, with a diameter of 6¼″. Scored for ¼″ diameter wire.

14. The bee hole or clevis for the sheave is cut in an angle of about 7 degrees so as to clear the track on the after side of mast.

15. Sheave pin of ½″ Tobin bronze about 5¾″ long before forging head. The head is bent over and flattened to take a 1″ wood screw.

MASTHEADS

The masthead fittings for the Marco Polo are patterned after the latest racing practice, not only to secure great strength for the weight, but principally to achieve neatness and to reduce

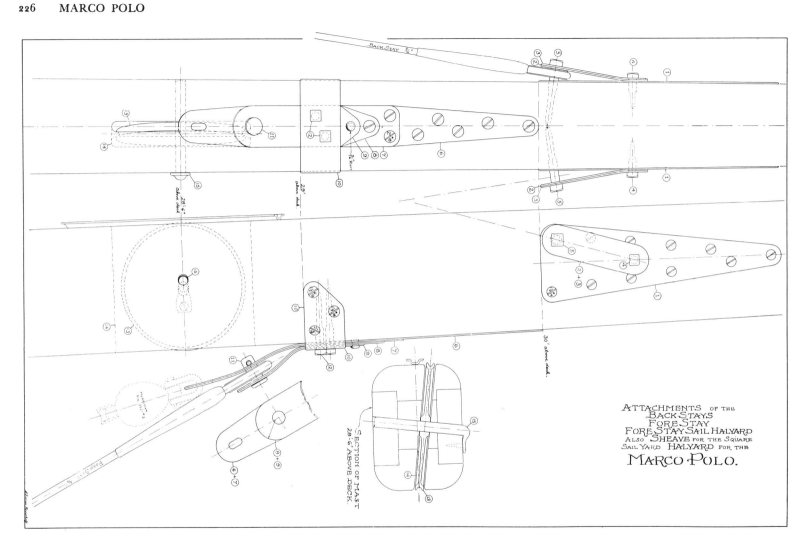

ATTACHMENTS of the
BACK STAYS
FORE STAY
FORE STAY SAIL HALYARD
ALSO SHEAVE for the SQUARE
SAIL YARD HALYARD for the

MARCO POLO.

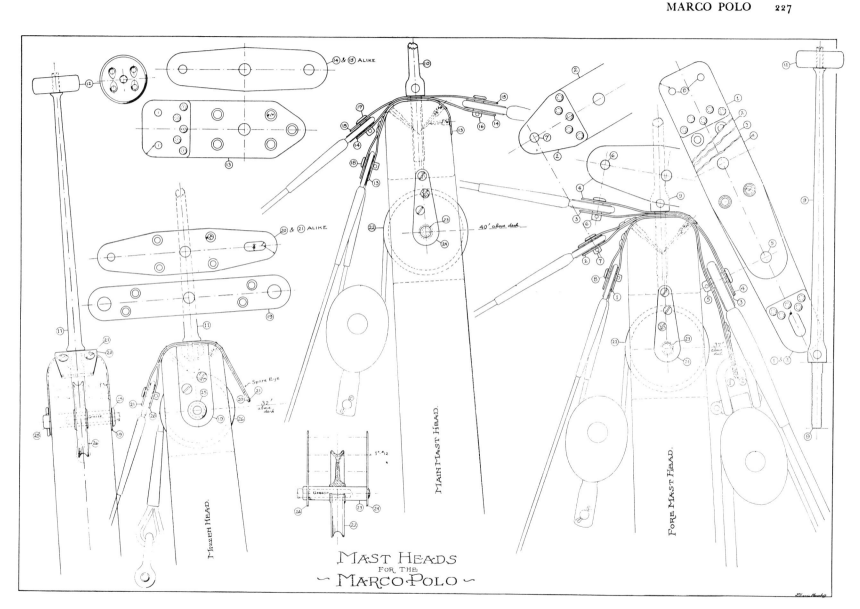

MAST HEADS
FOR THE
~ MARCO POLO ~

wind resistance when driving under power or when laying at anchor in strong winds.

All of these fittings can be made by any mechanic who is capable of laying out work, and amount mostly to trimming plates to size, drilling and countersinking holes, and turning pins.

The foremast head attachments may at first seem a little complicated, but when one considers that this fitting secures seven pieces of rigging, it might be realized that it will be easier to make that than seven separate attachments, and almost no other arrangement will secure all these parts at the very masthead.

The flagstaffs are one of the most difficult parts to make; the procedure in turning similar ones has been to use a lathe with a hollow headstock and only have a short length of the rod to be turned extend beyond the chuck. In this way a short section can be turned at a time and there will be no danger of the rod springing. The small, or upper, end should be turned first; then, with the slide rest set at about one degree, the required taper will be made. After the taper has been roughed out, it can be finished off in the lathe with a file. During this latter operation, the whole length of the tapered part can extend beyond the chuck and the small end can be supported by the center rest.

The trucks themselves on the upper ends of the flag staffs should be made of lignum vitae and threaded on as shown. This arrangement makes the most satisfactory flag hoist, which at times may be important on a seagoing vessel.

All of the sheet metal parts are 1/16″ thick, or thicker, phosphor bronze, Tobin bronze, Everdur, or Monel metal, all semi-hard rolled. Steel can be used, but as it will have to be galvanized after making up it would cost more in the end.

The numbered description is as follows:

1. Bronze plate, 1/16 by 2⅝ by 14¼″, with clip riveted to after end 1/16 by 2⅝ by 2⅞″.

2. Bronze plate, 1/16 by 2⅝ by 13¾″, with reinforcements on forward end 1/16 by 2¼ by 2¾″, and clip riveted to after end 1/16 by 2⅜ by 3″.

3. Bronze plate, 1/16 by 2⅜ by 9⅝″.

4. Bronze plate, 1/16 by 2⅜ by 9⅝″.

5. Tobin bronze pin, ½″ diameter, head ¾″, length overall 1½″.

6. Tobin bronze pin, 7/16″ diameter, head ⅝″, length overall 1″.

7. Tobin bronze pin, ⅜″ diameter, head ⅝″, length overall ⅞″.

8. Two Tobin bronze pins, 5/16″ diameter, head ½″, length overall ⅞″.

9. Flagstaff of Tobin bronze rod, ⅞″ diameter, about 17½″ overall before turning. 13½″ between shoulders; lower three inches ½″ diameter and threaded for about 2½″ with about 12 threads per inch. The upper end is threaded with about 5/16″ 20 thread. There is a ⅜″ tommy hole near the base for screwing the staff in. In boring the masthead, first a ½″ bitt should be used for about ½″ depth and the remainder of the hole bored with a 7/16″ bitt.

10. The same as nine except 1½″ longer, or about 19″ long before turning, and 15″ between shoulders.

11. Mizzen flagstaff of Tobin bronze rod, ⅞″ diameter, about 13⅝″ long before turning, and 12″ between shoulders. Fitted with a ½″ nut at the lower end.

12. The three masthead trucks are all alike of lignum vitae 2¼″ diameter by ¾″ thick with four ¼″ holes well chamfered off on top for the flag halliards.

13. Bronze plate, 1/16 by 2⅝ by 7⅝″, with clip riveted to after end 1/16 by 2⅝ by 2¼″.

14. Bronze plate, 1/16 by 2 by 7½″.

15. Bronze plate, 1/16 by 2 by 7½″.

16. Tobin bronze pin, ⅞″ diameter, head ⅝″, LOA 1″.

17. Tobin bronze pin, 3/8″ diameter, head 5/8″, LOA 7/8″.

18. Two Tobin bronze pins, 5/16″ diameter, head 1/2″, length overall 7/8″.

19. Bronze plate, 1/16 by 1½ by 9½″.

20. Bronze plate, 1/16 by 2 by 8½″.

21. Bronze plate, 1/16 by 2 by 8½″.

22. The sheaves for both the fore and mainmasts are alike, of bronze, 3/4″ wide at hub, 5/8″ wide at rim, 4″ diameter at rim, 3½″ diameter at score.

23. The sheave pins for both the fore and mainmasts are alike, of phosphor or Tobin bronze, 5/8 by 3⅛″; one end is shouldered down to 3/8″ and riveted to clip No. 24. The other end is drilled out as shown for a grease reservoir, with 1/8″ hole feeding sheave bearing. Wooden plug in outer end as shown.

24. The clips at both ends of the sheave pins are alike, but two are drilled and countersunk for 3/8″ rivet while two have straight 5/8″ hole. Each clip is secured to the mast with three 1″ No. 12 flat-headed bronze screws. The clips are 1/16 by 1¼ by 3½″. Make 4.

25. The mizzen sheave pin can be turned from either phosphor or Tobin bronze, 5/8″ diameter with 7/8″ head. Length overall 3⅜″. There is a cotter pin at one end and cavity at the other with wooden plug as shown.

26. The mizzen halliard sheave is 5/8″ wide at hub, 1/2″ wide at rim, 3½″ diameter at rim, 3⅛″ diameter at score.

The drawing of these mastheads is so complete that any mechanic should be able to make the metal work without difficulty. I have purposely avoided giving many dimensions, as a slight variation in the size of most parts will not affect their usefulness and, as the blueprint will be full size, all required dimensions can be taken from it. If this drawing is followed carefully, the parts will be nearly as scientific as the parts of an aeroplane.

SQUARESAIL GEAR AND LIFE RAILS

Most of the parts which have to do with the squaresail of the Marco Polo have purposely been left off previous drawings, for it is believed that many owners of these little ships will not need a squaresail, particularly if they are only to do coastal cruising, and I myself am not at all sure that a squaresail is necessary on a craft that has as much auxiliary power as the Marco Polo. One thing is certain, and that is that if the whole squaresail rigging is not included with the yacht as built, there will be a certain saving in cost and general simplification. However there are many who would like to play around with a squaresail. The procedure in setting it can be as follows:

When the yard is lying on deck in a fore and aft position, the squaresail can be slid onto the track. After the heads of the sail have been lashed to the ends of the yard the sail should be neatly stopped up as you would a balloon jib or spinnaker, using stops of easily broken twine every two or three feet depending on the wind that is blowing. Then the yard can be attached to the crane. (The crane slides on both the track on the mast and the yard.) Next, the yard lifts and braces should be attached and the sheets made fast to the clews. During these operations it probably will be best to have the crane on the mast slide and held up about four feet off the deck by belaying the yard halliard for this point. Now when everything is clear and the braces lead outside of all the shrouds and backstays, if the yard is hoisted smartly so that the end that was forward goes up first to a nearly perpendicular position, the after and lower end can be dipped around the rigging so that the yard is forward of all of the shrouds. After the lifts and braces are adjusted the sail can be broken out.

The procedure for taking in the squaresail can be nearly the reverse of the above, but as the sail will not be stopped up it may take at least three pairs of hands to take it in. The squaresail, yard, and all, can also be lowered away in a horizontal position, when the yard will have to be nearly athwartships. After the sail has been furled, after a fashion, the yard can be detached from the crane, when the yard can be carried forward enough so that its after end can dip inside the shrouds. Perhaps this can be done best with the foremost lift taking most of the weight of the yard and the men doing the work could stand on the main deck near the foremast. There are a great many other ways to rig a squaresail, but all of them that I know of entail several more ropes or necessitate leaving the yard up aloft, which is a disadvantage when turning to windward under either sail or power.

The numbered description is as follows:

1. One-inch track, 25′ long on forward side of foremast (and previously shown on the spar plan), but this track can be dispensed with on Marco Polos which will not set a squaresail.

2. 1″ track about 24″ long for attaching crane to yard.

3. 12 cast bronze slides with slot for track, milled for loose fit and 33/64″ holes drilled for ½″ rod. Five.

4. Cast bronze trunions with ⅝″ neck and 33/64″ hole. Make two. Machine where shown.

5. Tobin bronze rod about 20⅞″ long with ⅛″ grooves cut in it about 1/16″ deep. Grooves spaced about as shown on drawing or to give slides slight clearance. Make two.

6. Cast bronze vertical crane. Ends drilled 33/64″; middle section drilled ⅝″. No external machining.

7. Cast bronze horizontal crane. This piece is exactly like No. 6. In other words, make two.

8. 13/64″ hole for pin of 5/16″ shackle. These holes are intended for the shackle of the halliard, but should be in all four ends as shown, for the crane, being symmetrical, can be put on the mast slide four different ways.

9. Split rings to act as spacers on No. 5. Of Tobin bronze ⅛″ thick. I.D. ⅜″. O.D. ¾″. Twelve required.

10. Split rings to act as stops on No. 4. Of Tobin bronze, ⅛″ thick. I.D. ½″. O.D. ⅞″. Two required. Both Nos. 9 and 10 can be made by holding a piece of Tobin bronze rod in the lathe and drilling the required size hole and then cutting off the ⅛″ wide rings. Then saw out the gap for the mouth with a hacksaw.

11. Ratchet-type stops on the yard for the crane so the latter can be quickly removed. Make two. Made of ⅛″ thick bronze plate about 1½″ by 3¾″ and fastened to the yard with a 5/16″ lag screw, 1½″ long. Also a 1¼″ No. 14 round-headed screw in a slot as shown.

12. Yard halliard of ¼″ 6 by 19 wire, 29′ long; tailed out with 32 feet of 1¾″ circumference manila.

13. Clip attachments for the yard lifts and braces, of ⅛″ thick strong bronze plate, 2½″ by 5⅝″, secured with ten 1½″ No. 14 flat-headed screws. These clips are intended to take 5/16″ shackles and must be shaped about as shown to clear the sail track on the yard.

The yard lifts can be of 1¾″ manila about 80′ long each and can run through blocks similar to Merriman Figure 365, No. 2, and can be attached to the mast with snug fitting wire rope eyes riding on the top of the sail track or shackling into bronze eye plates like Merriman Figure 416, No. 2.

The yard braces can be 1¾″ circumference manila about 55′ long. The sheets can be 1½″ manila about 40′ long.

14. ⅞″ sail track 24′ long attached about one inch up from the lower forward face of the yard so as to clear No. 13.

15. The yard itself is 25 feet long overall and made hollow for lightness. The forward and after staves are 1″ thick rabbeted out ¼″ to take the upper and lower staves which are ¾″ thick. Rift-grain fir of fine texture would be good for the yard.

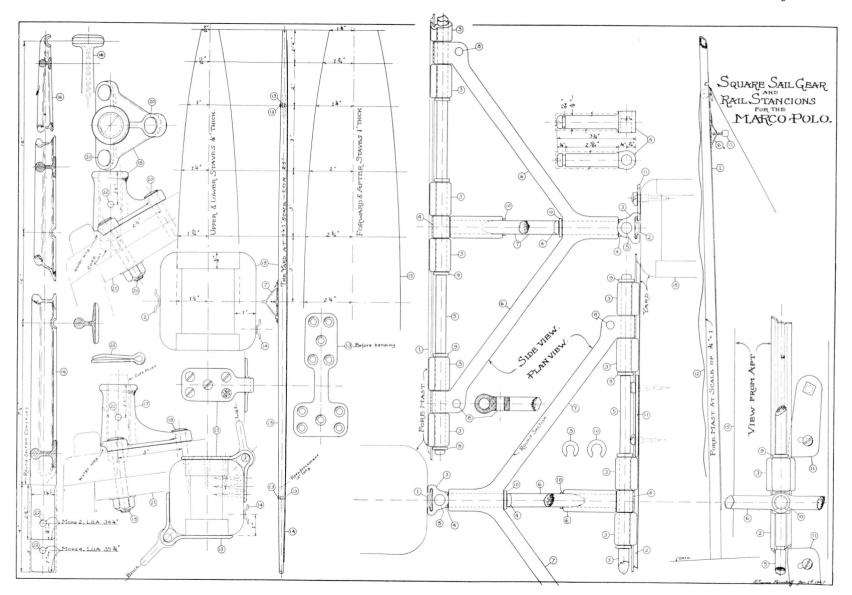

SQUARE SAIL GEAR
AND
RAIL STANCIONS
FOR THE
MARCO POLO.

UPPER & LOWER STAVES ¼" THICK.

FORWARD & AFTER STAVES ⅛" THICK

THIS YARD AT 1¼" SCALE OR L.O.A. 25'

Before bending

Reinforcement 12' long

SIDE VIEW.

PLAN VIEW.

FORE MAST

Round Section

YARD

FORE MAST AT SCALE OF ¾" = 1

VIEW FROM AFT

DECK

Make 2, L.O.A. 34¼"

Make 4, L.O.A. 35¾"

Bride

Besides the plugs at the ends the only other reinforcements are abreast the fittings (No. 13).

There should be holes drilled through the ends of the yard for the head outhaul lashings.

While the life rails on a boat like the Marco Polo are no more necessary than the squaresail, and in fact would only be a nuisance in coastal cruising, still good high rails give one a comfortable feeling in night sailing, so some may prefer them. Also they are desirable when and if children are aboard. But high life rails on a sailboat can never be very simple affairs, for at times where a sheet or other rope will chafe on them they must be let down.

On the Marco Polo there are pelican hooks in several places for this reason. This requires a rather different type of rail stanchion than is usual, for where a plain hole through a stanchion is used, the life line will render so that the rest of the rail is slacked up or becomes useless. Also with the usual stanchions the life lines cannot be unroved because the thimbles and pelican hooks will not pass through the eyes. For these reasons the life lines on the Marco Polo are seized to grooves on the stanchions the way a shroud is seized into a spreader tip. Of course the life lines on the Marco Polo are seized to the upper shrouds in places, so that they may as well be seized to the rail stanchions also. In fact a properly made seizing is a most satisfactory fastening, for it can easily be put on and quickly removed with a knife. This type of upper end on a stanchion is also a great improvement over the usual one, for if you should fall on it, it will not hurt you as much as the small eye type has in some cases.

The sockets of most removable rail stanchions are not strong enough or properly secured to the deck, and one of the reasons they give out or get started in the deck is because various lines are often secured to them. That is the reason these sockets are unusually heavy. The stanchions themselves are of T-section above the socket simply to reduce the amount of bronze used in the casting. The only machine work is at the cylindrical part that fits in the sockets, which can be turned by holding the stanchions in a hollow headstock lathe that has an independent jaw chuck.

The only machine work or finish on the sockets is boring the hole for the stanchions, and it is thought that this can be accomplished by holding the sockets in the chuck with the base outward. The bore of the sockets should all be about the same size so the stanchions are interchangeable. For this reason I have not given the exact dimensions, since it is presumed that a machine shop will prefer to finish these holes with some reamer they have, but the approximate size should be about $1\frac{1}{8}''$ and the diameter of the stanchion approximately five-thousandths less, or a loose running fit.

The numbered description is as follows:

16. Life rail stanchions of cast manganese bronze of a rather stiff composition. Cast six, four for the main deck $35\frac{3}{4}''$ overall, and two for the fore deck shortened up to $34\frac{1}{2}''$ overall because of the difference in deck levels.

17. Stanchion sockets for main deck. Make four of strong cast bronze. Bolts spaced about $3''$ both athwartships and fore and aft. Groove in outer edge for waterway and drain to socket hole.

18. Stanchion sockets for fore deck. Make two of strong cast bronze. Bolts spaced $2\frac{1}{2}''$ athwartship and $3''$ fore and aft.

19. Hold-down bolts for main deck sockets of $\frac{1}{2}''$ strong bronze; forged heads as shown, machined down to $\frac{3}{4}''$ at crown. These bolts should be about $3\frac{1}{2}''$ long. Make twelve with nuts and washers.

20. Hold-down bolts for fore deck sockets, same as above but $3\frac{1}{4}''$ long. Make six with nuts and washers.

21.   Reinforcing block of oak, ⅞ by 5½ by 9″ long under each socket.

22.   Holes for ¼″ diameter or larger cotter pins. If the cotter pins are bent as shown before they are inserted, their ends will not have to be opened, and thus they can be removed and replaced conveniently.

DINGHY

A good tender is one of the most difficult things to design, for it must possess several features which are somewhat conflicting. If she is light, she is easy to haul on deck, but quick moving underneath you until you are seated. The light boat also is generally more easily damaged. If her freeboard is high she will be drier and perhaps abler, but she will stick up high on deck and interfere with the vision of the helmsman. If a tender has a straight run aft and a large stern, she will go well with an outboard motor, but will be very hard to row when loaded. The large stern and straight run will also make her extremely difficult to tow, for in a following sea she will run up on her painter and yaw off in first one direction and then the other, while the tender with just the right turn-up aft will hold back in place and keep her painter tight. While it is conceded that the tender with the large stern tows easiest at six or eight miles an hour, still at these speeds the drag of the tender is of little consequence, for the yacht which is doing the towing is developing so much power then that the drag of the tender is negligible, and no doubt holds the yacht back less than the jerks in various directions of a poor towing tender.

A small tender should be an exceptionally good sea boat with only one aboard, and so arranged that she can be rowed handily in the strongest breezes, for she may have to carry out a kedge

A Marco Polo dinghy making knots despite trailing her weather leeboard, to say nothing of a stray line over the stern.

anchor or run a line to another vessel or save the life of someone who has fallen overboard, in which case the swimmer should be hauled in over the center of the stern, which will be depressed with the combined weights of the actors so that it is not too difficult, particularly if it has been practiced several times beforehand in rough weather with a good swimmer. The reason the center of the transom is the best point from which to haul in a swimmer is that during the operation the tender will head dead to leeward and thus be much steadier. When the rescued has been hauled in to a point about six inches below the navel, it is best to roll him over so the legs will flex upward. This is the most awkward moment in the operation, and the rescuer should be crouched down and ready to balance the tender at this moment. With practice this can all be accomplished with one sudden jerk if the rower has a good hold on his victim.

In rowing a small tender in rough water with two aboard, the

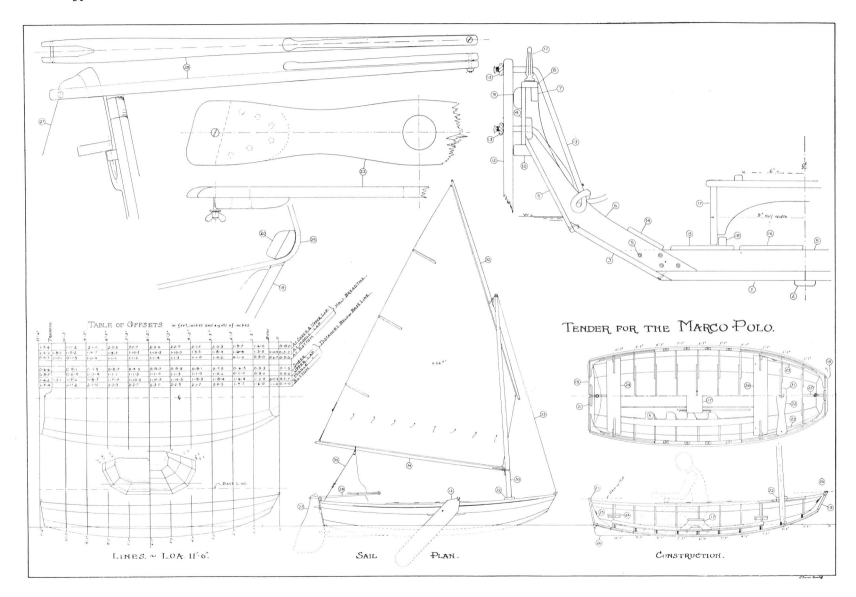

TABLE OF OFFSETS   in feet, inches and eights of inches

LINES. ~ L.O.A. 11'-6".

SAIL   PLAN.

CONSTRUCTION.

TENDER FOR THE MARCO POLO.

passenger should sit on the bottom with his face nearly up to where the rower's hands will come at the beginning of the stroke. All small tenders should have a scull hole, for not only is it convenient to propel the dinghy at times by sculling, but steering with an oar when sailing is the best arrangement in shallow water. The scull hole is also necessary when carrying out an anchor, for the anchor should hang over the stern with the bight of the anchor warp laying in the scull hole from whence it passes forward, to be secured by the pressure of the rower's heel against the rowing brace. In this way the rower can cast off and let fall the anchor by simply reducing the pressure of the heel. He can do this at the very instant he wants to without stopping rowing or shifting his position, so there is no danger of capsizing or drifting out of position.

This tender, of course, can be built without sail, rudder, leeboards, or mast partner, for some will only want to row while others will prefer her for sailing, rowing, and outboard motor. The lugsail is adopted because all of the spars will stow below the gunwale and because this is the simplest sail to rig (although not always the easiest to take in during a squall). However, outside of lace lines and tack rope the only ropes to handle are the mainsheet and halliard, the latter also acting as a forestay and reeves through a bee hole in the fore transom, then leading aft and belaying to the pin for that purpose in the forward thwart.

The tender has to have a removable mast partner and midships thwart because she rests over hatches when in position upside down on the deck of the Marco Polo, but both the removable mast partner and the sliding seat have advantages. A fixed mast partner would be in the way of the forward rower, and the shifting rowing seat that acts as middle thwart can be moved to trim the dinghy correctly for different combinations of positions of the rower or rowers, and there are oarlock sockets to correspond to these various positions.

A centerboard box also would come in the same region as the main hatch, with the tender stowed, so that leeboards are used, but with no centerboard box and the middle thwart removed there is a large comfortable space for the passenger to sit when sailing, which is not so in many dinghies.

Although this tender may sail wind abeam as fast as many another of her size, she is not intended for racing, and it is believed that leeboards secured with ropes as shown will be quite satisfactory. In fact in cruising many times only the leeward one need be used. The leeboards are secured by two lanyards of about $\frac{1}{2}''$ diameter rope; the forward and upper one passes through an oarlock and then belays on a pin in frame 4' 3''. The after and lower lanyard goes through a $\frac{1}{2}''$ hole in the sheer strake and belays on a pin in frame 5'. 3''.

Mast. If the mast is used without shrouds (as shown) it is much the most convenient, but it must be about $3\frac{1}{8}''$ at mast partner and $2\frac{1}{2}''$ at lower end. If shrouds are used it can be much smaller, say $2\frac{1}{4}''$. The brass strap over the clevis for the sheave at the upper end of the mast must be well made, for there is at times a side strain on the halliard of a lugsail.

The numbered description is as follows:

1.   Bottom planks. If soft pine or cedar, $\frac{7}{8}''$ thick. If mahogany or cypress, $\frac{3}{4}''$ thick. Each plank about 10'' wide with seam on centerline.

2.   False keel of hard wood to cover seam of bottom planks.

3.   Lower plank of soft pine, cedar, or mahogany, $\frac{1}{2}''$ thick.

4.   Middle plank and sheer strake of soft pine, cedar or mahogany, $\frac{3}{8}''$ thick.

5.   Floor timbers of oak, molded 2'', sided $\frac{5}{8}''$; fastened to frames with copper rivets or wood screws spaced as shown.

6.   Frames. Oak, sided $\frac{5}{8}''$, molded about as shown. Two inches at heels, $1\frac{1}{4}''$ at heads.

7.   Gunwale strip, or inwale. Oak, $\frac{5}{8}''$ by $1\frac{1}{4}''$.

8. Reinforcement for oarlock sockets. Oak, 1½" by 9/16" by 4' 2".

9. Wale or rubbing strake. Oak, 2 by ¾" amidships, tapered as shown to about 1 by ½" at ends.

10. Leeboard bearing strip. Oak, about 1¾" by 1" by 1' 10".

11. Oarlocks and sockets, similar to Wilcox-Crittenden Figure 429. Plain bronze, 8 sockets, 4 oarlocks.

12. Leeboards. Oak, ⅞" by 9" by 4' 3". Lower ends tapered to about ⅜" thick.

13. Ropes for securing leeboard. ½" diameter. Upper rope reeves through throat of oarlock and belays on pin in frame 4' 3". Lower rope reeves through hole in planking and belays on pin in frame 5' 3". Both ropes about 3' long.

14. Outer floor board, ⅜ by 3¾". Cedar.

15. This floor board to have cutouts to act as foot bracer for the rower, and there must be reinforcing cleats on the under side so the floor boards will not split.

16. Center floor boards. Cedar, ⅜" by 6" with ½" between boards.

17. Removable box-shaped seat to act as thwart for rower, with small cleats on top to prevent rower from slipping sideways. The top board can be ⅜ by 9 by 18¾". The side pieces ⅝ by 5¼ by 18".

18. Guide runner for seat box. Oak ¾" by ¾" by 3' 6".

19. Bow and stern transom. Oak, 1" or ⅞" thick. Tops curved downward to fit crown of Marco Polo's deck.

20. Reinforcement on bow transom for main halliard lead. Oak about ⅞ by 3 by 6".

21. Reinforcement on after transom for outboard motor. Oak, about ⅞ by 5 by 12".

22. Removable mast partner. Oak, 1 by 6 by 44", with oak cleats on outer ends well secured as shown, and 5/16" flathead stove bolts, 3" long with butterfly nuts and washers.

23. Lodging piece for mast partner. Oak, 1" deep, 1½" wide at middle, straight inside; outside tapered to fit gunwale.

24. Forward and after thwarts of semi-hard wood ⅝" by 8" set on cleats at planking and supported by gunwale knees about ⅝" thick. If necessary, there can also be a support under the middle of thwart.

25. Bow and stern knees of hackmatack or other suitable wood, about 1" thick; both knees to have hoisting rings similar to Wilcox-Crittenden, Fig. 274, No. 2. Forward ring also used for securing painter.

26. Deadwood of oak, 1" thick. Well secured.

27. Rudder of oak or mahogany, 1" thick. Made from plank 15" wide. Head shaped like detail shown to take removable tiller. Pintles and gudgeons, Wilcox-Crittenden 460, 462, 463. Size ¾.

28. Hardwood tiller, shaped like half-size detail with No. 14 bronze stove bolt across after end to act as locking pin. If desired the forward end of tiller can have a swinging extension as shown. Secured with No. 12 stove bolt and washers.

29. Showing the manner in which the main halliard reeves through the bee hole in the bow transom. Make the hole about ⅝".

30. Mast, round solid spruce, 10' 9" overall including tongue. Diameter at mast partner 3⅛"; diameter above tongue, 2⅛"; diameter of tongue, 1⅝"; diameter at head, 1½". Sheave for ½" diameter rope.

31. Mast step, oak, about 1½ by 3 by 8", well secured to floor timber and bottom.

32. Yard. Round solid spruce about 2¼" diameter at middle, and 1" at ends.

33. Main halliard. Strong hard-layed manila. 1½" circumference, ½" diameter. About 30' long. Secured to yard at upper end with rolling hitch.

34. Boom. Round solid spruce with neat jaws and leather strap for tack strap. Diameter at forward end 1⅜″; diameter at middle 1½″; diameter at after end 1″.

35. Mainsheet. About ⅜″ diameter (12 thread) cotton 20′ long with snap hook on end to run on wire rope traveler as shown. Small neat block, similar to Wilcox-Crittenden, Figure 952, size 1, lashed to boom.

I have gone to some length in describing the Marco Polo dinghy because there is no good stock dinghy built at present — none that will stand some abuse, tow well, and row easily when loaded. There are even few people today who know a good dinghy when they see one, and this is very evident from the wretched care they usually take of them. A good dinghy will never be cheap and there will never be light and strong ones made of materials heavier than wood. There are, however, some canvas-covered dinghies built that will stand hot sun without leaking, but it is doubtful if they would fit over the Marco Polo's hatches and not stick up too high. The Marco Polo dinghy, which is built like a dory, is strong enough for landing on rocky beaches, and she can be kept tight in tropical suns by having a canvas cover to spread over her bottom. This cover should be made of loose-woven canvas, and in dry weather a bucket of sea water can be poured over it every watch.

The Marco Polo dinghy will be quite heavy, and this may sometime be appreciated when you are on the other side of the world, but she can be hoisted aboard with fish tackles attached to the spreaders. When lowering or hoisting, the tender is held out sideways by the third person pushing on an oar whose blade bears against the inside of the farther side of the dinghy. The Marco Polo's dinghy can be made lighter if planked of thinner laminated wood, and although such a dinghy will remain tighter in dry weather, still she will have to be handled with kid gloves and kept in cotton batting or else the thin outer layers of this material will soon be worn through and splintered out. The laminated wood boat will definitely have a short life if used much.

The round bottom lapstrake dinghy is, of course, the best where lightness is paramount, but these are expensive and hard to repaint or repair, so that on the whole the old fashioned dory construction is the cheapest in the end and will stand the most abuse. Its only real disadvantage is from shrinking and cracking if allowed to dry out.

10   VALUES IN CRUISING BOATS

When the boys gather in front of our fireside here at Marblehead on winter nights, an argument frequently arises as to just what is the best type of cruising yacht. Each one seems to have his favorite type, whether it be deep cutter or wide tub, although generally he cannot give his reasons for his choice.

On one occasion we got together and tried to make up a score card, something on the idea of the score cards used by committees in judging horses, dogs, or poultry. While this does not sound very seagoing, it is, however, an interesting way of tallying the value of the different cruising qualities. Of course, no two people will agree on the exact value of the points, but an effort was made to have most of the points measurable in some unit. In the case of speed, cost and fuel consumption, these have to be more or less guessed at on "dream ships."

I have tried, therefore, to arrange the qualities that enter into the successful cruiser in columns of plus and minus, so that they come opposite each other, for it is well known in designing that each element exaggerated in a design is generally at the expense of some other quality. The result is always a compromise.

In the following table, covering the designs of six boats of widely different rig and type, the nine qualities considered are given below. No two people will agree on the plus and minus values I have assigned to the different designs, but they at least offer some means of measuring the design as a whole.

1.   On this first line length and cost are opposite each other, as the larger the boat the greater the cost.

2.   This is self explanatory.

3.   These balance, for deep boats of any size have small deckhouses; hence can carry a boat easily.

4.   On this line flat wide boats, which might have several berths are scored against if they lack head room.

5.   This balance is obvious.

6.   Here the advantages of non-inflammable fuel are balanced by cost.

7.   On this line things do not balance, but boats with slack bilges usually drive easily but heel more when aground.

8.   Here the large engine for speed is scored against on the basis of economy.

9.   Of course speed under sail is one of the most desired qualities, but to prevent the larger and faster type boats from

scoring too much here the rating is a negative quality.

The rating might be taken as that given by any rule which uses the standard time allowance tables, but I have used a rule especially developed for cruising boats, for it is generally considered that all of the existing rules for measuring racing yachts are unsatisfactory for cruisers.

In the following plans I have tried to show boats of quite varying type and size. The only actual existing ones shown are:

No. 4, *Har*, designed and built by S. H. Brown.

No. 6, *Walrus*, owned by Commodore C. A. Welch.

It is interesting and surprising to me to see how some of the boats score, and the resulting figures seem a quite accurate indication of the true value *for the money* for coastal cruising. Why not try to fill out some of the scores, giving your own valuation of the points indicated for the type of cruiser you prefer? Maybe they will rate better than any shown.

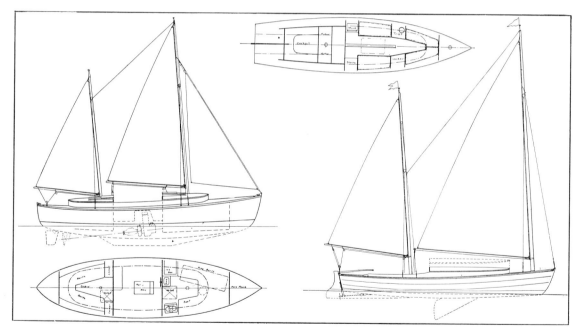

No. 1. Small auxiliary. Dimensions: 30' x 27½' x 8' x 2½'. Sail area, 235 sq. ft. 8 h.p. Diesel

No. 2. Sharpie. Dimensions: 40' x 37' x 10' x 1'. Sail area, 630 sq. ft. Two Flexifour Universals.

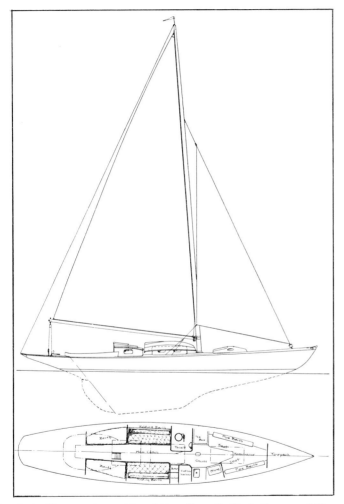

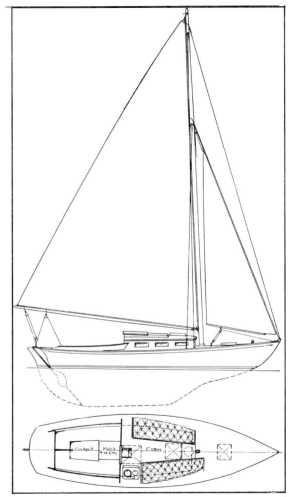

No. 3. Sailing cruiser, 44' x 33' x 9' x 6' 1". Sail area, 642 sq. ft.   *No. 4. Sloop "Har," 23' 10" x 19' 3" x 7' 1" x 3' 8". Sail area, 300 sq. ft.*

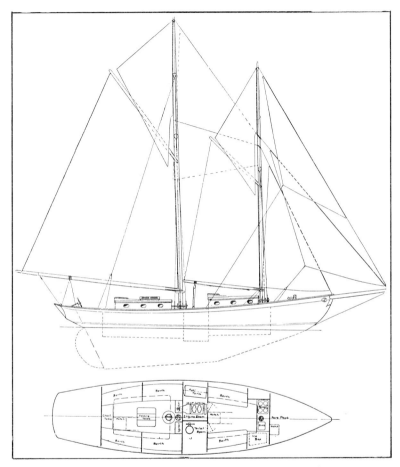

No. 5. Small schooner, 45' x 36' x 11½' x 6½'. Sail area, 1145 sq. ft. 12 h.p. gasoline motor

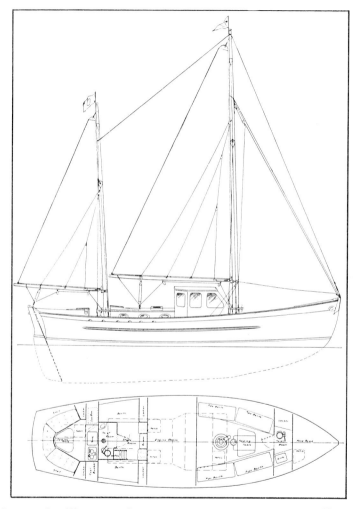

No. 6. Auxiliary "Walrus," 50' x 45' x 14½' x 6'. Sail area, 755 sq. ft. Two 65 h.p. gasoline motors.

PLUS QUALITIES —	No. 1	No. 2	No. 3	No. 4	No. 5	No. 6
1. Each foot over 20 l.w.l.	7.5	17.0	13.0	−0.8	16.0	25.0
2. 10 points for each mast	20.0	20.0	10.0	10.0	20.0	20.0
3. Ability to carry a boat on deck	0	0	5.0	0.0	5.0	0.0
4. Number of berths	3.0	4.0	6.0	2.0	6.0	8.0
5. Number of sails that can be set	3.0	2.0	3.0	3.0	9.0	3.0
6. 10 points if engine uses heavy oil	10.0	0.0	——	0.0	0.0	0.0
7. Fuel cruising radius 1 for each 50 N.M.	15.0	4.0	——	1.5	6.0	10.0
8. Speed under power N.M.P.H.	5.0	7.0	——	6	5.5	9.0
9. Speed under sail No. 3 wind abeam	4.0	6.0	8.0	5	7.5	4.0
Total Plus Points	67.5	60.0	45.0	27.5	75.0	79.0

MINUS QUALITIES +	No. 1	No. 2	No. 3	No. 4	No. 5	No. 6
Price complete, each $1,000	5.5	4.0	11.0	2.8	14.0	16.0
Number of men required to get under way quickly	2.0	2.0	2.0	1.0	3.0	3.0
Feet of draft	2.5	1.0	6.1	3.7	6.5	6.0
Each foot less than 6' headroom	1.5	1.3	.3	1.5	——	0.0
Number of running ropes	6.0	6.0	6.0	5.0	32.0	12.0
Cost of engine (units of $100.)	8.0	6.0	——	3.5	7.0	40.0
Each 5° heel when aground	7.0	0.0	10.0	9.0	9.0	8.0
Cents per mile for fuel	1.0	5.0	——	3.0	4.5	24.0
Each foot of rating	11.5	19.2	21.0	14.2	30.0	19.0
Total Minus Points ..	45.0	44.5	56.4	43.7	106.0	128.1
Point Result....	+22.5	+15.5	−11.4	−17.0	−31.0	−49.1

A PORTFOLIO OF L. FRANCIS HERRESHOFF'S SENSIBLE CRUISING DESIGNS

APPENDIX

In this appendix, we present a complete array of L. Francis Herreshoff's cruising designs. Through the kindness of Mrs. Muriel Vaughn, Mr. Herreshoff's secretary, we were allowed the run of Mr. Herreshoff's fascinating, upstairs workshop at The Castle in Marblehead. Going through all of the original drawings of the great designer and draftsman to select the cruising designs was a rare treat. For purposes of this book, we stayed away from power craft (but included motorsailers) and racing boats (except for a pair of racing canoes we couldn't resist). All of the cruising designs are on the following pages. We only regret that Mr. Herreshoff's passing necessitated that the brief commentaries on the designs be in our words rather than in his.

Roger C. Taylor

RACING KAYAK

Here is as long and slim a hull as one could desire. Fine though she is, her waterline is convex, not hollow, at the ends. She would be slippery in the water, including a certain tenderness, although she has just enough flare in the topsides to prevent the skillful paddler from capsizing. She would be ideal for glassy water, and, if it were shoal enough for the paddler to see the bottom racing by, would be quite exciting.

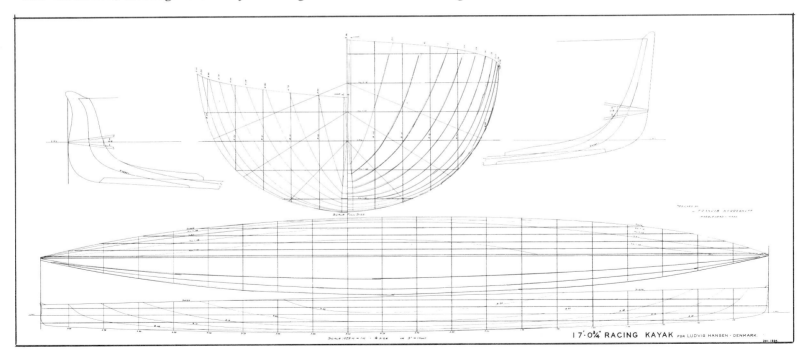

17'·0¾" RACING KAYAK FOR LUDVIG HANSEN · DENMARK

RACING WHITE WATER CANOE

This canoe, designed for rougher going than the previous boat, has a flatter floor than the racing kayak, and so greater stability. With this greater bulk amidships, fineness has been achieved by hollowing out the ends; her waterlines are concave at bow and stern. Her freeboard is higher than that of the kayak, and note the considerable flare high on the bow to throw spray out and away.

She would be fun to paddle either in the white water of an inland stream or that of a bay or river mouth on a rough day. With care and the patience to wait for a real smooth, she might even be launched from an open beach on a quiet day.

It should perhaps be mentioned again for the record that the scales on these plans apply, of course, to Mr. Herreshoff's original drawings, not to these reductions of them.

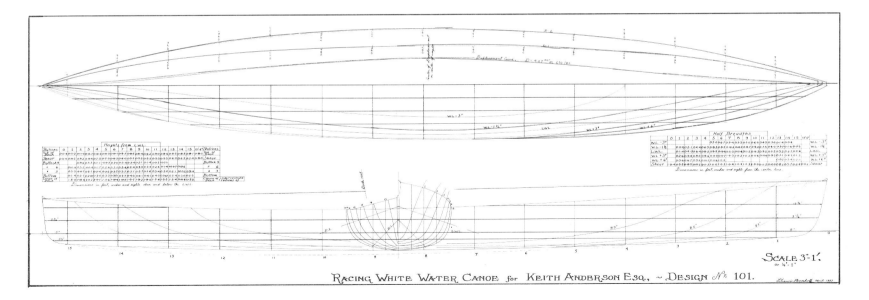

RACING WHITE WATER CANOE for KEITH ANDERSON ESQ., ~ DESIGN N° 101.

ROB ROY CANOE

Here, as the name implies, is a real cruising canoe. Her flat floor, relatively high freeboard, flared ends, and considerable deck area fenced off with a low coaming all indicate she was designed to be able to carry something of a load in fairly rough water. What a great boat she would be for a single-handed cruise along a complex coast like the west coast of Sweden or the eastern shore of the Chesapeake Bay.

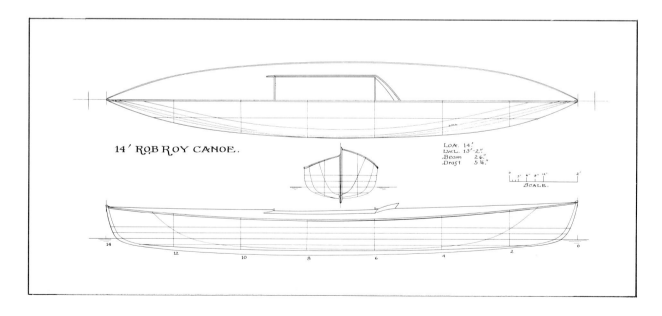

14' ROB ROY CANOE.

LOA. 14'
LWL. 13'-2"
Beam 2'6"
Draft 5'4"

SCALE.

MADOC DUCK BOAT

You wouldn't necessarily have to be a duck hunter to enjoy this boat. She would be an admirable sailing craft for lake or river, a perfectly adequate pulling boat, and good at exploring with a small outboard motor. Thus her great asset is versatility.

Once the centerboard and rudder were removed, she would take kindly to extremely shallow water, or the shore itself. The unusual shape of the centerboard is an ingenious method of putting its trunk way forward where knees won't bump it, yet keeping the lateral resistance of the board itself back where it should be. When running with the board raised, one would have to remember to lower it before jibing. One would also have to be careful not to run aground with the board down, for it might jam in its trunk, unlike a board that pivots from its forward end.

The boat's rig is simple and effective, with all three spars being short enough to stow inside. There are two rowing positions, one for single-handed work, and one for carrying a passenger. The hand rails at the gunwale are convenient for carrying the boat, for it's far easier to carry a small boat by her sides than by her ends.

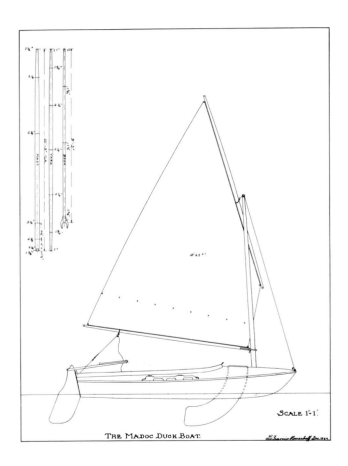

THE MADOC DUCK BOAT.

SCALE 1"=1'

TABLE OF OFFSETS, In feet, inches and eigths of inches, above and below L.W.L. and out from center line.

	STATION NOS.	12'	10'	8'	6'	4'	2'	1'	6"	0
HEIGHTS	CENTER OF DECK	1-2-6	1-7-1	1-9-4	1-7-0	1-6-0	1-3-5	1-2-5	1-2-2	1-2-0
	SHEER LINE	0-9-0	0-8-4	0-8-4	0-9-0	0-10-0	0-11-4	1-0-6	1-1-2	1-2-0
	BUTTOCK 1	0-0-5	0-1-6	0-2-4	0-2-6	0-1-2	+0-5-2	0-11-5		
	PROFILE	0-1-4	0-2-2	0-3-0	0-3-2	0-3-2	-0-2-2	+0-1-2	0-6-0	1-2-0
	DIAGONAL	1-11-4	2-2-3	2-3-2	2-2-4	2-0-0	1-6-0	1-0-6	0-9-6	
WIDTH	SHEER LINE	1-9-0	2-1-0	2-3-1	2-3-0	2-0-3	1-6-3	1-1-0	0-8-7	
	W.L. + 6"	1-8-0	2-0-3	2-2-5	2-2-0	1-9-6	1-0-4	0-5-5	0-0-0	
	W.L. + 3"	1-5-7	1-11-2	2-1-2	2-0-0	1-7-4	0-9-2	0-2-3		
	L.W.L.	1-1-5	1-7-7	1-9-7	1-8-3	1-3-1	0-5-5			

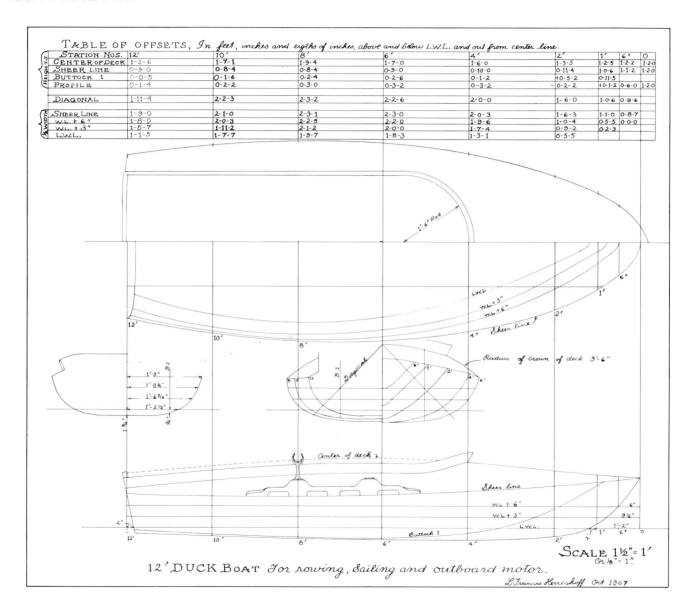

SCALE 1½" = 1'
Or ⅛" = 1"

12' DUCK BOAT For rowing, Sailing and outboard motor.

L. Francis Herreshoff Oct 1967

BEACH CRUISER

The little drawing to the right should conjure up all kinds of dreams, plans, and actions. The sketch of the Beach Cruiser, at rest on her crew's chosen shore, with her sail, its spars, and an oar ingeniously transformed into a tent with six-foot head room at its apex, should be sufficient, by itself, to create a great resurgence of cruising in the smallest craft. Or perhaps it already has.

In any case, this would be an ideal boat in which to explore sheltered shores. She would sail well and could be rowed readily if the wind should fail.

The shape of her topsides is compatible with her leeboards, an alternate method of providing lateral resistance without cluttering up the living space of a very small cruising boat with a centerboard trunk.

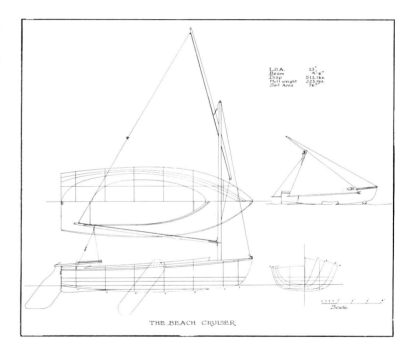

L.O.A.   13'
Beam   4'-6"
Disp   512 lbs.
Hull weight   225 lbs.
Sail Area   76"

Scale.

THE BEACH CRUISER

11'5" SAILING DINGHY

This is a high-performance boat, the kind of dinghy that wants to be sailed flat to windward by the crew hiking out (note the hiking stick on the tiller) and that will plane in a good breeze once the sheet is started. There is little in her underbody to hold her back, and her wide, flat quarters help keep her upright and at her best. She is small enough to row well, and would make a good cruising dinghy for a larger boat, especially for the man who likes to anchor in an interesting harbor and then explore it in a dinghy that will really sail well.

The centerboard trunk has been kept low enough for the crew to climb over easily, and the board is fitted with a dory-type lever, probably the simplest known mechanism for lowering and raising a centerboard. Her stern sheets are ample enough to provide the comfort usually found only in open boats of considerably larger size.

The gunter rig allows a triangular sail with a luff taller than the boat is long, yet with spars that will stow inside the boat.

The original idea behind this design was to start a racing class, beginning with five boats, one of which was to be sailed by the designer.

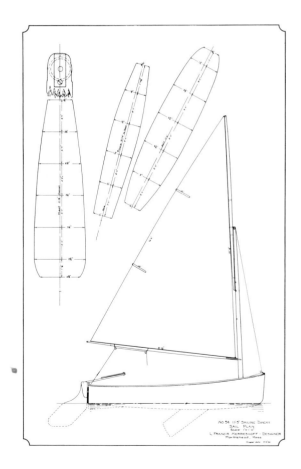

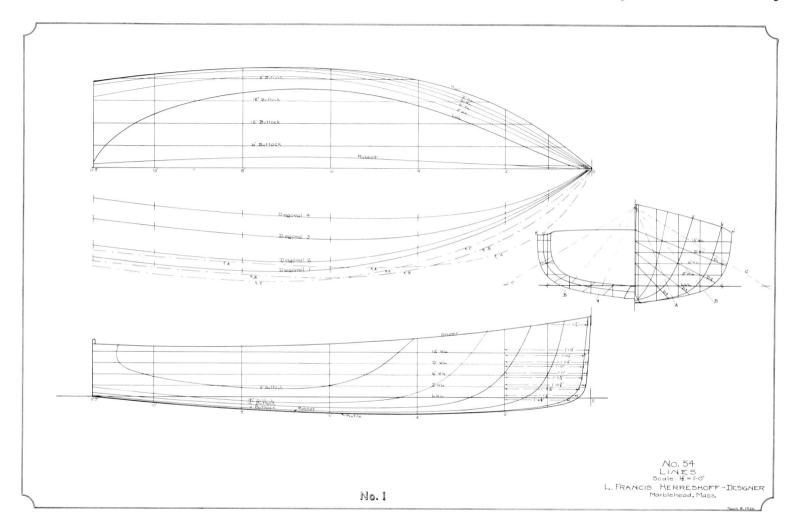

No. 54
LINES
Scale: 1½″ = 1′-0″
L. FRANCIS HERRESHOFF — DESIGNER
Marblehead, Mass.

No. 1

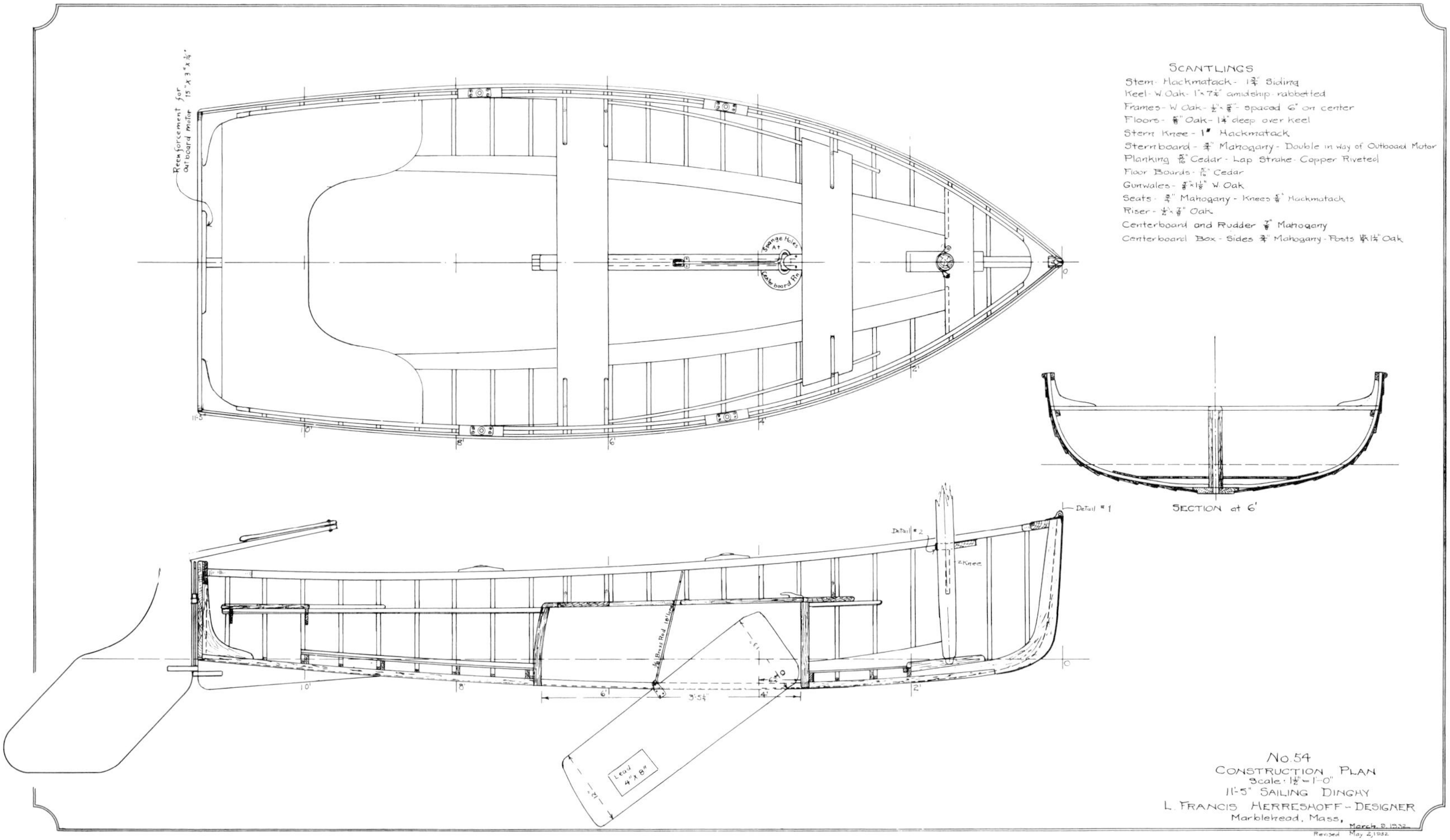
SCANTLINGS
Stem- Hackmatack- 1¾" Siding
Keel- W. Oak- 1"×7¼" amidship- rabbetted
Frames- W. Oak- ½"×⅝"- spaced 6" on center
Floors- ⅝" Oak- 1¼" deep over keel
Stern Knee- 1" Hackmatack
Sternboard- ¾" Mahogany- Double in way of Outboard Motor
Planking 5/16" Cedar- Lap Strake- Copper Riveted
Floor Boards- 5/16" Cedar
Gunwales- ⅝"×1⅛" W. Oak
Seats- ¾" Mahogany- Knees ⅝" Hackmatack
Riser- ½"×⅝" Oak
Centerboard and Rudder ⅞" Mahogany
Centerboard Box- Sides ¾" Mahogany- Posts ⅝×1¼" Oak
Reenforcement for outboard motor
SECTION at 6'
Detail #1
Detail #2
Lead 4"×8"
No. 54
CONSTRUCTION PLAN
Scale: 1½" = 1'-0"
11'-5" SAILING DINGHY
L. FRANCIS HERRESHOFF - DESIGNER
Marblehead, Mass.
March 8, 1932
Revised May 2, 1932

SO AND SO

This fast-looking, 15-foot sailing dinghy was designed by L. Francis for his own use. The finished sail plan is the one with an area of 72 square feet. The dotted line on the sail plan represents an alternate gunter rig of 99 square feet. The boat's mast can pivot to swing down above the rail, as if in a tabernacle, and the spar can be seen to be jointed about four feet above the rail. This was so the top section of the mast, about 14 feet long, would stow on deck without over-hanging.

There are a number of interesting features to be studied on the construction plan on the next page. Note, for example, that the boat has air tanks tucked away under her narrow side decks, running nearly her full length. In a cap-size, the leeward tank would provide considerable flotation in a position to exert self-righting force once the crew started her back up from 90 degrees of heel. The heavy, metal cen-terboard provides ballast for this fine, narrow hull.

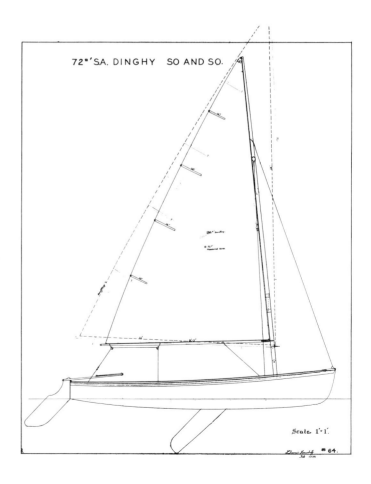

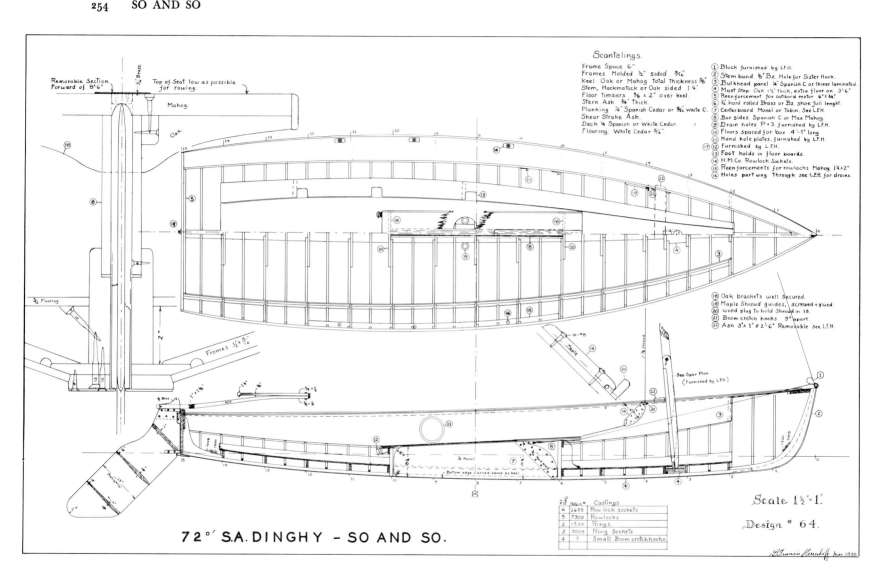

Scantelings.

Frame Space 6"
Frames Molded ½" sided 9/16"
Keel Oak or Mahog Total thickness ⅞"
Stem, Hackmatack or Oak sided 1¼"
Floor Timbers ⅝ x 2" over keel.
Stern Ash ¾" Thick.
Planking ¼" Spanish Cedar or 9/32 white C.
Shear Strake Ash.
Deck ⅛ Spanish or White Cedar.
Flooring, White Cedar 3/16"

1. Block furnished by L.F.H.
2. Stem band ⅜" Bz. Hole for Sister Hook.
3. Bulkhead panel ⅛" Spanish C or thiner laminated.
4. Mast Step. Oak 1½" thick, extra floor on 3'-6".
5. Reenforcement for outboard motor 6" x ¾".
6. ¼" hard rolled Brass or Bz. shoe full lenght.
7. Centerboard Monel or Tobin. See L.F.H.
8. Box sides Spanish C or Mex Mahog.
9. Drain holes P+S furnished by L.F.H.
10. Floors spaced for box 4'-1" long
11. Hand hole plates, furnished by L.F.H.
12. Furnished by L.F.H.
13. Foot holds in floor boards.
14. H.M.Co. Rowlock Sockets.
15. Reenforcements for rowlocks Mahog 1¾ x 2".
16. Holes part way through see L.F.H for drains.

18. Oak brackets well secured.
19. Maple Shroud guides, screwed + glued.
20. Wood plug to hold Shroud in 19.
21. Boom crotch hooks 9" apart.
22. Ash 3"x 1" x 2'-6" Removable see L.F.H.

Removable Section Forward of 8'-6"
Top of Seat low as possible for rowing.
Mahog.
Oak
Stern Ash ¾ Thick
Flooring
Frames ½ x 9/16

No. Req	Pattern	Castings
6	2685	Rowlock sockets
5	7309	Rowlocks
2	1520	Rings
2	7009	Ring Sockets
4	?	Small Boom crotch hooks

72 o' S.A. DINGHY - SO AND SO.

Scale 1½"= 1'.

Design # 64.

L Francis Herreshoff Mar 1935

BUZZARDS BAY 14 FOOTER

This is Francis Herreshoff's enlargement of his father's famous 12½ footer. These are waterline lengths, of course.
The 12½ footer, also known as the Buzzard Bay Boy's Boat,
the Bullseye, and the Dough Dish, was an extremely popular,
able, and handsome small daysailer built by the dozens at
the Herreshoff Manufacturing Company, Bristol, Rhode
Island, to the design and under the supervision of Nathanael
Greene Herreshoff.

Llewellyn Howland, a great admirer of the Herreshoffs,
father and son, and the man responsible for the creation of
the Concordia yawl, wanted a slightly larger version of the
12½-footer for daysailing on his beloved Buzzards Bay. This
design was the result. Nathanael Herreshoff also designed
a still larger version, the Fish Class, 16 feet on the waterline.

All these boats are amazingly able in rough water. They
were designed to cope with the hard sou'westers of the typical summer afternoon on Buzzards Bay and with the steep,
cresting chop that inevitably results, especially when the tide
is ebbing. We have seen one of the 12½ footers sailing comfortably under such conditions with six people aboard and
full sail set. This is a true little yacht.

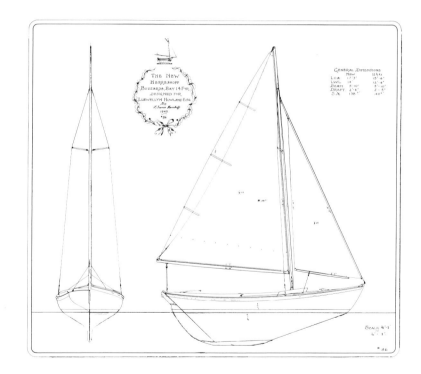

	18'	16'-6"	15'	13'-6"	12'	10'-6"	9'	7'-6"	6'	4'-6"	3'	1'-6"	0	
Top of Deck at Sides	1-9-1	1-6-5	1-4-6	1-3-5	1-3-1	1-3-4	1-3-4	1-4-4	1-5-6	1-7-4	1-9-4	2-0-0	2-3-0	Top of Deck
Buttock 24"		1-3-0	0-7-1	+0-2-3	~0-0-7	-0-2-7	-0-3-2	-0-2-1	0-1-2	0-9-3	2-2-4			B 24"
" 18"	+1-6-4	+0-10-1	+0-3-7	-0-0-6	-0-5-7	-0-5-7	-0-6-7	-0-6-1	-0-3-5	0-1-6	1-1-2	2-10-2		B 18"
" 12"	+1-3-1	+0-7-5	+0-1-5	-0-3-2	-0-6-7	-0-9-5	-0-10-2	-0-7-4	-0-3-4	0-4-0	1-10-3			B 12"
" 6"	+1-1-2	+0-6-0	-0-0-1	-0-6-1	-0-10-6	-1-1-7	-1-1-7	+1-3-2	-0-11-7	-0-8-3	-0-2-2	0-11-1	2-11-7	B 6"
Rabbet			-0-3-0	-1-4-0	-2-0-0	-1-10-4	-1-9-0	-1-7-4	-1-6-0	-1-1-1	-0-7-4	0-1-3	2-4-0	Rabbet
Face		+1-0-0	-0-6-0	-2-0-0	-2-5-5	-2-5-0+	-2-4-4	-2-1-4	-1-7-0	-1-1-5	-0-8-2	0-0-0	2-3-0	Face
At Deck	1-9-0	2-2-0	2-5-5	2-8-2	2-10-1	2-11-0	2-11-0	2-10-2	2-8-2	2-4-2	1-10-0	1-1-0	0-0-5	Deck
WL + 18"										2-3-7	1-8-4	0-9-6		WL+18"
" + 12"	0-1-4	1-8-7	2-4-0	2-7-5	2-9-6	2-10-6	2-10-5	2-6-5	2-1-4	1-5-2	0-6-4			WL+12"
" + 6"		0-6-4	1-10-3	2-4-5	2-7-6	2-9-2	2-8-6	2-7-2	2-3-6	1-9-5	1-1-2	0-3-4		WL+6"
LWL		0-1-1	0-6-4	1-1-4	2-1-6	2-4-0	2-4-2	2-2-6	1-10-6	1-4-0	0-8-2	0-0-2		LWL
WL - 6"			0-0-6	0-6-2	1-1-7	1-5-7	1-7-2	1-6-2	1-2-2	0-8-6	0-2-2			WL-6"
" " - 12"			0-0-3	0-1-7	0-4-5	0-7-6	0-9-4	0-8-4	0-6-0	0-1-7				WL-12"
" " - 18"			0-0-2	0-1-1	0-2-6	0-3-4	0-4-4	0-3-5	0-1-0					WL-18"
" " - 24"				0-0-6	0-1-5	0-2-5	0-2-7	0-1-5						WL-24"
Face	1-9-2		0-0-6	0-0-6	?	?	?	?	0-0-3	0-0-2	0-0-2	0-0-2	0-0-5	Face
Diagonal 1				0-2-0	0-3-7	0-5-6	0-6-7	0-6-2	0-4-4	0-1-4				D 1
" 2			0-3-3	0-8-6	1-0-3	1-2-4	1-3-4	1-3-0	1-1-2	0-8-3	0-6-0	0-0-2		D 2
" 3	0-0-4	0-9-2	1-4-4	1-9-4	2-1-1	2-2-3	2-3-4	2-0-3	1-8-0	1-2-1	0-6-0			D 3
" 4	1-4-6	2-0-5	2-6-2	2-10-0	3-0-3	3-1-4	3-1-3	3-0-0	2-9-1	2-4-1	1-9-0	0-11-3		D 4

$\bar{C} D = 31.5''$ or 2,000 lbs

Lead = 1,27 $\frac{1}{2}$'' or 900 lbs or 45 % of D.

SCALE 1½ = 1.

#86.

BUZZARDS BAY 14 FTR
DESIGNED FOR
LLEWELLYN HOWLAND ESQ. ~ SOUTH DARTMUTH,
MASSACHUSETTS.

NARRAGANSETT BAY BOAT

This is a very early Francis Herreshoff design, done when he was still at Bristol. Like her Buzzards Bay cousins, she would be an able boat in rough water. Her rig is somewhat reminiscent of that of Captain Nat's S boats, with its curved mast and small jib. Note the three-quarter-length jib club, a favorite Captain Nat rig. Also note the long battens in the mainsail, with the top one running from leech to luff. At first glance, her sail plan looks too far aft, as if she would carry a weather helm, but her lateral plane is also well aft.

She looks to be a boat eminently well suited for the fine sailing waters of Narragansett Bay.

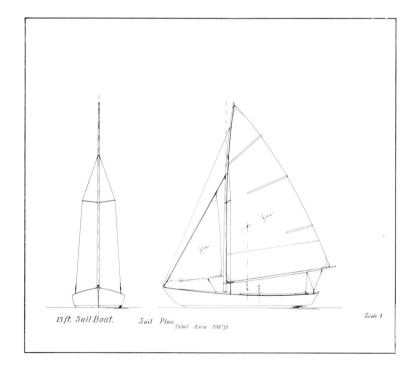

15 ft. Sail Boat.   Sail Plan
Total Area 208 ft   Scale t

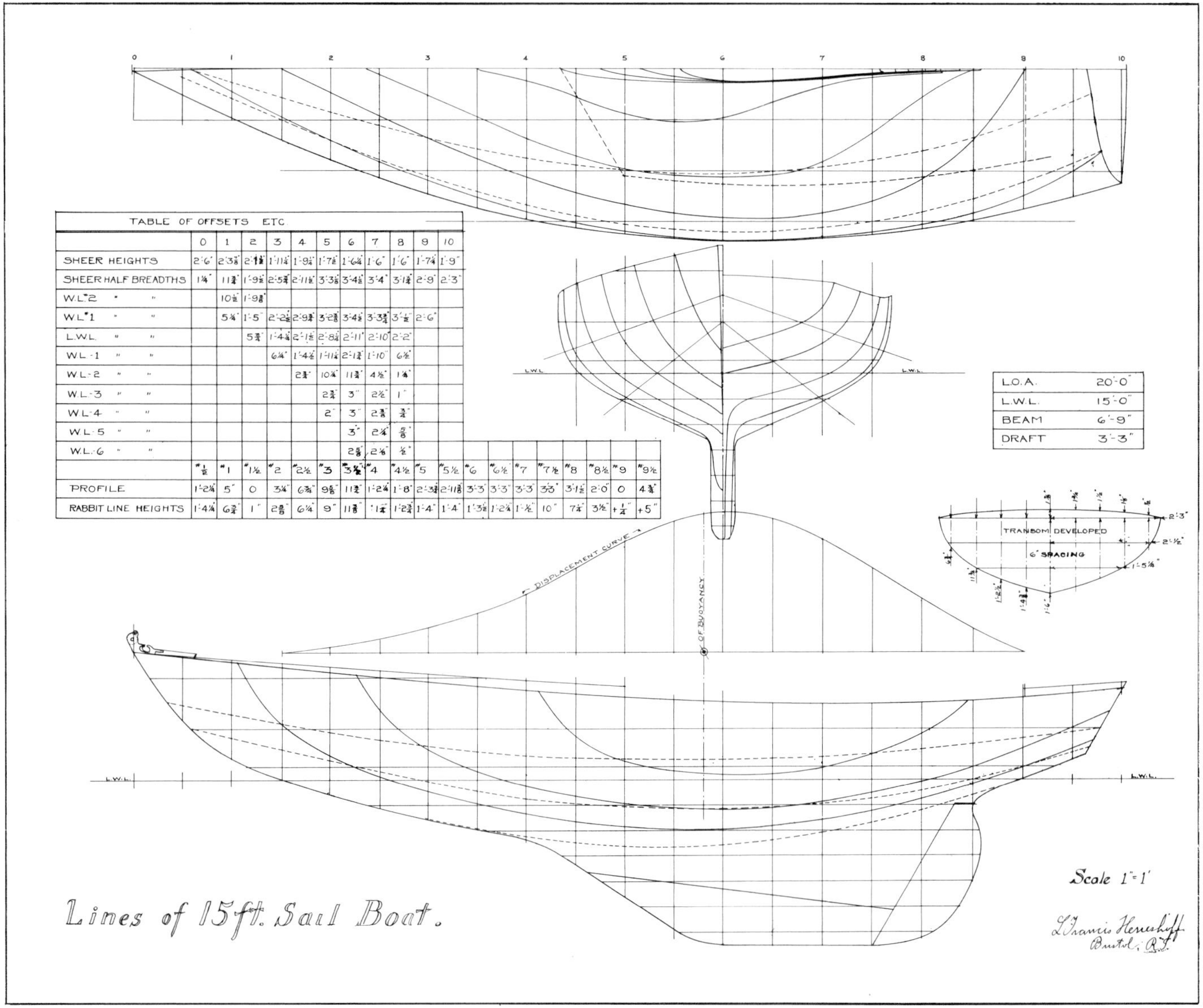
L.W.L.
DISPLACEMENT CURVE
C OF BUOYANCY
TRANSOM DEVELOPED
6" SPACING
Scale 1"=1'
Lines of 15ft. Sail Boat.
L. Francis Herreshoff
Bristol, R.I.

TABLE OF OFFSETS ETC.

	0	1	2	3	4	5	6	7	8	9	10
SHEER HEIGHTS	2'-6"	2'-3 7/8"	2'-1 1/2"	1'-11 1/4"	1'-9 1/4"	1'-7 1/2"	1'-6 1/4"	1'-6"	1'-6"	1'-7 1/4"	1'-9"
SHEER HALF BREADTHS	1 1/4"	11 3/4"	1'-9 1/2"	2'-5 3/4"	2'-11 1/2"	3'-3 3/8"	3'-4 1/2"	3'-4"	3'-1 3/4"	2'-9"	2'-3"
W.L.#2 " "		10 1/2"	1'-9 3/8"								
W.L.#1 " "		5 1/4"	1'-5"	2'-2 1/2"	2'-9 3/4"	3'-2 3/8"	3'-4 1/2"	3'-3 3/4"	3'-1/2"	2'-6"	
L.W.L. " "			5 3/4"	1'-4 1/4"	2'-1 1/2"	2'-8 1/4"	2'-11"	2'-10"	2'-2"		
W.L.-1 " "				6 1/4"	1'-4 1/2"	1'-11 1/4"	2'-1 3/4"	1'-10"	6 1/2"		
W.L.-2 " "					2 3/4"	10 1/4"	11 3/4"	4 1/2"	1 1/4"		
W.L.-3 " "						2 3/4"	3"	2 1/2"	1"		
W.L.-4 " "						2"	3"	2 3/8"	3/4"		
W.L.-5 " "							3"	2 1/4"	5/8"		
W.L.-6 " "							2 5/8"	2 1/8"	1/2"		

	#1/2	#1	#1 1/2	#2	#2 1/2	#3	#3 3/4	#4	#4 1/2	#5	#5 1/2	#6	#6 1/2	#7	#7 1/2	#8	#8 1/2	#9	#9 1/2
PROFILE	1'-2 1/4"	5"	0	3 1/4"	6 3/4"	9 5/8"	11 3/4"	1'-2 1/4"	1'-8"	2'-3 3/4"	2'-11 3/8"	3'-3"	3'-3"	3'-3"	3'-3"	3'-1 1/2"	2'-0"	0	4 3/4"
RABBIT LINE HEIGHTS	1'-4 1/4"	6 3/4"	1"	2 5/8"	6 1/4"	9"	11 3/8"	1 1/4"	1'-2 3/4"	1'-4"	1'-4"	1'-3 1/2"	1'-2 1/4"	1'-1/2"	10"	7 1/4"	3 1/2"	+1/4"	+5"

L.O.A.	20'-0"
L.W.L.	15'-0"
BEAM	6'-9"
DRAFT	3'-3"

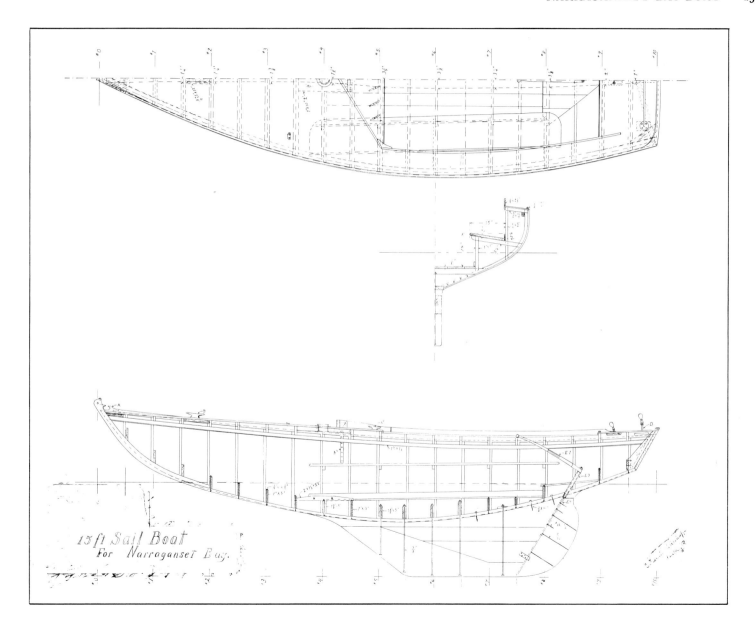

15 ft Sail Boat
For Narraganset Bay.

CENTERBOARD KNOCKABOUT

This 17-footer draws all of four inches when light. With generous sail plan and almost nonexistent underbody, she should be a real flyer if the crew could keep her reasonably upright. She would want to be reefed in a breeze, and the crew would have to make use of her nicely curved, double-yoke tiller to steer from a position well out on the weather rail when going to windward. If top speed weren't the objective, though, she would still sail very well and comfortably under short rig. Such a fast boat gives her crew a choice of whether to sail fast and work hard, or sail at a more moderate speed and take it easy. The crew of a boat designed solely for comfort and ease of handling has no such choice.

The shape of the bow of this boat is particularly interesting. The profile shows a knuckle just above the waterline that became typical of many Francis Herreshoff designs. And note the shapes of the forward ends of the waterlines. The load waterline (with the boat light) is convex, as is the waterline up near the deck, but the waterlines between these two, especially the one three inches above the load waterline, are very hollow. Of course when sailing, these waterlines would often be immersed.

This design seems to exude pure speed.

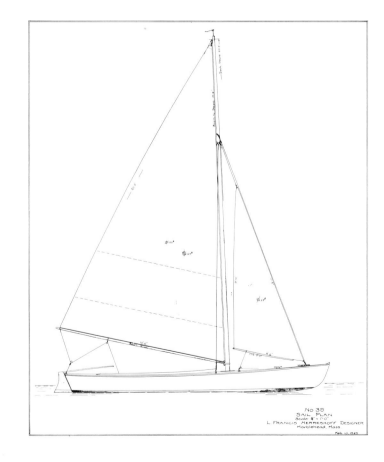

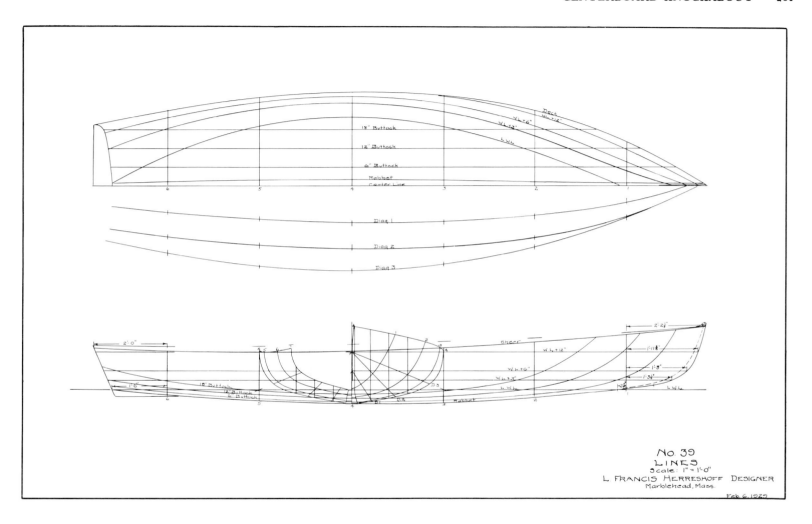

No. 39
LINES
Scale: 1" = 1'-0"
L. FRANCIS HERRESHOFF DESIGNER
Marblehead, Mass.
Feb. 6, 1929

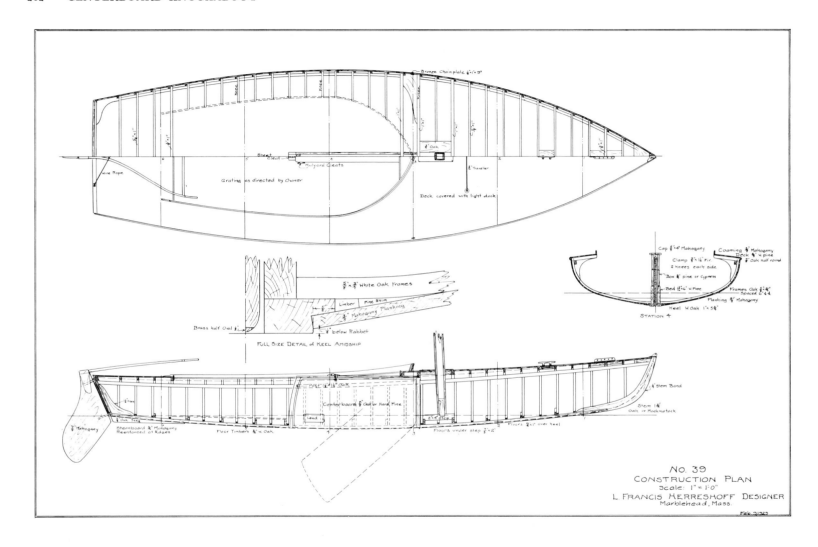

Bronze Chainplate ⅛"×1"×9"

Knee

Knee

Knee

Knee

Sheet Cleat

Halyard Cleats

⅞" Oak

⅜" Traveller

Wire Rope

Grating as directed by Owner

Deck covered with light duck

Cap ⅝"×4" Mahogany   Coaming ¾" Mahogany
Clamp ⅞"×1½" Fir   Deck ¾" W.pine
2 knees each side   ¾" Oak half round
Box ⅞" pine or Cypress
Bed 1⅞"×6" W.Pine   Frames Oak ⅝"×¾"
                            Spaced 6" c.c.
Keel W.Oak 1"×5¾"   Planking ½" Mahogany

STATION 4

⅝"×¾" White Oak Frames

Limber   Pine Shim
½" Mahogany Planking

Brass half Oval ⅜"

¾" below Rabbet

FULL SIZE DETAIL of KEEL AMIDSHIP

⅝" Stem Band

Stem 1⅝"
Oak or Hackmatack

Centerboard ⅝" Oak or Hard Pine

2"×4" Step

¾" Mahogany
Sternboard ¾" Mahogany
Reenforced at Edges

Oak Seat

Floor Timbers ⅞" W.Oak

Lead

Floors under step ⅝"×2"   Floors ⅝"×1" over keel

NO. 39
CONSTRUCTION PLAN
Scale: 1" = 1'-0"
L. FRANCIS HERRESHOFF DESIGNER
Marblehead, Mass.

Feb. 21,1920

CENTERBOARD CRUISING SLOOP

This is the original Prudence, the ancestor of the H-23, whose plans appear in the introduction to this book and whose portrait is on the dust jacket.

This boat's hull, with its handsome lapstrake planking, looks wholesome and able. With her fine ends and easy run she should have a good turn of speed. Her two-foot draft would allow plenty of interesting exploring.

The dotted line on the sail plan showing additional draft on the underwater profile is a modification suggested by the designer for another client ten years after the drawing of the original design.

The rig is straightforward. The lazyjacks on the jib club make a handy arrangement, and the bowsprit would serve well as an anchor derrick.

The layout is practical, and the centerboard trunk is really less of an obstruction than it appears in the drawings. Nonetheless, we wonder if Mr. Herreshoff might have designed this boat with leeboards later in his career. We are reasonably sure that the large engine taking up most of the cockpit of this boat was specified by the owner, not L. Francis.

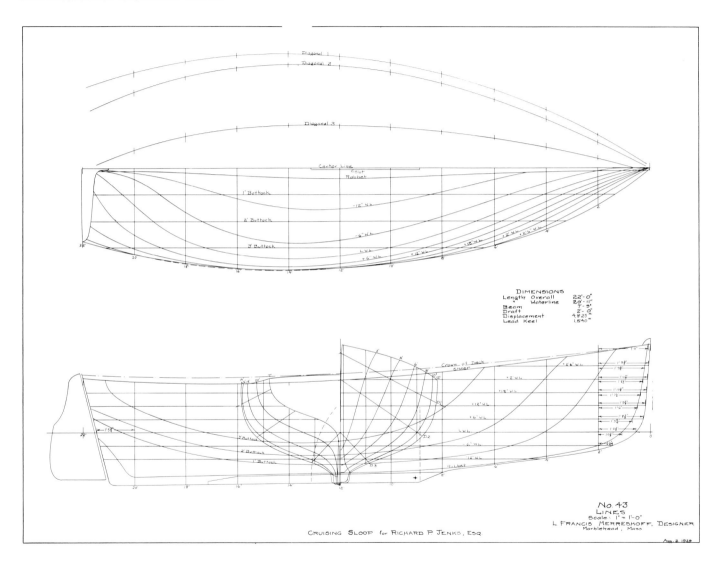

DIMENSIONS
Length Overall   22'-0"
   "   Waterline   20'-11"
Beam   7'-9"
Draft   2'-0"
Displacement   4,825
Lead Keel   1,540

No. 43
LINES
Scale 1" = 1'-0"
L FRANCIS HERRESHOFF, DESIGNER
Marblehead, Mass

CRUISING SLOOP for RICHARD P JENKS, ESQ

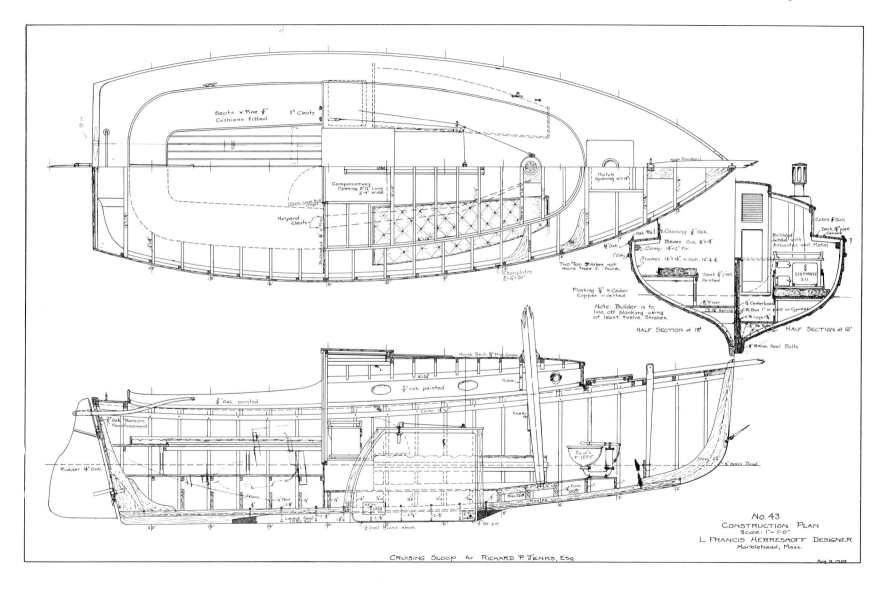

HALF SECTION at 18'

HALF SECTION at 12'

No. 43
CONSTRUCTION PLAN
Scale: 1" = 1'-0"
L. FRANCIS HERRESHOFF DESIGNER
Marblehead, Mass.

CRUISING SLOOP for RICHARD P. JENKS, ESQ.

BLOCK ISLAND BOAT

In this design, L. Francis refined the famous and traditional double-ended fishing craft developed at Block Island, Rhode Island, to make an able cruising boat. The boat was designed for W. J. Strawbridge, an oft-repeating client of Mr. Herreshoff's, but unfortunately was never built. She would have been a most interesting craft.

This boat is narrower and deeper than the working craft from which she derived, and a bit of curve has been introduced into the stem. The deadwood has been cut away a bit to make her handier in stays, a device employed by L. Francis on other designs of traditional yachts. Also, by comparison with the working Block Island boats, this vessel has finer, more hollow ends, less flare to the topsides, a bit more freeboard, and less sheer, especially forward. The end result is a boat with less extremes than the Block Island boats and one that would sail faster and be drier on deck than boats that had to work off the beach and fish for a living.

The traditional Block Island boat rig has been retained, although the foremast has been moved aft a trifle and the main boom shortened a bit. The boat carries less sail than did her ancestors. Standing rigging has been added, a complexity the Block Islanders did without. A pencilled after-thought to this design which doesn't appear, was a large balloon jib setting to a portable bowsprit. With this sail set she spread 1,629 square feet of sail. Her mainsail is 695 square feet, and the foresail, 562 square feet.

As these large sails indicate, this was a sizeable vessel, considerably bigger than she seems to be in the sail plan, probably because of her simplicity of rig and accoutrements. She is 51 feet long on deck, with a waterline length of 44 feet, a beam of 14'6", and a draft of 7 feet.

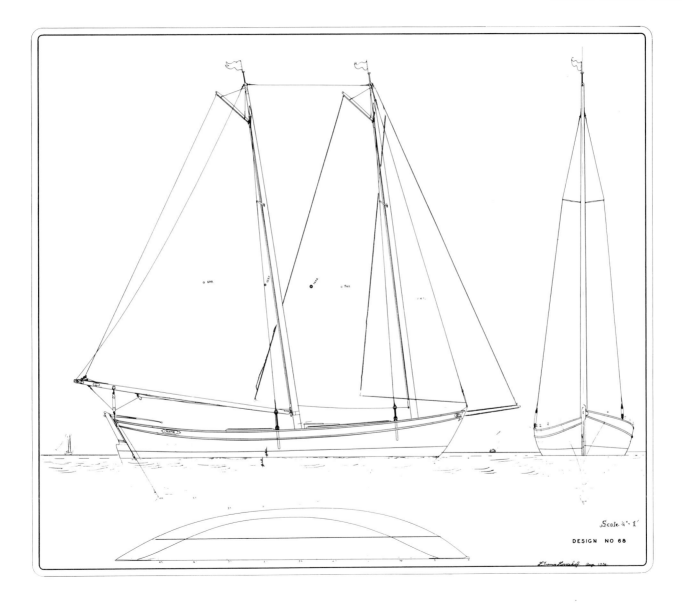

Scale ¼"–1'

DESIGN NO 68

L. Francis Herreshoff   Aug 1936

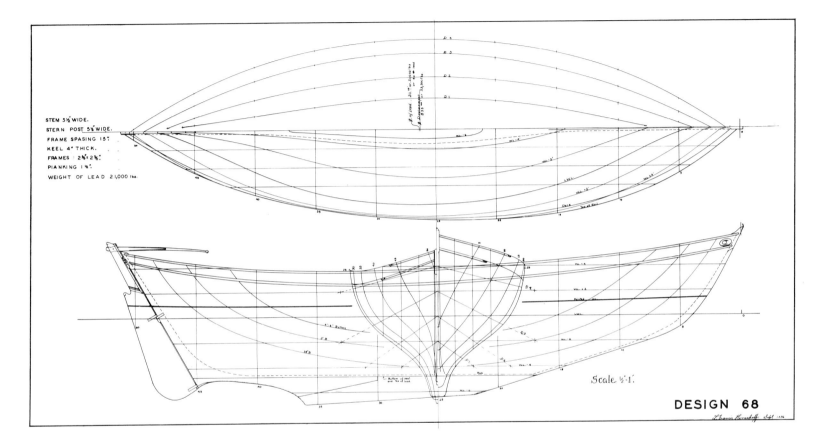

STEM 5½" WIDE.
STERN POST 5½" WIDE.
FRAME SPASING 15".
KEEL 4" THICK.
FRAMES 2⅜" 2⅜".
PLANKING 1½".
WEIGHT OF LEAD 21,000 lbs.

Scale ½"-1'.

DESIGN 68

CANOE YAWL

This great little cruising vessel is the original design of the fictitious canoe yawl that L. Francis wrote about in his delightful cruising stories published in *The Rudder* and later in book form in his *The Compleat Cruiser*. Thus she is the direct ancestor of the *Rozinante* of Chapter 4.

Long and slim, she has an exceptionally easily driven hull and so would be a good performer in all conditions without having to carry a great deal of sail. The divided rig is easily handled, and the boat will sail very well under jib and mizzen, or reach off nicely under mainsail alone.

Although the client wanted an engine in his boat, Mr. Herreshoff's original concept for this design was that she could be rowed with a ten-foot sweep. One of the reasons for the long cockpit was so that a standing oarsman could pull when he got tired of pushing, and vice versa. With her balanced rudder, she would be unusually easy to steer. Her deep-V sections indicate a boat with considerable stiffness and power. Under the house, she has a double berth forward and a galley aft.

This boat dimensions are: length on deck, 28'9"; length on the waterline, 24 feet; beam, 7 feet; and draft, 3'9". Her sail area is 342 square feet, with 164 square feet in the mainsail, 69 square feet in the mizzen, and 109 square feet in the jib.

In *The Compleat Cruiser,* the *Rozinante's* owner, Mr. Weldon, explained how he came by his boat: "After searching for a boat several years and finding nothing worth considering, I went to Old Fussbudget, the yacht designer. I went to him because he was one of the few left who could design a boat which was a good sailer and still had romance in her looks.

"I thought he was an old crank," remarked Coridon.

"I can imagine he would be," said Weldon, "if someone asked for impractical things in the design, but my requirements were so simple that he was very enthusiastic about the work."

"Just what did you ask for?" inquired Goddard.

"I told him I wanted a boat I could have peace and freedom in . . . ."

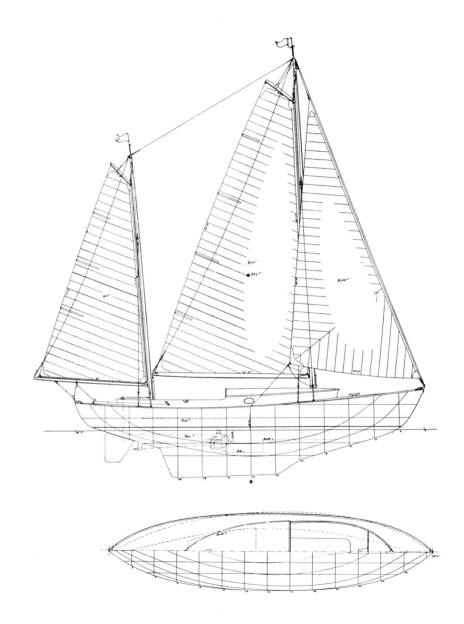

DULCINEA

This able double-ender could perhaps be considered a stout ancestor of the *Rozinante,* for she was designed some years prior to the canoe yawl. Her easily driven hull should slip along well, and she would certainly stand up to her moderate rig in most kinds of weather. Her design suggests an ability to make extended cruises in unfrequented waters. With her snug rig, she also has the look of a good cold-weather cruiser.

She has plenty of freeboard and a strong sheer. She would be quite "corky," and shouldn't take much solid water on deck. One can envision her picking her way nimbly through a heavy seaway.

Since the purpose of the design is clearly safety and comfort, even in blowing weather, some might prefer a club on the jib to make it self-tending. Not that a jib of 97 square feet should cause too much trouble, but it's just the bother of having to shift the sheet over when tacking. Her mainsail has 143 square feet, and the mizzen, 81 square feet, for a total area of 321 square feet.

Below, the boat has four pipe berths, L. Francis' favorite kind of bed afloat. The galley is at the forward end of the house, and there is a small enclosed head.

The engine specified is a Gray-430, a good-sized power plant to compensate for the boat's moderate rig in light airs, or shove her along in a calm.

The photograph shows a boat built to this design ready to go overboard into a Swiss lake. She was built in Zurich.

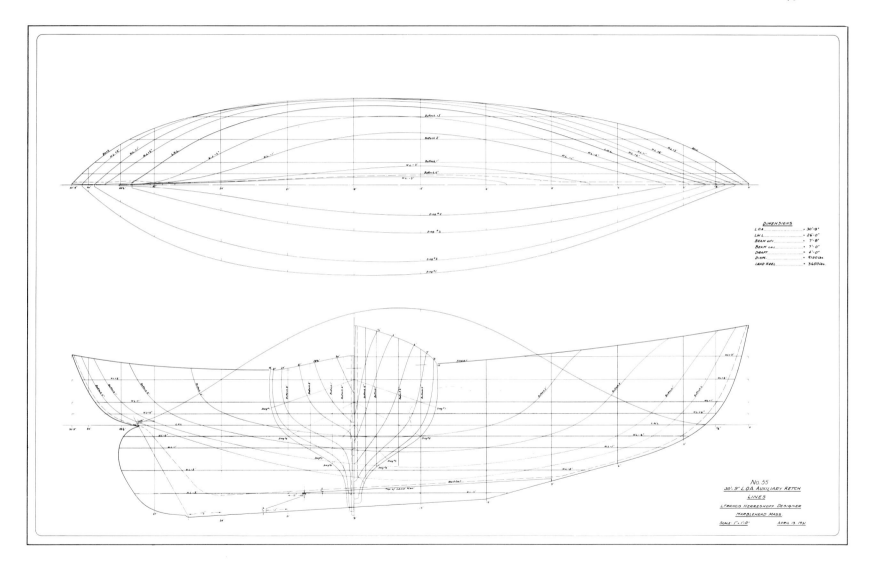

DIMENSIONS
L.O.A. .... = 30'-9"
L.W.L. .... = 26'-0"
BEAM OVER .... = 7'-8"
BEAM L.W.L. ..... = 7'-0"
DRAFT .... = 4'-0"
DISPL. .... = 9100 Lbs.
LEAD KEEL .... = 3650 Lbs.

No. 55
30'-9" L.O.A. AUXILIARY KETCH
LINES
L. FRANCIS HERRESHOFF DESIGNER
MARBLEHEAD MASS.
SCALE 1"-1'-0"   APRIL 13 1931

274   DULCINEA

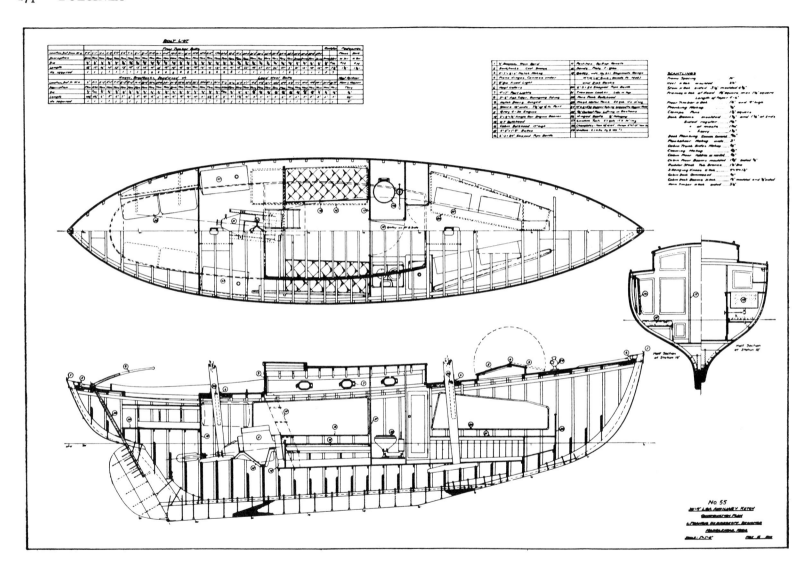

WAGON BOX

One of the owner's requirements for the design of this fine little ketch was that he be able to stow his dinghy on deck. One trusts that with the pram stowed athwartships he rigged lifelines aft from the main rigging for something to hang onto when clambering over her bow or stern. This boat, about the same size as the *Dulcinea,* carries a bit more sail and has a bit more power to carry it with her somewhat greater beam and draft. Because of these factors and her rather low freeboard, the *Wagon Box* would probably be a better performer to windward than would *Dulcinea.* The sail plan shows a masthead Genoa jib with an area of 214 square feet. The sail is evidently to be used for reaching, for it would indeed be hard to pass it between the stays when tacking. For chasing away before the wind, there are twin spinnakers, each with an area of about 135 square feet.

Because the deadrise is moderate, the engine and propeller have been kept low, advantages both as to ballasting and efficient propeller operation.

As is usual with Herreshoff designs, the diagonals are extremely fair. Not all designers agree as to the importance of fair diagonals, but the water must follow their curves, just as it follows the curves of waterlines and buttock lines, so if the diagonals are lumpy, the hull must cause turbulence. If there are problems with the diagonals, then it would appear that the designer needs to do more work with his model to get it truly fair all over.

The sheer line on this design is particularly pleasing, and her low freeboard would make her fun to sail in coastal waters. The freeboard amidships is only a bit over 18 inches; at the stern it is $2\frac{1}{2}$ feet, and at the bow, $3\frac{1}{2}$ feet. In a low-sided boat, you always seem to be going faster than you really are, because you are closer to the bubbles going by. And according to Mr. Weldon, the owner of the *Rozinante* in *The Compleat Cruiser,* seven-eighths of the adventure and romance of sailing his boat took place in his mind, just as did the adventures of Don Quixote, which, of course, was why he had named his little vessel after the Don's steed.

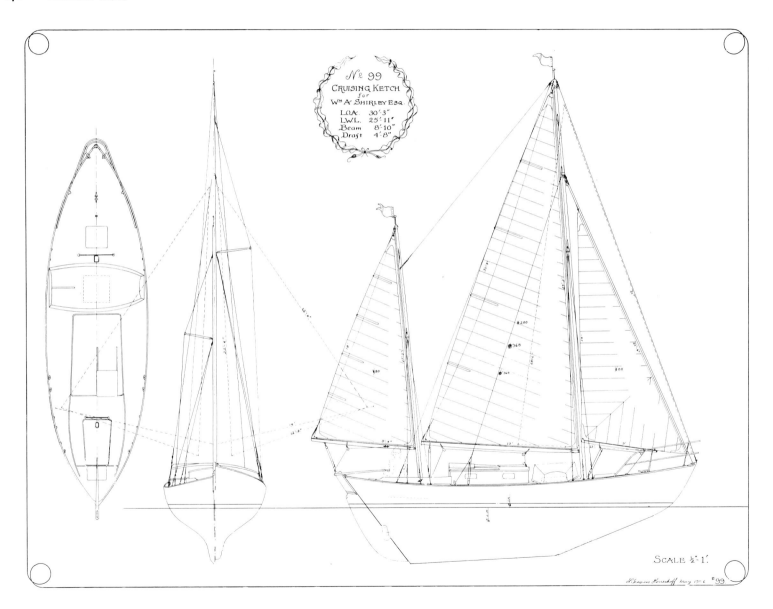

Nº 99
CRUISING KETCH
for
Wᵐ Aᵗ Shirley Esq.

L.O.A. 30' 3"
L.W.L. 25' 11"
Beam   8' 10"
Draft   4' 8"

SCALE ½"-1'.

Station numbers	30	28	26	24	22	20	18	16	14	12	10	8	6	4	2	0	Station numbers
Top of Deck at Sides	2-7-0	2-3-1	2-0-3	1-10-4	1-9-4	1-9-0	1-9-0	1-9-5	1-10-4	1-11-7	2-1-4	2-3-6	2-6-3	2-9-4	3-1-2	3-5-5	Top of deck at sides
Top of Lead			4-0-0	3-9-5	3-7-2	3-4-7	3-3-5			2-4-0							Lead
Rabbet	2-4-3	-0-0-0	2-9-0	4-0-2	3-9-6	3-6-0	3-5-0	3-2-5	3-0-1	2-9-6	2-4-2	1-4-6	0-3-2	10-6-4	3-7-4	Rabbet
Profile	2-3-4	-0-3-0	2-9-6	4-8-0	4-6-6	4-5-2	4-4-0	4-2-5	4-1-2	4-0-0	3-2-6	2-5-4	1-8-1	0-10-6	10-2-7	3-5-5	Profile
Buttock 1	3-7-0	2-1-7	-0-3-1	1-1-4	1-8-1	2-1-0	2-4-3	2-7-0	2-7-1	2-5-1	2-0-3	1-5-4	0-8-3	10-4-2	2-4-3	4-6-2	Buttock 1
B 2		2-8-4	0-7-1	-0-4-2	0-11-0	1-4-0	1-7-4	1-8-7	1-8-4	1-6-1	1-1-3	10-5-7	1-4-4	1-10-0	3-11-0		B 2
B 3			2-3-0	0-3-0	-0-3-0	0-11-2	1-0-0	0-8-6	0-2-2		10-7-0					B 3
Deck at sides	0-4-1	1-10-0	2-9-7	3-6-0	3-11-4	4-2-7	4-4-4	4-5-2	4-5-3	4-4-3	4-2-1	3-10-1	3-4-0	2-7-0	1-6-1	0-1-0	Deck at sides
WL+2'		1-7-6	2-9-7			4-1-4	4-4-6		4-3-6	4-1-7	3-8-5	3-0-7	2-1-1	0-9-6		WL+2'
WL+1'			0-10-2	2-4-0	3-3-9	3-3-0	3-11-0	4-0-0	3-10-7	3-7-6	3-9-4	2-5-6	1-5-3	0-4-2		WL+1'
LWL			0-2-3	1-3-6	2-5-4	3-3-0	3-8-4	4-0-0	3-7-6	3-2-0	2-6-0	1-8-0	0-9-0			LWL
WL-1'			0-5-0	1-1-2	1-10-4	2-6-4	3-0-7	3-0-0	2-8-1	1-5-6	0-9-0				WL-1'
WL-2'			0-1-7	0-4-6	1-0-5	1-0-5	1-4-2	1-7-1	1-7-0	1-0-5	0-5-5				WL-2'
WL-3'				0-2-2	0-4-0	0-5-7	0-7-6	0-8-7	0-8-7	0-2-7				WL-3'
WL-4'				0-1-4	0-2-5	0-3-7	0-4-4	0-4-6							WL-4'
Rabbet	0-1-7	0-1-7	0-1-7	0-1-7	0-2-5	0-4-1	0-5-5	0-6-7	0-7-3	0-7-0	0-4-1	0-1-7	0-1-7	0-1-7	0-1-7	Rabbet
Face	0-1-0	0-1-0	0-1-5	0-1-1	0-2-2	0-3-0	0-3-0	0-1-4	0-1-2	0-0-7	0-0-6	0-0-5	0-0-4	0-1-0	Face

Dimensions in feet, inches, and eights of inches above and below the L.W.L. and out from center line.
Planking thickness, between 1" and 1¼".
½ siding of Stem and Stern post 1⅜".

SCALE 1"=1'

CRUISING KETCH for Wm A. Shirley Esq.   DESIGN No 99 ~ SHEET 2

DOUBLE-ENDED SLOOP

Here is a design very similar to that of the *Wagon Box,* this boat being just a shade smaller all over. Unlike the *Wagon Box,* her deadwood has been cut away, and she has been given a shoaler, broader rudder. This boat carries more sail again than does the *Wagon Box,* her area of 399 square feet being made up of a mainsail of 283 square feet and a jib of 116 square feet. With the greater sail area and the sloop rig instead of the ketch, she would certainly be a faster boat under sail than the *Wagon Box.*

Note that the backstay makes down on the after end of the rudder head, this to bring it far enough aft so that the main boom will clear it no matter how high it may lift during a jibe. The generous jumper struts, stayed well forward, not only keep the masthead straight, but transfer some of the pull of the backstay directly to the point where the headstay meets the mast, thus eliminating the need for running backstays opposite the headstay.

This boat was designed for cruising in Maine with a family of two adults and two children. Below, she has two bunks on each side of the cabin, with the galley aft. No engine was put into the boat when she was built, though the design provided for later installation of a power plant if it was wanted.

She would be very smart under sail and quick in stays in any case, and it is easy to imagine her wriggling her way through a narrow passage between two Maine islands or working up to the very head of an intricate Maine cove.

N° 93
DOUBLE ENDED YACHT
for
JOHN M. GARBER, Esq.
L.O.A.   30'
L.W.L.   25' 10"
Beam   8' 9"
Draft   4'
S.A.   399

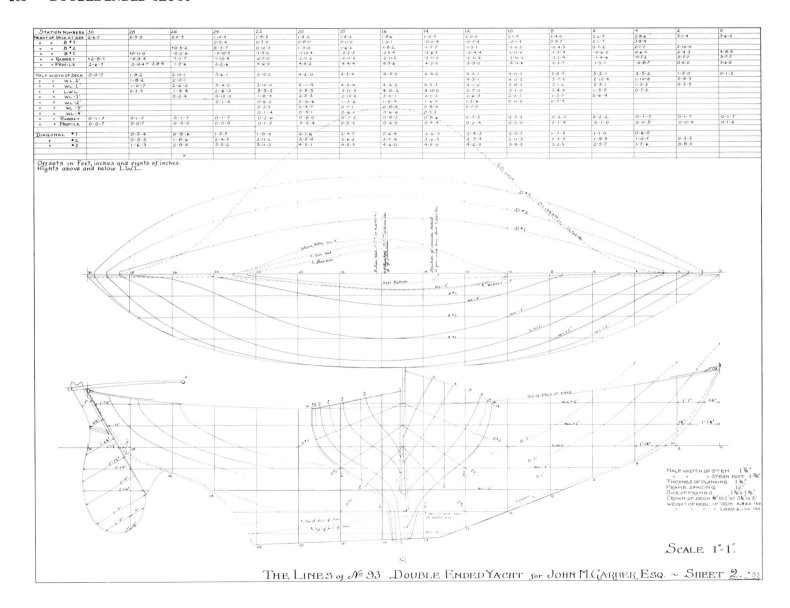

STATION NUMBERS	30	28	26	24	22	20	18	16	14	12	10	8	6	4	2	0
HEIGHT OF DECK AT SIDE	2-6-7	2-3-0	2-0-3		1-10-5	1-9-5	1-9-2	1-8-6		2-0-0	2-1-5		2-6-5	2-9-6	3-1-4	3-6-0
" B #3			10-5-2	0-5-4	0-3-0	0-0-0	0-11-0	1-0-1	-0-11-4	-0-7-4	-0-1-3	0-9-7	2-1-7	3-9-4		
" B #2		10-11-0		-0-2-6	-0-10-5	-1-5-2	-1-10-4	-2-2-5	-2-6-3	-2-4-4	-1-11-0	-1-3-4	-0-6-2	0-6-3	2-4-3	4-8-3
" B #1	+2-9-1	-0-3-4		-1-1-7	-1-10-4	-2-7-0	-2-11-2	-2-11-2	-2-1-4	-2-10-2	-2-10-2	-2-1-4	-1-4-6	-0-7-2	0-7-7	3-7-7
" RABBET	+2-9-1	-0-3-4		-1-1-7	-1-10-4	-2-7-0	-2-11-2	-2-11-2	-2-1-4	-2-10-2						
" PROFILE	2-6-7	0-10-4 3-8-4	1-3-6	2-2-6	4-6-0	4-3-2	4-4-4	4-3-6	4-3-0	3-9-0	2-11-6	2-3-7	1-5-7	-0-8-7	-0-5-0	3-6-0
HALF WIDTH OF DECK	0-0-7	1-9-2	2-10-1	3-6-1	3-10-2	4-2-0	4-4-0	4-4-0	4-3-1	4-3-1	4-0-2	3-8-5	3-2-1	2-5-2	1-5-0	0-1-2
" W.L. 2'		1-8-2	2-10-1		3-4-0	3-10-0	4-1-4	4-3-4	4-3-3	4-1-0	4-0-3	3-7-2	2-10-4	1-10-6	0-9-3	
" W.L. 1'		1-0-7	2-6-2	3-4-0	3-8-5	4-1-4	4-3-3	4-2-0	4-0-2	3-7-0	3-8-3	3-1-0	2-3-1	1-3-3	0-3-5	
" L.W.L.		0-3-3	1-4-4	2-6-0	3-8-5	3-1-0	4-0-2	3-10-0	3-7-0	2-4-4	2-4-4	1-5-5	0-7-2			
" W.L. -1'			0-2-4	0-10-0	1-8-4	2-5-3	2-10-2	3-0-1	2-11-2	2-6-3	2-0-1	1-3-7	0-6-4			
" W.L. -2'				0-6-2	0-10-6	1-2-6	1-5-4	1-4-0	0-11-0	0-3-4						
" W.L. -3'				0-2-5	0-4-7	0-7-1	0-7-1	0-8-4	0-8-4							
" W.L. -4'				0-1-4	0-4-1	0-6-1	0-6-4	0-5-3								
" RABBET	0-1-7	0-1-7	0-1-7	0-1-7	0-2-0	0-5-0	0-7-2	0-8-7	0-3-3	0-3-3	0-2-0	0-1-4	0-2-2	0-1-7	0-1-7	0-1-7
" PROFILE	0-0-7	0-0-7	0-0-0	0-0-0	0-1-3	0-3-4	0-5-5	0-6-0	0-4-4	0-2-4	0-2-0	0-1-4	0-1-0	0-0-5	0-0-4	0-1-2
DIAGONAL #1		0-3-4	0-9-6		2-1-6	2-4-7	2-6-3	2-6-3	2-4-3	2-0-7	1-7-5	0-6-0				
" #2		0-9-5	1-8-6	2-4-5	2-11-2	3-8-4	3-8-2	3-7-4	3-6-5	3-3-4	2-11-3	2-5-3	1-9-3	1-0-7	0-3-3	
" #3		1-6-3	2-8-4	3-5-2	3-11-2	4-3-1	4-5-3	4-6-0	4-5-0	4-2-0	3-9-3	3-2-5	2-5-7	1-7-6	0-8-3	

Offsets in Feet, inches and eights of inches.
Hights above and below L.W.L.

HALF WIDTH OF STEM   1 7/8"
   "   "   " STERN POST 1 7/8"
THICKNESS OF PLANKING   1 1/8"
FRAME SPACING   12"
SIZE OF FRAMES   1 7/8" x 1 7/8" in 9'
CROWN OF DECK   3/8" TO 1' or 3 1/2 in 9'
WEIGHT OF KEEL IF IRON 4,840 lbs
   "   "   "   LEAD 6,100 lbs

SCALE 1"=1'.

THE LINES of No 93   DOUBLE ENDED YACHT for JOHN M. GARBER. ESQ ~ SHEET 2. No 93

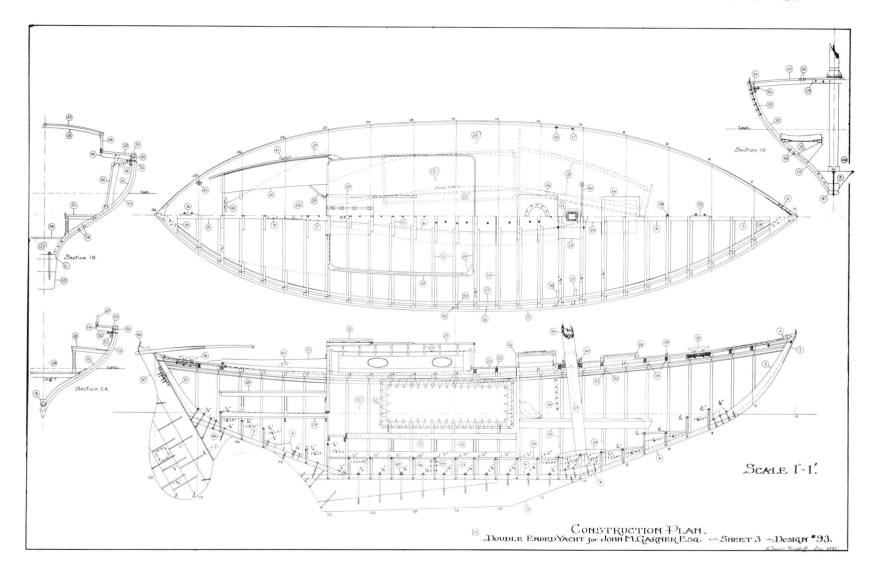

Section 10

Section 18

Section 24

SCALE 1"=1'

CONSTRUCTION PLAN.
DOUBLE ENDED YACHT for JOHN M. GARNER ESQ. ~ SHEET 3 ~ DESIGN #93.

DIDDIKAI

Several boats were built to the design of the *Diddikai,* including a pair in California and one in South Africa. The photo shows the latter sailing in her home waters in a good breeze with a single reef in her mainsail. She is, in a sense, an enlarged version of the *Dulcinea,* though the canoe stern and submerged rudder have been replaced by a stern planked to a straight stern post with an outboard rudder.

The *Diddikai* is 36'6" long on deck, with a waterline length of 31 feet, a beam of 8'8", and a draft of 4'9". Her displacement is 17,843 pounds. Her sail area is 510 square feet and, like her smaller sister, she looks well able to cope with very heavy weather. Her hull is narrow and fine enough to be easily driven, yet her midsection, with its fairly hard bilges and high topsides, shows considerable power.

In the cabin, the galley is aft on the starboard side with the engine opposite. The panelling around the engine dismantles for access. There are two pipe berths in the main cabin and two built-in berths forward. Up in the eyes of her, there is a good forepeak for gear stowage. We suppose a head could be installed in the forepeak by any owner too fastidious for the famed L. Francis Herreshoff cedar bucket. Note the hoisting eyes bolted through the keel so the vessel can be lifted by a crane. The after sling goes through a deck plate in the roof of the house. It would seem a shame, though, to ship the *Diddikai* off on the deck of a steamer; she looks fully capable of going anywhere on her own that a steamer could go.

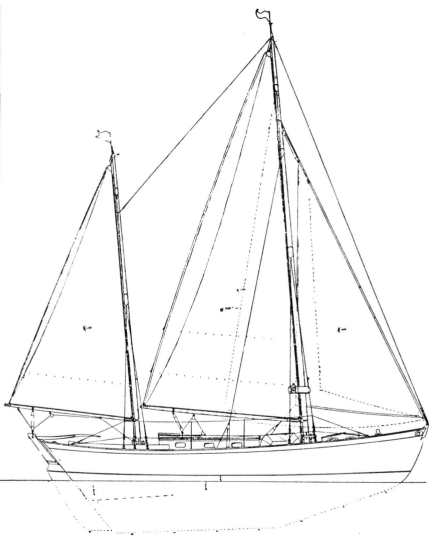

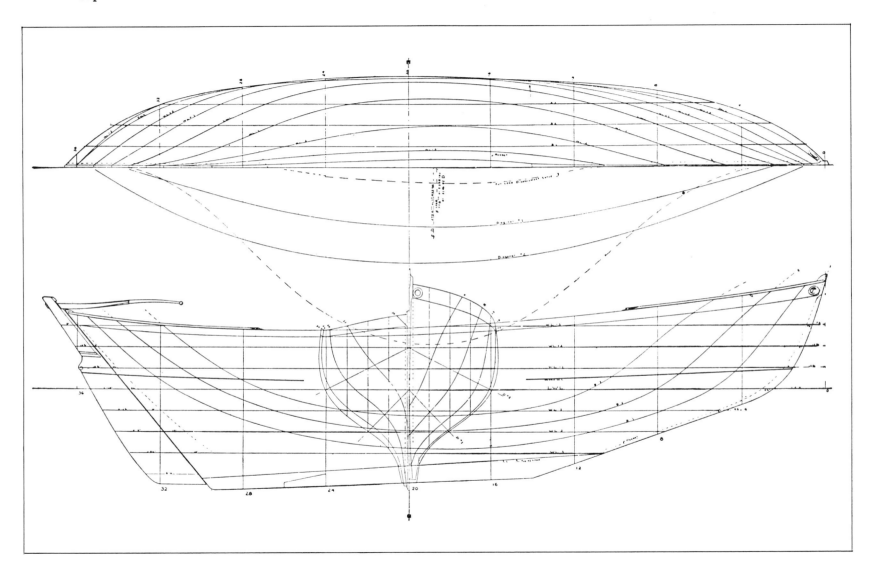

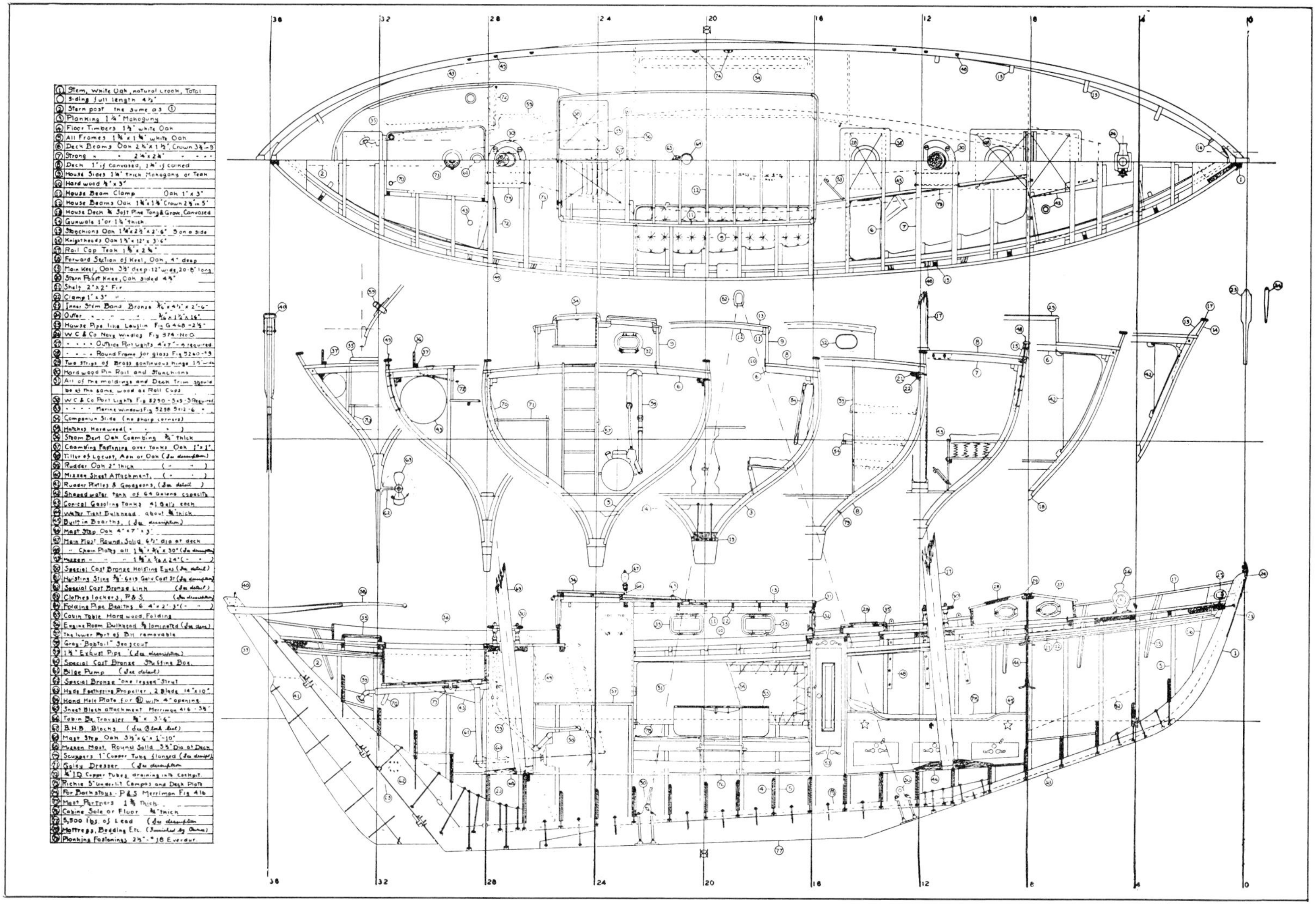
1 Stem, White Oak, natural crook, Total
siding full length 4 1/2"
2 Stern post the same as 1
3 Planking 1 1/4" Mahogany
4 Floor Timbers 1 1/2" white Oak
5 All Frames 1 3/4" x 1 3/4" white Oak
6 Deck Beams Oak 2 1/4" x 1 1/2", Crown 3 1/2" in 9'
7 Strong " " 2 1/4" x 2 1/4" " " "
8 Deck 1" if canvased, 1 1/4" if calked
9 House Sides 1 1/4" thick Mahogany or Teak
10 Hard wood 1/2" x 3"
11 House Beam Clamp Oak 1" x 3"
12 House Beams Oak 1 1/4" x 1 1/4" Crown 2 1/2" in 5'
13 House Deck 3/4 Soft Pine Tong & Grove, Canvased
14 Gunwale 1" or 1 1/4" thick
15 Stanchions Oak 1 3/4" x 2 1/2" x 2'-6" 9 on a side
16 Knightheads Oak 1 1/2" x 12" x 3'-6"
17 Rail Cap Teak 1 1/8" x 2 1/4"
18 Forward Section of Keel, Oak, 4" deep
19 Main Keel, Oak 3 1/2" deep-12" wide, 20'-8" long
20 Stern Post Knee, Oak sided 4 1/2"
21 Shelf 2" x 2" Fir
22 Clamp 1" x 3" "
23 Inner Stem Band Bronze 3/16" x 4 1/2" x 2'-6"
24 Outer " " " 3/16" x 1 1/4" x 16"
25 Hawse Pipe like Laughlin Fig G 468 - 2 1/2"
26 W C & Co Navy Windlass Fig 374 - No 0
27 " " " " Outside Port Lights 4" x 7" - 4 required
28 " " " " Round Frame for glass Fig 5260 - 9
29 Two strips of Brass continuous hinge 1 1/2" wide
30 Hard wood Pin Rail and Stanchions
31 All of the moldings and Deck Trim should
be of the same wood as Rail Caps
32 W C & Co Port Lights Fig 5290 - 5x9 - 3 Required
33 " " " " Marine windows Fig 5298 5x12 - 6 "
34 Companion Slide (no sharp corners)
35 Hatches Hardwood (" " ")
36 Steam Bent Oak Coaming 3/4" thick
37 Coaming Fastening over Tanks Oak 1" x 1"
38 Tiller of Locust, Ash or Oak (See description)
39 Rudder Oak 2" thick (" ")
40 Mizzen Sheet Attachment, (" ")
41 Rudder Pintles & Gudgeons, (See detail)
42 Shaped water tank of 64 Galons capacity
43 Conical Gasoline Tanks 41 Gal's each
44 Water Tight Bulkhead about 3/4" thick
45 Built in Berths, (See description)
46 Mast Step Oak 4" x 7" x 3'
47 Main Mast Round, Solid 6 1/2" dia at deck
48 " Chain Plates all 1 1/2" x 3/16" x 30" (See description)
49 Mizzen " " " 1 1/4" x 3/16" x 24" (" ")
50 Special Cast Bronze Hoisting Eyes (See detail)
51 Hoisting Sling 5/8" - 6x19 Galv Cast St (See description)
52 Special Cast Bronze Link (See detail)
53 Clothes lockers, P & S. (See description)
54 Folding Pipe Berths 6' 4" x 2' 3" (" ")
55 Cabin Table Hard wood, Folding
56 Engine Room Bulkhead 5/8 laminated (See desc)
57 The lower Part of Bh removable
58 Gray-"Bobtail" Sea Scout
59 1 1/2" Exhaust Pipe (See description)
60 Special Cast Bronze Stuffing Box.
61 Bilge Pump (See detail)
62 Special Bronze "one legged" Strut
63 Hyde Feathering Propeller, 2 Blade 14" x 10"
64 Hand Hole Plate for 41 with 4" opening.
65 Sheet Block attachment Merriman 416 - 3 1/2"
66 Tobin Br. Traveler 5/8" x 3'-6"
67 B.H.B. Blocks (See Block list)
68 Mast Step Oak 3 1/2" x 6" x 1'-10"
69 Mizzen Mast, Round Solid 3 1/2" Dia at Deck.
70 Scuppers 1" Copper Tube flanged (See descrip)
71 Galey Dresser (See description
72 3/4" I.D. Copper Tubes draining into Cockpit.
73 Richie 5" Underlit Compass and Deck Plate
74 For Backstays - P & S Merriman Fig 416
75 Mast Partners 1 3/4 thick
76 Cabine Sole or Floor 3/4" thick
77 5,500 lbs. of Lead (See description
78 Mattress, Bedding Etc. (Furnished by Owner)
79 Planking Fastenings 2 1/2" - #18 Everdur.

RESTRICTED SAIL AREA CRUISER

This boat was designed to be a cruising vessel with the ultimate performance that might be obtained from a sail area of 1,000 square feet. Actually, the jib shown, with its area of 300 square feet, somewhat exceeds the measured area of the fore triangle, so with that sail set, the ketch spreads 1,016 square feet of sail. None of her sails is too big to be handled by one man, if one is willing to follow the rule of thumb that a man can handle a sail of 500 square feet by himself. And the boat's largest sail, her mainsail of 495 square feet, is well inboard where it is easiest to set, hand, or reef.

This long, narrow ketch should be fast and weatherly. With her rather shapely cut-away forefoot and rudder quite far forward, she might be a bit hard to steer under some conditions. But standing up to her wheel and just watching her eat her way to windward in a breeze would be quite an experience. If it were calm and somebody had to get somewhere, her big Scripps F-4 would make the miles short.

Below, there is plenty of space in the ends of her for stowage, and she has five berths.

With her long waterline, this boat's hull speed should be very close to ten knots. And with her fine lines and easy run, sailing at hull speed or nearly so would hardly be a unique experience for her. She might or might not break a few port-to-port records, but her average passages over a period of years would be hard to beat. Perhaps even more important, she has great grace and beauty. Watching her go, either from on board or from off the boat, it would be hard to catch her in an awkward pose.

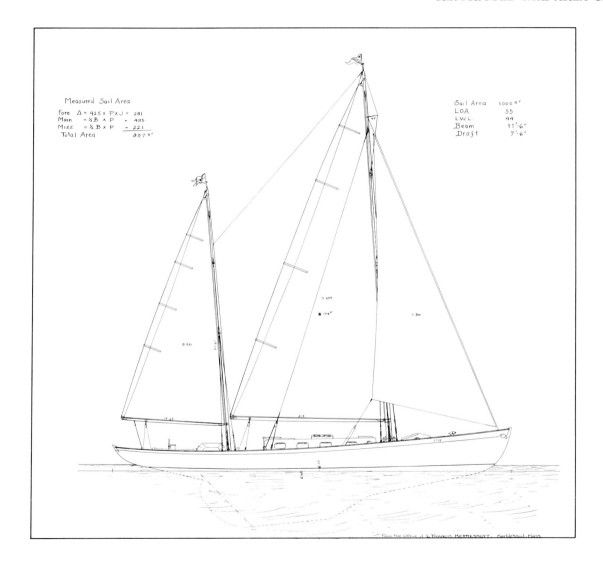

Measured Sail Area

Fore Δ = 425 x P x J = 281
Main = ½ B x P = 485
Mizz = ½ B x P = 221
  Total Area   997 □'

Sail Area   1000 □'
L O A   55
L W L   44
Beam   11'-6"
Draft   7'-6"

From the Office of L. FRANCIS HERRESHOFF, Marblehead, Mass.

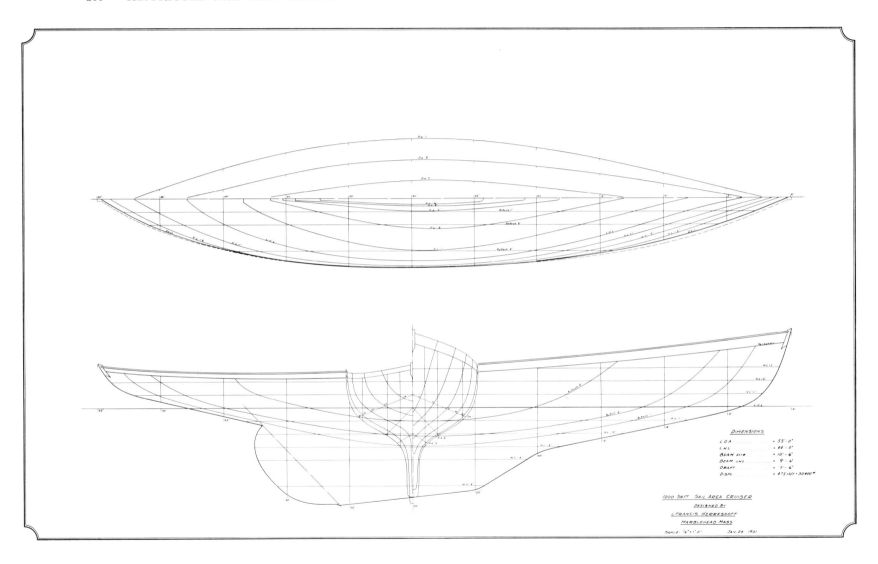

DIMENSIONS

L O A	= 55'-0"
L W L	= 44'-0"
BEAM EXTR	= 10'-6"
BEAM L W L	= 9'-6"
DRAFT	= 7'-6"
DISPL	= 475 cu.ft = 30400ᵈ

1000 Sq.Ft SAIL AREA CRUISER

DESIGNED BY

L.FRANCIS HERRESHOFF

MARBLEHEAD MASS

SCALE: 1/8" = 1'-0'   JAN. 24 1931

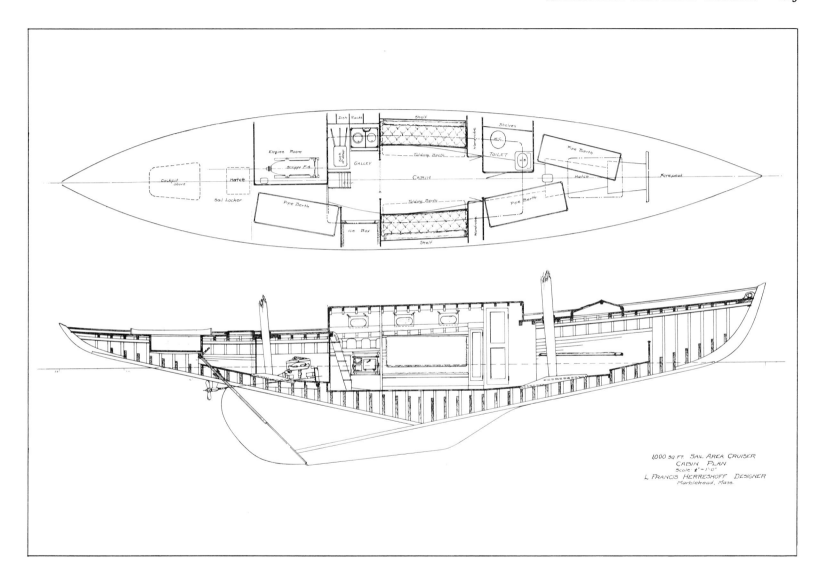

1,000 sq.ft. SAIL AREA CRUISER
CABIN PLAN
Scale ¾"=1'-0"
L FRANCIS HERRESHOFF DESIGNER
Marblehead, Mass.

CAT YAWL

Some who feel a tendency toward calling the *Rozinante* a canoe ketch, may also want to call this design a cat ketch, but L. Francis wrote, "First of all, as to the name of the rig: all vessels without headsails but having two masts with the after one the smaller are cat yawls. The term 'cat ketch' is incorrect and never used until recently. [He was writing in 1957.] The cat yawl was one rig quite common in America, particularly in southern New England and much of my first sailing was done in them."

The thought behind this design was to have a small cruising boat with many of the advantages of the catboat and a minimum of the disadvantages. L. Francis listed among the chief catboat advantages retained: general simplicity and roominess. He felt this design minimized the following catboat drawbacks: difficulty of maneuvering in certain situations, hard steering at times, tendency to run the bow under if pushed hard when running before a strong breeze and rough sea; and the necessity of having a very heavy mast in the bow.

Mr. Herreshoff designed this little craft as a keel boat to eliminate the problems and complexities associated with the centerboard. Yet he was able to retain a draft of only three feet. With this moderate draft and her easy sections, she would have a pleasant motion in a seaway. She is very fine forward and fine on the waterline aft, but her broad transom would quickly give her bearing as she began to heel.

Her sails set on mast tracks to allow the most advantageous placement of the standing rigging. Note the strap on the mizzen mast to counteract the thrust of the boom. Taking in the mizzen would be the equivalent of taking a good deep reef in the mainsail of a catboat. The mizzen has 62 square feet of area, while the mainsail has 173 square feet, for a total of 235 square feet.

The interior of the cat yawl is arranged as is that of the *Rozinante,* with a wide double berth forward and the galley area at the after end of the house. The V shape of the forward end of the house allows more working deck space forward than is found on most catboats.

All in all, she is a roomy and able little cruiser.

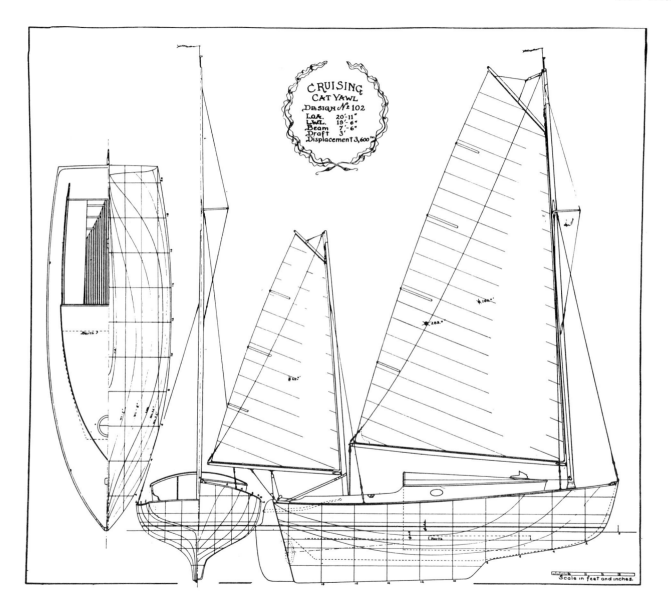

CRUISING
CAT YAWL
DESIGN Nº 102
L.O.A.   20'-11"
L.W.L.   19'-6"
Beam   7'-6"
Draft   3'-6"
Displacement 3,600 lbs

Scale in feet and inches.

SOLITAIRE

This heavy, able sloop can be considered an enlarged version of the *Prudence*, H-23. The *Solitaire* is 28'3" long on deck, with a waterline length of 23'3", a beam of 9'3", and a draft of 4'10". Her sail area is 446 square feet, with 306 square feet in the mainsail and 140 square feet in the jib. A club jib is also shown in dotted lines with an area of 119 square feet; the Genoa shown has 210 square feet.

The boat has a wholesome looking hull with fair, easy curves throughout. With only a moderate hollow in the garboards, wetted surface has been kept low; the boat would have a good turn of speed. Her flat transom, characteristic of L. Francis, would be a boon to her builder. Its rake and wineglass sections keep its flatness from giving the stern a clumsy look. Note that the section at station 2 just abaft the stem is a perfectly straight line. Most of L. Francis' designs show a bit of flare just below the rail at this station.

The *Solitaire's* rig is moderate and efficient. She wouldn't have to be reefed very often.

Remembering the great abilities of the Buzzards Bay 12½-footers and their larger cousins, it is interesting to compare the *Solitaire's* lines with those of the Buzzards Bay 14-footer on page 256. The marked similarities are at once apparent, and so we might expect great things of the *Solitaire*. She would undoubtedly do just beautifully in the Buzzards Bay chop.

Station Numbers	Top of Deck at Side	Buttock 1'	Buttock 2'	Buttock 3'	Buttock 4'	Rabbet	Top of Lead	Profile	At Deck	WL +2'	WL +1'	LWL	WL -1'	WL -2'	WL -3'	WL -4'	Rabbet	Top of Lead	Face	#1	#2	#3	Station Numbers
	ELEVATIONS above and below L.W.L.								HALF BREADTHS.											DIAGONALS.			
0	3-7-5					3-9-7		3-7-5	0-1-2								0-2-0		0-1-2				0
2	3-4-5	2-8-0				0-10-2		0-6-7	1-3-5	0-8-2	0-2-7						0-2-0		0-0-3		0-2-5	0-7-4	2
4	3-2-0	0-6-7	2-5-7			-0-6-1		-0-7-7	2-3-3	1-9-2	1-3-0	0-7-0					0-2-0		0-0-4	0-5-4	1-0-5	1-7-0	4
6	2-11-5	-0-7-6	0-7-0	2-8-2		-1-4-5		1-6-2	3-1-0	2-8-5	2-2-6	1-6-6	0-7-4				0-2-0		0-0-5	1-1-7	1-10-1	2-5-2	6
8	2-9-5	-1-5-4	-0-6-1	0-9-6		-2-2-6		2-4-2	3-8-1	3-5-6	3-1-0	2-5-3	1-5-7	0-4-2			0-2-0		0-0-7	1-8-7	2-6-2	3-2-2	8
10	2-7-7	-2-0-4	-1-2-3	-0-3-0	1-11-4	-2-9-1	2-9-6	3-3-0	4-1-3	4-0-0	3-8-4	3-2-2	2-2-6	1-0-2	0-2-4		0-3-0	0-2-7	0-2-0	2-2-3	3-0-5	3-9-3	10
12	2-6-3	-2-4-4	-1-6-5	-0-9-5	0-6-4	-2-11-3	3-0-0	4-3-0	4-4-7	4-4-4	4-1-7	3-8-4	2-9-0	1-4-6	0-5-3	0-3-4	0-5-4	0-5-3	0-3-0	2-5-4	3-2-5	4-2-4	12
14	2-5-1	-2-6-1	-1-8-6	-1-0-4	-0-0-1	-3-1-6	3-2-4	4-4-2	4-6-7	4-6-4	4-4-6	4-0-1	3-0-4	1-7-2	0-7-2	0-5-0	0-6-2	0-6-1	0-4-4	2-7-3	3-7-3	4-5-6	14
16	2-4-1	-2-5-6	-1-8-1	-1-0-4	-0-2-3	-3-4-0	3-4-7	4-5-5	4-7-4	4-7-5	4-6-4	4-1-6	3-1-1	1-6-3	0-7-3	0-4-7	0-5-5	0-5-4	0-4-3	2-6-5	3-7-6	4-7-0	16
18	2-3-5	-2-2-4	-1-5-5	-0-10-5	-0-0-6	-3-6-2	3-7-1	4-6-6	4-7-3	4-7-4	4-6-2	4-0-5	2-10-0	1-2-6	0-5-6	0-3-7	0-4-2	0-4-1	0-3-2	2-4-4	3-6-0	4-6-2	18
20	2-3-0	-1-8-7	-1-1-2	-0-6-5	+0-2-5	-3-8-7	3-9-4	4-7-7	4-5-7	4-6-0	4-4-5	3-9-4	2-2-2	0-8-6	0-3-3	0-2-4	0-2-5	0-2-4	0-1-6	2-0-3	3-1-7	4-3-6	20
22	2-2-6	-1-1-0	-0-6-7	0-0-6	0-9-0	-3-0-0	4-0-0	4-9-0 / 4-8-0	4-3-4	4-3-3	4-1-2	3-1-3	1-0-2	0-4-1	0-2-0		0-2-0	0-1-2	0-1-0	1-5-6	2-8-0	3-11-0	22
24	2-3-0	-0-3-4	0-0-6	0-6-0	2-3-0	-1-5-3		4-2-6	4-0-0	4-0-0	3-7-2	1-10-0	0-3-2	0-1-2	0-1-2		0-2-0		0-1-0	0-10-0	1-11-2	3-4-1	24
26	2-3-5	0-4-7	0-8-3	1-2-0		0-0-0		2-1-2	3-6-7	3-6-4	2-8-4	0-2-0					0-2-0		0-2-0	0-2-2	1-1-2	2-7-4	26
28	2-4-7							1-4-0	3-0-7														28
Transom	2-5-0	0-7-5	1-0-0	2-5-0				1-7-5	3-0-0	2-11-4	2-0-0	0-2-0									0-10-2	2-2-6	Transom

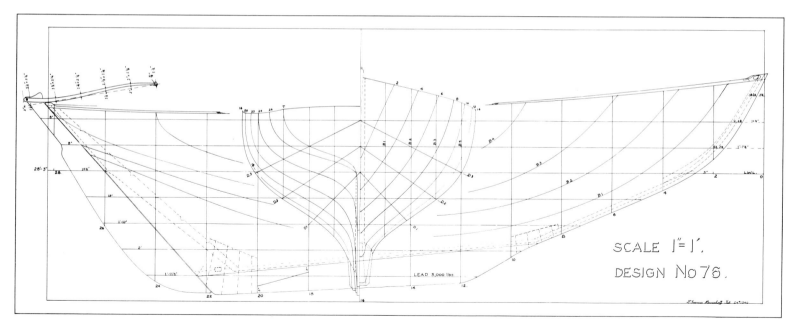

SCALE 1" = 1'.

DESIGN No 76.

LEAD 5,000 lbs

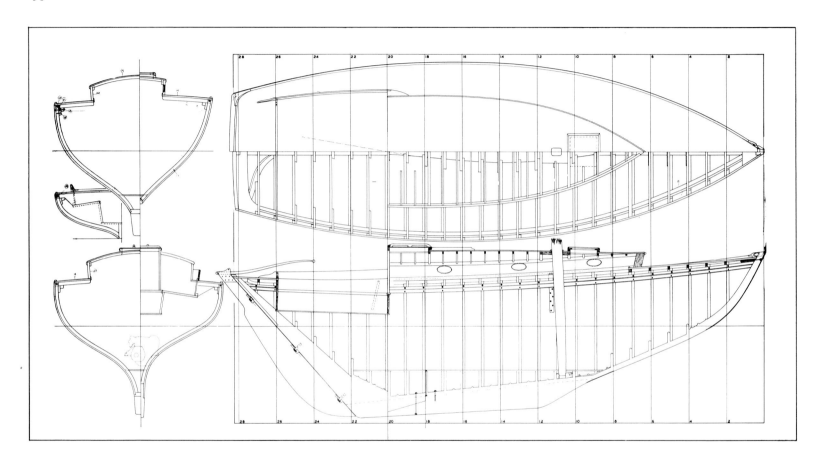

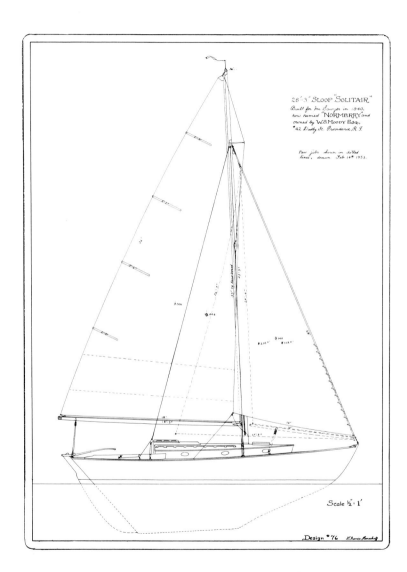

28'-3" Sloop "SOLITAIR."

Built for Mr Sawyer in 1940,
now named "NORMERRY" and
owned by W.S. Moody Esq.,
*42 Dudly St. Providence, R. I.

New jibs shown in dotted
lines, drawn Feb 14th 1953.

Scale ½" = 1'

Design #76   N. Herreshoff

SANTEE

This husky sloop, designed by Mr. Herreshoff early in his career when he was working in the offices of Burgess, Swasey, and Paine, naval architects, of Boston, Massachusetts, shows also the influence of the Buzzards Bay boats. Being far bigger, with a waterline length of 28′6″, she is naturally narrower in proportion, but the basic hull shape is similar to Captain Nat's 12½-footer. The transom, in particular, is narrower.

The boat looks quite deep and powerful, as she would need to be, for her sail plan is rather generous in keeping with the style of the mid-Twenties. Her length on deck was 33′6″, her beam, 9′6″, and her draft, as originally designed, 5′2″. Her sail area was 735 square feet, with 550 square feet in the mainsail, and 185 square feet in the jib. The plans show a sizeable 8-horsepower Kermath under the bridge deck and cockpit, but with her big sails, the *Santee* could be sailed smartly and handily even in light weather, and it was not intended that the engine be cranked up every time the wind dropped below a moderate breeze or the night's anchorage began to be approached. A generous sail area gives the cruising boat skipper a broad array of choices. When it blows hard, he can drive his boat to the limit, or ease her along; in light going, he can keep his vessel moving under sail if that is his desire.

The arrangement plan shows, among other things, an enclosed head taking up half of the most valuable end of the cabin, an oddity in a Francis Herreshoff boat, and one for which perhaps we should look to the Messrs. Burgess, Swasey, and Paine.

33'6" OA ~ 28'6" LWL.
Auxilary Sloop.
for
J.C.Hartwell Esq.

March 20th 1924.
Scale ⅜=1
Drawn by L.F.Herreshoff.

Stations	1	2	3	4	5	6	7	8	9	10	11	12	13	14	15	16	17
Deck	0-11-2	1-8-3	2-4-5	3-0-0	3-6-2	3-11-4	4-3-5	4-6-4	4-8-2	4-9-0	4-8-4	4-6-6	4-3-6	3-11-2	3-5-1	2-9-2	2-0-0
W L 1	0-4-5	1-2-6	2-0-5	2-9-1	3-4-3	3-10-1	4-2-4	4-5-4	4-6-4	4-8-4	4-8-0	4-6-2	4-3-0	3-10-2	3-3-3	2-5-6	
" 2		0-9-3	1-7-3	2-4-5	3-0-5	3-7-2	4-0-2	4-3-6	4-6-0	4-7-0	4-6-3	4-4-0	4-0-2	3-6-0	2-6-5	2-10-4	
" 3		0-3-2	0-11-7	1-9-0	2-6-2	3-2-0	3-7-7	3-11-6	4-2-1	4-2-7	4-1-7	3-10-6	3-4-2	2-4-2	0-11-4		
" 4			0-3-6	1-0-0	1-8-1	2-3-7	2-10-0	3-2-4	3-5-0	3-5-4	3-3-2	2-9-6	2-0-1	0-11-0	0-2-2		
" 5				0-1-5	0-8-5	1-3-3	1-8-6	2-0-1	2-2-2	2-2-1	1-10-6	1-4-0	0-8-5	0-4-0			
" 6						0-5-1	0-9-3	1-0-1	1-1-2	1-0-1	0-10-0	0-7-2	0-4-4	0-2-0			
" 7							0-3-1	0-5-7	0-7-0	0-7-0	0-6-3	0-5-0	0-3-3	0-1-2			
Keel Bottom	0-0-2	0-0-2	0-0-2	0-0-2	0-0-2	0-0-2	0-0-2	0-2-1	0-5-0	0-5-4	0-4-7	0-3-4	0-1-5	0-1-2	0-1-2	0-9-2	
Rabbet	0-2-0	0-2-0	0-2-0	0-2-0	0-2-3	0-4-0	0-6-5	0-7-7	0-7-4	0-6-6	0-5-6	0-4-3	0-2-3	0-2-4	0-2-4		
Sheer	3-7-2	3-5-3	3-3-4	3-1-6	3-1-2	2-10-6	2-9-3	2-8-0	2-7-1	2-6-4	2-6-0	2-5-7	2-6-1	2-6-5	2-7-4	2-8-6	2-10-4
Buttock #1			1-10-2	0-4-0	0-7-6	1-3-4	1-8-6	2-0-3	2-0-2	2-1-7	1-10-4	1-7-2	1-0-0	0-3-1	0-6-2	1-6-6	2-6-0
Rabbet	1-4-4	0-2-2	1-2-3	1-11-4	2-7-7	3-1-3	3-4-6	3-7-2	3-9-6	4-0-2	4-2-6	4-5-3	4-6-0	3-3-0	1-0-6		
Keel Bottom	1-0-6	0-5-4	1-4-3	2-2-0	2-11-5	3-9-0	4-6-4	5-1-5	5-1-5	5-1-5	5-1-5	5-1-5	5-1-5	4-0-4	1-6-4	0-11-4	
Diag #1	0-7-6	1-5-4	2-2-6	2-11-3	3-6-7	4-1-2	4-6-3	4-10-1	5-0-3	5-1-0	5-0-0	4-9-2	4-4-4	3-9-6	3-1-1	2-3-0	
2		0-8-3	1-4-3	2-0-2	2-7-5	3-2-1	3-7-2	3-10-5	4-0-3	4-0-7	3-11-5	3-8-0	3-1-7	2-5-5	1-7-2	0-7-0	
3			0-3-0	0-10-1	1-4-7	1-10-7	2-3-6	2-7-5	2-10-0	2-11-3	2-11-2	2-9-3	2-5-7	2-0-0	1-4-2	0-7-2	
4			0-3-0	0-8-7	1-2-3	1-7-1	1-11-0	2-1-3	2-2-3	2-1-6	1-11-5	1-7-6	1-2-4	0-8-5	0-2-3		
5				0-1-3	0-6-5	0-11-2	1-3-1	1-5-0	1-6-0	1-5-2	1-3-3	1-0-2	0-8-1	0-4-4			
6																	

Dimensions in Feet, Inches and Eighths to Outside of Plank.   Heights given from L.W.L.

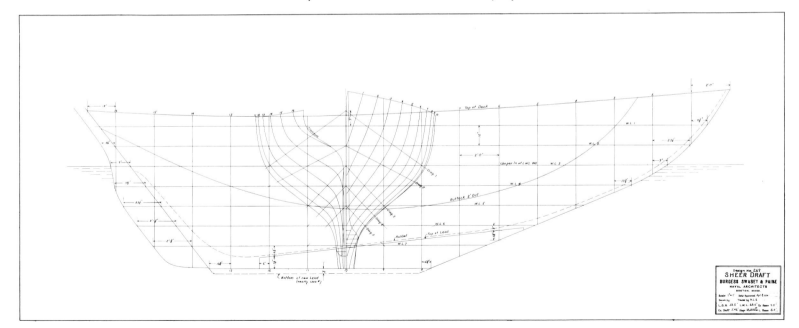

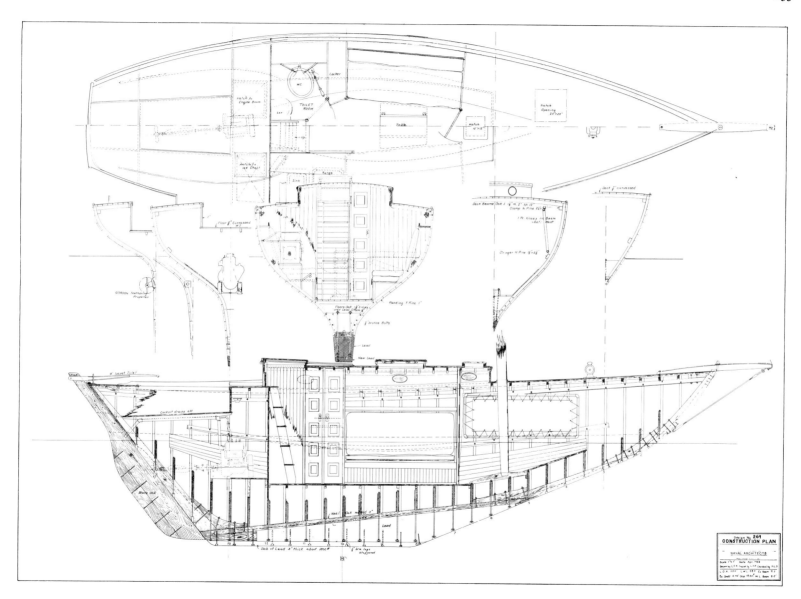

LANDFALL

Paul Hammond's great 71-foot ketch may perhaps be considered the ultimate development of the Buzzards Bay Boat line. Yet she really is considerably finer, with a good deal more hollow in the garboards, having been designed for ocean racing. And the dotted lines on her lines drawing on page 302 show what might have happened to her stern had the rating rule for racing not decreed that it be chopped off. The *Landfall* would have made a magnificent 77-foot double-ender.

What with her draft of nearly 11 feet, her working sail area of just over 3,000 square feet, her spare steering station at the deckhouse, her 18 bunks, and her gigantic saloon, the *Landfall* was quite a vessel. Uffa Fox, the great English designer contemporary with L. Francis, gave a complete description of the *Landfall* together with an account of her performance in the 1931 Transatlantic Race (she finished second to the well-sailed *Dorade* and was sixth out of ten on corrected time) in his book, *Sailing, Seamanship, and Yacht Construction.*

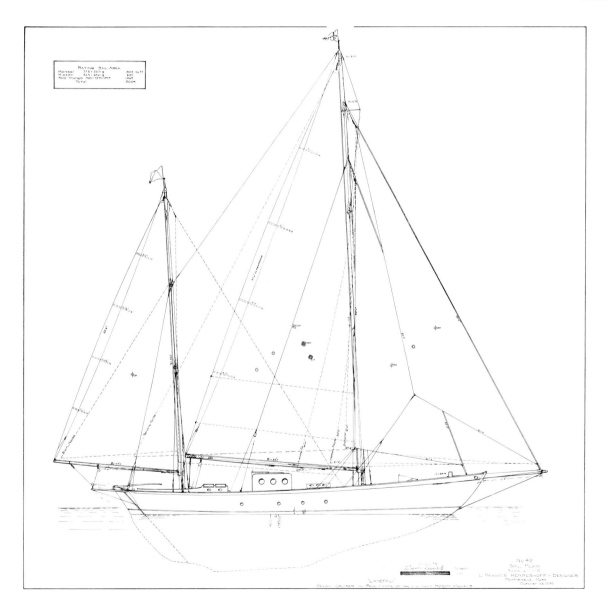

RATING SAIL AREA

Mainsail	77.5 × 33.7 ÷	1305 sq ft
Mizzen	52.5 × 24.2 ÷	635
Fore Triangle	92.5 × 72.7÷.7÷÷	1064
Total		3004

'LANDFALL'
OCEAN CRUISER — REG. CONSTRUCTION — FOR ROGER WILLIAMS

No.49
SAIL PLAN
SCALE ¼" = 1'0"
L. FRANCIS HERRESHOFF — DESIGNER
MARBLEHEAD MASS.
OCTOBER 26, 1930

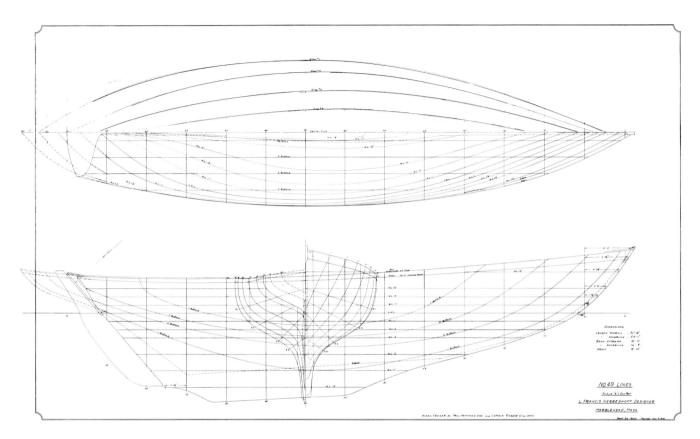

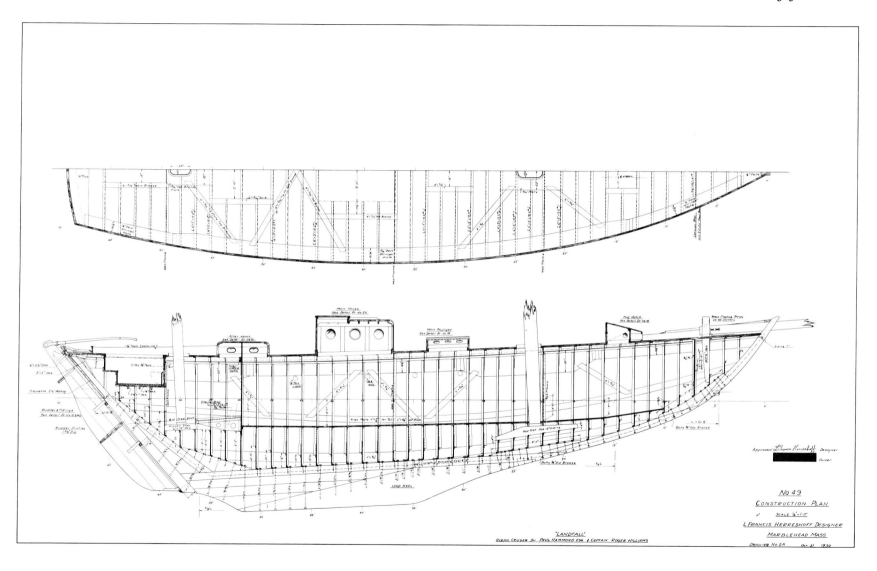

'LANDFALL'
OCEAN CRUISER for PAUL HAMMOND Esq & CAPTAIN ROGER WILLIAMS

No 49
CONSTRUCTION PLAN
SCALE ⅝"=1'-0"
L FRANCIS HERRESHOFF DESIGNER
MARBLEHEAD MASS
DRAWING No 5A   OCT 31 1930

Approved L Francis Herreshoff Designer
Owner

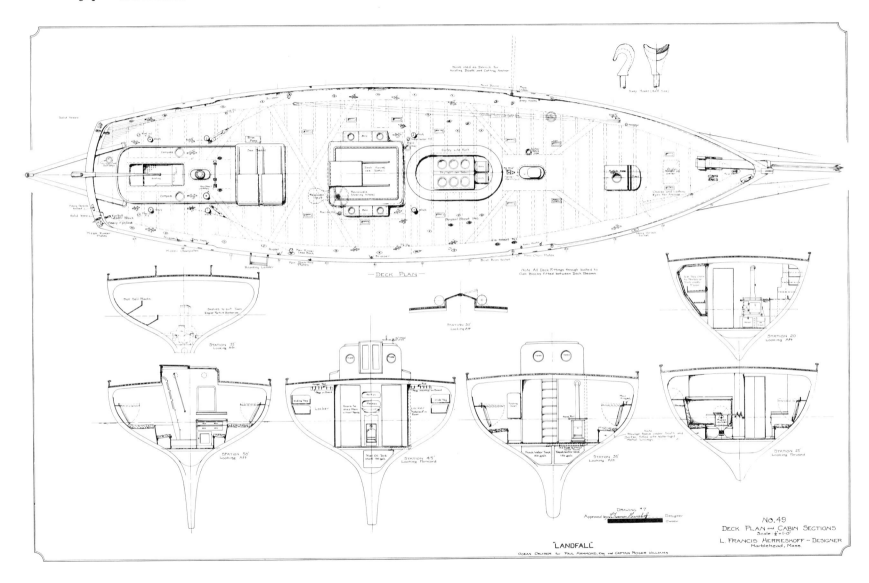

DECK PLAN

'LANDFALL'
OCEAN CRUISER for PAUL HAMMOND, Esq and CAPTAIN ROGER WILLIAMS

No. 49
DECK PLAN and CABIN SECTIONS
Scale ¾" = 1'-0"
L. FRANCIS HERRESHOFF — DESIGNER
Marblehead, Mass.

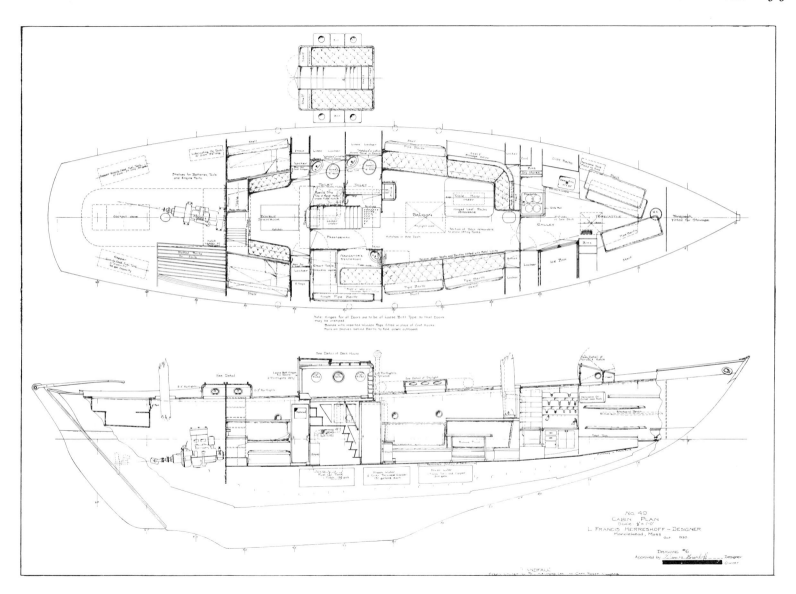

QUIET TUNE

This fast, light-displacement ketch was designed for daysailing in Maine. She has the same sail plan as the H-28, described in Chapter 3, but the *Quiet Tune* is a much faster, lighter boat than the H-28, with much less room in her. She is 29′6″ long on deck, 25 feet on the waterline, with a beam of 7′10″, and a draft of 4′6″.

In this design, we see again the influence of Captain Nat Herreshoff on his son, for this boat could be considered a narrower, deeper version of Captain Nat's 25-foot-waterline racing class for Buzzards Bay. The well-proportioned ketch rig is, of course, purely the trademark of L. Francis himself. Some minor differences in *Quiet Tune's* rig compared to the H-28 are that she has jumper struts instead of a headstay, double main backstays leading to the quarters, and a roller reefing boom on the mainsail.

She certainly looks to be a most handy and smart little vessel, ideal for her intended purpose, or for short cruises with two people. It's always good to be able to turn an intended day sail into an overnight cruise if the breeze proves irresistible.

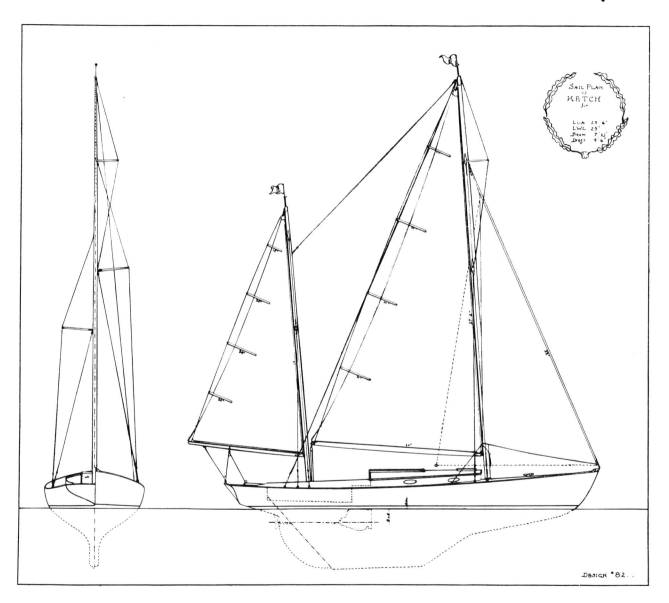

DESIGN *82*

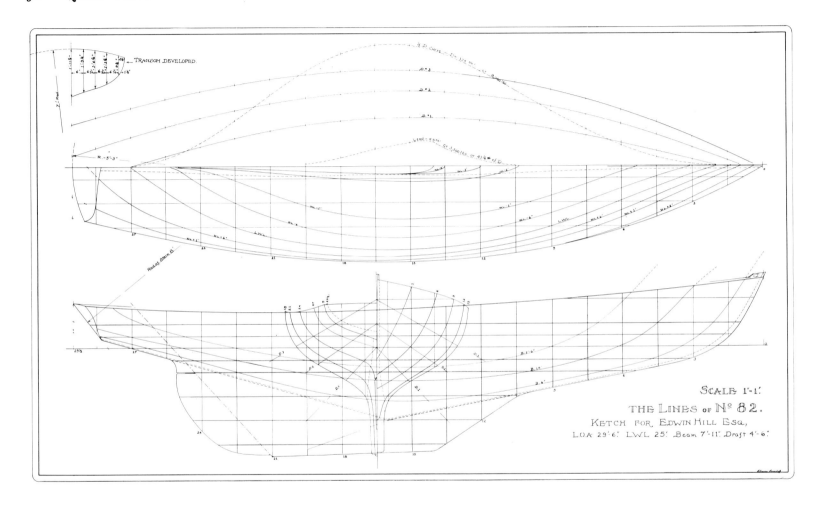

SCALE 1"-1'

THE LINES of Nº 82.

KETCH FOR EDWIN HILL ESQ,

L.O.A 29'-6", LWL 25', Beam 7'-11", Draft 4'-6".

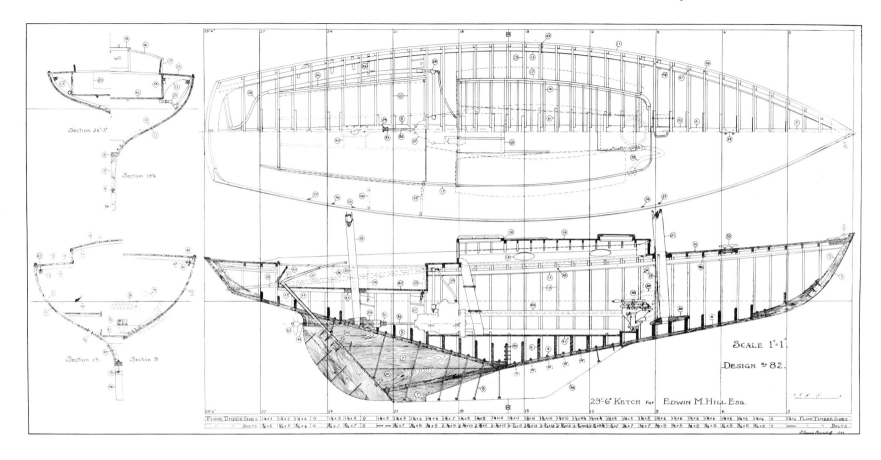

SCALE 1"=1.

DESIGN № 82.

29'-6" KETCH for EDWIN M. HILL Esq.

Section 26'-3"

Section 19½

Section 15   Section 9

FLOOR TIMBER SIZES	1¼×3	1¼×3	1¼×4	O	1¼×5	1¼×5	O	1¼×5	1¼×6	1¼×6	1¼×7	1¼×8	1¼×9	1¼×10	1½×11	1½×10	1½×10	1½×9½	1½×6½	1½×5	1¼×5	1½×6	1½×6½	1¼×6	1¼×6	1¼×6	1¼×6	O	1¼×6 FLOOR TIMBER SIZES
BOLTS	⅜×5	⅜×5	⅜×6	O	⅜×7	⅜×7	O	⅜×7	⅜×8	⅜×8	⅜×9	½×10	½×11	½×12	½×13	½×12	½×12	½×12	½×8	⅜×7	⅜×7	⅜×7	⅜×8	⅜×8	⅜×8	⅜×8	⅜×8	O	BOLTS

ALBACORE

This centerboard ketch has been cruising with great success for the last 45 years. She has evidently been well cared for during that time, for at this writing she looks to be in perfect condition. The people who sail her take obvious pride and delight in their vessel and it is a pleasure to observe them cruising in her.

The *Albacore* is 41′3″ long on deck, with a waterline length of 32′3″, a beam of 12′3″, and a draft of 4′3″. With her generous rig and fine lines forward she would have a good turn of speed. Her sail area is 832 square feet, with 400 square feet in the mainsail, 251 in the mizzen, and 181 in the jib. The mizzen is somewhat larger than Mr. Herreshoff used on most of his later ketches. The running backstays on the mizzen would only need to be used when reaching in a fresh breeze or to support the head of the mainmast via the springstay when plunging into a head sea or if a balloon jib were set on the headstay.

This boat was to be a full-powered auxiliary, and the engine originally specified was a big Lathrop of 40 horsepower. She could make a fast passage under power or push into a head wind of some strength if her owner desired.

Her standard arrangement plan is sensible, and she is beamy enough to allow berths outboard of the settees in the saloon, always a nice arrangement. Note the deck hatch directly above the icebox to simplify the loading chore.

It's no wonder the *Albacore* has been well cared for; clearly, she deserves nothing less. May she sail for many more decades.

NO. 36
SAIL PLAN
Scale ⅜"=1'0"
L.FRANCIS HERRESHOFF DESIGNER
Marblehead , Mass   Oct. 1928

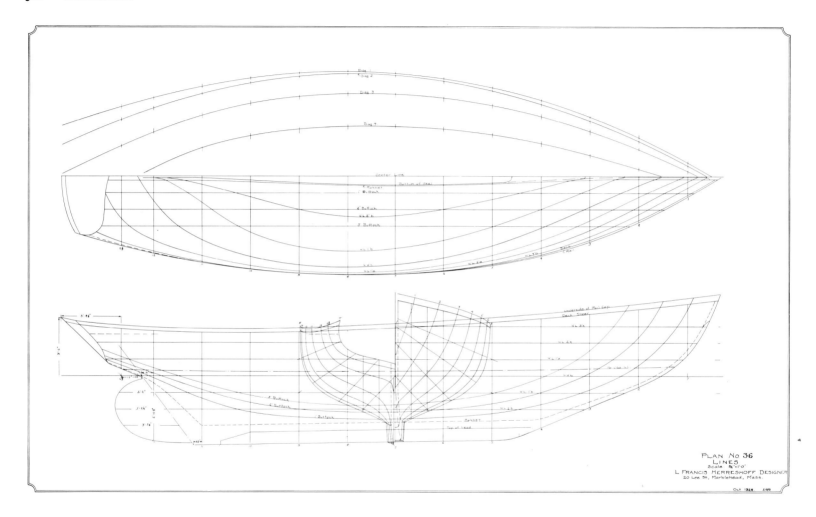

PLAN No 36
LINES
Scale ¾"=1'0"
L FRANCIS HERRESHOFF DESIGNER
20 Lee St, Marblehead, Mass.

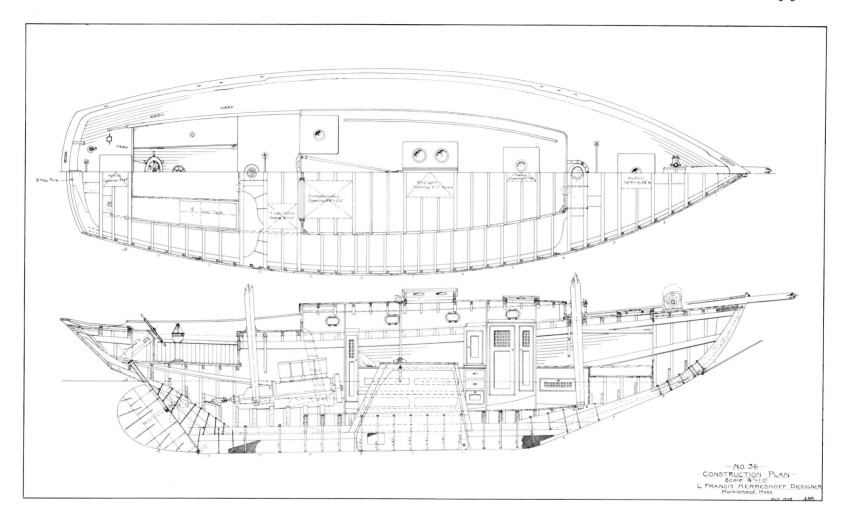

—NO. 36—
—CONSTRUCTION PLAN—
Scale ¾"=1'-0"
L FRANCIS HERRESHOFF DESIGNER
Marblehead, Mass.

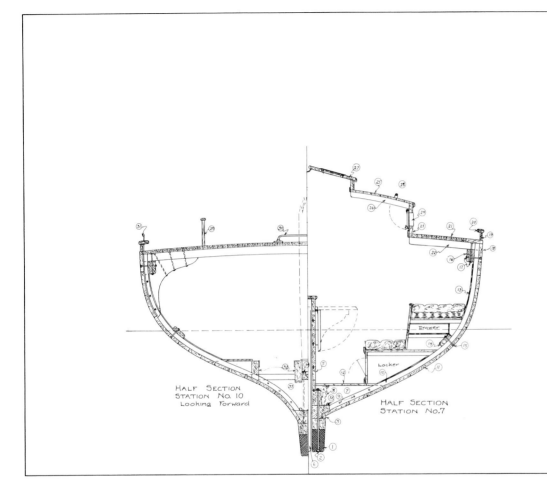

HALF SECTION
STATION NO. 10
Looking Forward

HALF SECTION
STATION NO.7

BILL MATERIAL

1	Lead keel about 7,500 lbs.
2	Keel Bolts 1" diam, ⅜" diam abreast C.B., Tobin Bronze
3	Oak Keel, 5"x17" amidship, tapered with Rabbet
4	C.B. Bed Logs, Oak 4"x6"
5	C.B. Trunk 1½" W. Pine or Cypress.
6	Centerboard Oak or Hard Pine, 2", ½" Dowells, Weighted with Lead
7	Floor Timbers, Oak 1¾", Heavy Floors under Engine
8	" Bolts to Keel ½" galv. iron
9	" " " Frames ⅜" galv. iron
10	Frames, White Oak 1¾"x 2", spaced 12" on center
11	Planking, 1¼" Oregon Pine, fastened with galv. screws.
12	Cabin Floor, rift Hard Pine, ⅞" thick, Hatches as needed
13	Ceiling, ⅝" W. Pine or Cypress.
14	Bilge Stringer, Oregon Pine 1⅜"x5¾"
15	" Bolts ⅜" galv. iron
16	Clamp, Oregon Pine 3"x5"
17	" Bolts ⅜" galv. iron
18	Gold Stripe
19	Rail Teak 1" dowelled to Covering board and Sheer Strake
20	" Cap Teak 1¾"x3", 1¾"x4" at Chainplates.
21	Deck 1¼"x2" rift sawn, W. Pine or Fir, Teak Covering board
22	" Beams, Oak 2½"x3" and 1¾"x3', Crown 4" in 12
23	House Sides 1⅛" Teak
24	Portlights 5"x9" Torrey Roller Bushing - Screens
25	House Deck 1" W. Pine tongue + Groove, covered with 8oz. Duck
26	" Beams White Oak 1⅜"x2", 2"x2" at Openings
27	Skylight Teak - 4 - 8" Deadlights, Bronze Hinges and Raisers
28	Grab Rail Teak
29	Coaming Teak 1", Cap 1"x2" Teak
30	Travellers Main ⅝"x24", Mizzen ⅝"x14", Jib ⅝"x40"
31	Chainplates
32	Engine Bed
33	" Floor Timbers
34	Mizzen Mast Step
35	Limber Holes with Brass Chain

PLAN NO. 36
CONSTRUCTION   SECTIONS
Scale: 1"=1'-0"

L. FRANCIS HERRESHOFF ~ DESIGNER
Marblehead, Mass.

Oct. 1928   L.F.H.

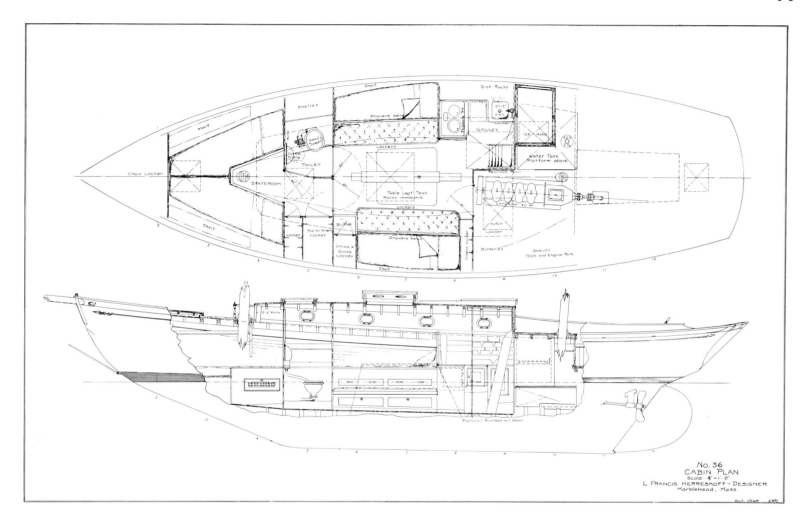

No. 36
CABIN PLAN
Scale ¾"=1'-0"
L. FRANCIS HERRESHOFF—DESIGNER
Marblehead, Mass

Oct. 1927   LFH

PERSEPHONE

This lovely yawl shows the influence, probably imparted by her owner, W. J. Strawbridge, rather than by her designer, of the Cruising Club of America rule for rating racing yachts. A good many pretty and able yawls of this general type were designed, along with *Persephone,* in the mid-Thirties, two other fine examples of the type being the *Stormy Weather,* designed by Olin Stephens, and the *Roland von Bremen,* designed by Henry Gruber. While the *Persephone* has the rather deep, narrow hull with moderate overhang forward, long fine counter, and rounded topsides of moderate height, along with the seven-eighths headstay and tiny mizzen, characteristic of these ocean racing yawls of forty years ago, she also has certain details that mark her unmistakably as a Francis Herreshoff creation. There is the knuckle in the stem profile just above the waterline, the shippy looking hawse-hole in the rail, the diamond-shaped chain plates, and the streamlined fo'c'sle hatch.

This is a big boat that would sail well under a great variety of conditions and would make fast passages at sea. She is 55 feet long on deck, 40 feet long on the waterline, with a beam of 12'7'''', and a draft of 7'9''. Her sail area with the slightly overlapping jib shown is 1,421 square feet, with 796 square feet in the mainsail, 135 in the mizzen, and 490 in the jib. Note the permanent main backstay lead to the end of the mizzen jumper strut.

The cabin plan on page 320 shows a standard layout for a boat of this size. The details at the top of the drawing show exactly how the frames for her canvas berths were to be made up and how the berths were to be attached.

The *Persephone* would be a joy to sail in almost any weather. But for her handkerchief mizzen, dictated by the rating rule, she would be an exceedingly beautiful yacht.

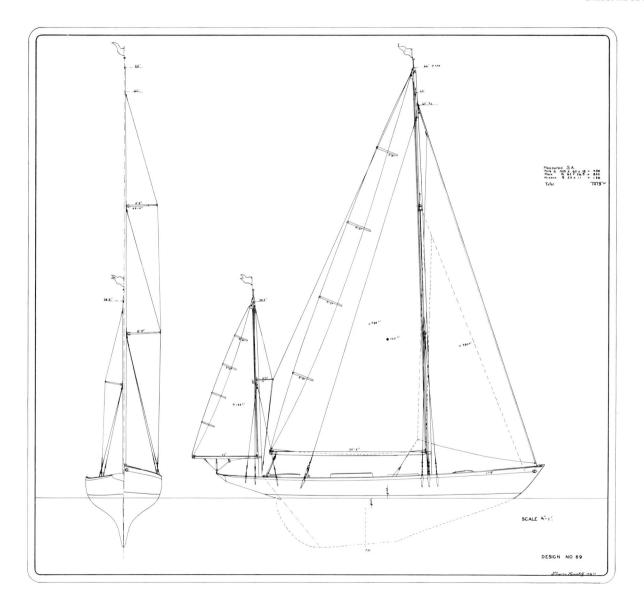

SCALE ¼"=1'

DESIGN NO 69

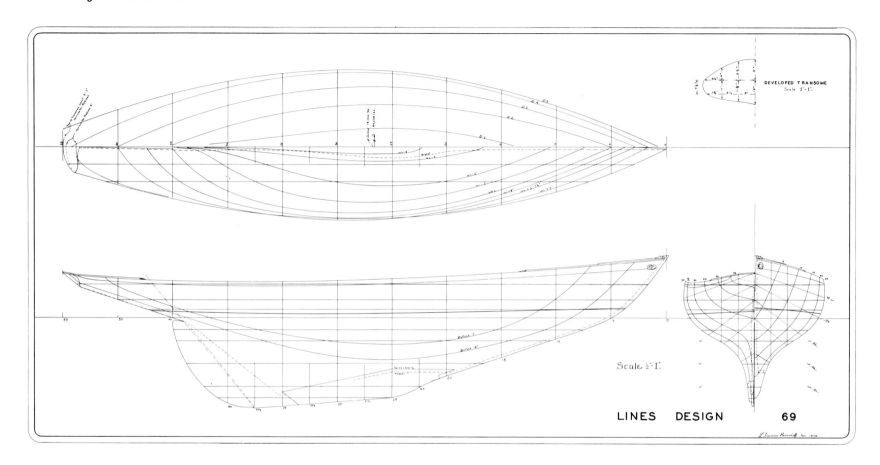

DEVELOPED TRANSOME
Scale 1"=1'.

Scale ½"=1'.

LINES   DESIGN   69

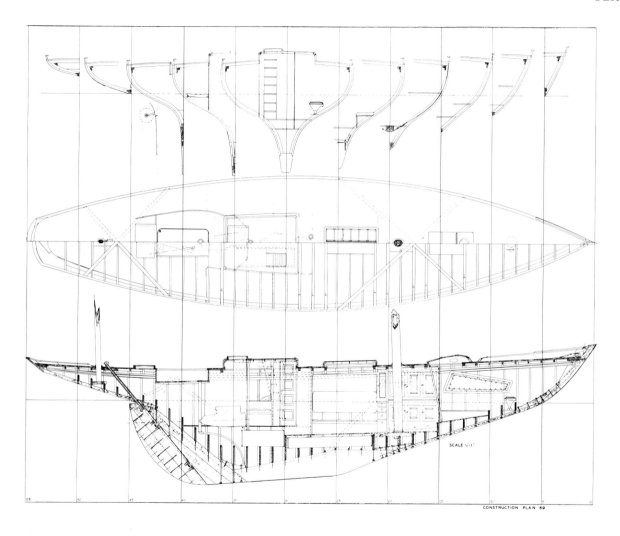

CONSTRUCTION PLAN 69

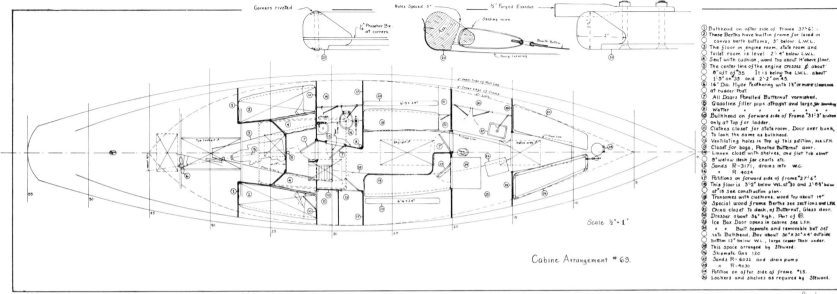

Scale ½" - 1'

Cabine Arrangement # 69.

① Bulkhead on after side of Frame 37'-6½".
② These Berths have built in frame for laced in
   canvas berth bottoms, 3" below L.W.L.
③ The floor in engine room, state room and
   toilet room is level 2'-4" below L.W.L.
④ Seat with cushion, wood top about 14"above floor.
⑤ The center line of the engine crosses ₵ about
   8" aft of #35   It is below The L.W.L. about
   1'-5" on 35 and 2'-2" on 45.
⑥ 16" Dia. Hyde Feathering with 1½" or more clearance
   at rudder Post.
⑦ All Doors Panelled Butternut varnished.
⑧ Gasoline filler pipe Straight and large for
   Water   "   "   "   "   "
⑨ Bulkhead on forward side of Frame #31'-3" broken
   only at top for ladder.
⑩ Clothes closet for state room, Door over bunk,
   To look the same as bulkhead.
⑪ Ventilating holes in Top of this partition, see L.F.H.
⑫ Closet for bags, Panelled Butternut door.
⑬ Linnen closet with shelves, and flat top about
   9" below deck for charts etc.
⑭ Sands R-3171, drains into W.C.
     "   R 4024
⑮ Patitions on forward side of frame #27'-6".
⑯ This floor is 3'-2" below WL. at #30 and 2'-8¾" below
   at #15 see construction plan.
⑰ Transomes with cushions, wood top about 14"
⑱ Special wood frame Berths see section and L.F.H.
⑲ China closet To deck, of Butternut, Glass door.
⑳ Dresser about 36" high, Part of ⑲.
㉑ Ice Box Door opens in cabine See L.F.H.
    "   " Built seperate and removable but Set
   into Bulkhead. Box about 30"x 30"x 4' outside
   bottom 12" below W.L., large copper Tank under.
㉒ This space arranged by Steward.
㉓ Shipmate Gas 120
㉔ Sands R-6022 and drain pump
     "   R-4030
㉕ Patition on after side of frame #15.
㉖ Lockers and shelves as required by Steward.

Corners riveted

¼" Phosphor Bz.
at corners.

Holes Spaced 8"
Sewing wire

½" Forged Everdur

Berth Bottom

Fancy Covering

Persephone

AUXILIARY KETCH

This design is somewhat reminiscent of Claud Worth's gaff cutter, later rerigged to a gaff ketch, *Tern III*. The chief difference is in the bow, for where the English cutter was nearly plumb bowed with convex waterlines forward and a deep forefoot, this ketch has a bit more overhang and has a fine, hollow bow with the forefoot somewhat cut away. The ketch is deep-bodied and powerful and would certainly be a wonderful sea boat.

Her double-head rig would be very handy indeed. In a hard breeze she would sail well under main and fore staysail, or with mizzen and both headsails. She would also run off well in a strong breeze under mainsail alone. She could set a variety of light weather headsails to augment her moderate sail area in light weather. Her sail area is 1,454 square feet, with 636 square feet in the mainsail, 322 in the mizzen, 236 the fore staysail, and 260 in the jib.

As can be seen in the construction plan on page 324, her 40-horsepower Red Wing motor is placed off center and quite far forward in its own engine room handy to the companionway. In an auxiliary craft, where the engine is a real working part of the vessel, it's just as well to give it space and a position of some prominence. This boat is roomy enough to do just that. The ketch has ten berths in her, but on a cruise of any length, her crew would probably be cut to five, for which her layout is very well suited.

No boat was ever built to this design, but perhaps someday one will be.

No. 42
SAIL PLAN
Scale ⅜″=1′0″
L. FRANCIS HERRESHOFF — DESIGNER
Marblehead, Mass.

AUXILIARY KETCH for EDMUND S. PARSONS, Esq.

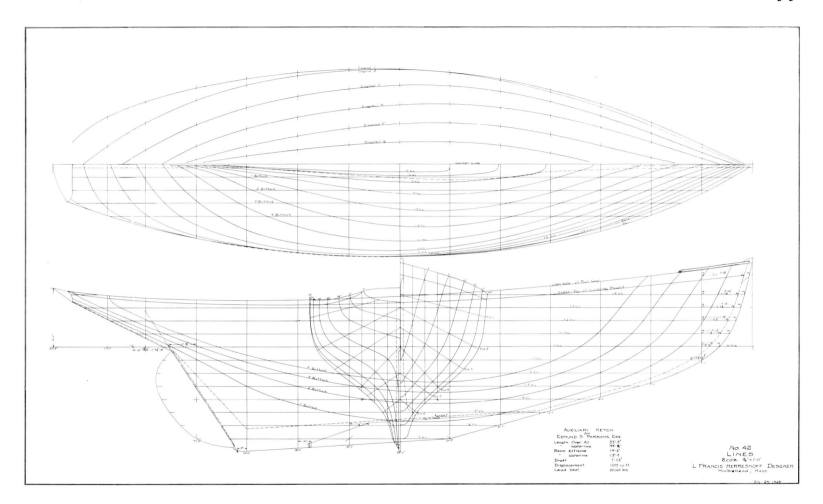

AUXILIARY KETCH
for
EDMUND S. PARSONS, Esq.

Length Over All	55'-2"
Waterline	44'-4"
Beam Extreme	14'-5"
" Waterline	13'-3"
Draft	7'-11 1/2"
Displacement	1105 cu. ft.
Lead Keel	20,160 lbs.

No. 42
LINES
Scale 3/4" = 1'-0"
L. FRANCIS HERRESHOFF, DESIGNER
Marblehead, Mass.

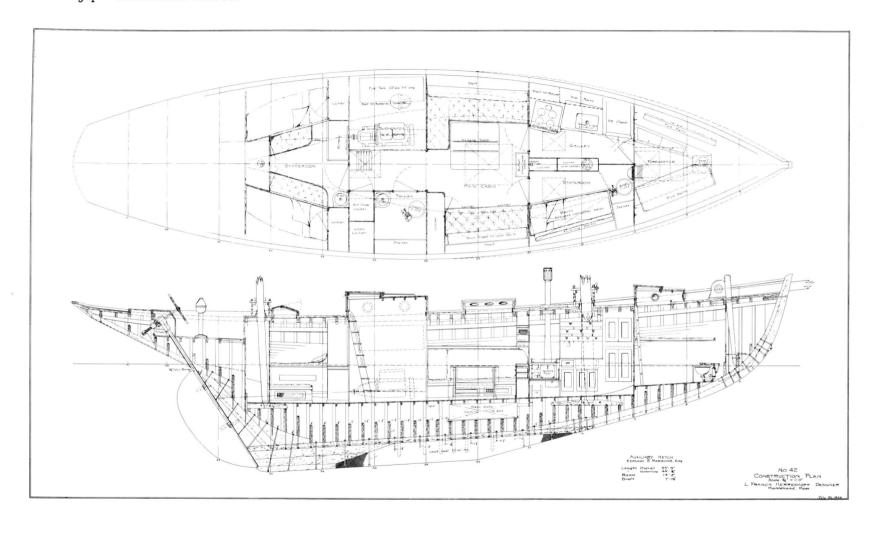

AUXILIARY KETCH
EDMUND S. PARSONS, Esq.

Length Overall   35' 3"
  Waterline   44' 6"
Beam   14' 2"
Draft   7' 11"

No 42
CONSTRUCTION PLAN
Scale: 3/4" = 1'-0"
L FRANCIS HERRESHOFF DESIGNER
Marblehead, Mass.

July 30, 1925

OCEAN RACING KETCH

Dudley Wolfe selected Frank Paine's design for the *Highland Light* over this Francis Herreshoff design for an ocean racer. While the great *Light's* performance over the years eliminates any quarrel with Wolfe's decision, yet it is a great pity that no boat has been built from this design.

She is a refined and lengthened version of the auxiliary ketch just preceding. This boat is 64 feet long on deck, with a waterline length of 50 feet, a beam of 15 feet, and a draft of 9 feet. By comparison with the smaller ketch, she has a bit more fineness and overhang at both bow and stern, a slightly deeper and narrower hull, easier bilges, and a bigger rig. She would certainly be a wonderful performer under sail, and it would have been most interesting to see how she would have fared racing against such boats as the *Highland Light,* or the great W. Starling Burgess design, the staysail schooner *Niña*.

Though this ketch was designed for ocean racing, she would also be an admirable cruiser, of course; forty years ago the rating rules for handicapping ocean racing boats encouraged rather wholesome vessels.

The construction plan and cabin arrangement plan on pages 328 and 329 show different layouts on deck and below.

For both racing and cruising, the arrangement suggested in the construction plan might be somewhat preferable, with the chart table and head right aft immediately accessible to the cockpit, rather than forward of the after stateroom. In any event, there is plenty of room in this big ketch for all the amenities. The great difficulty if this boat were built in this day and age might be to follow L. Francis' advice and keep her simple.

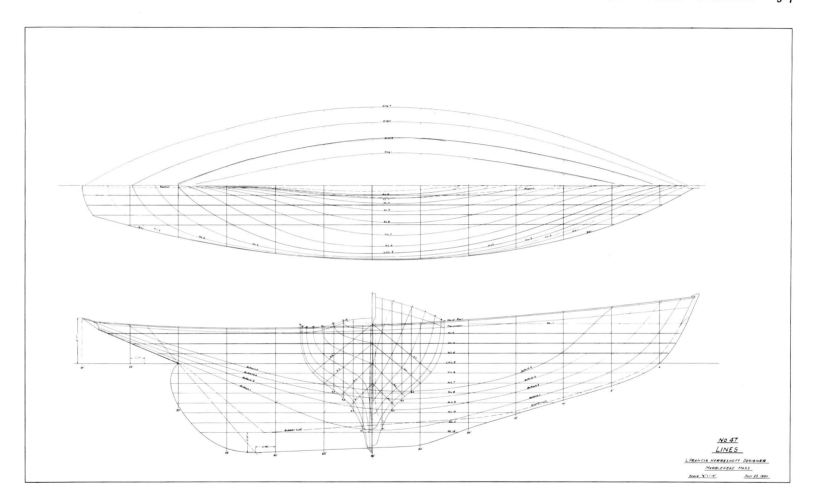

NO 47
LINES

L FRANCIS HERRESHOFF DESIGNER
MARBLEHEAD MASS

SCALE ⅜'·1·0'   JULY 25 1930

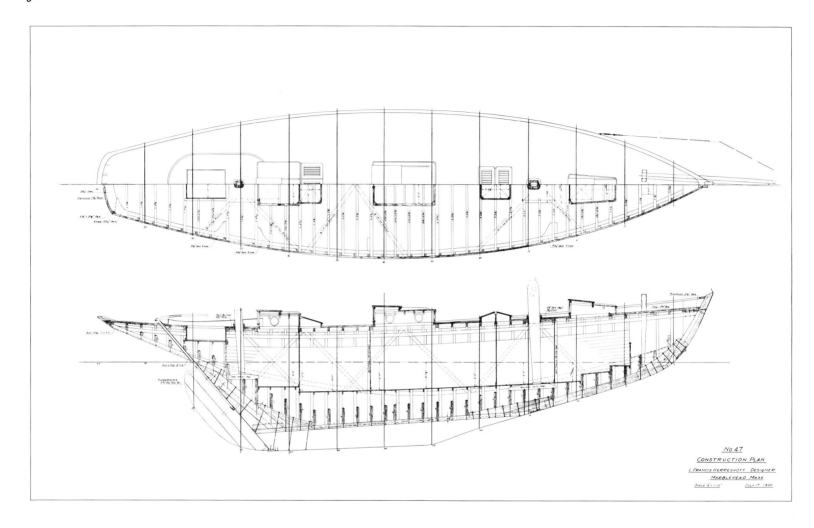

No 47
CONSTRUCTION PLAN
L FRANCIS HERRESHOFF DESIGNER
MARBLEHEAD MASS
SCALE ¾"=1'-0"   JULY 17 1930

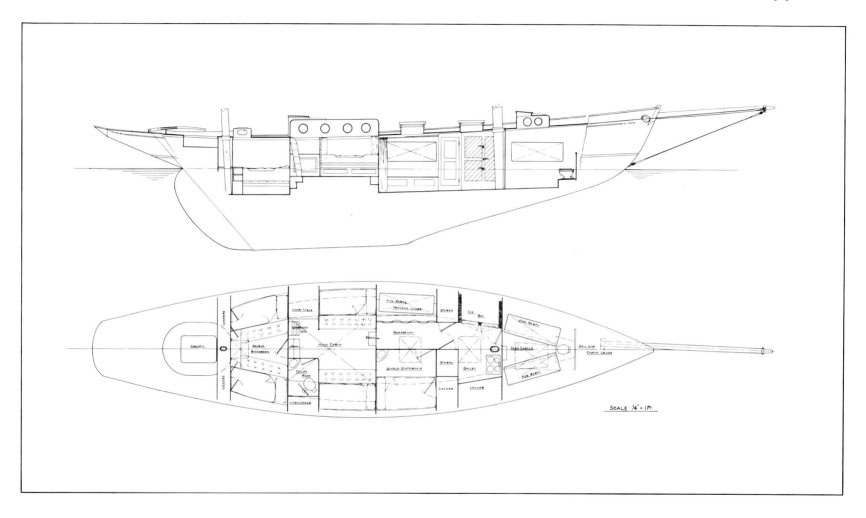

SCALE ¼" = 1 FT

LEEBOARD KETCH

This shallow-draft ketch, designed in 1963, was the last full-fledged yacht design of L. Francis Herreshoff. She is an admirable cruising boat, able to take her crew easily and comfortably wherever there is three feet of water. Her underbody is rather fine, and this characteristic together with her long, flat run should make her quite fast. Her leeboards leave the saloon uncluttered and provide sufficient lateral resistance, even though at first glance they look too small. We have to remember that, unlike a centerboard, the leeboard provides lateral plane throughout its submerged area, rather than just on that part of it that projects below the bottom of the keel. Her transom is shapely, and has enough deadrise to stay clear of the water until it is really needed for bearing as the boat heels well down.

Her rig looks short, but she has the kind of slippery hull that would not need to be driven hard. The sail area is 602 square feet, with 314 square feet in the mainsail, 152 in the mizzen, and 136 in the jib. The overlapping jib has 220 square feet. As shown by the combined center of effort of jib and mizzen on the sail plan, she would balance best under this combination if the mizzen had its reef tucked in. Some might prefer jib-headed sails in place of the short gaffs, but they do reduce the mast heights a bit, and also give the skipper a way to adjust the curvature of the leeches of his sails.

Everyone might not agree with the L. Francis method of stowing the dinghy; it's just a question of whether you want to trip over it occasionally or put it on top of the house and be peering around it constantly.

Her arrangement plan is straightforward with the engine under the bridge deck, the galley aft, and the saloon and forward stateroom separated by a head to port and closet to starboard. The boat is long enough to have, in addition, a sizeable forepeak for stowage.

It would indeed be wonderful if someone would build this last sensible cruising design of Mr. Herreshoff's, not out of sentiment, though there would be nothing wrong with that, but because she would be such a fine cruising boat.

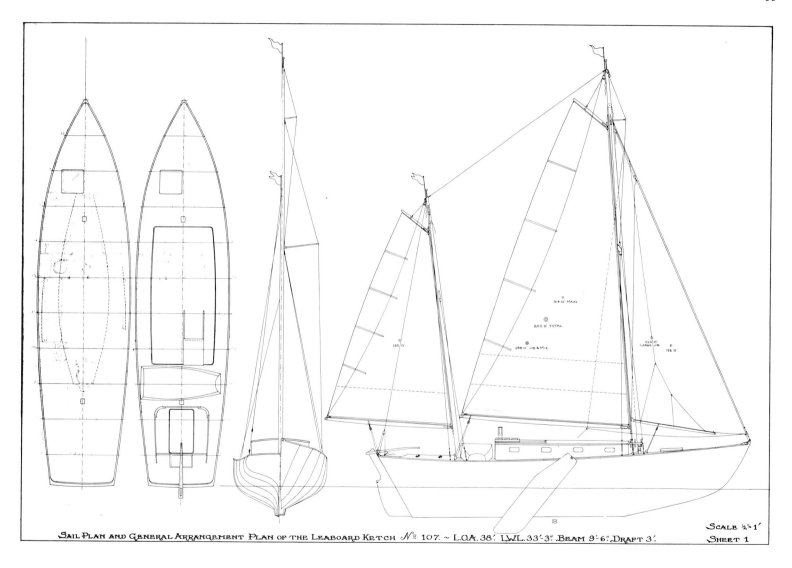

SAIL PLAN AND GENERAL ARRANGEMENT PLAN OF THE LEEBOARD KETCH №107. ~ L.O.A. 38'. L.W.L. 33'-3". BEAM 9'-6". DRAFT 3'.

SCALE ½" = 1'

SHEET 1

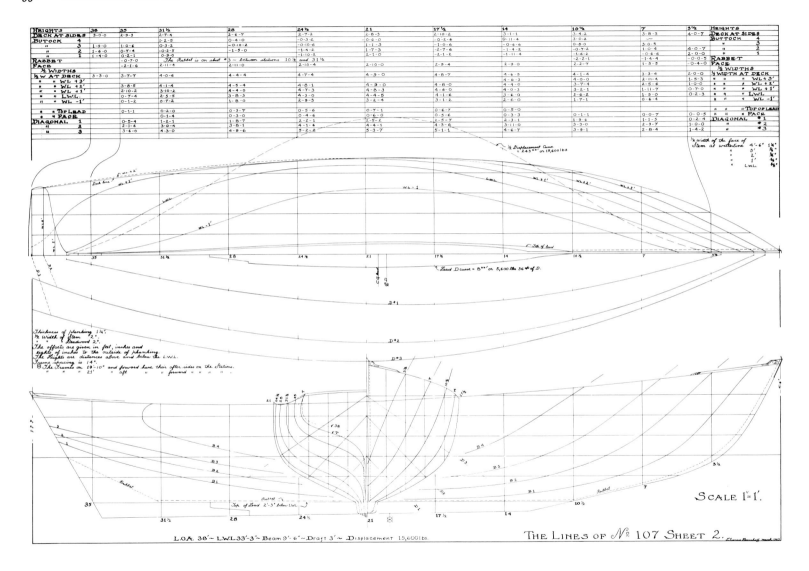

HEIGHTS	38	35	31½	28	24½	21	17½	14	10½	7	3½	HEIGHTS
DECK AT SIDES	3-0-0	2-9-3	2-7-4	2-6-7	2-7-2	2-8-3	2-10-2	3-1-1	3-4-2	3-8-3	4-0-7	DECK AT SIDES
BUTTOCK 4			1-2-5	0-4-0	-0-3-2	-0-6-0	-0-2-6	0-11-4	3-0-2	~		BUTTOCK 4
" 3	1-9-0	1-0-6	0-3-2	-0-10-6	-1-0-6	-1-1-3	-0-6-6	0-8-0	3-0-5			" 3
" 2	1-6-0	0-7-4	-0-2-5	-1-5-0	-1-4-2	-1-7-3	-1-4-2	-0-7-2	1-0-4	4-0-7		" 2
" 1	1-4-0	0-2-1	-0-9-0		-1-10-2	-2-1-0	-2-1-1	-1-6-2	-0-6-6	2-0-0		" 1
RABBET		-0-7-0	The Rabbet is on sheet #3 ~ between stations 10½ and 31½						-2-2-1	-1-4-4	-0-0-5	RABBET
FACE		-2-1-6	2-11-4	2-11-4	2-10-4	2-10-0	2-9-4	2-9-0	2-2-7	1-5-5	-0-4-0	FACE
½ WIDTHS												½ WIDTHS
½ W AT DECK	3-3-0	3-7-7	4-1-4	4-4-4	4-7-4	4-9-0	4-8-7	4-6-5	4-1-4	3-3-4	2-0-0	½ WIDTH AT DECK
" WL 4 3'								4-6-3	4-0-0	2-11-4	1-5-3	" WL 4 3'
" WL 4 2'		3-8-5	4-1-4	4-5-4	4-8-1	4-9-0	4-8-0	4-4-0	3-7-4	2-5-6	1-0-0	" WL 4 2'
" WL 4 1'		2-10-2	3-10-2	4-4-0	4-7-3	4-8-3	4-6-0	4-0-3	3-2-1	1-11-7	0-7-0	" WL 4 1'
" L.W.L.		0-7-4	2-5-5	3-8-3	4-3-0	4-4-5	4-1-6	3-6-0	2-6-2	1-5-0	0-2-3	" L.W.L.
" WL -1'		0-1-2	0-7-2	1-8-0	2-9-3	3-2-4	2-6-0	1-7-1	0-6-4			" WL -1'
" TOP OF LEAD		0-1-1	0-2-0	0-3-7	0-5-6	0-7-1	0-6-7	0-5-0				" TOP OF LEAD
" FACE			0-3-0	0-4-6	0-5-6	0-5-6	0-3-3		0-1-1	0-0-7	0-0-5	" FACE
DIAGONAL 1		0-5-4	1-2-5	1-8-7	2-2-1	2-5-7	2-5-7	1-9-6	1-1-5	0-2-4	DIAGONAL #1
" 2		2-1-6	3-0-4	3-8-1	4-1-6	4-4-1	4-3-6	3-11-0	3-0-0	2-3-7	1-0-0	" #2
" 3		3-6-0	4-3-0	4-9-6	5-2-2	5-3-7	5-1-1	4-6-7	3-9-1	2-8-4	1-4-2	" #3

½ width of the face of Stem at waterline 4'-6" 1¼"
" 3' ⅞"
" 2' ½"
" 1' ¾"
" L.W.L. ⅝"

½ Displacement Curve = 2.43°° or 15,600 lbs.

Lead D curve = 8°° or 5,600 lbs. 36 % of D.

Thickness of planking 1¼".
½ Width of Stem 2".
" " Deadwood 2".
The offsets are given in feet, inches and eighths of inches to the outside of planking.
The Heights are distances above and below the L.W.L.
Frame spacing is 14".
The frames on 10-10" and forward have their after sides on the Stations.
" " 21 aft " " forward "

Top of Lead 2'-3" below L.W.L.

SCALE 1"=1'.

L.O.A. 38'~ L.W.L. 33'-3"~ Beam 9'-6"~ Draft 3'~ Displacement 15,600 lbs.

THE LINES OF N° 107 Sheet 2.

PROPOSED SHALLOW DRAFT CRUISER

Here is another idea for a sizeable cruising ketch with but three feet of draft. The drawing shows she has full headroom for an average-sized man to stand up to his work of planning the next day's run with his shipmate. The boat would be fast under both sail and power. Sail would be used with a leading breeze, and the two engines would be brought into play, either in conjunction with the sails or by themselves, when it was necessary to make a passage to windward. She would be highly maneuverable under power, for with one engine going ahead and the other astern, she could be held in position and twisted in her own length. And there is no question that if power is to be used much, the tremendous increase in reliability gained with a second engine is well worth its extra cost. Moreover, it is easier to place in an out-of-the-way position two small engines than one big one, especially in a shallow-draft hull.

The openness of her interior arrangement is appealing; with the curtain between saloon and sleeping cabin pulled back, the clear area between the bulkheads in the cabin is 17 feet long.

This would be a fine boat for serious coastal exploration, for with her shoal draft and great maneuverability, she could venture into many an unfrequented nook and cranny, and with sails and engines to keep her going at a good speed, her passages between coastal points of interest would be fast enough to satisfy all but the most impatient expedition leader.

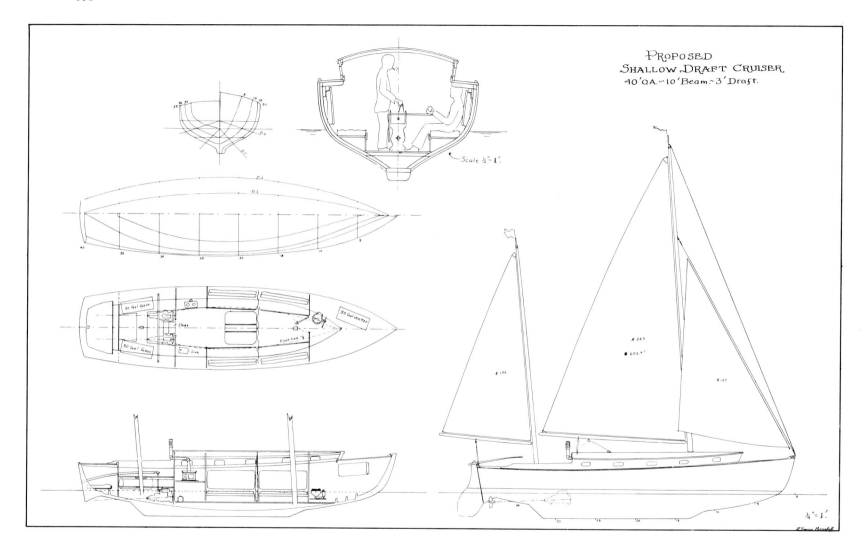

PROPOSED
SHALLOW DRAFT CRUISER
40'OA.~10'Beam~3'Draft.

Scale ½" = 1'.

¼" = 1'.

MAÑANA

An early design for a shallow-draft cruiser by Mr. Herreshoff was that for the big gaff schooner, *Mañana,* done while he was at Burgess, Swasey, and Paine. She draws only 3'9″ on a waterline length of 47 feet. The boat was doubtless not intended to be a great performer to windward; the construction plan on page 338 shows a big engine in way of the mainmast to port. She evidently was intended to be under sail in a breeze of wind, however, for the sail plan shows in dotted lines a small gaff foresail, a main trysail to be set over the furled mainsail, and a storm jib set well up off the deck. Even before it was necessary to get out these storm sails, her knockabout schooner rig would be handy enough. Her sail area was 1,391 square feet, with 716 square feet in the mainsail, 421 in the foresail, and 254 in the jib.

The construction plan shows what must, indeed, be a unique arrangement. The schooner's mainmast is stepped right on top of her centerboard trunk. It is enough to make one wish for a time machine to go back to the B, S, and P offices in 1924 and listen in on the discussion of that particular construction arrangement that must have ensued at some point between the three principals of the office and Mr. Herreshoff. Perhaps the centerboard trunk should have been offset beside the keel. If this would have infringed upon the vastness of the ship's great lavatory, so be it. The details to be seen in the cabin plan of upholstery, locker doors, shelf railings, leaded glass, and stovepipe joints, not to mention wood grain in the ship's backbone, are fascinating and revealing of both L. Francis' great drafting talent and of the time and patience to apply it.

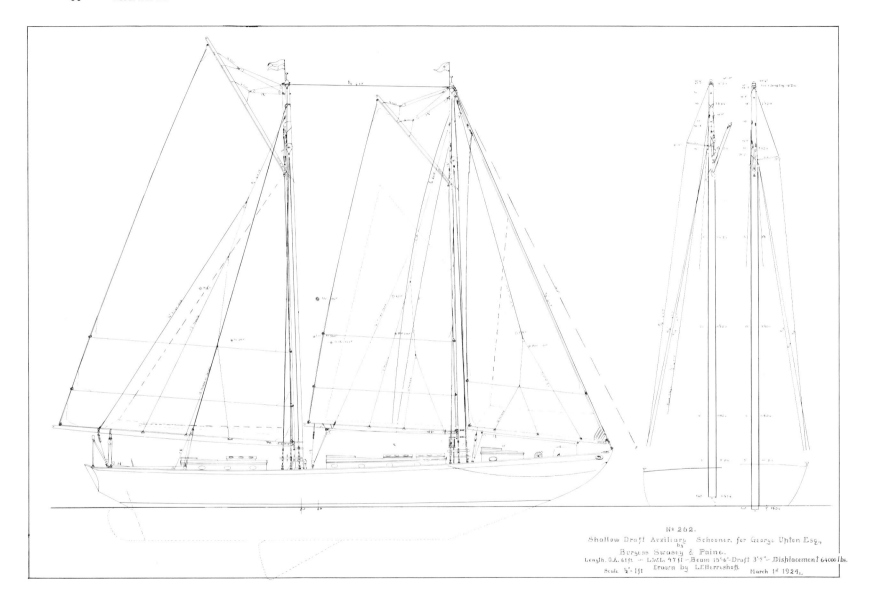

Nº 262.
Shallow Draft Auxiliary Schooner, for George Upton Esq.,
by
Burgess Swasey & Paine.
Length. O.A. 61ft. — L.W.L. 47ft — Beam 15'6" — Draft 3'8" — Displacement 64000 lbs.
Scale ½"=1ft   Drawn by L.F. Herreshoff.   March 1ª 1924.

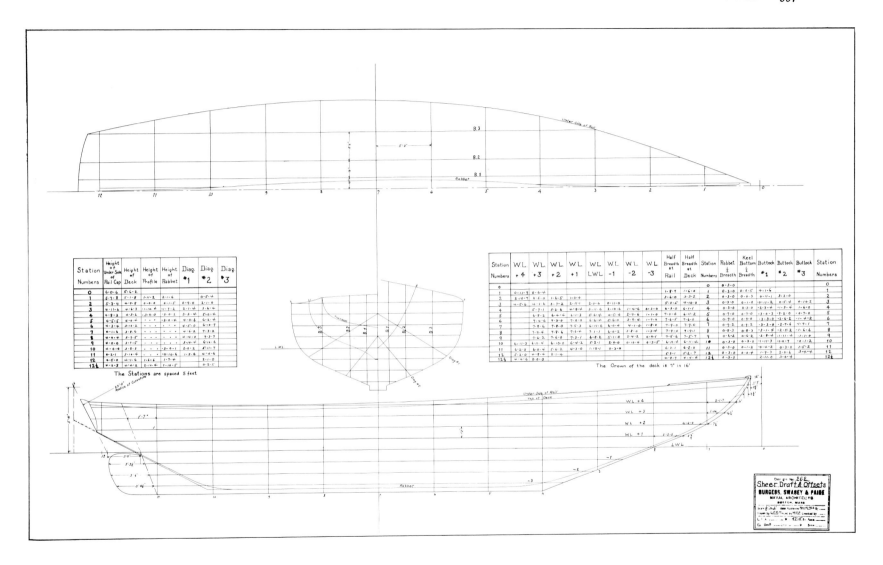

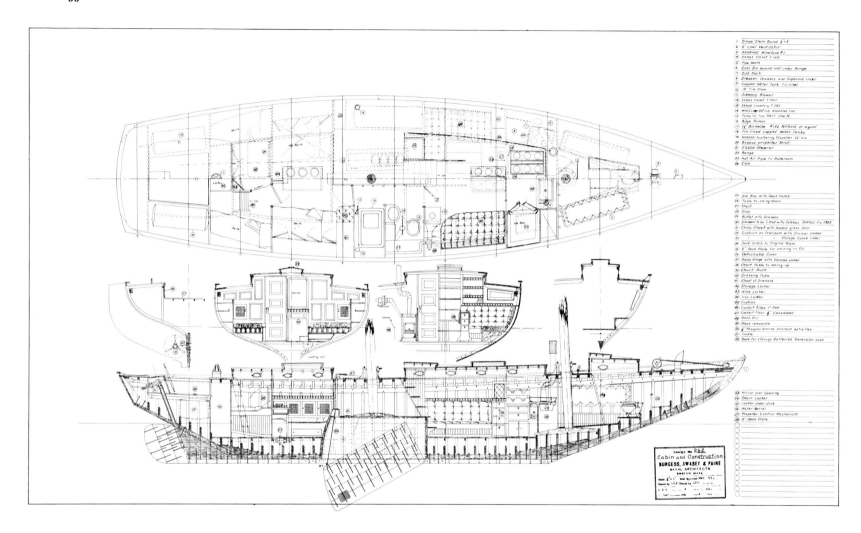

LIFEBOAT KETCH

Occasionally one hears of a man who wants a boat "able to go out in anything." Few of us really want to do that, but occasionally we may dream of having a craft able to put to sea even in a winter gale. This design represents the sort of craft such dreams are often made of. Although her motion would certainly be lively — in fact violent under the worst conditions — she would be as safe and dry in a heavy seaway as one could expect to be in a boat. She has tremendous buoyancy.

Although the rig is modest enough, one would expect to see more reef bands shown, along with some storm sails. Her mainsail has 303 square feet, the mizzen 175, and the jib 110, for the total of 588 square feet. Her power is a pair of 30-horse Lathrops.

For those who want to cruise in waters and seasons where heavy weather is often expected, this is the sort of design that makes sense.

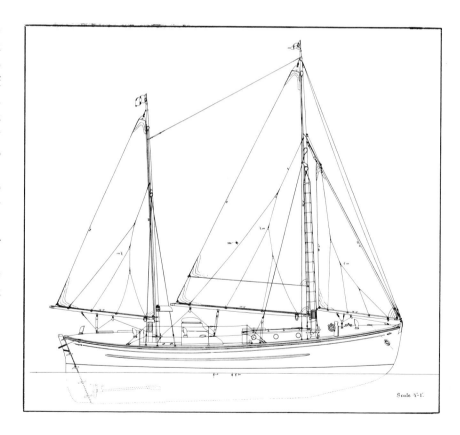

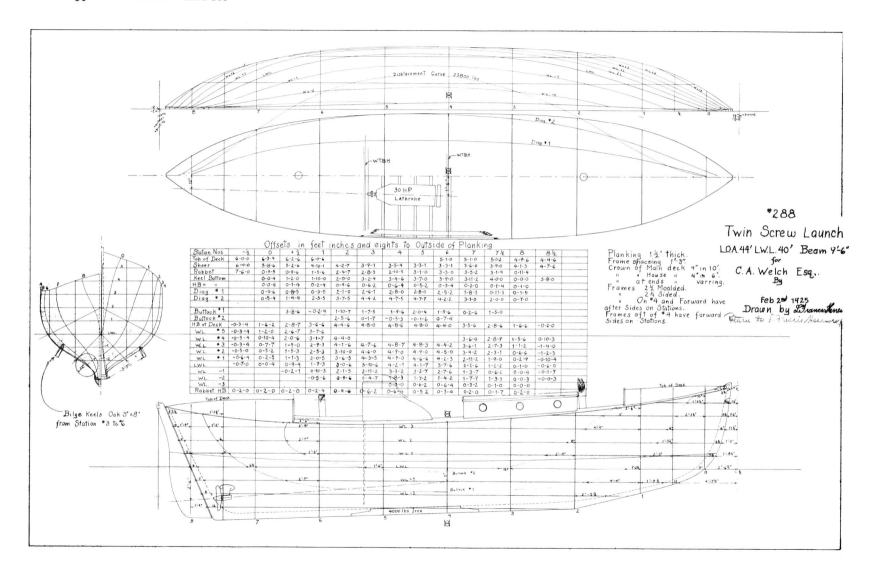

OCEAN CRUISER

This design was prepared for William A. Robinson, who had made long ocean voyages in the little Alden ketch, *Svaap,* and who wanted a vessel for ocean cruising to use after World War II. In fact, Robinson decided on a larger vessel, which was designed by Starling Burgess with the rig designed by Mr. Herreshoff. That craft was the interesting brigantine, *Varua.* But this design for an ocean cruising ketch has so far remained that of a dream ship.

She has as powerful a midsection as any L. Francis drew. Her bilges are full and low and would provide great stability. Yet her run is not abrupt and her ends are fine; she would not be a slow boat.

The rig is moderate, and the mainsail has been kept unusually small in comparison to the other sails. Its area is 381 square feet. That of the mizzen is 276 square feet, the fore staysail has 202 square feet and the jib 253, for a total of 1,112. The squaresail shown has an area of 513 square feet.

The vessel has an interesting arrangement, as shown in dotted lines in the construction plan on page 344. The deckhouse abaft the mizzen mast would be a most handy chart house and shelter for the watch on deck. The engine room is just forward of the mizzen mast. The companionway to the main living quarters is on the starboard side of the house, and this allows a big U-shaped settee extending right across the boat in the saloon. The head and galley are forward of this to port with a stateroom opposite.

She looks to be a fine design for making extended ocean passages.

DESIGN NUMBER 81
LOA 49'   LWL 42'
BEAM 12'5" DRAFT 6'3"
DISPLACEMENT 53,760 lbs

1942

SCALE ⅛"=1.

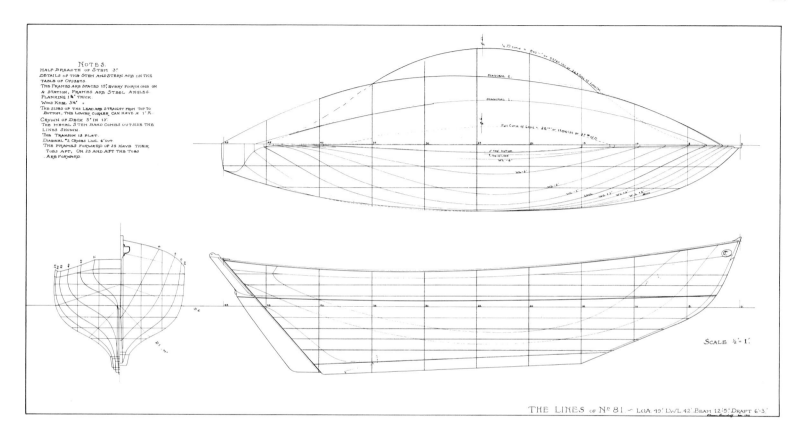

SCALE ½" = 1'.

THE LINES OF Nº 81 — LOA 49' LWL 42' BEAM 12'5" DRAFT 6'3'

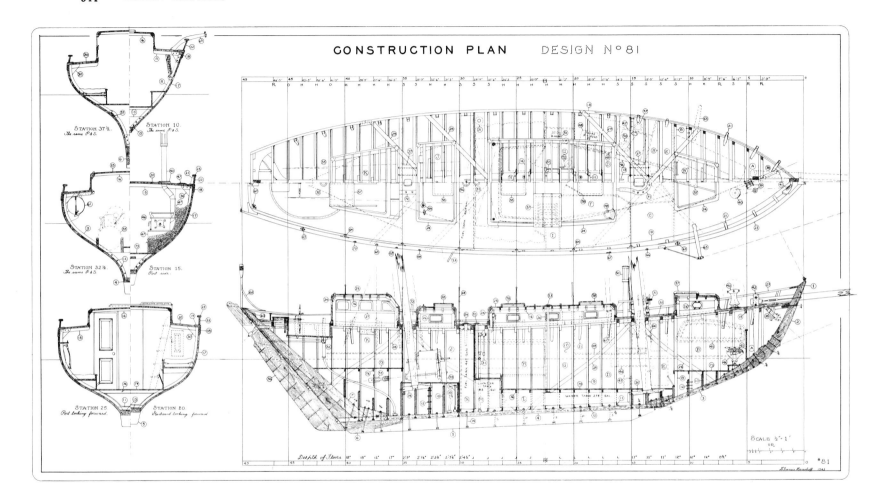

CONSTRUCTION PLAN   DESIGN N° 81

Station 37½.
The same P & S.

Station 10.
The same P & S.

Station 32½.
The same P & S.

Station 15.
Port side.

Station 25
Port looking forward.

Station 20.
Starboard looking forward.

Depth of Irons

Scale ½" = 1'
OR.

*81

WALRUS

Here is a design for a twin-engine power vessel with enough sail area and lateral plane to get where she wants to go under sail alone, if that is her owner's need or wish. She could be called a 50-50 cruiser or motorsailer, but she really seems to be a power craft with auxiliary sails. This makes a fine type of cruising vessel, for she can make good passages in any ordinary weather, and her rig will keep her steady, add to her speed on many runs, and make her far more interesting and fun to handle than is the out-and-out power craft.

Her hull lines are easy throughout, and she would be an excellent sea boat with a smooth motion. The rig would be versatile and easy to handle. Her power is a pair of 40-horse Lathrops, as her engines are labelled in the cabin plan, or two 65-h.p. gasoline engines of unspecified make, as noted on the outboard profile.

The cabin plan on page 350 shows her unusual arrangement. The big, four-man saloon forward is entered through a hatch in the forward starboard corner of the wheelhouse. There is a large, comfortable double stateroom with its own washroom abaft the engines, and tucked in the very stern under the turtleback is the galley and wardroom, entered through a separate hatch over a vertical ladder.

The *Walrus* seems clearly to be a man's boat. She would be an admirable cold-weather cruiser, with her big, pot-bellied stove in the saloon, her snug galley and wardroom aft, and her enclosed wheelhouse.

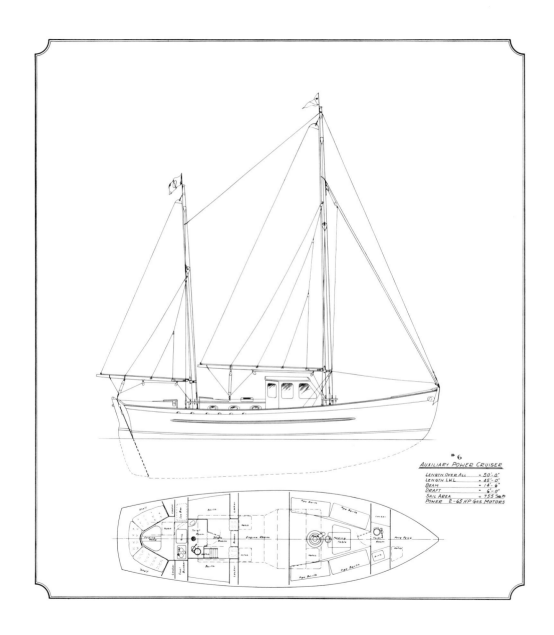

6

AUXILIARY POWER CRUISER

LENGTH OVER ALL	= 50'-0"
LENGTH L.W.L.	= 45'-0"
BEAM	= 14'-6"
DRAFT	= 6'-0"
SAIL AREA	= 755 Sq Ft
POWER	2-65 H.P. GAS MOTORS

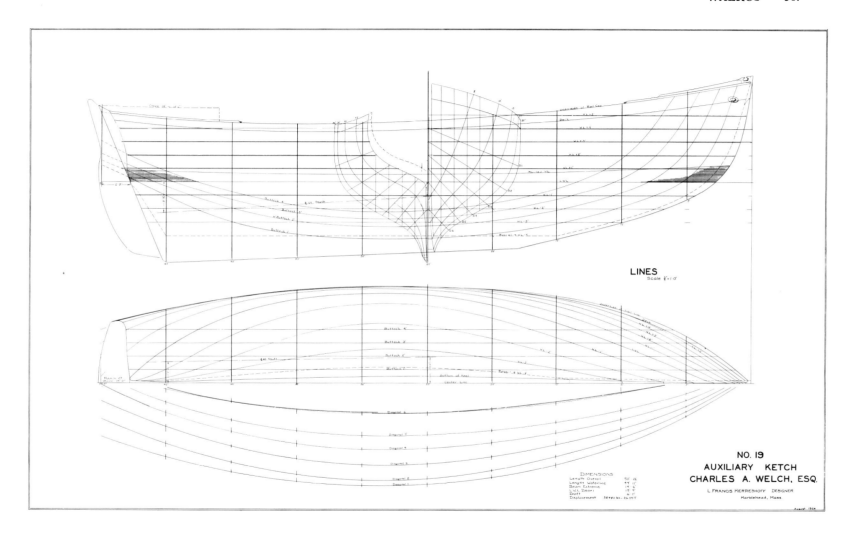

LINES
Scale ⅜"=1'-0"

NO. 19
AUXILIARY   KETCH
CHARLES A. WELCH, ESQ.

L FRANCIS HERRESHOFF DESIGNER
Marblehead, Mass

NO. 19 OFFSET TABLE

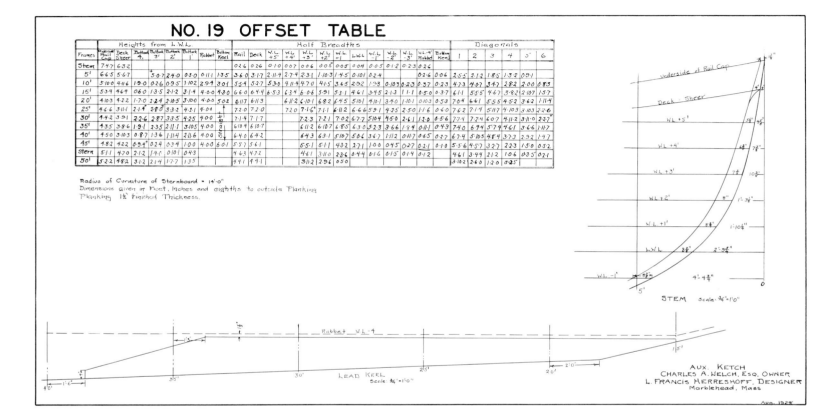

Frames	Heights from L.W.L.								Half Breadths													Diagonals					
	Underside Rail Cap	Deck Sheer	Buttock 4'	Buttock 3'	Buttock 2'	Buttock 1'	Rabbet	Bottom Keel	Rail	Deck	W.L +5'	W.L +4'	W.L +3'	W.L +2'	W.L +1	L.W.L	W.L -1'	W.L -2'	W.L -3'	W.L -4' Rabbet	Bottom Keel	1	2	3	4	5	6
Stem	7.4.7	6.3.2							0.2.6	0.2.6	0.1.0	0.0.7	0.0.6	0.0.5	0.0.5	0.0.4	0.0.5	0.1.2	0.2.3	0.2.6							
5'	6.6.5	5.6.7		5.0.7	2.4.0	0.3.0	0.11.1	1.3.5	3.6.0	3.1.7	2.11.4	2.7.4	2.3.1	1.10.3	1.4.5	0.10.1	0.2.4			0.2.6	0.0.6	2.5.5	2.1.2	1.8.5	1.3.2	0.9.1	
10'	5.10.0	4.11.6	1.9.0	0.2.6	0.9.5	1.10.2	2.9.4	3.0.1	5.5.4	5.2.7	5.3.0	4.11.4	4.7.0	4.1.5	3.6.5	2.9.2	1.9.3	0.10.3	0.2.3	0.3.7	0.2.3	4.7.3	4.0.7	3.4.7	2.8.2	2.0.0	0.8.3
15'	5.3.4	4.6.4	0.6.0	1.3.5	2.1.2	3.1.4	4.0.0	4.3.0	6.6.0	6.4.4	6.5.3	6.3.4	6.0.6	5.9.1	5.3.1	4.6.1	3.4.5	2.1.3	1.1.1	0.5.0	0.3.7	6.1.1	5.5.5	4.6.7	3.8.2	2.10.7	1.5.7
20'	4.10.3	4.2.2	1.7.0	2.2.4	2.10.5	3.10.0	4.0.0	5.0.2	6.11.7	6.11.3		6.11.2	6.10.1	6.8.2	6.4.5	5.10.1	4.10.1	3.4.0	1.10.1	0.10.3	0.5.3	7.0.4	6.6.1	5.5.5	4.5.2	3.6.2	1.11.4
25'	4.6.6	3.11.1	2.1.4	2.8.0	3.3.2	4.2.1	4.0.0		7.2.0	7.2.0		7.2.0	7.1.6	7.1.1	6.11.2	6.6.6	5.9.1	4.2.5	2.5.0	1.1.6	0.6.0	7.6.2	7.1.4	5.11.7	4.10.3	3.10.3	2.2.6
30'	4.4.2	3.9.1	2.2.6	2.8.7	3.3.5	4.2.5	4.0.0		7.1.4	7.1.7		7.2.3	7.2.1	7.0.2	6.7.7	5.10.4	4.5.0	2.6.1	1.2.0	0.5.6		7.7.4	7.2.4	6.0.7	4.11.2	3.11.0	2.2.7
35'	4.3.5	3.8.6	1.9.1	2.3.5	2.11.1	3.10.5	4.0.0		6.10.4	6.10.7		6.11.2	6.10.7	6.8.5	6.3.0	5.2.3	3.6.6	1.8.4	0.11.1	0.4.3		7.4.0	6.9.4	5.7.4	4.6.1	3.6.6	1.11.7
40'	4.5.0	3.10.3	0.8.7	1.3.6	1.11.4	2.11.6	4.0.0		6.4.0	6.4.2		6.4.3	6.3.1	5.10.7	5.0.6	3.6.7	1.11.2	0.11.7	0.6.5	0.2.7		6.7.4	5.10.5	4.8.4	3.7.3	2.9.2	1.4.7
45'	4.8.2	4.2.2	0.9.4	0.2.4	0.3.4	1.0.0	4.0.0	6.0.1	5.5.7	5.6.1		6.5.1	5.11.1	4.3.2	2.7.1	1.0.0	0.4.5	0.2.7	0.2.1	0.1.0		5.5.6	4.5.7	3.2.7	2.2.3	1.5.0	0.5.2
Stern	5.1.1	4.7.0	2.1.2	1.4.0	0.10.1	0.4.3			4.6.3	4.7.2		4.6.1	3.11.0	2.3.6	0.4.4	0.1.6	0.1.5	0.1.4	0.1.2			4.6.1	3.4.9	2.1.2	1.0.6	0.3.5	0.2.1
50'	5.2.2	4.8.2	3.1.2	2.1.4	1.7.7	1.3.5			4.9.1	4.9.1		3.11.2	2.9.6	0.5.0								3.10.2	2.6.0	1.2.0	0.2.5		

Radius of Curvature of Sternboard = 14'-0"
Dimensions given in Feet, Inches and eighths to outside Planking
Planking 1¼" finished Thickness.

Underside of Rail Cap
Deck Sheer
W.L +5'
W.L +4'
W.L +3'
W.L +2'
W.L +1'
L.W.L
W.L -1'
5'

STEM   Scale: ¾"=1'-0"

Rabbet W.L -4

LEAD KEEL   Scale ¾"=1'-0"

AUX. KETCH
CHARLES A. WELCH, ESQ. OWNER
L. FRANCIS HERRESHOFF, DESIGNER
Marblehead, Mass

Aug. 1928

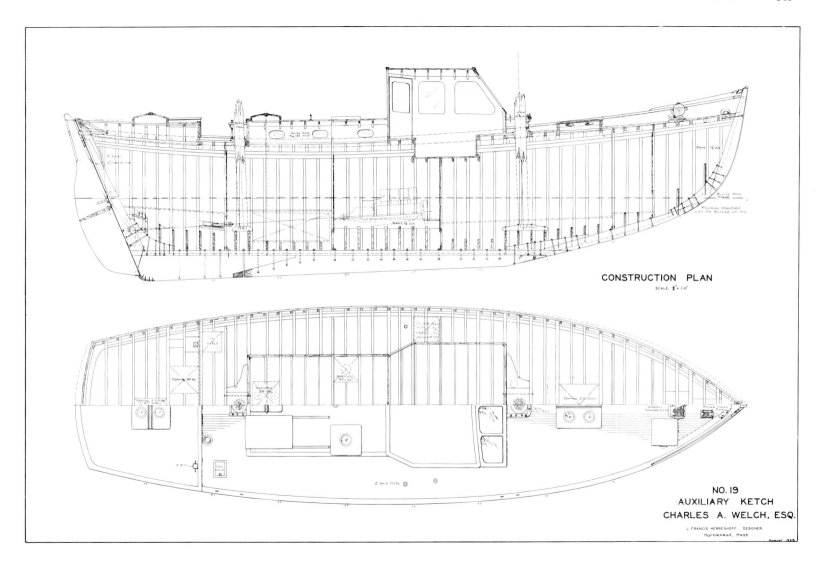

CONSTRUCTION PLAN
SCALE: ¾"= 1'-0"

NO. 19
AUXILIARY KETCH
CHARLES A. WELCH, ESQ.

L. FRANCIS HERRESHOFF DESIGNER
Marblehead, Mass

AUGUST 1928

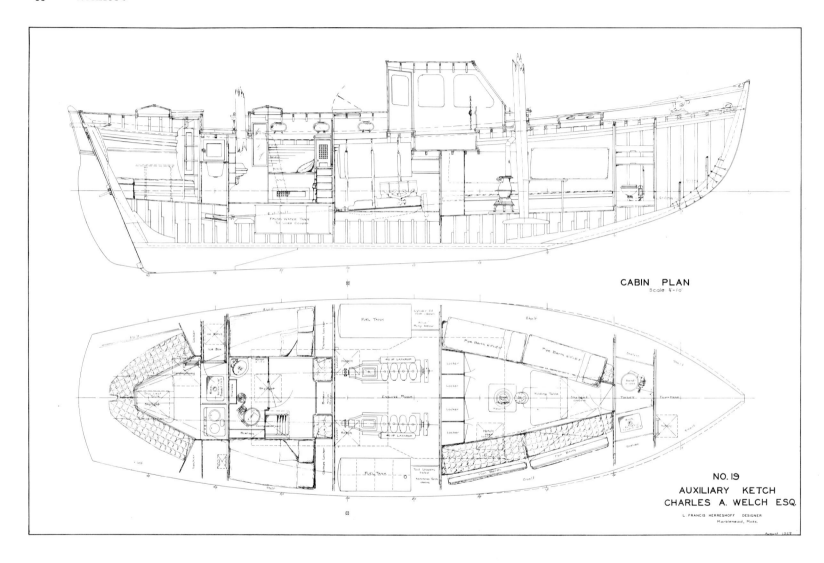

CABIN PLAN
Scale ¾"=1'0"

NO. 19
AUXILIARY KETCH
CHARLES A. WELCH ESQ.

L. FRANCIS HERRESHOFF DESIGNER
Marblehead, Mass.

CARPENTER

Naturally the *Carpenter* is the tender for the *Walrus*. She is a sort of cross between a whaleboat and a dory, for she is whaleboat-shaped above the waterline, but has the narrow, flat bottom of the dory. The combination would make an admirable sea boat, whether loaded or light, yet a boat that would also take kindly to being beached. The latter was obviously intended, for her heavy duty bottom was to be entirely sheathed with 1/16-inch bronze plate. The boat was to be planked lapstrake. She is 18 feet long over-all, 16′3″ on the waterline, with a beam of 4′6″, and a draft (light) of 5 inches.

The *Carpenter* would obviously carry quite a load through rough water with considerable ease. The turtlebacks fore and aft provide dry stowage space and extra buoyancy in a hard chance.

The rig is extremely versatile, for, as can be seen in the construction plan on page 354, there is an additional mast position at the forward end of the centerboard trunk, which would allow sailing her as a catboat with either the big sail or the small one. Running her off in a real breeze with only the 19-square-foot sail set would be some fun. In anything but a flat calm, she would have to be rowed double-banked, and if three oarsmen could get together in her, they could make her fly.

Towed astern of the *Walrus*, she would make an excellent secondary cruising boat for exploring small waters within range of the *Walrus'* anchorage. In fact it might become something of a question as to which boat was tending which.

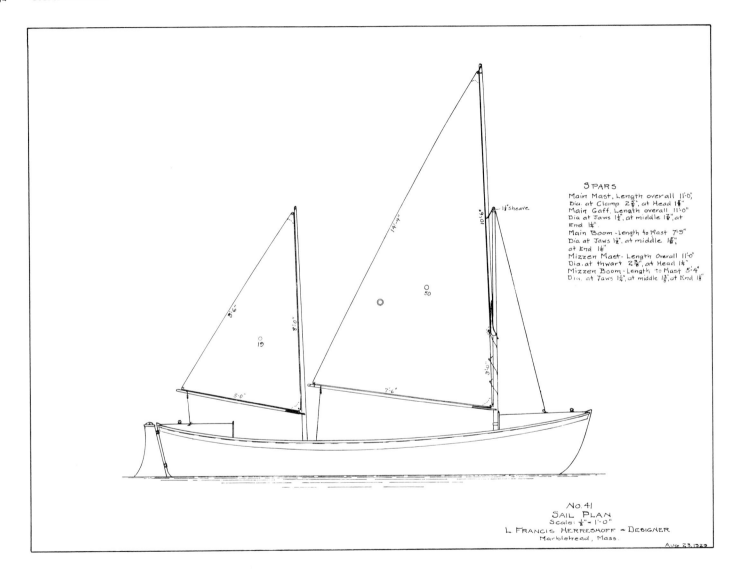

SPARS

Main Mast, Length overall 11'-0",
Dia. at Clamp 2⅜", at Head 1⅞"
Main Gaff, Length overall 11'-0"
Dia at Jaws 1½", at middle 1⅞", at
End 1¼".
Main Boom - Length to Mast 7'-5"
Dia. at Jaws 1½", at middle 1⅞",
at End 1¼"
Mizzen Mast - Length Overall 11'-0"
Dia. at thwart 2⅜", at Head 1¼"
Mizzen Boom - Length to Mast 5'-4"
Dia. at Jaws 1½", at middle 1⅜", at End 1⅛"

No. 41
SAIL PLAN
Scale: ½" = 1'-0"
L. FRANCIS HERRESHOFF ~ DESIGNER
Marblehead, Mass.

AUG. 23, 1922

No. 41 Offset Table

L. Francis Herreshoff – Designer   Marblehead, Mass. June 1929

	Heights from L.W.L.		Half Breadths								Diagonals		
	Sheer	Rabbet	Deck	+18"W.L.	+12"W.L.	+6"W.L.	+3"W.L	L.W.L.	-3"W.L.	Rabbet	1	2	3
Stem	2.6.0		0.0.3	0.0.1+	0.0.1+	0.0.1+	0.0.1+	0.0.1+		0.0.7			
1'-6"	2.2.0	+0.1.3	1.0.3	0.7.7	0.5.1+	0.2.7	0.1.4	0.0.3+		0.0.7	0.7.1+	0.4.7	0.2.6
4'-0"	1.9.4	0.3.7	1.10.4	1.8.3+	1.5.3	1.1.7+	0.11.6	0.8.7	0.5.0	0.3.5	1.6.2	1.3.0	0.10.4+
6'-6"	1.6.5+	0.4.6	2.2.0	2.1.6	1.11.7	1.9.3+	1.7.5	1.4.5+	1.0.0	0.8.4	2.0.5	1.9.1	1.2.7
9'-0"	1.5.2+	0.5.0	2.2.7+		2.2.2	2.1.0	1.11.5+	1.9.2+	1.4.3+	0.11.0	2.3.4+	2.0.2	1.4.4
11'-6"	1.5.0	0.4.7	2.2.5		2.2.1	2.0.5	1.11.1	1.8.6	1.4.0	0.10.3	2.3.1+	1.11.7	1.4.2
14'-0"	1.6.0	0.4.1	1.11.0	1.11.0	1.9.6	1.7.2	1.5.0+	1.1.6+	0.8.7	0.6.6	1.10.5	1.7.1	1.1.1
16'-6"	1.9.3+	0.2.3	1.1.0+	0.11.7	0.9.5	0.6.5	0.4.7	0.2.6		0.0.7	0.11.1	0.8.6	0.5.6
Stern	2.1.0		0.0.3	0.0.1+	0.0.1+	0.0.1+	0.0.1+	0.0.1+		0.0.7			

Dimensions are given in Feet, Inches and Eighths to outside of Planking
Take off 3/8" for Planking
Bottom projects 1/4" below Rabbet, Bottom 1 3/8" thick

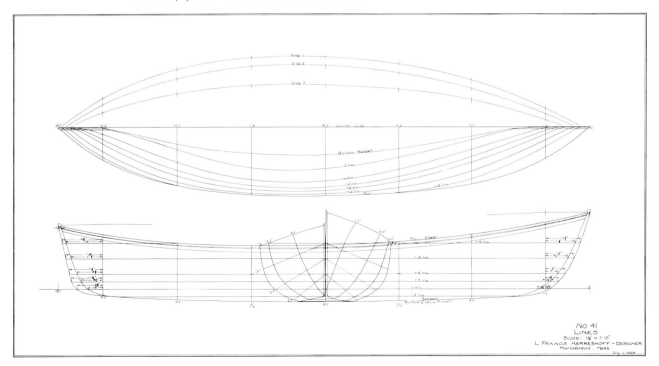

No. 41
LINES
Scale: 1 1/2" = 1'-0"
L. Francis Herreshoff – Designer
Marblehead, Mass.

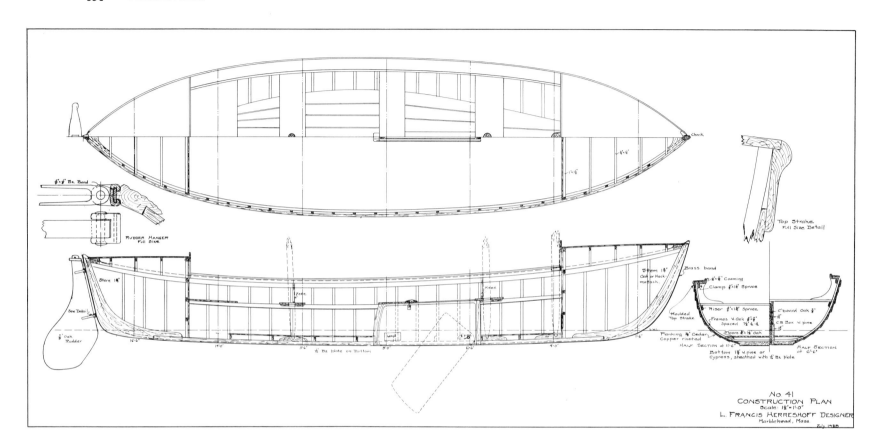

Chock

⅜" x ⅜" Bs. Band

RUDDER HANGER
Full Size

Top Strake
Full Size Detail

⅜" Bs. Band

See Detail

⅜" Oak
Rudder

Stern 1⅛"

Knee

Knee

16'0"

14'0"

11'6"

⅜" Bs. plate on Bottom

9'0"

6'6"

1'6"

4'0"

Stem 1⅛"
Oak or Hack
mataak

Brass band

⅜" x ⅜" Coaming

Clamp ⅜" x 1⅛" Spruce

Moulded
Top Strake

Riser ⅜" x 1⅛" Spruce

Frames W. Oak ⅜" x ⅞"
Spaced 7½" & ⅜

C'board Oak ⅜"

C.B. Box W pine

Floors ⅜" x 1⅜" Oak

Planking ⅜" Cedar
Copper riveted

HALF SECTION at 11'6"

Bottom 1⅜" W pine or
Cypress, sheathed with ⅜" Bs. plate

HALF SECTION
at 6'6"

No 41
CONSTRUCTION PLAN
Scale: 1½" = 1'0"
L. FRANCIS HERRESHOFF DESIGNER
Marblehead, Mass.
July 1928

ALBATROSS

For anyone who wants the ultimate dream ship in a motor-sailer, here is a worthy candidate, and she is virgin, for no vessel has yet been built to this design. The hull is that of a lovely double-ender, and there is no reason why she shouldn't sail quite well. The total sail area is 1,829 square feet, with 673 square feet in the mainsail, 515 in the mizzen, 290 in the fore staysail, and 351 in the jib.

The fore-and-aft lines of her hull are extremely fine, for she is very long. She has powerful bilges and just enough hollow in the garboards and depth of keel to hang on well going to windward. She is not designed to make passages to windward under sail alone, but, even in a motorsailer, some real windward ability is a great thing to have. It allows less than complete dependence on the machinery, and it also allows the boat really to get somewhere when pinched up into the wind under both sail and power.

The arrangement plan is a stretched-out version of that of the *Walrus*. The extra length of the *Albatross* has been used to add a fo'c'sle forward of the saloon and a full-width hold between the engines and the stateroom.

If anyone wants to go swordfishing, here is the vessel for it. Her two crow's nests, high on the mainmast, are ready to be manned; the harpoon can be hurled in an instant from the pulpit; the dory can be swung overboard slung from the main sheet block; and the fish hold is ready to receive the catch.

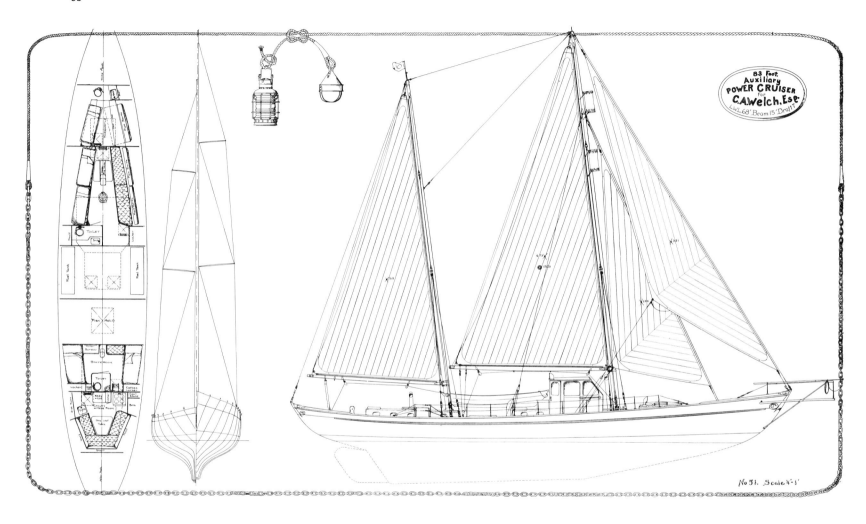

83 Foot
Auxiliary
POWER CRUISER
For
C.A.Welch.Esq.
L.W.L. 68' Beam 15' Draft 7

No 51. Scale ¼=1'

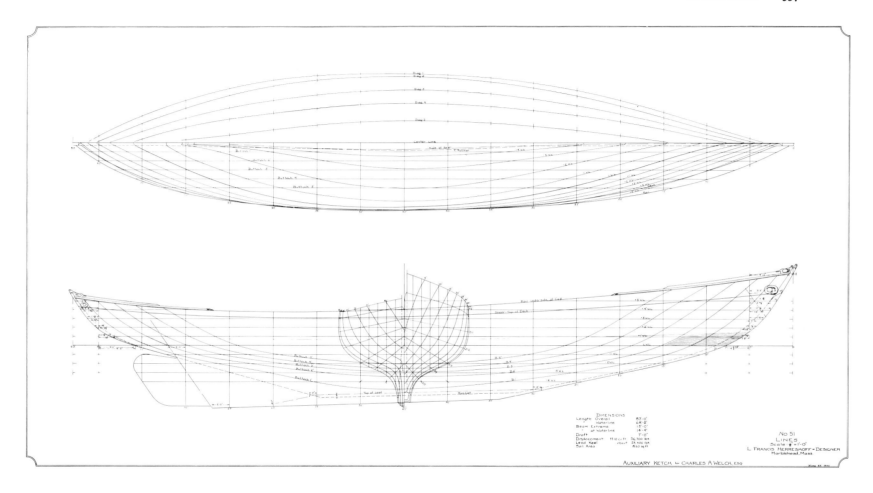

DIMENSIONS
Length Overall   83'-0"
        Waterline   65'-8"
Beam Extreme   15'-0"
      at Waterline   14'-4"
Draft   7'-0"
Displacement   1310 cu ft   36,700 lbs
Lead Keel   about   23,400 lbs
Sail Area   1820 sq ft

No 51
LINES
Scale ¼"=1'-0"
L. FRANCIS HERRESHOFF - DESIGNER
Marblehead, Mass.

AUXILIARY KETCH for CHARLES A WELCH, ESQ

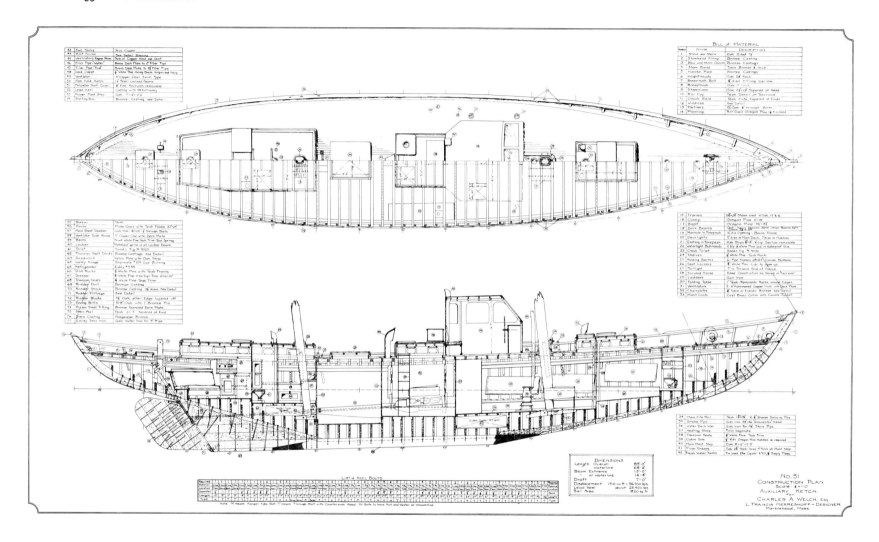

	BILL of MATERIAL

No. 51
CONSTRUCTION PLAN
Scale ¾"=1'0"
AUXILIARY KETCH
CHARLES A. WELCH, Esq
L. FRANCIS HERRESHOFF ~ DESIGNER
Markblehead, Mass.

A PAIR OF THREE-MASTERS

This design and the one on the next page indicate that L. Francis was thinking about long, narrow, seaworthy double-enders with three leg o'mutton sails long before he designed the *Marco Polo,* described in Chapter 9. The 130-footer on this page was designed in 1931, and the 100-footer on the following page, in 1922. Like the *Marco Polo,* these big vessels were designed with extreme seaworthiness, ease of handling, and moderate draft in mind, the objective being the creation of a boat suited for worldwide cruising.

It was in these early designs for large vessels that L. Francis worked on the basic concepts later used in the *Marco Polo.* In all three designs, we see the extremely buoyant, easily-driven hull and the very versatile rig. In the 100-footer, the rig details are especially interesting. We find the same cross-cut mainsail and vertical-cut foresail and mizzen as used in the *Marco Polo.* The former was to be a sail for light and moderate weather, whereas the latter were to be able to stand some real breeze. Note the boom on the foot of the squaresail.

Perhaps if the sailing cruise ship business turns oceanic, these designs will be brought out and dusted off.

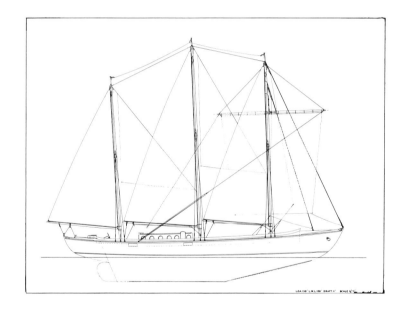

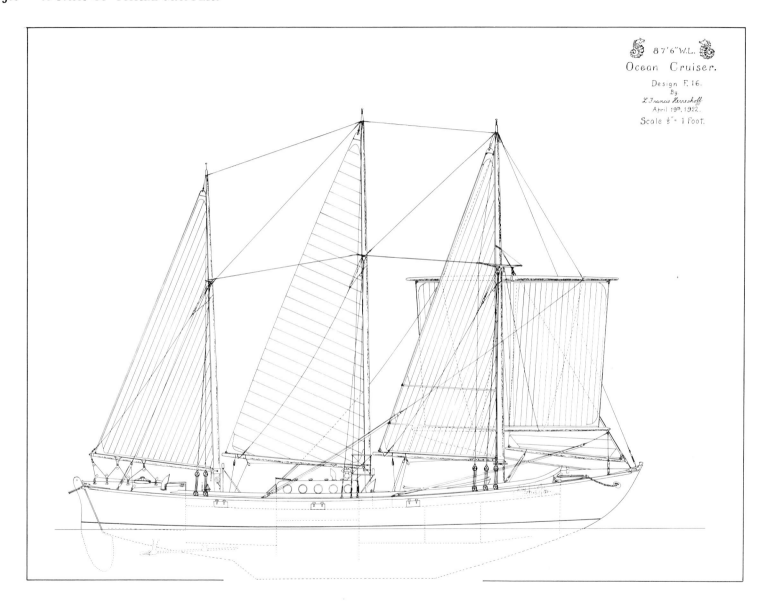

87'6"W.L.
Ocean Cruiser.
Design F. 16.
By.
L. Francis Herreshoff
April 19th, 1922.
Scale ⅛" = 1 Foot.

SLOOP WITH CLIPPER BOW

We use the sail plan of this handsome 32-foot cruising sloop to introduce a series of designs, each of which has what has become perhaps the best known trademark of L. Francis, his beautiful clipper bows. This version of what we might call the *Ticonderoga* type, for obvious reasons, has a transom stern and outboard rudder. Her waterline length is 27'9", her beam 10'3", and her draft 4'6". Her sail area is 563 square feet, with 324 square feet in the mainsail, 119 in the fore staysail, and 120 in the jib.

She seems to be a boat whose performance would be able to keep pace with her good looks.

ARAMINTA

The *Araminta* is the successor to the *Quiet Tune* both being day boats for Maine. She is very similar to *Quiet Tune* in hull and rig, but is an enlarged version, being 3'3" longer on the waterline. And the *Araminta* has the clipper bow, whereas the *Quiet Tune* had a spoon bow. The *Araminta* has also been given a more generous sail plan, with quite a tall mainsail. Her mainsail has an area of 295 square feet, the mizzen has 94, and the jib 193, for a total of 582.

This design approaches the ultimate for daysailing and short-range cruising. She is beautiful to look at, a very fast sailer, and an all-around delightful boat in which to spend days sailing on the coast of Maine.

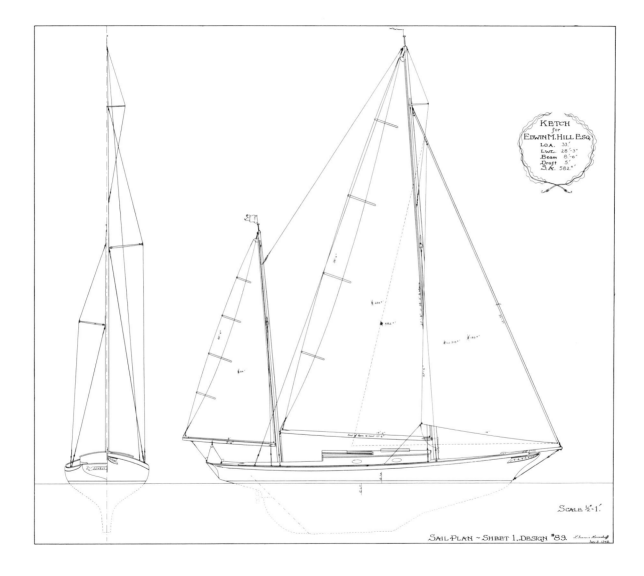

KETCH
for
EDWIN M. HILL ESQ.
L.O.A.   33'
L.W.L.   28'-3"
Beam   8'-6"
Draft   5'
S.A.   582□'

SCALE ½-1'.

SAIL PLAN ~ SHEET 1. DESIGN #89.

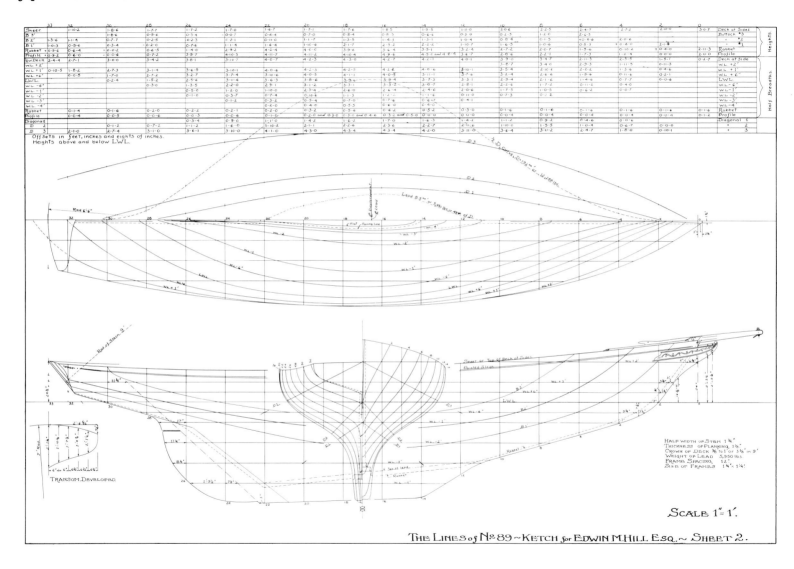

Offsets in feet, inches and eights of inches.
Heights above and below L.W.L.

TRANSOM DEVELOPED.

Half width of Stem 1¼"
Thickness of Planking 1⅛"
Crown of Deck ⅜ to 1 or 3⅜ in 9'
Weight of Lead 5,350 lbs.
Frame Spacing 12"
Size of Frames 1⅛" x 1¼"

SCALE 1"=1'.

THE LINES OF № 89 ~ KETCH for EDWIN M. HILL ESQ. ~ SHEET 2.

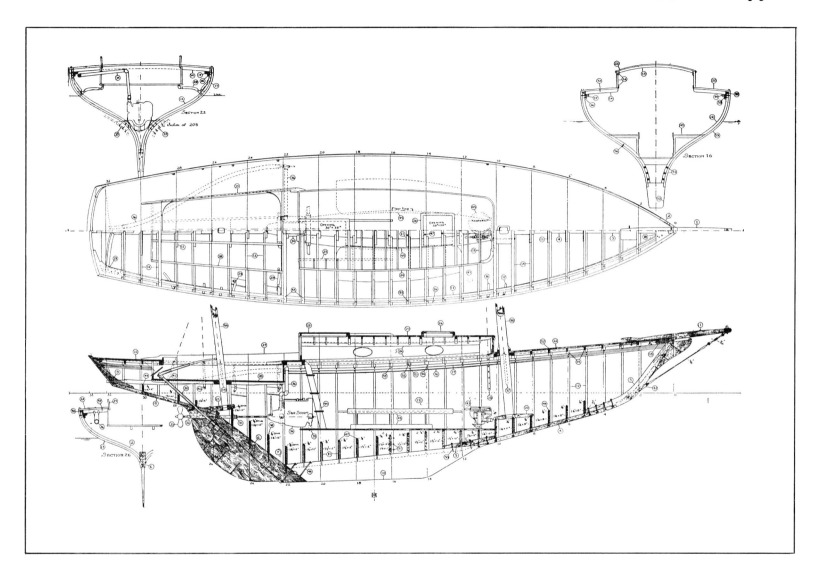

JOANN

This is a traditional schooner yacht designed by L. Francis early in his career. She is quite a heavy, full boat, though the draft has been kept moderate and she has a nice run. No great performer to windward, she would kick up her heels and go once her sheets were started. She has as full a bow as any boat Mr. Herreshoff designed; there is just the slightest hint of hollow at the forward end of the load waterline. Her hull has many of the essential characteristics of later, well-known Francis Herreshoff designs, such as the *Nereia* described in Chapter 7 and the *Mobjack* of Chapter 8.

The *Joann's* schooner rig looks old-fashioned to us today. The deadeyes and lanyards, elaborate lazyjacks, and lug foresail with its brails all seem outmoded, yet all of this is cruising gear that has proved its value in terms of making sail handling easier over a period of many years. Her mainsail has 614 square feet, the foresail 496, and the jib 312, for a total of 1,442. Note the deep reefs available to snug her right down.

The schooner's arrangement can be seen in the construction plan on page 370. In the after house, there is a chart table to port and the galley is to starboard, with the saloon immediately forward of these. In the forward house, the engine room with its work bench is to port, the head to starboard, with a sleeping cabin forward. There is a heating stove at the forward end of this cabin.

The *Joann* smacks of tradition and wholesome good looks. She could be counted on to behave herself at sea or along the shore; even today she is an appealing cruising vessel.

№ 257.

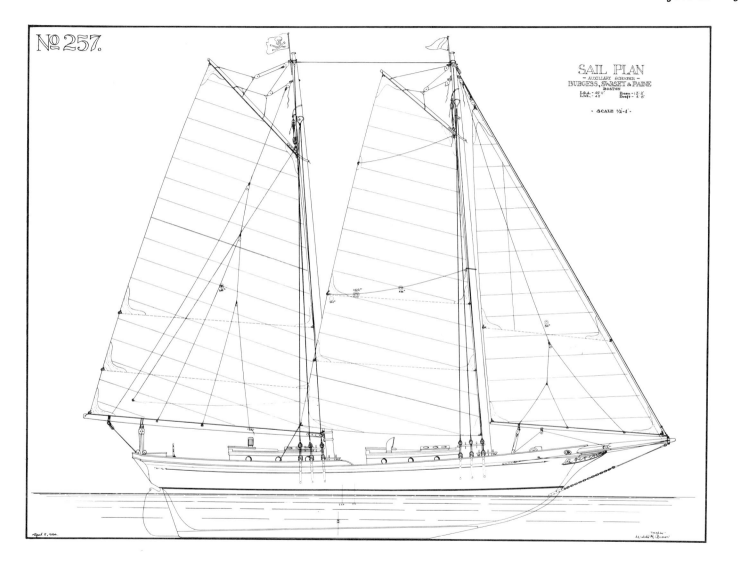

SAIL PLAN
— AUXILIARY SCHOONER —
BURGESS, SWASEY & PAINE
BOSTON

| L.O.A. - 49' 11" | Beam - 13' 2" |
| L.W.L. - 42' | Draft - 4' 6" |

- SCALE ½"-1' -

TABLE OF No. 257.

Design No. 257.
Aux. Schooner
BJS. . . . .
NA . . . ARCHITECTS
. . . R, MASS.
L.O.A. 49'-11" — W.L. 43'— Beam 13'2"
Draft 4'8" — Disp. 22.5 tons

OFFSETS

DIMENSIONS ARE
— GIVEN IN —
FEET — INCHES — EIGTHS

(Outside of Planking)

	Section No.	36	33	30	27	24	21	18	15	12	9	6	3	0	-3
HEIGHTS	Rail Cap, Under Side	3-9-1	3-4-4	3-1-4	2-11-6	2-10-6	2-11-0	3-0-2	3-2-0	3-4-7	3-8-3	4-0-6	4-5-5	4-11-2	5-5-2
	Deck Shear, at Rail	3-5-6	3-0-6	2-9-4	2-7-7	2-7-1	2-7-2	2-8-2	2-9-7	2-11-4	3-2-7	3-4-5	3-8-4	4-1-2	4-4-7
	Buttock # 6	—	—	+1-7-3	+0-6-3	-0-1-0	-0-3-4	+0-0-2	+1-5-7	—	—	—	—	—	
	B # 5		+1-8-0	0-4-5	0-5-3	-0-10-7	-1-1-5	-1-0-6	-0-7-4	+1-0-4	—	—	—	—	
	B # 4	—	+2-0-2	+0-10-0	-0-2-3	-1-0-0	-1-6-0	1-8-6	1-8-4	1-5-0	0-8-0	+1-5-0	—		
	B # 3	+3-1-2	+1-8-3	+0-5-0	-0-8-0	1-5-4	1-11-1	2-2-2	2-2-7	2-1-4	1-7-4	-0-3-6	+2-9-2	—	
	B # 2	+2-11-6	+1-5-4	0-0-0	1-2-4	2-0-0	2-4-4	2-8-1	2-8-7	2-7-4	2-2-7	-1-4-6	+0-7-7	+4-7-0	
	B # 1	+2-10-7	+1-2-4	-0-8-0	2-3-0	2-11-4	3-3-2	3-3-7	3-3-1	3-1-6	2-10-7	2-3-5	-1-10-7	+2-6-5	
	Rabbet	+2-8-7	+1-0-0	-3-7-1	3-9-6	3-8-5	3-7-4	3-6-3	3-5-2	3-4-1	3-3-2	2-11-3	-1-11-5	+0-7-0	
HALF-BREADTHS	Rail Cap, Under Side	3-2-4	4-3-1	5-2-0	6-0-0	6-3-5	6-6-1	6-6-4	6-5-2	6-2-3	5-8-3	4-11-1	3-9-0	2-1-6	
	W.h. # 4									—	4-10-5	3-5-7	1-7-5		
	W.h. # 3		4-5-0	5-2-6			—	6-6-6	5-5-6	6-2-1	5-6-5	4-6-4	3-1-1	1-2-3	
	W.h. # 2			3-10-1	5-2-7	6-0-2	6-5-2	6-7-2	6-7-2	6-5-7	6-1-3	5-4-1	4-2-3	2-7-3	0-9-3
	W.h. # 1			0-3-6	4-3-5	5-7-0	6-2-6	6-5-4	6-5-1	6-3-1	5-10-0	5-0-6	3-9-4	2-2-3	0-5-0
	L.W.L.	—	—	1-11-2	4-4-0	5-6-4	6-0-4	6-1-6	5-11-3	5-4-6	4-5-7	3-2-4	1-7-4	0-0-6	
	W.h. # -1	—	0-1-5	0-8-3	2-4-6	3-0-0	4-10-0	5-2-1	5-0-4	4-6-2	3-7-5	2-3-7	0-11-0	—	
	W.h. # -2	—	0-1-5	0-5-1	1-1-7	2-0-2	2-9-7	3-4-0	3-5-1	3-0-7	2-3-4	1-3-2	0-3-0	—	
	W.h. # -3	—	0-1-5	0-3-6	0-7-2	0-11-0	1-3-0	1-5-2	1-5-4	1-3-0	0-9-6	0-3-6	—		
	Rabbet	—	0-1-5	0-3-4	0-5-2	0-6-6	0-7-5	0-8-0	0-7-5	0-6-5	0-5-2	0-4-1	0-3-0	0-3-2	0-4-4
	Keel Bottom		—	0-3-4	0-5-2	0-6-6	0-7-5	0-8-0	0-7-5	0-6-5					
DIAGONALS	D. # 1		—	1-1-6	2-1-7	2-9-3	3-2-3	3-5-4	3-6-5	3-5-3	3-1-0	2-4-2	1-3-7	—	
	D. # 2	—	1-2-2	2-9-1	3-11-4	4-8-5	5-1-6	5-4-1	5-4-1	5-1-6	4-7-4	3-9-2	2-5-7	0-10-1	
	D. # 3	—	1-11-5	3-6-4	4-9-0	5-6-5	6-0-3	6-2-3	6-1-4	5-9-1	5-1-2	4-1-3	2-8-4	1-0-0	
	D. # 4	0-4-4	3-0-6	4-6-4	5-8-0	6-4-5	6-9-2	6-10-0	6-8-0	6-2-5	5-5-3	4-4-0	2-10-1	1-1-1	

— Waldo H. Brown —

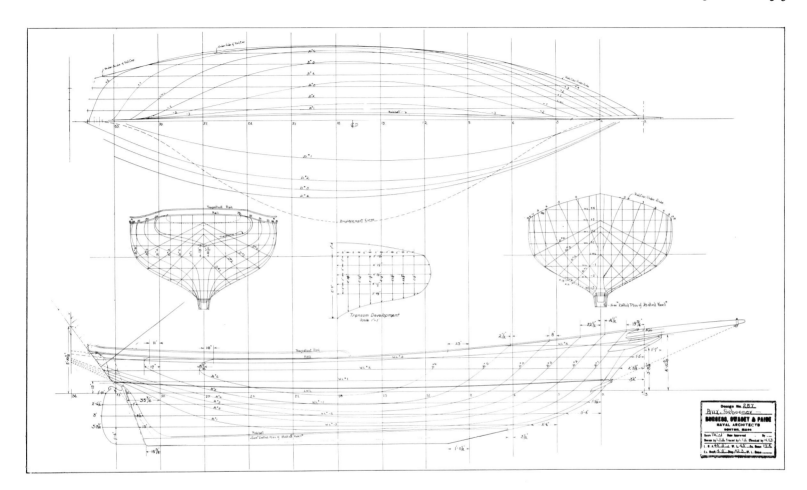

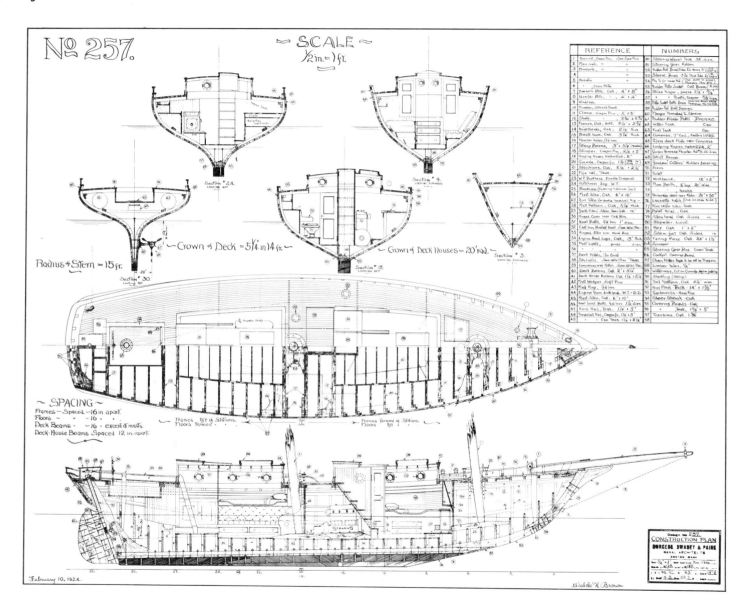

MISTRAL

This big schooner can be considered a refined, modernized version of the *Joann*. The hull is finer and more shapely, and the rig has been modernized. She still has a traditional air about her, with her handsome clipper bow, topgallant rail, and exposed, curved rudder head.

The *Mistral's* draft has been kept moderate, only 6′3″ on a waterline length of 54′9″, with the result that the buttock lines are easy and sweeping throughout. She would be a fine sea boat with a good turn of speed.

The Marconi mainsail is less attractive than the gaff sail in the *Joann,* but is probably somewhat easier to handle. Certainly the self-tending foresail, though less efficient than its loose-footed, overlapping ancestor, would be, by comparison, a joy to crew members. Note the vang on its gaff to take the twist out of the tall, narrow sail.

We don't mean to imply that the *Mistral* came full-blown into existence directly descended from the *Joann.* For in between the *Joann* and *Mistral,* L. Francis designed ketches with the same general hull form, as we shall see in the following pages.

The cabin plan on page 375 shows that the *Mistral* was somewhat chopped up below decks. Yet, while there are many small compartments, her saloon would be roomy and cheerful enough with its generous skylight and good fireplace. Note the separate companionway on the starboard side of the house just abaft the mainmast. She has adequate accommodations for eight, which would certainly be plenty to handle her straightforward rigging and sails.

Her total sail area is 1,972 square feet, with 895 square feet in the mainsail, 517 in the foresail, 260 in the fore staysail, and 300 in the jib. She is a big schooner well suited to take her crew either coasting or off soundings.

SAIL PLAN — SCHOONER YACHT FOR THEODORE W. LITTLE ESQ. — DESIGN NO 73. SHEET 1.

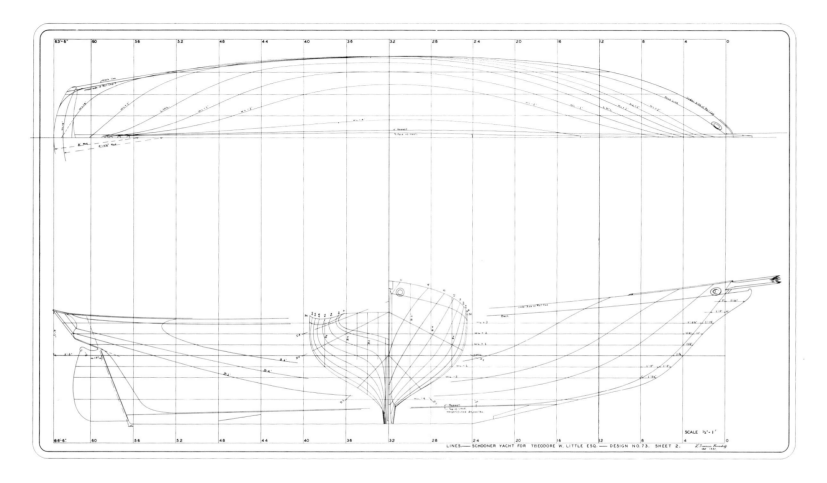

SCALE ½" = 1'

LINES.— SCHOONER YACHT FOR THEODORE W. LITTLE ESQ.— DESIGN NO. 73. SHEET 2.

DESIGN Nº 73   TABLE OF OFFSETS.

Stations	HEIGHTS above and below L.W.L.							HALF BREADTHS.											DIAGONALS.			Stations
	RAIL under side of Cap.	Sheer at Deck	6' Buttock	4' Buttock	2' Buttock	Rabbet	Profile	Rail	Deck	WL+3'	WL+2'	WL+1'	L.W.L.	WL-1	WL-2'	WL-4'	Rabbet	Face of stem of keel	1.	2.	3.	
0	6-8-4	5-8-1				5-8-1	3-9-0	1-0-4	0-3-2									0-1-0				0
4	6-1-6	5-2-2			4-2-0	0-11-6	0-0-0	3-9-0	2-9-4	1-3-2	0-9-0	0-4-0	0-0-4				0-3-4	0-0-4	0-0-6	1-7-3		4
8	5-7-7	4-9-1	4-0-0	1-2-0	-2-1-0	-2-8-2		5-3-4	4-6-2	3-3-0	2-6-4	1-9-5	1-3-4	0-8-7	0-4-0		0-3-4	0-1-2	1-2-0	3-3-2		8
12	5-2-7	4-4-6	4-10-4	1-6-7	-1-0-6	-3-4-6	-3-7-7	6-2-6	5-8-6	4-10-4	4-3-2	3-7-0	2-10-3	2-0-0	1-3-1		0-3-4	0-1-4	2-2-7	4-8-4		12
16	4-10-1	4-0-6	2-11-0	-0-4-4	-2-3-3	-4-2-0	-4-6-2	6-9-6	6-6-0	6-0-2	5-6-5	5-0-4	4-3-7	3-4-2	2-3-2	0-6-2	0-4-6	0-1-7	3-0-3	5-10-4		16
20	4-6-0	3-9-4	0-10-0	-1-6-2	-3-1-7	-4-6-2	-5-4-6	7-2-0	6-8-5	6-9-0	6-5-5	6-1-0	5-5-7	4-6-7	3-4-3	0-11-4	0-6-4	0-2-5	3-8-2	6-9-3		20
24	4-2-6	3-6-4	-0-3-6	-2-2-0	-3-6-2	-4-7-6	-6-3-0	7-4-5	7-3-2	7-2-0	7-0-4	6-9-0	6-3-0	5-4-1	4-2-3	1-4-0	0-7-4	0-3-4	4-1-3	7-4-7		24
28	3-11-7	3-4-1	-0-10-4	-2-6-2	-3-8-5	Straight	Straight	7-6-0	7-5-2	7-4-6	7-4-0	7-1-7	6-8-4	5-10-3	4-8-6	1-6-4	0-8-0	0-4-6	4-4-2	7-9-5		28
32	3-9-3	3-2-1	-1-1-2	-2-7-0	-3-9-3	Straight	Straight	7-6-0	7-6-0	7-6-0	7-5-6	7-3-4	6-10-4	6-0-6	4-10-6	1-7-6	0-8-1	0-5-0	4-4-4	7-11-2		32
36	3-7-4	3-0-5	-1-0-6	-2-4-6	-3-3-0	Straight	Straight	7-4-2	7-4-6	7-4-6	7-5-2	7-3-4	6-10-7	6-0-2	4-7-4	1-5-4	0-7-4	0-5-0	4-2-3	7-11-6		36
40	3-5-5	2-11-2	-0-9-0	-2-0-0	-2-6-4	Straight	Straight	7-2-1	7-2-7	7-2-6	7-3-4	7-2-2	6-8-6	5-8-0	4-0-0	1-2-4	0-6-4	0-4-4	3-10-1	7-10-2		40
44	3-4-5	2-10-4	-0-1-6	-1-4-4	-1-8-3	Straight	Straight	6-10-5	6-11-6	6-11-4	7-0-6	6-4-4	6-1-6	4-8-2	2-9-6	0-10-0	0-5-5	0-4-0	3-3-3	7-6-0	7-6-0	44
48	3-3-2	2-10-2	0-6-4	-0-7-0	-0-6-3	-5-1-6		6-6-0	6-7-4	6-7-3	6-8-1	5-5-4	5-2-0	3-1-5	1-7-3	0-7-0	0-4-4	0-3-1	2-7-0	7-0-4	7-1-4	48
52	3-4-3	2-10-6	1-6-4	0-3-4	0-6-3	-5-3-0		6-0-0	6-2-0	6-1-3	6-1-7	3-5-3	3-1-0	1-5-0	0-10-0	0-4-5	0-3-5	0-2-3	1-9-2	6-4-0	6-7-2	52
56	3-5-3	3-0-4		1-2-4	1-7-2	-3-3-0	-6-3-0	5-4-6	5-7-1	5-7-1	5-3-2	0-1-7	1-0-3	0-5-7	0-4-2	0-3-1	0-3-4	0-1-6	0-10-4	5-4-2	6-0-0	56
60	3-7-4	3-3-7		2-1-6	2-6-2	1-0-6	0-11-3	4-7-2	4-11-1	4-11-2	3-6-4		0-0-0	0-1-4	0-1-6	0-1-6	0-3-4	0-0-0		4-3-2	5-3-4	60
63'-6"	3-11-0	3-8-0		3-0-0		2-3-5	2-3-4	4-0-0	4-4-1	3-11-0							0-3-4			3-0-0	4-7-0	63'-6"

L. Francis Herreshoff

SHEET 3   # 73

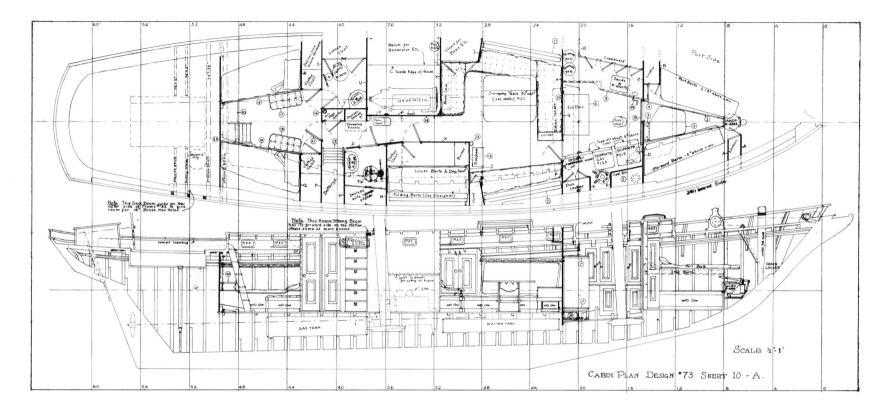

CABIN PLAN DESIGN #73 SHEET 10 - A.

SCALE ½"=1'

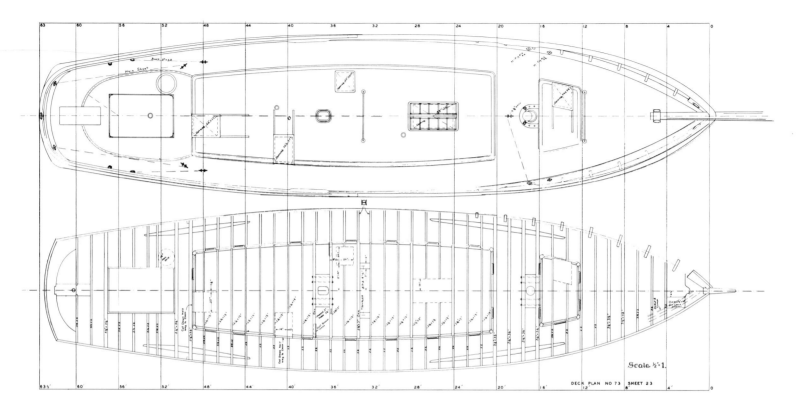

Scale ½"=1.

DECK PLAN NO 73   SHEET 23

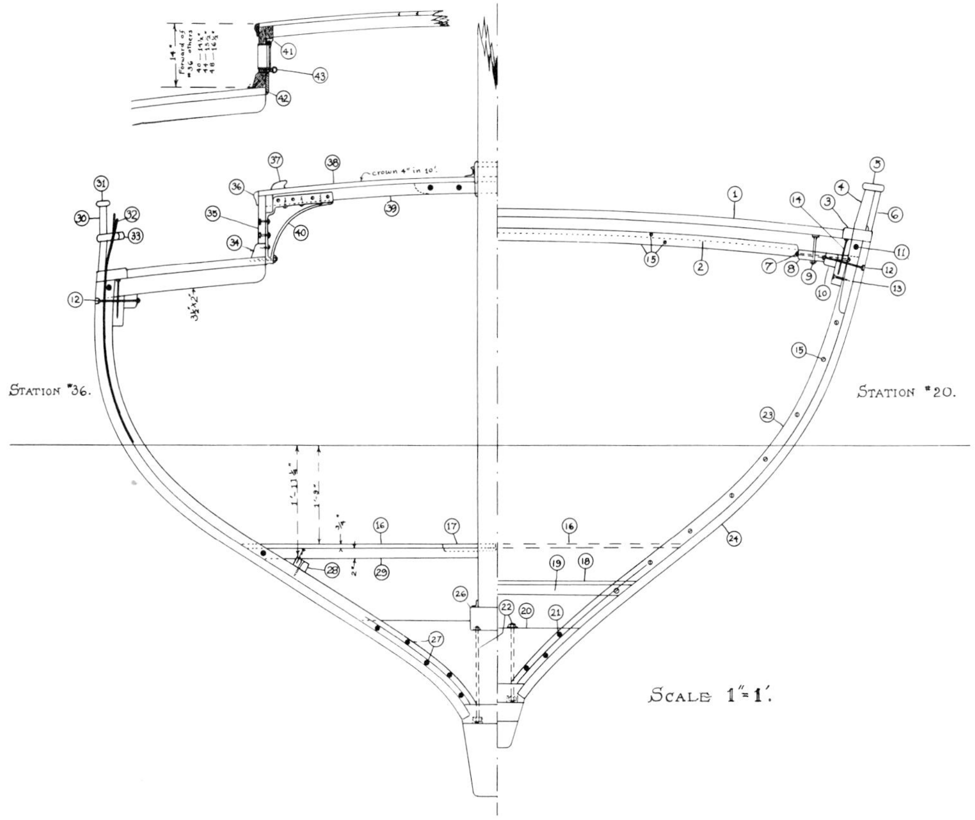

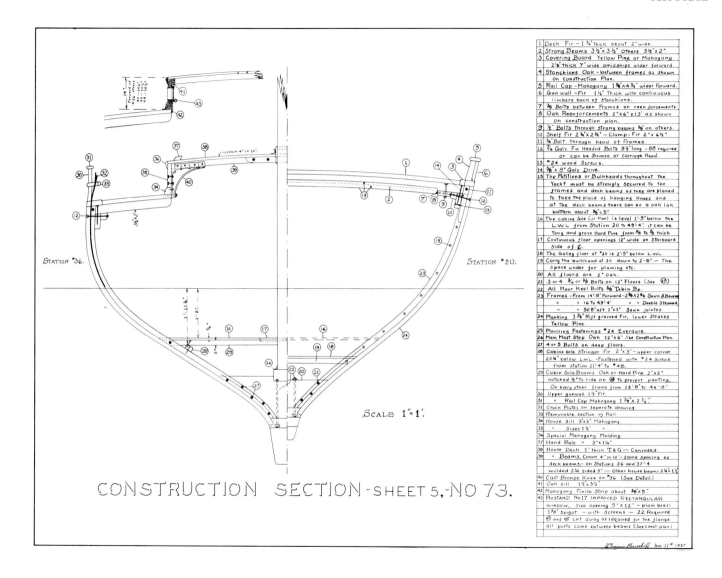

CONSTRUCTION SECTION - SHEET 5, - NO 73.

1	Deck Fir - 1 3/4" thick about 2" wide.
2	Strong Beams 3 1/2" x 3 1/2" Others 3 1/2" x 2".
3	Covering Board Yellow Pine or Mahogany 2 1/8" thick 7" wide amidships wider forward.
4	Stanchions Oak - between frames as shown on construction Plan.
5	Rail Cap - Mahogany 1 5/8" x 4 3/4" wider Forward.
6	Gun wall - Fir 1 1/2" Thick with continuous limbers back of stanchions.
7	3/8 Bolts between Frames on reenforcements.
8	Oak Reenforcements 2" x 6" x 13' as shown on construction plan.
9	1/2" Bolts through strong beams 3/8" on others.
10	Shelf Fir 2 3/4" x 2 3/4" - Clamp - Fir 2" x 6 1/2".
11	3/8" Bolt through head of Frames.
12	7/16 Galv. Fin Headed Bolts 9 1/2" long - 88 required or can be Bronze or carriage Head.
13	#24 wood Screws.
14	3/8" x 8" Galv Drive.
15	The Patitions or Bulkheads throughout the Yacht must be strongly secured to the frames and deck beams as they are planed to take the place of hanging knees and at the deck beams thare can be a oak lak battern about 5/8" x 5".
16	The cabine Sole (or Floor) is level 1'-9" below the L.W.L from Station 20 to 49'-4". it can be tong and grove Hard Pine from 5/8 to 7/8 thick
17	Continuous floor openings 12" wide on Starboard side of ℄.
18	The Galley floor at #20 is 2'-5" below L.W.L.
19	Carry the bulkhead at 20 down to 2'-8". - The space under for pluming etc.
20	All floors are 2" oak.
21	3 or 4 5/16 or 3/8 Bolts on 12" Floors (See (27))
22	All Floor Keel Bolts 5/8" Tobin Bz.
23	Frames - From 14'-8" Forward - 2 5/8 x 2 5/8 Sawn & Beveled " " 16 To 49'-4' " " Double Steamed " " 50'-8" aft 2" x 3" Sawn jointed.
24	Planking 1 7/8" Rift grained Fir, lower Strakes Yellow Pine.
25	Planking Fastenings #24 Everdure.
26	Main Mast Step Oak 12" x 6" See Construction Plan.
27	4 or 5 Bolts on deap floors.
28	Cabine sole stringer Fir 2" x 3" - upper corner 23 1/4" below L.W.L. - Fastened with #24 screws from station 21'-4" to #48.
29	Cabin Sole Beams Oak or Hard Pine 2" x 2" notched 1/2" to ride on (28) to prevent panting, On every other frame from 23'-8" to 46'-8".
30	Upper gunwall 1 1/2" Fir.
31	" Rail Cap Mahogany 1 3/8" x 2 3/4".
32	Chain Plates on seperate drawing.
33	Removable section of Rail
34	House sill 3" x 3" Mahogany.
35	" Sides 1 1/2" "
36	Special Mahogany Molding.
37	Hand Rale " 3" x 1 1/4"
38	House Deck 1" thick T & G - Canvased.
39	" Beams, Crown 4" in 10' - same spacing as deck beams, - on Stations 36 and 37'-4 molded 2 1/4 sided 3" — Other house beams 2 1/4" x 1 1/2"
40	Cast Bronze Knee on #36 (See Detail.)
41	Oak sill 1 1/2" x 3 1/2".
42	Mahogany Finish Strip about 3/8" x 5".
43	ROSTAND No 17 IMPPOVED RECTANGULAR WINDOW, size opening 5" x 12" - plain brass 1 5/8" spigot - with screens — 22 Required (41) and (42) cut away as required for the flange all ports come between beams (See const. plan.)

L. Francis Herreshoff Nov 11th 1937

TIOGA AND BOUNTY

This pair of lovely, clipper-bowed ketches makes a fascinating study, for both were built to exactly the same design except for the depth of the keel and the height of the rig . The *Tioga* was a centerboard boat drawing 4′7″ and carrying 1,324 square feet of sail; the *Bounty* was a keel boat drawing 6′2″ and carrying 1,519 square feet of sail. The sail plans are superimposed on each other on page 380. In the lines drawing on page 381, the underwater profile of the *Tioga* is the solid line, while that of the *Bounty* is the dotted line. Both photographs are of the *Tioga*. The *Bounty* is still sailing, recently having been given a new lease on life by the expert boatbuilder and great friend and admirer of Mr. Herreshoff, O. Lie-Nielsen.

These hulls are beautifully modelled with lovely sweeping curves everywhere. They are very easily driven, so that their rigs, which look a bit on the scant side at first, are really perfectly adequate. All of which makes for a fast sailing boat that is easy on herself and easy on her crew. And these, of course, are prime requisites of a cruising vessel.

On page 382, the cabin plan is that of the *Tioga*. The *Bounty* has her saloon aft with two berths outboard of the transoms. Forward of this there is a passage to starboard with a transom berth, opposite which is a double stateroom and a head. Her galley is just abaft the mainmast, and forward there is a fo'c'sle with two pipe berths.

The design of these ketches seems timeless. They are as fresh and beautiful looking today as they were when they were created forty and more years ago. Nor will these cruising vessels appear dated in the future, for once a cruising boat has been designed that is thoroughly harmonious with her environment, she must remain so.

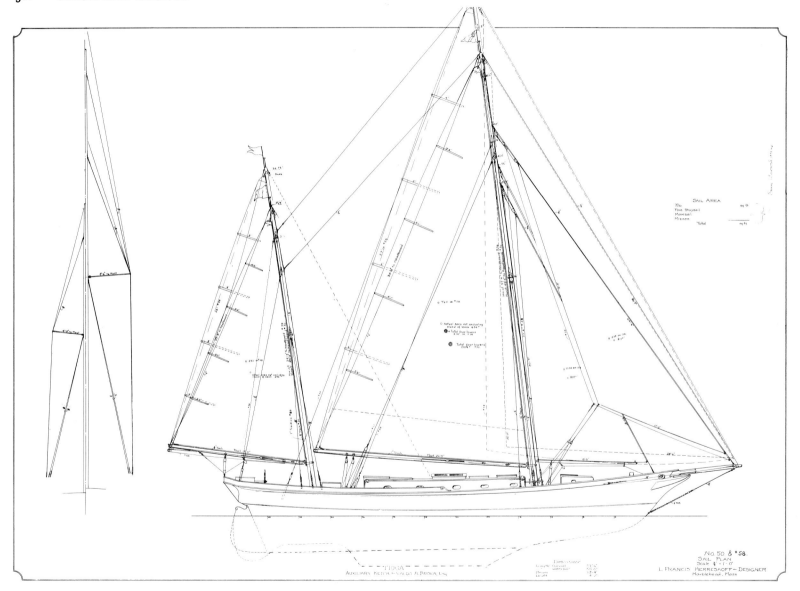

SAIL AREA

Jib
Fore Staysail
Mainsail
Mizzen
        Total

TIOGA
AUXILIARY KETCH · VALDO H. BROWN, ESQ.

No. 50 & *58.
SAIL PLAN
Scale ⅜' = 1'-0"
L. FRANCIS HERRESHOFF — DESIGNER
Marblehead, Mass

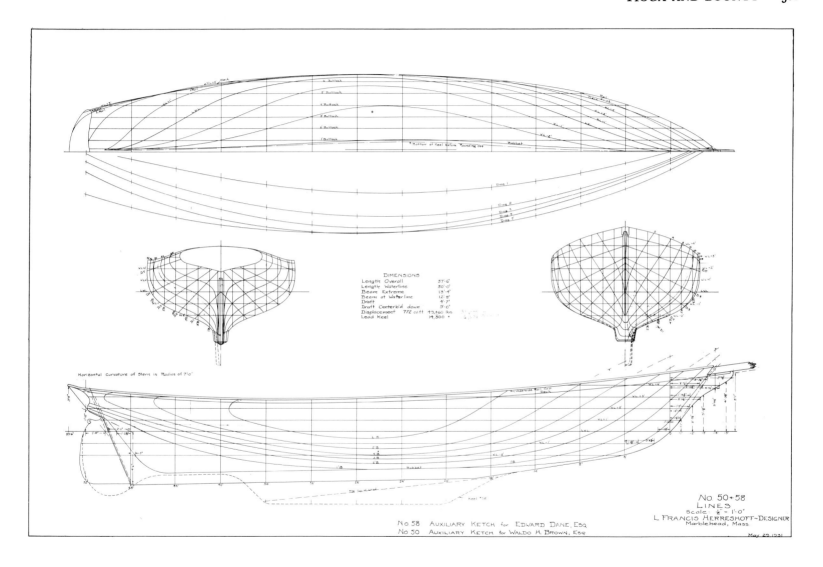

DIMENSIONS

Length Overall 57'6"
Length Waterline 50'0"
Beam Extreme 13'4"
Beam at Waterline 12'8"
Draft 4'7"
Draft Centerb'd down 9'0"
Displacement 772 cu.ft 49,460 lbs
Lead Keel 14,300 "

No 50 + 58
LINES
Scale: 3/8" = 1'-0"
L FRANCIS HERRESHOFF ~ DESIGNER
Marblehead, Mass

No 58 AUXILIARY KETCH for EDWARD DANE, ESQ
No 50 AUXILIARY KETCH for WALDO H. BROWN, ESQ

May 29 1931

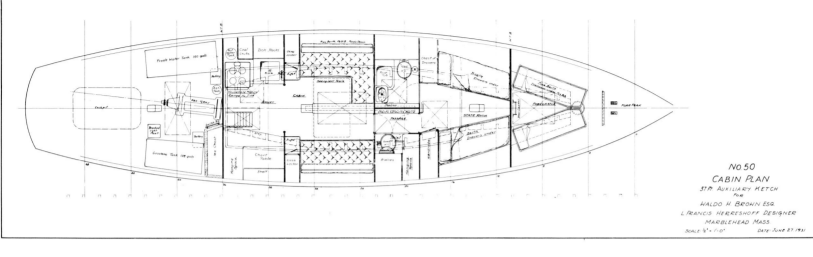

No. 50
CABIN PLAN
57 Ft. Auxiliary Ketch
for
Waldo H. Brown Esq.
L Francis Herreshoff Designer
Marblehead Mass.
Scale ½" = 1'-0"   Date June 27 1931

DESIGN NO. 50 TABLE of OFFSETS
AUXILIARY KETCH for WALDO H. BROWN, ESQ.
L. FRANCIS HERRESHOFF ~ DESIGNER

Stations	HEIGHTS above and below L.W.L.										HALF BREADTHS											DIAGONALS					Stations
	Rail underside of cap	Sheer	6' Buttock	5' Buttock	4' Buttock	3' Buttock	2' Buttock	1' Buttock	Rabbet	Profile	Rail	Deck	W.L.+4	W.L.+3	W.L.+2	W.L.+1	L.W.L.	W.L.-1	W.L.-2	Rabbet	Keel	5	4	3	2	1	
Stem		5·1·0									0·1·4	0·1·8	0·1·0	0·0·5	0·0·4	0·0·4	0·0·4	0·0·4	0·0·4	0·3·0							Stem
0	5·0·2	4·4·2					4·3·2	2·7·7	0·10·4	0·0·0	2·6·4	2·0·5	1·9·4	1·2·0	0·7·4	0·3·2				0·3·0	0·0·4	1·6·7	1·0·2	0·9·5	0·7·5		0
4	4·6·4	3·11·2			4·5·1	2·11·5	1·5·2	0·2·3	1·6·3	1·11·5	4·0·6	3·7·6	3·8·2	3·0·0	2·4·2	1·8·3	1·1·2	0·6·3		0·3·0	0·0·4	3·2·2	2·6·2	2·2·6	2·0·3	1·0·0	4
8	4·1·4	3·6·6		4·0·5	2·1·6	0·7·6	0·6·3	1·7·2	2·4·6	2·7·2	5·0·5	4·9·1	5·0·0	4·5·0	3·10·4	3·2·6	2·5·3	1·6·4	0·7·4	0·3·6	0·1·3	4·5·4	3·10·0	3·6·0	3·2·0	1·10·0	8
12	3·9·0	3·3·2			1·9·4	0·1·1	0·10·3	1·7·4	2·4·4	2·10·0	5·8·6	5·7·0		5·5·6	5·1·0	4·7·4	3·11·0	2·9·6	1·5·4	0·6·0	0·3·4	5·6·0	4·11·7	4·7·2	4·1·4	2·6·2	12
16	3·5·3	3·0·0	2·7·0	0·0·0	1·0·0	1·8·2	2·3·1	2·10·5	3·0·0	3·9·6	6·1·4	6·0·6		6·0·5	5·10·5	5·7·1	5·0·0	4·0·0	2·5·3	0·9·2	0·6·3	6·2·4	5·10·4	5·5·1	4·10·0	3·0·5	16
20	3·2·2	2·9·5	0·6·0	0·11·7	1·7·7	2·1·6	2·7·2	3·1·0	↑	4·1·0	6·5·2	6·5·0		6·5·0	6·4·0	6·1·7	5·9·2	4·11·6	3·3·6	1·0·0	0·9·0	6·7·7	6·6·0	6·1·0	5·3·7	3·4·6	20
24	2·11·7	2·7·4	0·4·5	1·5·1	1·11·5	2·4·0	2·8·6	3·2·4			6·6·4	6·6·4		6·6·4	6·5·5	6·2·2	5·6·2	3·10·6	1·0·5	0·10·0		6·10·1	6·10·5	6·5·3	5·7·2	3·6·6	24
28	2·10·0	2·6·2	0·6·7	1·5·1	1·11·2	2·3·4	2·8·0	3·2·4	Straight		6·7·0	6·7·1		6·7·5	6·7·2	6·4·4	5·7·4	3·9·7	0·11·0	0·9·1		6·11·3	7·0·0	6·5·7	5·7·0	3·6·0	28
32	2·8·7	2·5·4	0·3·5	1·2·1	1·7·7	2·0·3	2·5·6	3·0·0		Straight	6·5·6	6·6·0		6·6·4	6·6·1	6·2·2	5·3·0	3·0·5	0·9·0	0·7·4		6·10·7	6·10·4	6·3·0	5·3·5	3·2·6	32
36	2·8·6	2·5·4	0·5·4	0·6·4	1·0·6	1·6·2	2·0·0	2·9·0			6·2·4	6·3·0		6·3·6	6·2·5	5·8·0	4·1·0	1·11·4	0·6·4	0·5·4		6·8·0	6·5·0	5·8·0	4·8·6	2·10·0	36
40	2·9·4	2·6·4		0·3·5	0·3·0	0·8·6	1·2·7	2·0·0			5·9·4	5·10·3		5·11·3	5·8·0	4·6·1	2·5·1	1·0·0	0·4·1	0·4·0		6·3·3	5·9·0	4·10·0	3·11·6	2·2·4	40
44	2·11·3	2·8·7		1·4·5	0·7·6	0·2·4	0·2·6	1·0·0	3·6·4		5·2·1	5·2·7		5·3·4	4·6·6	2·5·7	1·0·0	0·5·6	0·3·0	0·3·0		5·7·2	4·9·7	3·10·0	3·0·4	1·5·2	44
48	3·2·6	3·0·3			1·10·0	1·4·0	1·0·1	0·6·2	1·5·4	4·7·0	4·4·5	4·5·6		4·6·0	4·2·1	1·10·6	0·6·4	0·4·0	0·2·6	0·3·0	0·1·6	4·9·1	3·6·2	2·6·4	1·9·6	0·7·2	48
Stern	3·8·4	3·5·4				2·5·3	2·2·1	1·11·5	1·9·2	1·8·4		3·5·4			3·7·3	1·0·4				0·3·0		3·8·5	1·10·4	0·11·4	0·3·4		Stern

Intersections of Diagonals and Center Line above L.W.L. ————————————————→	5	4	3	2	1
	4·0·0	3·0·0	2·6·0	2·0·0	0·0·0

Intersections of Diagonals and Water Lines out from Center Line ————————→					
	W.L.+2	L.W.L.	W.L.-1	W.L.-2	W.L.-2
	6·0·0	6·0·0	5·0·0	4·0·0	2·0·0

Station Numbers are distances in Feet from "0"

Dimensions are given in Feet, Inches and Eighths to Outside of Hull - Planking thickness 1¾"

Curvature of Stern Transom is a Radius of 7'0" parallel to Water Line

UNICORN

This big, husky, ocean cruising version of the clipper-bowed ketches was designed by L. Francis as late as 1960. Her hull is not as fine as those of her cousins, and though she would be stiffer, and probably drier on deck than they, she would not be quite so fast. She has a very powerful hull and she would need it to stand up to her generous rig. Her sail area of 2,417 square feet is made up of 1,092 square feet in the mainsail, 462 in the mizzen, 360 in the fore staysail, and 503 in the jib. The *Unicorn's* proposed square rig is interesting. The course has an area of 688 square feet, the topsail 430, and the raffee 308, for a total of 1,426. She would undoubtedly do some real rolling with the weight of her yards aloft. Her mizzen staysail might come in handy under such circumstances, for when sheeted flat it would dampen the roll a bit.

The general arrangement plan calls for a chartroom to port of the main companionway aft with a large washroom opposite. Next forward is a generous stateroom to starboard with head and sailroom opposite. Just forward of the deckhouse are the engine room to starboard and generator room to port with a passage between. Forward of these, the main saloon, galley, and fo'c's'le take the full width of the vessel.

This big ketch has some shippy features to her, aside from her square rig. Note her catheads, generous deckhouse, high monkey rail, and stern davits for the pram. She looks fully capable of taking her owner and his party in comfort and safety to the coast of Norway, the Galapagos, or the Strait of Magellan.

TIOGA II

This ketch is perhaps the most famous yacht built to a design of Francis Herreshoff. He was justifiably proud of her sailing performance. *Tioga II*, renamed *Ticonderoga,* and often spoken of as "Big Ti," has won a tremendous number of racing honors in her nearly four decades of life, including the setting of many race course records. And she is still going strong. Among the many entries in the 1973 Marblehead to Halifax Race, she stood out easily as far and away the handsomest vessel in the fleet.

Like all in this series of clipper-bowed ketches, Big Ti's draft has been kept moderate. It seems amazing that a boat 63′10″ long on the waterline and drawing only 7′9″, can sail to windward really well. Or that she is stiff enough with her ballast only moderately low and a beam of only 16 feet to carry her rig of over 2,800 square feet. Her working sails have areas as follows: mainsail, 1,271 square feet; mizzen, 500; fore staysail, 376; jib, 394; and jib topsail, 264. Yet all is in balance in this design, and fly she does.

The cabin plan shows her huge open saloon, a room that would be a delight both in port and at sea. She has berths for a dozen people and enough room on deck and below so that they wouldn't be crowded.

Big Ti is a magnificent yacht that well deserves her splendid reputation. Here is a great design and perhaps the crowning achievement of L. Francis Herreshoff.

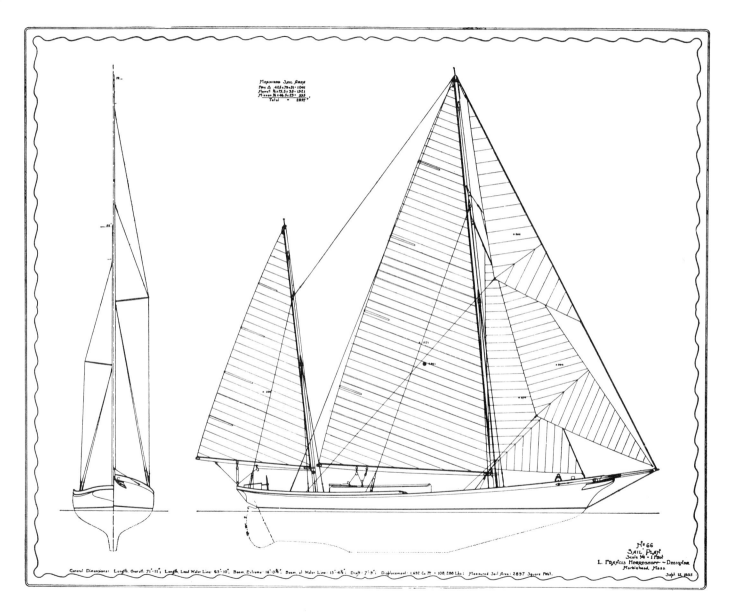

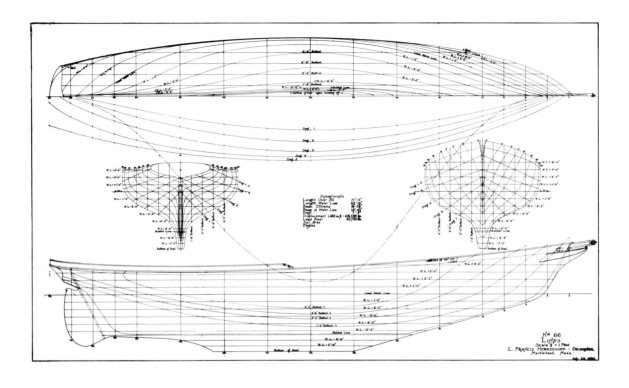

No 66
LINES
Scale ½ = 1 Foot
L. FRANCIS HERRESHOFF - Designer
Marblehead, Mass.

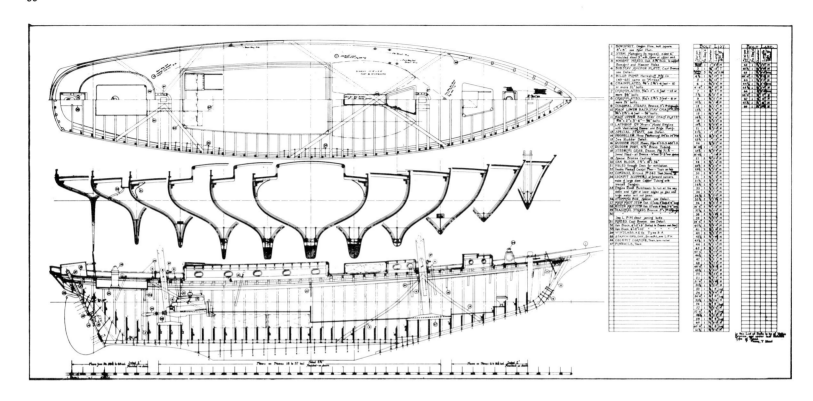

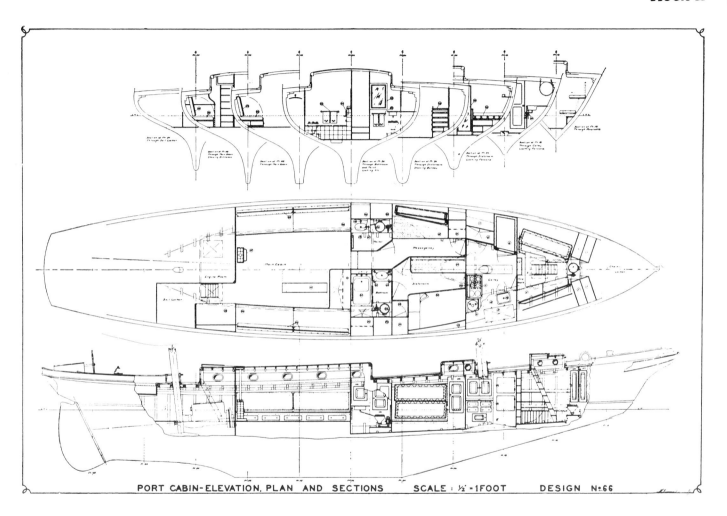

PORT CABIN-ELEVATION, PLAN AND SECTIONS   SCALE : ½'-1FOOT   DESIGN N:66

EPILOGUE

We cannot resist rounding out this collection of L. Francis' cruising designs with a sort of ultimate cruiser, ultimate, at least, in terms of size and ocean cruising possibilities. Here is a 110-foot version of *Ticonderoga,* if you will, a craft of such size that a third mast has been added to keep the sails down to a reasonable size. Her overlapping foresail and mainsail would really pull, as would her square-rigged sails on foremast and mainmast. She would be quite a vessel to sail.

Note the round skylight in the top of her house, probably letting in light and air to a grand saloon. Note also the big tender stowed on deck forward, reminiscent of the whaleboat-dory, *Carpenter,* described on pages 351 through 354.

This big three-master could mount all sorts of interesting and worthwhile expeditions to the far corners of the watery world. She would be an expensive yacht to sail, of course, just because of her size. But perhaps the day may be coming when a number of factors will converge to make it possible again for a fast, handsome sailing vessel, such as could be designed by L. Francis Herreshoff, to earn her way at sea. Perhaps this design is that of the clipper ship of the future.

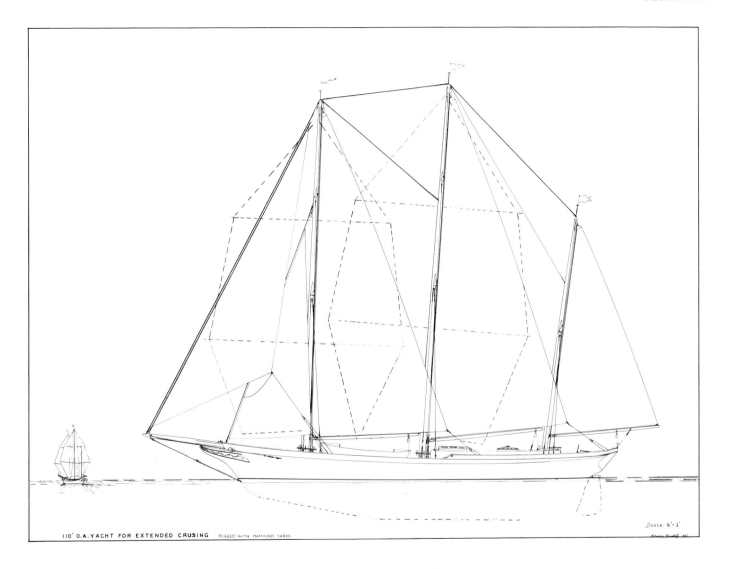

110' O.A. YACHT FOR EXTENDED CRUSING   RIGGED WITH HAMMOND YARDS

Scale ⅛" = 1'

INDEX OF DESIGNS